C0-AKQ-345

THE CORRESPONDENCE OF MARX AND ENGELS

Karl Marx AND *Frederick Engels*

Selected Correspondence

1846 - 1895

WITH EXPLANATORY NOTES

Translated by Dona Torr

INTERNATIONAL PUBLISHERS, NEW YORK

PRINTED IN THE U.S.A.

PUBLISHER'S NOTE

Of the letters exchanged between Marx and Engels more than fifteen hundred are printed in the *Gesamtausgabe* (Collected Edition) of the Marx-Engels-Lenin Institute; those written by them to other correspondents number many hundreds. From this treasure house a selection of the most important passages has been made and annotated under the editorship of V. ADORATSKY, Director of the Marx-Engels-Lenin Institute, and has already been published in German (1934). The present volume is the English translation of this *Selected Correspondence*. It includes everything contained in the German edition and in addition, by permission of the Marx-Engels-Lenin Institute, sixteen further letters, or extracts from letters, of particular interest to students of the English and American working-class movements. Notes, including some additional extracts, have been supplied to these letters and a few notes for the use of English-speaking readers have been added elsewhere. In a few cases also the extracts in the text have been lengthened to include passages on the English movement. Lists of the letters dealing specially with England and America will be found in the index.

Eleven of the letters here included were written in English, and these, with one exception (see Letter 155) are given in their original form and indicated by footnotes; the letters to Danielson (Nikolai-on) and to Florence Kelley (Wischnewetsky) have been taken from the photo-copies of the originals in the possession of the Marx-Engels-Lenin Institute. The English words and phrases which Marx and Engels sometimes introduced with such vivid effect into their German letters to each other have all been retained, but to have indicated them typographically would have introduced false emphasis. Students interested in questions of translation are asked to note that the letters from Marx and Engels to each other have been translated from the text of the *Gesamtausgabe*, the only existing printed edition which gives the letters entirely unaltered and with "foreign" words left untranslated; the letters to Bebel, Liebknecht, Kautsky and other German Social-Democrats have been translated from the text (Vol. I) published by the Marx-Engels-Lenin Institute in 1933, and other letters have in most cases been translated from photo-copies of the originals. With one exception (see Letter 230) letters and quoted passages originally written in French have been translated from the French and not from the frequently used German versions, and are indicated by footnotes. The letters to Kugelmann and Letter 185 on the death of Marx are taken from the English translations published by International Publishers.

With reference to the use of the word "nigger" which occurs in this book: Marx used the word while living in England, in the last century. The word does not have the same connotation as it has now in the United States and should be read as "Negro" whenever it occurs in the text.

PREFACE

THE idea of publishing the selected letters of Marx and Engels comes from Lenin. He repeatedly stressed the great scientific and political value of the correspondence of the founders of scientific Communism.

In 1913, Lenin wrote with regard to the correspondence between Marx and Engels, which had then just been published (V. I. Lenin, *Selected Works,* Vol. XI):

"In this correspondence it is not merely that Marx and Engels here stand out before the reader in striking relief and in all their greatness. The extremely rich theoretical content of Marxism is unfolded most vividly, since Marx and Engels again and again return in the letters to the most diverse aspects of their teaching, emphasising and explaining—at times discussing with each other and proving to each other—the most recent (in relation to previous views), most important and most difficult points.

"The history of the labour movement throughout the world, at its most important moments and in the most essential points, passes before the reader with striking vividness. Even more valuable is the history of the *politics* of the working class. Prompted by most diverse occurrences, in various countries, in the old world and in the new, and at different historical moments, Marx and Engels would discuss what was most fundamental in the formulation of questions concerning the *political* tasks of the working class. Now the epoch covered by the correspondence was just the epoch when the working class became demarcated from bourgeois democracy, the epoch of the rise of an independent labour movement, the epoch when the basic principles of proletarian tactics and policy were being determined. The more frequently one observes nowadays how the labour movement in various countries suffers from opportunism, in consequence of the stagnation and decay of the bourgeoisie, in consequence of the fact that the labour leaders are engrossed in the trivialities of the day, etc.—the more valuable becomes the great wealth of material contained in the correspondence, displaying as it does the most profound understanding of the fundamental revolutionary aims of the proletariat and an unusually flexible definition of any given problem of tactics, from the point of view of these revolutionary aims and without the slightest concession to opportunism or revolutionary phraseology.

" If one were to attempt to define in one word, so to say, the focus of the whole correspondence, the central point around which the entire network of the ideas, expressed and discussed, turns—that word would be : *dialectics*. The application of materialist dialectics to the restatement of all political economy from its foundations, to history, natural science, philosophy and the policy and tactics of the working class—that is what interested Marx and Engels above all. It is here that they made the most important and novel contribution and herein lies the stride forward made by their genius in the history of revolutionary thought."

A special character attaches to the correspondence of Marx and Engels with third persons, with various political leaders with whom the founders of scientific Communism maintained connection. In these letters Marx and Engels appear above all as leaders of the working class and leaders of the Communist Party. Lenin, in giving an estimate of the theoretical content of the correspondence of Marx and Engels with Sorge, once again stresses both the immense scientific value of these letters and their political significance. The letters to Sorge for the most part fall within the period after the Paris Commune:

Referring to the correspondence with Sorge, Lenin writes :

" In these letters Marx and Engels most frequently dealt with the burning questions of the English-American and of the German labour movements. This is comprehensible since they were Germans, living at that time in England and corresponding with their American comrades. On the French labour movement, and particularly on the Paris Commune, Marx expressed himself much more frequently and in greater detail in the letters which he wrote to the German Social Democrat Kugelmann.

"It is exceedingly instructive to compare how Marx and Engels dealt with the questions of the English-American and of the German labour movements. This comparison acquires especially great significance when we consider that Germany on the one hand, and England and America on the other, represent different stages of capitalist development, different forms of domination of the bourgeoisie as a class in the whole of the political life of these countries. From a scientific point of view we here see a model example of materialist dialectics, an ability to bring to the fore and to emphasise the various points, various aspects of a question in application to the concrete peculiarities of one or other of the political and economic conditions. From the point of view of the practical policy and tactics of a workers' party, we here see a model example of the way in which the creators of *The Communist Manifesto* defined the tasks of the struggling proletariat in application to the different stages of the national labour movement in various countries."

The present collection contains letters and portions of letters dealing with questions both of theory and policy. The theoretical questions discussed in the letters relate to the most varied spheres: to political economy, philosophy, natural science and to the study of the history of various countries at various periods, beginning with the history of the European countries and America at the time of Marx and Engels and ending with questions of ancient and primitive history. The reader will find in the letters dealing with questions of the policy, strategy and tactics of the proletarian party a series of examples of how Marx and Engels fought for and carried through the policy of revolutionary Marxism, a series of characteristic examples of their struggle against all varieties of opportunism and class conciliation, examples of the fight on two fronts.

The present collection of letters, covering a period of almost half a century [1846-95] reflects the struggle and the scientific work conducted by Marx and Engels as leaders of the proletariat. The collection forms a supplement to the selected works of Marx in two volumes.* The letters are given in chronological order. To facilitate reference, a subject index is appended and the letters are provided with notes giving the reader necessary information relating to the persons and events mentioned in the letters.

V. Adoratsky.

* Karl Marx, *Selected Works,* Vol. I and II, International Publishers.

CONTENTS

1. Engels to the Communist Correspondence Committee in Brussels

(Committee Letter [No. 3])

Paris, 23 October, 1846.

About the business with the Straubingers here there is not much to be said. The main thing is that the various points of difference which I have had to fight out with the lads up till now have been settled ; Grün's chief follower and pupil, Papa Eisermann, has been turned out, the influence of the rest over the mass of them has been completely overthrown and I got a resolution against them carried unanimously.

Briefly, this is what happened :

The Proudhon Associations' scheme was discussed for three evenings. At first I had nearly the whole clique against me, but at the end only Eisermann and the other three followers of Grün. The chief point was to prove the necessity for revolution by force and in general to demonstrate that Grün's "true socialism," which has derived new life from the Proudhon panacea, is anti-proletarian, petty-bourgeois, Straubingerish. In the end I got furious at the perpetual repetition of the same arguments by my opponents and made a direct attack on the Straubingers, which excited great indignation among the Grünites but enabled me to lure the noble Eisermann into an *open attack* on Communism. Whereupon I gave him such a merciless hiding that he never returned to the charge.

I now made use of the handle which Eisermann had given me—the attack on Communism—all the more so as Grün was intriguing the whole time, running round the workshops, summoning people to his place on Sundays, etc., etc., and on the Sunday after the aforementioned session had *himself* had the unbounded stupidity to attack Communism in front of eight or ten Straubingers. I therefore announced that before I took part in further discussion we must vote whether we were to meet here as Communists or not. In the first case, care would have to be taken that attacks on Communism like that made by Eisermann did not occur again; in the second case, if they were simply stray individuals discussing there anything that might come into their heads, I did not give a damn for them and should not come again. This greatly horrified the Grünites—they met together "for the good of mankind," for their own enlightenment, they were progressive spirits, not one-sided, doctrinaires, etc., etc., and surely it was impossible to call worthies like themselves "stray individuals." Moreover *they must first know* what Communism really was (these hounds who have been calling themselves Communists for years and have only deserted from fear of Grün and Eisermann, who had sneaked in among them with Communism as their pretext!). Naturally I did not let myself be trapped by their engaging request that I should tell them, the ignorant, what Communism is in two or three words. I gave them an extremely simple definition. It covered no more than the particular points at issue and, by positing community of goods, *ruled out* peaceableness, tenderness or consideration towards the bourgeoisie, including the Straubingers, and, finally, the Proudhon joint stock company with its retention of individual *property* and what follows from it. Moreover, it contained nothing which could give any opportunity for digressions and evasion of the proposed vote. I therefore defined the objects of the Communists in this way: (1) To achieve the interests of the proletariat in opposition to those of the bourgeoisie; (2) To do this through the abolition of private property and its replacement by community of goods; (3) To recognise no means of carrying out these objects other than a democratic revolution by force.

This was discussed for two evenings. On the second, the best of the three Grünites, observing the mood of the majority, came completely over to my side. The other two were contradicting each other the whole time without noticing it. Several chaps who had never spoken before suddenly got their mouths open and declared themselves quite decidedly for me. Up till then only Junge had done this. Some of these new men, although they were trembling in deadly terror of getting stuck, spoke quite nicely and in general seem to possess quite healthy intelligences. In short, when it came to the vote, the meeting declared itself Communist in the sense of the above definition by thirteen votes against the two still-faithful Grünites—of whom one also explained later that he had the greatest longing to be converted.

This has at last cleared the ground and one can now start to make something out of the chaps, so far as that is possible. Grün, who easily got out of his money trouble because his principal creditors were these same Grünites, his chief followers, now stands very low with the majority and even with a section of his followers, and despite all his intrigues and experiments (*e.g.*, going in a cap to meetings at the *barrières*,* etc., etc.) has come a first-class crash with his Proudhon Society. Even if I had not been there our friend Ewerbeck would have rushed into it bald-headed. . . .

¶ In order to further the enlightenment of the German workers and journeymen living in Paris, of whom there were a large number in the 'forties, and to win them for the new Marxian ideas of scientific socialism and the proletarian class struggle, Engels was commissioned by the Communist Correspondence Committee in Brussels to transfer himself to Paris in the second half of 1846.

"STRAUBINGERS" : Handicraftsmen and workers whose class consciousness was backward and undeveloped, who were full of petty-bourgeois prejudices and who could only with difficulty pass beyond the limitations of the old craft point of view. Marx and Engels had to carry on a hard fight to awaken proletarian class consciousness in elements of this kind too, as Engels' letter bears witness. The chief task was to overcome the influence of Proudhon and of the German "true socialists,"

* *Barrières* : The districts just outside the gates and fortifications of Paris were the favourite resort of the workers for amusements, meetings, etc., on Sundays. [*Ed. Eng. ed.*]

especially of Karl Grün. Wilhelm Weitling, the first German proletarian writer, who, however, stood for a Utopian-revolutionary form of socialism with the petty-bourgeois slogan of "equality" as its chief motto, also played a great part in these groups, especially as he was himself a journeyman. (See Letter 166, Note.)

In a letter to Marx written from Paris in October 1846 (about October 23), Engels says:

"I think I shall be able to pull it off with the Straubingers here. These fellows are indeed appallingly ignorant and utterly unprepared by their conditions of life; there is no competition whatever among them, their wages always piss on at the same level, struggles with the master do not turn on the question of wages at all but on 'the journeyman's pride,' etc. The ready-made clothing shops are having a revolutionary effect on the tailors now. If only it were not such a rotten trade.

"Grün has done a fearful lot of harm. He has turned everything definite for the fellows into mere day-dreams, efforts for humanity, etc. Under the pretence of attacking Weitling and other forms of abstract communism he has stuffed their heads full of vague literary and petty-bourgeois phrases and declared everything else to be system-mongering. Even the joiners, who were *never* Weitlingers—or at any rate only one or two individuals among them were—have got a superstitious terror of the bogey of 'bread and butter communism' and—at least *before* the decision was taken—would rather associate themselves with the most visionary dreams, plans for peace and happiness, etc., than this 'bread and butter communism.' The confusion which reigns here is endless. I have recently sent Harney a mild attack upon the peacefulness of the Fraternal Democrats and have also written him that he should remain in correspondence with you all."

PROUDHON: For his theories and practical proposals see Letters 2 and 72.

HARNEY: See Note to Letter 18.

GRÜN, KARL (1813-87). Writer. From 1842 onwards Editor of the bourgeois-radical newspaper, *Mannheimer Abendzeitung*. After 1844 one of the chief representatives of "true socialism." (See Marx and Engels, *German Ideology* and the *Communist Manifesto* IIIc.) Engels, in the postscript to his translation of Fourier's *Fragment on Trade*, * writes with regard to the theoretical content of " true socialism " : " Something about ' humanity,' as the thing has been recently labelled, something about the ' realisation ' of this humanity or rather— monstrosity; a little about property, taken from Proudhon—at third or fourth hand—some moans about the proletariat; the organisation of labour, miserable associations for the improvement of the lower classes of the people, all combined with boundless ignorance of political economy and actual society— that is the whole story, which, moreover, theoretical impartiality, the ' absolute calm of thought,' drains of its last drop of blood, its last trace of energy and elasticity." And in his *Ludwig Feuerbach* Engels wrote : " But what we ought not to forget is that it was just to these two weaknesses of Feuerbach's [the ' fine writing and in places even bombastic style' and the ' extravagant glorification of love '] that the ' true socialism,' which spread like a plague throughout ' educated ' Germany from 1844 onwards, attached itself, substituting literary phrases for scientific knowledge and in place of the emancipation of the proletariat by the economic transformation of production putting the liberation of mankind through ' love.' In short it lost itself in the disgusting literary phrase-making and suffocating sentimentality of which Herr Karl Grün was the type."

PAPA EISERMANN. German handicraft worker in Paris.

JUNGE, ADOLF FRIEDERICH : a Communist of Cologne, an emigrant in Paris.

EWERBECK, AUGUST HERMANN (1816-60). Author. Emigrant in Paris. Member of the Communist League.

2. MARX TO P. V. ANNENKOV†

Brussels, 28 December, 1846.

You would long ago have received my answer to your letter of November 1 but for the fact that my bookseller only sent me Monsieur Proudhon's book, *The Philosophy of Misery*, last week. I have gone through it in two days in order to be able to give you my opinion about it at once. As I have read the

* Marx-Engels, *Gesamtausgabe I*, Bd. IV, S. 457.
† This letter was written in French.

book very hurriedly, I cannot go into details but can only tell you the general impression it has made on me. If you wish, I could go into details in a second letter.

I must frankly confess to you that I find the book as a whole bad, and very bad. You yourself laugh in your letter at the " imprint of German philosophy " which M. Proudhon parades in this obscure and formless work, but you supppose that the economic argument has not been infected by the philosophic poison. I too am very far from imputing the faults in the economic argument to M. Proudhon's philosophy. M. Proudhon does not give us a false criticism of political economy because he is the possessor of an absurd philosophic theory, but he gives us an absurd philosophic theory because he fails to understand the social situation of to-day in its *engrenement* [concatenation], to use a word which like much else M. Proudhon has borrowed from Fourier.

Why does M. Proudhon talk about God, about universal reason, about the impersonal reason of humanity which never errs, which remains the same throughout all the ages and of which one need only have the right consciousness in order to know truth ? Why does he produce feeble Hegelianism to give himself the appearance of a bold thinker ?

He himself provides you with the clue to this enigma. M. Proudhon sees in history a certain series of social developments ; he finds progress realised in history ; finally he discovers that men, as individuals, did not know what they were doing and were mistaken about their own movement; that is to say their social development seems at the first glance to be distinct, separate and independent from their individual development. He cannot explain these facts, and in a moment the hypothesis of the universal reason revealing itself is produced. Nothing is easier than to invent mystical causes, that is to say phrases which lack common sense.

But when M. Proudhon admits that he understands nothing about the historical development of humanity—he admits this by using such high sounding words as : Universal Reason, God, etc.—is he not implicitly and necessarily admitting that he is incapable of understanding economic development ?

What is society, whatever its form may be? The product of men's reciprocal activity. Are men free to choose this or that form of society for themselves? By no means. Assume a particular state of development in the productive forces of man and you will get a particular form of commerce and consumption. Assume particular stages of development in production, commerce and consumption and you will have a corresponding social order, a corresponding organisation of the family and of the ranks and classes, in a word a corresponding civil society.* Presuppose a particular civil society and you will get particular political conditions which are only the official expression of civil society. M. Proudhon will never understand this because he thinks he is doing something great by appealing from the State to society—that is to say from the official summary of society to official society.

It is superfluous to add that men are not free to choose their *productive forces*—which are the basis of all their history—for every productive force is an acquired force, the product of former activity.

The productive forces are therefore the result of practical human energy; but this energy is itself conditioned by the circumstances in which men find themselves, by the productive forces already won, by the social form which exists before they do, which they do not create, which is the product of the former generation. Because of this simple fact that every succeeding generation finds itself in possession of the productive forces won by the previous generation which serve it as the raw material for new production, a connection arises in human history, a history of humanity takes shape which has become all the more a history of humanity since the productive forces of man and therefore his social relations have been extended. Hence it necessarily follows: the social history of men is never anything but the history of their individual development, whether they are conscious of it or not. Their material relations are the basis of all their relations. These material relations

* Civil society. Any form of society based on division of labour and classes. [*Ed. Eng. ed.*]

are only the necessary forms in which their material and individual activity is realised.

M. Proudhon mixes up ideas and things. Men never relinquish what they have won, but this does not mean that they never relinquish the social form in which they have acquired certain productive forces. On the contrary, in order that they may not be deprived of the result attained, and forfeit the fruits of civilisation, they are obliged, from the moment when the form of their intercourse [Fr. *commerce*] no longer corresponds to the productive forces acquired, to change all their traditional social forms. I am using the [French] word *commerce* here in its widest sense, as we use *Verkehr* in German. For example: The institution and privileges of guilds and corporations, the regulatory regime of the Middle Ages, were social relations corresponding only to the acquired productive forces and to the social condition which had previously existed and from which these institutions had arisen. Under the protection of this regime of corporations and regulations capital was accumulated, overseas trade was developed, colonies were founded. But the fruits of this would themselves have been forfeited if men had tried to retain the forms under whose shelter these fruits had ripened. Hence came two thunderclaps—the revolutions of 1640 and 1688.* All the old economic forms, the social relations corresponding to them, the political conditions which were the official expression of the old civil society, were destroyed in England. Thus the economic forms in which men produce, consume, exchange, are *transitory and historical*. When new productive forces are won men change their method of production and with the method of production all the economic relations which are merely the necessary conditions of this particular method of production.

This is what M. Proudhon has not understood and still less demonstrated. M. Proudhon, incapable of following the real movement of history, produces a phantasy which presumptuously claims to be dialectical. He does not feel it necessary to speak of the seventeenth, the eighteenth or the nineteenth

* In England.

century, for his history proceeds in the misty realm of imagination and rises far above space and time. In short it is not history but Hegelian *vieillerie* [old junk], it is not profane history—the history of man—but sacred history—the history of ideas. From his point of view man is only the instrument of which the Idea or the eternal reason makes use in order to unfold itself. The *evolutions* of which M. Proudhon speaks are understood to be evolutions such as are accomplished within the mystic womb of the absolute Idea. If you tear the veil from this mystical language what it comes to is that M. Proudhon is offering you the order in which economic categories arrange themselves inside his own mind. It will not require any great exertion on my part to prove to you that it is the order of a very disorderly mind.

M. Proudhon starts his book with a dissertation on *value*, which is his pet subject. I will not begin an examination of this dissertation to-day.

The series of the economic evolutions of the eternal reason begins with *division of labour*. To M. Proudhon division of labour is a perfectly simple thing. But was not the caste regime also a particular division of labour? Was not the regime of the guilds another division of labour? And is not the division of labour under the system of manufacture, which in England begins in the middle of the seventeenth century and comes to an end in the last part of the eighteenth, totally different from the division of labour in large-scale modern industry?

M. Proudhon is so far from the truth that he neglects what even the profane economists attend to. When he talks about division of labour he does not feel it necessary to mention the world market. Good. Yet must not the division of labour have been fundamentally different in the fourteenth and fifteenth centuries, when there were still no colonies, when America did not as yet exist for Europe, and Eastern Asia only existed for her through the medium of Constantinople, from what it was in the seventeenth century when colonies were already developed?

And that is not all. Is the whole inner organisation of nations with all their international relations anything other than the expression of a particular division of labour? And must not these change when the division of labour changes?

M. Proudhon has so little understood the problem of the division of labour that he never even mentions the separation of town and country, which was taking place in Germany, for instance, from the ninth to the twelfth centuries. For M. Proudhon, since he knows neither its origin nor development, this separation becomes an eternal law. All through his book he speaks as if this creation of a particular mode of production would endure until the end of time. Everything that M. Proudhon says about the division of labour is only a summary, and moreover a very superficial and incomplete summary, of what Adam Smith and a thousand others have said before him.

The second evolution is *machinery*. The connection between the division of labour and machinery is entirely mystical to M. Proudhon. Each kind of division of labour had its specific instruments of production. Between the middle of the seventeenth and the middle of the eighteenth centuries, for instance, everything was not made by hand. There were implements, and very complicated ones, such as looms, ships, levers, etc.

Thus there is nothing more absurd than to derive machinery from division of labour in general.

I may also remark, by the way, that since M. Proudhon has not understood the development of machinery he has still less understood its historical origin. One can say that up to the year 1825—the period of the first general crisis—the general demands of consumption increased more rapidly than production, and the development of machinery was a necessary consequence of the needs of the market. Since 1825, the invention and application of machinery has been simply the result of the war between workers and employers. And this is only true of England. As for the European nations, they were driven to adopt machinery owing to English competition both in their home markets and on the world market. Finally, in North America the introduction of machinery was due both to competition with other countries and to lack of hands, that is, to the disproportion between the population of North

America and its industrial needs. From these facts you can see what sagacity Monsieur Proudhon develops when he conjures up the spectre of competition as the third evolution, the antithesis to machinery !

Finally and in general it is altogether absurd to treat *machinery* as an economic category, on a level with division of labour, competition, credit, etc.

Machinery is no more an economic category than the ox which draws the plough. The application of machinery in the present day is one of the conditions of our present economic system, but the way in which machinery is utilised is totally distinct from the machinery itself. Powder remains the same whether it is used to wound a man or to dress his wounds.

M. Proudhon surpasses himself when he allows competition, monopoly, taxes or police, balance of trade, credit and property to develop inside his head in the order in which I have quoted them. Nearly all credit institutions had been developed in England by the beginning of the eighteenth century, before the discovery of machinery. Public credit was only a fresh method of increasing taxation and satisfying the new demands created by the rise of the bourgeoisie to power.

Finally, the last category in M. Proudhon's system is constituted by *property*. In the real world, on the other hand, the division of labour and all M. Proudhon's other categories are social relations forming as a whole what is to-day known as property : outside these relations bourgeois property is nothing but a metaphysical or juristic illusion. The property of a different epoch, feudal property, develops in a series of entirely different social relations. M. Proudhon, by establishing property as an independent relation, commits more than a mistake in method : he clearly shows that he has not grasped the bond which holds together all forms of *bourgeois* production, that he has not understood the *historic and transitory* character of the forms of production in a particular epoch. M. Proudhon, who does not regard our social institutions as an historical product, who understands neither their origin nor their development, can only produce dogmatic criticism of them.

M. Proudhon is also obliged to take refuge in a *fiction* in order to explain development. He imagines that division of labour, credit, machinery, etc., were all invented to serve his fixed idea, the idea of equality. His explanation is sublimely naive. These things were invented in the interests of equality but unfortunately they turned against equality. This constitutes his whole argument. In other words, he makes a gratuitous assumption and then as the actual development contradicts his fiction at every step he concludes that there is a contradiction. He conceals from you the fact that the contradiction exists solely between his fixed ideas and the real movement.

Thus M. Proudhon, mainly because he lacks the historical knowledge, has not perceived that as men develop their productive forces, that is, as they live, they develop certain relations with one another and that the nature of these relations must necessarily change with the change and growth of the productive forces. He has not perceived that *economic categories* are only the *abstract expressions* of these actual relations and only remain true while these relations exist. He therefore falls into the error of the bourgeois economists who regard these economic categories as eternal and not as historic laws which are only laws for a particular historical development, a development determined by the productive forces. Instead, therefore, of regarding the political-economic categories as abstract expressions of the real, transitory, historic, social relations, Monsieur Proudhon only sees, thanks to a mystic transposition, the real relations as embodiments of these abstractions. These abstractions themselves are formulæ which have been slumbering in the heart of God the Father since the beginning of the world.

But here our good M. Proudhon falls into severe intellectual convulsions. If all these economic categories are emanations from the heart of God, are the hidden and eternal life of man, how does it come about, first, that there is such a thing as development, and second, that M. Proudhon is not a Conservative ? He explains these contradictions by a whole system of antagonism.

To throw light on this system of antagonism let us take an example.

Monopoly is a good thing, because it is an economic category and therefore an emanation of God. Competition is a good thing because it is also an economic category. But what is not good is the reality of monopoly and the reality of competition. What is still worse is the fact that competition and monopoly devour each other. What is to be done? As these two eternal ideas of God contradict each other, it seems obvious to him that there is also a synthesis of them both within the heart of God, in which the evils of monopoly are balanced by competition and *vice versa*. As a result of the struggle between the two ideas only the good side will come into view. One must extract this secret idea from God and then apply it and everything will be for the best; the synthetic formula which lies hidden in the darkness of the impersonal reason of man must be revealed. M. Proudhon does not hesitate for a moment to come forward as the revealer.

But look for a moment at real life. In the economic life of the present time you find not only competition and monopoly but also their synthesis, which is not a *formula* but a *movement*. Monopoly produces competition, competition produces monopoly. But this equation, far from removing the difficulties of the present situation, as the bourgeois economists imagine that it does, results in a situation still more difficult and confused. If therefore you alter the basis on which present-day economic relations rest, if you destroy the present *method of production*, then you will not only destroy competition, monopoly and their antagonism, but also their unity, their synthesis, the movement which is the real equilibrium of competition and monopoly.

Now I will give you an example of Monsieur Proudhon's dialectic.

Freedom and *slavery* constitute an antagonism. I need not speak of the good and bad sides of freedom nor of the bad sides of slavery. The only thing that has to be explained is the good side of slavery. We are not dealing with indirect slavery, the slavery of the proletariat, but with direct slavery, the slavery of the black races in Surinam, in Brazil, in the Southern States of North America.

Direct slavery is as much the pivot of our industrialism to-day as machinery, credit, etc. Without slavery no cotton ; without cotton no modern industry. Slavery has given their value to the colonies ; the colonies have created world trade ; world trade is the necessary condition of large-scale machine industry. Before the traffic in Negroes began, the colonies only supplied the Old World with very few products and made no visible change in the face of the earth. Slavery is thus an economic category of the highest importance. Without slavery North America, the most progressive country, would be transformed into a patriarchal land. You have only to wipe North America off the map of the nations and you get anarchy, the total decay of trade and of modern civilisation. But to let slavery disappear is to wipe North America off the map of the nations. And therefore, because it is an economic category, we find slavery in every nation since the world began. Modern nations have merely known how to disguise the slavery of their own countries while they openly imported it into the New World. After these observations what will be M. Proudhon's attitude toward slavery ? He will look for the synthesis between freedom and slavery, the golden mean or equilibrium between slavery and freedom.

Monsieur Proudhon has very well grasped the fact that men produce cloth, linen, silks, and it is a great merit on his part to have grasped this small amount. What he has not grasped is that these men, according to their powers, also produce the *social relations* amid which they prepare cloth and linen. Still less has he understood that men, who fashion their social relations in accordance with their material method of production, also fashion *ideas* and *categories*, that is to say the abstract, ideal expression of these same social relations. Thus the categories are no more eternal than the relations they express. They are historic and transitory products. For M. Proudhon, on the contrary, abstractions and categories are the primordial cause. According to him they, and not men, make history. The *abstraction*, the *category taken as such*, i.e. apart from men and their material activities, is of course immortal, unmoved, unchangeable, it is only one form of the being of pure reason ; which is only another way of saying that the abstraction as such is abstract. An admirable *tautology!*

Thus, regarded as categories, economic relations for M. Proudhon are eternal formulæ without origin or progress.

Let us put it in another way : M. Proudhon does not directly state that *bourgeois existence* is for him an *eternal verity* ; he states it indirectly by deifying the categories which express bourgeois relations in the form of thought. He takes the products of bourgeois society for independent eternal existences, endowed with a life of their own, as soon as they present themselves to his mind in the form of categories, in the form of thought. So he does not rise above the bourgeois horizon. As he is operating with bourgeois ideas, the eternal truth of which he presupposes, he seeks a synthesis, an equilibrium for these ideas and does not see that the method by which they reach equilibrium at present is the only possible one.

Indeed he does what all good bourgeois do. They all tell you that in principle, that is as abstract ideas, competition, monopoly, etc., are the only basis of life, but that in practice they leave much to be desired. They all want competition without its tragic effects. They all want the impossible, namely, the conditions of bourgeois existence without the necessary consequences of those conditions. None of them understands that the bourgeois form of production is historic and transitory, just as the feudal form was. This mistake arises from the fact that the bourgeois-man is to them the only possible basis of every society ; they cannot imagine a society in which men have ceased to be bourgeois.

M. Proudhon is therefore necessarily a *doctrinaire.* The historic movement which is turning the world upside down to-day reduces itself for him to the problem of discovering the correct equilibrium, the synthesis, of two bourgeois ideas. And so the clever fellow is able by his cunning to discover the hidden thought of God, the unity of two isolated thoughts—which are only isolated because M. Proudhon has isolated them from practical life, from present-day production, that is, from the union of realities which they express.

In place of the great historic movement arising from the

conflict between the productive forces already acquired by men and their social relations, which no longer correspond to these productive forces; in place of the terrible wars which are being prepared between the different classes within each nation and between different nations; in place of the practical and violent action of the masses by which alone these conflicts can be resolved—in place of this vast, prolonged and complicated movement Monsieur Proudhon supplies the evacuating motion of his own head. So it is the men of learning, the men who know how to get God's secret thoughts out of him, who make history. The common people have only to apply their revelations. You will now understand why M. Proudhon is the declared enemy of every political movement. The solution of present problems does not lie for him in public action but in the dialectical contortions of his own mind. Since to him the categories are the moving force, it is not necessary to change practical life in order to change the categories. On the contrary, change the categories and the result will be the transformation of the actual social order.

In his desire to reconcile the contradictions Monsieur Proudhon does not even ask himself if the basis of those contradictions must not itself be overthrown. He is exactly like the political doctrinaire who will have it that the king, the chamber of deputies and the chamber of peers are integral parts of social life, eternal categories. All he is looking for is a new formula by which to establish an equilibrium between these forces (whose equilibrium depends precisely on the actual movement in which one force is now the conqueror and now the slave of the other). Thus in the eighteenth century a number of mediocre minds were busy finding the true formula which would bring the social orders, king, nobility, parliament, etc., into equilibrium, and they woke up one morning to find that there was in fact no longer any king, nobility or parliament. The true equilibrium in this antagonism was the overthrow of all the social conditions which served as a basis for these feudal existences and their antagonisms.

Because M. Proudhon places eternal ideas, the categories of pure reason, on the one side and human beings and their practical life, which according to him is the application of these categories, on the other, one finds with him from the beginning a *dualism* between life and ideas, soul and body, a dualism which recurs in many forms. You can see now that this antagonism is nothing but the incapacity of M. Proudhon to understand the profane origin and history of the categories which he deifies.

My letter is already too long for me to speak of the absurd case which M. Proudhon puts up against Communism. For the moment you will grant me that a man who has not understood the present state of society can still less understand the movement which is tending to overthrow it, or the literary expression of this revolutionary movement.

The sole point on which I am in complete agreement with Monsieur Proudhon is in his dislike for sentimental socialistic day-dreams. Before him I have already drawn much enmity upon myself by ridicule of this sentimental, utopian, mutton-headed socialism. But is not M. Proudhon strangely deluding himself when he sets up his petty-bourgeois sentimentality, I am referring to his declamations about home, conjugal love and all such banalities, in opposition to socialist sentimentality, which in Fourier, for example, goes much deeper than the pretentious platitudes of our worthy Proudhon? He himself is so thoroughly conscious of the emptiness of his arguments, of his utter incapacity for speaking about these things, that he hurls himself head over heels into explosions of rage, vociferation and righteous wrath, foams at the mouth, curses, denounces, cries shame and murder, beats his breast and boasts before God and man that he is unspotted by these socialist infamies! He does not seriously criticise socialist sentimentalities, or what he regards as such. Like a holy man, a Pope, he excommunicates poor sinners and sings the glories of the petty bourgeoisie and of the miserable patriarchal and amorous illusions of the domestic hearth. And this is no accident. From head to foot M. Proudhon is the philosopher and economist of the petty bourgeoisie. In an advanced society the *petty bourgeois* is necessarily from his very position a socialist on the one side and an economist on the other; that is to say, he is dazed by the magnificence of the big bourgeoisie and his sympathy for the sufferings of the people. He is at once both bourgeois and man of the people. He inwardly flatters himself that he is impartial and has found the right equilibrium, which claims to be something different from mediocrity. A petty bourgeois of this type glorifies *contradiction* because contradiction is the basis of his existence. He is himself nothing but social contradiction in action. He must justify in theory what he is in practice, and M. Proudhon has the merit of being the scientific interpreter of the French petty bourgeoisie—a genuine merit, because the petty bourgeoisie will form an integral part of all the impending social revolutions.

I wish I could have sent you my book on political economy with this letter, but it has so far been impossible for me to get this work, and the criticism of the German philosophers and socialists of which I spoke to you in Brussels, printed. You would never believe the difficulties which a publication of this kind comes up against in Germany, from the police on the one hand and from the booksellers, who are themselves the interested representatives of all the tendencies I am attacking, on the other. And as for our party, it is not merely that it is poor, but a large section of the German Communist Party are also angry with me for opposing their Utopias and declamations.

¶ ANNENKOV, P. W. (1812-87). Russian man of letters who lived a great deal abroad, where he became acquainted with Marx. Except for this acquaintance he had no connection with socialism whatever. In his recollections, *A Remarkable Decade* (*Vestnik Yevropy* [*European Messenger*], 1880), he describes the meeting and conversation between Marx and Weitling in Brussels, March 30, 1846. In the same memoirs he also gives a literary portrait of Marx as reflected in the consciousness of a liberal Russian gentleman of the 'forties.

This letter of Marx, written in French, was published in and is here taken from the *Correspondence of M. M. Stassulevich*

(Edited by M. K. Lemke, Vol. III, p. 455) where the following description is given of its external aspect :

" The letter is written in Marx's characteristic handwriting, sloping towards the left and astonishingly small but legible ; thanks to its microscopic nature he was able to write the whole on four sides of a large sheet of notepaper. There is scarcely an erasure in the letter." This letter is a brilliant example of dialectical thought and scientific criticism.

PROUDHON, PIERRE JOSEPH (1803-65). Theoretician of the petty bourgeoisie and one of the theoreticians of anarchism. A detailed estimate of Proudhon is also given in Marx's letter to Schweitzer (No. 72 of this volume). The ideas of Proudhon had a great influence, above all on the French workers, for a fairly long time ; this influence was still considerable even at the time of the Paris Commune in 1871. The anarchism of Bakunin, against which Marx and Engels had to fight hard in the First International, was also partly based on Proudhonist theories. In his letter to Marx on September 18, 1846, Engels describes the nature of one of Proudhon's " practical " proposals.

" Proletarians are to save up small shares. From these in the first place (no beginning is made at all, of course, with anything less than 10,000 to 20,000 workers) one or more workshops would be set up for one or more handicrafts, a section of the shareholders employed there and the products : (1) sold at the price of the raw material plus the labour to the shareholders (who thus do not have to pay any profit) and (2) in the case of any surplus, sold at current prices in the world market. As the capital of the society is increased by new members or by further savings on the part of the old shareholders, it will be employed to set up new workshops and factories, etc., etc., until—*all* proletarians are employed, *all* the productive forces existing in the country have been bought up and thus the capital in the hands of the bourgeoisie has lost its power to command labour and make profit ! . . . These people have got nothing more or less in mind than to *buy up*, for the time being, the whole of *France*, and later on perhaps the rest of the world as well, with the savings of the proletariat and by renouncing profit and the interest on their capital. Was such a splendid plan ever invented, and if one wants to go in for a *tour de force* would it not be much quicker simply to coin five franc pieces out of the silver moonshine? And these silly lads the workers here, I mean the Germans, *believe* in the rubbish; they, who cannot keep six halfpence in their pockets so as to be able to go to a wineshop on the evening of their meeting, want to buy up all *la belle France* with their savings. Rothschild and Co. are mere amateurs compared to these colossal sharks. It is enough to give one epilepsy. Grün has messed the fellows up so much that the most senseless phrase has more meaning for them than the simplest fact employed in an economic argument. Really it is shameful that one should still have to be haranguing against such barbarous nonsense. But one must be patient and I am not going to let go of the fellows until I have driven Grün from the field and cleared their muddled heads for them."

Proudhon could not get beyond petty-bourgeois ideas: "Like a real Frenchman he limits the association to the factory because he has never met a Moses and Co. or a Midlothian farmer. The French peasant and the French cobbler, tailor and merchant seem to him eternally fixed quantities, which have to be accepted. But the more I have to do with this rubbish the more I become convinced that the reform of agriculture, and therefore also of the *Eigentumscheisse* [filthy property system] based upon it, is the beginning and end of the coming upheaval. Without that Father Malthus would prove to be right...." (Marx to Engels, August 14, 1851.)

3. ENGELS TO MARX

Paris, 23-24 November, 1847.

... Think over the confession of faith* a bit. I believe we had better drop the catechism form and call the thing: Communist *Manifesto*. As more or less history has got to be related in it the form it has been in hitherto is quite unsuitable. I am bringing what I have done here with me,† it is simply a narrative, but miserably put together in fearful haste. I begin: What is Communism? And then straight to the proletariat—history of its origin, difference from former workers, develop-

* The draft of the *Communist Manifesto*.

† Engels met Marx in Ostend, November 27, on their way to London for the Second Congress of the Communist League, November 29. [*Ed. Eng. ed.*]

ment of the contradiction between proletariat and bourgeoisie, crises, results. In between this all sorts of secondary matters and in conclusion the Party policy of the Communists, in so far as it can be made public. What I have here has not yet all been submitted for endorsement, but, apart from a few quite small details, I mean to get it through in a form in which there will at least be nothing contrary to our views. . . .

¶ Among the advanced workers, members of the League of the Just, renamed in June 1847 the Communist League, a great need was felt for a small pamphlet giving a short account of the fundamental ideas of the Communists in a form which could be generally understood. Various drafts were produced for this "confession of faith," as it was then called. One of them originated from Moses Hess. About this draft Engels wrote to Marx on October 25-26, 1847:

"Hellish confusion among the Straubingers. A few days before my arrival the last Grünites were thrown out—a whole commune*—of whom, however, half will return. We are now only thirty strong. I have immediately organised a propaganda commune and am rushing round in an awful way, holding forth. I was at once elected to the circle and have been given the correspondence. From twenty to thirty candidates are proposed for membership. We shall soon be stronger again. *Quite between ourselves* I have played a devilish trick on Mosi [Moses Hess]. He had actually put through the most absurd revised confession of faith. Last Friday I went through this in the circle, question by question, and before I had got halfway people announced that they were satisfied. *Without any opposition* I got myself commissioned to draft a new one, which will now be discussed in the circle next Friday, and, *behind the backs of the communes*, sent to London. But of course not a soul must notice this or we shall all be deposed and there will be a deadly row." The draft of a "confession of faith" of this kind, written by Engels, was only published for the first time in 1913

* Commune (*Gemeinde*). By the provisional constitution of the Communist League, agreed to at its first Congress (London, June 1847) and endorsed at the Second Congress (November–December 1847), the League had been organised in communes (three to twenty members), circles (two to ten communes), leading circles, Central Committee and Congress. [*Ed. Eng. ed.*]

—twenty years after his death. For particulars about the origin of the *Communist Manifesto* and the history of the Communist League, see Engels' preface to Marx's *Enthüllungen über den Kommunistenprozess zu Köln* (*Revelations Concerning the Communist Trial in Cologne*).

HESS, MOSES (1812-75). One of the representatives of "true socialism." He was a collaborator of the *Rheinische Zeitung* on which Marx began his career as journalist and politician. Hess was at first on friendly terms with Marx and Engels, but after the publication of the *Communist Manifesto* a breach took place between its authors and Hess, as Hess took his stand increasingly on the side of "true socialism" (see Letter 1, Note) which was finally exposed in the *Manifesto* as a reactionary, petty-bourgeois theory. Later Hess attached himself to Lassalle's movement and came out against Marx and Engels. He was one of the theoreticians of the reactionary Jewish Zionist movement.

With regard to the activities of Hess in the workers' circles, Engels wrote to Marx on November 23-24, 1847:

"For a long time now I have been absolutely unable to understand why you have not stopped Moses' chatter. It produces the devil of a confusion for me here and the most long-winded counter-speeches from the workers. Whole circle meetings have been wasted over it, and it is not even possible to make a decisive attack on this stale nonsense in the communes—it could not be thought of before the election, especially."

[Engels is referring to the approaching Second Congress of the Communist League (London, November 29 to December 10, 1847) at which the programmatic principles and tactics of Marx and Engels were at length accepted and Marx was commissioned to draw up the *Communist Manifesto* (published February 1848). *Ed. Eng. Ed.*]

4. ENGELS TO MARX IN COLOGNE

Barmen, 25 April, 1848.

. . . We can count damned little on shares from this place. Blank, to whom I had already written on the subject and who is still the best of the lot, has become a bourgeois in practice, and the others even more so now that they are established and have come into collision with the workers. People shun any discussion of social questions like the plague; they call it incitement. I have squandered the finest flowers of speech and exerted every possible form of diplomacy, but have always got wavering replies. I am now going to make one more final attempt, if that fails everything is at an end. In two or three days you will hear definitely what has come of it. At bottom the thing is that these radical bourgeois here too see in us their main future enemies and do not want to put any weapons into our hands which we should very soon turn against them.

¶ After the beginning of the revolution in Germany (Berlin rising, March 18, 1848) Engels returned to his country from Paris in order to collect subscriptions to shares for the publication of a newspaper from those of his acquaintances who sympathised with democracy and Communism. Blank was one of the former friends of Engels who had been enthusiasts for Communism. Until the revolution great enthusiasm for Communism had existed among the bourgeois youth. In the revolution, however, real class interests came to light. The "Communists" of yesterday revealed their real class nature.

Engels wrote to Marx on May 9, 1848:

"The two sorts of people who make the most difficulties are, first, the young republicans in yellow gloves who are afraid for their money and scent Communism, and secondly, the local bigwigs who regard us as competitors."

On June 1, 1848, the first Marxist newspaper, the *Neue Rheinische Zeitung*, was published in Cologne. Of this paper Lenin wrote in 1914 in his essay *Karl Marx* (*Collected Works*, English ed., Vol. XVIII, p. 48) that "to this very day it remains the best and unsurpassed organ of the revolutionary proletariat." During the period of martial law, proclaimed at the end of September 1848, the paper was prohibited, but it soon came out again and appeared until May 19, 1849, when it was finally suppressed. In a letter to Bernstein (February 2, 1881) Engels in giving him advice as to how the *Sozial-Demokrat*, at that time the central organ of German Social-Democracy, should be edited, writes:

" As you have the *Neue Rheinische Zeitung* you would do well to read it occasionally. The contempt and mockery with which we treated our opponents was just what brought us in nearly 6,000 subscribers in the six months ending with the declaration of martial law, and although we started again from the beginning in November we had the same number and more by May 1849."

5. ENGELS TO JENNY MARX

Vevey, 25 July, 1849.

. . . The same day that I wrote to Marx (from Kaiserslautern) the news came that Homburg had been occupied by the Prussians and communications with Paris therefore cut. So I could no longer despatch the letter and went to Willich. In Kaiserslautern I had steered clear of any concern with the so-called revolution ; but when the Prussians arrived I could not resist the desire to be in the war too. Willich was the only officer who was any good, and so I went to him and became his adjutant. I was in four engagements, of which two were fairly important, especially the one at Rastatt, and discovered that the much-vaunted courage of flinging oneself into battle is the very commonest quality that anyone could have. The whistling of the bullets is quite a small affair and despite a lot of cowardice I did not see a dozen people throughout the whole campaign who behaved in a cowardly fashion during *the fighting*. But there was all the more " brave stupidity." To conclude, I came through all right everywhere, and taking it all together it is a good thing that someone from the *Neue Rheinische Zeitung* was present, for all the democratic rabble from Baden and the Palatinate were there and are boasting of the heroic deeds they never did. We should have heard the same tale again : the gentlemen of the *Neue Rheinische Zeitung* are too cowardly to fight. But of all the democratic gentlemen Kinkel and I were the only ones who fought. Kinkel enlisted in our corps as a musketeer and did quite well ; he took part in the first engagement, where a bullet grazed his head and he was taken prisoner.

After our corps had covered the retreat of the Baden Army we moved, 24 hours later than all the rest, into Switzerland and yesterday arrived here in Vevey.

¶ Engels gives an excellent detailed account of the insurrection in Baden and the Palatinate in 1849 in his series of articles on *Die Deutsche Reichsverfassungskampagne* (*The Campaign for a German Constitution.*)

On May 18, 1849, Marx received an order of expulsion from Cologne, and on May 19 the last number of the *Neue Rheinische Zeitung* appeared—printed in red. After leaving Cologne Marx and Engels went first to Baden and then to the Palatinate. They there convinced themselves that no military preparations had been made by the revolutionary organisations in these districts, which were supposed to be affected by the rising. The frontier was not guarded and no measures had been taken for extending the insurrection. The leaders of the movement were petty-bourgeois democrats who predominated both in the " Committees of Public Safety " and in the " Provisional Governments " but did nothing there but talk. Marx went to Paris because decisive events were to be expected there. Engels remained and took part in the war. He was thus able to observe the petty bourgeoisie and their rôle in the revolution in practice and he summed up the results of his experiences in the above-named articles. On the petty bourgeoisie he writes there :

" The history of all the political movements since 1830 in Germany, as well as in France and England, invariably shows us this class talking big, making loud protestations and sometimes even using extreme phrases, so long as they see no danger ; nervous, cautious and conciliatory as soon as the smallest danger approaches ; amazed, anxious, vacillating, as soon as the movement they excited is seized upon by other classes and taken seriously ; betraying the whole movement for the sake of their petty-bourgeois existence as soon as it comes to taking up arms and fighting—and finally, thanks to their indecision, always specially well cheated and ill-treated when the reactionary party has triumphed. . . . " But behind the bulk of the petty bourgeoisie stand other classes and groups which come out more energetically: the proletariat and the mass of the peasantry, as well as the more advanced section of the petty bourgeoisie. "These classes, with the proletariat of the bigger towns at their head, took the loudly protested assurances in favour of the national constitution more seriously than the petty-bourgeois agitators liked. If the petty bourgeoisie, as they swore every other minute, were going to sacrifice 'their property and their blood' for the national constitution, the workers, and, in many districts, the peasants too, were ready to do the same, on the condition—perfectly well known to all parties though not mentioned—that once the victory had been won the petty bourgeoisie would have to defend that same national constitution against those very same proletarians and peasants."

Engels, summarising the results of the political struggles of these years of revolution, wrote in 1850:

"Now that it [the campaign for a national constitution] has been lost, the only possibility of victory lies either with the slightly constitutionalised feudal-bureaucratic monarchy, or with a genuine revolution. And the revolution in Germany can no longer be brought to an end until it is ended by the complete domination of the proletariat."

An excellent analysis of the experiences of the revolutionary struggles is also given in the *Address of the Central Committee of the Communist League* issued to its members in March 1850.

Engels returned to the question of petty-bourgeois democracy and its rôle in the revolution in a letter to Bebel, December 11, 1884 (193 in this volume).

WILLICH, AUGUST (1810-78). Former Prussian artillery officer. As a convinced republican he retired in 1846. He took an active part in the Revolution of 1848-49. After the suppression of the rising he emigrated to London. With Schapper he was the leader of the "Left" fraction of the Communist League. To get some means of livelihood he learned the trade of carpenter. Went to America in 1853 and at first worked there as a carpenter. In 1858 he became a journalist. During the Civil War of North against South (1861-65) he fought on the side of the Northerners, distinguished himself and was made a general. After the war he went into the government service and occupied high positions in Cincinnati. In 1870 he came for a time to Germany. He died in the United States.

In his concluding Note to the *Revelations concerning the Communist Trial in Cologne* Marx writes: "In the Civil War in North America Willich showed that he is more than a visionary." (See also Letter 31 and Note.)

KINKEL, GOTTFRIED (1815-82). German writer and poet, a bourgeois democrat who took part in the Revolution of 1848. He was arrested and sentenced to lifelong imprisonment in a fortress, but succeeded in escaping. As a refugee in London he played a ludicrous rôle and was one of the chief intriguers against Marx among the refugees, who occupied themselves with fractional quarrels and mutual slander instead of with serious revolutionary work, and therefore fell into a condition of stagnation.

6. MARX TO ENGELS

London, 7 January, 1851.

I am writing to you to-day in order to lay a *questiuncula theoretica* [a little question of theory] before you, *naturae politico-economicae* [of a political-economic nature] of course.

You know, to begin from the beginning, that according to Ricardo's theory rent is nothing else but the difference between the cost of production and the price of the produce of the land, or, as he also expresses it, the difference between the price at which the worst land must sell in order to cover expenses (the farmer's profit and interest being always included in the expenses) and the price at which the best land can be sold.

The increase of rent proves, according to his own account of his theory:

(1) That ever poorer types of land are resorted to, or that the same amount of capital applied successively to the same land does not produce the same result. In a word: the soil deteriorates in the same measure that the population is obliged to demand more from it. It becomes relatively less fertile. This is where Malthus found the real ground for his theory of population and where his pupils now seek their final sheet anchor.

(2) Rent can only rise when the price of corn rises (with

economic legality, at least); it must fall with the fall of the latter.

(3) When the *rental of a whole country* rises this can only be explained by the fact that a very large mass of relatively poorer land has been taken into cultivation.

Now these three propositions are everywhere contradicted by history.

(1) There is no doubt that as civilisation progresses poorer and poorer types of land are taken into cultivation. But there is also no doubt that, as a result of the progress of science and industry, these poorer types of land are relatively good in comparison with the former good types.

(2) Since 1815 the price of corn has dropped—irregularly but steadily—from 90 shillings to 50 shillings and lower—this before the repeal of the Corn Laws. Rent has steadily risen. Thus in England. On the Continent, allowing for the difference of conditions, everywhere the same.

(3) In every country we find, as Petty had already noticed, that when the price of corn dropped the total rental of the country rose.

The main point in all this remains to square the law of rent with the progress of the fertility of agriculture in general; this is the only way by which the historical facts can be explained and the only way of superseding Malthus' theory of the deterioration, not merely of the labour force but of the land.

I think the matter can be simply explained in the following way:

Assume that in a given stage of agriculture the price of wheat is seven shillings a quarter and an acre of land of the best quality, paying a rent of ten shillings, produces 20 bushels. The yield of the acre therefore equals 20 by 7 or equals 140 shillings. In this case the costs of production are 130 shillings and therefore 130 shillings is the price of the product of the worst land taken into cultivation.

Assume that a general improvement in agriculture now takes place. In assuming this we are at the same time taking it for granted that science, industry and population are also growing. A general increase in the productivity of the soil, due to improvements, presupposes these conditions, as distinct from the productivity simply due to the accident of a favourable season.

Say the price of wheat falls from 7 to 5 shillings a quarter and that the best land, No. 1, which formerly produced 20 bushels, now produces 30 bushels. It now brings in, therefore, instead of 20 by 7 or 140 shillings, 30 by 5 or 150 shillings. That is to say a rent of 20 shillings instead of the former one of 10 shillings. The poorest land, which carries no rent, must produce 26 bushels, for, according to our assumption above, the necessary price of these is 130 shillings, and 26 by 5 equals 130. If the improvement, that is to say, the general progress of science, which goes hand in hand with the whole progress of society, population, etc., is not so general that the poorest land which has to be brought into cultivation can produce 26 bushels, then the price of corn cannot fall to 5 shillings a quarter.

As before, the 20 shillings of rent expresses the difference between the costs of production and the price of corn on the best land, or between the costs of production on the worst land and those on the best. Relatively the one piece of land remains just as infertile compared with the other as before. But the *general fertility* has increased.

All that is presupposed is that if the price of corn falls from 7 shillings to 5, consumption increases to the same degree, or that the productivity does not exceed the demand which can be expected at a price of 5 shillings. Utterly false as this assumption would be if the price had dropped from 7 to 5 shillings because of an exceptionally abundant harvest, it is an equally necessary one where the rise in the productivity is a gradual one promoted by the producers themselves. In any case we are only dealing here with the economic possibility of this hypothesis.

It follows that:

(1) Rent can rise although the price of the produce of the soil falls, and yet *Ricardo's law remains correct.*

(2) The law of rent, as laid down by Ricardo in its simplest

form, apart from its application, does not assume the diminishing fertility of the soil but (*in spite of the fact that the general fertility of the soil increases as society develops*) only presupposes *different* degrees of fertility in different pieces of land, or different results from the successive application of capital to the same land.

(3) The more general the improvement of the soil, the more kinds of land will it embrace, and the rental of the whole country may rise although the price of corn in general has fallen. Taking the above example, for instance, the only question will be how large an amount of land produces more than 26 bushels at 5 shillings without exactly having to produce 30; that is to say how much variety there is in the quality of the land lying between the best and the worst grades. This has nothing to do with the rate of the rent of the best land. It does not directly affect the rate of rent in general.

You know that the main point about rent is that it is produced by equalising the price of the results of different costs of production, but that this law of the market price is nothing but a law of bourgeois competition. But even if bourgeois production were done away with there would remain the crux that the soil becomes relatively less fertile and that the same labour produces successively less, although it would no longer be the case, as under the bourgeois system, that the produce yielded by the best land was as dear as that of the worst. According to what has been said above, this objection would fall to the ground.

Please give me your opinion on the matter.

¶ The "law of diminishing returns" which Marx mentions in this letter is one of the main pillars of bourgeois political economy. According to this law, each successive application of labour and capital to the soil produces not a corresponding but a diminishing yield, and with its aid bourgeois and especially also Social-Democratic economists attempt to prove that the industrialisation of agriculture is impossible and the backwardness of agriculture in comparison with industry an eternal law of nature. By supporting themselves on Malthus they try to represent unemployment, which results from the laws of the capitalist form of production, as an eternal phenomenon inherent in nature, against which it is impossible to struggle. Lenin, in his work on *The Agrarian Question and the Critics of Marx*, says of this law that it " does not at all apply to the case where technique is progressing and methods of production are changing ; it has only an extremely relative and conditional application to those cases where technique remains unchanged. That is why neither Marx nor the Marxists refer to this law." (Lenin, *Collected Works*, English edition, Vol. IV, 1, p. 185.)

The practical refutation of this " law " is found to-day on the one hand in the increasing industrialisation of agricultural production in capitalist countries, which became one of the main factors in the world crisis of agriculture, and on the other in the rapid building up of socialist mechanised agriculture in the Soviet Union. (See also Letters 7, 82.)

Marx is speaking here of differential rent only and not of absolute ground rent, the decisive part of his theory of ground rent, which he only developed later (see Letter 54).

RICARDO, DAVID (1772-1823). English banker and economist. The last great representative of classical political economy. Ricardo starts with the determination of value by labour time and " compels science . . . to deliver an account to itself . . . of how far the science . . . which only reproduces the forms in which the process appears, and how far these appearances themselves, correspond in general to the basis on which the inner connections, the real physiology of bourgeois society, rest. . . . This therefore is Ricardo's great historic importance for science." Bound up with this is the fact " that Ricardo exposes and openly declares the economic contradiction between the classes—as shown by the inner contradiction—and thus the roots of the historic struggle and process of development are grasped by political economy." (Marx.)

Ricardo, however, did not understand the historical character of the capitalist method of production and conceived it as eternal. (*Cf.* Letters 54, 56, 107, 131, 132, in this volume.)

7. ENGELS TO MARX

[Manchester], 29 January, [1851].

In any case your new stuff about ground rent is perfectly right. I never could convince myself about Ricardo's unproductivity of the land increasing as the population increases, nor could I ever find confirmation of his rising price of corn, but with my well-known laziness in matters of theory I took the inward growls of my better self quietly and never went to the bottom of the thing. There is no doubt that your solution is the right one and that you have thus acquired a new claim to the title of the economist of ground rent. If there were any right or justice left in the world the earth's total ground rent should now be yours for at least a year, and even that would be the least you would have the right to demand.

I never could get it into my head how it was that Ricardo in his simple definition represents ground rent as the difference in productivity between the different kinds of land, but in proof of this proposition: (1) recognises no other factor except the inclusion of ever poorer types of land, (2) totally ignores the progress of agriculture, and (3) ends by dropping practically entirely the point about bringing in the worse types of land and instead works all the time with the premise that the capital which is successively applied to a given field contributes continually less to the increase of the yield. The proposition to be proved was as clear as the reasons advanced for the proof were remote, and you will remember that in the *Deutsch-Französische Jahrbücher** I had already challenged the theory of increasing unproductivity, on the ground of the progress of scientific agriculture—of course very crudely and without any connected development. You have now cleared the thing up, and this is one more reason why you should hasten to complete and publish the *Economy*.† If an article by you on ground rent could be published in a translation in an English periodical it would attract enormous attention. Think about this; I will undertake the translation.

* *German–French Year-Books* (1843-44).
† Marx's *Critique of Political Economy*.

¶ At the end of 1843 Engels had written for the *Deutsch-Französische Jahrbücher* (*German-French Year-books*) edited by Marx and Ruge, an article, *Outlines of a Criticism of Political Economy*, which was of great importance in the development of Marx's economic theory. Marx refers in various parts of *Capital* to this article, in which as early as 1843 Engels had brilliantly formulated in brief outline all the important questions of economic theory. The passage referred to in Engels' letter is probably the following :

" The extent of land is limited. Very well. The amount of labour power which has to be applied to this area increases with the population ; let us even assume that the increase of the yield is not always proportionate to the increase of labour ; yet there still remains a third factor—which never counts for anything with the economists, it is true—namely science, and the advance of science is as limitless and at least as rapid as that of population. How much of the progress of agriculture in this century is due to chemistry alone, and indeed to two men alone—Sir Humphrey Davy and Justus Liebig ? But science multiplies itself at least as much as population : population increases in relation to the number of the last generation ; science advances in relation to the total amount of knowledge bequeathed to it by the last generation, and therefore under the most ordinary conditions in geometrical progression too—and what is impossible for science ? But it is ridiculous to talk about over-population while 'there is waste land enough in the valley of the Mississippi for the whole population of Europe to be transplanted upon,' and while in general only a third of the earth's surface can be regarded as cultivated and the production of this third part could itself be increased sixfold and more by the application even of the improved methods already known." (*Marx-Engels Gesamtausgabe* I. Vol. 2, pp. 400-401). Compare Letter 82.

8. ENGELS TO MARX

[Manchester], 5 February, 1851.

The Free-Traders here are making use of the prosperity, or semi-prosperity, to buy the proletariat, and John Watts is acting as broker. You know Cobden's new plan : a National

Free School Association to put through a bill empowering the townships to impose local taxation on themselves for the erection of schools. The thing is being pushed splendidly. In Salford a Free Library and Museum have already been established as well—lending library and reading-room gratis. In Manchester the Hall of Science—and here, as the Mayor of Manchester most graciously acknowledged, Watts was really the broker—has been bought up by public subscriptions (about £7,000 altogether) and will also be transformed into a Free Library. At the end of July the affair will be opened—with 14,000 volumes to begin with. All the meetings and assemblies held for these objects resound with the praises of the workers and especially of the worthy, modest, useful Watts, who is now on the best of terms with the Bishop of Manchester. I am already looking forward to the outburst of indignation at the ingratitude of the workers which will break loose from every side at the first shock.

¶ The "prosperity" which Engels here refers to was the opening of the period 1848-80 in which industrial capitalism reached its height in England. Engels later (see Note to Letter 207) referred to the period 1850-90 as the "forty years' winter sleep" of the English proletariat. See Note on the Chartist movement, Letter 31, and for other references to the British working-class movement in this period, Letters 35, 36, 41, 63, 71, 74, 88, 90, 91, 116, etc. [*Ed. Eng. ed.*]

COBDEN, RICHARD (1804-65). Manchester calico manufacturer who with John Bright (Letter 63) had led the agitation against the Corn Laws (see Note to Letter 31). The tariff on imported corn had been repealed in 1846 and the efforts of the "apostles of free trade" were now directed against other tariffs, towards measures of "financial reform" (taxes on landed estate) and extension of the franchise. To strengthen this agitation the Financial Reformers once more required the support of the working class. They won it largely through the franchise agitation of the next period. (See Letters 35, 63, 71, 74, 88, 90, 91, 116.) Marx and Engels have shown how the politics of Bright and Cobden represented the interests of the rising industrial bourgeoisie as opposed to those of the great landowners. The supporters of these "Liberals" included the most brutal exploiters of the workers. The "Free-Traders" had bitterly opposed the Ten-Hour Bill (limiting the day in English factories to ten hours) which was put through by the landowners (1847). See Engels, *The Condition of the Working Class in England in 1844*, *Die Englische Zehnstundenbill* [*The English Ten-Hour Bill*] and *The Ten-Hour Question* (1850), Marx, *Speech on Free Trade*, January 9, 1848, Marx, *Capital*, I, pp. 310-11, 742 (Kerr edition). [*Ed. Eng. ed.*]

"The Free-Traders (the men of the Manchester school, the Parliamentary and Financial Reformers)," wrote Marx in his article on the Chartists (August 10, 1852) in the *New York Tribune*, "are the *official representatives of modern English society*, the representatives of that England which rules the market of the world. They represent the party of the self-conscious bourgeoisie, of industrial capital striving to make available its social power as a political power as well and to eradicate the last arrogant remnants of feudal society. This party is led on by the most active and most energetic portion of the English bourgeoisie—the *manufacturers*. What they demand is the complete and undisguised ascendance of the bourgeoisie, the open, official subjection of society at large under the laws of modern bourgeois production and under the rule of those men who are the directors of that production. By free trade they mean the unfettered movement of capital freed from all political, national and religious shackles.

"The struggle of this party against the old institutions, products of a superannuated, an evanescent stage of social development, is resumed in the watchword: *Produce as cheap as you can and do away with all the 'faux frais' of production* (with all superfluous, unnecessary expense in production). And this watchword is addressed not only to the private individual but to the *nation at large* principally." Thus, says Marx, they opposed the Crown, the House of Lords, a large standing army, the State Church and its possessions, the routine of English law, and national wars, as superfluous "costs of production." ("England can exploit other countries more cheaply if she is at peace with them.")

But the reason why the bourgeoisie after their first victory over the aristocracy on the repeal of the Corn Laws had not gone forward in a more radical way was "because in every violent movement they are forced to appeal to the *working class*." And if the aristocracy is their vanishing opponent the working class is their arising enemy. "They prefer to compromise with the vanishing opponent rather than to strengthen the arising enemy to whom the future belongs, by concessions of a more than apparent importance." [*Ed. Eng. ed.*]

WATTS, JOHN. A former follower of Owen. Petty-bourgeois conciliator. Marx in *Capital*, Vol. I, chap. XXI (*Piece Wages*), Kerr edition, pp. 603, quotes in a note a passage from a pamphlet by John Watts in which the idea is put forward that piece work is better than time work for the worker and improves his conditions. "Piece workers are in fact their own masters even whilst working upon the capital of the employer." (John Watts, *Trade Societies and Strikes*, *Machinery and Co-operative Societies*, Manchester, 1865.) "I quote this little work," says Marx, "because it is a very sink of all long-ago-rotten apologetic commonplaces." In 1846 (September 16), Engels had written of Watts that his aim in life was now "to become respectable among the bourgeois despite his disrespectable atheism and socialism"; and on December 17, 1850: "He has now got a much bigger shop in Deansgate. . . . On the Educational Committees he sits in a brotherly way beside his former furious opponents the Dissenting parsons, and from time to time allows votes of thanks to be passed him for the very able address he delivered that evening." [*Ed. Eng. ed.*]

9. MARX TO ENGELS

London, 2 April, 1851.

The worst of it is I am now suddenly interrupted in my studies in the library.* I have got so far that I could be finished with the whole of the economic shit in five weeks. And that done I shall work out the economy at home and pitch into another science in the Museum. This is beginning to bore me. Fundamentally this science has made no more progress since A. Smith and D. Ricardo, although so much has been done in the way of particular and often super-delicate investigations.

* Marx worked in the British Museum Reading Room. The interruption was due to his wife's confinement and illness at a time of desperate financial straits. [*Ed. Eng. ed.*]

10. ENGELS TO MARX

[Manchester], 23 May, 1851.

. . . The more I think over the business the clearer it becomes to me that the Poles as a nation are done for and can only be made use of as an instrument until Russia herself is swept into the agrarian revolution. From that moment onwards Poland will have absolutely no more reason for existence. The Poles have never done anything in history except play at brave, quarrelsome stupidity. And one cannot point to a single instance in which Poland represented progress successfully, even if only in relation to Russia, or did anything at all of historic importance. Russia, on the other hand, is really progressive in relation to the East. For all its baseness and Slavonic dirt, Russian domination is a civilising element on the Black Sea, the Caspian Sea and Central Asia and among the Bashkirs and Tartars, and Russia has absorbed far more civilising and especially industrial elements than the Poles, whose whole nature is that of the idle cavalier. The mere fact that the Russian aristocracy—from the tsar and Prince Demidoff down to the lousiest fourteenth-class boyar, who is only *blahorodno*, " well-born "—manufactures, bargains, cheats, allows itself to be corrupted and carries on every possible kind of Christian and Jewish business, is in itself an advantage. Poland has never been able to nationalise foreign elements. The Germans in the towns are and remain Germans. Every German-Russian of the second generation is a speaking example of Russia's faculty for Russianising Germans and Jews. Even the Jews develop Slavonic cheek-bones there.

Napoleon's wars of 1807 and 1812 afford striking examples of the " immortality " of Poland. The only immortal thing about Poland was its habit of picking baseless quarrels. Added to which the largest section of Poland, the so-called White Russia, i.e., Byelostok, Grodno, Vilna, Smolensk, Minsk, Mohilev, Volhynia and Podolia, have with a few exceptions quietly allowed themselves to be governed by the Russians since 1772 ; except for a few burghers and noblemen here and there they have never stirred. A quarter of Poland speaks

Lithuanian, a quarter Ruthenian and a small section semi-Russian, while of the Polish section proper fully a third is Germanised.

Fortunately in the *Neue Rheinische Zeitung* we never undertook any positive obligations towards the Poles except the unavoidable one of their restoration with suitable frontiers—and that too only on condition of an agrarian revolution. I am certain that this revolution will come about completely in Russia before it does in Poland, owing to the national character and to Russia's more developed bourgeois elements. What are Warsaw and Cracow compared to Petersburg, Moscow, Odessa, etc !

Conclusion : To take away as much as possible from Western Poland, to occupy her fortresses, especially Posen, with Germans, under the pretext of defence, to let them make a mess of things for themselves, to drive them into the fire, to eat up their country, to feed them on hopes of Riga and Odessa, and, if the Russians can be got to move, to form an alliance with them and force the Poles to give way. Every inch of the boundary from Memel to Cracow conceded to the Poles completely ruins this already miserably weak frontier from a military point of view, and exposes the whole Baltic coast up to Stettin.

Moreover, I am convinced that when the next brawl occurs the whole Polish insurrection will be limited to the nobles in Posen and Galicia with a few adherents from the kingdom, for the country is so appallingly exhausted that it can do nothing more ; and the pretensions of these knights, unless they are supported by Frenchmen, Italians, Scandinavians, etc., and strengthened by a row in Czecho-Slovakia, will collapse as a result of their miserable performance. A nation which can raise at best twenty thousand to thirty thousand men does not count. And Poland can certainly not raise much more.

11. MARX TO ENGELS

London, 13 July, 1851.

. . . I rather gather from your letter that while the old man* was in Manchester you never learnt that a second document had been published in the *Kölnische Zeitung* [*Cologne Gazette*] under the heading : *The Communist League.* It was the address to the League which we drew up together—at bottom nothing but a plan of war against democracy. From one point of view its publication was good, as a contrast to Bürgers' document with its more or less absurd form and not very consoling matter. On the other hand several passages will make things more difficult for the present prisoners.†

I hear . . . from Cologne that Bürgers writes very gloomily from Dresden. On the other hand there is a general belief in Cologne that Daniels will be released ; there is nothing against him and all the shouters in the holy city are shouting for him. Naturally they regard him as incapable of such " tomfooleries."

Miquel has written from Göttingen. His house has been searched several times. Nothing was found. He has not been arrested. Five new emissaries—gentlemen—have left Göttengen for Berlin, etc. The persecution of Jews naturally increases the zeal and interest. The funniest thing about it is that the imbecile *Augsburger Allgemeine Zeitung* [*Augsburg General Gazette*] fathers the document we drew up on to Messrs. Mazzini and Ruge, beats itself repeatedly on the breast and can find no better way of expressing the mental shock produced by this monstrosity than by screaming, " Madness ! " a number of times. Madness ! Madness !

The Treves paper—i.e., Karl Grün—has of course got on its high horse and proved from the first document the material

* Engels' father.

† Eleven members of the Communist League in Germany had been arrested in May 1851. The address of Marx and Engels was published by the *Kölnische Zeitung* as evidence against the prisoners. The trial took place in Cologne in October–November 1852. Three of the prisoners were sentenced to imprisonment for six years (for " attempted high treason "), three to five years and one to three years. The rest were acquitted. Marx's pamphlet on the trial, *Revelations Concerning the Communist Trial in Cologne*, was published in February 1853. [*Ed. Eng. ed.*

but from the second the " spiritual " impotence of the Party. Of course there is no lack of enlightened and most extremely " anarchistic " phrases : Everything to be done from above ! A police state ! Those whose opinions differ to be formally excommunicated and excluded ! *Mon Dieu !* This is more than anyone can stand !

¶ The document referred to here is the *Address of the London Central Committee of the Communist League* (March 1850), in which Marx and Engels, analysing the results of the 1848-49 Revolution, explained their views on tactical questions to the members of the Party.

In answer to Marx's letter, Engels wrote on July 17, 1851 :

" The old document can only harm the prisoners by the one passage about ' excesses '—all the other passages are directed against the democrats and would make the prisoners' position more difficult only if they came before a semi-democratic jury ; but it looks as if they will be brought before a selected special or federal jury, if they are brought before any at all. And even these things had already been used again for the most part in Bürgers' document, which was drawn up right at the beginning. But in every other respect it is an enormous advantage that the thing has been published and reproduced in all the papers. The quiet isolated groups of growing Communists, quite unknown to us, which, to judge from past experiences, must be established in every part of Germany will get splendid support from it, and even the *Augsburger* article shows that the thing has produced quite a different effect from the first revelations. The way they interpret its contents shows that they have understood the ' madness ' only too well—it was in fact impossible to misunderstand it.

" Meanwhile the mad, blind onrush of feudal reaction is such that this whole scare agitation does not produce the faintest effect on the bourgeoisie. It is too funny to see how the *Kölnische Zeitung* is preaching every day now that *il faut passer par la mer rouge* [the 'red' sea must be crossed] and admitting all the mistakes of the 1848 constitutionalists. But really, with a man like Kleist-Retzow made *Oberpräsident* in Coblenz and the shameless *Kreuzzeitung* getting more and more abusive with its bad jokes and doggerel, what is the refined and sedate constitutional opposition to do! It is a pity that we have not got the *Kreuzzeitung* here. I see all sorts of extracts from it. One has no conception of the utterly low, gutter-snipe, stinkingly stupid Prussian style in which this little paper now falls upon the well-behaved, well-to-do and respectable constitutional bigwigs. If fellows like Beckerath and Co. could still be credited with a little self-respect and capacity for resistance they would certainly prefer the ill-treatment and abuse of a rascally Rhenish *Père Duchesne* and the whole Red terror to the treatment they have daily to enjoy at present from the Junkers and the *Kreuzzeitung*. . . ."

BÜRGERS, HEINRICH. Revolutionary. Collaborator in the Paris *Vorwärts* in 1844. Expelled from Paris in 1845, he settled in Cologne. When the *Neue Rheinische Zeitung* was started in 1848 (Letter 4) Bürgers was nominated to the editorial staff as the candidate of the Cologne democrats, but he only played an insignificant part on the paper. As a member of the Communist League he was arrested in May 1851 and sentenced in November 1852 at the Cologne Trial to six years' imprisonment.

12. ENGELS TO MARX

[Manchester, July *c.* 20, 1851.]

I like Miquel's letter. At least the fellow thinks, and he would no doubt turn out very well if he came abroad for a bit. His fears about the unfavourable effect our recently published document* will have on the democrats are no doubt quite justified in his district; but these primitive middle peasant democrats of Lower Saxony whose arses the *Kölnische Zeitung* has lately been kissing, offering them an alliance, are not up to much anyhow and stand far below the petty-bourgeois democrats of the big towns, by whom they are, however, dominated. And this petty-bourgeois, normal democracy, although obviously greatly annoyed by this document, is itself far too much squeezed and oppressed not to arrive much sooner, with the big bourgeoisie, at the necessity for crossing the 'red' sea. The fellows will resign themselves more and

* See previous letter.

more to the necessity for a temporary rule of terror by the proletariat :—after all it cannot last long, for the positive contents of the document are really so senseless that there can be no question of the permanent rule of such people or of the ultimate carrying out of such principles ! The big or middle peasant of Hanover, on the other hand, who has nothing but his land, whose house, land, barns, etc., are exposed to every danger by the ruin of all the insurance companies, to be foreseen in advance, and who, apart from this, has since Ernest Augustus' time already had a thorough taste of all the delights of lawful resistance—this German sturdy yeoman will take very good care not to go into the 'red' sea before he is obliged to. . . .

To return again to the effect of our document upon the democrats. Miquel should nevertheless remember that we have continuously and uninterruptedly harrassed these gentlemen in writings which were after all more or less Party manifestoes. Why all this outcry then about a programme which only summarises in a very quiet and, especially, a thoroughly impersonal way what has long ago been published already? Did our Continental followers disown us then, and commit themselves with the democrats further than Party policy and Party honour allowed? If the democrats screamed in such a revolutionary way from sheer lack of resistance, who is responsible for their lack of resistance? Not we, but at most the German Communists in Germany. And indeed that seems to be the snag. Every democrat with any intelligence must have known beforehand what he had to expect from our Party—the document could not have contained much that was new to him. If they made a temporary alliance with the Communists they were perfectly well aware of the conditions and duration of the alliance, and it would never have struck anybody but Hanoverian middle peasants and lawyers to suppose that since 1850 the Communists had been converted from the principles and policy of the *Neue Rheinische Zeitung*. Certainly Waldeck and Jacoby never allowed themselves to dream of such things. In any case no publications of this kind can do anything in the long run against " the nature of things " or against " the conception of relation," as Stirner would say, and democratic shouting and wire-pulling will soon be in full swing again and proceeding hand in hand with the Communists. And we knew long ago that the fellows will be playing some dirty tricks on the movement the next day all the same—no diplomacy can stop that.

On the other hand the fact that, as I assumed, small Communist groups are being formed everywhere on the basis of the *Manifesto* has given me great pleasure. Considering the weakness of our general staff up till now, this is just what we lacked. Soldiers can always be found if the situation is far enough developed, but it is very pleasant to have the prospect of a general staff not consisting of *Straubingers** and allowing of a larger choice than the existing one of only twenty-five men with any education at all. It would be a good thing to make a general recommendation that propaganda should be carried on among office workers. If one had to form an administration these chaps would be indispensable—they are used to hard work and intelligible bookkeeping, and commerce is the only practical school for serviceable clerks. Our lawyers, etc., are no good at it. Clerks for bookkeeping and office work, talented well-educated men for drawing up despatches, letters, documents, that is what we want. With six clerks I could organise an infinitely more simple, comprehensive and practical branch of administration than I could with sixty government councillors and financial experts. These latter cannot even write legibly and muck up all the books so that not a soul can make anything out of them. Seeing that one will be more and more obliged to prepare for this eventuality the matter is not unimportant. Besides, these office workers are used to continuous mechanical activity and make fewer demands ; it is easier to keep them from idling and to get rid of them if they are unsuitable.

¶ MIQUEL, JOHANN (1829-1901). In his youth a Communist, in the 'sixties became the leader of the National Liberals—

* *Straubingers*. See Letter 1.

the party of the big bourgeoisie in Germany. From 1890 to the end of his life he was Prussian Minister of Finance.

WALDECK (1802-70). German bourgeois politician. In 1848 he was elected to the Prussian National Assembly, where he belonged to the Left wing ; he was chairman of the commission for working out a constitution.

JACOBY, JOHANN (1805-77). Prussian politician. Bourgeois-democrat who distinguished himself by the consistency of his democracy. For this reason Marx and Engels respected him.

13. ENGELS TO MARX

[Manchester], 21 August, 1851.

. . . I have read Proudhon* half through and find your opinion greatly confirmed. His appeal to the bourgeoisie, his return to Saint Simon and a hundred other things, even in the critical section, prove that he regards the industrial class, bourgeoisie and proletariat, as really identical and only brought into opposition by the non-completion of the revolution. The pseudo-philosophic historical construction is obvious: before the revolution the industrial class-in-itself ; 1789-1848 in contradiction, negation ; then the Proudhon synthesis to wind up the whole with a flourish. The whole thing strikes me as a final attempt to retain the bourgeoisie theoretically ; our premises on the decisive historical initiative of material production, class struggle, etc., are to a large extent adopted, for the most part distorted, and upon this is based an attempt to produce by pseudo-Hegelian sleight-of-hand the appearance of a return of the proletariat within the bourgeoisie. The synthetic section I have not yet read. In the attacks upon L. Blanc, Robespierre, Rousseau, there are some nice things here and there, but taken as a whole one could read nothing more pretentiously superficial than his political criticism ; for instance, on democracy, where like the *Neue Preussische Zeitung* and the whole old historical school, he comes along counting heads and is not ashamed to construct systems from petty practical considerations worthy of a schoolboy. And what a great idea that

* Proudhon's *Idée Générale de la Révolution au* XIX *Siècle.*

power and liberty are irreconcilable contradictions and that no form of government can give *him* a sufficient moral ground for obeying it! What does one need power for at all then, by God?

14. MARX TO WEYDEMEYER

London, 11 September, 1851.

. . . I consider Mazzini's policy fundamentally wrong. By inciting Italy to a breach now he is working entirely in the interests of Austria. On the other hand he omits to appeal to that section of Italy which has been oppressed for centuries, the peasants, and thus prepares new resources for the counter-revolution. Mr. Mazzini only knows the towns with their liberal aristocracy and enlightened citizens. The material needs of the agricultural population of Italy—who like the Irish are sucked dry and systematically exhausted and stupefied—are of course too low for the heaven-in-words of his cosmopolitan-neo-catholic-ideological manifesto. But it would certainly have required some courage to have informed the bourgeoisie and aristocracy that the first step towards the independence of Italy is the complete emancipation of the peasants and the transformation of their system of semi-tenancy into free bourgeois property. Mazzini seems to consider it more revolutionary to get a loan of ten million francs than to win ten million men. I am very much afraid that in case of extreme need the Austrian government will itself alter the system of property in Italy and reform it in the "Galician" manner. . . .*

¶Marx and Engels attached great importance to the revolutionary struggle of the peasants and paid great attention to the peasant question. In his *Eighteenth Brumaire of Louis Bonaparte* (1852) Marx pointed out that with the development of capitalist conditions the interests of the peasants no longer harmonise with those of the bourgeoisie, of capital, but come into opposition to them. The peasants then "find their natural ally and

* Galician manner. See next letter.

leader in the *town proletariat*, whose task is the overthrow of the bourgeois order of society." (Chapter VII.) See also Engels' letters to Turati and to Sorge, Nos. 227, 228 of this volume.

At this time Italy was still in the manufacturing period, big industry was only just beginning. The working class was still far from having been fully expropriated and proletarianised. The town workers still possessed their own instruments of labour. On the land the small peasants and farmers carried on agriculture and industry at the same time. The proletariat had not yet become conscious of itself as a separate class and the revolutionary energy of the bourgeoisie was still unimpaired. The splitting up of Italy only arose from the foreign domination of Austria, under whose protection individual rich princes brought the country to the verge of ruin. Even the aristocracy were for unity and national independence. The unification of Italy was accomplished in a revolutionary way (Garibaldi's landing in Sicily). The House of Savoy saw how to make use of the revolution and in 1861 received the Italian Crown.

WEYDEMEYER, GEORG (died 1866). Prussian artillery officer. Writer. At first a supporter of "true socialism" he became, in 1845-46, a follower of Marx and Engels. He visited Marx in Brussels, stayed there for a time and attended Marx's lectures. There too he wrote out large parts of the manuscript of the *Deutsche Ideologie* (*German Ideology*) in a fair copy. Collaborated in socialist periodicals: the *Westphälisches Dampfboot* (*Westphalian Steamboat*) and the *Neue Rheinische Zeitung* (*New Rhenish Gazette*). In 1851 he emigrated from Germany to America and worked there as a journalist. He took part in the war against the Southern slave owners as colonel of a regiment in the Northern army.

MAZZINI, GUISEPPE (1805-72). Italian bourgeois politician who played a leading part in the bourgeois revolutionary movement (especially among the town intelligentsia and liberal aristocracy). He lived abroad as a refugee. In 1831-32 he founded "Young Italy," a revolutionary organisation aiming at the unification of Italy, which was at that time still split up into many different states. He took part in the revolutionary struggles of the year 1848 in Italy. After this he was again an *émigré* abroad (London), and there founded the European Democratic Committee, which was intended to unite the bourgeois revolutionary movements in the different countries. His republican programme demanded the independence and unity of Italy and a democratic republic ; his slogan was "*Dio i Popolo*" (God and the People). Marx criticised the inconsistent and anti-proletarian character of Mazzini's programme and carried on an energetic struggle against him and his Committee. (See Letters following and Letters 20 and 71.)

15. MARX TO ENGELS

London, 13 September, 1851.

The Italian Committee has split too. A considerable minority has resigned from it. Mazzini sorrowfully describes this event in the *Voix du Peuple* [*Voice of the People*]. The main reasons are said to be : in the first place God. They don't want God. Next, and this is more serious, they accuse Master Mazzini of working in the interests of Austria by preaching insurrection ; that is, by precipitating it. Finally, they insist on a direct appeal to the material interests of the Italian peasants, which cannot be made without attacking on the other side the material interests of the bourgeoisie and liberal aristocracy who form the main phalanx of Mazzini's supporters. This last point is very important. If Mazzini or any one else who puts himself at the head of the Italian agitation does not this time frankly and immediately transform the peasants from *métayers** into free landowners (the position of the Italian peasants is appalling ; I have now waded right through the filthy story) the Austrian government will, in case of a revolution, take refuge in Galician methods.† It has already threatened in Lloyd's "a complete change in the conditions of property holding" and "destruction of the turbulent nobility." If Mazzini's eyes are not open yet he is an ox. True, the

* *Métayer*. A share farmer under the system common in France and Italy. See Note on *mezzadria*, p 525. [*Ed. Eng. ed.*]

† "Galician methods." After the incorporation of Galicia into Austria the Austrian government abrogated a large part of the feudal privileges of the Galician aristocracy in order to play off the peasants against the rebellious aristocrats in a demagogic fashion and thus create a social basis for the exploitation of this province, which was still dominated by the big landowners. Austria had introduced a system of the bitterest national oppression in Northern Italy.

interests of the agitation have to be considered. Where is he to get his ten million francs from if he offends the bourgeosie? How is he to retain the services of the aristocracy if he has to inform them that the next question is their expropriation? These are difficulties for demagogues of the old school like himself. . . .

16. ENGELS TO MARX

Manchester, 23 September, 1851.

. . . The split among the Italians is wonderfully fine. It is splendid that such a very astute visionary as Mazzini should at last have been crossed by material considerations and that in his own country. One good result of the Italian revolution has been that there too the most isolated classes have been swept into the movement and that a new party, more radical than the old Mazzini *émigrés*, is now being formed which is gradually supplanting Mr. Mazzini.

According to newspaper reports too, *il Mazzinismo* seems to be getting into the bad books even of people who are neither constitutional nor reactionary and who are using what remains of the freedom of the press in Piedmont to make attacks on Mazzini—the bearing of which the government fails to understand. Otherwise the Italian revolution far surpasses the German in its poverty of ideas and wealth of phrases. It is fortunate that a country which instead of proletarians has practically nothing but *lazzaroni* [beggars] does at least possess *métayers*. The other reasons given by the Italian dissidents are also pleasing, and finally it is very good, too, that the one band of exiles which has hitherto remained, at least openly, unsplit, should now also be all at loggerheads. . . .

17. ENGELS TO MARX

[Manchester,] 3 December, 1851.

" *Représentants de la France, délibérez en paix !* "
[" Representatives of France, deliberate in peace ! "]

And where could the gentlemen deliberate more peacefully

than in the d'Orsay barracks, guarded by a battalion of *Chasseurs de Vincennes !**

The history of France has reached the stage of completest comedy. Could anything funnier be imagined than this travesty of the Eighteenth Brumaire carried out in a time of peace by the most insignificant man in the whole world, with the aid of discontented soldiers and, so far as one can judge at present, without meeting with any resistance whatever ?†

And how splendidly all the old asses have been caught ! The slyest fox in the whole of France, old Thiers, the smartest lawyer at the bar, M. Dupin, trapped as easily as the stark republican virtue of M. Cavignac and as the heroic talker Changarnier in the snare laid for them by the most notorious blockhead of the century. And to complete the picture, a rump parliament with Odilon Barrot as *Löwe von Calbe* and this same Odilon demanding to be imprisoned for such a breach of the constitution, but unable to succeed in getting himself hauled off to Vincennes ! The whole thing has been specially invented for the red Wolff; from now onwards only he can write the history of France. Was there ever a *coup d'état* made in the world with sillier proclamations than this one ? And the absurd Napoleonic apparatus, the anniversary of the coronation and of Austerlitz, the provocation against the consular constitution and so on—that such a thing could succeed if even for a day really does degrade our French gentlemen to an infantile level which has never been equalled.

The capture of the great spokesmen of order‡ was splendid, of little Thiers and of the bold Changarnier quite excellent. Splendid too was the session of the rump parliament in the tenth *arrondissement* with M. Berryer shouting " Long Live the Republic ! " out of the window, until in the end the whole lot

* This letter was written the day after Louis Bonaparte, President of the French Republic since December 1848, had carried out his *coup d'état*, dissolving the National Assembly and the Council of State. Louis Bonaparte was proclaimed Emperor (Napoleon III) in December 1852. [*Ed. Eng. ed.*]

† Eighteenth Brumaire (9 November, 1799). The day on which the later Emperor Napoleon I overthrew the Directory and achieved supreme power as First Consul. He was proclaimed Emperor in 1804.

‡ The Party of Order was the royalist coalition of landowners, financiers, and big industrialists by means of which Louis Napoleon had governed after becoming President in 1848. [*Ed. Eng. ed.*]

were taken and shut up with soldiers in a barracks' square. And then stupid Napoleon, who immediately packs up to move into the Tuileries. If one had plagued oneself for a whole year one could not have invented a finer comedy.

And in the evening, when stupid Napoleon had at last flung himself into the long-yearned-for bed in the Tuileries, then the silly blockhead must really have begun to wonder what he was up to. The Consulate without the First Consul? No greater internal difficulties than had been usual for the last three years, no exceptional financial stringency—even in his own purse—no coalition at the frontiers, no St. Bernard to cross, no Marengo to win! Enough to drive one to desperation, really. And now no longer even a National Assembly to bring to nought the great schemes of the misunderstood man; no, for to-day at any rate the ass is so free, so unfettered, so absolutely like the old man on the evening of the Eighteenth Brumaire, so completely unrestrained that he can't help exposing his asinine self in all directions. Appalling perspective of no resistance!

But the people, the people!—The people does not care a damn about all this business, is as pleased as a child at its boon of the franchise and will probably use it like a child too. What can come of the ridiculous elections on Sunday week if they ever happen at all? No press, no meetings, martial law in abundance, and on the top of it all the order to provide a deputy in fourteen days.

But what is to come of the whole business? "If we regard it from the standpoint of world history" a splendid subject for declamation presents itself. For instance: it remains to be seen if the Prætorian regiments of the Roman Empire, which presupposed a widely extended state organised throughout on military lines, a depopulated Italy and the absence of a modern proletariat, is possible in a geographically concentrated, thickly populated country like France, with a large industrial proletariat. Or: Louis Napoleon has no party of his own; he has trodden the Orleanists and Legitimists under foot, he must now make a turn to the Left. A turn to the Left implies an amnesty, an amnesty implies a collision, etc. Or again: universal franchise is the basis of Louis Napoleon's power, he cannot attack it, and universal franchise is *now* incompatible with a Louis Napoleon. And other similarly speculative themes which could be spun out splendidly. But after what we saw yesterday, the people cannot be relied on for anything and it really seems as if old Hegel in his grave were acting as World Spirit and directing history, ordaining most conscientiously that it should all be unrolled twice over, once as a great tragedy and once as a wretched farce, with Caussidière for Danton, Louis Blanc for Robespierre, Barthélemy for St. Just, Flocon for Carnot, and the mooncalf [Louis Napoleon] with the first dozen debt-encumbered lieutenants to hand for the Little Corporal [Napoleon I] and his Round Table of marshals. And so we should already have arrived at the Eighteenth Brumaire.

The behaviour of the people of Paris was childishly stupid. It's not our business : if the president and the assembly are murdering each other—what does it matter to us ! But that the army should take on itself to present France with a government—and with such a government into the bargain—that surely does concern them, and the mob will begin to wonder what sort of a " free " universal suffrage this is which it is now to exercise " for the first time since 1804 ! "

How much further the World Spirit, who is obviously very much annoyed with humanity, will conduct this farce, whether we shall see Consulate, Empire, Restoration, etc., passing before our eyes in the course of a year, whether the Napoleonic dynasty too will have to be thrashed in the streets of Paris before it becomes impossible in France, the devil only knows. But it looks to me as if the thing would take a remarkably crazy turn and as if the *Crapauds** were going to meet with a marvellous humiliation.

Granted even that Louis Napoleon consolidates himself for the moment, such silly nonsense cannot last after all, even if the French have sunk to the lowest possible depths. But what then ? There is damned little Red in the outlook, that is pretty clear, and if M. Blanc and Ledru-Rollin packed up their

* *Crapauds*. Literally toads. Slang nickname for the French bourgeois used by Marx and Engels.

baggage yesterday afternoon* they can only unpack it again to-day. The thunderous voice of the people has not recalled them as yet.

¶This letter gives an extraordinarily clear and correct estimate of Louis Bonaparte's *coup d'état* on December 2, 1851, which was confirmed by subsequent events. In a letter written to Marx on April 26, 1853, Engels gave the following description of the economic consequences of Napoleon's *coup d'état*:

"... In France commerce already seems to be on the downgrade. There is a special decline in the direct imports of cotton from America. The American exports are as follows, from September 1 to April 6 of each year:

	1853	*1852*	*1851*	*1850*
To England ..	1,100,000	930,000	757,000	592,000
To France ..	257,000	302,000	246,000	192,000
To all other countries ..	204,000	189,000	163,000	105,000

"So that France is the *only* country which, in spite of the enormous American harvest, has taken *less* than last year and scarcely more than in the year of political depression, 1851, when order and society were about to be engulfed in the abyss of socialism. In 1852 the imports show the temporary magical effect of the *coup d'état*: 1853 shows the reverse. Something was always being sent from Liverpool to Havre, but no longer so much as formerly. In other respects too, French industry does not seem to be exactly flourishing. This time the thing seems to be really serious and to be particularly due to the fact that French goods are being supplanted in the foreign markets by home manufactures. The enormous expulsion of workers in 1851-52 is beginning to bear fruit; I am convinced that it has very specially contributed to the extension and improvement of the English and American manufacture of Parisian goods, bronzes, etc. To-day law and order are still driving the proletariat across the frontiers with impunity, though a thousand times less than formerly. Even in a time of

* In order to return to France from London where they were living as political refugees.

the most perfect peace this method of government by the continual exploitation of conspiracy, with its perpetually renewed banishment of proletarians, would be bound to drive French industry to the devil; the English and the Yankees certainly know how to take advantage of the useful side of it!"

The collapse of 1870 was the immediate result of the events of the years 1850-51. In estimating the political situation resulting from the *coup d'état* Engels wrote on December 11, 1851: "... it cannot be denied that if, during a revolutionary development, the revolutionary party begins to let decisive turning points pass without having a word to say, or if it intervenes without gaining the victory, that party can be fairly certainly regarded as having gone to pieces for a time. Witness the insurrections after Thermidor* and after 1830; and the gentlemen who are now saying so loudly that 'the real people is only awaiting its opportunity' are in danger of gradually landing in the same boat as the impotent Jacobins of 1795-99 and the Republicans of 1831-39 and greatly discrediting themselves."

Later, in his notes on *The Dialectics of Nature and Natural Science*, 1873-76, Engels wrote regarding the events of 1848 and 1851:

"In history it is in all the critical epochs of leading nations that movement through contradiction comes out really clearly. At such moments a nation only has the choice between two horns of a dilemma: Either—Or! And indeed the question is always put in a totally different way from that desired by the amateurs of politics among the philistines of every period. Even the liberal German philistine of 1848 found himself in 1849 suddenly, unexpectedly and against his own will faced by the question: Return to the old reaction in a more acute form, or, advance of the revolution to a republic, perhaps even to the one and indivisible republic with a socialistic background. He did not stop long to think and helped to create the Manteuffel reaction as the fruit of German liberalism. In just the same way the French bourgeois of 1851 found himself faced by a dilemma which he had certainly never expected—namely: Caricature of empire, Prætorian rule, and France exploited by

* One of the months in the calendar of the French Revolution. On the 9th Thermidor (July 27), 1794, the dictatorship of the petty bourgeoisie (Jacobins) was overthrown by the bourgeois counter-revolution. (See Letter 198 of this volume.)

a gang of blackguards, or, a social-democratic republic. And he prostrated himself before the gang of blackguards so that he might continue his exploitation of the workers under their protection." (*Marx-Engels Archiv.*, Bd. II, S 190.)

For the social basis of Bonapartism see Marx : *The Eighteenth Brumaire of Louis Bonaparte*, and Engels : *The Housing Question.*

THIERS, LOUIS ADOLPHE (1797-1877). French historian, bourgeois politician and business man. From 1832 onwards Minister in Louis-Philippe's government. In 1871 head of the Versailles Government, the butchers of the Paris Commune. Until May 24, 1873, President of the Third Republic. In Marx's *Civil War in France* he is characterised as " the complete intellectual expression of the class corruption of the French bourgeoisie," " a master of petty government knavery, a virtuoso in perjury and treachery," " consistent only in his greed for riches and his hatred for those who produce them."

DUPIN, ANDRÉ MARIE J. J. (1783-1865). Lawyer and business man. In 1830 Louis Philippe appointed him Public Prosecutor in the Court of Appeal. He was an opponent of Thiers not on principle but from rivalry. For eight years from 1832 he was president of the Chamber of Deputies. On February 24, 1848, having faithfully served Louis Philippe, he recognised the Republic, declaring that for a long time already the administration of justice had been conducted in the name of the French people. But in 1851 he was one of the first to support Bonaparte when he saw that the latter's success was assured. After the *coup d'état* of December 2 he retained his position as Public Prosecutor.

CAVAIGNAC, LOUIS EUGÈNE (1802-57). Bourgeois-democratic general. Executioner of the Parisian proletariat in the year 1848. He made his military career in Africa (he was Governor of the French Colony of Algiers). In 1848 he was Minister for War in the Provisional Government. In the June days of 1848 he organised the brutal suppression of the Paris workers' rising, when artillery was employed in street fighting for the first time. He unsuccessfully opposed Louis Bonaparte in the Presidential elections.

CHANGARNIER, NICOLAS (1793-1877). French general, General Governor of Paris after the February Revolution of 1848, then member of the National Assembly. As he was an Orleanist, Napoleon removed him in 1851 from his post as

Commander-in-Chief of the National Guard and of the military division of Paris.

BARROT, ODILLON (1791-1873). Lawyer and bourgeois politician. Made Premier—at the head of the " Party of Order "—for the first year after Louis Bonaparte became President in 1848.

LÖWE VON KALBE (1814-66). A doctor. In 1848 became a member of the Frankfurt Parliament, in which he belonged to the Left. In 1849 elected as first Vice-President. When the Left " rump parliament " transferred itself to Stuttgart he was elected as its Speaker. After the revolution he emigrated.

WOLFF, FERDINAND—" Red Wolff." Nicknamed " Red " from his red beard and radical views. A revolutionary close to Marx, a member of the editorial staff of the *Neue Rheinische Zeitung*. Emigrated and lived in England. In the year Marx died Wolff was head of an educational institution.

18. MARX TO WEYDEMEYER

London, 5 March, 1852.

... Your article against Heinzen, which Engels unfortunately sent me too late, is very good, both brutal and subtle—a combination which should be found in any polemic worthy of the name. I gave this article to Ernest Jones, and enclosed you will find a communication for you from him intended for publication. As Jones writes very illegibly, with abbreviations, and as I assume that you are not an out-and-out Englishman as yet, I am sending you together with the original a copy made by my wife, and at the same time the German translation, as you must have them both printed side by side, original and translation. After the letter from Jones you can make the following addition: With regard to George Julian Harney, who is also one of Herr Heinzen's authorities, Harney published our *Communist Manifesto* in English in his *Red Republican* with a note saying that it was " the most revolutionary document ever given to the world," and in his *Democratic Review* he translated the articles I wrote in the *Neue Rheinische Zeitung* on the French revolution, Heinzen's " discarded " wisdom. In an article on Louis Blanc he refers his readers to these articles as the "true criticism" of the French affair. For the rest, in England there is no need to support oneself only upon the "extremists." If a member of Parliament in England becomes a Minister he has to be re-elected, so *Disraeli*, the new Chancellor of the Exchequer, writes to his electors on March 1:

"We shall endeavour to put an end to a class struggle which in recent years has had such a harmful effect on the well-being of this kingdom."

On which *The Times* comments on March 2: "If anything could divide the classes in this country up to a point which would make further reconciliation impossible, it would be a tax on foreign corn."

And in case a chap like Heinzen, with his ignorant faith in "characteristics," should imagine that the aristocracy are *for* and the bourgeoisie *against* corn laws, because the former want "*monopoly*" and the latter "*freedom*"—a worthy of this sort only sees contradictions in this abstract form—it is to be noted that in the eighteenth century the English aristocracy were for "freedom" (of trade) and the bourgeoisie for "monopoly"—the same relative position that we find at this very moment between these two classes in Prussia with regard to "corn laws." The *Neue Preussische Zeitung* is the most violent free-trader.

Finally, in your place I should in general remark to the democratic gentlemen that they would do better first to acquaint themselves with bourgeois literature before they presume to yap out their contradictions of it. For instance, these gentlemen should study the historical works of Thierry, Guizot, John Wade, etc., in order to enlighten themselves as to the past "history of classes." Before they try to criticise the criticism of political economy they should acquaint themselves with the first foundations of political economy. One has only to open Ricardo's great work, for example, to find these words on the first page: "The produce of the earth—all that is derived from its surface by the united application of labour, machinery and capital—is divided among three classes of the community, namely, the proprietor of the land, the owner of the stock or capital necessary for its cultivation, and the labourers by whose industry it is cultivated."*

That bourgeois society in the United States has not yet developed far enough to make the class struggle obvious and comprehensible is most strikingly proved by *C. H. Carey* (of Philadelphia), the only American economist of importance. He attacks *Ricardo*, the most classic representative (interpreter) of the bourgeoisie and the most stoical adversary of the proletariat, as a man whose works are an arsenal for anarchists, socialists, and all the enemies of bourgeois society. He reproaches not only him but Malthus, Mill, Say, Torrens, Wakefield, McCulloch, Senior, Wakley, R. Jones, etc., the master-minds among the economists of Europe, with rending society and preparing civil war because they show that the economic bases of the different classes are bound to give rise to a necessary and ever-growing antagonism. He tries to refute them, not indeed like the fatuous Heinzen by deriving the existence of classes from the existence of *political* privileges and *monopolies*, but by attempting to make out that *economic* conditions—rent (landed property), *profit* (capital), and wages (wage labour) instead of being conditions of struggle and antagonism are rather conditions of co-operation and harmony. All he proves, of course, is that he is taking the "undeveloped" conditions of the United States for "normal conditions."

And now as to myself, no credit is due to me for discovering the existence of classes in modern society nor yet the struggle between them. Long before me bourgeois historians had described the historical development of this class struggle and bourgeois economists the economic anatomy of the classes. What I did that was new was to prove: (1) that the *existence of classes* is only bound up with *particular, historic phases in the development of production*; (2) that the class struggle necessarily leads to the *dictatorship of the proletariat*; (3) that this dictatorship itself only constitutes the transition to the *abolition of all classes* and to a *classless society*.

Ignorant louts like Heinzen who deny not merely the class

* David Ricardo, *On the Principles of Political Economy and Taxation*. 1817. Author's Preface.

struggle, but even the existence of classes, only prove that, despite all their blood-curdling yelps and the humanitarian airs they give themselves, they regard the social conditions under which the bourgeoisie rules as the final product, the *non plus ultra* [final limit] of history, and that they are only the slaves of the bourgeoisie. And the less these clowns themselves understand even of the greatness and temporary necessity of the bourgeois regime the more disgusting is their servitude.

From the above notes take anything you think suitable. For the rest, Heinzen has adopted "centralisation" from us in place of his "federative republic." When the views which we are now spreading about the classes have become platitudes and a part of the furniture of the "ordinary human mind," then the lout will announce them with a lot of noise as the latest product of "his own penetration" and start barking against our further development. So by "his own penetration" he yelped against the Hegelian philosophy as long as it was progressive. Now he is feeding himself on the stale fragments of it which have been spewed out undigested by Ruge.

¶Weydemeyer (Note to Letter 14) had written an article against Heinzen in an American periodical, *The Democrat.* Marx's letter deals with this article. In the letter which Marx enclosed from Ernest Jones to Weydemeyer, Jones wrote that it was impossible for anyone with the faintest knowledge of English conditions to ignore the class war.

HEINZEN, KARL (1809-80). A doctor by profession. Bourgeois democrat. Editor of several German-American papers. Opponent of Marx and Engels. A narrow-minded petty bourgeois who held that the despotic powers of the German princes were the root of all evil—hence he got the nickname of "the prince-killer." He regarded the "class struggle" as a mad idea of the Communists. In support of his views he had cited the Chartist leader, Ernest Jones.

JONES, ERNEST (1819-69). [Son of a British officer]. Educated in Germany. Called to the Bar. Became a Chartist in 1846. A first-class orator who rapidly became famous. At the Chartist Convention of 1848 he was a delegate from Halifax and was elected a member of the Executive Committee of the Chartist Party. In July 1848 he was sentenced to two years' imprisonment for his revolutionary activities. After his release in 1850 he became the leader of the Left wing of the Chartists. From 1852 onwards he edited the Chartist *People's Paper*, of which the first number appeared in May 1852. (See Letter 31.) The paper continued until 1858. [See also Note (Schulze-Delitzsch) p. 149.] Jones's best period was 1851-53 when he was under the influence of Marx. (For Jones and Marx's breach with him see Letters 35, 36, 41.)

HARNEY, GEORGE JULIAN (1817-97). Radical Chartist leader (1842-48). Editor of the Chartist paper *The Northern Star*. In this capacity he came into close connection with Marx and Engels. He came out in favour of the use of force ("physical force man") and a revolutionary representation of the people. At the Chartist Convention he opposed the exclusive use of legal methods of struggle. It was Harney who maintained the contact between the Chartists and the Continental workers and revolutionaries.

["We were in contact with the revolutionary section of the English Chartists through Julian Harney, editor of the central organ of the movement, *The Northern Star*, to which I contributed," writes Engels in his preface (1885) to the *Cologne Trial*. Besides the articles contributed by Engels (1846-48) there was also published in *The Northern Star* (July 25, 1846) an *Address of the German Democratic Communists of Brussels to Mr. Feargus O'Connor*, congratulating him on his success in the Nottingham election and signed by Marx, Engels and Ph. Gigot. In 1845 Harney founded a London branch of the international society known as the Fraternal Democrats (See Letter 1): Marx and Engels both spoke at a meeting organised by this society in Drury Lane, London, on November 29, 1847, the anniversary of the Polish revolution of 1830. Harney was a member of the Communist Correspondence Committee set up in London. Harney and Jones met Marx in Paris in March 1848 after Marx's expulsion from Belgium. The first English translation of the *Communist Manifesto*, to which Marx refers above, was published in *The Red Republican* in 1850. Owing to proceedings taken against it under the Stamp Act, this paper changed its name to *The Friend of the People* in December 1850.] [*Ed. Eng. ed.*]

Later on Harney became a member of the First International but was not further prominent politically. In his letter to Engels on February 23, 1851, Marx gives the following characterisation of Harney : " He likes theatrical effect. He is unquestionably eager for applause, I will not say vain. There is no doubt that he is himself deeply dominated by phrases and develops a very rich assortment of emotional gas. Is all the more deeply involved in democratic rubbish because he likes to take the floor. He has a double spirit : one made for him by Friedrich Engels, another which is all his own. The first is a kind of strait-jacket to him. The other is himself naked and unadorned."

(For Marx and Engels on the Chartist movement see Note to Letter 31.)

19. ENGELS TO MARX

[Manchester], 24 September, 1852.

The *crapauds** are doing well. With the temporary prosperity, and prospects of the glory of an empire, the workers seem to have become completely bourgeois after all. It will take a severe chastisement by crises if they are to become good for anything again *soon*. If the next crisis is a mild one Bonaparte may be able to steer through it. But it looks as if it was going to be damned serious. No crisis is worse than one in which over-speculation in production is slowly developing, for it requires as many years to develop its results as a crisis in the trade in products and stocks and shares requires months. And with old Wellington has been buried not only the common sense of old England but old England itself, in the person of its sole surviving representative. What remains are inconsequent sporting characters like Derby and Jewish swindlers like Disraeli—who are as much caricatures of the old Tories as Monsieur Bonaparte is of his uncle.

¶WELLINGTON, DUKE OF (1769-1852). Fought in India 1796-1805, first in Mysore and then in the Mahratta War. Led

* See footnote, Letter 17.

forces which defeated Napoleon's armies in Spain and Portugal 1808-14. Commanded allied forces at Waterloo, 1815, where Napoleon's army was defeated. Prime Minister 1828-30. Opposed (franchise) Reform Bill but withdrew opposition when he saw it was hopeless. Opposed abolition of flogging in the army. Organised military forces against the great Chartist demonstrations in April 1848. [*Ed. Eng. ed.*]

Of Wellington Engels had written in a letter to Marx on April 11, 1851 :

" I am also gradually beginning to get clearer about Wellington. A self-willed, tough, obstinate Englishman with all the good sense and all the resourcefulness of his nation ; slow in his deliberations, cautious ; never, despite the most colossal luck, reckoning on a lucky accident ; he would be a genius if common sense were not incapable of soaring into genius. Everything he does is a model, nothing a masterpiece. A general like himself might have been created for the English army, in which every soldier, every sub-lieutenant is a little Wellington in his own sphere."

20. Marx to Engels

[London] 23 February, 1853.

. . . You have seen that Kossuth, through an American filibuster, Captain Mayne Reid, has disowned his alleged Milan proclamation. Now yesterday Szemere writing to me from Paris says he knows *positively* that the proclamation was *authentic*. As a matter of fact that was already obvious from its contents. The " *Leader* " (Mazzinist) " deems it his duty to caution his readers that this affair lies entirely between Mr. Kossuth and Mr. Mazzini and that the latter is *absent* from England."* You will have read Della Rocca's declaration in the *Daily News* yourself—aimed directly against Agostini and indirectly also against Kossuth. The noble pair of brothers seems to be divided. Kossuth is as false as he is cowardly. . . .

While the Milan affair is a wretched finale to Mazzini's eternal conspiracies and while I am strongly of opinion that he has damaged himself personally, it seems equally certain to

* Quoted in English.

me that this event is on the whole favourable to the revolutionary movement. Especially because of the brutal way in which the [Austrians]* plunder. If Radetsky† had followed Strassoldo's example, praised the citizens of Milan for their "exhibition of order," described the whole thing as the miserable *putsch* of a few "miscreants" and in token of his confidence allowed the reins to be slackened in appearance, then the revolutionary party would have been discredited before God and the world. But by introducing a complete system of plunder he turns Italy into that "crater of revolution" which Mazzini has never been able to conjure forth by his declamations.

And another thing. Would any one of us have believed that after their four years of victory, war preparations and boasting, the reactionary forces would feel so immeasurably feeble that they would let fly a regular scream of terror at the first *putsch*? The faith of these fellows in the revolution is unshakable. They have now once more provided the whole world with evidence of their insecurity. While the *émigrés* are in reality completely bankrupt and can't say boo to a goose, their power is being trumpeted through all the government newspapers and the belief sown that a web of conspiracies is being woven around good citizens on every side.

¶The Milan revolt took place in 1853; it was only a flash in the pan and ended unsuccessfully.

KOSSUTH, LUDWIG (1802-94). Hungarian nationalist. Dictator in the year 1848. Chairman of the Committee of National Defence. After the defeat at Temeszvar he abdicated his dictatorial powers to General Gorgei (August 11, 1849). Emigrated to England. Marx accuses this hero of the bourgeoisie of cowardice, because after the failure of the revolution he disavowed his proclamations calling for revolution. For the attitude of Marx after the defeat of the Paris Commune see *The Civil War in France* and Letters 155, 160, etc.

* Paper damaged here.

† Radetsky. Field-Marshal commanding the Austrian forces. [*Ed. Eng. ed.*]

21. ENGELS TO MARX

[Manchester, *about* 18 May, 1853].

Yesterday I read the book on Arabian inscriptions which I spoke to you about. It is not uninteresting stuff, although the parson and Bible apologist peeps out everywhere in a revolting way. His greatest triumph is that he is able to demonstrate a few blunders made by *Gibbon* in ancient geography and from this to conclude that Gibbon's theology is also to be rejected. The thing is called : *The Historical Geography of Arabia*, by the Reverend Charles Forster. The best that one gets out of it is that :

(1) The alleged genealogy of Noah, Abraham, etc., given in Genesis is a fairly exact enumeration of the then existing Bedouin tribes according to the greater or less degree of kinship between their dialects, etc. It is well known that the Bedouin tribes to this day always call themselves Beni Saled, Beni Jussuf, etc., that is, the sons of so-and-so. This nomenclature, arising from the old patriarchal form of existence, finally results in that sort of genealogy. The enumeration in Genesis is more or less confirmed by the old geographers, while more modern travellers prove that the old names still mostly exist in an altered dialect. But all this reveals the fact that the Jews themselves are nothing more than a small Bedouin tribe like the rest —brought into opposition to the other Bedouins by local conditions, agriculture, etc.

(2) With regard to the great Arab invasion which we spoke about before : the Bedouins, just like the Mongols, made periodical invasions ; the Assyrian and Babylonian empires were founded by tribes of Bedouins on the same spot as was later the Khilafat of Baghdad. The founders of the Babylonian Empire, the Chaldeans, still exist in the same district under the same name, Beni Chaled. The rapid establishment of great cities, Nineveh and Babylon, took place in exactly the same way as the creation, only 300 years ago, of similar gigantic cities—Agra, Delhi, Lahore, Multan—in East India, as a result of the Afghan or Tartar invasions. This deprives the Mohammedan invasion of much of its distinctive character.

(3) Where they settled down, in the South-West, the Arabs seem to have been just as civilised a people as the Egyptians, Assyrians, etc. ; their buildings prove that. This also explains much in the Mohammedan invasion. So far as the religious swindle is concerned, from the ancient inscriptions in the South, in which the old national Arab tradition of monotheism, of which the Hebrew tradition is only a *small part*, still predominates (as among the American Indians), it appears that Mohammed's religious revolution, like *every* religious movement, was *formally a reaction*, an alleged return to the old, the simple.

It is now perfectly clear to me that the so-called sacred writings of the Jews are nothing more than the record of the old Arabian religious and tribal tradition, modified by the early separation of the Jews from their tribally related but nomadic neighbours. The circumstance that on the Arabian side Palestine is surrounded by nothing but desert, Bedouin land, explains the separate development. But the old Arabian inscriptions and traditions and the Koran, added to the facility with which all the genealogies, etc., can now be unravelled, prove that the main content was Arabian, or rather Semitic in general—in the same relation as our German heroic sagas bear to the Edda.

22. MARX TO ENGELS

London, 2 June, 1853.

About the Hebrews and Arabians your letter interested me very much. For the rest : (1) A *general* relationship can be proved among all Oriental tribes, between the settlement of one section of the tribe and the continuance of the other in nomadic life, since history began. (2) In Mohammed's time the trade route from Europe to Asia had been considerably modified and the cities of Arabia, which took a great part in the trade to India, etc., were in a state of commercial decay ; this in any case contributed to the impulse. (3) As to religion, the question resolves itself into the general and therefore easily answered one: why does the history of the East *appear* as a history of religions?

On the formation of Oriental cities one can read nothing more brilliant, vivid and striking than old François Bernier (nine years physician to Aurengzebe): *Voyages contenant la description des états du Grand Mogol, etc.* [*Travels Containing a Description of the States of the Great Mogul, etc.*]. He also describes the military system, the way these great armies were fed, etc., very well. On these two points he remarks, among other things: "The cavalry forms the principal section, the infantry is not so big as is generally rumoured, unless all the servants and people from the bazaars or markets who follow the army are confused with the real fighting force; for in that case I could well believe that they would be right in putting the number of men in the army accompanying the king alone at 200,000 or 300,000 and sometimes even more, when for example it is certain that he will be a long time absent from the principal town. And this will not appear so very astonishing to one who knows the strange encumbrance of tents, kitchens, clothes, furniture and quite frequently even of women, and consequently also the elephants, camels, oxen, horses, porters, foragers, provision sellers, merchants of all kinds and servitors which these armies carry in their wake; or to one who understands the particular state and government of the country, namely that the *king is the sole and only proprietor of all the land** in the kingdom, from which it follows by a certain necessary consequence that the whole of a *capital city** like Delhi or Agra lives almost entirely on the army and is therefore obliged to follow the king if he takes the field for any length of time. For these towns are and cannot be anything like a Paris, *being properly speaking nothing but military camps*,* a little better and more conveniently situated than in the open country."

On the occasion of the march of the Great Mogul into Kashmir with an army of 400,000 men, etc., he says: "The difficulty is to understand whence and how such a great army, such a great number of men and animals, can subsist in the field. For this it is only necessary to suppose, what is perfectly

* Underlined by Marx.

true, that the Indians are very sober and very simple in their food, and that of all that great number of horsemen not the tenth nor even the twentieth part eats meat during the march. So long as they have their *kicheri*, or mixture of rice and other vegetables over which when it is cooked they pour melted butter, they are satisfied. Further it is necessary to know that camels have extreme endurance of work, hunger and thirst, live on little and eat anything, and that as soon as the army has arrived the camel drivers lead them to graze in the open country where they eat everything they can find. Moreover, the same merchants who keep the bazaars in Delhi are forced to maintain them in the country too, likewise the small merchants, etc. . . . And finally with regard to forage, all these poor folk go roaming on all sides in the villages to buy and to earn something, and their great and common resort is to scrape whole fields with a sort of small trowel, to crush or cleanse the small herb which they have scratched up and to bring it to sell to the army. . . ."*

Bernier rightly considers that the basic form of all phenomena in the East—he refers to Turkey, Persia, Hindustan—is to be found in the fact that *no private property in land existed.* This is the real key, even to the Oriental heaven.

¶BERNIER, FRANÇOIS (1625-88), of whose seventeenth-century French work Marx here makes such brilliant use, travelled in Syria and Egypt before settling for twelve years in India as physician to the great Mogul Emperor—Aurengzebe. In 1685 he visited England. He was well known in the literary circles of Paris in Louis XIV's time. [*Ed. Eng. ed.*]

23. ENGELS TO MARX

[Manchester,] 6 June, [1853.]

The absence of property in land is indeed the key to the whole of the East. Here lies its political and religious history.

* Quoted from the French.

But how does it come about that the Orientals do not arrive at landed property, even in its feudal form? I think it is mainly due to the climate, together with the nature of the soil, especially with the great stretches of desert which extend from the Sahara straight across Arabia, Persia, India and Tartary up to the highest Asiatic plateau. Artificial irrigation is here the first condition of agriculture and this is a matter either for the communes, the provinces or the central government. And an Oriental government never had more than three departments: finance (plunder at home), war (plunder at home and abroad), and public works (provision for reproduction). The British government in India has administered numbers 1 and 2 in a rather more formal manner and dropped number 3 entirely, and Indian agriculture is being ruined. Free competition discredits itself there completely. This artificial fertilisation of the land, which immediately ceased when the irrigation system fell into decay, explains the otherwise curious fact that whole stretches which were once brilliantly cultivated are now waste and bare (Palmyra, Petra, the ruins in the Yemen, districts in Egypt, Persia and Hindustan); it explains the fact that one single devastating war could depopulate a country for centuries and strip it of its whole civilisation. Here too, I think, comes in the destruction of the Southern Arabian trade before Mohammed, which you very rightly regard as one of the chief factors in the Mohammedan revolution. I do not know the trade history of the first six centuries after Christ thoroughly enough to be able to judge how far general material world conditions caused the trade routes through Persia to the Black Sea and through the Persian Gulf to Syria and Asia Minor to be preferred to the route over the Red Sea. But in any case the relative security of the caravans in the ordered Persian Empire of the Sassanids was not without considerable effect, while between the years 200 and 600 the Yemen was almost continuously subjugated, invaded and plundered by the Abyssinians. The cities of Southern Arabia, which were still flourishing in the time of the Romans, were sheer ruined wastes in the seventh century; within five hundred years the neighbouring Bedouins had adopted purely mythical, fabulous traditions of their origin (see the Koran and the Arabian historian Novaïri), and the alphabet in which the inscriptions in that part are written was almost totally unknown, *although there was no other*, so that even *writing* had actually fallen into oblivion. Things of this sort imply, besides a " superseding " caused by some kind of general trade conditions, some absolutely direct and violent destruction which can only be explained by the Ethiopian invasion. The expulsion of the Abyssinians took place about forty years before Mohammed and was obviously the first act of the awakening Arabian national consciousness, which was also spurred by Persian invasions from the North, pushing forward almost to Mecca. I am only starting on the history of Mohammed himself in the next few days ; up till now, however, the movement has seemed to me to have the character of a Bedouin reaction against the settled but degenerate fellahin of the towns, who at that time had also become very decadent in their religion, mingling a corrupt nature-cult with corrupt Judaism and Christianity.

Old Bernier's things are really very fine. It is a real delight once more to read something by a sober old clear-headed Frenchman, who keeps hitting the nail on the head without appearing to notice it. . . .

24. MARX TO ENGELS.

London, 14 June, 1853.

Carey, the American national economist, has published a new book, *Slavery at Home and Abroad.* Under 'slavery' are here included all forms of servitude, wage slavery, etc. He has sent me his book and has quoted me repeatedly (from the *Tribune*). Sometimes as " a recent English writer," sometimes as " Correspondence of the *New York Tribune*." I told you before that in this man's previously published works the " harmony " of the economic foundations of the bourgeois system was described and all the mischief was attributed to superfluous interference by the State. The State was his bogey. Now he is singing another tune. The root of all evil is the centralising effect of big industry. But this centralising effect is England's fault again, because she turns herself into the workshop of the world and forces all other countries back to the rudest agriculture, divorced from manufacture. For the crimes of England the Ricardo-Malthus theory and especially Ricardo's theory of ground rent are in their turn responsible. The necessary consequences alike of Ricardo's theory and of industrial centralisation would be Communism. And in order to avoid all this, to oppose centralisation by localisation and a combination of factories and agriculture scattered all over the country, the final recommendation of our ultra free-trader is—*protective tariffs*. In order to escape the effects of bourgeois industry, for which he makes England responsible, he resorts like a true Yankee to hastening this development in America itself by artificial means. His opposition to England, moreover, throws him into *Sismondian* praise of the petty bourgeoisie of Switzerland, Germany, China, etc. This is the same fellow who used to sneer at France for its likeness to China. The only thing of positive interest in the book is the comparison between the former English Negro slavery in Jamaica, etc., and the Negro slavery of the United States. He shows that the main body of Negroes in Jamaica, etc., always consisted of newly imported barbarians, as under English treatment the Negroes were not only unable to maintain their population but lost two-thirds of the number annually imported ; the present generation of Negroes in America, on the other hand, is a native product, more or less Yankee-ised, English speaking, etc., and therefore *fit for emancipation.*

The *Tribune* is of course trumpeting Carey's book with all its might. Both indeed have this in common, that under the guise of Sismondian philanthropic socialistic anti-industrialism they represent the Protectionists, *i.e.*, the industrial bourgeoisie of America. This also explains the secret why the *Tribune* in spite of all its " isms " and socialistic humbug, can be the " leading journal " in the United States.

Your article on Switzerland was of course a direct smack at the leader in the *Tribune* (against centralisation, etc.), and *their* Carey. I have continued this hidden warfare in a first article on India, in which the destruction of the native industry by England is described as *revolutionary*. This will be very shocking to them. For the rest the whole rule of Britain in India was swinish, and is to this day.

The stationary character of this part of Asia—despite all the aimless movement on the political surface—is fully explained by two mutually dependent circumstances: (1) the public works were the business of the central government; (2) beside these the whole empire, not counting the few larger towns, was resolved into *villages*, which possessed a completely separate organisation and formed a little world in themselves. . . .

These idyllic republics, which jealously guarded only the *boundaries of their village* against the neighbouring village, still exist in a fairly perfect form in the North-western parts of India which have but recently fallen into English hands. I do not think one could imagine a more solid foundation for the stagnation of Asiatic despotism. And however much the English may have Irelandised the country, the breaking up of those stereotyped primitive forms was the *sine qua non* [essential condition] for Europeanisation. The tax-gatherer alone was not the man to achieve this. The destruction of their archaic industry was necessary in order to deprive the villages of their self-supporting character.

In Bali, an island on the east coast of Java, this Hindu organisation, together with Hindu religion, is still complete—its traces, moreover, like those of Hindu influence, are to be found throughout Java. As to the *question of property*, this is a very *vexed question* among the English writers on India. In the broken hill-country south of Crishna, property in land and soil does seem to have existed. In Java, on the other hand, Sir Stamford Raffles, former *English* Governor of Java, states in his *History of Java* that the sovereign was absolute landlord of the whole surface of the land "where rent to any considerable amount was attainable." In any case it seems to have been the Mahommedans who first mainly established the principle of "no property in land" throughout the whole of Asia.

About the villages mentioned above I notice also that they

already figure in Manu* and that the basis of the whole organisation is according to him : ten under a superior collector, then a hundred and then a thousand.

¶Besides a scathing account of a parliamentary debate on India (June 3) Marx wrote his three articles on India for the *New York Tribune* at this time : *The British Rule in India* (June 10), *The East India Company—Its History and Results* (June 24), *The Future Results of British Rule in India* (July 22). In these articles he exposed not only the horrors and brutalities of British rule, but the revolutionary rôle which the development of capitalism had to play in India. [*Ed. Eng. ed.*]

CAREY, HENRY (1793-1879). American economist, originally a bookseller. Opponent of Ricardo's theory of rent ; at first a free-trader, later a protectionist. For his economic theory see also Letters 129, 131 of this volume.

25. MARX TO ENGELS

London, 27 July, 1854.

. . . A book that has interested me very much is Thierry's *Histoire de la Formation et des Progrès du Tiers état* (*History of the Formation and Progress of the Third Estate*), 1853. Remarkable how indignant this gentleman—the father of the " class-struggle " in French historical writing—waxes in his preface at the " new " writers who now see an antagonism between the bourgeoisie and the proletariat also, and would even detect traces of this opposition in the history of the third estate before 1789. He takes a lot of trouble to prove that the third estate includes all ranks and conditions except the clergy and nobility, and that the bourgeoisie plays its part as the representative of all these other elements. He quotes, for instance, from the reports of the Venetian Embassy : " Those who are called the estates of the realm are of three orders of individuals : the clergy, the nobility, and the remaining order of those

* The Code of Manu. The laws of ancient Hindu Society (Brahmanic). [*Ed. Eng. ed.*]

persons who by common consent may be called the *people.*" * If M. Thierry had read our things he would know that the definite opposition of the bourgeoisie to the people naturally only begins when the bourgeoisie ceases to be opposed to the clergy and nobility as the third estate. As to the " roots in history," " of an antagonism *born only yesterday*,"* his book provides the best proof that these " roots " came into existence as soon as the third estate came into existence. This critic—otherwise clever in his own way—would be obliged to conclude from the *Senatus populusque Romanus* [Senate and people of Rome] that there was never any other opposition in Rome except that between the Senate and the people. What has interested me is to see in the documents he quotes that the word " *catalla, capitalia* "—capital—appears with the rise of the communes.† Moreover, he has proved against his will that nothing did more to retard the French bourgeoisie in their victory than the fact that they did not decide until 1789 to make common cause with the peasants. He describes well, if not as a connected whole : (1) How from the first, or at least after the rise of the towns, the French bourgeoisie gets too much of its influence by constituting itself the parliament, the bureaucracy, etc., and not as in England merely through commerce and industry. This is certainly still characteristic even of France at the present day. (2) From his account can be excellently demonstrated how the class arises, as the different forms in which its main gravity lies at different times, and the various fractions which gain influence through these forms, break down. This series of metamorphoses, leading up to the domination of the class, has never in my opinion—at any rate so far as the material is concerned—been thus presented before. Unfortunately, in dealing with the corporations, guilds, etc.—with the forms, in short, in which the industrial bourgeoisie developed—he has confined himself almost entirely to general and generally known phrases, although here too he alone knows the

* Underlined by Marx. Quoted in Italian.

† " *Commune* was the name taken, in France, by the nascent towns even before they had conquered from their feudal lords and masters local self-government and political rights as ' the Third Estate.' " Engels : Footnote to *The Communist Manifesto*, English edition 1888. [*Ed. Eng. ed.*]

material. What he develops and emphasises well is the conspiratorial and revolutionary character of the municipal movement in the twelfth century. The German emperors—Frederick I and Frederick II for instance—issued edicts against these "*Communiones*" [communes], *conspirationes* [conspiracies], "*Conjurationes*" [sworn confederacies], quite in the spirit of the German Federal Diet ; *e.g.*, in 1226 Frederick II takes on himself to declare all "Consulates" and other free municipal constituencies in the cities of Provence null and void : "It has recently come to our knowledge that the guilds of certain cities, market-towns and other places, have, of their own will, constituted tribunals, authorities, offices, administrations and certain other institutions of this kind, . . . and because among many of them . . . such things have already developed into abuse and malpractices . . . we hereby in virtue of our imperial power revoke these jurisdictions, etc., and also the concessions in regard to them obtained by our sure knowledge through the Counts of Provence and of Forcalquier, and declare them null and void."*

Further : "We prohibit, also, all conventions and sworn confederacies within and without the cities : between city and city, between person and person or between city and person, of whatsoever kind they may be," (Peace Decree of Frederick I).*

"That no city and no market-town may organise communes, constitutions, unions, leagues or sworn confederacies of any kind, no matter what they may call themselves, and that we neither can nor ought to allow, without the agreement of their lord, the cities and markets formed in our empire the right to establish communes, constitutions or conspiracies of any kind no matter by what name they may call themselves." (Decree of King Henry against City Communes.)*

Is not this exactly the same stiff German professorial style which used to fulminate in later days from the "Central Commission" of the Confederation ? The *Commune jurée* [sworn commune] penetrated no further into Germany than Treves, and there Kaiser Frederick I made an end of it in

* Quoted in Latin.

1161 : " Every union of the citizens of Treves which is also called sworn confederacy and which we have abolished in the city . . . but which as we have heard was nevertheless later established, shall be dissolved and declared null and void."*

This policy of the German emperors was utilised by the French kings, who gave secret support to the " sworn confederacies " and " communes " in Lorraine, Alsace, Dauphiné, Franche-Comté, Lyonnais, etc., in order to detach them from the German Empire : " According to the information which has reached our Highness, the king of France . . . is seeking to corrupt the sincerity of your loyalty." (Rudolph I, letter to the citizens of Besançon.*) Just the same policy which these fellows adopted to make the Italian cities Guelph.

It is often funny how the word " *communio* " [commune, community] is heaped with abuse just as Communism is to-day. The parson Guilbert of Rayon, writes, for instance : " *Communio* is a new and extremely bad name."†

There is frequently something quite pathetic about the way in which the burghers in the twelfth century invite the peasants to escape to the cities, to the sworn communes. So for instance in the Charter of St. Quentin :

" They " (the citizens of St. Quentin) " have sworn together each to give common aid to his confederate, to have common counsel, common responsibility and common defence. In common we have determined that whoever shall enter our commune and give us his aid whether by reason of flight either from the power of his enemies or for other offence . . . shall be allowed to enter the commune, *for the door is open to all*,‡ and if his lord has unjustly detained his goods and will not hold them rightfully we will execute justice on that account."§

¶THIERRY, AUGUSTIN (1795-1856). French bourgeois historian. Settled in Paris in 1814, got to know Saint Simon and became his secretary. Parted from him in 1817. From 1817-20

* Quoted in Latin.
† " *Communio novum ac pessimum nomen.*"
‡ Underlined by Marx.
§ Quoted in French.

he worked hard at French history in order to combat the theories of the aristocracy and to prove the illegitimacy of their reactionary claims. He published his work in the collection *Ten Years of Historical Study* (1834). In 1821 he published his *Letters on the History of France* and in 1825 his *History of the Conquest of England by the Normans.* He became blind in 1826 and from that time onwards withdrew from public activity. But he did not give up his work. Towards the end of his life he published three volumes of his *Collection of Unpublished Documents on the History of the Third Estate.* The book to which Marx refers in his letter was a sort of introduction to this collection. (See also page 56.)

26. MARX TO ENGELS

London, 14 December, 1855.

... You would never guess who came to see me the day before yesterday, in the evening—Edgar Bauer, whom I had not seen for about a year, and with him—Bruno [Bauer]. Bruno has already been here a fortnight and wants to stay about six months, " in order to put his assertion to the test "—a test which certainly cannot fail, considering the way he is setting about it. The man has visibly aged ; his forehead has developed and he now more or less gives the impression of a pedantic old professor. For the moment he is lodging with Edgar—in a shack somewhere about the end of Highgate—and there he sits in the midst of the deepest petty-bourgeois misery, seeing and hearing nothing, too. This he believes to be London, imagining that except for thirty thousand privileged persons all Englishmen live like Edgar Bauer. His hatred and " contempt " for the country are therefore enormous. He feels as if he were living " in Treuenbrietzen."* London is a regular " prison " when you come from " Berlin." It also came out incidentally that his present ideal is the " East Friesian," " Altenburgian " and partly the " Westphalian " peasant—those true aristocrats. He is also convinced that no amount of subtle argument will do away with these louts—they are the

* Treuenbrietzen, a suburb of Potsdam.

rocks on which the modern levelling nonsense bemoaned by the " dissolutionist " will come to grief. It is very curious to hear the " *Critique* " [" *Criticism* "] confess that ultimately its real basis is Berthold Auerbach. In his opinion, with the exception of a few " purely commercial cities," the towns are decaying in Germany, but the "country " is flourishing magnificently. He did not know a thing about the growth of industry but quietly lamented all the same that they were doing nothing now in Germany but make " improvements."

The " English language " is " miserable," completely Latinised. Hereupon I proceeded to point out to him as a consolation that the Dutch and the Danes say the same about the German language and that the only genuine fellows who have not been corrupted by foreign tongues are the Icelanders. The old boy has occupied himself a great deal with languages. He *speaks* Polish and therefore declares that the *Polish language* is the " most beautiful of all." His language studies seem to have been very uncritical. Considers Dobrovski much " more important " than Grimm, for instance, and calls him the father of comparative philology. He has also allowed the Poles in Berlin to stuff him up with a tale that old Lelewel, in one of his latest works, has demolished Grimm's *History of the German Language*.

¶During his student period in Berlin (1836-41) Marx was associated with the circle of Left Hegelians and was a member of the Young Hegelians' Club. Of the members of this club, Bruno Bauer and Karl Friedrich Koppen had a great influence on the young Marx.

BAUER, BRUNO (1809-82). Was one of the leaders of the Young Hegelians in Berlin ; owing to his criticism of religion he was removed from his position as a lecturer at Bonn University. He was the author of numerous critical works on religion. Later on, he lived in very bad circumstances and at times had to support himself by small farming. Marx and Engels criticised Bauer, who did not move beyond the idealistic Hegelian philosophy. Bauer fought fiercely against the materialist philosophy of Feuerbach, and especially against Marx and Engels when by their materialistic "turning upside down" of the Hegelian dialectic they had developed the narrow, undialectic materialism of Feuerbach into dialectical historical materialism and on the basis of this theoretical realisation had taken a practical part in revolutionary struggle, while the Young Hegelians with Bauer at their head contented themselves with phrases. Marx and Engels made a criticism of Bauer, who with idealistic presumption called himself "*the* critic," "*the* criticism," above all in their polemical work *The Holy Family, or a Criticism of the Critical Criticism* (1845) and also in the *German Ideology*. (*Marx-Engels Gesamtausgabe*, I, 3, and 5.) Marx's letters give a lifelike portrait of the ageing professor who had spent all his life in the backward, limited, petty-bourgeois conditions of Germany and had not passed beyond the confines of bourgeois thought.

BAUER, EDGAR. Bruno Bauer's brother, who also belonged to the Young Hegelians and wrote several works of religious and political criticism of a bourgeois-liberal character.

AUERBACH, BERTHOLD (1812-82). German writer. Author of romantic and idealised stories of peasant life. [*Ed. Eng. ed.*]

GRIMM, JACOB (1785-1863). Famous German philologist and Germanic scholar. From 1830 Professor of German Language and Literature in Gottingen. Dismissed in 1837 for his protest against the abrogation of the Hanoverian Constitution. Elected member of the Berlin Academy of Sciences in 1840. Author of the *German Grammar*, *History of the German Language*, of the great *German Dictionary* and of many other works on the history of language ; also published collections of historical, legal and literary documents from original sources.

27. MARX TO ENGELS

London, 18 January, 1856.

. . . Have seen Bruno again several times. Romanticism reveals itself more and more as the "presupposition" of the critical criticism. In political economy he rhapsodises over the physiocrats, whom he misunderstands, and believes in the beneficent effects of landed property. Added to this he has a great opinion of the economic fantasies of Adam Müller, the German romantic. In military science his highest authority is the "genius" Bülow. I told him that these latest disclosures of his enabled me fully to appreciate the arduous labour of his thought. As to Russia, he declares that the old order of things in the West must be done away with: this can only happen from the East because only the Oriental possesses real hatred, namely, against the Western peoples, and Russia is the only compact power in the East, besides being the only country in Europe where "coherence" still exists. As for our illusions about internal class struggles: (1) the workers have no "hate"; (2) have never accomplished anything with such hate as they do possess; (3) are a "mob" (without interest for *synoptikers*) which can only be tamed and led by force and cunning; (4) give them a penny rise and "everything" is settled. No one, moreover, who does not belong to the "descendants of the conquerors" can play any part in world history—except in the theoretical field. And here something actually has been done in the last sixteen years, but only in Germany, and indeed only by Bruno. He has brought things to such a point that "scientific" theology has ceased to exist in Germany, the only place where it did exist, and that "Tholuck does not write any more." What an immense result! Otherwise a pleasant old gentleman. Thinks of stopping a year in England. I believe he is speculating on *introducing* the "scientific theology" which has ceased to exist in Germany, *into England*. Humboldt he calls a complete ass, because he fraudulently appropriated the renown abroad which should belong to Bruno. . . .

¶MÜLLER, ADAM (1799-1829). Philosopher with a reactionary theory of the state and romantic economist who serves to-day as the main source for Fascist theoreticians. In *Capital*, Vol. III, Chap. XXIV (Kerr edition, p. 467), Marx says of Müller's romantic economics: "It is made up of current prejudices, skimmed from the most superficial semblance of things. This false and trivial substance is then supposed to be uplifted and rendered poetical by a mystifying mode of expression."

BÜLOW, F. W., FREIHERR VON (1755-1816). Prussian general in the period of the Prussian wars of liberation, 1813-15.

THOLUCK, FRIEDRICH AUGUST (1799-1877). Theologian.

HUMBOLDT, ALEXANDER VON (1769-1859). German scientist who did important work in natural science and geography and travelled extensively.

28. MARX TO ENGELS

London, 12 February, 1856.

. . . Have seen Bruno [Bauer] again once or twice since. The fellow obviously has a plan, as he came to his dear brother without a halfpenny. He is an old bachelor through and through, anxiously concerned about his conservation and preservation and not without some secret misgivings about his relation to the present time. By degrees he is beginning to find out that London is a remarkable place, that there are even " contrasts between rich and poor " there, and other similar " discoveries." His superior airs and done-with-the-world pose on the one hand and his childish curiosity and rustic surprise at everything and anything on the other form a contrast anything but refreshing. He is now mainly grinding away at English. As soon as I have another meeting with him I will give you a report of it.

29. MARX TO ENGELS

London, 5 March, 1856.

Levy. Sent here by the Düsseldorf workers on a *double* commission. (1) *To denounce Lassalle*. And after a *very sharp* examination I think *they are right*. Lassalle quite transformed since the Countess got her 300,000 talers*—deliberately repulsing the workers, a sybarite, coquetting with the Blues. They further accuse him of having constantly exploited the party for his *Privatdreck* [wretched private affairs], even of having tried to use the workers for *personal crimes* in the interests of the case. The

* A taler, 3 marks.

case came to an end in this way: Count Hatzfeld's estate agent, Stockum, who, as you know, was later sentenced to five years' hard labour at the Assizes, had fallen out with the Count. He let Lassalle know that he had documents in his possession which would land the Count in chains for perjury, forgery, etc. Lassalle promised him 10,000 talers and then persuaded the Chief Prosecutor, Kösteritz (who has been forced to resign owing to this affair) to let the Count know that a charge lay against him. Hatzfeld is already dashing to Paris when Lassalle hands him the compromising documents and withdraws the charge on condition *he signs the agreement* with the Countess. (Kösteritz of course merely acted as his tool.) Thus it was not his *legal* acumen but a regular low intrigue which brought about the sudden end of the case. He did not pay Stockum the 10,000 talers and the workers say quite rightly that such a breach of faith could only be forgiven if he had handed over the money to the party instead of embezzling it for the Countess. They tell of a mass of dirty personal dealings which I cannot repeat because I forget them one after the other. Among others: Lassalle speculated in foreign government bonds with a Düsseldorf man, Scheuer, who advanced him the money for this. They lost. In the meantime Scheuer went bankrupt. Lassalle wins the case. Scheuer demands the money he advanced Lassalle. Lassalle mockingly refers him to a Paragraph 6 of the Code,* which forbids speculation on foreign exchanges. The workers say they allowed everything Lassalle did to pass on the excuse that he was involved in the case as a matter of honour. Now, when he has won, instead of letting the Countess pay him for his work and making himself independent, he lives shamefully under her yoke as a kept man, without any pretext whatever. He always boasted about what he was going to do as soon as the case was won. Now in a deliberately provocative way he flings the workers aside as superfluous tools. He attended one more (private) meeting, on New Year's Day, because a French colonel was present. To the general amazement he spoke before sixty workers of nothing but the "struggle

* Code Napoléon. The French bourgeois statute book which was also in force in the Rhine Provinces.

of civilisation against barbarism," of the western powers against Russia. They say his plan was to go to Berlin, play the great gentleman there and open a "*salon.*" On his return from there he promised the Countess in Levy's presence to create a "court of literary men" for her. He constantly, also in Levy's presence, expressed his "longing for dictatorship," etc., etc. (he seems to have quite a different idea of himself from what we have of him, he regards himself as a world-compeller because he was reckless in a personal intrigue, as if a man of real importance would sacrifice ten years to such a trifle). To show how dangerous he is, moreover: in order to smuggle a man from the workers' party into the police as a sham spy he *gave* the man one of *my letters* and told him to establish his credentials by saying he had stolen it from Lassalle. The workers say further that with his diplomatic ways he would never have come out so sharply against them if he did not directly intend to go over to the bourgeois party. At the same time he credits himself with enough influence to be able to talk them over at the moment of an insurrection, if he gets up on a table and harangues the masses, etc. The hate against him is so great, Levy says, that whatever we might decide, the workers would massacre him if he was in Düsseldorf when a movement took place. They are convinced, moreover, that he will choose the right moment to betake himself elsewhere if anything suspicious comes to his ears.

All these are only separate details of what I listened to and in patches retained. The *whole* has made a *definite* impression on Freiligrath and me, though I was much prejudiced in favour of Lassalle and greatly though I mistrust workers' gossip. I have told Levy that of course it is impossible to come to a decision on a report from one side only; in any case suspicion was useful; they should continue to watch the man but for the time being avoid any open break; we should perhaps find an opportunity of forcing Lassalle to take up a clear position, etc., etc.

What do you think of it? I should also like to know Lupus's* opinion.

* Lupus—Wilhelm Wolff, to whom Vol. I of *Capital* was dedicated. [*Ed. Eng. ed.*]

2. The second object of Levy's mission was to give me information about the position of the workers in the Rhine province. The Düsseldorf workers are still in contact with the workers of Cologne, where there are no longer any "gentlemen." But the chief propaganda is now among *the factory workers in Solingen, Iserlohn and district, Elberfeld, and the mining district of Westphalia.*

In the iron districts the chaps want to take to force and are only to be restrained by the prospect of a French revolution and because "the Londoners do not think the time has come yet." If the thing drags on much longer Levy thinks it will be difficult to prevent a rising. But in any case an insurrection in Paris would be the signal. These people seem to be firmly convinced that *we and our friends will hasten to them from the very first moment.* Naturally they feel the need of political and military leaders. Nobody can blame them for that. But I am afraid that with their highly naturalistic plans they would have been smashed up four times over before we had perhaps even been able to leave England. In any case it is due to them that one should explain from the military point of view exactly what can and what can not be done. I have told them, of course, that *if circumstances permitted* we would come and join the Rhenish workers ; that any rising on their own, without initiative in Paris, Vienna or Berlin, would be senseless ; that if Paris does give the signal, it would be well to risk everything in any case, for then even a momentary defeat could only have bad consequences for the moment ; that I would seriously consult my friends on the question of what can be directly done by the working-class population of the Rhine Province itself, and that after a while they should send someone to London again, but that they should do *nothing* without previous agreement. . . .

¶LASSALLE, FERDINAND (1825-64). Lawyer. Founder of reformism in the German labour movement.

In 1857 he published his philosophical work, *The Philosophy of Heraclitus the Dark of Ephesus*, with which Marx deals in Letter 37. His pamphlet, *The Italian War and Prussia's Task*, which Marx mentions in Letter 46, appeared in 1859 and his *System of Acquired Rights* in 1861 (Letters 51, 52). On May 23, 1863 was founded the *Allgemeine Deutsche Arbeiterverein* (General Association of German Workers) in which Lassalle played the leading part. In the *Open Letter to the Workers' Committee of the Leipzig Workers' Association*, which Lassalle had already written in February 1863, he laid down the two main demands of the Association : universal suffrage and state credits for producers' co-operatives. (Letter 63.) Lassalle led the Association along the path of compromise with the Prussian Junker state and in secret negotiations with Bismarck promised him the support of the workers. (See Letters 73, 80, 81.)

In July 1864 Lassalle went for a holiday to Switzerland and there became engaged to Helene von Dönniges. When she was obliged by her parents to give him up he became involved in a duel with her fiancé which led to his death. (See Letters 69, 70.)

Lassalle's historical service was that he " converted the working class from an appendage of the liberal bourgeoisie into an independent political party." (Lenin, *Collected Works*, Russian edition, Vol. II, p. 480.) But " Lassalle and the Lassalleans, in view of the weak chances of the proletarian and democratic way [of the bourgeois revolution in Germany] pursued a vacillating policy and adapted themselves to the hegemony of the Junker Bismarck. Their mistakes amounted to a deviation of the workers' party on to the Bonapartist-state-socialist path." (Lenin, *Collected Works*, Russian edition, Vol. XVI, p. 547.) A detailed characterisation of Lassalle as a politician will be found in Letter 81.

LEVY, GUSTAV. Düsseldorf merchant, one of the most active agitators in the *Allgemeine Deutsche Arbeiterverein.*

HATZFELD, SOPHIE VON, COUNTESS (1805-89). Had much to suffer from her husband, Count Hatzfeld ; Lassalle conducted the proceedings for her divorce for ten years and finally won the case. [See Letter 81 etc. for her later rôle.]

30. ENGELS TO MARX

Manchester, 14 April, 1856

Now the last phase of the swindle is beginning : Russia is importing capital and speculation, and with such distances and railways hundreds of miles long the swindle will no doubt develop so well that in a short time it will break its neck. When first we hear of the Grand Irkutsk Trunk Line, with branches to Pekin, etc., then it will be time to pack up our traps. This time the crash will beat anything known before ; all the factors are there : intensity, universal extension, entanglement of all possessing and ruling social elements. The most amusing thing about it is the English gentlemen who are nourishing themselves on the belief that with the " healthy " trade that exists here nothing of this kind can occur. It is clear enough that no big swindle can be carried out in industrial *production,* where it is well known that by a small capital investment in direct production all the markets can be glutted within a year, and especially while such a colossal demand exists for capital to be invested in means of communication. But industrial production too is being increased considerably beyond its normal proportions by the communications swindle, only more slowly than in 1833-36 and 1842-45, for instance. This year cotton prices are soaring rapidly in view of an unprecedented harvest of 3,500,000 bales, which seems no bigger this year, than, for instance, 2,500,000 bales would have seemed to be in 1850. Added to this the Continent is taking nearly three times as much in comparison with England this year as it did five years ago, as the following table of exports from America, September 1 to April 1 of each year, shows:

	In thousands of bales			
Exports for 7 months	*1856*	*1855*	*1854*	*1853*
To England ..	1,131,000	963,000	840,000	1,100,000
To France ..	354,000	249,000	229,000	255,000
To other European ports	346,000	167,000	179,000	204,000

Thus the Continent, which in 1853 imported an amount equal to $\frac{45}{110}$ or one-third of the English imports, in 1856 took $\frac{70}{113}$ or five-eighths. To this must also be added the exports to the Continent from England. You can see that Continental industry has increased quite out of all comparison with English industry, and Messrs. the Britons, being rather on the decline, have every reason not to over-trade in their cotton industry. The best comparison, however, is between 1853 and 1856, because in both these years the harvest was very big—3,300,000 and 3,500,000 bales. The large export to France is only apparent, for part of it goes from Havre to Switzerland, Baden, Frankfort, and Antwerp. But it is in this enormous growth of Continental industry that the most vital germ of the English revolution is to be found. . . .

¶Marx and Engels attached great importance to crises because they regarded them as the crudest expression of the conflict between the powerfully developed productive forces and the narrow productive relations in capitalist society. Hence they carefully studied the signs of the approach of crises and their course. In a letter to Bernstein, 25 January, 1882, Engels wrote :

" That crises are one of the most powerful levers of revolutionary upheaval was already stated in *The Communist Manifesto* and was treated in detail up to 1848 inclusive in the review in the *Neue Rheinische Zeitung*, where, however, it was shown too that returning prosperity also breaks revolutions and lays the basis for the victory of reaction."

In 1856-57 signs of the approach of a crisis called forth hopes of a revolution. Marx writes to Engels on September 1856 : " This time, moreover, the thing is on a European scale never reached before and I do not think we shall be able to sit here as spectators much longer. Even the fact that I have at last got to the point of furnishing a house again and sending for my books proves to me that the ' mobilisation ' of our persons is at hand."

In a letter to Marx on 15 November, 1857, Engels in analysing the course of the crisis, writes : " It would be desirable for this ' improvement ' to have merged into the chronic crisis before a second and decisive blow falls. Chronic pressure is necessary for a while in order to warm up the populations. The proletariat will then strike better, with better consciousness of its cause and more unity, just as a cavalry attack succeeds much better if the horses have first to trot 500 paces in order to come within charging distance of the enemy. I would not like anything to happen too soon, before all Europe is completely involved—the struggle afterwards would be harder, more tedious and more fluctuating. May or June would still be almost too early. The masses must have got damned lethargic after such long prosperity."

In the same letter Engels writes of the joy with which he awaits the revolution :

" From the time the swindle crashed in New York I had no more peace in Jersey* and feel in magnificent form amidst this general downbreak. The bourgeois filth of the last seven years had stuck to me to a certain extent after all, if it is washed away now I shall feel another fellow again. The crisis will do me as much good physically as a sea-bathe, I can see that already. In 1848 we said : Now our time is coming—and in a certain sense it came, but now it is coming altogether, now it will be a fight for life. This makes my military studies more practical at once. I am instantly throwing myself into the existing organisation and elementary tactics of the Prussian, Austrian, Bavarian and French armies, and beyond that into nothing but riding, that is, fox hunting, which is the real school." These statements show how Marx and Engels studied crises, not from the point of view of abstract theoretical research, but as revolutionaries.

31. MARX TO ENGELS

London, 16 April, 1856

The day before yesterday there was a little banquet to celebrate the anniversary of the *People's Paper*. On this occasion I accepted the invitation, as the times seemed to demand it of me, and all the more since I *alone* (as announced in the paper) of all the refugees had been invited and the first toast also fell to me, and I was to speak for the sovereignty of the proletariat in all countries. So I made a little English speech which I shall not allow to be printed.† The aim which I had in mind was achieved. Herr Talandier, who had to buy his ticket for 2s. 6d., and the rest of the French and other refugees, have convinced

* Where he had gone to recover from a serious illness. [*Ed. Eng. ed.*]
† Marx's speech. See page 90.

themselves that we are the only "intimate allies" of the Chartists and that though we refrain from public demonstrations and leave open flirtation with Chartism to the Frenchmen, we have it in our power to reoccupy at any time the position already historically due to us. This had become all the more necessary because at the meeting I mentioned on 25 February, under Pyat's chairmanship, the German *Knote** *Scherzer* (old boy) came forward and in truly awful Straubinger style,† denounced the German "men of learning," the "intellectual workers" who had left them (the *Knoten*) in the lurch and forced them to discredit themselves among the other nations. You know this Scherzer from Paris days. I have had some more meetings with friend *Schapper* and have found him a very repentant sinner. The retirement in which he has lived for the last two years seems rather to have sharpened his mental powers. You will understand that in any eventuality it may always be good to have the man at hand, and still more out of Willich's hands. Schapper is now furious with the *Knoten* at the Windmill. . . .‡

I fully agree with you about the Rhine province. The fatal thing for us is that I see something looming in the future which will smack of "treachery to the fatherland." It will depend very much on the turn of things in Berlin whether we are not forced into a position similar to that of the Mainz Clubbists in the old revolution. That will be hard. We who are so enlightened about our worthy brothers on the other side of the Rhine! The whole thing in Germany will depend on the possibility of covering the rear of the proletarian revolution by a second edition of the Peasants' War. Then the affair will be splendid.

* *Knote*. Handicraftsman, journeyman. Marx and Engels had their own frequent uses for this word between themselves, and no one English word conveys all they meant by it. The *Knote* not only has the narrow and backward mentality of the German handicraftsman in a period of rising capitalism (*cf. Straubinger*), but is in general essentially a non-proletarian, petty-bourgeois, philistine diehard. [*Ed Eng. ed.*]

† *Straubinger*. See Letter 1, Note.

‡ Great Windmill Street, London, where the house was in which the meetings of the German Workers' Educational Society took place.

¶Chartism was the first independent political movement of the working class. " Great Britain, of all other countries, has seen developed on the greatest scale the despotism of capital and the slavery of labour. In no other country have the intermediate stations between the millionaire commanding whole industrial armies and the wage slave living only from hand to mouth so, gradually, been swept away from the soil. There exist here no longer as in continental countries, large classes of peasants and artisans almost equally dependent on their own property and labour. A complete divorce of property from labour has been effected in Great Britain. In no other country, therefore, the war between the two classes that constitute modern society has assumed so colossal dimensions and features so distinct and palpable." (From Marx's Letter of 9 March, 1854, to the " Labour Parliament " in Manchester—published in the *People's Paper*, 18 March, 1854.)

After years of struggle against the capitalists, the working class of England arrived at a consciousness of their position as a class and strengthened their organisation. With the development of large-scale industry the antagonism between the bourgeoisie and the aristocracy also became increasingly acute, especially as the tariffs on corn imposed in the interests of the big landowners added enormously to the workers' cost of living. In order to prosecute their struggle against these Corn Laws, which had necessitated some rise in the workers' wages, the bourgeoisie had to break the parliamentary monopoly held by the great landowners. In their struggle they made use of the indignation and discontent of the workers and in 1832 (First Reform Act) attained their aim—the great landowners were forced to alter the franchise system. Needless to say the workers were betrayed. Not only did they not get the vote, but by the compromise come to between the bourgeoisie and the big landowners the Corn Laws remained in force for the time being. From that moment onwards began the independent working-class movement, and this received a still stronger impulse from the Poor Law of 1834, which robbed the poor of support and drove them into prison-like workhouses. During the trade crisis of 1836-37 the slogan of a struggle for influence in Parliament in order to improve their position spread among the workers and found its first expression in the " Charter " of the London Workingmen's Association, the six points of which comprised a demand for universal male suffrage, secret ballot, annual Parliament, equal electoral districts and payment of members. Enormous masses of the working class quickly joined in the agitation.

"In Chartism it is the whole working class which arises against the bourgeoisie and attacks, first of all the political power, the legislative rampart with which the bourgeoisie has surrounded itself. . . . These six points . . . harmless as they seem, are sufficient to overthrow the whole English Constitution, Queen and Lords included. The so-called monarchical and aristocratic elements of the Constitution can maintain themselves only because the bourgeoisie has an interest in the continuance of their sham existence; and more than a sham existence neither possesses to-day." (Engels, *The Condition of the Working Class in England in 1844.*)*

Chartism was only in form a purely political movement, in reality it was the class movement of the workers against capitalist exploitation. "*Chartism is of an essentially social nature*, a class movement. The 'Six Points' which for the Radical bourgeois are the beginning and end of the matter, which are meant, at the utmost, to call forth certain further reforms of the Constitution, are for the proletarian a mere means to further ends. . . . The 'knife and fork question' of the preacher Stephens was a truth for a part of the Chartists only, in 1838; it is a truth for all of them in 1845." (Engels, *ibid.*) The more strongly this social character came to expression in the movement, the more widely did Socialism spread among the Chartists. After 1848 the decay of the movement began (see Letters 8, 35, 36, 41), especially owing to the rapid growth of industry, in the course of which unemployment decreased and, thanks to England's monopoly in the world market, the upper stratum of the English working class received higher wages. The era of reformism, the development of the co-operative movement, and the co-operation of working-class leaders with the bourgeoisie now began. (See Letters 8, 63, 71, 74, etc.) From the beginning of their acquaintance with the English working class Marx and Engels were always in close contact with the Chartists, especially with Julian Harney and Ernest Jones. (See Letter 18 and Notes.)

* Translated by Florence Kelley Wischnewetzky. With Preface by Engels. English edition, 1892.

[MARX'S SPEECH, referred to in this letter, was made in response to the toast, "The proletarians of Europe," proposed by Ernest Jones. The supper took place at the Bell Hotel, Strand, and was attended by the compositors and staff of the paper and by a number of political refugees. *Ed. Eng. ed.*] The speech as published in the Chartist *People's Paper* of 19 April, 1856, was as follows :

"The so-called revolutions of 1848 were but poor incidents, small fractures and fissures in the dry crust of European society. However, they denounced the abyss. Beneath the apparently solid surface, they betrayed oceans of liquid matter, only needing expansion to rend into fragments continents of hard rock. Noisily and confusedly they proclaimed the emancipation of the proletarian, i.e., the secret of the nineteenth century, and of the revolution of that century. The social revolution, it is true, was no novelty invented in 1848. Steam, electricity and the self-acting mule were revolutions of a rather more dangerous character than even Citizens Barbès, Raspail, and Blanqui !* But, although the atmosphere in which we live weighs upon everyone with a twenty-thousand-pound force, do you feel it ? No more than European society before 1848 felt the revolutionary atmosphere enveloping it and pressing it from all sides. There is one great fact characteristic of this our nineteenth century, a fact which no party dares deny. On the one hand there have started into life industrial and scientific forces which no epoch of the former human history had ever suspected. On the other hand there exist symptoms of decay, far surpassing the horrors recorded of the latter times of the Roman Empire. In our days, everything seems pregnant with its contrary. Machinery, gifted with the wonderful power of shortening and fructifying human labour, we behold starving and overworking it. The newfangled sources of wealth, by some strange, weird spell, are turned into sources of want. The victories of art seem bought by the loss of character. At the same pace that mankind masters nature, man seems to become enslaved to other men or to his own infamy. Even the pure life of science seems unable to shine but on the dark background of ignorance. All our invention and progress seem to result in endowing material forces with intellectual life, and in stulti-

* *Barbès* and *Blanqui*—French revolutionaries, who took part in all the French struggles and conspiracies of their time. *Raspail* : a doctor and bourgeois democrat.

fying human life into a material force. This antagonism between modern industry and science, on the one hand, and modern misery and dissolution, on the other hand; this antagonism between the productive forces and the social relations of our epoch is a fact, palpable, overwhelming, and not to be controverted. Some may wail over it; others may wish to get rid of modern arts, in order to get rid of modern conflicts. Or they may imagine that so signal a progress in industry wants to be completed by as signal a regress in politics. For our part, we do not mistake the shape of the shrewd spirit that continues to mark all these contradictions. We know that if the newfangled forces of society are to work satisfactorily, they need only be mastered by newfangled men—and such are the working men. They are as much the invention of modern time as machinery itself. In the signs that bewilder the middle class, the aristocracy, and the poor prophets of regression, we recognise our old friend Robin Goodfellow, the old mole that can work in the earth so fast, that worthy pioneer—the revolution. The English working men are the firstborn sons of modern industry. Certainly, then, they will not be the last to aid the social revolution produced by that industry—a revolution which means the emancipation of their class all over the world, which is as universal as capital-rule and wage slavery. I know the heroic struggles the English working class has gone through since the middle of the last century; struggles not the less glorious because they are shrouded in obscurity and burked by middle-class historians. To take vengeance for the misdeeds of the ruling class there existed in the Middle Ages in Germany a secret tribunal called the *Vehmgericht*. If a red cross was seen marked on a house, people knew that its owner was doomed by the *Vehm*. All the houses of Europe are now marked by the mysterious red cross. History is the judge; its executioner, the proletarian."

SCHAPPER, KARL (1813-70). German revolutionary. Member of the Communist League. In his preface to Marx's pamphlet, *Revelations Concerning the Communist Trial in Cologne* (1853), Engels gives the following characterisation of him:

"A giant in size, resolute and energetic, always ready to stake bourgeois life and existence, he was the model of the professional revolutionary who played a part in the thirties."

Schapper was one of the leaders of the "Left" fraction in the Communist League.

The study of this fractional struggle is still of great importance to-day: in the minutes of the London Central Committee of the Communist League, 15 September, 1850, Marx's own words are thus recorded:*

"The minority† substitutes dogmatism for the standpoint of criticism, and idealism for materialism. It treats *pure will* as the motive power of revolution instead of actual conditions. While we say to the workers: 'You have got to go through fifteen, twenty, fifty years of civil wars and national wars not merely in order to change your conditions but in order to change yourselves and become qualified for political power,' you on the contrary tell them, 'We must achieve power immediately, otherwise we may as well lie down and go to sleep.' While we specially point out the undeveloped nature of the German proletariat to the German workers, you flatter the national feelings and craft prejudices of the German handicraftsman in the crudest way, which is of course more popular. Just as the democrats turned the word '*people*' into a sacred being, so you have done with the word '*proletariat*.' Like the Democrats you substitute revolutionary phrases for revolutionary development, etc."

The importance which Marx attributed to the fight against the "Left" fraction is shown by the following observation which he made in his concluding note to the *Communist Trial* (London, January 8, 1875): "In moments of crisis, to lose one's head becomes a crime against the Party which demands public expiation."

MAINZ CLUBBISTS: Members of the Jacobin Club in Mainz (Germany) in 1792 who stood for the declaration of a Rhineland Republic and for its union with the revolutionary French Republic.

32. ENGELS TO MARX

Manchester, 23 May, 1856.

In our tour in Ireland we came from Dublin to Galway on the west coast, then twenty miles north inland, then to Lime-

* Quoted by Marx in his pamphlet *Revelations Concerning the Communist Trial in Cologne.*

† Schapper-Willich "Left" fraction.

rick, down the Shannon to Tarbert, Tralee, Killarney and back to Dublin. A total of about four to five hundred English miles in the country itself, so that we have seen about two-thirds of the whole country. With the exception of Dublin, which bears the same relation to London as Düsseldorf does to Berlin and has quite the character of a small one-time capital, all English-built too, the whole country, and especially the towns, has exactly the appearance of France or Northern Italy. Gendarmes, priests, lawyers, bureaucrats, squires in pleasing profusion and a total absence of any and every industry, so that it would be difficult to understand what all these parasitic growths found to live on if the misery of the peasants did not supply the other half of the picture. " Strong measures " are visible in every corner of the country, the government meddles with everything, of so-called self-government there is not a trace. Ireland may be regarded as the first English colony and as one which because of its proximity is still governed exactly in the old way, and here one can already observe that the so-called liberty of English citizens is based on the oppression of the colonies. I have never seen so many gendarmes in any country, and the drink-sodden expression of the Prussian gendarme is developed to its highest perfection here among the constabulary, who are armed with carbines, bayonets and handcuffs.

Characteristic of this country are its ruins, the oldest from the fifth and sixth centuries, the latest from the nineteenth—with every intervening period. The most ancient are all churches ; after 1100, churches and castles ; after 1800 the houses of peasants. The whole of the west, but especially in the neighbourhood of Galway, is covered with these ruined peasant houses, most of which have only been deserted since 1846. I never thought that famine could have such tangible reality. Whole villages are devastated, and there among them lie the splendid parks of the lesser landlords, who are almost the only people still living there, mostly lawyers. Famine, emigration and clearances together have accomplished this. There are not even cattle to be seen in the fields. The land is an utter desert which nobody wants. In County Clare, south of Galway, it is rather better, here there are at least some cattle, and the hills toward Limerick are excellently cultivated, mostly by Scottish farmers, the ruins have been cleared away and the country has a bourgeois appearance. In the south-west there are a lot of mountains and bogs but also wonderfully rich forest growth, beyond that again fine pastures, especially in Tipperary, and towards Dublin land which is, one can see, gradually coming into the hands of big farmers.

The country has been completely ruined by the English wars of conquest from 1100 to 1850 (for in reality both the wars and the state of siege lasted as long as that). It is a fact that most of the ruins were produced by destruction during the wars. The people itself has got its peculiar character from this, and despite all their Irish nationalist fanaticism the fellows feel that they are no longer at home in their own country. Ireland for the Saxon ! That is now being realised. The Irishman knows he cannot compete with the Englishman, who comes with means in every respect superior ; emigration will go on until the predominantly, indeed almost exclusively, Celtic character of the population is all to hell. How often have the Irish started to try and achieve something, and every time they have been crushed, politically and industrially ! By consistent oppression they have been artificially converted into an utterly demoralised nation and now fulfil the notorious function of supplying England, America, Australia, etc., with prostitutes, casual labourers, pimps, thieves, swindlers, beggars and other rabble. This demoralised character persists in the aristocracy too. The landowners, who everywhere else have taken on bourgeois qualities, are here completely demoralised. Their country seats are surrounded by enormous, wonderfully beautiful parks, but all around is waste land, and where the money is supposed to come from it is impossible to see. These fellows ought to be shot. Of mixed blood, mostly tall, strong, handsome chaps, they all wear enormous moustaches under colossal Roman noses, give themselves the sham military airs of retired colonels, travel around the country after all sorts of pleasures, and if one makes an inquiry, they haven't a penny, are laden with debts, and live in dread of the Encumbered Estates Court.

¶The history of English colonial rule is an unbroken chain of bloody wars and brutal exploitation. The use of military force and oppression was a necessary condition of England's world monopoly in the nineteenth century. It insured the exploitation of millions of workers and peasants and made it possible for the bourgeoisie to split the working-class. A particularly crass example of this is afforded by English rule and policy in Ireland.

Marx and Engels regarded the Irish question as of decisive importance for the revolutionary struggle of the English proletariat for freedom. (See Letters 101, 102, 128, 130, 133-36, 141.)

Besides the letters contained in this volume the reader is referred to the Circular of the General Council of the International (January 1, 1870) to the *Comité Fédéral Romand* in Geneva (given in Marx's letter to Kugelmann of March 28, 1870)* and to Lenin's pamphlet on *The Right of Nations to Self-Determination*.

33. MARX TO ENGELS

London, 2 December, 1856.

What has decided me definitely for Poland, on the basis of my latest studies of Polish history, is the historical fact that the intensity and vitality of all revolutions since 1789 can be gauged pretty accurately by their relation to Poland. Poland is their "external" thermometer. This can be demonstrated in detail from French history. It is obvious in our short German revolutionary epoch, and equally so in the Hungarian.

Of all the revolutionary governments, including that of Napoleon I, "the Committee of Public Safety" forms an exception only because it refused intervention not from weakness but from "mistrust." In 1794 they summoned the agent of the Polish insurgents before them and put the following questions to this "citizen":

"How is it that your Kosziuscko is a popular dictator and yet suffers a king alongside of him, who, moreover, as Kosziuscko must be aware, has been put on the throne by Russia?

* *The Letters of Marx to Kugelmann*. Martin Lawrence 1934.

Why does your dictator not dare to carry out the mass mobilisation of the peasants, for fear of the aristocrats who do not want ' hands ' to be withdrawn from labour ? How is it that his proclamations lose their revolutionary tone in proportion to the distance which his line of march removes him from Cracow ? Why did he *immediately* punish the people's insurrection in Warsaw with the gallows, while the aristocratic ' traitors to their country ' wander freely about or are sheltered behind the lengthy formalities of a trial. Answer ! " To which the Polish " citizen " could only remain silent.

What do you say to Neufchâtel and Valangin ? This case has led me to supplement my highly defective knowledge of Prussian history. Indeed and indeed the history of the world has never produced anything more sordid. The long history of how the nominal kings of France became real kings is also full of petty struggles, treachery, and intrigues. But it is the history of the origin of a nation. Austrian history, which shows how a vassal of the German Empire establishes the power of his own house, becomes interesting from the circumstance that, thanks to the entanglements with the East, Bohemia, Italy, Hungary, etc., the vassal imposes himself as Kaiser ; and ultimately because the power of this house assumes such dimensions that Europe fears it will become a universal monarchy. Nothing of this sort in Prussia. Prussia never subjugated a single powerful Slav nation and in five hundred years was never even able to succeed in getting hold of Pomerania until she finally got it by " exchange." In fact, the Margraviate of Brandenburg—as it was in the hands of the Hohenzollerns—never made any real *conquests* except *Silesia*. As this is its *only* conquest, Frederick II is doubtless the " Unique " ! Petty thieving, bribery, direct purchase, underhand dealings with inheritances, etc.—all this shabby business is what the history of Prussia amounts to. And what is usually interesting in feudal history—the struggle between overlord and vassals, trickery with the towns, etc.—is here all caricatured to a dwarfish scale because the towns are petty and boring, the feudal lords are insignificant louts, and the sovereign himself is a nonentity. In the Reformation, as in the French Revolution, vacillating perfidy, neutrality, separate peace treaties. The snapping up of a few morsels thrown to it in the course of the various partitions instituted by Russia—so with Sweden, Poland, Saxony. Added to this, in the succession of regents never any but three types of character following one another as night follows day, with irregularities which only change the sequence but never introduce a new type—pietist, sergeant-major and clown. What has kept the state on its legs through all this has been *mediocrity*—golden mediocrity—accurate book-keeping, avoidance of extremes, precision in drill, a certain home-bred meanness and " church order." Disgusting ! . . .

¶In 1856 a clique of Neufchâtel noblemen carried through a monarchist *Putsch* in order to restore their vanishing privileges. These nobles proclaimed the restoration of the right of the Prussian kings to be princes of Neufchâtel (a right destroyed by the revolution of 1848). The Swiss authorities quickly suppressed the revolt and arrested all the participants (about sixty men). From this arose a conflict which threatened to lead to war. Mobilisation was on the point of taking place in Prussia.

Marx published an article in the Chartist *People's Paper* of December 13, 1856, *The Right Divine of the Hohenzollerns*, in which he showed how the Hohenzollerns had really attained their " divine rights " over various possessions—Brandenburg, Prussia, the rank of *Kurfürst* and finally the rank of king, " by the divine right of bribery, open purchase, petty larceny, legacy hunting, and treacherous partition treaties."

A characterisation of German history by Engels is to be found in his letter to Mehring of July 13, 1893 : " In studying German history, which is simply one long continuous misery, I have always found that one only gets the right proportion by comparing it with the corresponding French periods, because what happens there is the exact opposite of what happens with us. There the construction of a national state from the scattered members of the feudal state, at the very moment where with us the chief decay sets in. There a rare objective logic in the whole course of the process, with us an arid and ever increasingly arid confusion. There foreign intervention is represented by the intervention of the English conquerors in the Middle Ages on the side of the Provençal nationality as against the northern French. The English wars represent the Thirty Years' War, so to speak, which ends, however, with the driving out of the foreign invaders and the subjection of the south to the north. Next comes the struggle between the central power and its Burgundian vassal, the latter supporting itself on foreign possessions and playing the part of Brandenburg-Prussia; here again the central power is victorious and finally establishes the national state. And it is exactly at the same moment that with us the national state breaks down completely (so far as the 'German Kingdom' within the Holy Roman Empire can be called a national state) and the plundering of German territory begins on a large scale. It is a comparison of the most intensely humiliating order for the Germans, but all the more instructive for that very reason, and since our workers have brought Germany into the front rank of the historical movement we can swallow the disgrace of the past rather more easily. Very specially characteristic of the German development is the fact that the two component states, which ultimately divided up the whole of Germany between them, were neither of them purely German, but both colonies on conquered Slav territory—Austria a Bavarian and Prussia a Saxon colony—and that they only acquired power in Germany by supporting themselves on foreign, non-German possessions—Austria on Hungary (to say nothing of Bohemia) and Brandenburg on Prussia. This sort of thing did not take place on the western frontier, the most threatened frontier; on the northern frontier the Danes were left to protect Germany from the Danes, and in the south there was so little to protect that the guardians of the frontier, the Swiss, were able to tear themselves free even from Germany."

34. MARX TO ENGELS

[London], 25 September, 1857.

... The history of the *army* brings out more clearly than anything else the correctness of our conception of the connection between the productive forces and social relations. In general, the army is important for economic development. For instance, it was in the army that the ancients first developed a complete wages system. Similarly among the Romans the *peculium castrense** was the first legal form in which the right of others than fathers of families to movable property was recognised. So also the guild system among the corporation of *fabri* [smiths]. Here too the first use of machinery on a large scale. Even the special value of metals and their use as money appears to have been originally based—as soon as Grimm's stone age was passed—on their military significance. The division of labour *within* one branch was also first carried out in the armies. The whole history of the forms of bourgeois society is very strikingly epitomised here. When you can find time you must work the thing out from this point of view.

In my opinion, the only points which have been overlooked in your account are: (1) The first complete appearance of mercenary troops on a large scale and at once among the Carthaginians. (For our private use I will look up a book on the Carthaginian army written by a Berlin man, which I only came to know later.) (2) The development of the army in Italy in the fifteenth and the beginning of the sixteenth centuries. Tactical tricks, at any rate, were developed here. Extremely humorous too is Machiavelli's description (which I will copy out for you) in his *History of Florence* of the way the Condottieri fought one another. (No, when I come to you at Brighton (when?) I would rather bring the volume of Machiavelli with me. The *History of Florence* is a masterpiece.) And finally, (3) Asiatic military organisation as it first appeared among the Persians and then, though modified in a great variety of ways, among the Mongols, Turks, etc.

¶Marx is referring to Engels' article *Army*, written by him for the *New American Cyclopædia*, edited by George Ripley and A. Dana, New York (1860-62). Other articles on military questions, which Engels wrote for Marx, were also published there. The articles had to be written at great speed by the given date demanded by the publisher. In his letter Marx

* The separate property (as distinguished from family property) which the Roman soldier acquired in camp.

praises the article but says how much it troubles him that Engels should have to work so hard. " Especially if I had known that you would be working into the night I would rather have let the whole thing go to hell."

Marx and Engels always regarded questions relating to war as of great importance ; hence they often occupied themselves with military questions. Evidence of this is also afforded by the following passage from Engels' letter to Marx of January 7, 1858, where he says :

" Among other things I am now reading Clausewitz on war. A strange way of philosophising but very good on his subject. To the question whether war should be called an art or a science, the answer given is that war is most like trade. Fighting is to war what cash payment is to trade, for however rarely it may be necessary for it actually to occur, everything is directed towards it and eventually it must take place all the same and be decisive."

Lenin also studied Clausewitz on war. V. Sorin, in No. 111 of *Pravda* (1923) reported the following remark of Lenin's about Clausewitz : " Political tactics and military tactics are what is called in German *Grenzgebiet* [borderland] and Party workers might profitably study the works of Clausewitz, the great German military theoretician." (*Leninsky Sbornik*, Vol. XII, p. 390.)

35. MARX TO ENGELS

[London], 24 November, 1857.

. . . Jones is behaving very stupidly.* You know that long before the crisis—with no definite aim except to find some pretext for agitation in this lukewarm time—he had arranged for a Chartist conference, to which bourgeois radicals (not only Bright† but even fellows like Cunningham) were also to be invited. In general, a compromise was to be come to with the bourgeoisie by which *they* were to get the ballot‡ if they would concede manhood suffrage to the workers. This proposal gave

* Jones. See Letter 18, Note.
† John Bright. See Letter 63.
‡ The secrecy of the ballot was not established in England until 1872. [*Ed. Eng. ed.*]

rise to divisions in the Chartist party which in their turn involved Jones more deeply in his scheme.

Now instead of using the crisis to replace a badly selected pretext for agitation by real agitation, he clings firmly to his nonsense and shocks the workers by preaching co-operation with the bourgeoisie, while he is far from inspiring the latter with the slightest confidence. Some of the radical papers are cajoling him in order to ruin him completely. In his own paper that old ass, Frost, whom he himself had boosted as a hero and whom he had nominated president of his conference, has come out against him with a most brutal letter in which he says among other things : If Jones considers the co-operation of the middle class necessary—and *nothing* can be done *without* it—he should come out for it *bona fide* [in a genuine way]. Who gave him the right to draw up the programme of the conference *without* their allies ? Who gave him the right to nominate Frost President and to play the dictator himself, etc. ?

So now he is in a hole, and for the first time is playing not merely a *stupid* but an *ambiguous* part. I have not seen him for a long time, but will now visit him. I consider him honest, and as in England no *public character* can become impossible because he does stupid things, etc., it is only a question of his extricating himself as quickly as possible from his own snare. The ass should first *form* a party, for which he must go to the factory districts. Then the radical bourgeoisie will come and ask him for compromises.

¶FROST, JOHN (1785-1877). Chartist. In 1837 Mayor of Newport. After the march on Newport (November 4, 1839), in which he took a leading part, he was one of those sentenced to death. The sentence was commuted to transportation for life to Australia. He was amnestied in 1856 and returned to London. [*Ed. Eng. ed.*]

36. MARX TO ENGELS

[London] 14 January, 1858.

. . . I am getting some nice developments. For instance, I have thrown over the whole doctrine of profit as it has existed up to now. In the *method* of treatment the fact that by mere accident I have again glanced through Hegel's *Logic* has been of great service to me—Freiligrath found some volumes of Hegel which originally belonged to Bakunin and sent them to me as a present. If there should ever be time for such work again, I should greatly like to make accessible to the ordinary human intelligence, in two or three printer's sheets,* what is *rational* in the method which Hegel discovered but at the same time enveloped in mysticism. . . .

What do you say to friend Jones? That the fellow has sold himself I am not yet willing to believe. His experience in 1848 may lie heavy on his stomach. With his great belief in himself he may think himself capable of exploiting the middle class or may imagine that if only Ernest Jones were got into Parliament, one way or another, the history of the world would be bound to take a new turn. The best of it is that Reynolds has now come out in his paper as a furious opponent of the middle class and of all compromise—of course out of spite against Jones. Mr. B. O'Brien, likewise, has now become an irrepressible Chartist at any price. The only excuse for Jones is the inertia which at present pervades the working class in England. However this may be, he is at present on the way to becoming a dupe of the middle class or a renegade. The fact that he, who used anxiously to consult me about every bit of rubbish, is now equally anxious to avoid me, shows anything but a good conscience. . . .

¶HEGEL, G. F. W. (1770-1831). The most important representative of classical German philosophy; he represented an objective idealism; a brilliant investigator of the laws of dialectic, which he was the first consciously to apply. In the Hegelian system " the whole world of nature, of history and of

*Drückbogen: one sheet = 16 printed pages [*Ed. Eng. ed.*]

the mind is for the first time—and that is a great merit—represented as a process. . . . Hegel freed the conception of history from natural mysticism; he made it dialectical." (Engels.) And Marx writes in his preface to the second edition of *Capital* (Book I) :

" The mystification which dialectic suffers in Hegel's hands by no means prevents him from being the first to present its general form of working in a comprehensive and conscious manner. With him it is standing on its head. It must be turned right side up again if you would discover the rational kernel within the mystical shell."

REYNOLDS, GEORGE WILLIAM (1814-79). Chartist. Editor of *Reynolds' Weekly Newspaper.*

O'BRIEN, JAMES BRONTERRE (1805-64). One of the chief Chartist writers in the period of the 'thirties ; after 1848 withdrew from the movement and propagated land nationalisation and currency reform. [*Ed. Eng ed.*]

37. MARX TO ENGELS

London, 1 February, 1858.

Heraclitus the Dark by Lassalle the Bright is at bottom a very feeble compilation. With each of the many images by which Heraclitus works out for himself the unity of affirmation and negation, in steps Lassalle and takes the opportunity of treating us—always at full length—to some extract from Hegel's *Logic*, which hardly gains by this process. He does it like a schoolboy who has got to prove in his exercise that he has thoroughly learned his " essence," " appearance " and " dialectical process." And if that is what the schoolboy is speculating upon one can be sure that he will only after all be able to conduct this process of thought according to the prescribed recipe and in the sacred forms. Exactly the case with our Lassalle. The chap seems to have tried to make Hegel's *Logic* clear to himself through Heraclitus and never to have got tired of perpetually starting this process afresh. So far as erudition is concerned there is an enormous exhibition of it. But every expert knows how easy it is, when one has time and money, and, like Mr. Lassalle, can have the Bonn University library sent direct to his home whenever he likes, to put together this sort of exhibition of quotations. One can see what a wonderful swell the fellow seems to himself in this philological tinsel, moving with all the grace of a chap who for the first time in his life is wearing fashionable dress. As most philologists have *not* the speculative conception which predominates in Heraclitus, every Hegelian has the indisputable advantage of understanding what the philologist does not understand. (It would, by the way, be strange if just because a fellow had learnt Greek he became a philosopher in *Greek* when he was not one in *German.*) But instead of simply taking all this for granted Mr. Lassalle treats us in a sort of Lessing manner. In long-winded legal phraseology the Hegelian interpretation is justified against the misconstructions made by the philologists owing to their lack of special knowledge. So that we have the double pleasure, first of seeing dialectical things which we had almost forgotten reconstructed for us in full amplitude, and secondly of having this " speculative heritage " vindicated against the unspeculative philologists as the particular philological and juridical smartness and learnedness of Mr. Lassalle. Moreover, despite the fellow's boast that Heraclitus has up to now been a book with seven seals, he has added *absolutely nothing new*, where the main point is concerned, to what Hegel says in his *History of Philosophy*. He only brings it out in detail, which could of course have been done quite amply enough in a couple of printer's sheets.* Still less does it occur to the fellow to betray any critical reflections on the dialectic itself. If all the fragments of Heraclitus were printed together they would hardly fill half a printer's sheet. Only a fellow who prints books at the expense of the awful "hussy" [Countess Hatzfeld] would think of giving two volumes of sixty sheets to the world on such a pretext.

There is a saying of " Heraclitus the Dark " where, in order to explain the transformation of all things into their opposites, he says: " So gold transforms itself into all things and all things transform themselves into gold." Gold, says Lassalle, is here money (which is correct) and money is value. It is therefore the Ideal, the Universal, the One (value) and things

* *Drückbogen.* See p. 102.

are the Real, the Particular, the Many. He utilises this startling piece of penetration in order to give us, in a long note, an earnest of his discoveries in the science of political economy. Every word is a blunder, but declaimed with remarkable pretentiousness. I can see from this one note that the fellow is proposing to present political economy in the Hegelian manner in his second great work. He will learn to his cost that to bring a science by criticism to the point where it can be dialectically presented is an altogether different thing from applying an abstract ready-made system of logic to mere inklings of such a system.

But as I wrote to you immediately after his first self-intoxicated letter, the old Hegelians and philologists must really have been pleased to find such an old-fashioned mind in a young man who passes for a great revolutionary.

38. MARX TO ENGELS

[London], 2 April, 1858.

Following is a short outline of the first part. The whole *Scheisse* [shit] is to be divided into six books: I. Capital; II. Landed property; III. Wage labour; IV. State; V. International trade; VI. World market.

I. *Capital* contains four sections: A. Capital in general (*this is the material of the first part*); B. *Competition*, or the action of the many capitals upon one another; C. *Credit*, where capital appears as the general element in comparison with particular capitals; D. Share capital as the most complete form (passing over into Communism) together with all its contradictions.

The transition of capital to landed property is also historical, as the modern form of property in land is a product of the effect of capital upon feudal, etc., landed property. Similarly the transition of landed property to wage labour is not only dialectical but historical, since the final product of modern landownership is the general institution of wage labour, which in turn appears as the basis of the whole shit. Well (it is difficult for me to write to-day), we now come to the *corpus delicti* [evidence for the crime].

I. *Capital. First section : Capital in General.* In the whole of this section it is assumed that the wages of labour are constantly equal to their lowest level. The movement of wages themselves and the rise or fall of the minimum come under the consideration of wage labour. Further, landed property is taken as =0 ; that is, nothing as yet concerns landed property as a particular economic relation. This is the only possible way to avoid having to deal with everything under each particular relation.

(1) *Value.* Purely reduced to quantity of labour. Time as the measure of labour. Use value—whether considered subjectively as usefulness of the work, or objectively as utility of the product—appears here simply as the material presupposition of value, which for the time being drops completely out of the determination of the economic form. Value as such has no other " material " but labour itself. This determination of value, first indicated by Petty, clearly worked out by Ricardo, is merely the most abstract form of bourgeois wealth. In itself already presupposes : the dissolution of (1) primitive communism (India, etc.) ; (2) of all undeveloped, pre-bourgeois modes of production not completely dominated by exchange. Although an abstraction, this is an historical abstraction which could only be adopted on the basis of a particular economic development of society. All objections to this definition of value are either derived from less developed conditions of production, or are based on a confusion by which the more concrete economic determinations (from which value is abstracted and which, from another point of view, can therefore also be regarded as a further development of it) are set up in opposition to value in this abstract undeveloped form. Considering the lack of clarity among Messrs. the Economists themselves as to how this abstraction is related to the later and more concrete forms of bourgeois wealth, these objections were more or less justified.

From the contradiction between the general character of value and its material existence in a particular commodity, etc.—these general characteristics are the same which later appear in money—arises the category of money.

(2) *Money.* Something about the precious metals as the medium of money relations.

(a) *Money as measure.* Some notes on the *ideal* measure of Stewart, Attwood, Urquhart ; put forward in a more comprehensible form by the advocates of labour-money (Gray, Bray, etc. Some hits on occasion at the Proudhonists). The value of the commodity translated into money is its *price*, which for the time being still only appears in this *purely formal* differentiation from value. According to the general law of value, a particular quantity of money merely expresses a particular quantity of embodied labour. So long as money is measure, the variability of its own value makes no difference.

(b) *Money as a means of exchange, or simple circulation.* Here only the simple form of this circulation itself is to be considered. All the circumstances which further determine it lie outside of it and are therefore only considered later. (They presuppose more developed conditions.) If we call the commodity C and money M, simple circulation does, it is true, exhibit the two circular movements or circuits : C—M—M—C and M—C—C—M (the latter constitutes the transition to Section c), but the point of departure and the point of return in no way coincide, or, if so, only accidentally. Most of the so-called laws laid down by the economists treat money circulation, not within its own limits, but as included under and determined by higher movements. All this to be done away with. (Comes partly under the theory of credit ; but part must also be dealt with at points where money comes up again, but more fully defined.) Here then money as a means of circulation (*coin*). But at the same time as the *realisation* (not merely disappearing) of price. From the simple determination that the commodity, fixed as a *price*, is already ideally exchanged for money, before it is actually exchanged, arises of itself the important economic law that *the amount of the circulating medium is determined by the price and not vice versa.* (Here something historical on the controversy relating to this point.) It follows further that velocity can replace mass, but that a *definite mass* is necessary for the simultaneous acts of exchange, in so far as these are not related to one another as + and — ; this equalisation and the consideration of it are however only to be touched on at this point in anticipation. I will not now go into further details of the further development of this section but will only remark that the falling apart of C—M and M—C is the most abstract and superficial form in which the possibility of crises is expressed. The development of the law that price determines the mass of circulation shows that presuppositions are here involved which by no means apply to all stages of society; it is absurd, therefore, to take, for instance, the influx of money from Asia to Rome and its influence on Roman prices, and simply to put it beside modern commercial conditions. The most abstract determinations, when more carefully examined, always point to a further definite concrete historical basis. (Of course—since they have been abstracted from it into these determinations.)

(c) *Money as money*. This is the development of the form M—C—C—M. Money as the independent existence of value, apart from circulation; the material existence of abstract wealth. Shows this in circulation, in so far as money does not merely appear as a means of circulation but as the realisation of price. In its capacity as (c), where (a) and (b) appear only as functions, money is the general commodity of contracts (here the variability of its value, due to the determination of value by labour time, is important) and an object of hoarding. (This function is still important in Asia and was important in the ancient world and Middle Ages generally. Exists now only as a subordinate part of the banking system. In times of crisis money in this form is again important. A consideration of money in this form and of the delusions it has produced in the course of world history. Destructive properties, etc.) Money as the realisation of all the higher forms in which value will appear; definite forms in which all value relations are externally limited. Money fixed in this form, however, ceases to be an economic relation—the form is lost in its material medium, gold and silver. On the other hand in so far as money comes into circulation and is again exchanged for C, the final process, the consumption of the commodity, again falls outside the economic relation. Simple money circulation does not contain the principle of self-reproduction within itself and therefore points beyond itself. Money, as the development of its determinations shows, contains within itself the demand for value which will enter into circulation, maintain itself during circulation and at the same time establish circulation—that is, for *capital.* This transition historical also. The antediluvian form of capital is trade capital, which always develops money. At the same time, real capital arises from that money or merchants' capital which gains control of production.

(d) This simple circulation, considered in itself—and here we have the surface of bourgeois society, obliterating the deeper operations from which it arises—reveals no difference between the objects of exchange, except formal and temporary ones. This is the *realm of freedom and equality and of property based on "labour."* Accumulation, which here appears in the form of hoarding, is therefore only greater thriftiness, etc. Next, on the one hand the absurdity of the economic harmonists and modern free traders (Bastiat, Carey, etc.) who assert this most superficial and abstract aspect as *their* truth applying to the more developed productive relations and their antagonisms. On the other hand the absurdity of the Proudhonists and similar socialists who try to apply ideas of equality corresponding to this exchange of equivalents (or to what is assumed as such) to the inequalities, etc., from which the exchange arises and to which it returns. As the law of appropriation in this sphere there appears appropriation by labour, an exchange of equivalents, so that the exchange merely returns the same value in a different material form. In short everything is "lovely," but will very soon come to a horrible end, and indeed owing to the law of equivalence.

We now come, namely, to

(3) *Capital.* This is really the most important part of the first section, about which I most need your opinion. But I cannot go on writing to-day. This filthy jaundice makes it difficult for me to hold my pen and bending my head over the paper makes me giddy. So—for next time.

¶On the first part of the *Critique of Political Economy* which Marx sent Engels to read through, the latter wrote on April 9, 1858 : " The study of your abstract of the first half part* has kept me very busy. *It is a very abstract abstract indeed*,† which could not be avoided in the short form, and I often have trouble in searching for the dialectical transitions, as all abstract reasoning has become very foreign to me. This arrangement of the whole in the six books could not possibly be better and pleases me exceptionally, although I do not yet clearly see the dialectical transition from landed property to wage labour. The development of the account of money is also very fine; Here again there are particulars which I am not yet clear about, as I often have first to hunt up the historical basis for myself. However, I think that as soon as I have the conclusion of the chapter in general I shall see the line better, and I will then write to you in greater detail about it. The abstract dialectical tone of this epitome will of course disappear in the working out."

In the above letter Marx gives the first plan of his economic work. *Capital* was not fixed in its form from the beginning. In the course of the years 1858 to 1867, as Marx kept penetrating more deeply into his material, he was always giving it a new shape, until he found the form of presentation which most clearly reflected the dialectical content of this, the chief work of Marxism. (See also paragraph 3 of the Introduction to the *Critique of Political Economy*: " The Method of Political Economy.")

39. MARX TO LASSALLE

London, 10 June, 1858.

You would have received a full answer to your letter, but I thought it good—not in order to formulate my own opinion but because three make a collegium—to send the case to Manchester for Engels and Lupus [Wilhelm Wolff] to report their judgment upon. As their views coincide in every point with my own you can regard the following as our common opinion.

* The *Critique of Political Economy* was published in parts. See Letter 43. [*Ed. Eng. ed.*]

† Engels' English.

(1) *On the question of the duel.* It is as clear as daylight that both the gentlemen—the *Intendanturrat and Assessor* [Commissariat Councillor and Assistant]—have put themselves completely on the cudgelling level by their low street attack, and that the only duel in which one *could* possibly engage with lads of this sort has already taken place in the scuffle. If two fellows lie in wait for a third and *both* attack him we do not believe that any code of duelling *in the world would permit* one still to fight a duel with such a gang. If Herr Fabriz wished by his demonstration with the riding whip to provoke a duel by force, then Herr B. should either have been present as a purely passive *witness* or else was altogether superfluous. But where two men fall both together upon a third, and one even operates behind the person assaulted—in the rear—one has to do with scum who have shown that it is impossible to have a proper duel with them, an honourable fight between two persons.

(2) *The principle of the duel.* We are not of the opinion, speaking generally, that such a relative affair as a duel can be classified in the category of *good* or *bad*. There is no doubt that the duel in itself is irrational and the relic of a past stage of culture. At the same time the result of the one-sidedness of *bourgeois* society is that certain individualistic feudal forms assert their rights in opposition to it. The most striking proof of this is to be found in the civil right of duelling in the United States of America. Individuals can get into such unbearable collisions with one another that the duel seems to them to be the only solution. But such deadly tension is really not possible in relation to an indifferent subject like an *Intendanturrat* or *Assessor* or a lieutenant. An important personal relation must be involved, otherwise the duel is a pure farce. It is always a farce when it takes place out of consideration for so-called "public opinion."

(3) Thus in our view the duel depends entirely on circumstances and as an exceptional *emergency resort* may be adopted in exceptional circumstances. But in the present case all the circumstances are decisively against it; even if the street attack had not put it altogether out of the question.

(4) The first decisive circumstance is that you are not only

opposed to all duelling on principle but have also declared this principle, and in the presence of Fabriz. You would therefore discredit yourself if, despite this, you fought a duel from fear of "public opinion."

(5) In the present case the duel could have no possible point except as the fulfilment of a *conventional* form recognised by certain privileged orders. Our party must set its face resolutely against these ceremonials of rank and reject with the utmost cynical contempt the presumptuous demand that it should submit to them. The times are far too serious now to allow one to become involved in such childishness; and it would be pure childishness to fight a duel with Herr Fabriz, because he is an *Intendanturrat* and belongs to the clique entitled to fight duels, when if, say, a tailor or a cobbler attacked you in the street you would simply hand him over to the law courts without any injury to your "honour." In the present case you would not be fighting a duel with Herr Fabriz, who as an individual is indifferent to you, but with the *Intendanturrat*—which would be an absurd manœuvre. In general the demand of these fellows that any collision with them must be settled by duelling, as a privilege which is their due—and this applies to all fashionable duels—must be treated with utter derision. To recognise it would be directly counter-revolutionary.

¶Fabriz had met Lassalle at the house of the publisher and liberal bourgeois politician Franz Duncker. From dislike and envy of Lassalle, Fabriz challenged him to a duel for no reason, taking offence at some smile of Lassalle's. After his challenge Fabriz armed himself with a riding whip, and, together with his friend Borman, fell upon Lassalle in the street with the intention of thrashing him. Lassalle naturally, defended himself, and indeed used his stick with considerable success.

40. ENGELS TO MARX

Manchester, 14 July, 1858.

. . . Do send me Hegel's *Philosophy of Nature* as you promised. I am now doing some physiology and shall combine it with comparative anatomy. There are some highly speculative things here, all of which have only recently been discovered, however ; I am very eager to see if the old man did not scent something of them. This much is certain ; if he had a philosophy of nature to write *to-day* the facts would fly into his hands from every side. Moreover, one has absolutely no conception of the progress made by the natural sciences in the last thirty years. For physiology the decisive factors have been, first, the tremendous development of organic chemistry, and secondly, the microscope, which has only been properly used for the last twenty years. The microscope has led to even more important results than chemistry : the main thing which has revolutionised the whole of physiology and for the first time made comparative physiology possible is the discovery of the cell—in plants by Schleiden and in animals by Schwann (about 1836). Everything is a cell. The cell is Hegel's " Being-in-itself " and its development exactly follows the Hegelian process, resulting finally in the " idea " i.e., each completed organism.

Another result which would have pleased old Hegel is in physics the correlation of forces : the law that under given conditions mechanical motion, that is, mechanical force (produced, e.g., by friction), is changed into heat, heat into light, light into chemical affinity, chemical affinity (e.g., in the Voltaic pile) into electricity, electricity into magnetism. These transitions can also take place differently, backwards or forwards. It has now been proved by an Englishman, whose name I cannot at the moment remember, that the transformation of these forces into one another takes place under quite definite quantitative conditions, so that, for instance, a certain quantity of one, say electricity, corresponds to a certain quantity of each of the others—e.g., magnetism, light, heat, chemical affinity (positive or negative, of combination or dissociation) and motion. The idiotic theory of latent heat is thus superseded.

But is this not a splendid material proof of the way in which the *Reflexionsbestimmungen* [the determinations of thought] are resolved into one another?

So much is certain; comparative physiology gives one a withering contempt for the idealistic exaltation of man over the other animals. At every step one bumps up against the most complete uniformity of structure with the rest of the mammals, and in its main features this uniformity extends to all vertebrates and even—less clearly—to insects, crustaceans, earthworms, etc. The Hegelian business of the qualitative leap in the quantitative series is also very fine here. Finally, among the lowest infusoria one reaches the primitive form, the simple, independently existing cell, which in turn, however, is not to be distinguished in any perceptible way from the lowest plants (fungi consisting of single cells—the fungi of the potato and the vine diseases, etc.) or from the germs of the higher stages of development up to the human ovum and spermatozoon inclusive, and which also looks just like the independent cells of the living body (blood corpuscles, the cells of the epidermis and mucous membrane, the secretion cells of the glands, kidneys, etc.). . . .

¶Marx, and especially Engels, always showed that dialectic is the universal law of movement in nature and society. While they definitely combated the narrow, unhistorical materialism derived from natural science alone, they constantly studied with equal thoroughness the results of research in the natural sciences, which provided them with the richest material for the confirmation of their conception of the world. " For in nature nothing happens alone. Everything has an effect on something else and vice versa, and it is mostly forgetfulness of this general movement and interaction which prevents our investigators of nature from seeing the simplest things clearly." (Engels, " Work as a Factor in the Development of Apes into Human Beings.")

Engels has left us extensive studies on natural science and its results (*Anti-Dühring* and the great manuscript on *The Dialectics of Nature*). The struggle for the demonstration " that the laws of dialectic are real laws of natural development and therefore apply also to the theoretical study of natural science " (Engels) was continued by Lenin, who attacked above all the idealistic falsification of dialectical materialism in natural science. In his book, *Materialism and Empirio-Criticism*, he writes :

" In a word, the ' physical ' idealism of to-day, just like the ' physiological ' idealism of yesterday, merely signifies that one school of natural scientists in one branch of science has succumbed to reactionary philosophy, without being able to rise directly and immediately above metaphysical materialism and to arrive at dialectical materialism. Modern physics has made and will continue to make this step, but it reaches the only true method and the only true philosophy of natural science, not directly but through zigzag progress, not consciously but instinctively, not clearly aware of its ' final goal ' but continually drawing nearer to it, through groping, vacillating, even retrogressive motion. Modern physics is in a state of confinement ; it is giving birth to dialectical materialism." (Lenin, *Collected Works*, Eng. ed., Vol. XIII (1927), p. 268.) The enormous growth of technique and of the natural sciences in the Soviet Union, the decay of technique and of the natural sciences in capitalist countries, have revealed the conditions in which a full and consistent application of dialectical materialism to research in the natural sciences is possible and can be carried out on the widest scale.

41. ENGELS TO MARX

Manchester, 7 October, 1858.

The business with Jones is very disgusting. He has held a meeting here and spoken entirely along the lines of the new alliance. After this affair one is really almost driven to believe that the English proletarian movement in its old traditional Chartist form must perish completely before it can develop itself in a new form, capable of life. And yet one cannot foresee what this new form will look like. For the rest, it seems to me that Jones's new move, taken in conjunction with the former more or less successful attempts at such an alliance, is really bound up with the fact that the English proletariat is becoming more and more bourgeois, so that this most bourgeois of all nations is apparently aiming ultimately at the possession of a bourgeois aristocracy and a bourgeois proletariat *as well as* a bourgeoisie. For a nation which exploits the whole world this is of course to a certain extent justifiable. The only thing that would help here would be a few thoroughly bad years, and since the gold discoveries these no longer seem so easy to come by. I must say all the same, however, that the way the mass of over-production which brought about the crisis has been absorbed is by no means clear to me; such a rapid ebb after such a violent flood tide has never occurred before.

¶At the end of the Chartist movement Jones went over more and more to the bourgeoisie. Marx therefore finally broke off relations with him. He wrote to Weydemeyer on February 1, 1859:

"I have broken with Ernest Jones. Despite my repeated warnings, and although I had predicted to him exactly what has happened—namely that he would ruin himself and disorganise the Chartist Party—he involved himself in attempts to come to an agreement with the bourgeois radicals. He is now a ruined man, but the harm he has done the English proletariat is enormous. Of course the damage will be repaired, but a very favourable moment for action has been lost. Imagine an army whose general goes over to the enemy on the day of battle!"

On the death of Jones, Engels wrote to Marx (January 29, 1869):

"To-morrow, with an enormous procession, Jones is to be buried in the same churchyard where Lupus* lies. The fellow is really a loss. His bourgeois phrases were only hypocrisy after all, and here in Manchester there is no one who can take his place with the workers. They will become completely disintegrated again and fall right into the net of the bourgeosie. Moreover, he was the only *educated* Englishman among the politicians who was, at bottom, entirely on our side." (See Letters 18, 35, 36.)

* Wilhelm Wolff.

42. MARX TO ENGELS

London, [8 October], 1858.

With the favourable turn of world trade at this moment (although the enormous accumulation of money in the banks of London, Paris and New York shows that things must still be very far from all right) it is at least consoling that in Russia *the revolution* has *begun*, for I regard the convocation of the "notables" to Petersburg as such a beginning. In Prussia likewise things are worse than in 1847 and the absurd delusions as to the middle-class propensities of the Prince of Prussia will be dissolved in fury. It will do the French no harm if they see that the world can move without them.* At the same time there are exceptionally big movements among the Slavs, especially in Bohemia, movements which are indeed counter-revolutionary but still add to the ferment.

The Russian war of 1854-55, wretched though it was and little as its results harmed the Russians (Turkey, rather, was the only one harmed), has nevertheless obviously hastened the present turn of things in Russia. The one circumstance which made the Germans in their revolutionary movement such complete satellites of France was the attitude of Russia. With an internal movement in Muscovy this bad joke will come to an end. As soon as the business there develops rather more perceptibly we shall be able to prove how far the worthy State Councillor Haxthausen† allowed himself to be taken in by the "authorities" and by the peasants drilled by the authorities.

We cannot deny that bourgeois society has experienced its sixteenth century a second time—a sixteenth century which will, I hope, sound the death-knell of bourgeois society just as the first one thrust it into existence. The particular task of bourgeois society is the establishment of the world market, at least in outline, and of production based upon the world market. As the world is round, this seems to have been com-

* *Dass die Welt auch ohne sie "mov't" (pennsylvanisch).* Marx here uses the English verb "move" in a German construction, adding "Pennsylvanian" as a joking explanation. [*Ed. Eng. ed.*]

† August von Haxthausen (1792-1867) a Prussian State Councillor, who wrote several books about Russia and Transcaucasia, based on his travels.

pleted by the colonisation of California and Australia and the opening up of China and Japan. The difficult question for us is this : on the Continent the revolution is imminent and will also immediately assume a socialist character. Is it not bound to be crushed in this little corner, considering that in a far greater territory the movement of bourgeois society is still on the ascendent?

As to what specially concerns China, I have assured myself by an exact analysis of the movement of trade since 1836, *first*, that the increase of English and American exports (1844-46) proved in 1847 to be a pure fraud, and that also in the following ten years the average remained nearly stationary, while the imports into England and America from China grew enormously ; *secondly*, that the opening up of the five ports and the seizure of Hong-Kong only resulted in the trade passing from Canton to Shanghai. The other " emporiums " do not count. The chief reason for the failure of this market appears to be the opium trade, to which in fact any increase in the export trade to China is continually limited ; but added to this is the internal economic organisation of the country, its minute-scale agriculture, etc., which will take an enormous time to break down. England's present treaty with China, which in my opinion was worked out by Palmerston in conjunction with the Petersburg cabinet and given to Lord Elgin on his journey, is a mockery from beginning to end.

¶This letter shows how Marx and Engels studied the development of the capitalist method of production and all its new manifestations as practical revolutionaries. About China Engels wrote to Sorge (in New York) on November 10, 1894 : " The Chinese war [with Japan] has given the death-blow to the old China. Isolation has become impossible, the introduction of railroads, steam engines, electricity, large-scale industry has already become a necessity for purposes of military defence. But with this the old economic system of small peasant cultivation, where the family also makes its industrial products for itself, falls to pieces too, and with it the whole of the old social system, under which a relatively dense population was possible. Millions will be turned out of their homes and forced to emigrate; and these millions will find their way as far as Europe and that in masses. But Chinese competition, once it is on a mass scale, will rapidly bring things to a head both for you [in the U.S.A.] and for us, and so the conquest of China by capitalism will at the same time give an impetus to the overthrow of capitalism in Europe and America."

43. MARX TO WEYDEMEYER

London, 1 February, 1859.

My *Critique of Political Economy* will be published in parts (the first part in eight or ten days from now) by Franz Duncker (Besser's publishing house) in Berlin. It is only thanks to Lassalle's extraordinary zeal and powers of persuasion that Duncker has been persuaded to take this step. Even then he has provided himself with a way of escape—*the definite contract is to depend on the sale of the first parts.* I divide the whole political economy into six books:

Capital; Landed Property; Wage Labour; State; Foreign Trade; World Market.

Book I on capital is divided into four sections. *Section I: Capital in general*, is divided into three chapters: (1) *The Commodity;* (2) *Money or Simple Circulation;* (3) *Capital.* (1) and (2), about ten sheets, form the contents of the parts which are appearing first. You understand the *political* reasons which have moved me to hold back the third chapter, on "Capital," until I have got a footing again. . . .

In these two chapters the foundation is also destroyed of the Proudhonist socialism now fashionable in France, which wants to leave private property in existence *but to organise* the exchange of private products; which wants *commodities* but not *money.* Above all things Communism must rid itself of this "false brother." But, apart from any polemical aim, you know that the analysis of the simple money-forms is the hardest, because it is the most abstract part of political economy.

44. MARX TO ENGELS

[London], 25 February, 1859.

Po and Rhine is an excellent idea, which must immediately be put into operation. You must get down to it *at once*, as time is *everything* here. I have written to Lassalle to-day already and am sure Jüdel Braun* will put it through.

The pamphlet (how many sheets?—on this point reply *by return*) must first appear *anonymously*, so that the public thinks the author is a great general. In the *second* edition, which you will undoubtedly see if the thing appears at the right moment, you will reveal yourself in a six-line preface. This will then be a triumph for our party. I have done you some honour in my Preface† and so it will be all the better if you yourself appear upon the stage immediately afterwards.

The dogs of democrats and the liberal scoundrels will see that we are the only fellows who have not been stupefied by this appalling period of peace.

¶Engels proposed to write a pamphlet, entitled *Po and Rhine*, on the forthcoming Austro-Italian war.

The Austro-Italian war was prepared with the participation of the Russian government. In July 1858 Bonaparte had a meeting with Cavour [the minister of King Victor Emmanuel of Piedmont and Sardinia] and between them they concluded an agreement, which included a war against Austria and the following division of spoils: to France—Savoy and Nice; to Piedmont—Lombardy, Venice, Modena, Parma, Tuscany and part of the Papal territory.

The war began in April 1859 and was ended at the river Mincio in June of the same year. On July 11, 1859, peace was concluded at Villafranca. Sardinia (Piedmont) received additional territories and France got Savoy and Nice, that is, the boundaries of 1807 were again restored. Thus Italy remained ununified. (See Letter 14.)

Marx and Engels stood for the revolutionary way of unifica-

* Nickname for Lassalle.

† Preface to the *Critique of Political Economy* (1859).

tion for Germany, which was directed against both France and Russia. The view that Germany required the line of the Mincio as a protection against France, supported by the theory of "natural" frontiers, only served reactionary ends and represented "that theory of a Central European Great Power which would like to turn Austria, Prussia and the rest of Germany into a federal state under the predominant influence of Austria, to Germanise Hungary and the Slav-Rumanian Danube countries by colonisation, schools and quiet force, to transfer by this means the centre of gravity of this complex of countries more and more towards the South-East, towards Vienna, and incidentally also to reconquer Alsace and Lorraine. The 'Central European Great Power' is to be a sort of rebirth of the Holy Roman Empire of the German nation and appears among other things to aim at incorporating into itself the former Austrian Netherlands as well as Holland, as vassal states. . . . In this way German moral earnestness combined with the youthful Central European Great Power cannot fail shortly to seize for the latter world domination by sea and land, and to inaugurate a new historic era in which Germany will at length, after so long, again play first fiddle while the other nations dance to her tune." (Engels, *Po and Rhine.*) Engels proved that this chauvinistic theory would not hold water from a military point of view, and with the greatest emphasis advocated the revolutionary unification of Germany. (See also Letters 45, 46, 89, 90, 144, 145 of this volume.)

45. MARX TO LASSALLE

London, 25 February, 1859.

Engels is intending to publish, at first anonymously, a small pamphlet entitled *Po and Rhine*.

Main contents: proof according to military science that all the reasons which are adduced to show that the Austrians must have the line of the Mincio in order to protect *Germany*, can be exactly applied to show that France must have the Rhine frontier in order to protect herself; further that while *Austria* certainly has a great interest in the Mincio line, Germany as a united power has none whatever, and that Italy, from the military point of view, will always be dominated by Germany unless the whole of Switzerland becomes French. The thing is chiefly directed against the strategy of the *Augsburger Allgemeine Zeitung*. Otherwise, of course, nationally against Mr. Bonaparte. . . .

46. MARX TO ENGELS

[London], 18 May, 1859.

Lassalle's pamphlet is an enormous blunder. The appearance of your "anonymous" pamphlet* kept him awake at nights. The position of the revolutionary party in Germany is certainly difficult at the moment, but, with some critical analysis of the circumstances, clear nevertheless. As to the "governments," it is obvious from every point of view, if only for the sake of Germany's *existence*, that the demand must be put to them *not to remain neutral*, but, as you rightly say, to be *patriotic*. But the *revolutionary* point is to be given to the affair simply by emphasising the antagonism *to Russia* more strongly than the antagonism against Boustrapa.† This is what Lassalle should have done in answer to the anti-French screams of the *Neue Preussische Zeitung*. *This* is also the point which, as the war goes on, will in practice land the German governments in a betrayal of the Empire and where they will be got by the throat. For the rest, if Lassalle takes upon himself to speak in the name of the Party, he must in future either make up his mind to be publicly disowned by us, for the situation is too important for personal considerations, or else, instead of pursuing his mixed inspirations of passion and logic, must previously come to an understanding with the views held by other people besides himself. We must absolutely insist on party discipline now or everything will go to the dogs. . . .

Messrs. the *Knoten*‡ have . . . had a very nice lesson. That old-Weitlinger ass Scherzer thought *he* could nominate Party

* *Po and Rhine* (Letter 44).

† Napoleon III.

‡ *Knoten*. See Note on page 87. The allusion in this paragraph is to some petty groups of political refugees in London who gave themselves such names as "Communist Association," etc. [*Ed. Eng. ed.*]

representatives. When *I* met a deputation of the *Knoten* (I have refused to join any association, but Liebknecht [was nominated] chairman of one and the Lapp [Anders] of the other) I told them straight out: We had received our appointment as representatives of the proletarian party from nobody *but ourselves* It was, however, endorsed by the exclusive and universal hatred consecrated to us by all the parties and fractions of the old world. You can imagine how staggered the blockheads were. . .

¶Lassalle's pamphlet was entitled *The Italian War and Prussia's Task.* In this pamphlet he put forward the demand that the nationalist policy of Bonaparte, *i.e.*, the incorporation of Italian territory in the south, should be countered by a similar policy in the north, *i.e.*, the annexation of Schleswig-Holstein. Actually, therefore, he yielded to Bismarck, for in place of the demand of Marx and Engels for the revolutionary unification of Germany against France and Russia he put a nationalist demand for annexation which furthered Bismarck's interests. "During the period from 1864 to 1870, in which the epoch of the bourgeois-democratic revolution in Germany was being completed, in which the exploiting classes of Prussia and Austria were fighting for this or that method of completing the revolution *from above*, Marx . . . condemned Lassalle for coquetting with Bismarck. . . . Marx insisted upon revolutionary tactics . . . which would not be adapted to suit the 'victor,' the Prussian *Junker*, but by which the struggle with him would forthwith be renewed *upon the very basis* created by the Prussian military successes." (Lenin, *The Teachings of Karl Marx.* See Little Lenin Library, Vol. I, p. 36.) As a means of carrying on the struggle against reaction in Germany, Marx and Engels put the struggle against Russia, at that time the shield of reaction, in the forefront, and attached decisive importance to it. The "point" against Russia was at the same time the point against reaction in Prussia. Hence Marx and Engels also followed internal events in Russia with great attention. (Compare Letters 47, 48, 60, 62, 65.)* At the end of his pamphlet, *Savoy, Nice and the Rhine*, Engels wrote: "In the meantime we have gained an ally in the Russian serf. The struggle which has

* See Subject Index, "Russia."

now broken out in Russia between the ruling classes of the rural population and the ruled is already undermining the whole system of Russian foreign policy. The system was only possible so long as Russia had no internal political development. But that time is past. The industrial and agricultural development which the government and the aristocracy have promoted in every possible way has thriven to such a degree that it can no longer be reconciled with the existing social conditions. Their abolition is a necessity on the one hand and an impossibility —unless they are changed by force—on the other. Together with the Russia which existed from Peter the Great to Nicholas, there falls also the foreign policy of that Russia. It looks as if it had been reserved for Germany to make this fact clear to Russia not only with the pen but with the sword."

47. MARX TO ENGELS

London, 13 December, 1859.

In Russia the movement is advancing faster than in all the rest of Europe. The struggle for a constitution for one thing—of the nobles against the tsar and of the peasants against the nobles. Alexander has also at last discovered that the Poles will have nothing to do with assimilation into a Slav-Russian nationality and has made a lot of fuss. All this more than counterbalances the extraordinary successes of Russian diplomacy during the last fifteen years and especially since 1849. When the next revolution comes Russia will be so kind as to revolutionise as well.

48. MARX TO ENGELS

[London], 11 January, 1860.

In my opinion, the biggest things that are happening in the world to-day are on the one hand the movement of the slaves in America, started by the death of John Brown, and on the other the movement of the serfs in Russia. You will have seen that the Russian aristocracy have thrown themselves directly into agitation for a constitution and that two or three people from the chief families have already found their way to Siberia. At the same time Alexander has spoilt things with the peasants by the latest Manifesto, which declares in so many words that the "communistic principle" must cease with emancipation. Thus the "social" movement has started in the West and in the East. This added to the prospective downbreak in Central Europe will be grandiose. . . .

¶BROWN, JOHN (1800-59). American revolutionary, opponent of slavery. Leader of partisan troops in the partisan war against the slave owners in Kansas, 1854-58. He tried to form an army of runaway slaves. On October 16, 1859, he took the arsenal at Harper's Ferry by a daring attack and wanted to arm the slaves in the neighbourhood but did not gain any support. On October 18, 1859, government troops recaptured the arsenal from him. He was executed on December 2, 1859.

49. MARX TO LASSALLE

London, 16 January, 1861.

Darwin's book is very important and serves me as a basis in natural science for the class struggle in history. One has to put up with the crude English method of development, of course. Despite all deficiencies, not only is the death-blow dealt here for the first time to "teleology" in the natural sciences but their rational meaning is empirically explained.

¶DARWIN, CHARLES (1809-82). Famous natural scientist who brought about a revolution in biology by his theory of the development of the animal world, the struggle for existence, adaptation and the "survival of the fittest." He particularly investigated how the transformation of organisms takes place. "Darwin," as Marx wrote, "has interested us in the history of Nature's technology." (*Capital*, I, chap. XV [1], Kerr edition, p. 406, note 2.) The work referred to in Marx's letter, *On the*

Origin of Species by Means of Natural Selection or the Preservation of Favoured Races in the Struggle for Life, was published in 1859.

Marx wrote to Engels on December 19, 1860:

"During my time of trial, these last four weeks,* I have read all sorts of things. Among others Darwin's book on Natural Selection. Although it is developed in the crude English style, this is the book which contains the basis in natural history for our view."

50. MARX TO ENGELS

[London,] 27 February, 1861.

The Cologne people have made a nice mess of my library. The *whole* Fourier is stolen, ditto Goethe, ditto Herder, ditto Voltaire and, what is the most awful to me, the *Économistes du 18me Siècle* (quite new, cost me about 500 francs) as well as many volumes of the Greek classics, many single volumes of other works. If I come to Cologne I shall have a word to say about this with Mr. National Union Bürgers.† Hegel's *Phenomenology* and *Logic* ditto. . . .

As a relaxation in the evenings I have been reading Appian on the Roman Civil Wars, in the original Greek text. A very valuable book. The chap is an Egyptian by birth. Schlosser says he has "no soul," probably because he goes to the roots of the material basis for these civil wars. Spartacus is revealed as the most splendid fellow in the whole of ancient history. Great general (no Garibaldi), noble character, real representative of the ancient proletariat.

Pompeius, *reiner Scheisskerl* [an utter rotter]; got his undeserved fame by snatching the credit, first for the successes of Lucullus (against Mithridates), then for the successes of Sertorius (Spain), etc., and as Sulla's "young man," etc. As a general he was the Roman Odilon Barrot. As soon as he had to show what he was made of—against Cæsar—a lousy good-for-nothing. Cæsar made the greatest possible military mistakes —deliberately mad—in order to bewilder the philistine who

* He had been nursing his wife through a severe illness.

† Bürgers (See Letter 11, Note). For the "*National Verein*" (National Union), see page 218, Note on Bennigsen. Bürgers had become a National Liberal. [*Ed. Eng. ed.*]

was opposing him. An ordinary Roman general—say Crassus—would have wiped him out six times over during the struggle in Epirus. But with Pompeius everything was possible. Shakespeare, in his *Love's Labour Lost*, seems to have had an inkling of what Pompey really was.

¶Marx had touched on the same question in his letter of March 8, 1855: "A little time ago I went through Roman history (ancient) again up to the Augustan era. The internal history simply resolves itself into the struggle of small versus large landed property, *specifically modified*, of course, by slave conditions. The debt relations, which play such a great part from the very beginning of Roman history, figure merely as the inevitable *consequence* of small landownership."

51. MARX TO ENGELS

[London,] 7 May, 1861.

Lassalle, dazzled by the reputation he has made in certain learned circles by his Heraclitus and in a certain circle of spongers by his good wine and cookery, is naturally unaware that he is discredited among the public at large. Then there is his insistence on being always in the right, his fixed attachment to the "speculative conception" (the lad is even dreaming of writing a new Hegelian philosophy raised to the second power), his infection with old French liberalism, his bombastic writing, his self-assertiveness, tactlessness, etc. Lassalle could be of service as one of the editors, under strict discipline. Otherwise would only bring discredit. But you see the great friendship he showed me made it very embarrassing for me to come out with this in so many words. I therefore remained altogether indefinite, saying that I could decide nothing without previous discussion with you and Lupus [Wilhelm Wolff].

¶Lassalle had proposed to Marx, who had been staying with him in Berlin, that they should start a paper to be edited by himself, Marx and Engels; Lassalle's vote on one side was to be counted as equivalent to the combined vote of Marx and Engels on the other. (See also Letter 55.)

52. ENGELS TO MARX

[Manchester, 2 December, 1861].

These last days I have at length been reading Lassalle.* The stuff about retrospective action is very plausible but won't work; witness, for instance, the divorce laws where one might also say, as many a Berlin philistine has in fact said: If I had known they would make divorce so difficult for me I would never have married. Moreover, it is really deeply superstitious of the fellow that he should still believe in the "idea of justice," absolute justice. His objections to Hegel's philosophy of law are for the most part perfectly correct, but all the same he himself has still not got well under way with his new philosophy of mind. Even from the philosophical point of view he ought at least to have got far enough to conceive the process only, and not its mere temporary result, as the absolute, and in that case the only idea of justice which could have resulted would have been just the historical process itself. The style is nice, too. The "hand-wringing despair of the contradictions," etc. And then the preface. Smart Ephraim† all over. I am not likely to get much further with it unless I find I can use it as a course of Roman law, in which case I shall read it through.

53. MARX TO ENGELS

[London,] 9 December, 1861.

I agree with your strictures on Itzig‡ (who has written to me from Florence that he had "a *very* interesting meeting" with

* Lassalle's book *The System of Acquired Rights* (1861).
† *Ephraim Gescheit*—nickname for Lassalle.
‡ Itzig ("Ikey"), a nickname for Lassalle.

Garibaldi, etc.). The second volume is more interesting, because of the Latin quotations for one thing. The ideologising pervades everything and the dialectical method is *falsely* applied. Hegel never called dialectics the subsumption of a mass of " cases " under a general principle.

54. MARX TO ENGELS

[London,] 2 August, 1862.

It is a real marvel that I have still been able to carry on as I have done with the theoretical work.* I now intend after all to bring the theory of rent already into this volume as a supplementary chapter, *i.e.*, as an " illustration " of a principle laid down earlier. I will tell you in a few words what is a *lengthy and complicated story when worked out*, in order that you may *give me your opinion*.

You know that I distinguish two parts of capital : *constant capital* (raw material, *matières instrumentales* [auxiliary materials], machinery, etc.) whose value merely *reappears* in the value of the product, and, second, *variable capital*, *i.e.*, the capital laid out in wages, which contains less embodied labour than the worker gives in return for it. *E.g.*, if the daily wage = 10 hours and if the worker works 12, he replaces the variable capital + $\frac{1}{5}$ (2 hours). This latter surplus I call *surplus value*.

Assume a given *rate of surplus value* (namely the length of the working day and the surplus of the labour above that necessary for the reproduction of the worker's pay) and say it equals 50 per cent. In this case, with a working day of, *e.g.*, 12 hours, the worker would work 8 hours for himself and 4 hours ($\frac{8}{2}$) for the employer. And assume this for all trades, so that any differences in the average working time are simply compensation for the greater or less difficulty of the work, etc.

In these circumstances, with *equal* exploitation of the worker in *different* trades, different capitals of *the same size* will yield very *different* amounts of surplus value in different spheres of production and therefore *very different rates of profit*, since profit is nothing but the proportion of the surplus value to the total

* In a time of desperate financial difficulty.

capital advanced. This will depend on the *organic composition* of the capital, *i.e.*, on its division into constant and variable capital.

Assume, as above, that the surplus labour = 50 per cent. Then if, *e.g.*, £1 = 1 working day (it makes no difference if you think of the length of the day as a week), the working day = 12 hours and the necessary labour (for reproduction of the pay) = 8 hours, the wages of 30 workers (or working days) would therefore = £20 and the value of their work = £30; the variable capital for one worker (daily or weekly) = $\frac{2}{3}$ £ and the value he produces = £1. The amount of surplus value produced in different trades by a capital of £100 will be very different according to the proportions of constant and variable capital into which this capital is divided. Call the constant capital *c*, the variable *v*. If in the cotton industry, for instance, the composition were *c* 80, *v* 20, the value of the product would = 110 (given 50 per cent. surplus value or surplus labour). The amount of surplus value = 10 and the rate of profit = 10 per cent., since the profit = the relation of 10 (the surplus value) : 100 (the total value of the capital expended). Assume that in wholesale tailoring the composition is *c* 50, *v* 50, then the product = 125, surplus value (at a rate of 50 per cent. as above) = 25 and rate of profit = 25 per cent. Take another industry, where the proportion is *c* 70, *v* 30, then the product = 115, and the rate of profit = 15 per cent. And finally an industry where the composition = *c* 90, *v* 10, then the product = 105 and the rate of profit = 5 per cent.

We have here, with *equal exploitation* of labour, very different amounts of surplus value for equal sums of capital invested in different trades, and hence very different rates of profit.

But if we take the above four capitals together we get:

		Value of the Product		*per cent.*	
(1)	*c* 80, *v* 20	110	Rate of profit =	10	*Rate of surplus value in all cases = 50 per cent.*
(2)	*c* 50, *v* 50	125	,, ,, ,, =	25	
(3)	*c* 70, *v* 30	115	,, ,, ,, =	15	
(4)	*c* 90, *v* 10	105	,, ,, ,, =	5	
	Capital	400	Profit =	55	

On 100 this gives a rate of profit of 13¾ per cent.

Regarded as the *total capital* of the *class* (400) the rate of profit would = 13¾ per cent. And capitalists are brothers. Competition (transfer of capital or withdrawal of capital from one trade to another) brings it about that *equal sums* of capital in *different* trades, despite their different organic composition, yield the *same average* rate of profit. In other words: the *average* profit which a capital of £100, for instance, makes in a certain trade is not made as the application of this particular capital, nor related, therefore, to the particular aim with which the surplus value is produced, but is made as an *aliquot part* of the total capital of the capitalist class. It is a share on which, in proportion to its size, dividends are paid from the total sum of surplus value (or unpaid labour) which the total variable capital (laid out in wages) of the class produces.

Now in order that 1, 2, 3, 4, in the above illustration shall make the same *average profit*, each one of them must sell his commodities at £113⅓. 1 and 4 sell them *above their value*, 2 and 3 *below* their value. Price regulated in this way = the expenses of capital + the average profit; for instance, 10 per cent. is what Smith calls the *natural price*, *cost price*, etc. It is to this average price that competition between the different trades reduces the prices in different branches (by transfer or withdrawal of capital). Competition does *not* therefore reduce commodities to their *value*, but to their *cost price*, which is *above*, *below* or *equal* to their *value*, according to the organic composition of the respective capitals.

Ricardo confuses *value* with *cost price*. He therefore believes that if *absolute rent* existed (*i.e.*, a rent *independent* of the different productivity of different kinds of land) agricultural produce, etc., would always be sold *above its value*, because it would be sold *above* its cost price (the capital advanced + the average profit). This would overthrow his fundamental law. So he denies the existence of absolute rent and only assumes differential rent.

But his identification of the *value* of commodities with their *cost price* is fundamentally false and traditionally accepted from A. Smith.

The fact is this :

Assume that the *average* composition of all *not* agricultural capital is *c* 80, *v* 20, so that the product (at 50 per cent. rate of surplus value) = 110 and the rate of profit = 10 per cent.

Assume further that the average composition of *agricultural capital* is = *c* 60, *v* 40. (This figure is statistically fairly correct for England ; the pasture rents, etc., make no difference to this question because they are determined by the corn rents and not by themselves.) The product, with equal exploitation of labour as above, then = 120 and the rate of profit = 20 per cent. If therefore the farmer sells his produce *at its value*, he sells it for 120, and not at 110, its *cost price*. But *landed property* prevents the farmer, the equivalent of the brother capitalists, from adjusting the *value* of the product to its *cost price*. Competition between the capitals cannot enforce this. The landowner intervenes and extracts the *difference between value and cost price*. In general a low proportion of constant to variable capital is the expression of a low (or relatively low) development of the productive forces of labour in a particular sphere of production. Therefore if the average composition of agricultural capital, for instance, is *c* 60, *v* 40, while that of non-agricultural capital is *c* 80, *v* 20, this proves that agriculture has not yet reached the same stage of development as industry. (Which is very easy to explain, for, apart from everything else, the presupposition of industry is the older science of mechanics, the presupposition of agriculture the entirely new sciences of chemistry, geology and physiology). If the proportion in agriculture equals *c* 80, *v* 20 (as assumed above) *absolute rent* disappears. There only remains *differential rent*, which, however, I develop in such a way that Ricardo's assumption of the continual deterioration of agriculture is revealed as most ridiculous and arbitrary.

In the above determination of *cost price* as distinct from *value* it must also be noted that in addition to the distinction between constant and variable capital, which arises from the *immediate process of production* in which the capital is involved, there is also a distinction between *fixed* and *circulating* capital, which arises from the *process of the circulation* of capital. But the formula would become too complicated if I tried to insert this in the above as well.

Here you have—roughly, for the thing is rather complicated—the criticism of Ricardo's theory. This much you will admit, that attention to the *organic composition of capital* does away with a mass of what have seemed hitherto to be contradictions and problems. . . .

¶This letter, in which Marx gives a brilliant sketch of what he later presented in detail in Vol. III of *Capital*, is important because bourgeois economists, in order to hide their failure to understand the nature of the Marxian method, industriously attempt to manufacture a contradiction between the first and third volumes of *Capital*. This letter is a documentary proof that Marx already had the skeleton of his whole theory complete long before Vol. I of *Capital* was published. Here too in his theory of rent, he has already got the theory of absolute rent worked out, which in 1851 (see Letter 6) he had not as yet developed. (See also Letters 56 and 85.)

The manuscripts belonging to the year 1862 remain preserved to us ; here there are actually long and detailed passages on rent which Marx in the final arrangement of *Capital* relegated to Volume III.

SMITH, ADAM (1723-90). Economist and philosopher. He gave to classical economy its developed form. Marx calls him the economist of the manufacturing period. His theories of the division of labour, of productive labour and of surplus value were of great importance. According to his doctrine the true wealth of nations does not consist in money, as the mercantilists maintained, but in useful labour productive of exchange values. According to Adam Smith surplus value was produced not only by agricultural labour, as maintained by the physiocrats, but also by industrial labour. " The important thing about A. Smith's contradictions is that they contain problems which he does not indeed solve but which he gives expression to by contradicting himself." (Marx.) The main fault in his theory of reproduction, exposed by Marx, is his failure to take constant capital into account, his resolution of the value of commodities into wages and surplus value. (*Cf.* Letter 67.)

55. MARX TO ENGELS

London, 7 August [1862].

Itzig [Lassalle] also told me that he may perhaps start a paper if he goes back in September. I told him that for *good pay* I would be its English correspondent, without in any way taking on any other responsibility or political partnership, since politically we agree in nothing except in some far-distant ultimate ends.

I do not entirely share your views on the American Civil War. I do not think that all is up. The Northerners have been dominated from the first by the representatives of the border slave states, who also pushed McClellan, that old partisan of Breckinridge, to the top. The Southerners, on the other hand, acted as one man from the beginning. The North itself has turned the slaves into a military force on the side of the Southerners, instead of against them. The South leaves productive labour to the slaves and could therefore put its whole fighting strength into the field without disturbance. The South had unified military leadership, the North had not. That no strategic plan existed was already obvious from all the manœuvres of the Kentucky army after the conquest of Tennessee. In my opinion all this will take another turn. In the end the North will make war seriously, adopt revolutionary methods and throw over the domination of the border slaves statesmen. A single nigger regiment [*ein einziges niggerregiment*]* would have a remarkable effect on Southern nerves.

The difficulty of getting the 300,000 men seems to me purely political. The North-West and New England wish to and will force the government to give up the diplomatic method of conducting war which it has used hitherto, and they are now making terms on which the 300,000 men shall come forth. If Lincoln does not give way (which he will do, however) there will be a revolution.

As to the lack of military talent, the method which has prevailed up till now of selecting generals purely from considerations of diplomacy and party intrigue is scarcely designed to

* See footnote, page 136.

bring talent to the front. General Pope seems to me to be a man of energy, however.

With regard to the financial measures, they are clumsy, as they were bound to be in a country where up to now no taxes for the whole state have in fact existed; but they are not nearly so idiotic as the measures taken by Pitt and Co. The present depreciation of money is due, I think, not to economic but to purely political reasons—distrust. It will therefore change with a different policy.

The long and short of the business seems to me to be that a war of this kind must be conducted on revolutionary lines, while the Yankees have so far been trying to conduct it constitutionally.

¶After the election of Abraham Lincoln to the presidency of the United States in 1860, when the chief political power passed to the industrial capitalists of the North, the Southern slave-owners, who were in no position to compete with industry based on wage labour, decided to organise their own state, which would guarantee the chief political power to the slave-owning class.

At the beginning of 1861, the slave-owning South announced its secession from the Union and established its own Confederation (hence the troops of the Southern States were known as the Confederates, the troops of the Northern States as the Federalists). Jefferson Davis was elected President of the Southern Confederation. The Civil War which now arose between the slave-owning South and the industrial North lasted about five years, 1861 to 1865.

The Southern States had prepared themselves for war beforehand and already possessed a number of generals, soldiers by profession: Beauregard, Bragg, Johnston, Jackson, Lee, etc. The Federal government of the North, on the other hand, was not prepared for war, and attempted to settle the conflict peacefully along constitutional lines. Added to this there were among the Northerners elements from the border states who sympathised with the Southerners, which naturally impeded the activity of the Federal government. The first engagements did not end favourably for the North (the storming of Fort Sumter and the battle of Bull Run).

The North could only give its army a hurried and extremely inadequate training and was obliged several times to change its Commander-in-Chief—McDowell, McClellan, Burnside. But it was able to organise constant new reinforcements, the army gained experience in battle and in the end the industrial North was victorious. Towards the end of the war the North had excellent generals like Grant and Sherman. Many German emigrants who had taken part in the revolution of 1848 and had had military experience fought on the side of the North. Both fractions of the Communist League—Willich, Weydemeyer, Steffen, etc.—also took part in the war on the side of the North.

Marx was sure the whole time that the North would win. On September 10, 1862, he wrote to Engels:

"As for the Yankees, I am as certain as ever in my opinion that the North will win in the end. . . . The way the North is conducting war is only what might have been expected from a *bourgeois* republic, where fraud has been enthroned king so long. The South, an *oligarchy*, is better adapted to it, especially an oligarchy where the whole productive work falls on the niggers,* and the four millions of 'white trash' are professional filibusters. All the same I would bet my head that these fellows will get the worst of it, in spite of 'Stonewall Jackson.' It is possible, of course, that before this things may come to a sort of revolution in the North itself."

In the Preface to the first edition of *Capital* (1867) Marx wrote:

"As in the eighteenth century the American War of Independence sounded the tocsin for the European middle class, so in the nineteenth century the American Civil War sounded it for the European working class." (See also Letters 57, 58.)

POPE (1822-92). Was placed at the head of the army of the North on June 27, 1862. Resigned after the defeats in August, 1862.

LINCOLN, ABRAHAM (1809-65). Sixteenth President of the United States. One of the best representatives of bourgeois democracy.

* Marx's letters on the American Civil War are crowded with English words and phrases reproduced from the newspapers he was so intensively studying; the ironic force of these reproductions—*e.g.*, 'nigger' for Negro—tends to be weakened in a purely English version. See page v (Publisher's Note). [*Ed. Eng. ed.*]

PITT, WILLIAM (the younger) (1759-1806). One of the most reactionary English statesmen, Prime Minister at the time of the French Revolution. He organised the war of intervention against the revolution and the wars against Napoleon I. He suppressed the Irish rebellion of 1798 and carried out a series of reactionary measures against the workers' movement.

BRECKINRIDGE (1821-76). Candidate of the Democratic Party in the presidential election of 1860 and a fanatical supporter of slavery.

56. MARX TO ENGELS

[London], 9 August, 1862.

With regard to the *theory of rent*, I must first, of course, wait for your letter.* But in order to simplify the "debate," as Heinrich Bürgers would say, I send the following:

(I) The only thing I have got to prove *theoretically* is the *possibility* of absolute rent, without violating the law of value. This is the point around which the *theoretical* conflict has turned from the days of the physiocrats up till now. Ricardo denies this possibility, I maintain it. I also maintain that his denial is based upon a theoretically false dogma taken over from Adam Smith—the pre-supposed identity between the *cost price* and the *value of commodities*. Further, that where Ricardo illustrates the point by *examples* he always presupposes conditions in which there is either no capitalist production or *no landed property* (actually or legally). But the whole point is to investigate the law when these things exist.

(II) As to the *existence* of absolute ground rent, that is a question which would have to be solved *statistically* in each country. But the importance of the purely theoretical solution is due to the fact that all the statisticians and practical men in general have been maintaining the existence of absolute rent for the last 35 years, while the (Ricardian) theoreticians have been trying to demonstrate it out of existence by very arbitrary and theoretically feeble abstractions. Up to now in all such quarrels I have always found the theoreticians in the wrong.

* Engels had written on August 8: "The existence of 'absolute' rent is by no means clear to me, for after all you have still got to prove it." [*Ed. Eng. ed.*]

(III) I show that, even assuming the existence of absolute ground rent, it by no means follows that under all circumstances the worst cultivated land or the worst mine pays a rent, but that very possibly they have to sell their products at market value, though *below* their *individual* value. In order to prove the opposite Ricardo always assumes—what is theoretically false—that under all conditions of the market the commodity produced under the most *unfavourable* conditions determines the market value. You already gave the right reply to this in the *Deutsch-Französische Jahrbücher*.

57. MARX TO ENGELS

[London,] 29 October, 1862.

As for America, I believe that the Maryland campaign was decisive in so far as it showed that even in this section of the border states most sympathetic to the South support for the Confederates is weak. But the whole struggle turns on the border states. Whoever gets them dominates the Union. At the same time the fact that Lincoln issued the forthcoming Emancipation Act at a moment when the Confederates were pushing forward in Kentucky, shows that all consideration for the loyal slave-owners in the border states has ceased. The emigration of the slave-owners from Missouri, Kentucky and Tennessee to the South, with their black chattels, is already enormous, and if the war is prolonged for a while, as it is certain to be, the Southerners will have lost all hold there. The South began the war for these territories. The war itself was the means of destroying its power in the border states, where, apart from this, the ties with the South were becoming weaker every day because a market can no longer be found for the breeding of slaves and the internal slave trade. In my opinion, therefore, for the South it will only be a matter now of the defensive. But their sole possibility of success lay in an offensive. If the report is confirmed that Hooker is getting the active command of the Potomac army, that McClellan is being "retired" to the "theoretical" post of Commander-in-chief and that Halleck is taking over the chief command in the West, then the conduct of the war in Virginia may also take on a more energetic character. Moreover the most favourable time of year for the Confederates is now past.

There is no doubt at all that morally the collapse of the Maryland campaign was of the most tremendous importance.

As to finance, the United States know from the time of the War of Independence, and we know from observation of Austria, how far one can go with depreciated paper money. It is a fact that the Yankees never exported more corn to England than they have this year, that the present harvest is again far above the average and that the trade balance was never more favourable for them than it has been for the last two years. As soon as the new system of taxation (a very ridiculous one, it is true, exactly in Pitt's style) comes into operation, the paper money which up to now has only been continually *emitted* will also at last begin to *flow back again*. An extension of the paper issue on the present scale will therefore become superfluous and further depreciation will thus be checked. What had made even the present depreciation less dangerous than it was in France, and even in England, in similar circumstances, has been the fact that the Yankees never prohibited *two prices*, a gold price and a paper price. The actual mischief done resolves itself into a state debt for which the proper equivalent has never been received and a premium on jobbing and speculation.

When the English boast that their depreciation was never more than 11½ per cent. (other people's belief is that it was more than double this during some time), they conveniently forget that they not only continued to pay their old taxes but every year paid new ones as well, so that the return flow of the banknotes was assured from the beginning, while the Yankees have actually carried on the war for a year and a half *without taxes* (except the greatly diminished import duties), simply by repeating the issue of paper. In a process of this kind, of which the turning point has now been reached, the actual depreciation is still comparatively small.

The fury with which the Southerners have received Lincoln's Acts proves their importance. All Lincoln's Acts appear like the mean pettifogging conditions which one lawyer puts to his opposing lawyer. But this does not alter their historic content, and indeed it amuses me when I compare them with the drapery in which the Frenchman envelops even the most unimportant point.

Of course, like other people, I see the repulsive side of the form the movement takes among the Yankees ; but I find the explanation of it in the nature of "bourgeois" democracy. The events over there are a world upheaval, nevertheless, and there is nothing more disgusting in the whole business than the English attitude towards them.

58. ENGELS TO MARX

Manchester, 5 November, 1862.

As regards America I also think, of course, that the Confederates in Maryland have received an unexpected moral blow of great significance. I am also convinced that the *definite* possession of the border states will decide the result of the war. But I am by no means certain that the affair is going to proceed along such classic lines as you appear to believe. Despite all the screams of the Yankees, there is still no sign whatever available that the people regard this petty business as a real question of national existence. On the contrary, these election victories of the Democrats go to prove rather that the party which has had enough of the war is growing. If there were only some proof or some indication that the masses in the North were beginning to rise as they did in France in 1792 and 1793, then it would all be very fine. But the only revolution to be expected seems rather to be a democratic counter-revolution and a rotten peace, including the partition of the border states. That this would not be the end of the affair by a long way—granted. But for the moment it would be the end. I must say I cannot work up any enthusiasm for a people which on such a colossal issue allows itself to be continually beaten by a fourth of its own population, and which after eighteen months of war has achieved nothing more than the discovery that all its generals are asses and all its officials rascals and traitors. After all the thing must happen differently, even in a bourgeois republic, if it is not to end in utter failure. I entirely agree with what you say about the meanness of the English way of looking at the business. . . .

59. MARX TO ENGELS

[London,] 28 January, 1863.

I am adding something to the section on machinery.* There are some curious questions here which I ignored in my first treatment. In order to get clear about it I have read through all my notebooks (extracts) on technology again and am also attending a practical course (experimental only) for workers, by Professor Willis (at the Geological Institute in Jermyn Street, where Huxley also used to give his lectures). It is the same for me with mechanics as it is with languages. I understand the mathematical laws, but the simplest technical reality demanding perception is harder to me than to the biggest blockheads.

You may or may not know, for in itself the question does not matter, that there is a great dispute as to what distinguishes a *machine* from a *tool*. The English (mathematical) mechanists, in their crude way, call a tool a simple machine and a machine a complicated tool. The English technologists, however, who pay rather more attention to economics (and who are followed by many, by most, of the English economists) base the distinction between the two on the fact that in one case the motive power is derived from human beings, in the other from a natural force. The German asses, who are great at these small things, have therefore concluded that, for instance, a *plough* is a machine, while the most complicated spinning-jenny, etc., in so far as it is worked by hand, is not. But now if we look round at the *elementary* forms of the machine there is no question at all that the industrial revolution starts, not from the *motive power* but from that section of machinery which the English call

* See *Capital*, Vol. I, Chap. XV, Section 1, "The Development of Machinery."

the *working machine*. Thus, for instance, the revolution was no due to the substitution of water or steam for the action of th foot in turning the spinning-wheel, but to the transformatio of the immediate process of spinning itself and to the displace ment of that portion of human labour which was not merely th "exertion of power" (as in working the treadle of the wheel but was directly applied to the working up of the raw material On the other hand, it is equally certain that when it is a ques tion, not of the *historical* development of machinery but o machinery on the basis of the present method of production the *working machine* (for instance, the sewing-machine) is th only determining factor; for as soon as this process has beer mechanised everyone nowadays knows that the thing can b moved by hand, water-power or a steam-engine according tc its size.

To pure mathematicians these questions are indifferent, bu they become very important when it is a case of proving th connection between the social relations of human beings anc the development of these material methods of production.

The re-reading of my technical-historical extracts has led m to the opinion that, apart from the discoveries of gunpowder the compass and printing—those necessary pre-requisites o bourgeois development—the two material bases on which th preparations for machine industry were organised withir manufacture during the period from the sixteenth to th middle of the eighteenth century (the period in which manu facture was developing from handicraft into actual large scale industry) were the *clock* and the *mill* (at first the corr mill, that is, a water-mill). Both were inherited from th ancients. (The water-mill was introduced into Rome from Asia Minor at the time of Julius Cæsar.) The clock is the firs automatic machine applied to practical purposes; the whole theory of the *production of regular motion* was developed through it. Its nature is such that it is based on a combination of half artistic handicraft and direct theory. Cardanus, for instance, wrote about (and gave practical formulæ for) the construction of clocks. German authors of the sixteenth century called clockmaking "learned handicraft" (*i.e.*, not of the guilds) and it would be possible to show from the development of the clock how entirely different the relation between theoretical learning and practice was on the basis of the handicraft from what it is, for instance, in large-scale industry. There is also no doubt that in the eighteenth century the idea of applying automatic devices (moved by springs) to production was first suggested by the clock. It can be proved historically that *Vaucanson's* experiments on these lines had a tremendous influence on the imagination of the English inventors.

The *mill*, on the other hand, from the very beginning, as soon as the water-mill was produced, supplies the essential distinctions in the organism of a machine: the mechanical driving power—prime motor—on which it depends; the transmitting mechanism; and, finally, the working machine, which deals with the material—each with an existence independent of the others. The *theory of friction*, and with it the investigations into the mathematical forms of wheel-work, cogs, etc., were all developed at the mill; here first ditto the theory of measurement of the degree of motive power, of the best way of employing it, etc. Almost all the great mathematicians after the middle of the seventeenth century, so far as they occupied themselves with practical mechanics and its theoretical side, started from the simple corn-grinding water-mill. And indeed this was why the name *mill* came to be applied during the manufacturing period to all mechanical forms of motive power adapted to practical purposes.

But with the mill, as with the press, the forge, the plough, etc., the actual work of beating, crushing, grinding, pulverisation, etc., was performed from the very first *without* human labour, even though the moving force was human or animal. This kind of machinery is therefore very ancient, at least in its origins, and actual mechanical propulsion was formerly applied to it. Hence it is also practically the only machinery found in the manufacturing period. The *industrial revolution* begins as soon as mechanism is employed where from ancient times onwards the final result has always required human labour; not, that is to say, where, as with the tools just mentioned, the actual material to be dealt with has *never*, from *the beginning*, been dealt with by the human hand, but where, from the nature of the thing, man has not from the very first merely acted as *power*. If one is to follow the German asses in calling the use of animal power (which is just as much *voluntary movement* as human power) machinery, then the use of this kind of locomotive is at any rate much older than the simplest handicraft tool.

¶CARDANUS (1501-76). Famous Italian man of science and doctor. Made researches in mathematics, physics and medicine.

VAUCANSON, JACQUES DE (1709-82). Mastered the mechanism of the clock as a child and made himself a wooden clock. The automatic machines he constructed made him famous (among others a flute player, first shown in Paris in 1738, and a hissing snake which threw itself on the breast of Cleopatra). He was made Royal Inspector of Silk Manufactures by Cardinal Fleury. Vaucanson perfected many machines for this industry.

60. MARX TO ENGELS

[London], 13 February, 1863.

What do you say to the Polish business ? This much is certain —the era of revolution has now fairly opened again in Europe. And the general position of things is good. But the comfortable delusions and the almost childish enthusiasm with which we hailed the era of revolution before February 1848 have all gone to hell. Old comrades like Weerth, etc., are gone, others have dropped out or become demoralised and new blood is not visible, at any rate as yet. Added to which we now know what a part stupidity plays in revolutions, and how they are exploited by scoundrels. For the rest, the " Prussian " enthusiasts for nationality, for " Italy " and " Hungary," are already getting into a fix. The " Prussians " will not renounce their Russianism. Let us hope that this time the lava will flow from east to west and not the other way round, so that we may be spared the " honour " of French initiative.

¶In January 1863 a rising took place in Poland. The insurrection spread over the whole country and led to the formation of a national government. This revolt, however, was under the leadership of the lesser nobility, who were not capable of drawing the masses into the movement, and it was suppressed when the power passed to the big landowners; these latter, hoping for diplomatic intervention on the part of France and England, came to an "honourable" agreement with the tsar, who naturally broke the agreement as no intervention took place.

Marx and Engels regarded Poland as the barrier separating Germany from the barbaric despotism of Russia—a barrier which they held to be necessary for the free development of capitalism in Germany. (See also Letters 62, 65.)

WEERTH, GEORG (1822-56). Member of the Communist League, one of the editorial staff of the *Neue Rheinische Zeitung*, a revolutionary poet. He died in Havana.

61. MARX TO ENGELS

[London], 21 February, 1863.

What I am most afraid of in the Polish affair is that the swine Bonaparte will find an excuse for coming to the Rhine and once more wangling himself out of his horrid position.

Send me (as you have more material to hand about it) a few notes (exact) on the behaviour of Frederick William the Just in the year 1813 after Napoleon came to grief in Russia. This time it is a case of really coming to grips with the barren House of Hohenzollern.

62. MARX TO ENGELS

[London], 24 March, 1863.

The political standpoint I have reached is the following: that Bismarck and Vincke do in fact *truly* represent the principle of the Prussian State; that the "State" of Prussia (a very different creature from Germany) can exist neither *without* the present Russia nor *with* an independent Poland.

The whole of Prussian history leads to this conclusion, at which the Herren Hohenzollern (including Frederick II) arrived long ago. This instinct of the paternal ruler is far superior to the limited vassal's mind of the Prussian Liberals. As therefore the existence of Poland is necessary to Germany but impossible alongside of Prussia, this State of Prussia must be demolished. In other words, the Polish question is only a fresh occasion for proving that it is impossible to further German interests so long as the Hohenzollern dynastic state exists.

¶VINCKE, GEORG ERNST (1811-75). Leader of the Prussian Liberals at the turn of the 'fifties. Marx gave the following picture of Vincke in a letter to Engels on May 10, 1861: "I have even idealised the fellow. . . . In a bad farce of Freytag's, called *The Journalists*, which I saw in Berlin, there was a fat Hamburg philistine and wine merchant, called Piepenbrink. Vincke is the very image of this Piepenbrink. Repulsive Hamburg-Westphalian dialect, rapidly mumbled words, no sentence properly constructed or quite finished."

63. MARX TO ENGELS

[London], 9 April, 1863.

Itzig [Lassalle] has already published two pamphlets about his case again, which, fortunately, he has *not* sent me. On the other hand he sent me the day before yesterday his open *letter in answer* to the Workers' Central Committee for the Leipziger workers' (read *Knoten*) Congress.* His attitude—very important, flinging about phrases borrowed from us—is quite that of the future workers' dictator. He resolves the question between wage-labour and capital "as easily as in play" (verbatim). The workers, that is to say, are to agitate for *universal suffrage* and then send people armed, like himself, with the "shining sword of science" to the Chamber of Representatives. Then

* *Knoten.* Note on page 87. For Lassalle's open letter, etc., see Letter 29, Note. [*Ed. Eng. ed.*]

they will establish workers' factories, for which the *State* will advance the capital, and by and by these institutions will embrace the whole country. This is at any rate surprisingly new! . . .

. . . I attended the meeting held by Bright at the head of the trade unions. He looked quite like an Independent and every time he said, "In the United States no kings, no bishops," there was a burst of applause. The workers themselves spoke *excellently*, with a complete absence of bourgeois rhetoric and without in the least concealing their opposition to the capitalists (whom Father Bright, by the way, also attacked).

How soon the English workers will free themselves from their apparent bourgeois infection one must wait to see.* For the rest, where the main points in your book† are concerned, they have been confirmed down to the smallest detail by the later development since 1844. I have myself compared the book again with my notes on the later period. Only the little German *Spiessgesellen* [petty-bourgeois], who measure world history by the yard and the latest "interesting news in the paper," could imagine that in developments of such magnitude twenty years are more than a day—though later on days may come again in which twenty years are embodied.

Re-reading your book has made me regretfully aware of our increasing age. How freshly and passionately, with what bold anticipations and no learned and scientific doubts, the thing is still dealt with here! And the very illusion that the result itself will leap into the daylight of history to-morrow or the day after gives the whole thing a warmth and jovial humour—compared to which the later "gray in gray" makes a damned unpleasant contrast.

¶BRIGHT, JOHN (1811-89). [Manufacturer and liberal bourgeois politician, who with Richard Cobden led the fight of the

* Engels had written to Marx the day before (April 8, 1863): "All revolutionary energy has faded practically entirely away from the English proletariat and the English proletarian is declaring his complete agreement with the rule of the bourgeoisie." [*Ed. Eng. ed.*]

† *The Condition of the Working Class in England in* 1844.

rising industrial capitalists in England against the feudal landowners. See Letter 8, Notes, and Letters 71, 74. Bright was now in the midst of his nine years' campaign (1858—1867) for the extension of the franchise, a campaign in which the workers were also enlisted. See Letters 71, 88, 90, 91. *Ed. Eng. ed.*]

Bright in his speeches also attacked the capitalists. While of course this may have been partly pure demagogy it may also have sometimes had a real background. "The bourgeoisie never rules as a whole," wrote Engels in his *Campaign for the German Constitution;* "apart from the feudal castes, who have still retained some part of their political power, even the big bourgeoisie, as soon as it has defeated feudalism, splits into a ruling and an opposition party—which are usually represented by the bank on the one side and the manufacturers on the other. The oppositional, progressive fraction of the big and middle bourgeoisie then has common interests with the petty bourgeoisie against the ruling fraction, and unites with it in a common struggle."

64. ENGELS TO MARX

Manchester, 21 April, 1863.

What is to be done with Lassalle it is hard to say; after all, I should assume that it would be beneath the dignity of the great Itzig [Lassalle] to bring out the heavy artillery of a formal denial against such petty gossip as that of Meyen. Let the fellow get out of his own dirty mess himself; if he can do anything he will not need any testimonial from you, and why should you compromise yourself after once having told him that he cannot go with us all the same, or we with him. What stupidity, to start with, to mix himself up in the Schulze-Delitzsch *Knoten** business and to attempt to form a party there, of all places, on the basis of our former work. We can only welcome the fact that Schulze-Delitzsch and other rabble are trying during this bourgeois period to raise the *Knoten* to the heights of the bourgeois point of view, for otherwise we should have had this business to wade through during the revolution, and in Germany, where everything is so much complicated by

* See footnote, page 87.

the mentality of the petty state, this small beer might have been held up to us as something new and practical. That is finished with now; we have got our opponents in the right position and the *Knote* has become conscious and so transferred himself to the ranks of the petty-bourgeois democracy. But to regard these chaps as representatives of the proletariat! It takes Itzig to do that.

¶SCHULZE-DELITZSCH (1808-83). Bourgeois politician and economist, organiser of consumers' co-operatives for handicraft workers, which were to prevent the decay of their class. Marx wrote to Engels on November 4, 1864: "By chance a few numbers of E. Jones' *Notes to the People* (1851, 1852) have come into my hands again; these, so far as the main points of the economic articles are concerned, were written under my immediate guidance and partly also with my direct co-operation. Well! What do I find there? That at that date we were conducting against the co-operative movement (in so far as in its present limited form it pretended to rank as something *final*) the same polemic—only better—as Lassalle carried on ten or twelve years later in Germany against Schulze-Delitzsch." "A cloak for reactionary humbug," Marx called unions of the Schulze-Delitzsch type. (*Capital*, Vol. I, Chap. X [7], Note on Robert Owen, Kerr edition, p. 327.)

65. ENGELS TO MARX

Manchester, 11 June, 1863.

The business in Poland no longer seems to be going so well of late. The movement in Lithuania and Little Russia is obviously weak, and the insurgents in Poland do not seem to be advancing either. All the leaders fall in the fighting or else are taken prisoner and shot, which seems to show that they must have to expose themselves greatly in order to get their people to advance. The quality of the insurgents is no longer what it was in March and April, the best fellows have been used up. These Polacks are quite incalculable, however, and the business may still turn out well all the same, although the prospects are less. If they hold out they may yet be involved in a general European movement which will save them ; on the other hand if things go badly Poland will be finished for ten years—an insurrection of this kind exhausts the fighting strength of the population for many years.

A European movement seems to me very probable, because the bourgeois has now once more lost all his fear of the Communists and if necessary will again attack with them. The French elections prove this, and so do the events in Prussia since the last elections. I hardly think a movement of this kind will start in France. The election results in Paris were really *too* bourgeois, the workers, where they put up special candidates, were defeated, and had not even the strength to force the bourgeoisie at least to elect radicals. Added to which Bonaparte knows the way to keep big cities in check.*

In Prussia they would still be chattering if the worthy Bismarck had not turned the lock on them. However the business there may turn out, peaceful constitutional development is at an end and the philistine must prepare himself for a row. This means a lot already. Much as I despise the valour of our old friends the Democrats, it seems to me that the largest amount of inflammable matter is concentrated here, and, as it is scarcely possible that the Hohenzollerns will not entangle themselves in the greatest stupidities in their foreign policy, it might well come about that the troops, divided half on the Polish frontier and half on the Rhine, left Berlin free, and that a coup followed. Bad enough for Germany and Europe if Berlin arrived at the head of the movement.

What surprises me most is that no peasant movement breaks out in Great Russia. The Polish rising seems actually to have an unfavourable effect there.

* See Letter 145, note on Haussman. [*Ed. Eng. ed.*]

66. MARX TO ENGELS

British Museum, 12 June, 1863.

Itzig [Lassalle] has sent me (and perhaps you too) his speech in court on *indirect taxation*. There are some good points in it but, in the first place, the whole thing is *written*, in an unbearably self-assertive and loquacious way, with the most ludicrous, learned and pompous airs. Moreover, it is after all essentially the compilation of a "*pupil*" who is in a desperate hurry to boost himself as a "thoroughly learned man" carrying on independent research. Hence it swarms with historical and theoretical blunders. One example will suffice (in case you have not read the stuff yourself). In order to impress the court and the public he wishes to give a sort of retrospective history of the polemic against indirect taxation, and so he goes back and takes quotations from all over the place—beyond Boisguillebert and Vauban to Bodenus, etc. And here the typical pupil reveals himself. He omits the *physiocrats*, being obviously unaware that everything that Adam Smith, etc., said on the subject was copied from them and that in general they were the heroes of this "question." Equally after the fashion of the pupil he treats "indirect taxes" as "bourgeois taxes," which they were "in the Middle Ages" but are not to-day (at least not where the bourgeoisie is developed) as he could learn further from Messrs. R. Gladstone and Co. in Liverpool. The ass does not seem to know that the polemic against "indirect" taxation is one of the slogans of the English and American friends of Schulze-Delitzsch and Co. and therefore cannot be a slogan against them, I mean the free-traders. Just like a *schoolboy* too is the way he *applies* a statement of Ricardo's to the Prussian Land Tax. (Absolutely wrong, that is to say.) How touching when he communicates to the court the discoveries "*he*" has derived from "deepest science and truth" and terrible "night hours," namely,

that in the Middle Ages landed property dominated,
in modern times, capital, and now
the "*principle* of the *estate* of labour," "*labour*" or "the *moral principle of labour*"; and on the very day he communi-

cated this discovery to the *Knoten*,* *Oberregierungsrat* [Chief Government Councillor] Engel (without knowing about him) disclosed it to a more refined public in the *Singakademie*. He and Engel mutually congratulated each other " by letter " upon their " simultaneous " scientific results.

The " *estate* of labour " and the " moral principle " certainly are achievements on the part of Itzig [Lassalle] and the Chief Government Councillor.

I have not been able to bring myself to write to the fellow since the beginning of this year. For me to criticise his stuff would be waste of time, besides he appropriates every word to himself as a " discovery." To bring him up against his plagiarism would be absurd, for I will not deprive him of our things in the form into which he has messed them up. To recognise his boasting and *tactlessness* would not do either. The chap would make use of that at once.

So there is nothing for it but to wait until at last his wrath breaks forth. I shall then have a very good excuse in the fact that he (like Chief Government Councillor Engel) always remarks : this is not " *Communism*." I shall answer him, therefore, that these repeated asseverations of his would have forced me, if I was to take any notice of him at all, to show the public (1) where and how he had copied from us ; (2) where and how we dissociate ourselves from his nonsense. In order, therefore, not to prejudice " Communism " or to damage him I had completely ignored him.

¶Engels had written to Marx on June 11, 1863, saying that Lassalle was " now working purely in the service of Bismarck and it may happen one day, if Monsieur Bismarck is tired of him, that he will be flung into prison and will make acquaintance with the Prussian Land Law, which he always seems to confuse with the *Code* [*Code Napoléon*—the French bourgeois Statute book]. For the rest it is nice that after his appearance in the Vogt affair *he* should now be under the ægis not only of the *Augsburger* [newspaper] but also of the *Kreuzzeitung*."

* *Knoten*. Note page 87.

R. GLADSTONE & CO. Robertson Gladstone (1809-98). A rich Liverpool merchant, brother of W. E. Gladstone, the statesman, and one of the leaders of the group of Liverpool "Financial Reformers" (industrial bourgeoisie) who agitated for a progressive income tax directed against the big landowners. Marx, in his *Critique of the Gotha Programme* (1875), pointed out that the German Social-Democratic Party, by including in their programme the demand for a single progressive income-tax "as an economic basis of the state," were asking just the same as these "bourgeois individuals." [*Ed. Eng. ed.*]

67. MARX TO ENGELS

London, 6 July, 1863.

If you find it possible in this heat, look with some care at the enclosed *Tableau économique** which I substitute for Quesnay's Table, and tell me of any objections you may have to it. It embraces the whole process of reproduction.

You know that according to A. Smith the "*natural*" or "*necessary*" *price* is composed of wages, profit (interest), rent—and is thus entirely resolved into revenue. This nonsense was taken over by Ricardo, although he excludes rent, as merely accidental, from the catalogue. Nearly *all* economists have accepted this from Smith and those who combat it fall into some other imbecility.

Smith himself is conscious of the absurdity of resolving the *total product* for society *merely into revenue* (which can be annually consumed), while in *every separate* branch of production he resolves price into *capital* (raw materials, machinery, etc.) and *revenue* (wages, profit, rent). According to this, society would have to start afresh, *without capital*, every year.

Now with regard to my table,† which will figure as a *summary* in one of the last chapters of my book, it is necessary to understand the following:

(1) The figures indifferent, represent millions.

* *Economic table.*

† Facing page 154.

(2) Under *means of subsistence** is to be included *everything* which goes annually into the *consumption fund* (or which could go into the consumption fund *without accumulation*, this being *excluded* from the table).

In Class I (means of subsistence) the *whole product* (700) consists of *means of subsistence* which by their nature do *not* enter into *constant capital* (raw material and machinery, buildings, etc.). Similarly in Class II the *whole product* consists of commodities which constitute *constant capital*, *i.e.*, which enter into the process of reproduction again as raw material and machinery.

(3) *Ascending* lines are *dotted*, *descending* lines are *plain*.

(4) *Constant capital* is that part of capital which consists of raw material and machinery. *Variable capital* that part which is exchanged for labour.

(5) In agriculture, for instance, one part of the same product (*e.g.*, wheat) constitutes means of subsistence, another part (*e.g.*, wheat) enters in its natural form (*e.g.*, as *seed*) into reproduction again as raw material. But this makes no difference. For such branches of production figure in the one quality in Class II and in the other in Class I.

(6) The point of the whole business is therefore this :

CATEGORY I. MEANS OF SUBSISTENCE.

Working materials and machinery equal, say, £400 (*i.e.*, that portion of *these* which is included in the yearly product as *depreciation* ; the part of the machinery, etc., which is not used up does *not* appear in the table at all). The variable capital exchanged for labour = 100 and is reproduced as 300, of which 100 replaces the wages in the product and 200 represents the surplus value (*unpaid surplus labour*). The product = 700, of which 400 represents the value of the constant capital, the whole of which has, however, entered into the product and must therefore be replaced.

In this relation between variable capital and surplus value it is assumed that the worker works one-third of the working day for himself and two-thirds for his natural superiors.

* Marx uses here throughout the word " *Lebensmittel* " (means of subsistence) instead of the word "*Konsumtionsmittel* " (means of consumption) used when he developed the above account in *Capital*, II, Chap. XX, " Simple Reproduction." [*Ed. Eng. ed.*]

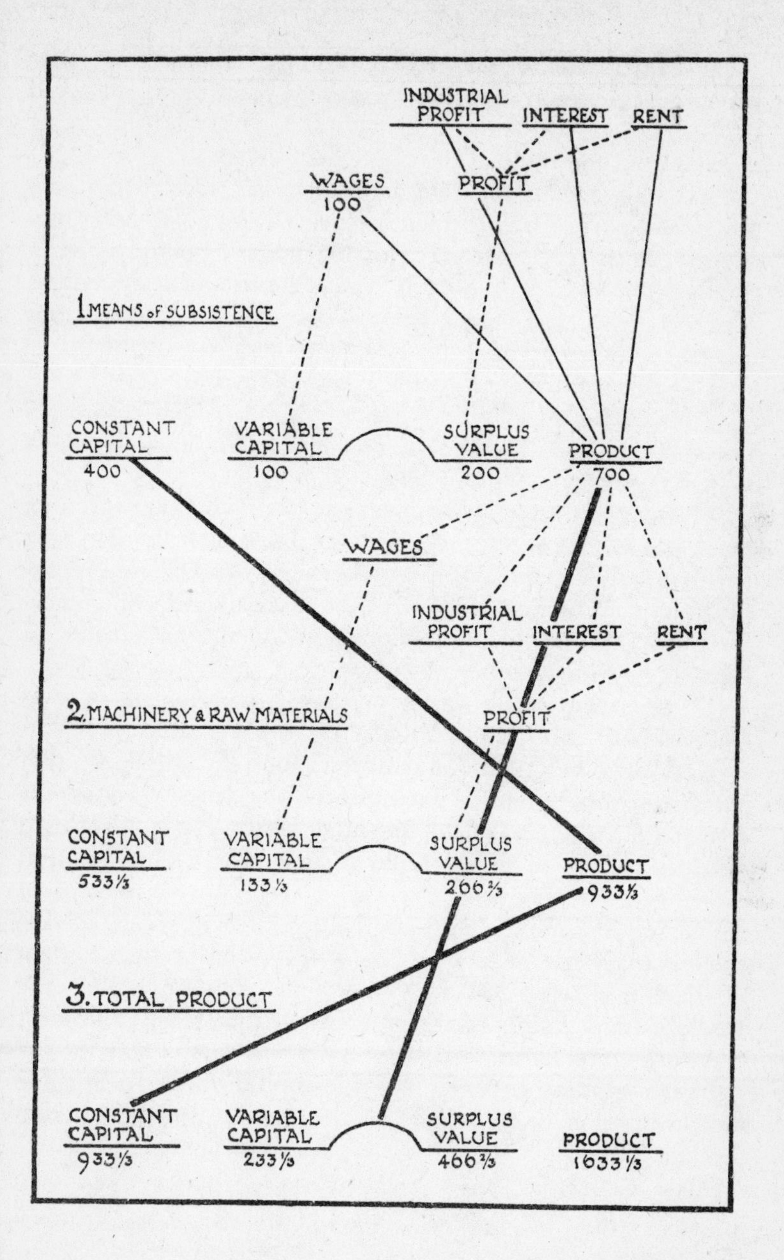

Facing page 154

100 (variable capital) is therefore paid out in money as wages, as indicated by the dotted line; with this 100 (indicated by the descending line) the worker buys the *product* of this class, *i.e.*, means of subsistence for 100. Thus the money flows back again to the capitalist Class I.

The surplus value of 200 in its general form = profit, which is split up, however, into *industrial* (including *commercial*) *profit*, into *interest*, which the capitalist pays in money, and into rent, which he also pays in money. The money thus paid out for industrial profit, interest and rent flows back again (indicated by the descending lines) because it is spent on the product of Class I. Thus the whole of the money laid out by the industrial capitalist within Class I flows back to him again, while 300 of the product 700 is consumed by the workers, employers, monied men and landlords. There remains in Class I a *surplus*, 400, of the product (in means of subsistence) and a deficit of 400 in the constant capital.

CATEGORY II. MACHINERY AND RAW MATERIALS.

As the *total product of this category* (not only that part of the product which replaces the constant capital but also that which represents the equivalent of the wages and surplus value) consists of *raw materials* and *machinery*, the revenue of this category cannot be realised in its own product, but only in the product of Category I. But setting aside accumulation, as we do here, Category I can only buy from Category II the amount required to replace its constant capital, while Category II can only expend the part of its product which represents wages and surplus value (*revenue*) on the product of Category I. The workers of Category II therefore spent their money = 133⅓ on the product of Category I. The same takes place with the surplus value of Category II, which, like that of I, is split up into industrial profit, interest and rent. Thus 400 in money flows back from Category II to the industrial capitalists of Category I, who in return dispose of the remainder of their product = 400 to the former.

With this 400 money Class I buys the necessary 400 replacement of its constant capital from Category II, to whom the money spent in wages and consumption (by the industrial capitalists themselves, the monied men and the landlords) thus flows back again. There remains therefore to Category II, 533⅓ of its total product, with which it replaces its own used-up constant capital.

The movement, partly within Category I, partly between Categories I and II, shows at the same time how the money with which they pay new wages, interest and ground rent flows back to the respective industrial capitalists of both categories.

CATEGORY III represents the whole process of reproduction. The total product of Category II here appears as the constant capital of the whole of society, and the total product of Category I as that part of the product which replaces the variable capital (the wage fund) and the revenues of the classes who share out the surplus value.

¶QUESNAY, FRANÇOIS (1694-1774). French doctor and economist, founder of the physiocratic theory, which " transferred the investigation into the origin of surplus value from the sphere of circulation to the sphere of immediate production itself, and by so doing laid the foundations for the analysis of capitalist production." (Marx.) According to the physiocrats, ground rent was the only form of surplus value and agricultural labour was therefore the only productive labour. But this " apparent glorification of landed property turns into its economic negation and into the confirmation of capitalist production " (Marx), since the physiocrats wanted to throw the whole weight of taxation on to ground rent, demanded that industry should be freed from state tutelage and preached free competition. We have specially to thank the physiocratic doctrine for the famous *Economic Table* (*Tableau Economique*) of Quesnay, in which he represented the process of reproduction of social capital as a whole. This table, " in the first third of the eighteenth century, when political economy was in its infancy . . . was incontestably the most brilliant idea of which political economy had hitherto been guilty." (Marx. See *Theorien über den Mehrwert*, Bd. I.)

68. MARX TO ENGELS

[London,] 15 August, 1863.

My work (the manuscript for the printer) is getting on well in one respect. In the final working out the things are taking on, as it seems to me, a bearably *popular* form, except for some unavoidable M—C and C—M.* On the other hand, although I write the whole day, the thing does not get on in the way my own impatience, after this long trial of patience, desires. Anyhow it will be 100 per cent. easier to understand than No. I.† For the rest, when I look at this compilation now and see how I have had to turn everything round and how I had to make even the *historical* part out of material of which some was quite unknown, then Itzig [Lassalle] really does seem funny to me, with "*his*" economy already in the making, though all the stuff he has hawked out so far reveals him as a sixth-form schoolboy who with the most revolting and bombastic old wives' chatter trumpets abroad—as his latest discovery—principles which—ten times better—we were already distributing as small change among our partisans twenty years ago. The same Itzig otherwise also collects in his manure factory the party excrements we dropped twenty years ago, with which world history is to be fertilised.

69. ENGELS TO MARX

Manchester, 4 September, 1864.

You can imagine how the news surprised me.‡ Whatever Lassalle may have been personally, or from the literary and scientific point of view, politically he was undoubtedly one of the most important fellows in Germany. For us he was at the moment a very uncertain friend, and in the future would have been a fairly certain enemy, but all the same it hits one hard to see how Germany breaks everyone in the extreme party

* M=money, C=commodity. For this formula see *Capital*, Vol. I, Chap. III Section 2.

† *The Critique of Political Economy* (1859).

‡ The news of Lassalle's death. (See Letter 29, note.)

with any degree of capacity. What rejoicing will reign among the factory owners and the Progressive swine—Lassalle was after all the only chap they were afraid of in Germany itself.

But what an extraordinary way to lose one's life! To fall seriously in love with the daughter of a Bavarian ambassador—this would-be Don Juan—to want to marry her, to come into collision with a rejected rival, who is in addition a Wallachian swindler, and to get oneself shot dead by him. This could only have happened to Lassalle, whose strange mixture of frivolity and sentimentality, of Judaism and would-be chivalry, was peculiar to himself alone. How could a politician like himself engage in a duel with a Wallachian adventurer?

70. MARX TO ENGELS

[London], 7 September, 1864.

Lassalle's misfortune has been damnably in my head these days. After all he was still one of the old guard and the enemy of our enemies. And then the thing came as such a surprise that it is hard to believe such a noisy, stirring, pushing person is now as dead as a mouse and has got to keep his mouth shut altogether. You are quite right about the pretext for his death. It was one of the many tactless acts which he committed in his life. But for all that I am sorry that in the last years our relations were clouded, though he was to blame for this. On the other hand I am very glad that I resisted the provocations from various sides and made no attack on him during his "jubilee year."

The devil knows, the squad is always getting smaller, nothing new is added to it. For the rest I am convinced that if Lassalle had not been in Switzerland, in the company of the military adventurers and revolutionaries in yellow gloves, this catastrophe would never have come about. But this Coblenz of the European revolution had exercised a fatal attraction upon him again and again.

The "daughter of a Bavarian ambassador" is none other than the daughter of the Berliner, Dönniges, a fellow-demagogue of Rutenberg and Co. at the university, originally one of little dwarf Ranke's young gents, or rather, as they were no gentlemen, young people, who used to publish awful old annals of the German emperors under his direction.. What the bouncing little root-grubber Ranke regarded as the spirit of history—facile anecdote-mongering and the attribution of all great events to petty and mean causes—was strictly forbidden to these young men from the country. They were to confine themselves to "objectivity" and leave the spirit to their master. Our friend Dönniges was regarded in some respects as a rebel because he disputed Ranke's monopoly of the spirit, in practice at least, and demonstrated in various ways that he was as much a born "valet" to "history" as Ranke.

¶COBLENZ. A town on the Rhine which during the great French Revolution was a centre for counter-revolutionary aristocratic refugees who had fled from France.

RANKE, LEOPOLD (1795-1886). German historian.

71. MARX TO ENGELS

[London], 4 November, 1864.

... (2) THE WORKINGMEN'S INTERNATIONAL ASSOCIATION.

Some time ago London workers had sent an address about Poland to Paris workers and summoned them to common action in this matter.

The Parisians on their part sent over a deputation headed by a worker called *Tolain, the real workers' candidate at the last election in Paris*, a very nice fellow. (His companions too were quite nice lads.) A public meeting in St. Martin's Hall was summoned for September 28, 1864, by Odger (shoemaker, President of the Council here of All London Trades Unions* and also especially of the Trade Unions Suffrage Agitation Society, which is connected with Bright) and Cremer, mason and

* The London Trades Council.

Secretary of the Masons' Union. (These two organised the big meeting of the Trade Unions in St. James's Hall for North America, under Bright, ditto the Garibaldi demonstrations.) A certain *Le Lubez* was sent to ask me if I would take part on behalf of the German workers, and especially if I would supply a German worker to speak at the meeting, etc. I provided them with Eccarius, who came off splendidly, and ditto was present myself as a mute figure in the platform. I knew that this time real "powers" were involved both on the London and Paris sides and therefore decided to waive my usual standing rule to decline any such invitations.

(Le Lubez is a young Frenchman, *i.e.*, in the thirties, who has however grown up in Jersey and London, speaks English excellently and is a very good intermediary between the French and English workers.) (Music teacher and French lessons.)

At the meeting, which was packed to *suffocation* (for there is now evidently a revival of the working classes taking place),* Major Wolff (Thurn-Taxis, Garibaldi's adjutant) represented the London *Italian* Workingmen's Society. It was decided to found a "Workingmen's International Association," of which the General Council should be in London and should act as an "intermediary" between the workers' societies in Germany, Italy, France and England. Ditto that a General Workingmen's Congress should be summoned in Belgium in 1865. A Provisional Committee was appointed at the meeting; Odger, Cremer and many others, some of them old Chartists, old Owenites, etc., for England; Major Wolff, Fontana and other Italians for Italy; Le Lubez, etc., for France; Eccarius and I for Germany. The committee was empowered to co-opt as many members as it chose.

So far so good. I attended the first meeting of the Committee. A *sub-committee* (including myself) was appointed to draft a declaration of principles and provisional statutes. Being unwell I was prevented from attending the meeting of the sub-committee and the meeting of the whole committee which followed.

In these two meetings which I had missed—that of the sub-

* These words in parenthesis were written in English.

committee and the subsequent one of the whole committee—the following had taken place:

Major Wolff had handed in the *réglement* [statutes] of the *Italian Workers' Societies* (which possess a central organisation but, as later transpired, are really associated benefit societies) to be used for the new Association. I saw the stuff later. It was evidently a compilation of Mazzini's, so you already know the spirit and phraseology in which the real question, the workers' question, was dealt with. Also how nationalities were shoved in.

In addition an old Owenite, Weston*—now a manufacturer himself, a very amiable and worthy man—had drawn up a programme of indescribable breadth and full of the most extreme confusion.

The subsequent general committee meeting instructed the sub-committee to remodel Weston's programme, ditto Wolff's regulations. Wolff himself left in order to attend the Congress of Italian Workingmen's Associations in Naples and get them to decide on joining the London Central Association.

Another meeting of the sub-committee—which I again failed to attend, because I was informed of the *rendezvous* too late. At this a "declaration of principles" and a new version of Wolff's statutes were put forward by Le Lubez and accepted by the committee for submission to the general committee. The general committee met on October 18. As Eccarius had written me that delay would be dangerous I appeared, and was really frightened when I heard the worthy Le Lubez read out an appallingly wordy, badly written and utterly undigested preamble, pretending to be a declaration of principles, in which Mazzini could be detected everywhere, the whole being crusted over with the vaguest tags of French socialism. Added to this the Italian statutes were taken over in the main, and these apart from all their other faults, aim at something which is in fact utterly impossible, a sort of central government of the *European* working classes (with Mazzini in the background, of course). I put up a mild opposition and after a lot of talking backwards and forwards Eccarius proposed that the sub-committee should submit the thing to further "editing." On

* Weston. See Letter 83.

the other hand the " sentiments " contained in Lubez' declaration were voted for.

Two days later, on October 20, Cremer (for the English), Fontana (Italy), and Le Lubez assembled in my house. (Weston was prevented.) Hitherto I had never had the documents (those of Wolff and Le Lubez) in my hand so could not prepare anything, but was firmly determined that if possible not one single line of the stuff should be allowed to stand. In order to gain time I proposed that before we " edited " the preamble we should " discuss " the rules. This took place. It was an hour after midnight by the time the first of forty rules was agreed to. Cremer said (*and this was what I had aimed at*) : We have nothing to put before the committee, which meets on October 25. We must postpone the meeting till November 1. But the sub-committee can get together on October 27 and attempt to reach a definite conclusion. This was agreed to and the " papers " " left behind " for my opinion.

I saw that it was impossible to make anything out of the stuff. In order to justify the extremely strange way in which I intended to present the " sentiments " already " voted for," I wrote *An Address to the Working Classes* (which was not in the original plan : a sort of review of the adventures of the Working Classes since 1845) ; on the pretext that everything material was included in this *Address* and that we ought not to repeat the same things three times over I altered the whole preamble, threw out the declaration of principles and finally replaced the forty rules by ten. In so far as international politics come into the address, I speak of countries, not of nationalities, and denounce Russia, not the lesser nations. My proposals were all accepted by the sub-committee. Only I was obliged to insert two phrases about " duty " and " right " into the Preamble to the Statutes, ditto " truth, morality and justice," but these are placed in such a way that they can do no harm.

At the meeting of the general committee my address, etc., was agreed to with great enthusiasm (unanimously). The discussion on the method of printing, etc., takes place next Tuesday. Le Lubez has a copy of the address to translate into French and Fontana one to translate into Italian. (For a start there is a weekly paper called the *Beehive*, edited by Potter, the Trade Unionist, a sort of *Moniteur*.) I myself am to translate the stuff into German.

It was very difficult to frame the thing so that our view should appear in a form acceptable from the present standpoint of the workers' movement. In a few weeks the same people will be holding meetings for the franchise with Bright and Cobden. It will take time before the reawakened movement allows the old boldness of speech. It will be necessary to be *fortiter in re, suaviter in modo* [bold in matter, mild in manner]. As soon as the stuff is printed you will get it.

(3) *Bakunin* sends you greetings. He has left to-day for Italy, where he lives (Florence). Yesterday I saw him again for the first time for sixteen years. I must say I liked him very much and better than formerly. About the Polish movement he says that the Russian government has used the movement to keep Russia itself quiet, but never reckoned on an eighteen months' struggle. It provoked the business in Poland for that purpose. Poland came to grief for two reasons : the influence of Bonaparte and secondly the hesitation of the Polish aristocracy in proclaiming *peasant socialism* openly and unambiguously from the very beginning. In future, after this failure of the Polish business, Bakunin is only going to take part in the socialist movement.

On the whole he is one of the few people whom after sixteen years I find to have developed further instead of backwards. I also talked over the Urquhart denunciations with him. (By the way, the International Association will no doubt cause a breach between these friends and me!) He asked much after you and Lupus. When I told him of the latter's death he said at once that the movement had lost an irreplaceable man.

¶Marx is here reporting the foundation of the International Workingmen's Association (First International) and the origin of its programme, the famous *Inaugural Address*. The foundation and leadership of the First International are a model of Marx's revolutionary activity. From the varied mixture of most widely different tendencies expressed in the workers' movement in the different countries Marx and Engels succeeded in creating a united international party with a clear proletarian-revolutionary line, and in working out tactics which were to serve as a model to the whole later working-class movement. During the existence of the First International the following congresses took place:

LONDON CONFERENCE (September 25-29, 1865). On the agenda were the questions of the trade union movement, the rôle of Russian tsarism in Europe, the restoration of Poland, standing armies. The speeches showed that, except in England, the workers' movement was everywhere only in its first stage of development.

GENEVA CONGRESS (September 3-8, 1866). The statutes and fundamental principles of the programme were ratified. At this Congress conflicts arose with the Proudhonists. (See Letter 91, Marx to Kugelmann, 9 October, 1866.)

LAUSANNE CONGRESS (September 2-8, 1867). At this Congress, the function of the state, the political tasks of the proletariat, the question of war and the question of the international policy of the proletariat were dealt with.

BRUSSELS CONGRESS (September 6-15, 1868): was a turning point in the development of the First International. The Proudhonists suffered a defeat. At this Congress the representatives of the big workers' organisations and especially of the German workers were present for the first time.

BASLE CONFERENCE (September 6-12, 1869). Bakuninism [anarchism] made its first appearance (see Note below).

LONDON CONFERENCE (September 12-23, 1871): the main question was the division in the International; the split finally took place at the

HAGUE CONGRESS (September 2, 1872), when Bakunin and Guillaume were expelled from the International. (See Letter 157.) A resolution was also adopted on the basis of which the General Council was transferred to New York. On the reasons for this decision, Marx wrote to Sorge on September 27, 1873:

"According to my view of conditions in Europe, it will be thoroughly useful to let the formal organisation of the International withdraw into the background for a time, only, if possible, keeping some control over the centre in New York in order to prevent idiots like Perret or adventurers like Cluseret getting hold of the leadership and compromising the cause. Events themselves and the inevitable development and complexity of things will ensure the resurrection of the International in an improved form. Meanwhile it will be enough if we do not allow the connection with the most active workers in the different countries to slip entirely out of our hands; for the rest, however, we shall not care a straw for the local decisions of Geneva—simply ignore them. This course of action will be facilitated by the one good decision come to there, to postpone the Congress for two years. Moreover, it will upset the calculations of the governments on the Continent that at the very moment when their *crusade of reaction* is about to begin the spectre of the International should refuse its services for the time being, and that indeed the bourgeoisie everywhere should believe the ghost to have been successfully laid."

The Hague Congress concluded with a public meeting at which Marx, in the course of his speech, said:

"One day the working class must hold political power in its hands in order to establish a new organisation of labour; it must overthrow the old political system which maintains the old institutions in being, unless it wishes, like the early Christians, who despised and neglected such action, to renounce 'the kingdom of this world'."

As the fundamental principle of the International Marx put the solidarity of the proletariat in all countries, saying: "The revolution must be made with solidarity; we learn this from the Paris Commune, which only fell because just this solidarity was lacking among the workers of the other countries." (*Volksstaat*, October 2, 1872.) [For the history of the International see Letters 156, 157, 159, 160 and *Index*].

BAKUNIN, M. (1814-70). Russian revolutionary. One of the founders of anarchism. In the 'thirties a follower of Hegel's philosophy. In 1848 he took part in the German revolution (the rising in Dresden). He was arrested (1849), handed over to the Russian government and sentenced to life imprisonment. After the death of the Tsar Nicholas I, Bakunin was exiled to Siberia (1857). In 1861 he escaped and came to London.

Bakunin did not at once join the International. He was at first a member of the bourgeois League of Peace and Freedom. At the Berne Congress of this League (1868) he and his supporters (E. Réclus, Aristide Rey, Jaclard, Fanelli, N. Joukovsky,

V. Mratchkovsky and others) being left in a minority, seceded from the League and established their own International Alliance of Socialist Democracy. In 1869 this Alliance was affiliated to the International. (See Letter 121.) In the International Bakunin was an opponent of Marx. For his anarchist theories see Letters 156, 157, 186.

In *Ludwig Feuerbach and the Exit of Classical German Philosophy* Engels says that Bakunin combined Stirner with Proudhon and christened this amalgam "anarchism." Plekhanov showed the unclarity and the eclectic character of Bakunin's theory in *Our Differences*. There Plekhanov says: "Bakuninism is not a system. It is a mixture of the socialist theories of the 'Latin countries' with Russian 'peasant ideals,' of Proudhon's People's Bank with communal property in land, of Fourier with Stenka Razin." (Plekhanov, *Works*, Vol. II, p. 320.)

ODGER, GEORGE (1820-77). Shoemaker (one of the leaders of a small union of skilled shoemakers, the Ladies' Shoemakers' Society) and for ten years (1862-72) secretary of the London Trades Council (founded 1860). Actively supported the great building trades' strikes, 1859-60. Member of the committee which sent the address to the Paris workers mentioned at the beginning of Marx's letter. Odger had a great reputation as the most radical of democratic republicans and, consequently, great influence with the London workers. Like Cremer (see below) and Applegarth (Letter 133, Note) he was identified with the "new model" trade unionism of the 'fifties and 'sixties; with Applegarth he was a leading member of the so-called "Junta." After the extension of the franchise gained in 1867, Odger and his friends had no longer the same interest in supporting the International, they looked to Parliament to change the laws hampering the activities of the trade unions and they were jealous of the revolutionary influence of Marx (Letter 100). Odger's attitude is clearly revealed in connection with the Irish debate (Letter 133, Note). He was one of the first working-class candidates nominated at the elections held after the (franchise) Reform Act of 1867, but withdrew on three occasions in favour of the Liberals. He was President of the General Council of the International in 1866 (Marx having refused to be nominated) and was so much offended when, on Marx's proposal, this office was abolished in 1867 that he gave the Council "the cold shoulder" for a year, later asking its support for his candidature in Chelsea. (Marx to Engels, January 11, October 10, 1868.) He violently attacked the Address of the General Council on the Paris Commune written by Marx (*The Civil War in France*) and declared his resignation from the Council (June 1871) on this account. See also Letter 160, note on the *Beehive* below and notes to Letter 133. [*Ed. Eng. ed.*]

CREMER, W. R. (1838-1908). Joiner. First secretary of the General Council of the International. Cremer was an active member of the strike committee in the first great London building trades' strike, July 1859 to February 1860. (For Marx's reference to this strike see *Capital*, Vol. I, "The Working Day," and for his reference to the London building industry, Vol. II, chap. XII.) Original member of first London Trades Council (1860) and a founder of the Amalgamated Society of Carpenters and Joiners (1860), the second great trade union founded on the "new model." At the first Congress of the International (Geneva, September 1866), which voted for the abolition of standing armies and the general arming of the people, he took a pacifist line. After the Congress he failed, to his great surprise and disgust, to secure re-election as secretary (Marx to Engels, September 26, 1866) ; he resigned from the Council and was not re-elected at the 1867 Congress. Identified himself with various pacifist organisations (secretary of the "Workmen's Peace Association"). Liberal M.P. for Haggerston, 1885-95 and 1900-08. (See Engels' Letter, 197.) He was knighted—Sir Randall Cremer—and in 1903 received the Nobel Peace Prize. [*Ed. Eng. ed.*]

ECCARIUS. A taïlor by trade. German member of the Communist League (1848-52). He came as a refugee to London, settled there and took part in the British workers' movement. Member of the London Trades Council. Secretary of the General Council of the International. In 1871 he resigned his secretaryship and broke with Marx. Engels wrote of him (to Liebknecht, May 24-28, 1872) that he had been utterly demoralised by his intercourse with "English agitators and trading politicians and trades unions paid secretaries, who are all bought by the middle class here now or else begging to be bought by them." [*Ed. Eng. ed.*]

THE "BEEHIVE" (1862-76). Was founded after the second building workers' strike (1861) by a group of trade unionists, including Odger, as "a weekly newspaper of general intelligence and trades, friendly society and co-operative journal"; it was the official organ of the London Trades Council and its "avowed object" was "reporting the proceedings of trade societies and other bodies of working men shut out from the columns of the speculating and other middle-class newspapers." Its first editor was George Trupp, its second Robert Hartwell, a former Chartist and later a member of the General Council of the International. George Potter (Bricklayers' Trade Union) secretary of the building workers' committee 1858-59, and strike committee (1859-60), and till 1868 an opponent of the "Junta," was its publisher and manager. In 1863 the *Beehive* altered its sub-title and became "A Journal of general intelligence advertising industrial interests." Marx in the first months of the International tried to gain the *Beehive* as its real organ, but failed owing to the mutual enmities of Odger and Potter and their respective fractions.* The International therefore, had no organ of its own but continued to use the *Beehive* until in 1869 it was bought by the astute woollen manufacturer and Liberal M.P., Samuel Morley (see Letter 155). Applegarth and Odger, both members of the General Council of the International, had remained members of the editorial committee of the *Beehive* after it was sold to Morley, but through Marx's determination the decision to "sever our connection with the *Beehive* and *to publish* that resolution" was nevertheless carried by a unanimous vote of the Council. "Mr. Applegarth sat opposite to me, while I explained my motion, with a diminished head. . . . I denounced the paper as sold to the bourgeoisie (S. Morley, etc.), specially mentioned its treatment of our Irish resolutions and debates, etc." (Marx to Engels, April 28, 1870.) Various complaints about suppression of reports by the *Beehive* occur in the letters of Marx and Engels ("Last Sunday the *Beehive* had nothing about the International but of course an account of the wedding of the Duke of Abercorn's daughter instead"—Engels, November 17, 1869), and Engels wrote on July 30, 1869: "It is surely a disgrace that after nearly forty years of a political working-class movement in England the only working-class paper which

* Potter's hostility to Odger was in the main the reflection of that of the smaller, localised trade unions to the line of national amalgamation pursued by the "Junta," whose aim was to use the trade union organisation almost exclusively for parliamentary agitation.

exists can be bought up by a bourgeois like S. Morley. Unfortunately, however, it seems to be a law of the proletarian movement everywhere that a section of the workers' leaders should become demoralised." [*Ed. Eng. ed.*]

72. MARX TO SCHWEITZER

London, 24 January, 1865.

Yesterday I received a letter in which you demand from me a detailed judgment of Proudhon. Lack of time prevents me from fulfilling your desire. Added to which I have none of his works by me. However, in order to show you my good will I am hastily jotting down a brief sketch. You can complete it, add to it or cut it—in short do anything you like with it.*

Proudhon's earliest efforts I no longer remember. His school work about the *Langue Universelle* [*Universal Language*] shows how little he hesitated to attack problems for the solution of which he lacked the first elements of knowledge.

His first work, *Qu'est ce que la Propriété?* [*What is Property?*], is undoubtedly his best. It is epoch-making, if not from the novelty of its content at least by the new and audacious way in which everything is said. Of course "property" had been not only criticised in various ways but also "*done away with*" in the utopian manner by the French socialists and communists whose works he knew. In this book Proudhon's relation to St. Simon and Fourier is about the same as that of Feuerbach to Hegel. Compared with Hegel, Feuerbach is very poor. All the same he was epoch-making *after* Hegel, because he laid stress on certain points which were disagreeable to the Christian consciousness but important for the progress of criticism, and which Hegel had left in mystic semi-obscurity.

This book of Proudhon's has also, if I may be allowed the expression, a strong muscular style. And its style is in my opinion its chief merit.

Even where he is only reproducing old stuff, one can see that Proudhon has found it out for himself, that what he is saying is

* "We considered it best to give the article *unaltered*," stated an editorial note in the *Social Demokrat*.

new to him and ranks as new. The provocative defiance, laying hands on the economic " holy of holies," the brilliant paradox which made a mock of the ordinary bourgeois mind, the withering criticism, the bitter irony, and, revealed here and there behind these, a deep and genuine feeling of indignation at the infamy of the existing order, a revolutionary earnestness —all these electrified the readers of *What Is Property?* and produced a great sensation on its first appearance. In a strictly scientific history of political economy the book would hardly be worth mentioning. But sensational works of this kind play their part in the sciences just as much as in the history of the novel. Take, for instance, Malthus' book *On Population*. In its first edition it was nothing but a " sensational pamphlet " and *plagiarism* from beginning to end into the bargain. And yet what a *stimulus* was produced by this *libel on the human race!*

If I had Proudhon's book before me I could easily give a few examples to illustrate his *first manner*. In the passages which he himself regarded as the most important he imitates Kant's treatment of the *antinomies*—Kant, whose works he had read in translations, was at that time the only German philosopher he knew—and he leaves one with a strong impression that to him, as to Kant, the resolution of the antinomies is something " beyond " the human understanding, *i.e.*, something about which his own understanding is in the dark.

But in spite of all his apparent iconoclasticism one already finds in *What is Property?* the contradiction that Proudhon is criticising society on the one hand from the standpoint and with the eyes of a French small peasant (later petty bourgeois) and on the other from the standards imposed on him by his inheritance from the socialists.

The deficiency of the book is indicated by its very title. The question was so falsely formulated that it could not be answered correctly. *Ancient* " *property relations* " were swallowed up by *feudal* property relations and these by " *bourgeois* " property relations. Thus history itself had practised its criticism upon past *property relations*. What Proudhon was actually dealing with was *modern bourgeois property* as it exists to-day. The question of what this is could only have been answered by a critical analysis of "*political economy*," embracing these *property relations* as a whole, not in their *legal* expression as *voluntary relations* but in their real form, that is, as *relations of production*. But as he entangled the whole of these economic relations in the general juristic conception of "*property*," Proudhon could not get beyond the answer which *Brissot*, in a similar work, had already, before 1789, given in the same words: "Property is theft."

The most that can be got out of this is that the bourgeois juristic conceptions of "*robbery*" apply equally well to the "*honest*" gains of the bourgeois himself. On the other hand, since theft as a violent violation of property *presupposes the existence of property*, Proudhon entangled himself in all sorts of fantasies, obscure even to himself, about *true bourgeois property*.

During my stay in Paris in 1844 I came into personal contact with Proudhon. I mention this here because to a certain extent I am also to blame for his "*sophistication*," as the English call the adulteration of commercial goods. In the course of lengthy debates, often lasting all night, I infected him to his great injury with Hegelianism, which, owing to his lack of German, he could not study properly. After my expulsion from Paris Herr *Karl Grün* continued what I had begun. As a teacher of German philosophy he also had the advantage over me that he understood nothing about it himself.

Shortly before the appearance of Proudhon's second important work, *Philosophie de la Misère, etc.* [*The Philosophy of Poverty, etc.*], he announced this to me himself in a very detailed letter in which he said, among other things: "I await your stern criticism." This soon fell upon him (in my *Misère de la Philosophie, etc.* [*Poverty of Philosophy, etc.*], Paris 1847) in a fashion which ended our friendship for ever.

From what I have already said you can see that Proudhon's *Philosophie de la Misère ou Système des Contradictions économiques* [*Philosophy of Poverty or System of Economic Contradictions*] first actually contained his answer to the question *What is Property?* In fact it was only after the publication of this latter work that he had begun his economic studies; he had discovered that the questions he had raised could not be answered by invective, but only by an *analysis* of modern "*political economy*." At the same time he attempted to present the *system* of economic categories dialectically. In place of Kant's insoluble "*antinomies*" the Hegelian "*contradiction*" was to be introduced as the method of development.

For an estimate of his book, which is in two fat volumes, I must refer you to the work I wrote as a reply. There I showed, among other things, how little he has penetrated into the secret of scientific dialectic and how, on the contrary, he shares the illusions of speculative philosophy in his treatment of the *economic categories*; for instead of conceiving them as *the theoretical expression of historic relations of production, corresponding to a particular stage of development in material production*, he garbles them into pre-existing *eternal ideas* and in this roundabout way arrives once more at the standpoint of bourgeois economy.

I also show further how very deficient and sometimes even schoolboyish his knowledge is of the "political economy" which he undertook to criticise, and how he and the utopians are hunting for a so-called "*science*" by which a formula for the "solution of the social question" is to be excogitated *a priori*, instead of deriving their science from a critical knowledge of the historic movement, a movement which itself produces the *material conditions of emancipation*. But especially I show how confused, wrong and superficial Proudhon remains with regard to *exchange value*, the basis of the whole thing, and how he even mistakes the utopian interpretation of *Ricardo's* theory of value for the basis of a new science. With regard to his general point of view I made the following comprehensive judgment:

"Every economic relation has a good and a bad side; this is the only point on which Mr. Proudhon does not contradict himself. He sees the good side stressed by the economists and the bad side denounced by the socialists. From the economists he borrows the necessity of eternal relations, from the socialists the illusion that in poverty there is nothing to be seen but poverty (instead of recognising the revolutionary, destructive aspect of it which will overthrow the old society). He agrees with them both and in this attempts to support himself on the authority of science. Science reduces itself for him to the dwarfish dimensions of a scientific formula; he is a hunter after formulæ. Mr. Proudhon accordingly flatters himself that he has made a criticism both of political economy and of communism—he stands far below both. Below the economists, because as a philosopher equipped with a magic formula he thinks he can exempt himself from going into purely economic details; below the socialists, because he has neither enough courage nor enough insight to lift him, if only in speculation, above the bourgeois horizon. . . . He wants to soar as the man of science above the bourgeoisie and the proletariat; he remains nothing but the petty bourgeois perpetually tossed about between capital and labour, between political economy and communism."*

Severe though the above judgment sounds I must still endorse every word of it to-day. At the same time, however, it must be remembered that at the time when I declared his book to be the petty-bourgeois code of socialism and proved this theoretically, Proudhon was still being branded as an extreme arch-revolutionary alike by the political economists and by the socialists. That is why I also never joined in the outcry later on about his "*treachery*" to the revolution. Originally misunderstood by others as well as by himself, it was not his fault if he failed to fulfil unjustified hopes.

In *The Philosophy of Poverty* all the defects of Proudhon's method of presentation stand out very unfavourably in comparison with *What is Property?* The style is often what the French call *ampoulé* [bombastic]. High-sounding speculative jargon, supposed to be German-philosophical, appears regularly on the scene when his Gallic acuteness of understanding fails him. A self-advertising, self-glorifying, boastful tone and especially the twaddle about "*science*" and sham display of it which are always so unedifying, are continually screaming in one's ears. Instead of the genuine warmth which glowed in his first attempt, here certain passages are systematically worked up into a momentary heat by rhetoric. Add to this the clumsy, unpleasant erudition of the self-taught, whose primitive pride in his own original thought has already been broken and who now, as a *parvenu* of science, feels it necessary to bolster him-

* Marx, *The Poverty of Philosophy*, Chap. II (French).

self up with what he is not and has not. Then the mentality of the petty bourgeois who in an indecently brutal way—and neither acutely nor profoundly nor even correctly—attacks a man like *Cabet*, to be respected for his practical attitude towards the proletariat, while he flatters a man like *Dunoyer* (a State Councillor, it is true). Yet the whole importance of this Dunoyer lay in the comic zeal with which, throughout three fat, unbearably boring volumes, he preached the rigourism characterised by Helvetius as "*On veut que les malheureux soient parfaits*" [the demand that the unfortunate should be perfect].

The February Revolution certainly came at a very inconvenient moment for Proudhon, who had irrefutably proved only a few weeks before that "the *era of revolutions*" was past for ever. His coming forward in the National Assembly, however little insight it showed into existing conditions, was worthy of every praise. After the June insurrection it was an act of great courage. In addition it had the fortunate consequence that M. Thiers, by his speech opposing Proudhon's proposals, which was then issued as a special publication, proved to the whole of Europe on what a pedestal of infantility this spiritual pillar of the French bourgeoisie was based. Indeed, compared to *M. Thiers*, *Proudhon* expanded to the size of an antediluvian colossus.

Proudhon's discovery of "*crédit gratuit*" [free credit] and the "*banque du peuple*" [people's bank] based upon it, were his last economic "deeds." In my book, *A Critique of Political Economy* . . . will be found the proof that the theoretical basis of his idea arises from a misunderstanding of the first elements of bourgeois "political economy," namely of the relation between *commodities* and *money;* while the practical superstructure is simply a reproduction of much older and far better developed schemes.

That under certain economic and political conditions the credit system can serve to hasten the emancipation of the working class, just as, for instance, in the beginning of the eighteenth and again at the beginning of the nineteenth century in England, it served towards transferring the wealth of one class to another, is quite unquestionable, self-evident. But to regard *interest-bearing capital as the main form of capital* while trying to use a special form of credit, the alleged abolition of interest, as the basis for a transformation of society, is a thoroughly *petty-bourgeois* fantasy. Hence indeed this fantasia, eked out further, is already to be found among the *economic spokesmen of the English petty bourgeoisie in the seventeenth century*. Proudhon's polemic with Bastiat (1850) about interest-bearing capital is on a far lower level than the *Philosophy of Poverty*. He succeeds in getting himself beaten even by Bastiat and breaks into burlesque bluster when his opponent drives his blows home.

A few years ago Proudhon—instigated I think by the government of Lausanne—wrote a prize essay on *Taxation*. Here the last flicker of inspiration is extinguished. Nothing remains but the petty bourgeois pure and simple.

So far as his political and philosophical writings are concerned they all show the same contradictory, dual character as the economic works. Moreover their value is confined to France. Nevertheless his attacks on religion, the church, etc., were of great merit in his own country at a time when the French socialists thought it desirable to show by their religiosity how superior they were to the bourgeois Voltaireanism of the eighteenth century and the German godlessness of the nineteenth. If Peter the Great defeated Russian barbarism by barbarity, Proudhon did his best to defeat French phrasemongering by phrases. His work on the *coup d'état*, in which he flirts with Louis Bonaparte and, in fact, strives to make him palatable to the French workers, and his last work, written against *Poland*, in which for the greater glory of the tsar he expresses the most imbecile cynicism, must be characterised as not merely bad but base productions ; of a baseness which corresponds, however, to the petty-bourgeois point of view.

Proudhon has often been compared to *Rousseau*. Nothing could be more mistaken. He is more like *Nicolas Linguet*, whose *Théorie des lois civiles* [*Theory of Civil Law*], by the way, is a very brilliant book.

Proudhon had a natural inclination for dialectic. But as he never grasped really scientific dialectic he never got further than sophistry. In fact this hung together with his petty-bourgeois point of view. Like the historian *Raumer*, the petty bourgeois is composed of On The One Hand and On The Other Hand. This is so in his economic interests and *therefore* in his politics, in his scientific, religious and artistic views. It is so in his morals, in everything. He is a living contradiction. If, like Proudhon, he is in addition a gifted man, he will soon learn to play with his own contradictions and develop them according to circumstances into striking, ostentatious, now scandalous, now brilliant paradoxes. Charlatanism in science and accommodation in politics are inseparable from such a point of view. There only remains one governing motive, the *vanity* of the subject, and the only question for him, as for all vain people, is the success of the moment, the attention of the day. Thus the simple moral sense which always kept a Rousseau, for instance, far from even the semblance of compromise with the powers that be, is necessarily extinguished.

Perhaps future generations will sum up the latest phase of French development by saying that Louis Bonaparte was its Napoleon and Proudhon its Rousseau-Voltaire.

¶SCHWEITZER, J. B. VON (1833-75). Lassalle's successor in the leadership of the *Allgemeine Deutsche Arbeiterverein* (General Association of German Workers). A Frankfort lawyer, originally a National Liberal, became a follower of Lassalle in the early 'sixties. In 1865, in Berlin, Schweitzer founded the central organ of the Lassalleans, the *Social-Demokrat*, for which he received subsidies from Bismarck.

Schweitzer tried to turn the political party which has to lead the class movement of the proletariat into a sect, and opposed the unification of the German workers' movement. He was a representative of Bismarck's policy, a " Royal Prussian Social-Democrat." (Marx.) (See further Letters 75, 77, 81, 113.)

LINGUET, SIMON NICOLAS HENRI (1736-94). French author who conducted a polemic " against the bourgeois-liberal ideals of his contemporaries of the Enlightenment, against the opening rule of the bourgeoisie." (Marx.)

ROUSSEAU, JEAN JACQUES (1712-78). The most important representative of the ideology of the revolutionary petty bourgeoisie before the great French revolution. Himself under the influence of the ideas of the period of Enlightenment, he turned at the same time against their rationalism. He glorifies the natural state of primitive equality. According to him the development of civilisation leads to the extreme height of inequality in absolute monarchy and precisely through this to the new equality of the social contract (*contrat social*), this being with him only the ideological expression of the relations of capitalist commodity production, which are formally only contractual relations. He bases the rights of the people on the forcible expulsion of despots. His pedagogic and political writings exercised a great influence on his contemporaries. The Jacobins, *e.g.*, Robespierre, regarded him as their theoretical precursor.

VOLTAIRE, FRANCOIS MARIE AROUET (1694-1778). Famous French rationalist, representative of the ideology of the rising revolutionary French bourgeoisie. His historic rôle lies in the critical writings and satires in which he made violent attacks upon the feudal-aristocratic government, the morals of his time and especially the Catholic church ; through these he exercised a great influence on the revolutionary development in France and also abroad. He was severely persecuted for his writings.

73. ENGELS TO MARX

Manchester, 27 January, 1865.

I am sending the chaps* the little Danish folksong about the *Tidmann* who is struck dead in the *Thing* [parliament] by the old man because he lays new taxes upon the peasants. This is revolutionary without being punishable and above all it is against the feudal aristocracy, and the paper *absolutely must come out* against them. I add a few remarks to it on that account. The article on the organisation of the army I shall probably be able to do as soon as I have the new army Bill, etc. I am writing telling them to send them to me ; I am also telling them that I shall come out against the government—past and present—as much as against the Progressives, and that if they will not accept this the article is *not to be printed*. . . .

* The *Social-Demokrat*, edited by Schweitzer.

The worthy Lassalle is being gradually unmasked as just a common rogue after all. We have never started to judge people by what they imagined they were but always by what they were, and I do not see why we should make an exception for the late Itzig. Subjectively his vanity may have represented the thing plausibly to him, objectively it was a blackguardly act, a betrayal of the whole workers' movement to the Prussians. And the silly conceited ass never seems to have extracted any reciprocity, anything definite, to say nothing of guarantees, from Bismarck, but simply to have relied on the fact that he *was bound* to over-reach Bismarck, just as he could not fail to shoot Rakowitz dead. Baron Itzig [Lassalle] all over.

¶The supposition which Engels here expresses was fully confirmed in the year 1928 by the chance discovery of the correspondence between Lassalle and Bismarck. In a letter dated June 8, 1863, Lassalle writes to Bismarck, in sending him the statutes of the recently formed Workers' Association: "But this miniature picture [the statutes] will clearly convince you how true it is that the working class feels an instinctive inclination towards a dictatorship, if it can first be rightly persuaded that the dictatorship will be exercised in its interests; and how much, despite all republican views—or rather precisely because of them—it would therefore be inclined, as I told you only recently, to look upon the Crown, in opposition to the egoism of bourgeois society, as the natural representative of the social dictatorship, if the Crown for its part could ever make up its mind to the—certainly very improbable—step of striking out a really revolutionary line and transforming itself from the monarchy of the privileged orders into a social and revolutionary people's monarchy."

When the questions of universal suffrage and of the Schleswig-Holstein war came up, Lassalle was prepared to support Bismarck, who was proposing to utilise universal suffrage for his own reactionary ends—against the bourgeoisie—and pointed out to him that the introduction of universal suffrage, which would in fact have meant a *coup d'état* against the bourgeois-progressive majority of the Prussian Parliament, must, whatever happened, take place before the war. "Why can you do anything you like in peace time?" Lassalle asks Bismarck in a letter written at the end of January or the beginning of February 1864. "Why did I admit to you as long ago as last May that, so long as no external conflict arose, our country would quietly acquiesce even in the most severe absolutism? ... In peace time the interests of *private life* completely predominate and reduce the mood of the people to one of indifference, whatever conditions may be." At the same time Lassalle placed all his literary activities at Bismarck's disposal. He sent Bismarck, for instance, the proof-sheets of his *Bastiat-Schulze* before it appeared and asked Bismarck to protect him from judicial confiscation of a book which "will lead ... to the *most thorough* destruction of the progressive party and of the whole liberal bourgeoisie." (Letter of February 5, 1864; this and the preceding quotations from letters are taken from Gustav Mayer's pamphlet, *Bismarck und Lassalle*, Berlin 1928.) The mistrust felt by Marx and Engels for Lassalle, their constant struggle against his false theory of the state, derived from Hegel, are brilliantly justified by this correspondence. Lassalle may not have regarded himself as such, but objectively he was undoubtedly an agent of Bismarck in the camp of the working class, a traitor to the workers' movement. [For Bismarck, see Letter 86.]

74. MARX TO ENGELS

[London], 1 February, 1865.

Cremer, our Honorary General Secretary, had received a written invitation for the "Council," as well as a private visit, on behalf of a Provisional Committee which is meeting *privately* in the London Tavern next Monday. Object: Monster meeting for manhood suffrage. *President—Richard Cobden!*

The point is this. As E. Jones had already told us, the fellows had had a complete failure in Manchester. Consequently they adopted a broader platform, in which, however, in place of manhood suffrage, *registration* "for paying poor-rate" figured. This is what is stated in the printed circular sent to us. Since, however, after various indications it became clear to them that nothing under manhood suffrage could attract any co-operation whatever on the part of the working classes they announced that they would accept manhood suffrage. A *big* demonstration in London would lead to similar ones in the provinces, write the provincials " yet once again," they having " all ready " arrived at the realisation that they are incapable of setting the ball agoing.

The next point, which was discussed yesterday, was this: should our Society, *i.e.*, Council, agree to the wish of these fellows (who include all the old sham City agitators like Sam Morley, etc.) and send some delegates who would attend the transactions of their provisional committee as "observers?" Secondly, if these fellows *directly* pledge themselves to the slogan of manhood suffrage and call the public meeting in its name, should we give our support? This *last* point is just as decisive for these chaps as it was in the American business.* Without the trade unions no mass meeting is possible and without us the trade unions are not to be had. This is also the reason why the gentlemen are applying to us.

Opinions were *very* divided, largely as a result of *Bright's* latest imbecility in Birmingham.

On my motion it was decided: (1) To send the deputation merely as " observers " (in my motion I excluded foreigners, but Eccarius and Lubez were elected as " English " and as *silent* witnesses); (2) So far as the meeting is concerned, to act with them if, in the *first* place, manhood suffrage is directly and openly proclaimed in the programme, and, in the *second*, if people *elected by us* are brought on to the *regular* Committee, so that they can watch the fellows and when the *fresh treachery*, which, as I made clear to them all, is *certainly planned*, takes place, can compromise them. I am writing to E. Jones about the affair to-day.

¶This letter, with its evidence of the approach attempted by Cobden (the leader with Bright of the industrial bourgeoisie) to the General Council of the International, is also evidence of

* See page 160.

the power wielded by the International in England at this time. It further affords a brilliant example of the tactics by which Marx, while maintaining a completely uncompromising political line, utilised every opportunity of intensifying mass agitation. (Compare Letters 88, 91.) For Cobden, Bright, the franchise agitation, etc., see also Letters 8, 35, 63 and pp 160, 163. [*Ed. Eng. ed.*]

75. MARX TO ENGELS

[London] 3 February, 1865.

Enclosed are (1) Letter from Siebel giving a report of his meeting with Klings, which I had "ordered" him to have. On this I will merely remark that I shall mix *no further* in the affair. If Klings succeeds—*without* our help—together with the old bitch [Countess Hatzfeld] in removing B. Becker and his testatory importance I am agreed. Nothing can be done with the Workers' Association, as bequeathed by Baron Itzig [Lassalle]. The quicker it is dissolved the better.

(2) The *Rheinische Zeitung* with a leading article, apparently by Red Becker. It is an appeal for mercy on the part of the "Progressives."

My opinion is now that *we both* must make a declaration, and that this crisis gives us just the opportunity for resuming our "legitimate" position. I had written about ten days ago telling Schweitzer that he must make a front against Bismarck, that even the appearance of a flirtation with Bismarck on the part of the workers' party must be dropped. He has thanked me by "all ready" philandering with Pissmarck more than ever. "Yet once again" in No. 16 of the *Social-Demokrat*, where, adorned with misprints, my letter on Proudhon appears,* Moses Hess, for the second time "all ready," denounces the "International Association." I wrote a furious letter about this to Liebknecht yesterday and told him that he had now had the *very last* warning; that I did not give a farthing for "good intentions" which did the work of bad intentions; that I cannot make it clear to the members of the "International Committee" here that things of this kind are done in good

* See Letter 72.

faith out of sheer stupidity ; that their filthy rag, while it continues to glorify Lassalle, although they know now what treachery he was secretly harbouring, and while it flirts like a coward with Bismarck, has the shamelessness to accuse us here, through the Plon-plonist Hess, of Plon-plonism [Bonapartism].

My opinion is now as follows. We start from Moses' denunciation or insinuation in order to introduce in a few words a declaration of war against Bonaparte Plon-plon, taking the opportunity to give honourable mention also to Moses' friend, the Rabbi Ein-Horn [One-Horn]. . . . We then use this to declare ourselves ditto against Bismarck and against the knaves or fools who dream or drivel about an alliance with him for the working class. In conclusion, of course, the Progressive swine should also be told, on the one hand that they have got the thing stuck by their political cowardice and helplessness, on the other that if they demand an alliance with the working class against the government—and this is in fact the only correct step at the moment—then they must at least make concessions to the workers corresponding to their own principles of " free trade " and " democracy " ; namely, the repeal of the whole of the Exceptional Laws against the workers, including, in addition to the Combination Laws,* quite specifically the present Prussian Press laws. They must also at least express themselves as favourable to the restoration of universal suffrage, which was set aside in Prussia by *coup d'état.* This is the least which can be expected of them. On the military question there may also perhaps be something to put in. In any case the thing must be finished quickly. And you must jot down on paper your " ideas " about the whole declaration. I will then add mine, knead it together, send you the whole thing again and so forth. The moment seems to me favourable for this " *coup d'état.*" Neither out of consideration for Liebknecht nor for

† Combination Laws [" *Koalitionsgesetze* "]. Passed in 1845. Paragraph 181 prohibited combinations between bodies of employers, paragraph 182 combinations between bodies of workers ; paragraphs 183 and 184 prohibited every form of combination among factory workers of whatever grade and provided punishment by fines and imprisonment for " breach of civil contract " where workers were disobedient or rebellious. [*Ed. Eng. ed.*]

anybody else can we let this opportunity slip for our *restitutio in integrum* [restoration to our former position].

At the same time you must not fail to let the *Social-Demokrat* have your article on the military question as soon as possible.

With regard to the declaration I should of course write and tell them that if they themselves do *not* accept it in its entirety it will " all ready " appear in other papers.

If they take it, so far good, and it will not even do any harm if it gets them smashed up. (Although Bismarck will be careful to avoid forcible measures at the moment.) If they do not accept it we have a decent excuse for being rid of them. In any case the air must be purified and the party swept clean of this remaining Lassalle stink.

¶ The first number of the *Social-Demokrat* appeared under the editorship of Schweitzer on December 15, 1864. The names of Marx and Engels were included in the list of contributors. From January 4, 1865, the paper began to appear regularly three times a week. In February 1865 Marx and Engels withdrew from the circle of contributors to the *Social-Demokrat* because Schweitzer did not come out definitely enough against the Prussian government. (See Letters 78, 80.)

BECKER, BERNHARD. Died 1882. Lassalle's successor as leader of the *Allegemeine Deutsche Arbeiterverein* (General Association of German Workers). Marx wrote to Engels on November 4, 1864 : " Lassalle (like a reigning prince) has, by a deposition in his will, ' put in ' Bernhard Becker—the unfortunate fellow who was Juch's editor of *Hermann* for a time—as his successor in the dignity of President of the General Association of German Workers." Bernhard Becker, after stepping into office, quickly revealed his incapacity for the rôle and was replaced by Schweitzer.

HESS, MOSES. See Letter 3, Note.

" PLON-PLONISM." Plon-plon was the nickname of Napoleon III's cousin, Prince Jerome Napoleon ; he tried to make himself popular by radical speeches and came out in opposition to the Emperor. He and his followers made the Palais Royal their centre, as a sort of rival camp to the Tuileries but were equally representative of Bonapartism. See Letter 87. [*Ed. Eng. ed.*]

EIN-HORN—pseudonym Horn. A Liberal rabbi who sympathised with the organisation of workers' co-operatives under bourgeois influence.

KLINGS. A worker in Solingen, member of the General Association of German Workers.

SIEBEL. A relative of Engels.

LIEBKNECHT, WILHELM (1826-1900). One of the founders and chief leaders of German Social-Democracy. By profession a tutor, in his youth a revolutionary democrat, took part in the revolution of 1848 and the South German rising of 1849. In the years of reaction (up to 1862) he lived in London, where, under Marx's influence, he became a Socialist. In 1865, together with Bebel, he founded in Leipzig the Saxon *Volkspartei* [People's Party], in 1869 in Eisenach the *Deutsche Sozialdemokratische Arbeiter Partei* [German Social-Democratic Workers' Party]; 1869-75 he edited the *Volkstaat* [People's State]; he fought for the revolutionary way of unification for Germany. In 1870 he came out against the war credits and the annexation of Alsace-Lorraine, for which he was imprisoned 1870-71; in 1872, together with Bebel and Hepner, he was condemned to two years' imprisonment in a fortress on a charge of high treason (till April 1874). In 1875 he was the chief organiser of the union with the Lassalleans. Editor of *Vorwärts* (Forward), 1876-78; expelled from Leipzig 1881, he settled in Borsdorf; took an active part in the organisation of the Second International, 1889; editor of *Vorwärts* from 1891 till his death. He was many times elected a member of the Reichstag during the 'seventies, 'eighties and 'nineties.

Liebknecht was an energetic agitator, the author of numerous articles and pamphlets. Under the guidance of Marx and Engels he carried out a revolutionary, proletarian line on many of the most important questions, but he was unable to root out his petty-bourgeois notions of democracy; in his fight against opportunism he took a thoroughly conciliatory attitude. Marx and Engels submitted Liebknecht's vacillations to ruthless criticism in their letters (*e.g.*, 1866-71: his petty-bourgeois narrow-mindedness and his federalist tendencies; 1875: his capitulations to Lassallean opportunism; 1878-80: his reformist line in Parliament and liquidatory vacillations when the Party went into illegality; 1885: his attempts to come to a compromise with the Right; 1889: conciliatory mistakes at the foundation of the Second International; 1891: opportunist vacillations in the working out of the new programme; 1894: conciliation with regard to Vollmar, etc.). At the end of the 'nineties Liebknecht strongly opposed Millerandism [Socialists taking office in bourgeois governments] and Bernsteinism ['revising' away the revolutionary teaching of Marx].

76. ENGELS TO MARX

Manchester, 5 February, 1865.

I fully agree about the declaration. But you must do it yourself or I shall not get through with the military article. I am afraid the thing will be so long that it will only do as a pamphlet. I and II are ready (except for revision), III not yet. I have had a lot of interruption, Blank was here, etc. So do the declaration. Included in the Exceptional Laws are also the limitation of the right of association and meeting, all the laws about *journeymen's road books** and finally Article 100 of the Penal Code: Incitement of citizens to hatred and contempt (also an inheritance from Napoleon). Then, if it can be worked in, an indication that in a predominantly agricultural country like Prussia it is dastardly to make an exclusive attack on the bourgeoisie in the name of the industrial proletariat but never to devote a word to the patriarchal exploitation of the rural proletariat under the lash of the great feudal aristocracy. . . .

77. MARX TO ENGELS

[London], 6 February, 1865.

Fortunately in the *Social-Demokrat* which has arrived to-day your appeal for a death-blow to the aristocracy appears in the Feuilleton, after my article, which itself contains a condemnation of any "semblance of compromise."

I now think it better first to send in the few lines given below instead of the declaration I originally proposed. They will undoubtedly provide the *opportunity* for a *further declaration*. . . .

* Internal passport system for workers. [*Ed. Eng. ed.*]

TO THE EDITOR OF THE *Social-Demokrat*
DECLARATION

In No. 16 of your paper, Herr M. Hess, writing from Paris, makes insinuations about the *French members of the London Central Committee* of the International Workingmen's Association, who are entirely unknown to him, in these words: "Indeed one cannot see that it would matter *if some friends of the Palais Royal** *were also to be found in the London Society, as it is a public one,*" etc.

In an earlier number, in a little chat about the paper *L'Association*, the same Herr M. Hess made a similar insinuation against the Paris friends of the London Committee. We declare his insinuations to be a grotesque slander.

For the rest we are glad to see that this incident has justified our conviction that the Parisian proletariat is now as before irreconcilably opposed to Bonapartism in both its forms—the Tuileries form and the Palais Royal form—and has never for a moment entertained the project of selling its historic honour for a mess of pottage (or, instead of "*historic honour*," shall we say, "its historic right as firstborn to be the protagonist of revolution"?) We recommend this example to the German workers.

78. MARX TO ENGELS

[London], 11 February, 1865.

As to-day is Saturday I imagine you will not be sending off your thing† on the same day, in which case there will still be time for these "supplementary" proposals for alteration.

(1) In the place *where you ask, what do the workers want?* I should not answer as you do that the workers in Germany, France and England want so and so. For the answer sounds as if we accepted Itzig's [Lassalle's] slogans (at least it will be so *interpreted*). I should rather say:

It would seem that the demands put forward at the moment

* Friends of the Palais Royal, etc. See Note, page 183: "Plon-plonism." [*Ed. Eng. ed.*]

† Engels' pamphlet, "The Military Question in Prussia and the German Workers' Party."

by the most advanced workers in *Germany* were directed towards, etc. This does not involve you at all, which is all the better considering that later on you yourself criticise the demand for universal suffrage, if put forward without the necessary conditions. (The word " direct " moreover would indeed have no sense, *e.g.*, in England, etc., and is only the opposite to the " indirect " franchise invented by the Prussians.) The form in which the *Knoten** in Germany conceive of state intervention *à la* Lassalle is of such a kind that one must avoid identifying oneself with it at all. It is much more distinguished (and safe) if you take the *Knoten* at their word and *let them say* what *they* want for themselves. (I say the *Knoten*, because they are the really argumentative section, *under the influence of Lassalle.*)

(2) I should not say that the movement of 1848-49 failed because the bourgeois resisted *direct universal suffrage.* On the contrary, the latter was declared as a German right by the Frankfort parliament and proclaimed in every form by the viceregent of the *Reich.* (In my opinion, too, as soon as the thing comes to be discussed seriously, this franchise must be treated in Germany as part of the rightfully *existing* law.) As that is not the place for a longer exposition, I would help myself with the phrase that the bourgeoisie at that time preferred peace and servitude to the mere *prospect* of fighting and freedom, or something of the sort.

As a whole the thing is very good and I am specially tickled by the part where it is shown that the present *Knoten* movement only in fact exists by the favour of the police.

79. ENGELS TO MARX

[Manchester], 13 February, 1865.

Your suggestions came just in time yesterday and have both been used. How specially necessary the one about the demands of the *Knoten* was is brought home to me again by Nos. 20 and 21 of the *S*[*au*]-*Drecks*† which have arrived to-day.

* *Knoten.* See Note, page 87.

† The *Social-Demokrat.* See Note, page 183. "*Sau-Dreck,*" (literally swine-dung), " filthy muck," " rotten trash." [*Ed. Eng. ed.*]

For the rest, our attitude seems to be bearing fruit all the same. In No. 21 there is a certain revolutionary tone which was formerly entirely lacking. I have, however, written to Liebknecht that it is unnecessary to kick up a row ; they have only got to drop the flirtation with the reactionaries and also to let the aristocracy and the reaction have their share, but otherwise not to *abuse* them or the bourgeoisie, this is superfluous when things are quiet.

But one can see that Itzig [Lassalle] has given a Tory-Chartist character to the movement which will be hard to destroy, and has set going in Germany a tendency hitherto unknown among the workers. This revolting cringing to the reaction reveals itself everywhere. We shall have some trouble with that. You will see, the *Knoten* are going to say: What does Engels want? What has he been doing all the time? How can he speak in our name and tell us what we are to do? The fellow is sitting in Manchester exploiting the workers, etc. True, I don't care a damn about this, but it is sure to come and we have Baron Itzig to thank for it.

80. MARX TO ENGELS

[London], 18 February, 1865.

Enclosed are two letters from Liebknecht—one to you and one to me. Also an earlier one from Schweitzer.

My opinion is that :

Liebknecht having once given notice we must finish with the thing. If he had postponed the affair we could also have delayed it as your pamphlet is not completed.

I regard Schweitzer as incorrigible (probably in secret understanding with Bismarck).

What confirms me in this are :

(1) The passages which I have underlined in the enclosed letter of the 15th from him to me.

(2) The *moment* at which his *Bismarck III* appeared.

In order to justify both assertions I herewith give you a *literal transcript* of passages from my letter of February 13 to him :

'... As the correspondence of M. Hess in No. 21, received to-day, renders our declaration partly out of date, the matter may now be allowed to rest. True, our declaration also included another point, praise of the anti-Bonapartist attitude of the Parisian proletariat and a hint to the German workers to copy this example. This was more important to us than the attack on Hess. However, we shall express our views as to the relation of the workers to the Government of Prussia in detail elsewhere.

" In your letter of February 4 you say that I myself warned Liebknecht not to overstep the mark, in order that he should not get himself sacked. Quite true. But at the same time I wrote to him that it is possible to say *everything* if one hits on the right form. Even a form of polemic *against* the government " possible " for the meridian of Berlin is undoubtedly very different from flirtation or even the semblance of compromise with the government ! I wrote to you yourself that the *Social-Demokrat* must avoid even such a semblance.

" I see from your paper that the Ministry is expressing itself ambiguously and playing for time with regard to the repeal of the combination laws. A *Times* telegram reports, on the other hand, that it has given indication of a protective attitude towards a proposal for state support of the co-operative societies. It would not surprise me at all if for once, by way of an exception, *The Times* had telegraphed correctly !

" Coalitions with the trade unions, which have grown from the working class, are not only of the utmost importance as a means of organising the working class for struggle against the bourgeoisie—this importance is shown, for instance, in the fact that even workers of the United States, despite their franchise and their republic, cannot do without them—but the right of combination in Prussia and in Germany means also in general breaking through the rule of the police and bureaucracy and tearing to bits the *Gesindeordnung* and *Adelswirtschaft** in the rural districts. In short it is a measure for the emancipation of

† *Gesindeordnung*. Master and Servant Act. Rules and regulations of a feudal patriarchal character which the aristocracy had absolute powers to enforce on their estates. *Adelswirtschaft*—Control by the aristocracy. [*Ed. Eng. ed.*]

"vassals," which the Progressive Party, or any bourgeois opposition party in Prussia which was not crazy, could allow a hundred times sooner than the Prussian government, and above all the government of a Bismarck! Support for co-operative societies from the Royal Prussian government, on the other hand —and anyone who knows Prussian conditions knows beforehand its necessarily minute dimensions—is of no value whatever as an economic measure, while at the same time it extends the system of guardianship, corrupts a section of the workers and castrates the movement. The bourgeois party in Prussia discredited itself and produced its present misery chiefly because it seriously believed that with the "new era" the government, by the grace of the Prince Regent, had fallen into its lap. But the workers' party will discredit itself far more if it imagines that in Bismarck's era, or any other Prussian era, the golden apples will drop into its mouth by grace of the king. That disappointment will follow Lassalle's unlucky illusion concerning socialist intervention on the part of a Prussian government is beyond all doubt. The logic of things will speak. But the *honour* of the workers' party demands that it should reject fancy pictures of this kind even before their hollowness is exposed by experience. The working class is revolutionary or it is nothing."

Well! To this letter of mine on the 13th he replies with his of the 15th in which he demands that I should subordinate myself in all "practical" questions to *his* tactics—he replies with "*Bismarck III*" as a fresh specimen of these tactics. And indeed it seems to me now that the *obstinate* way in which he put the cabinet question, on the occasion of the declaration against Hess, was not due to tenderness for Hess but to a *fixed determination* that *in no circumstances* should our hint to the German workers be given any space in the *Social-Demokrat.*

As, therefore, we have got to break with the fellow all the same, it is better done at once. As to the German *Knoten*, let them scream as much as they like. The useful elements among them are bound to join us again sooner or later. If you agree with the declaration below, copy it out, sign it and send it to me. It has been hurriedly scribbled down, so alter what seems unsuitable to you or rewrite it entirely as you prefer.

DECLARATION

TO THE EDITOR OF THE *Social-Demokrat*

The undersigned promised their collaboration with the *Social-Demokrat* and allowed their names to be published as collaborators, on the express condition that the paper should be edited in the spirit of the short programme communicated to them. They never for a moment underestimated the difficult position of the *Social-Demokrat* and therefore made no demands unsuitable to the meridian of Berlin. But they repeatedly demanded that language at least as bold as that used against the Progressives should be adopted towards the Ministry and the feudal-absolutist party. The tactics pursued by the *Social-Demokrat* make their further collaboration with it impossible. The opinion of the undersigned with regard to Royal Prussian Government Socialism and the correct attitude of the workers' party to such a deceptive sham was already fully developed in No. 73 of the *Deutsche Brüsseler Zeitung* (September 12, 1847) in an answer to No. 206 of the *Rheinische Beobachter*, then appearing in Cologne, in which an alliance of the "proletariat" with the "government" against the "liberal bourgeoisie" had been proposed. Every word of the declaration *we* made then we still subscribe to to-day.

¶ In the article, *Bismarck III*, referred to above, Schweitzer wrote among other things: "If we bear in mind the fact that the real Prussia, as it actually exists, with its own history and its own spirit of government, carries and must carry within itself the *tendency towards expansion in Germany*, and that moreover it is precisely on the *glorious moments of its development* that this tendency is based, and if at the same time we recall the fact that Bismarck's Ministry gives unmistakable indications of doing justice to this tendency, we have reached the *heart of our investigation*. . . . A *Prussian* government, which, in the second half of the nineteenth century, begins to annex German land, a Prussian government which, *in face of the solemn and public declarations of Emperor, Kings and Princes that the political constitution of Germany is untenable, resumes the 'policy of Frederick the Great'* (as a Greater-German newspaper expressed it), cannot stand still after a small victory—it must move further along the path upon which it has entered—it must move forward, if necessary, with '*blood and iron.*' For to start from the proudest traditions of an historically mature state and then to shrink back like cowards from a decisive act would be to kill the inmost vital nerve of such a state. One can let traditions of this kind rest—but *one cannot take them up again in order to ruin them.* A Prussian Minister who adopted a policy *of this sort* for Prussia would fall a doomed victim to the wrathful shade of the great Frederick and to the *mockery of his own contemporaries.*" (See also Letter 113.)

The article from the *Deutsche Brüsseler Zeitung* [*Brussels German Newspaper*] mentioned in Marx' and Engels' declaration—*The Communism of the "Rhine Observer"* (September 12, 1847)—contains the following passage:

"If a certain fraction of German Socialists have perpetually attacked the liberal bourgeoisie, and in a way which was of no advantage to anyone except to the German governments, if government papers like the *Rheinische Beobachter* [*Rhine Observer*], supported by the phrases of these people, now maintain that it is not the liberal bourgeoisie but the government which represents the interests of the proletariat, the Communists have nothing in common either with the former or the latter. True, the attempt has been made to lay the responsibility for this upon the German Communists, they have been accused of an alliance with the government. This accusation is ridiculous. The government cannot ally itself with the Communists for the simple reason that of all the revolutionary parties in Germany the Communists are the most revolutionary, and because the government knows this better than anyone else. Are the Communists to ally themselves with a government which has declared them guilty of high treason and treated them accordingly? Are the government organs to propagate principles which in France are accounted anarchistic, incendiary, destructive of all social relations, and to which this same government perpetually attributes exactly the same qualities? There is no thought of such a thing. . . ." "The proletariat does not ask whether the welfare of the people is the main consideration for the bourgeois or only secondary, whether they *want* to use the proletariat as cannon fodder or not. The proletariat does not ask what the bourgeoisie only *want*, but what they are *obliged* to do. It asks whether the present political situation, where the bureaucracy rules, or that striven for by the Liberals, where the bourgeoisie would rule, offers it more means of attaining its own ends. . . ." "Of all political elements the most dangerous for a king is the people. . . . The genuine people—the proletarians, the small peasants and the mob—they are, as Hobbes says, *puer robustus sed malitiosus*, a stalwart and malicious boy, who will not let himself be made a fool of by lean kings or by fat ones. The people would force from His Majesty above all a constitution, besides universal suffrage, freedom of the press and of association and other unpleasant things. And when they had got all this they would with the greatest possible speed use it in order to declare the might, the dignity and the poetry of monarchy [superfluous]. (*Marx-Engels Gesamtausgabe*, Bd. I, 6.)

81. MARX TO KUGELMANN

London, 23 February, 1865.

First of all I shall briefly describe my attitude to Lassalle. During his agitation relations between us were suspended : (1) because of the self-flattering braggadocio to which he added the most shameless plagiarism from my writings, etc. ; (2) because I *condemned his political tactics* ; (3) because, even *before* he began his agitation, I fully explained and "proved" to him here in this country that direct *socialist* action by the "State of Prussia" was nonsense. In his letters to me (from 1848 to 1863), as in our personal encounters, he always declared himself an adherent of the party which I represent. As soon as he had convinced himself, in London (end of 1862), that he could not play his games *with me*, he decided to put himself forward as the "workers'" dictator *against* me and the old party. In spite of all that, I recognised his services as an agitator, although towards the end of his brief life even that agitation appeared to me of a more and more ambiguous character. His sudden death, old friendship, sorrowful letters from the Countess Hatzfeld, indignation over the *cowardly impertinence* of the bourgeois press towards one whom in his lifetime they had so greatly feared, all that induced me to publish a short statement against the wretched Blind, which did not, however, deal with the *content* of Lassalle's actions (Hatzfeld sent the statement to the *Nordstern*).

For the same reasons, and in the hope of being able to remove elements which appeared to me dangerous, Engels and I promised to contribute to the *Social-Demokrat* (it has published a translation of the *Address* and at the editors' request I wrote an article about Proudhon on the death of the latter); and, after Schweitzer had sent us a *satisfactory Programme of his editorial work*, we allowed our names to be given out as contributors. A further guarantee for us was the presence of *W. Liebknecht* as an unofficial member of the editorial board.

However, it soon became clear—the proofs fell into our hands—that *Lassalle* had in fact *betrayed* the party. He had entered into a formal contract with Bismarck (of course, *without having in his hand any sort of guarantees*). At the end of September 1864 he was to go to Hamburg and there (together with the crazy Schramm* and the Prussian police spy Marr) *force* Bismarck to annex Schleswig-Holstein, that is, he was to proclaim its incorporation in the name of the "workers," etc. In return for which Bismarck promised universal suffrage and a few socialist charlatanries. It is a pity that Lassalle could not play the comedy through to the end. The hoax would have made him look damned ridiculous and foolish, and would have put a stop for ever to all attempts of that sort.

Lassalle went astray because he was a "*Realpolitiker*" of the type of Herr Miquel, but cut on a larger pattern and with bigger aims. (By the bye, I had long ago seen sufficiently far through Miquel to explain his coming forward by the fact that the *National Verein* offered an excellent excuse for a petty *Hanoverian* lawyer to make his voice heard outside his own four walls by all Germany, and thus cause the enhanced "*reality*" of himself to react again on the Hanoverian homeland, playing the "*Hanoverian* Mirabeau" under Prussian protection. Just as Miquel and his present friends snatched at the "new era"

* Rudolf Schramm.

inaugurated by the Prussian prince regent, in order to join the *National Verein* and to fasten on to the "Prussian top," just as they developed their "civic pride" generally under Prussian protection, so Lassalle wanted to play the Marquis Posa* of the proletariat with Philip II of Uckermark, Bismarck acting as intermediary between him and the Prussian kingdom. He only imitated the gentlemen of the *National Verein*; but while these invoked the Prussian "reaction" in the interests of the middle class, Lassalle shook hands with Bismarck in the interests of the proletariat. These gentlemen had greater justification than Lassalle, in so far as the bourgeois is accustomed to regard the interest immediately in front of his nose as "reality," and as in fact this class has concluded a compromise everywhere, even with feudalism, whereas, in the very nature of the case, the working class must be sincerely *revolutionary*.

For a theatrically vain nature like Lassalle (who was not, however, to be bribed by paltry trash like office, a mayoralty, etc.), it was a most tempting thought: an act directly on behalf of the proletariat, and executed by Ferdinand Lassalle! He was in fact too ignorant of the real economic conditions attending such an act to be critically true to himself. The German workers, on the other hand, were too "demoralised" by the despicable "practical politics" which had induced the German bourgeoisie to tolerate the reaction of 1849-59 and the stupefying of the people, not to hail such a quack saviour, who promised to get them at one bound into the promised land.

Well, to pick up again the threads broken off above. Hardly was the *Social-Demokrat* founded than it became clear that old Hatzfeld wanted to execute Lassalle's "testament." Through Wagener (of the *Kreuzzeitung*) she was in touch with Bismarck. She placed the *Arbeiterverein* (*Allgemeine Deutscher*),† the *Social-Demokrat*, etc., at his disposal. The annexation of Schleswig-Holstein was to be proclaimed in the *Social-Demokrat*, Bismarck to be recognised in general as patron, etc. The whole pretty plan was *frustrated* because we had Liebknecht in Berlin and on

* Marquis Posa, the hero of a play by Schiller; he was convinced that he could persuade the tyrant Philip II of the justice of his cause.

† General Association of German Workers. See Note to Letter 29.

the editorial board of the *Social-Demokrat.* Although Engels and I were not pleased with the editing of the paper, with its lick-spittle cult of Lassalle, its occasional coquetting with Bismarck, etc., it was of course more important not to break publicly with the paper for the time being, in order to thwart old Hatzfeld's intrigues and the complete compromising of the workers' party. We therefore made *bonne mine a mauvais jeu* [put a good face on it], although privately we were always writing to the *Social-Demokrat* that Bismarck must be opposed just as much as the Progressives. We even put up with the intrigues of that affected coxcomb Bernhard Becker—who takes the importance conferred upon him in Lassalle's testament quite seriously—against the *International Workingmen's Association.*

Meanwhile Herr Schweitzer's articles in the *Social-Demokrat* became more and more Bismarckian. I had written to him earlier, that the Progressives could be *intimidated* on the coalition question, but that the *Prussian government would never* concede the complete abolition of the Combination Laws, because that would involve making a breach in the bureaucracy, would give the workers adult status, would shatter the *Gesindeordnung,** abolish the flogging regime of the aristocracy in the countryside, etc., etc., which Bismarck would never allow, which was altogether incompatible with the Prussian *bureaucratic state.* I added that if the Chamber rejected the Combination Laws, the government would have recourse to phrases (such phrases, for example, as that the social question demanded " more thorough-going " measures, etc.) in order to retain them. All this proved to be correct. And what did Herr von Schweitzer do? He wrote an article *for* Bismarck and saved all his heroics for such *infiniment petits* [infinitely small people] as Schulze, Faucher, etc.

I think that Schweitzer and Co. have honest intentions, but they are " *Realpolitiker.*" They want to accommodate themselves to *existing* circumstances and not to surrender this *privilege* of " real politics " to the exclusive use of Herr Miquel and Co. (The latter seem to want to keep for themselves the right of intermixture with the Prussian government.) They know

* See Note, page 189.

that the workers' press and the workers' movement in Prussia (and therefore in the rest of Germany) exist solely *par la grace de la police* [by the grace of the police]. So they want to take the circumstances as they are, and not irritate the government, just like our "*republican*" "*real politicians*," who are willing to "put up with" a Hohenzollern *emperor*.

Since I am not a "*Realpolitiker*," I have found it necessary to sever all connection with the *Social-Demokrat* in a public declaration signed by myself and Engels (which you will probably see soon in one paper or another). You will understand at the same time why at the present moment I can do *nothing* in Prussia. The government there has refused point blank to re-naturalise me as a Prussian citizen. I should only be allowed to *agitate* there in a form acceptable to Herr v. Bismarck.

I prefer a hundred times over my agitation here through the *International Association*. Its influence on the English proletariat is direct and of the greatest importance. We are making a stir here now on the General Suffrage Question, which of course has a *significance here quite different* from what it has in Prussia.

On the whole the progress of this "Association" is *beyond all expectation*, here, in Paris, in Belgium, Switzerland and Italy. Only in Germany, of course, Lassalle's successors oppose me, in the first place, because they are frantically afraid of losing their importance, and, secondly, because they are aware of my avowed opposition to what the Germans call "*Realpolitik*." (It is this sort of reality which places Germany so far behind all civilised countries.)†

¶WAGENER, HERMANN (1815-89). Reactionary German politician. Founded and conducted until 1854 the central organ of the Conservative Party, the *Kreuzzeitung*. He was the leader of that fraction of the *Junkers*' party which supported Bismarck.

† *Letters to Dr. Kugelmann* by Karl Marx. Martin Lawrence 1934. Page 27.

82. ENGELS TO F. A. LANGE

Manchester, 29 March, 1865.

Meanwhile my involuntary delay in answering you has given me the opportunity of getting your book on the labour question ; I have read it with much interest. I too was struck, the very first time I read Darwin, with the remarkable likeness between his account of plant and animal life and the Malthusian theory. Only I came to a different conclusion from yours : namely, that nothing discredits modern bourgeois development so much as the fact that it has not yet succeeded in getting beyond the economic forms of the animal world. To us so-called " economic laws " are not eternal laws of nature but historic laws which arise and disappear ; and the code of modern political economy, in so far as it has been drawn up with proper objectivity by the economists, is to us simply a summary of the laws and conditions under which alone modern bourgeois society can exist—in short the conditions of its production and exchange expressed in an abstract and summary way. To us also, therefore, none of these laws, in so far as it expresses *purely bourgeois conditions,* is older than modern bourgeois society ; those which have hitherto been more or less valid throughout all history only express just those relations which are common to the conditions of all society based on class rule and class exploitation. To the former belongs the so-called law of Ricardo, which is valid neither for feudal serfdom nor ancient slavery ; to the latter belongs what is tenable in the so-called Malthusian theory.

Like all his other ideas, Parson Malthus had stolen this theory direct from his predecessors; all that belongs to him is the purely arbitrary application of the two progressions. In England the theory itself has long ago been reduced to a rational scale by the economists ; the pressure of population is not upon the means of subsistence but upon the means of *employment ;* mankind is capable of increasing more rapidly than modern bourgeois society can stand. To us a further reason for declaring this bourgeois society a barrier to development which must fall.

You yourself ask how increase of population and increase in the means of subsistence are to be brought into harmony ; but except for one sentence in the preface I find no attempt to solve the question. We start from the premise that the same forces which have created modern bourgeois society—the steam-engine, modern machinery, mass colonisation, railways, steam-ships, world trade—and which are now already, through the permanent trade crises, working towards its ruin and ultimate destruction—these same means of production and exchange will also suffice to reverse the relation in a short time, and to raise the productive power of each individual so much that he can produce enough for the consumption of two, three, four, five or six individuals. Then town industry as it is to-day will be able to spare people enough to give agriculture quite other forces than it has had up to now ; science also will then at last be applied in agriculture on a large scale and with the same consistency as in industry ; the exploitation of the inexhaust-ible regions fertilised by nature herself in South-Eastern Europe and Western America will be carried out on an enormous scale hitherto quite unknown. If all these regions have been ploughed up and after that a shortage sets in, then will be the time to say *caveant consules* [to sound the alarm].

Too little is produced, that is the cause of the whole thing. But *why* is too little produced ? Not because the limits of pro-duction—even to-day and with present-day means—are ex-hausted. No, but because the limits of production are deter-mined not by the number of hungry bellies but by the number of *purses* able to buy and to pay. Bourgeois society does not and cannot wish to produce any more. The moneyless bellies, the labour which cannot be utilised *for profit* and therefore cannot buy, is left to the death-rate. Let a sudden industrial boom, such as is constantly occurring, make it possible for this labour to be employed with profit, then it will get money to spend, and the means of subsistence have never hitherto been lacking. This is the endless vicious circle in which the whole economic system revolves. One presupposes bourgeois condi-tions as a whole, and then proves that every part of them is a necessary part—and therefore an " eternal law."

I was much amused at your description of the Schulze co-operatives. All that sort of thing has existed here in its own way but is now more or less a thing of the past. Proletarian pride has yet to be acquired by the people in Germany.

I cannot leave unnoticed a remark you make about old Hegel, who you say lacked the more profound kind of mathematical and scientific training. Hegel knew so much mathematics that not one of his pupils was equal to the task of editing the numerous mathematical manuscripts he left behind. The only man I know who understands enough mathematics and philosophy to do this is Marx. The absurdities of detail in Hegel's *Philosophy of Nature* I grant you of course readily enough, but his *real* philosophy of nature is to be found in the second part of his *Logic*, in the doctrine of Essence, the true heart of the whole theory. But the modern scientific doctrine of the correlation of natural forces (first of all I think in Groves, 1838) is after all only another expression, or rather it is the positive proof, of the Hegelian development of cause, effect, interaction, force, etc. I am of course no longer a Hegelian, but I still have a great feeling of piety and devotion towards the colossal old chap.

¶LANGE, FRIEDRICH ALBERT (1828-75). A German bourgeois scientist and political writer. In the labour movement he showed himself a conciliator. Author of the well-known book, *The Labour Question: Its Significance for the Present and Future.**

Also the author of a *History of Materialism*, of which Plekhanov said that it had "contributed a great deal, not towards the criticism of materialism but towards spreading and strengthening among the public a wrong view of the historical development of materialism and of its importance for modern social science." (Plekhanov's preface to the Russian translation of *The Communist Manifesto*.)

Marx said of Lange in a letter to Engels (March 11, 1865): "Siebel has sent me Lange's pamphlet. Confused; Malthu-

* *Die Arbeiterfrage in ihrer Bedeutung für Gegenwart und Zukunft* (1865).

sianism mixed with Darwinism ; flirts with all sides—but there are some nice things against Lassalle and the bourgeois consumers' co-operative fellows."

Marx wrote to Kugelmann about Lange (June 27, 1870) : "Herr Lange (*Die Arbeiterfrage, etc.*, second edition) sings my praises loudly, but with the object of making himself important. Herr Lange, you see, has made a great discovery. The whole of history can be subsumed under a single great natural law. This natural law is the *phrase* (in this application Darwin's expression becomes nothing but a phrase) 'the struggle for life' and the content of this phrase is the Malthusian law of population or, rather, over-population. So, instead of analysing the struggle for life as represented historically in different definite forms of society, all that has to be done is to translate every concrete struggle into the phrase 'struggle for life' and this phrase itself into the Malthusian population fantasy. One must admit that this is a very impressive method—for swaggering, sham-scientific, bombastic ignorance and intellectual laziness. What the same Lange says about the Hegelian method and my application of it is really childish. First of all, he understands nothing about Hegel's method and secondly, as a consequence, far less, even, about my critical application of it. In one respect he reminds me of Moses Mendelssohn. That prototype of a windbag wrote to Lessing, asking how he could take the 'dead dog Spinoza' seriously. Similarly, Herr Lange wonders that Engels, I, etc., take the dead dog Hegel seriously when Büchner, Lange, Dr. Dühring, Fechner, etc., are agreed that they—poor deer* have buried him long ago. Lange is naive enough to say that I 'move with rare freedom' in empirical matter. He hasn't the least idea that this 'free movement in matter' is nothing but a paraphrase for the *method* of dealing with matter—that is, *the dialectic method*."†

MALTHUS, T. (1766-1834). English economist who became famous through his book, *Essay on Population*. He there developed the idea that population increases faster (in geometrical progression) than the means of subsistence (the production of which increased in arithmetical progression). This assertion is contradicted by facts. Engels in a letter to Danielson (Nicolai-on) remarks that the opposite is now the case—the

* This phrase was written in English.
† Marx : *Letters to Dr. Kugelmann*. Martin Laurence 1934, page 111.

means of subsistence are growing faster than the population. Marx (see Letter 72) called Malthus' pamphlet "a libel on the human race." But in spite of all the facts, the Malthusian law of population, in one form or another, still remains part of the permanent stock of bourgeois economics.

83. MARX TO ENGELS

[London], 20 May, 1865.

I am now working like a horse, as I must use the time in which it is possible to work and the carbuncles are still there, though now they only disturb me locally and not in the brain-pan.

Between whiles, as one cannot always be writing, I am doing some Differential Calculus $\frac{dx}{dy}$. I have no patience to read anything else. Any other reading always drives me back to my writing-desk.

This evening a special session of the International. A good old fellow, an old Owenist, *Weston* (carpenter) has put forward the two following propositions, which he is continually defending in the *Beehive* : (1) That a general rise in the rate of wages would be of no use to the workers ; (2) That therefore, etc., the trade unions have a *harmful* effect.

If these two propositions, in which *he* alone in our society believes, were accepted, we should be turned into a joke (*so wären wir Kladderadatsch*) both on account of the trade unions here and of the *infection of strikes** which now prevails on the Continent.

On this occasion—as non-members may be admitted to this meeting—he will be supported by a born Englishman, who has written a pamphlet to the same effect. I am of course expected to supply the refutation. I ought really therefore to have worked out my reply for this evening, but thought it more important to write on at my book† and so shall have to depend upon improvisation.

Of course I know beforehand what the two main points are :

* This phrase was written in English.
† *Capital*, Vol. I, published in 1867.

(1) That the *wages of labour* determine the value of commodities; (2) That if the capitalists pay 5 instead of 4 shillings to-day, they will sell their commodities for 5 instead of 4 shillings to-morrow (being enabled to do so by the increased demand).

Inane though this is, only attaching itself to the most superficial external appearance, it is nevertheless not easy to explain to ignorant people all the economic questions which compete with one another here. *You can't compress a course of political economy into one hour. But we shall do our best.**

¶Marx debated against Weston on the night of May 20 and again on the 23rd; on June 24, 1865, he wrote to Engels: "I have read a paper in the Central Council (it would make two printer's sheets, perhaps) on the question brought up by Mr. Weston as to the effect of a general rise of wages, etc. The first part of it was an answer to Weston's nonsense; the second a theoretical explanation, in so far as the occasion was suited to this. Now the people want to have this printed... In the second part the thing contains, in an extremely condensed but relatively popular form, much that is new, taken in advance from my book,† while at the same time it has necessarily to slur over all sorts of things."

The "paper" referred to is Marx's *Value, Price and Profit*, which he had read on June 20. He did not agree to its publication in 1865, when the fuller exposition in *Capital* had not yet been given to the world (see Letters 84, 98) and it was then forgotten until after Engels' death in 1895, when it was found by Marx's daughter, Eleanor Marx Aveling, who edited and published it in its original English form in 1898. [*Ed. Eng. ed.*]

WESTON, JOHN. A member of the General Council of the International from its formation. (See Letter 71.) As treasurer he was one of the signatories of the Address of the Council drawn up by Marx on the Paris Commune (*The Civil War in France*) May 30, 1871. "Our old Weston," as Marx called him (letter to Engels, November 7, 1867), supported Marx's

* The last two sentences were written in English.
† *Capital.*

line on the Irish question. (*Ibid.* and Letter 133 of this volume.) [*Ed. Eng. ed.*]

84. MARX TO ENGELS

London, 31 July, 1865.

Now as to my work I will tell you the unvarnished truth.* There are still three chapters to write in order to complete the theoretical part (the first three books). Then there is still the fourth book, the historical-literary one, to write, which is relatively the easiest part to me as all the problems have been solved in the first three books and this last is therefore more of a repetition in historical form. But I cannot bring myself to send off anything until I have the whole before me. Whatever shortcomings they may have, the merit of my writings is that they are an artistic whole, and that can only be attained by my method of never having them printed until they lie before me as a *whole*. This is impossible with the Jacob Grimm method, which is in general more suited to works not dialectically constructed.

85. MARX TO ENGELS

[London] 13 February, 1866.

As to this "damned" book, the position is as follows: it was *ready* at the end of December. According to the present arrangement the discussion of ground rent alone, the chapter before the last, takes up nearly one book. I went to the Museum in the daytime and wrote at nights. I had to wade through the new agricultural chemistry in Germany, especially Liebig and Schönbein, who are more important in this matter than all the economists put together, and also the enormous amount of material which the French have produced since I last occupied myself with this point. I ended my theoretical investigation of

* *Ich will dir reinen Wein einschenken.* Engels had written on July 15 to ask if the book was really nearly finished. "The first of September was absolutely the final date and as you know it is going to cost twelve bottles of wine." [*Ed. Eng. ed.*]

ground rent two years ago. And it is just in this interval that a lot has been done—entirely confirming my theory, moreover. The opening up of Japan was also important here (otherwise, except when obliged to do so professionally, I never read descriptions of travel as a rule). Hence the "shifting system" which the swine of English factory-owners used to apply to the *same* person in 1848-50 has been applied by me to myself.

Although finished, the manuscript, gigantic in its present form, could not be prepared for publication by anyone but myself, not even by you.

I began the copying out and the *polishing of the style* punctually on the first of January, and the thing proceeded very merrily, as I naturally enjoyed licking the infant clean after so many birthpangs. But then the carbuncle interfered again so that up till now I have not been able to get further, but have only really been able to fill out what was already finished according to the plan.

For the rest I agree with your view and shall give the first volume, as soon as it is ready, to Meissner. But to finish it I must at least be able to *sit down*.

¶LIEBIG, JUSTUS V. (1803-73). A pioneer of German chemistry, especially in the sphere of agriculture.

SCHÖNBEIN, CHRISTIAN FREDERICK (1799-1866). German chemist.

MEISSNER, OTTO. The publisher of *Capital*.

86. ENGELS TO MARX

[Manchester], 13 April, 1866.

So Bismarck has made his universal suffrage *coup*,* even though without his Lassalle. It looks as if the German bourgeois will agree to it after a little struggle, for after all, Bonapartism is the real religion of the modern bourgeoisie. It is always becoming clearer to me that the bourgeoisie has not the

* See Note to Letter 89.

stuff in it for ruling directly itself, and that therefore where there is no oligarchy, as there is here in England, to take over, in exchange for good pay, the management of state and society in the interests of the bourgeoisie, a Bonapartist semi-dictatorship is the normal form. The big material interests of the bourgeoisie carry this through, even against the opposition of the bourgeoisie, but allow the dictatorship no share in the real power. The dictatorship in its turn, on the other hand, is forced against its will to further these material interests of the bourgeoisie. So we now get Monsieur Bismarck adopting the programme of the National Union. To carry it out is something quite different, of course, but Bismarck is hardly likely to come to grief through the German bourgeoisie.

¶BISMARCK, OTTO VON (1815-98). Prussian Prime Minister and first Chancellor of the German Reich. By birth a *junker* of the East Elbe district and a bitter enemy of the working class. "Bismarck is Louis Napoleon, translated from the French adventurer and Royal pretender into the Prussian petty *junker* and German university 'corps' student . . . a man of great intelligence and great cunning, a born business man and a smart one. . . . But this well-developed intelligence in the sphere of practical life is often combined with corresponding limitations of vision, and here Bismarck surpasses his French predecessor. For the latter had at least worked out his 'Napoleonic ideas' for himself during his vagabond period—their quality being to match—while Bismarck . . . never produced even the trace of an original political idea but only took other people's ideas ready-made and combined them together for himself. But it was just this narrow-mindedness which was his good fortune. Without it he would never have succeeded in representing the whole of world history to himself from a specifically Prussian point of view. . . . Indeed, when in his own way he had fulfilled the particular mission assigned to him from without, he was also at the end of his resources; we shall see what antics he was driven to resort to as a result of his total lack of rational ideas and his utter incapacity for understanding the historical situation which he had himself created." (Engels, *Gewalt und Oekonomie bei der Gründung des Deutschen Reichs*).

Bismarck's historic significance lies in the fact that he carried through the unification of Germany, the key question of the German bourgeois revolution, in a reactionary way, involving the maintenance of the old apparatus of the *junker* state. By fulfilling the economic demands of the bourgeoisie he made it possible for their political demands to be realised in a manner *chosen by himself.*

"In politics there are only two decisive powers: the organised force of the state—the army—and the unorganised elemental force of the masses. After 1848 the bourgeoisie no longer knew any way of appealing to the masses, it feared them more than it feared absolutism. The army, on the other hand, was in no sense at its disposal but very much at Bismarck's disposal." . . . "A man in Bismarck's position and with Bismarck's past would be bound, if he had any insight into the state of affairs, to say to himself that the *junkers*, as they were, did not constitute a class capable of survival, that of all definite classes the bourgeoisie alone could lay claim to a future and that therefore (apart from the working class, of whose historic mission we will not ascribe to him any understanding) the more he gradually prepared his new empire for transition into a modern bourgeois state, the more secure would be its prospects of existence. . . . True, from the standpoint of the working class the fact revealed itself that it was already too late to establish a lasting bourgeois rule. . . . But even though it is too late for a peaceful and securely established bourgeois regime in Germany, in the year 1870 it was nevertheless the best policy for the interests of the possessing classes in general to aim at this bourgeois domination." (Engels, *Gewalt und Oekonomie bei der Gründung Deutschen Reiches* [*Force and Economics in the Foundation of the German Empire*]. See, too, Letters 89, and, for Bismarck's approach to Marx, 93, 94.)

87. MARX TO ENGELS

[London] 20 June, 1866.

Yesterday there was a discussion in the International Council on the present war.* It had been announced beforehand and our room was very full. The Italian gentlemen had also sent

* The Prussian-Austrian war of 1866.

us representatives once more. The discussion wound up, as was to be expected, with " the question of nationality " in general and the attitude we should take towards it. This subject was adjourned till next Tuesday.

The French, very numerously represented, gave vent to their cordial dislike for the Italians.

Moreover the representatives of " young France " (*non-workers*) came out with the announcement that all nationalities and even nations were " antiquated prejudices." Proudhonised Stirnerism. Everything to be dissolved into little " groups " or " communes " which will in their turn form an " association " but no state. And indeed this " individualisation " of mankind and the corresponding " mutualism " are to proceed while history comes to a stop in all other countries and the whole world waits until the French are ripe for a social revolution. They will then perform the experiment before our eyes, and the rest of the world, overcome by the force of their example, will do the same. Just what Fourier expected of his model phalanstery. Moreover, everyone who encumbers the " social " question with the " superstitions " of the old world is " reactionary."

The English laughed very much when I began my speech by saying that our friend Lafargue, etc., who had done away with nationalities, had spoken " French " to us, *i.e.*, a language which nine-tenths of the audience did not understand. I also suggested that by the negation of nationalities he appeared, quite unconsciously, to understand their absorption into the model French nation.

For the rest, the line is difficult now because one has equally to oppose the silliness of English pro-Italianism on the one hand and the false polemic of the French on the other, and must specially prevent any demonstration which would involve our Association in a one-sided direction.

¶The mistake of the Proudhonists in failing to understand the significance of the national question in the proletarian struggle for freedom was also repeated later on. (See the discussions on the national question, especially during the imperialist war; Lenin against Rosa Luxemburg, etc. Lenin, *Collected Works*, English edition, Vols. XVIII and XIX.)

STIRNER, MAX JOHANN (Caspar Schmidt) (1806-56). Petty-bourgeois post-Hegelian philosopher, who pushed individualism to its extreme point and on the basis of his idealistic point of view arrived at a complete negation of all social-historical interconnection. Marx and Engels criticised him in the *Deutsche Ideologie* as the philosophical expression of the German petty bourgeois and his ignorance of the world.

FOURIER, FRANÇOIS CHARLES (1772-1837). French utopian socialist. The strong side of his work is his criticism of the bourgeois social order. "In Fourier we find a criticism of existing social conditions made with true French wit but none the less penetrating on that account. He mercilessly exposes the moral and material misery of the bourgeois world. . . . But Fourier appears at his greatest in his conception of the history of society. . . . Fourier handles dialectic with the same mastery as his contemporary, Hegel." (Engels, *The Development of Socialism from Utopia to Science*.)

88. MARX TO ENGELS

[London] 7 July, 1866.

The workers' demonstrations in London, which are marvellous compared with anything we have seen in England since 1849, are purely the work of the "International." Mr. Lucraft, for instance, the leader in Trafalgar Square, is one of our Council. This shows the difference between *working* behind the scenes and disappearing in public and the Democrats' way of making oneself important in public and *doing nothing*. . . .

Is there anywhere where our theory that the *organisation of labour is determined by the means of production* is more brilliantly confirmed than in the human slaughter industry? It would really be worth while for you to write something about it (I have not the necessary knowledge) which I could insert under your name as an appendix to my book. Think this over. But if it is to be done it must be done for the first volume, where I deal with this subject *ex professo* [myself]. You will understand what great pleasure it would give me if you were also to appear as a direct collaborator in my chief work (hitherto I have only done small things) instead of merely through quotations.

I am also studying Comte now, as a sideline, because the English and French make such a fuss about the fellow. What takes their fancy is the encyclopædic touch, the synthesis. But this is miserable compared to Hegel. (Although Comte, as a professional mathematicisn and physicist, was superior to him, *i.e.*, superior in matters of detail, even here Hegel is infinitely greater as a whole.) And this Positivist rot appeared in 1832!

¶The workers' demonstrations in London were those demanding universal suffrage. The Reform Act of 1867 extended the franchise. See Letters 74, 90, 91, 116. BENJAMIN LUCRAFT, later a member of the London School Board. [*Ed. Eng. ed.*]

COMTE, AUGUSTE (1798-1857). French philosopher. Founder of Positivism, the characteristic intellectual tendency of the liberal-democratic bourgeoisie of the nineteenth century. His motto was: "Neither restoration nor revolution." (Compare Letter 155.)

89. ENGELS TO MARX

Manchester, 25 July, 1866.

The business in Germany seems to me fairly simple now. From the moment Bismarck carried out the Smaller-German scheme of the bourgeoisie, with the Prussian army and such colossal success, the development in Germany has taken this direction so decisively that we, like everyone else, must acknowledge the accomplished fact, we may like it or not. As to the *national* side of the affair, B[ismarck] will in any case establish the Smaller German Empire in the dimensions intended by the bourgeoisie, *i.e.*, including South-West Germany—for the phrases about the line of the Main and the optional separate South German Confederacy are no doubt intended for the French, and in the meantime the Prussians are marching on

Stuttgart. Moreover before very long the German-Austrian provinces will also fall to this empire, since Austria is bound now to become Hungarian, and the Germans will be the third nationality in the empire—still below the Slavs.

Politically B[ismarck] will be forced to depend on the bourgeoisie, whom he needs against the imperial princes. Not at the moment, perhaps, because the prestige and the army are still sufficient. But he will have to give something to the bourgeoisie even in order to secure for himself from Parliament the necessary conditions for the central power, and the natural course of the affair will always force him or his successors to appeal to the bourgeoisie again. So that if, as is possible, Bismarck does not concede more to the bourgeoisie than he is actually *obliged* to now, he will still be driven more and more into their arms.

The thing has this good side to it that it simplifies the situation ; it makes a revolution easier by doing away with the brawls between the petty capitals and will in any case hasten development. After all a German Parliament is something quite different from a Prussian Chamber. The whole of the petty states will be swept into the movement, the worst localising influences will cease and parties will at last become really national instead of merely local.

The chief disadvantage—a very great one—is the unavoidable flooding of Germany with Prussianism. Then there is the temporary separation of German Austria, which will result in an immediate advance of the Slav elements in Bohemia, Moravia and Carinthia. Unfortunately neither of these things can be helped.

In my opinion, therefore, all we can do is simply to accept the fact, without justifying it, and to use, so far as we possibly can, the greater facilities for *national* organisation and unification of the German proletariat which must now at any rate offer themselves.

¶After the triumph of the reaction in 1849, Germany remained disunited. Unification was necessary for the further free development of bourgeois conditions. It could have been obtained in three ways: (1) the revolutionary way—by the creation of a German republic; but the bourgeoisie would not take this path; (2) the unification of Germany under the rule of the Hohenzollerns; (3) unification under the rule of the Hapsburgs.

In 1864 the Austrians and Prussians acting together defeated the Danes near the town of Düppel and won Schleswig-Holstein from them. After the victory a conflict over this province arose between Austria and Prussia. In the summer of 1865 neither of the two foes felt quite prepared for fighting and so things did not come to a war. Prussia and Austria came to an agreement at Bad Gastein by which Holstein went to Austria and Schleswig to Prussia.

In September 1865 Bismarck paid a visit to Bonaparte and negotiated with him. Probably Bismarck promised Bonaparte a piece of German territory (a promise which he never kept). On April 8, 1866, a Prusso-Italian offensive alliance was concluded against Austria, with the tacit consent of Bonaparte, of course.

Bismarck concluded his war preparations by introducing, on April 9, 1866, a proposal for the convocation of an assembly elected on the basis of universal suffrage which should decide the question as to the reform of the constitution of the North German Federation. (See Letter 86.) The war was very short. On July 3, 1866, the Austrians were defeated at Königgrätz. Prussian predominance in Germany was assured.

Besides the letters given here, an estimate of the events of 1866 will also be found in Engels' preface to the second edition of his *Peasant War in Germany*.

In general, Marx and Engels considered that the bourgeois revolution in Germany was completed in 1866. (See Letter 190.) Thus the unity of Germany was accomplished in the second way. (See also letters following.)

90. MARX TO ENGELS

[London] 27 July, 1866.

I fully agree with you that one has got to accept the mess as it is. Still it is pleasant to be at a distance during this first period of love's young dawn. The arrogance of the Prussians, the folly of Handsome William,* who thinks that nothing has changed since the dream of triumph, except that he has become a Great Power, etc., will soon have their effect. The Austrians are now in the position where the Prague Slavophil fanatics wanted them to be in 1848. On the other hand their loss of Venice, their forced concentration of strength, is by no means favourable to Russia for the time being. As a pan-Slav empire themselves they will be all the more antagonistic to the Muscovites. Indeed the extreme decay of the Hapsburgs gives cause for fear that by and by they will allow themselves to be misled by the Russians into a common attack on Turkey.

For the workers everything which centralises the bourgeoisie is of course favourable. In any case the peace, even if it is concluded to-morrow, will be still more provisional than those of Villafranca and Zurich. As soon as the various belligerents have undertaken the " reform " of their " weapons of war " they will start " laying into one another again," as Schapper says. At any rate Bonaparte has also had a setback, although the formation of militaristic kingdoms to the right and left suits the Plon-plon scheme of " general democracy."

Here [in London] the government has nearly produced a rising. The Englishman first needs a revolutionary education, of course, and two weeks would be enough for this if Sir Richard Mayne† had absolute control. In fact the thing only depended on one point. If the railings—and it was touch and go—had been used offensively and defensively against the police and about twenty of the latter had been knocked dead, the military would have had to " intervene " instead of only parading. And then there would have been some fun. One thing is certain, these thick-headed John Bulls, whose brainpans seem to have been specially manufactured for the constables' bludgeons, will never get anywhere without a really bloody encounter with the ruling powers.

* Nickname for Wilhelm I, King of Prussia, later first Emperor of Germany.

† Commissioner of Police in London. The demonstration was for the franchise. See Letter 88. Compare the *Autobiography* of John Stuart Mill. [*Ed. Eng. ed.*]

91. MARX TO KUGELMANN

London, 9 October, 1866.

I had great fears for the first Congress at Geneva. On the whole, however, it turned out better than I expected. The effect in France, England and America was unhoped for. I could not, and did not want to go there, but wrote the programme for the London delegation. I deliberately restricted it to those points which allow of immediate agreement and concerted action by the workers and give direct nourishment and impetus to the requirements of the class struggle and the organisation of the workers into a class. The Parisian gentlemen had their heads full of the emptiest Proudhonist phrases. They babble about science and know nothing. They scorn all *revolutionary* action, *i.e.*, action arising out of the class struggle itself, all concentrated social movements, and therefore all those which can be carried through by *political means* (*e.g.*, the *legal* limitation of the working day). Under the *pretext of freedom*, and of anti-governmentalism or anti-authoritarian-individualism, these gentlemen—who for sixteen years have so calmly endured the most miserable despotism, and still endure it—actually preach the ordinary bourgeois science, only Proudhonistically idealised ! Proudhon has done enormous mischief. His sham criticism and sham opposition to the utopians (he himself is only a philistine utopian, whereas in the utopias of a Fourier, an Owen, etc., there is the presentiment and imaginative expression of a new world) attracted and corrupted first the " brilliant youth," the students, and then the workmen, particularly those of Paris, who, as workers in luxury trades, are strongly attached, without knowing it, to the old muck. Ignorant, vain, presumptuous, chattering, dogmatic, arrogant, they were on the point of spoiling everything, for they came to the Congress in numbers which bore no proportion whatever to the number of their members. I shall have a dig at them in the report without mentioning names.

I was very pleased with the American Workers' Congress at Baltimore which took place at the same time. The slogan there was organisation for the struggle against capital, and curiously enough most of the demands which I drew up for Geneva were also put forward there by the correct instinct of the workers.

The Reform movement* here, which our Central Council called into existence and *quorum magna pars fui* [in which I played a great part] has now reached immense and irresistible dimensions. I have kept behind the scenes all the time and do not trouble myself further about the affair since it has been set going.†

92. MARX TO KUGELMANN

London, 13 October, 1866.

Since my last letter but one to you, I have again had continual relapses and have therefore been constantly interrupted in my theoretical work (the practical work for the International Association goes on all the time, and there is a great deal of it, for really I have to lead the whole society). Next month I shall send the first sheets to Meissner and continue doing so until I bring the remainder to Hamburg myself. Then I shall visit you in any case.

My circumstances (physical and external interruptions‡ without intermission) make it necessary for the first volume to appear separately, not both volumes together, as I had at first intended. There will probably be three volumes after all.

The whole work is divided as follows :

Book I. The Production Process of Capital.
Book II. Circulation Process of Capital.
Book III. Form of the Process as a Whole.
Book IV. Contribution to the History of Economic Theory.

The first volume contains the first two books.

The third book will, I think, fill the second volume and the fourth book the third.

I considered it necessary to begin in the first book *ab ovo*,§ that

* For universal suffrage. See Letters 74, 88, 90.
† *Letters to Dr. Kugelmann* by Karl Marx. (Martin Lawrence 1934), p. 39.
‡ *i.e.* in consequence of domestic and financial troubles.
§ From the beginning.

is, to make in one chapter on commodities and money a *resumé* of my book which Duncker published.* I thought that necessary not only for the sake of completeness, but also because even people with quite good heads did not grasp the matter quite rightly, and there must therefore be something lacking in the first presentation, particularly in the *analysis of commodities*. Lassalle, for example, in his *Kapital und Arbeit*, where he is supposed to have given the " intellectual quintessence " of my development of the question, makes great blunders, which, it is true, always happens with him in his very unceremonious appropriation of my works. It is funny to hear him accuse me of literary and historical " errors," because I frequently quote from memory, without looking up the original. I have not yet quite made up my mind whether I should put in a few words in the preface about Lassalle's plagiarism. The shameless way in which his blind followers have come out against me would anyway justify my doing so.†

93. MARX TO ENGELS

Hanover, 24 April, 1867.

Kugelmann is a very eminent doctor in his special line, gynæcology. Virchow and the other authorities (among them a certain Meyer in Berlin, formerly Von Syboldt in Göttingen and until his insanity, Semmelweis of Vienna) correspond with him. If there is a difficult case in this line here he is always brought in as consultant. To give me a picture of the professional jealousy and local stupidity, he told me that at first he was blackballed—*i.e.*, not admitted to the doctors' association, because " gynæcology " was " immoral *schweinerei* " [filth]. Kugelmann also has a lot of technical talent. He has invented a heap of new instruments in this line.

He is, secondly, a fanatical supporter (and for my taste too Westphalian an admirer) of our theory and of us both personally. He sometimes bores me with his enthusiasm, which contradicts his dispassionateness as a medical man. But he

* *The Critique of Political Economy.*

† *Letters to Dr. Kugelmann* by Karl Marx. (Martin Lawrence 1934), p. 42.

understands, is sound through and through, uncalculating and self-sacrificing, and, the main thing, *convinced*. He has a nice little wife and a most delightful daughter of eight years old. He possesses a much better collection of our works than both of us put together. Here I also found *The Holy Family* again; he has presented it to me and will send you a copy. I was pleasantly surprised to find that we do not need to be ashamed of this work, although the cult of Feuerbach produces a very humorous effect upon one now.

The people, and in the capital, Hanover, even the bourgeoisie, are extremely *hostile to Prussia* (the same in *Hesse*) and express their opinion on every occasion. They openly speak of their wish—*for the French*. If anyone remarks to them that this is unpatriotic they say: "The Prussians did just the same. When they came through here they were boasting, with their officers at their head, about French help—in case of need." Wehner's father is very much respected here, is also reckoned a Guelph. Yesterday Bismarck sent one of his satraps to me, the lawyer Warnebold (this *between ourselves*). He wishes to utilise me and "my great talents in the interests of the German people." Von Bennigsen will call on me to-morrow.

We two have really got quite a different position in Germany, especially among the "educated" officialdom, from any we had an idea of. For instance the Superintendent of the Statistical Bureau here, Merckel, called on me and told me that for years he had studied the business about money in vain, but I had immediately made the thing clear once and for all. "Your twin-star, Engels," said he, "recently received recognition from my professional colleague Engel in Berlin, in the presence of the royal family." These are trivialities, but they are important for us. Our influence with this official world is greater than it is with the *Knoten*.*

I also received an invitation from the "European" Society. This is the name here for the Prussian-hating, North German National Unionists. Asses!

* *Knoten*, See Note, page 87.

¶ KUGELMANN, LUDWIG (1828-1902). A member of the First International. Developed great propagandist activity for the first volume of *Capital*.

BENNIGSEN, RUDOLF VON (1824-1902). Hanoverian National Liberal, founded the German *National Verein* [National Union], the political party of the German bourgeoisie, which stood for a German Federal State under Prussian leadership. Bennigsen was for many years the leader of the National Liberals and supported Bismarck, especially at the time of the "*Kultur-kampf*" [culture struggle—Bismarck's struggle with the Catholic Church].

ENGEL, ERNST (1812-96). Director of the German Statistical Bureau in Berlin.

94. ENGELS TO MARX

Manchester, 27 April, 1867.

I expected Bismarck to knock at your door, though scarcely with such rapidity. It is typical of the fellow's horizon and way of thinking that he judges everyone by himself. Well may the bourgeoisie admire the great men of to-day—it sees its own reflection in them. All the qualities by which Bonaparte and Bismarck achieved success are the qualities of the merchant: the pursuit of a definite end by waiting and experimenting until the right moment is hit upon, the diplomacy of the ever-open loophole of escape, the compromising and haggling, the swallowing of insults if interest demands it, the "do not let us be thieves"—in short, everywhere the merchant. Gottfried Ermen is just as great a statesman as Bismarck in his way, and if one follows all the tricks of these great men one always finds oneself back again on the Manchester Exchange. Bismarck thinks to himself: if I go on knocking at Marx's door I shall, after all, be sure to hit on the right moment in the end and then we will do a little business together. Gottfried Ermen all over.

¶ ERMEN, GOTTFRIED. Owner of the firm of cotton-spinners, Ermen and Engels. Engels was at first an employee and later a partner in this concern and by this means, during nearly twenty years, made it possible for Marx, despite all difficulties, to carry on his work on *Capital*.

95. MARX TO S. MEYER

Hanover, 30 April, 1867.

Why I never answered you? Because I was perpetually hovering on the verge of the grave. Therefore I had to use *every* moment in which I was capable of work in order that I might finish the task to which I have sacrificed my health, my happiness in life and my family. I hope this explanation requires no further supplement. I laugh at the so-called "practical" men and their wisdom. If one chose to be an ox one could of course turn one's back on the agonies of mankind and look after one's own skin. But I should really have regarded myself as *unpractical* if I had pegged out without completely finishing my book, at least in manuscript.

The first volume of the work will be published in a few weeks' time by *Otto Meissner* in Hamburg. The title is: *Capital, a Critique of Political Economy*. I have come to Germany in order to bring the manuscript across and am staying for a few days with a friend in Hanover on my way back to London.

Volume I comprises the "*process of capitalist production.*" Besides the general scientific development, I describe in great detail, from hitherto unused *official* sources, the condition of the English agricultural and industrial proletariat *during the last twenty years*, ditto *Irish* conditions. You will understand beforehand that all this only serves as an "*argumentum ad hominem.*"* I hope that in a year from to-day the whole work will have been published. *Volume II* gives the continuation and conclusion of the theories. *Volume III the history of political economy from the middle of the seventeenth century.*†

* Turning the weapons of the adversary (*i.e.*, of the English bourgeoisie) against himself.

† Marx intended to publish the continuation of the first volume of *Capital* in *one* volume; this volume grew into two. Consequently the volume which had been planned as Volume III [Theories of Surplus Value] was numbered IV. (See Engels' Preface to Vol. II of *Capital*.)

MEYER, SIEGFRIED (1840-72). German-American Socialist, member of the First International ; took part in the organisation of the German workers' movement in New York.

96. ENGELS TO MARX

Manchester, 16 June, 1867.

The second sheet* especially bears rather strong marks of the carbuncles, but that cannot be altered now and I do not think you should do any more about it in the additions, for, after all, the philistine is not accustomed to this sort of abstract thought, and will certainly not bother himself with it for the sake of the form of value.† At most the points here established dialectically might be demonstrated historically at rather greater length, the test to be made from history, so to speak, although what is most necessary in this respect has already been said. But you have so much material that you can certainly still make quite a good digression upon it, which will prove to the philistine from history the necessity for the development of money and of the process which takes place in connection with it.

In these more abstract developments you have committed the great mistake of not making the sequence of thought clear by a larger number of small sections and separate headings. You ought to have dealt with this part in the manner of Hegel's Encyclopædia, with short paragraphs, every dialectical transition marked by a special heading and so far as possible all excursuses and mere illustrations printed in special type. The thing would have looked rather like a school-book, but it would have been made much more easily comprehensible to a very large class of readers. For the populace, even the learned section, is no longer at all accustomed to this kind of thinking and one must facilitate it for them with every possible kind of help

Compared with the earlier account (Duncker)‡ the progress

* The second *Druckbogen* [printer's sheet] of *Capital*, Volume I.

† Marx, in sending some of the proof-sheets of *Capital* to Engels on June 3, had written : " You must tell me exactly which points in the account of the form of value you think should be specially popularised for the philistine in my additions." [*Ed. Eng. ed.*]

‡ The *Critique of Political Economy*, published by Duncker in 1859.

in the sharpness of the dialectical development is very marked, but in the account itself I like many things better in the first form. It is a great pity that it should be just the important second sheet which suffers from the carbuncle imprint. But there is nothing more to be done about this, and anyone capable of thinking dialectically will understand it all the same. The other sheets are very good and have given me much delight. . . .

Have read Hofmann.* The more recent chemical theory, with all its faults, a great advance on the former atomic one. The molecule as the smallest part of matter *capable of independent existence* is a perfectly rational category, a " node," as Hegel put it, in the infinite series of divisions, which does not conclude them but establishes a qualitative difference. The atom—formerly represented as the limit of possible division—is now nothing more than a *relation*, although Monsieur Hofmann himself falls back every other minute into the old idea of actual indivisible atoms. For the rest the progress of chemistry which the book records is really enormous, and Schorlemmer says that this revolution is still going on every day, so that one may expect new upheavals at any moment.

97. MARX TO ENGELS

[London] 22 June, 1867.

. . . Your satisfaction up to now is more important to me than anything the rest of the world may say of it. At any rate I hope the bourgeoisie will remember my carbuncles all the rest of their lives. Here is yet another proof what swine they are. You know that the Children Employment Commission has been functioning for five years. As a result of their first report, which appeared in 1863, " measures " were at once taken against the sections denounced. At the beginning of this session the Tory Ministry had introduced a Bill, through Walpole, the weeping willow, accepting all the proposals of the Commission, though on a very reduced scale. The fellows against whom measures would be taken, among them the big

* Hofmann, A. W., *Einleitung in die moderne Chemie* [*Introduction to Modern Chemistry*], 1866-67.

metal manufacturers and also especially the vampires of "home work," sat silent and humiliated. Now they are presenting a petition to Parliament and demanding *a fresh investigation!* They say the former one was prejudiced. They are calculating on the Reform Bill* absorbing all the public attention so that the thing can be smuggled through quite comfortably and privately while at the same time the trade unions have stormy weather to face themselves. The worst thing in the "*reports*" are the *statements of the fellows themselves.* And they know that a fresh investigation can only mean one thing, but it is just the thing "we bourgeois want"—a new term of five years' exploitation. Fortunately my position in the "International" enables me to disturb the tricky calculations of these curs. The thing is of the most enormous importance. It is a question of *abolishing the torture* of one and a half million human beings, not including the adult male working men!

As to the development of the *form of value* I have and have not followed your advice, in order to behave dialectically in this respect as well. That is to say I have (1) written an *appendix* in which I describe *the same thing* as simply and as much like a schoolmaster as possible, and (2) followed your advice and divided each step in the development into paragraphs, etc., *with separate headings.* In the *preface* I then tell the "non-dialectical" reader that he should skip pages x-y and read the appendix instead. This is not merely a question of the philistine, but of youth eager for knowledge, etc. Besides, the matter is too decisive for the whole book. Messrs. the economists have hitherto overlooked the extremely simple point that the form: *20 yards of linen = 1 coat* is only the undeveloped basis of *20 yards of linen = £2*, and that therefore the *simplest form of commodity*, in which the value is not yet expressed as a relation to all other commodities but only as *differentiated* from the commodity in its own natural form, contains the *whole secret of the money form* and with it in a nutshell *all the bourgeois forms of the product of labour.* In my first account (Duncker)† I avoid the difficulty of the development by only giving an actual analysis of the

* For the extension of the franchise. Passed in 1867.
† See Note to previous letter.

expression of value when it appears already developed and expressed in money.

You are quite right about Hofmann. You will also see from the conclusion of my chapter III, where the transformation of the handicraft-master into a capitalist—as a result of purely *quantitative* changes—is touched upon, that *in the text* I refer to the law Hegel discovered, of *purely quantitative changes turning into qualitative changes*, as holding good alike in history and natural science. In a *note* to the text (at that time I was just hearing Hofmann's lectures) I mention the *molecular theory* but not Hofmann, who discovered *nothing* of the affair, nothing *exceptional*, but instead I mention Laurent, Gerhardt and Wurtz, of whom the last is *the real man*.* Your letter brought a dim recollection of the thing to my mind and I therefore looked up my manuscript.

¶Marx began his economic studies in 1842-43: "... as editor of the *Rheinische Zeitung* I found myself for the first time under the embarrassing necessity of discussing so-called material interests with other things. The dealings of the Rhenish Landtag [Provincial Diet] in regard to timber thefts and the dividing up of landed property, the official polemic opened by Herr von Schaper, at that time *Ober-präsident* of the Rhine Province, with the *Rheinische Zeitung* on the conditions of the Moselle peasantry, and finally the debates about free trade and protection, provided the first incentive towards my occupation with economic questions." (Marx, Preface to the *Critique of Political Economy*.) And when the shareholders of the *Rheinische Zeitung*, frightened by its powerful revolutionary tone, dismissed Marx in order to avoid the suppression of the paper, Marx " eagerly " utilised the opportunity of " withdrawing from the public platform to the study." From this time onwards he began to make the study of political economy, the investigation and discovery of the laws of movement governing capitalist society, his lifework, not for purely scientific ends, but in order to forge a weapon for the proletariat by providing them with the theoretical basis of their struggle for freedom. Tens of years of

* See *Capital*, I, chapter XI [IX] (Kerr edition). Also the note added by Engels on this point, page 338. [*Ed. Eng. ed.*]

study, both of the reality and the theory of the capitalist method of production, were required to create the chief work of Marxism, *Capital*.

The difficulties with which Marx was faced in carrying out this work were gigantic, and without the faithful and constant help of Engels he could never have completed it. (See Letter 98.) In a letter to Lassalle (22 February, 1858) Marx wrote: "I will tell you how the economic work stands. I have in fact had the final working out in hand for some months.* But the thing makes very slow progress because as soon as one tries to come to a final reckoning with questions which one has made the chief object of one's studies for years, they are always revealing new aspects and demanding fresh consideration. Added to which I am not the master of my own time but rather a servant. I only have the night left over for myself and this night-work again is disturbed by very frequent attacks and recurrences of liver trouble. . . . After all, I have a presentiment that now, when after fifteen years of study I have got far enough to have the thing within my grasp, stormy movements from without will probably interfere. Never mind. If I get finished so late that I no longer find the world ready to pay attention to such things, the fault will obviously be my own."

The conditions which Marx mentions here were to accompany him until he had completed the first volume of *Capital*. In 1859, about sixteen years after he had begun his economic studies, was published the *Critique of Political Economy*, which was meant to be the first number in a series of pamphlets in which Marx intended to present the theory of the capitalist method of production. But the publication of the first number was not followed by the others; Marx continued his studies, altered his plan, and once more began to shape his formidable material and to give it the form in which we now have *Capital*. This constant wrestling with the material, with new facts which had to be dealt with and which produced new points of view, was one of the main difficulties accompanying the birth of *Capital*.

But in addition to this there were a number of external factors. Marx writes to Kugelmann on December 28, 1862: "The long delay is due to the following causes. First of all, the Vogt scandal in 1860 took up a great deal of my time, because

* The *Critique of Political Economy*.

I had to make many investigations into matters which were in themselves of no value, engage in litigation, etc. In 1861, because of the American Civil War, I lost my chief source of income, the *New York Tribune*. My contributions to that paper have been suspended up to the present moment. So I have been, and am, compelled to accept a lot of hackwork to keep myself and my family off the streets. I had even decided to become a ' practical man,' and was to have taken a position in a railway office early next year. Shall I call it good luck or bad ? I did not get the post because of my bad handwriting. So you see I had but little time and peace for theoretical work. It is probable that the same reasons will delay the final preparation of my work for the printers longer than I should wish."*

Perpetual anxiety as to means of existence were further intensified by Marx's illness. On August 23, 1866, he writes to Kugelmann, for instance : " I cannot work productively more than a very few hours a day without feeling the effect physically, and out of consideration for my family I must, however unwillingly, observe hygienic limits until I am completely restored to health. Besides that, my work is often interrupted by adverse external circumstances."†

Thus it was not in the assured calm of a professorial existence that *Capital* came into being : Marx was not spared the petty difficulties and hindrances of everyday life. But he was not the man to give way. (See Letter 95.) He fought against all the circumstances which obstructed and impeded his work and at every moment united his theoretical work with practical struggle, with the task of arousing the class consciousness of the working class and of organising them. He regarded his economic work as a means to be used in the immediate struggle of the proletariat. On December 21, 1857, he wrote to Lassalle : " The present commercial crisis has spurred me on to devote myself seriously to the working out of my principles of economics and also to prepare something on the present crisis." For Marx and Engels expected crises to lead to a further intensification of class contradictions which would be bound to give a powerful impulse to the workers' movement. " I am working like mad all through the nights at putting my economic studies together so that I may at least have the outlines clear before the deluge comes," he wrote on December 8, 1857, when he

* *Letters to Dr. Kugelmann*, Martin Lawrence, 1934 p. 23.

† Ibid, p. 37. Compare Letters 92, 95 in the present volume.

was expecting a new wave of the revolutionary movement. "As for my book, I am working twelve hours a day at writing out the fair copy." (Letter to Kugelmann, January 15, 1866.) When in 1864 this revival in the workers' movement began, when the International Workingmen's Association was formed under Marx's leadership, his theoretical work found its completion in the practical, political and organisational activity which it inspired, guided and directed. This union of theory and practice, the basis of Marxism, gave Marx the strength, despite all opposing forces, to bring his gigantic theoretical work to a conclusion.

98. MARX TO ENGELS

[London] 16 August, 1867
2 o'clock, night

Dear Fred,—Have just finished correcting the *last sheet* (49) of the book. The appendix—*form of value*—takes up 1¼ sheet in small print.

Preface ditto corrected and sent back yesterday. So *this volume is finished.* This has been possible thanks to *you* alone. Without your self-sacrifice for me I could never possibly have done the enormous work for the three volumes. I embrace you, full of thanks!

Enclosed two sheets of corrected proofs.

The £15 received with best thanks.

Greetings, my dear, beloved friend!

Your
K. MARX.

I shall only want the corrected proofs back *as soon as the whole book has appeared.*

99. MARX TO ENGELS

[London] 24 August, 1867.

The best points in my book are: (1) the *double character of labour*, according to whether it is expressed in use value or exchange value (*all* understanding of the facts depends upon this, it is emphasised immediately in the *first* chapter); (2) the treatment of *surplus value independently of its particular* forms as profit, interest, ground rent, etc. This will come out especially in the second volume. The treatment of the particular forms by classical economy, which always mixes them up with the general form, is a regular hash.

100. MARX TO ENGELS

[London] 11 September, 1867.

At the next Congress in Brussels I shall personally deal these fools of Proudhonists the finishing blow. I have managed the whole thing diplomatically and did not want to come out *personally* until my book was published and our Association had struck root. I will give them a hiding too in the official report of the General Council (despite all their efforts, the Parisian babblers could not prevent our re-election).

Meanwhile our Association has made great progress. The wretched *Star*, which tried to ignore us entirely, announced yesterday in a leading article that we were more important than the Peace Congress. Schulze-Delitzsch was not able to prevent his "Workers' Association" in Berlin from joining us. The swine among the English trade unionists, who thought we went too "far," are now coming running to us. Besides the *Courrier Français*, Girardin's *Liberté*, the *Siècle*, *Mode*, *Gazette de France*, etc., have given reports of our Congress. Things are moving. And in the next revolution, which is perhaps nearer than it appears, *we* (*i.e.*, you and I) will have this powerful engine *in our hands*. Compare this with the results of Mazzini's, etc., operations during the last thirty years! And without any financial means, moreover. With the intrigues of the Proudhonists in Paris, of Mazzini in Italy, of the jealous Odger, Cremer, and Potter in London, with the Schulze-Delitzschites and Lassalleans in Germany! We can be very well content.

¶As to the First International's need of money Marx wrote to Engels on October 19, 1867:

"What our Party lacks is money, as both the enclosed letters from Eccarius and Becker once more painfully prove. But for this deficiency we should still, despite our great and irreplaceable losses, be the strongest to-day, as we were in 1848."

101. MARX TO ENGELS

[London] 2 November, 1867

I used to think the separation of Ireland from England impossible. I now think it inevitable, although after the separation there may come *federation*. The way the English are going on is shown by the agricultural statistics for this year, published a few days ago. Then too the form of the evictions. The Irish Viceroy, Lord Abicorn* (this is *roughly* the name) has "cleared" his estate of thousands within recent weeks by forcible executions. Among the evicted are well-to-do farmers whose improvements and capital investments are confiscated in this fashion! There is no other European country in which foreign rule takes this direct form of native expropriation. The Russians only confiscate for political reasons; the Prussians in West Prussia buy out.

102. MARX TO ENGELS

London, 30 November, 1867.

What the English do not yet know is that since 1846 the economic content and therefore also the political aim of English domination in Ireland have entered into an entirely new phase, and that, precisely because of this, Fenianism is characterised by a socialistic tendency (in a negative sense, directed against the appropriation of the soil) and by the fact that it is a lower orders movement. What can be more ridiculous than to confuse the barbarities of Elizabeth or Cromwell,—who wanted to supplant the Irish by English colonists (in the Roman sense),—with the present system, which wants to supplant them by sheep, oxen and pigs! The system of 1801-46, with its rackrents and

* Lord Abercorn.

middlemen, collapsed in 1846. (During this period evictions were exceptional, occurring mainly in Leinster where the land is specially good for cattle raising.) The repeal of the Corn Laws, partly the result of or at any rate hastened by the Irish famine, deprived Ireland of its *monopoly* of England's corn supply in normal times. Wool and meat became the slogan, hence conversion of tillage into pasture. Hence from then onwards systematic consolidation of farms. The Encumbered Estates Act,* which turned a mass of previously enriched middlemen into landlords, hastened the process. The *clearing of the estate of Ireland!* is now the one idea of English rule in Ireland. The *stupid* English government in London itself knows nothing, of course, of this immense change since 1846. But the Irish know it. From *Meagher's Proclamation* (1848) down to the election manifesto of *Hennessy* (Tory and Urquhartite) (1866), the Irish have expressed their consciousness of it in the clearest and most forcible manner.

The next question is, what shall *we* advise the *English* workers? In my opinion they must make the *repeal of the Union* (in short the affair of 1783, only democratised and adapted to the conditions of the time) into an article of their *pronunziamento*. This is the only *legal* and therefore only possible form of Irish emancipation which can be admitted in the programme of an *English* party. Experience must show later whether a purely personal union can continue to subsist between the two countries. I half think it can if it takes place in time.

What the Irish need is:

(1) Self-government and independence from England.

(2) An agrarian revolution. With the best will in the world the English cannot accomplish this for them, but they can give them the legal means of accomplishing it for themselves.

(3) *Protective tariffs against England.* Between 1783 and 1801 every branch of Irish industry began to flourish. The Union, which overthrew the protective tariffs established by the Irish Parliament, destroyed all industrial life in Ireland. The little

* The Encumbered Estates Act enabled the inheritor of an estate encumbered with debt to compound with his creditors by surrendering part of the estate at a valuation. [*Ed. Eng. ed.*]

bit of linen industry is in no way a substitute. The Union of 1801 had just the same effect on Irish industry as the measures for the suppression of the Irish woollen industry, etc., taken by the English Parliament under Anne, George II, etc. Once the Irish are independent, necessity will turn them into protectionists, as it did Canada, Australia, etc. Before I bring my views before the General Council (next Tuesday, this time fortunately *without* the presence of reporters), I should be glad if you would send me a few lines with your opinion.

¶The English domination of Ireland began at the end of the twelfth century, but it was not until the sixteenth century that English oppression and exploitation developed into a permanent system. Up till then the forms of communal property had been completely preserved. (See Letter 133.) The Reformation was forced upon Ireland, her independence was more and more curtailed, and England embarked upon the policy of large-scale land-robbery which she pursued for centuries, thereby transforming the Irish people into one of the most bitterly oppressed of nations. At the end of the sixteenth century, Queen Elizabeth, after a bloody suppression of revolts, began systematically to settle English soldiery in Ireland, thus initiating a policy of colonisation which was further developed by the leader of the English bourgeois revolution, Cromwell, in the middle of the seventeenth century, and which, in conjunction with the grants of land to English nobles, forced the bulk of the Irish either to emigrate or to become tenant farmers exploited in the most unexampled way by the English landlords and their middlemen. After some temporary concessions which England was obliged to make during the American War of Independence (1782) and the French Revolution, there followed, in 1798, the bloody suppression of a fresh revolt and the forcible union of Ireland with England under the British Crown, by which the last traces of Irish independence were done away with. After the 'thirties, owing especially to the repeal of the Corn Laws, by which Irish corn production was left at the mercy of foreign competition, cattle-raising began to displace wheat-farming, and this resulted in a further mass emigration of Irish small farmers to America. As a result of this constant exploitation and oppression the history of Ireland includes a great number of revolutionary movements ; in the 'sixties a great part was played by the petty-bourgeois revolutionary Fenian movement, which was organised on illegal, semi-military lines. The main demands of the Fenian programme were a republic and the replacement of the tenant system by small peasant holdings.*

MEAGHER, THOMAS FRANCIS (1823-67). Irish revolutionary. One of the leaders of the 1848 rebellion, he was arrested and sentenced to death ; this sentence was commuted to transportation to Tasmania. In 1852 he escaped from Tasmania and went to America.

HENNESSY, JOHN POPE. Tory Catholic elected to the House of Commons with Fenian support against the Government candidate. Later a Nationalist. [*Ed. Eng. ed.*]

"THE AFFAIR OF 1783." By the "Renunciation Act" of 1783 Ireland received the right to be governed by the laws of her own parliament and courts, though the appointment of Ministers, etc., remained with the English. The Union (1800) put an end to the Irish parliament, and to the provisions of this Act. [*Ed. Eng. ed.*]

103. MARX TO ENGELS

[London], 8 January, 1868.

With regard to Dühring. It is a great deal from this man that he almost positively accepts the section on *Primitive Accumulation.* He is still young. As a follower of Carey, in direct opposition to the free-traders. Added to this he is *a university lecturer* and therefore not sorry that *Professor* Roscher, who blocks the way for all of them, should get some kicks. One thing in his account has struck me very much. Namely, so long as the determination of value by working time is itself left "undetermined," as it is by Ricardo, it does not make people shaky. But as soon as it is brought into exact connection with the working day and its variations, a very unpleasant new light

* The Fenian rising took place early in 1867 ; the trial and execution of the "Manchester martyrs" had just taken place when Marx wrote this letter. Marx had been most active in promoting agitation among the English workers on behalf of the Fenian prisoners and wrote with passionate indignation of English hypocrisy in refusing them treatment as political prisoners, but he realised the limitations of the movement and disapproved of its terroristic manifestations (blowing up of Clerkenwell prison, etc.) See also Letters 130, 133. [*Ed. Eng. ed.*]

dawns upon them. I believe one of Dühring's reasons for reviewing my book at all was rage against Roscher. Indeed his fear of being treated like Roscher is very easily perceptible. It is strange that the fellow does not realise the three fundamentally new elements of the book :

(1) That in contrast to *all* former systems of political economy, which *begin* by taking the particular fragments of surplus value with their fixed forms of rent, profit, and interest as already given, I first deal with the general form of surplus value, in which all these elements are still undifferentiated—in solution as it were.

(2) That, without exception, the economists have missed the simple point that if the commodity has a double character—use value and exchange value—then the labour represented in the commodity must also have a double character, while the mere bald analysis of labour, as in Smith, Ricardo, etc., is bound to come up everywhere against the inexplicable. This is, in fact, the whole secret of the critical conception.

(3) That for the first time wages are shown as the irrational form in which a hidden relation appears, and this is exactly represented in the two forms of wage payment—time wages and piece wages. (It was a help to me that similar formulæ are often found in higher mathematics.)

And as for Dühring's modest objections to the definition of value, he will be astonished when he sees in Volume II how little the determination of value "directly" counts for in bourgeois society. *No form* of society can indeed prevent the fact that, one way or another, the working time at the disposal of society regulates production. So long, however, as this regulation is accomplished not by the direct and conscious control of society over its working time—which is only possible under common ownership—but by the movement of commodity prices, things remain as you have already quite aptly described them in the *Deutsch-Französische-Jahrbücher*.

DÜHRING, KARL EUGEN (1833-1921). Petty-bourgeois philosopher and economist, lecturer in Berlin. Lost his position at the university as a result of a conflict with the authorities. Dühring represented an inconsistent form of materialism closely allied to idealism. He was a violent opponent of dialectics and of Marxism, and an anti-Semite. Engels wrote his *Anti-Dühring* in opposition to Dühring's ideas on science, which had found some disciples among the German Social-Democracts.

ROSCHER, WILHELM (1817-94). German economist, representative of vulgar economics. Vulgar economy in his case took on the "professorial form which sets to work in an historical fashion and with wise moderation seeks to bring together the 'best' everywhere, not troubling about contradictions but only about completeness. . . . As works of this kind first appear when political economy has completed its orbit as a science, they are at the same time the grave of this science." (Marx, *Theories of Surplus Value.*)

104. MARX TO ENGELS

[London] 11 January, 1868.

At the Museum, where I did nothing but glance through catalogues, I also discovered that *Dühring* is a great philosopher. For he has written a *Natural Dialectic* against Hegel's "unnatural" one. Hence these tears. The gentlemen in Germany (all except the theological reactionaries) think Hegel's dialectic is a "dead horse." Feuerbach has much to answer for in this respect.

105. MARX TO KUGELMANN

London, 6 March, 1868.

There is something touching about Thünen. A Mecklenburg *junker* (true, with a *German* training in thinking) who treats his estate at Tellow as *the land* and Mecklenburg-Schwerin as *the town*, and who, proceeding from these premises, with the help of observation, the differential calculus, practical accounting, etc., constructs for himself the Ricardian theory of rent. It is at once worthy of respect and at the same time ridiculous.

I can now understand the curiously embarrassed tone of

Herr Dühring's criticism. He is ordinarily a most bumptious, cheeky boy, who sets up as a revolutionary in political economy. He has done two things. He has published, firstly, (proceeding from Carey) a *Critical Foundation of Political Economy* (about 500 pages) and, secondly, a new *Natural Dialectic* (against the Hegelian). My book has buried him from both sides. He gave it notice because of his hatred for Roscher, etc. For the rest, half intentionally, and half from lack of insight, he commits deceptions. He knows very well that my method of development is not Hegelian, since I am a materialist and Hegel is an idealist. Hegel's dialectic is the basic form of all dialectic, but only after it has been stripped of its mystical form, and it is precisely this which distinguishes my method. As for Ricardo, it really hurt Herr Dühring that in my treatment of Ricardo the weak points in him, which Carey and a hundred others before him pointed out, do not even exist. Consequently he attempts, in *mauvaise foi* [bad faith], to burden me with all Ricardo's limitations. But never mind. I must be grateful to the man, since he is the first expert who has said anything at all.

In the second volume (which will certainly never appear if my health does not improve) property in land will be one of the subjects dealt with, competition only in so far as it is required for the treatment of the other themes.

During my illness (which I hope will soon cease altogether) I was unable to write, but I got down an enormous amount of "stuff," statistical and otherwise, which in itself would have been enough to make people sick who are not used to that sort of fodder and do not possess stomachs accustomed to digesting it rapidly.

My circumstances are very harassing, as I have been unable to do any additional work which would bring in money, and yet certain appearances must be maintained for the children's sake. If I did not have these two damned volumes to produce (and in addition to look for an English publisher) which can be done only in London, I would go to Geneva, where I could live very well with the means at my disposal.*

* From *Letters to Dr. Kugelmann* (Martin Lawrence), page 63.

¶THÜNEN, JOHANN HEINRICH VON (1783-1850). German economist. Landowner in Mecklenburg. He deduced differential ground rent by presupposing a town surrounded by a series of circles of different kinds of agricultural cultivation whose respective distance from the town was determined by the amount of human labour they required (*e.g.*, vegetable cultivation nearer, cattle-raising further off). In his book, *Der isolierte Staat* (*The Isolated State*) he raised the question of the nature of capitalist exploitation. Marx comments on this in *Capital*, Vol. I, Chap. XXV (1): " It is Thünen's merit to have asked this question. His answer is simply childish."

106. MARX TO ENGELS

[London,] 25 March, 1868.

With regard to Maurer. His books are exceptionally important. Not only primitive times but the whole later development of the free imperial cities, of the immunity of landowners, of public authority and of the struggle between free peasantry and serfdom is given an entirely new form.

Human history is like palæontology. Owing to a certain judicial blindness even the best intelligences absolutely fail to see the things which lie in front of their noses. Later, when the moment has arrived, we are surprised to find traces everywhere of what we failed to see. The first reaction against the French Revolution and the period of Enlightenment bound up with it was naturally to see everything as mediæval and romantic, even people like Grimm are not free from this. The second reaction is to look beyond the Middle Ages into the primitive age of each nation, and that corresponds to the socialist tendency, although these learned men have no idea that the two have any connection. They are therefore surprised to find what is newest in what is oldest—even equalitarians, to a degree which would have made Proudhon shudder.

To show how much we are all implicated in this judicial blindness :—right in *my own* neighbourhood, on the *Hunsrücken*, the old Germanic system survived up till the *last few years*. I now remember my father talking to me about it from a lawyer's point of view. Another proof: Just as the geologists, even th best, like Cuvier, have expounded certain facts in a completel distorted way, so philologists of the force of a Grimm *mistrans lated* the simplest Latin sentences because they were under the in fluence of Möser etc., (who, I remember, was enchanted tha "liberty" never existed among the Germans but tha "*Luft macht eigen*" [the air makes the serf]*) and others. *E.g.* the well-known passage in Tacitus: "*arva per annos* mutant e *superest ager*," which means, "they exchange the fields, *arva* (b lot, hence also *sortes* [lot] in all the later law codes of the bar barians) "and the common land remains over" (*ager* as publi land contrasted with *arva*)—is translated by Grimm, etc. "they cultivate fresh fields every year and still there is alway (uncultivated) land over!"

So too the passage: "Colunt *discreti ac diversi*" [their tillag is separate and scattered] is supposed to prove that from tim immemorial the Germans carried on cultivation on individua farms like Westphalian *junkers*. But the same passage con tinues: "*Vicos locant* non in nostrum morem *connexis et co haerantibus aedificiis*: suum quisque locum *spatio circumdat*;" [they do not lay out their villages with buildings connecte and joined together after our fashion: each surrounds hi dwelling with a strip of land]; and primitive Germanic village still exist here and there in Denmark in the form described Obviously Scandinavia must become as important for Germa jurisprudence and economics as for German mythology. An only by starting from there shall we be able to decipher ou past again. For the rest even Grimm, etc., find in Cæsar tha the Germans always settled as *Geschlechtsgenossenschaften*† an not as individuals: "*gentibus* cognationibusque qui uno coie reant" [according to clans and kindreds, who settled together]

But what would old Hegel say in the next world if he hear that the *general* [*Allgemeine*] in German and Norse mean nothing but the common land [*Gemeinland*], and the *particular Sundre*, *Besondere*, nothing but the separate property divided of

* A mediæval German saying meaning that merely because he lived an breathed the air on a certain spot a man was enslaved—a serf or bondsman tie to the soil. [*Ed. Eng. ed.*]

† *Geschlechtsgenossenschaft*—the *gens* or patriarchal joint family. [*Ed. Eng. ed.*]

from the common land? Here are the logical categories coming damn well out of "our intercourse" after all.

Climate and the Vegetable World throughout the Ages, a History of Both, by Fraas (1847)* is very interesting, especially as proving that climate and flora have changed in *historic* times. He is a Darwinist before Darwin and makes even the *species* arise in historic times. But he is also an agricultural expert. He maintains that as a result of cultivation and in proportion to its degree, the "damp" so much beloved by the peasant is lost (hence too plants emigrate from south to north) and eventually the formation of steppes begins. The first effects of cultivation are useful, later devastating owing to deforestation, etc. This man is both a thoroughly learned philologist (he has written books *in Greek*) and a chemist, agricultural expert, etc. The whole conclusion is that cultivation when it progresses in a primitive way and is not *consciously controlled* (as a bourgeois of course he does not arrive at this), leaves deserts behind it, Persia, Mesopotamia, etc., Greece. Here again another unconscious socialist tendency!

This Fraas is also interesting from a German point of view. First Dr. Med., then inspector and teacher of chemistry and technology. Now head of the Bavarian veterinary organisation, university professor, head of government experimental agriculture, etc. In his last things one notices his advanced age, but he is still a gay lad. Has knocked around a lot in Greece, Asia Minor, Egypt! His history of agriculture is important too. He calls Fourier "this pious and humanistic socialist." Of the Albanians, etc.: "every kind of abominable lewdness and rape."

It is necessary to look carefully at the new and newest things on agriculture. The *physical* school is opposed to the *chemical* school.

¶MAURER, G. L. (1790-1872). German jurist and historian. Distinguished for his investigations into the history of the

* "*Klima und Pflanzenwelt in der Zeit, eine Geschichte beider.*"

development of common property in land, the formation of towns in the Middle Ages and feudal relations.

TACITUS, PUBLIUS CORNELIUS (*c.* 55-120). Only a portion of the works of this Roman historian has been preserved to us, including the small work *Germania*, in which he gives a description of the old Germanic methods of production and social order.

107. MARX TO ENGELS

[London], 22 April, 1868.

I will only give you a short account now of a "little thing" which *occurred* to me as I was just glancing at the part of my manuscript dealing with the rate of profit. Thanks to it one of the most difficult questions is simply solved. The question is, namely, how it happens that when the value of money, *i.e.*, of gold, is falling, the *rate of profit* rises, while it falls when the value of money rises.

Say the value of money falls by $\frac{1}{10}$. Then the price of commodities, other circumstances remaining equal, rises by $\frac{1}{10}$. If, on the other hand, the value of money rises by $\frac{1}{10}$, the price of commodities falls, other circumstances remaining equal, by $\frac{1}{10}$.

If, when the value of money is falling, the price of labour does not rise to the same degree, then it *falls*, the rate of surplus value rises, and therefore, all other things remaining the same, the rate of profit also. The rise of the latter—so long as the ascendant oscillation in the value of money continues—is simply due to the fall in wages, and this fall is due to the fact that the change in wages only slowly accommodates itself to the change in the value of money. (So at the end of the sixteenth and seventeenth centuries.) If, on the contrary, when money rises in value wages do not fall in the same proportion, then the rate of surplus value falls, and therefore, other things being equal, the rate of profit.

These two movements, the rise in the rate of profit when money falls in value, and its fall when money rises in value, are, *in these circumstances*, both only due to the fact that the price of labour has not yet been adjusted to the new value of money.

These phenomena (their explanation has long been known) cease when the price of labour and the value of money are adjusted.

Here begins the difficulty. The so-called theoreticians say: As soon as the price of labour corresponds to the new value of money, *e.g.*, has risen when the value of money has fallen, both profit and wages are expressed in so much more money. *Their relation therefore remains the same.* Therefore there can be no change in the rate of profit. To this the specialists who concern themselves with the history of prices reply with facts. Their explanations are mere phrases. The whole difficulty arises from confusing *the rate of surplus value with the rate of profit.* Let us assume that the rate of surplus value remains *the same, e.g.,* 100 per cent. Then if the value of money falls $\frac{1}{10}$, wages of £100 (say for 100 men) rise to 110 and the surplus value likewise to 110. The same total quantity of labour which was formerly expressed in £200 is now expressed in £220. If therefore the price of labour has been adjusted to the value of money, no change in the value of money can cause the *rate of surplus value* to rise or fall. Assume, however, that the elements, or some elements, of the *constant* part of the capital fall in value owing to the growing productivity of labour, whose products they are. If the fall in their value is greater than the fall in the value of money, their price will fall, despite the fallen value of money. If their fall in value only corresponds to the fall in the value of money, their price remains unchanged. Let us assume the latter case.

For instance, in a certain branch of industry the capital of 500 is composed of 400 c + 100 v, so we have, with a *rate of surplus value* of 100 per cent.: 400 c + 100 v + 100 sv = $\frac{100}{500}$ = 20 per cent. *rate of profit.* (In Vol. II I am thinking of using 400 c etc., instead of $\frac{0}{400}$ etc., as it is less complicated. What do you think about this?) If the value of money falls $\frac{1}{10}$ then wages rise to 110 and ditto surplus value. If the money price of the *constant* capital remains the same, because as a result of the increased productivity of labour the value of its component parts has fallen $\frac{1}{10}$, then now: 400 c + 110 v + 110 sv or $\frac{110}{510} = 21\frac{29}{50}$ per cent. rate of profit, which would therefore have risen by about $1\frac{1}{2}$ per cent., while the rate of surplus value $\frac{110^{sv}}{110^{v}}$ remains as before 100 per cent.

The *rise in the rate of profit* would be greater if the value of the constant capital dropped faster than the value of money, and less if it dropped more slowly. The rise will continue, however, so long as any fall in the value of the constant capital is taking place—so long as the same quantity of the means of production does not cost £440 instead of as formerly £400.

It is, however, an historical fact and can be specially demonstrated from the years 1850-60, that the productivity of labour, especially in industry proper, receives a stimulus from the falling value of money, the mere inflation of money prices and the general international scramble for the increased mass of money.

108. MARX TO ENGELS

London, 30 April, 1868

For the case under discussion it does not matter whether s.v. (the surplus value) is *quantitatively* larger or smaller than the surplus value produced in the given branch of production itself. For instance, if $\frac{100^{sv}}{400^{c}+100^{v}} = 20$ per cent. and this, owing to the fall in the value of money by $\frac{1}{10}$, becomes $\frac{110^{sv}}{400^{c}+110^{v}}$ (assuming that the value of the constant capital falls), then it makes no difference if the capitalist producer only pockets half the surplus value he himself produces. For the rate of profit for him will then be $\frac{55^{sv}}{400^{c}+110^{v}}$ and greater than the former $\frac{50^{sv}}{400^{c}+100^{v}}$. I retain sv here in order to show *qualitatively* in the expression itself, where the profit comes from.

But it is proper that you should know the method by which the rate of profit is developed. I will therefore give you the *most general features* of the process. In Book II, as you know, the *process of the circulation* of capital is described on the basis of the premises developed in Book I. Hence the new determinations of form which arise out of the process of circulation, such as fixed and circulating capital, turnover of capital, etc. In Book I, finally, we content ourselves with the assumption that if in the process of realisation £100 becomes £110, the elements into which a further turnover will take place are *already present* in the market. But now we investigate the conditions under which these elements are found already in existence, namely the social intertwining of the different capitals, of the component parts of capital and of revenue (= sv).

In Book III we come to the transformation of surplus value into its different forms and separate component parts.

I. *Profit* is for us first of all only *another name* or another category of *surplus value*. As, owing to the form assumed by wages, the whole of the labour appears to be paid for, the unpaid part seems necessarily to come not from labour but from capital, and not from the variable part of capital but from the capital as a whole. In this way *surplus value* gets the form of *profit*, without any *quantitative* difference between the one and the other. This is only the illusory form in which surplus value appears.

Further, the part of capital consumed in the production of a commodity (the capital, constant and variable, advanced for its production *minus* the utilised but not actually consumed portion of the *fixed* capital) appears now as the *cost price* of the commodity ; for to the capitalist that part of the value of the commodity *he* has to pay for is the cost price of *the commodity*, while the unpaid labour it contains is not included in *its* cost price from his point of view. The surplus value = profit now appears as the *excess of the sale price over the cost price.* Let us call the value of the commodity v and its cost price c, then $v = c + sv$, therefore $v - sv = c$, therefore v is greater than c. This new category of cost price is very necessary for the details of the later development. It is evident from the outset that the capitalist can sell a commodity *below its value* at a profit (so long as he sells it above cost price) and this is the *fundamental law* explaining the equalisation effected by competition.

If, profit, then, is at first *only formally* distinguished from surplus value, the *rate of profit*, on the other hand, is at once really distinguished from the *rate of surplus value*, for in one case the formula is $\frac{sv}{v}$ and in the other $\frac{sv}{c+v}$ from which it follows from the outset, since $\frac{sv}{v}$ is greater than $\frac{sv}{c+v}$, that the rate of profit is less than the rate of surplus value—unless $c = 0$.

Taking into consideration the points developed in Book II, however, it follows that we cannot compute the rate of profit on any output of commodities we choose—*e.g.*, a weekly output —but that $\frac{sv}{c+v}$ here represents the surplus value produced *during the year* in relation to the capital *advanced* during the *year* (*i.e.*, as distinct from the capital *turned over*). The formula $\frac{sv}{c+v}$ stands here, therefore, for the *annual* rate of profit.

We next examine how variations in the *turnover* of capital (partly depending on the relation between the circulating and fixed portions of capital, partly on the amount of circulating capital turned over in a year, etc.) modify the *rate of profit* while *the rate of surplus value remains the same.*

Taking the turnover as given, and $\frac{sv}{c+v}$ as the yearly rate of profit, we examine how the latter can change, independently of the changes in the rate of surplus value and even in its total sum.

Since sv, the total sum of surplus value = *the rate of surplus value multiplied by the variable capital*, then, if we call the rate of surplus value r and the rate of profit p', p' = $\frac{r.v}{c+v}$. Here we have the four quantities p', r, v, c, with any three of which we can work, while always seeking the fourth as an unknown quantity. This covers all possible cases of movements in the rate of profit, in so far as they are distinct from the movements in the rate and to a certain extent even from those in the total sum, of surplus value. This has, of course, been *inexplicable* to everybody hitherto.

The laws thus discovered will be, *e.g.*, very important for understanding how the price of raw material influences the rate of profit and they hold good *no matter how* the surplus value may be later divided between the producer, etc.* This can only change the *form of appearance.* These laws, moreover, remain *directly* applicable if $\frac{sv}{c+v}$ is treated as the relation of the socially produced surplus value to the social capital.

II. What were treated in I as *movements*, whether of capital in a given branch of production or of social capital—movements changing the composition, etc. of capital—are now conceived as *differences* between the *sums of capital invested in the various branches of production.*

* [Meaning : between the producer and other capitalists.]

It next follows that *the rate of surplus value* (the exploitation of labour being assumed as *equal*), the production of value and therefore the production of surplus value and therefore *the rate of profit*, are *different* in different branches of production. But out of these different rates of profit a mean or general rate of profit is formed by competition. This rate of profit, expressed absolutely, can be nothing else than the *surplus value* produced (annually) by the *capitalist class* in relation to the total *social* capital advanced. For instance, if the social capital = 400 c + 100 v and the surplus value annually produced from it = 100 sv, then the composition of the social capital = 80 c + 20 v and that of the product (in percentages) = 80 c + 20 v || + 20 sv = 20 per cent. rate of profit. This is the *general rate of profit.*

What competition is striving to produce between the various masses of capital—differently composed and invested in different spheres of production—is *capitalist communism*, namely that the *mass of capital belonging to each sphere of production* should snatch an aliquot part of the total surplus value proportionate to the aliquot part of the total social capital which it forms.

This can only be achieved if in each sphere of production (assuming as before that the total capital = 80 c + 20 v and the social rate of profit = $\frac{20 sv}{80c+20v}$) the yearly output of commodities is sold at *cost price* plus 20 per cent. *profit* on the *capital value already advanced* (it makes no difference how much of the previously advanced fixed capital enters into the annual cost price or not). But this means that the *price determination* of the commodities will *not coincide with their value.* Only in those branches of production where the composition of the capital (in percentages) equals 80 c + 20 v, will the price c (cost price) + 20 per cent. coincide with the value of the capital advanced. Where the composition is higher (*e.g.*, 90 c + 10 v), the price is *above* the value ; where the composition is lower (*e.g.*, 70 c + 30 v) the price is *below* the value.

The price thus equalised, which divides up the social total of surplus value equally among the individual totals of capital in proportion to their size, is the *price of production* of commodities, the centre around which the oscillation of the market price moves.

Those branches of production which constitute natural *monopolies* are exempted from this equalisation process even if their rate of profit is higher than the social rate. This is important later for the development of *ground rent*.

In this chapter must be further developed the various *causes of equalisation* among the various capital investments, which appear to the vulgar conception as so many *original sources* of profit.

Further: the *changed form of appearance* now assumed by the previously developed and still valid laws of value and of surplus value *after the transformation of value into price of production*.

III. *The tendency of the rate of profit to fall as society progresses.* This already follows from what was developed in Book I on the *change in the composition of capital with the development of the social productive forces*. This is one of the greatest triumphs over the great *pons asini* [stumbling block] of all previous economics.

IV. Until now we have only dealt with *productive capital*. Now there arises modification through *merchant capital*.

According to our previous assumption the *productive capital* of society = 500 (whether millions or milliards makes no difference). And the formula was: 400 c + 100 v|| + 100 s.v. The general rate of profit, p', = 20 per cent. Now let the merchant capital = 100. The 100 sv has now to be calculated on 600 instead of 500. The general rate of profit is therefore reduced from 20 per cent. to 16⅔ per cent. The *price of production* (for the sake of simplicity, we will here assume that all 400 c, including the whole fixed capital, enters into the *cost price* of the yearly output of commodities) now = 583⅓. The merchant sells at 600 and realises therefore, if we ignore the fixed portion of his capital, 16⅔ per cent. on his 100, that is, as much as the producing capitalists; in other words, he appropriates to himself ⅙ of the social surplus value. The commodities—taken as a whole and on a social scale—are sold *at their value*. His £100 (apart from its fixed portion) only serves him as circulating money capital. Whatever more the merchant swallows up he gets either simply by trickery, or by speculation on the oscillations of commodity-prices, or, in the case of the actual retailers, as wages for labour—wretched unproductive labour though it is—all these appearing under the form of profit.

V. We have now reduced profit to the form in which it appears as actually given in practice, *i.e.*, according to our assumption, 16⅔ per cent. *Next comes the splitting up of this capital into entrepreneur's profit and interest. Interest-bearing capital. The credit system.*

VI. *Transformation of surplus profit into ground rent.*

VII. At last we have arrived at the *forms of appearance* which serve as the *starting point* in the vulgar conception : ground rent coming from the earth, profit (interest) from capital, wages from labour. But from our point of view the thing is now seen differently. The apparent movement is explained. Moreover, A. Smith's nonsense, which has become the *main pillar* of all economics hitherto, that the price of a commodity is derived from those three revenues, *i.e.*, only from variable capital (wages) and surplus value (ground rent, profit, interest), is overthrown. The whole movement takes place in this apparent form. Finally since these three (wages, ground rent, profit (interest)) constitute the respective sources of income of the three classes of landowners, capitalists and wage labourers, we have, in conclusion, the *class struggle*, into which the movement of the whole *Scheisse* [shit, business] is resolved.

109. MARX TO KUGELMANN

London, 11 July, 1868.

Thank you very much for the things you sent. Do *not* write to Faucher, otherwise that *mannequin piss** will think himself too important. All that he has achieved is to induce me, if there is a second edition, to make a few necessary thrusts at Bastiat in the part about the *magnitude of value*. This was not done before because the third volume will contain a separate

* The well-known fountain figure in Brussels.

and detailed chapter about the "vulgar economy" gentlemen. You will find it quite natural for Faucher and Company to deduce the "exchange value" of their scribbling not from the *quantity of labour power expended*, but from the *absence of such expenditure*, that is, from "*saved labour*." And the worthy Bastiat did not even himself make this "discovery," so welcome to those gentlemen, but, as was his custom, just "copied" many earlier authors. The sources he used are of course unknown to Faucher and Company.

As for the *Zentralblatt*, the man is making the greatest possible concession in admitting that, if one means anything at all by value, the conclusions I draw must be accepted. The unfortunate fellow does not see that, even if there were no chapter on value in my book, the analysis of the real relationships which I give would contain the proof and demonstration of the real value relation. The nonsense about the necessity of proving the concept of value arises from complete ignorance both of the subject dealt with and of the method of science. Every child knows that a country which ceased to work, I will not say for a year, but for a few weeks, would die. Every child knows too that the mass of products corresponding to the different needs require different and quantitatively determined masses of the total labour of society. That this necessity of distributing social labour in definite proportions cannot be done away with by the *particular form* of social production, but can only change the *form it assumes*, is self evident. No natural laws can be done away with. What can change, in changing historical circumstances, is the *form* in which these laws operate. And the form in which this proportional division of labour operates, in a state of society where the interconnection of social labour is manifested in the *private exchange* of the individual products of labour, is precisely the *exchange value* of these products.

The science consists precisely in working out *how* the law of value operates. So that if one wanted at the very beginning to "explain" all the phenomena which apparently contradict that law, one would have to give the science *before* the science. It is precisely Ricardo's mistake that in his first chapter on value he takes as given all possible categories, which have still to be developed, in order to prove their conformity with the law of value.

On the other hand, as you correctly assumed, *the history of the theory* certainly shows that the concept of the value relation has *always been the same,* whether more or less clear, hedged with illusions or scientifically precise. Since the thought process itself grows out of the conditions, is itself a *natural process*, thinking that really comprehends must always be the same, and can only vary gradually according to maturity of development, including that of the organ by which the thinking is done. Everything else is drivel.

The vulgar economist has not the faintest idea that the actual everyday exchange relations need not be directly identical with the magnitudes of value. The point of bourgeois society consists precisely in this, that *a priori* there is no conscious, social regulation of production. The reasonable and the necessary in nature asserts itself only as a blindly working average. And then the vulgar economist thinks he has made a great discovery when, as against the disclosures of the inner connection, he proudly claims that in appearance things look different. In fact, he is boasting that he holds fast to the appearance and takes it for the last word. Why, then, any science at all? But the matter has also another background. When the inner connection is grasped all theoretical belief in the permanent necessity of existing conditions breaks down before their practical collapse. Here, therefore, it is in the interest of the ruling classes to perpetuate this unthinking confusion. And for what other purpose are the sycophantic babblers paid, who have no other scientific trump to play, save that in political economy one should not think at all?

But *satis supraque.** In any case it shows what these priests of the bourgeoisie have come to, when workers and even manufacturers and merchants understand my book and find their way about in it, while these "scribes" (!) complain that I make excessive demands on their understanding.†

* Enough and more than enough.

† *Letters to Dr. Kugelmann.* (Martin Lawrence 1934), page 93.

¶Marx's *Critique of Political Economy* (published in 1859) received very little attention from the public. " The conspiracy of silence with which I am honoured by the German literary mob whenever they themselves notice that abuse will not settle the matter, affects the sale of my book unfavourably, apart from the tendency of my works," wrote Marx to Kugelmann on 28 December, 1862. And although Marx and Engels expected a special success with the publication of *Capital*, they thought it necessary to prepare the ground. Hence Engels wrote accounts of the first volume of *Capital* for a number of newspapers and periodicals, adapting himself in each case with great skill to the character and tendency of the paper; these articles he got published by the help of Party friends in Germany. (See Marx—Engels *Archiv.*, Bd. II, 1927, where some of the articles are reprinted.)

BASTIAT, FRÉDÉRIC (1801-50). French vulgar economist and free-trader, " the shallowest and therefore the most successful representative of the apologists of vulgar economics." (Marx.)

FAUCHER, JULIUS (1820-78). German vulgar economist, " a regular Münchhausen for lying," " a free-trader who does not even know what the bourgeoisie is." (Marx.) Faucher wrote an account of *Capital* in which he branded Marx as an unworthy pupil of Bastiat.

110. MARX TO ENGELS

London, 26 August, 1868.

The invitation which I received to the Congress of the General Association of German Workers (Hamburg, August 22 to 25) was signed by Schweitzer as President and by more than twenty workers from the various districts of Germany (members of the *Executive*). I had to take this latter fact into consideration in my reply. The reason I gave for not coming was the work of the Central Council of the International Workingmen's Association, and I said I was glad to see that the starting-points of any " serious " working-class movement—agitation for full political freedom, regulation of the working day and international co-operation of the working class—were emphasised in their *programme* for the Congress. In other words, that is to say, I congratulated them on having given up *Lassalle's programme*. Whether they will see the joke, remains to be seen. Schweitzer, the only one with a head in the whole Lassalle gang, will certainly be aware of it. But whether he will think it more advisable to show this or to pretend to be dense, we shall see.

111. MARX TO ENGELS

London, 26 September, 1868.

For the German working class the most necessary thing of all is that it should cease conducting its agitation by kind permission of the higher authorities. A race so schooled in bureaucracy must go through a complete course of "self-help." On the other hand they undoubtedly have the advantage of beginning the movement at a period when conditions are much more advanced than they were for the English and, being Germans, of having heads on their shoulders capable of generalising.

112. MARX TO ENGELS

London, 10 October, 1868.

When you were here last you saw the Blue Book on the land situation in Ireland 1844-45. By accident I have found in a small second-hand shop the *Report and Evidence on Irish Tenant Right, 1867* (House of Lords). This was a real find. While Messrs. the Economists treat the question whether ground rent is payment for natural differences in the land, or merely interest on the capital invested in the land, as a pure conflict of dogmas, we have here an actual life and death struggle between farmer and landlord on the question of *how far* the rent *should also* include, *in addition to* payment for the difference in the land, interest on the capital invested in it—not by the landlord but by the tenant. It is only by substituting for conflicting dogmas the conflicting facts and real contradictions which form their hidden background that we can transform political economy into a positive science.

113. MARX TO SCHWEITZER

London, 13 October, 1868 [Draft].

As for the Lassalle Association,* it was founded in a period of reaction. Lassalle—and this remains his immortal service—re-awakened the workers' movement in Germany after its fifteen years of slumber. But he committed great mistakes. He allowed himself to be too much governed by the immediate circumstances of the time. He made a small starting-point—his opposition to a dwarf like Schulze-Delitzsch—into the central point of his agitation—state aid versus self-help. In so doing he merely took up again the slogan which *Buchez*, the leader of French *Catholic* socialism, had given out in 1843 and the following years against the genuine workers' movement in France. Much too intelligent to regard this slogan as anything but a temporary makeshift, Lassalle could only justify it on the ground of its (alleged) immediate practicability. For this purpose he had to maintain that it could be carried out in the *near* future. Hence the "state" transformed itself into the Prussian State. And thus he was forced into concessions to the Prussian monarchy, the Prussian reaction (feudal party) and even the clericals.

With Buchez' state aid for associations he combined the Chartist cry of universal suffrage. He overlooked the fact that conditions in Germany and England were different. He overlooked the lessons of the Second Empire with regard to universal suffrage. Moreover from the outset, like everyone who declares that he has a panacea for the sufferings of the masses in his pocket, he gave his agitation a religious and sectarian character. Every sect is in fact religious. Further, just because he was the founder of a sect, he denied all natural connection with the earlier movement *both in Germany and outside*. He fell into the same mistake as Proudhon, and instead of looking among the genuine elements of the class movement for the real basis of his agitation, he tried to prescribe their course to these elements according to a certain dogmatic recipe.

Most of what I am now saying after the event I foretold to

* See Letter 29.

Lassalle in 1862, when he came to London and invited me to place myself with him at the head of the new movement.

You yourself have experienced in your own person the opposition between the movement of a sect and the movement of a class. The sect sees the justification for its existence and its "point of honour"—not in what it has in *common* with the class movement but in the *particular shibboleth* which *distinguishes* it from it. Therefore when at Hamburg you proposed the congress for the formation of trade unions you were only able to defeat the opposition of the sect by threatening to resign from the office of president. In addition, you were obliged to double yourself and to announce that in one case you were acting as the head of the sect and in the other as the organ of the class movement.

The dissolution of the General Association of German Workers gave you the historic opportunity to accomplish a great step forward and to declare, to prove if necessary, that a new stage of development had now been reached, and that the moment was ripe for the sectarian movement to merge into the class movement and make an end of all dependence. Where the true content of the sect was concerned it would, as with all previous working-class sects, be carried on into the general movement as an element which enriched it. Instead of this you actually demanded of the class movement that it should subordinate itself to the movement of a particular sect. Those who are not your friends have concluded from this that whatever happens you want to preserve your "own workers' movement."

114. ENGELS TO MARX

Manchester, 6 November, 1868.

It is difficult to come to an absolutely definite judgment about the thing [Dietzgen's manuscript]. As a philosopher the man is no child of nature, and added to that is only half self-taught. Some of his sources (*e.g.*, Feuerbach, your book, and various rubbishy popular works on natural science) can be immediately recognised from his terminology, but one cannot tell what else he has read. His terminology is of course still very confused—hence there is a lack of sharpness and frequent repetition in new terms. There is also some dialectic in it, but appearing more in flashes than as a connected whole. The account of the thing-in-itself as *Gedankending* [thing made of thought] would be very nice and even brilliant if one could be *sure* that he had discovered it *for himself*. There is a lot of wit and, despite the lack of grammar, a marked talent for style. On the whole, a remarkable instinct for arguing out so much correctly with such deficient preliminary training.

As I said, the repetitions are the result partly of the deficient terminology and partly of unfamiliarity with the discipline of logic. It will be very hard to get them all out. If the man absolutely insists on having his things printed I am not sure that to limit him to two printer's sheets would be the best for him—in any case it would give him the devil's own job as he is not conscious of his repetitions, and then I am not sure either whether two sheets would get any attention paid them at all. More likely six to eight. And he will never get it into a periodical.

¶DIETZGEN, JOSEPH (1828-88). A tanner. By independent thinking and reading he worked out a philosophical conception of the world for himself. His first philosophical work *Das Wesen der menschlichen Kopfarbeit* [*The Nature of Man's Mental Activity*] was published in 1869. Marx, in forwarding to Engels the manuscript which Dietzgen had sent him of this first work, wrote on October 4, 1868 : " My opinion is that J. Dietzgen would do best to condense all his ideas into two *printer's sheets* and have them published under his own name as a tanner. If he publishes them in the size he is proposing he will discredit himself by the lack of dialectical development and his way of going round in a circle." (For Dietzgen see Lenin : *Materialism and Empirio-Criticism*, *Collected Works*, English edition, Vol. XIII, pp. 91 *et seq.*, 201 *et seq.*, 204 *et seq.* See also Letters 115, 116 below.)

115. MARX TO ENGELS

London, 7 November, 1868.

Borkheim is translating the chief passages from the Russian book on the disintegration of agriculture for me, and has also given me a French book about it by the Russian, Shédo-Ferroti. The latter makes a great mistake—he is altogether quite a superficial fellow—when he says the Russian communal system first originated from the law prohibiting the peasant from leaving the land. The whole thing, *down to the smallest details*, is absolutely identical with the *primitive Germanic* communal system. What the Russians have added (and this is also found in a section *of the Indian communal system*, not in the Punjab but in the South) is (1) the *non-democratic* but *patriarchal* character of the commune leadership, and (2) the *collective responsibility* for taxes to the state, etc. It follows from the second point that the more industrious a Russian peasant is, the more he is exploited for the purposes of the state, not only for taxes, but for the supply of produce, horses, etc., during the continual passage of bodies of troops, for government couriers, etc. The whole foul mess is in process of collapse.

I regard Dietzgen's development, in so far as Feuerbach, etc.—in short, his sources—are not obvious, as entirely his own independent achievement. For the rest, I agree with everything you say. I will say something to him about the repetitions. It is bad luck for him that it is precisely Hegel that he has *not* studied.

116. ENGELS TO MARX

Manchester, 18 November, 1868.

What do you say to the elections in the factory districts? Once again the proletariat has discredited itself terribly. Manchester and Salford return three Tories to two Liberals, including moreover the milk-and-water Bayley. Bolton, Preston, Blackburn, etc., practically nothing but Tories. In Ashton it looks as if M[ilner] Gibson would go to the wall. Ernest

Jones nowhere, despite the cheering. Everywhere the proletariat are the tag, rag and bobtail of the official parties, and if any party has gained additional strength from the new voters, it is the Tories. The small towns, the half rotten boroughs are the salvation of bourgeois liberalism and the rôles will be reversed : the Tories will now be in favour of more members for the big towns and the Liberals for unequal representation.

Here the electors have increased from 24,000 to not quite 48,000, while the Tories have increased their voters from 6,000 to 14,000—15,000. The Liberals threw away a lot and Mr. Henry did a lot of harm, but it cannot be denied that the increase of working-class voters has brought the Tories more than their mere additional percentage and has improved their relative position. On the whole this is to the good. It looks at present as if Gladstone will get a *narrow* majority and so be compelled to keep the ball rolling and reform the Reform Act ; with a big majority he would have left it all to God as usual.

But it remains a hopeless certificate of destitution for the English proletariat, all the same. The *parson* has shown unexpected power and so has the cringing to respectability. Not a single working-class candidate had a ghost of a chance, but my Lord Tomnoddy or any *parvenu* snob could have the workers' votes with pleasure.

¶These elections were the first held under the Reform Act of 1867 which had granted a relatively wide extension of the franchise. Gladstone was returned to power. For the agitation preceding this "reform," and its influence on the workers' movement of the previous fifteen years, see Letters 35, 63, 74, 88 Notes on Odger and Cremer (Letter 71), and on the Irish debate (Letter 133). [*Ed. Eng. ed.*]

117. MARX TO KUGELMANN

London, 12 December, 1868.

I am also returning Dietzgen's portrait. The story of his life is not quite what I had imagined it to be, although I always had a feeling that he was " not a worker like Eccarius." It is true that the sort of philosophic outlook which he has worked out for himself requires a certain amount of peace and leisure which the everyday workman does not enjoy. I have got two very good workmen living in New York, A. Vogt, a shoemaker and Siegfried Meyer, a mining engineer, both from Berlin. A third workman who could give lectures on my book, is Lochner, a carpenter (common working man), who has been here in London about fifteen years.

Tell your wife I never suspected her of being one of Generaless Geck's subordinates. My question was only intended as a joke. In any case ladies cannot complain of the *International*, for it has elected a lady, Madame Law, to be a member of the General Council.

Joking aside, great progress was evident in the last Congress of the American " Labour Union " in that among other things, it treated working women with complete equality. While in this respect the English, and still more the gallant French, are burdened with a spirit of narrow-mindedness. Anybody who knows anything of history knows that great social changes are impossible without the feminine ferment. Social progress can be measured exactly by the social position of the fair sex (the ugly ones included).*

118. MARX TO ENGELS

[London], 14 December, 1868.

I have found little new in the Ténot† (Paris) except a few details—I have not yet read the *Provinces*. The enormous sensation the book has made in Paris and in France generally proves a very interesting fact, namely that the generation which has grown up under Badinguet‡ knows absolutely nothing of the history of the regime under which it is living. Now the fellows are rubbing their eyes and seem as if they had

* *Letters to Dr. Kugelmann* by Karl Marx. (Martin Lawrence 1934). Page 83.
† Eugene Ténot (1830-90), French writer. Author of two books on the Second Empire, *The Provinces in December* 1851 and *Paris in December* 1851.
‡ Nickname for Napoleon III.

just dropped from the clouds. If one may compare small things with great, have not we had just the same experience in our way? In Germany it is now spreading as a wonderful novelty that Lassalle was only one of our satellites and *did not discover* the "class war."

119. ENGELS TO MARX.

Manchester, 18 December, 1868.

Many thanks for Ténot and the Baudin trial. As soon as I have read the latter I will send them both back. You can keep the *Provinces* for I have ordered both volumes for myself from the bookseller, as one must possess a copy of a thing of this kind. It is a necessary result of every victorious reaction that the causation of the revolution and especially of the counter-revolution should pass into utter oblivion; the younger generation in Germany knows absolutely nothing about 1848 except the groans of the *Kreuzzeitung*, which were echoed by all the other papers from 1849-52; history suddenly comes to an end there in 1847.

120. MARX TO ENGELS.

London, 19 December, 1868.

Ténot's *Province* is much better. It gives us a lot of new details. If the Parisians had held out one or two days longer the empire would have been done for. The (republican) movement among the country people was much bigger than we knew.

121. MARX TO KUGELMANN

London, 3 March, 1869.

A very interesting movement is going on in France.

The Parisians are making a regular study of their recent revolutionary past, in order to prepare themselves for the business of the impending new revolution. First the *origin of the Empire*—then the *coup d'état of December*. This has been completely forgotten, just as the reaction in Germany succeeded in stamping out the memory of 1848-49.

That is why Ténot's books on the *coup-d'état* in Paris and the provinces attracted such enormous attention that in a short time they went through ten impressions. They were followed by dozens of other books on the same period. It was all the rage and therefore soon became a speculative business for the publishers.

These books were written by the opposition—Ténot, for example is one of the *Siècle* [Century] men (I mean the liberal bourgeois paper, not our "century"). All the liberal and illiberal scoundrels who belong to the official opposition patronise this movement. Also the republican democrats, people like, for example, Delescluze, formerly Ledru Rollin's adjutant, and now, as a republican patriarch, editor of the Paris *Réveil*.

Up to the present everybody has been revelling in these posthumous disclosures or rather reminiscences, everybody who is not Bonapartist.

But then came the other side of the medal. First of all the French government itself got the renegade Hippolyte Castille to publish *Les Massacres de Juin 1848* [The Massacres of June 1848.] This was a blow for Thiers, Falloux, Marie, Jules Favre, Jules Simon, Pelletan, etc., in short, for the chiefs of what is called in France *l'Union Liberale*,* who want to wangle the next elections, the infamous old dogs!

Then, however, came the Socialist Party, which "exposed" the opposition—and the republican democrats of the old style. Among others, Vermorel: *Les Hommes de 1848* and *L'Opposition*. [*The Men of 1848* and *The Opposition*].

Vermorel is a Proudhonist.

Finally came the Blanquists, for example G. Tridon: *Gironde et Girondins*.

And so the whole historic witches' cauldron is bubbling.

When shall *we* be so far !†

* *L'Union Liberale*. This was an alliance of all the Liberal parties in opposition to Napoleon III.

† *Letters to Dr. Kugelmann* (Martin Lawrence 1934), page 89.

122. MARX TO ENGELS.

[London], 5 March, 1869.

The enclosed little document* arrived *yesterday* (although dated February 27). You must send it back as soon as you have read it, as I have to lay it before the Council on Tuesday next. The gentlemen of the "Alliance" have taken a long time to achieve this *opus* [production].

As a matter of fact we would rather they had kept their "innumerable legions" in France, Spain and Italy for themselves.

Bakunin thinks to himself: if we approve his "radical programme" he can make a big noise about this and compromise us *tant soit peu* (just a little bit). If we declare ourselves against it we shall be decried as counter-revolutionaries. Moreover: if we admit them he will see to it that he is supported by some riff-raff at the Congress in Basle. I think the answer should be on the following lines:

According to Paragraph I of the Statutes every workers' association "aiming at the same end, viz, the protection, advancement and *complete emancipation of the working classes*" shall be admitted.

As the stage of development reached by different sections of workers in the same country and by the working class in different countries necessarily varies very much, the actual movement necessarily expresses itself in very various theoretical forms.

The community of action which the International Working-men's Association called into being, the exchange of ideas by means of the different organs of the sections in all countries, and, finally, the direct discussions at the General Congresses, will by degrees create for the general workers' movement its common theoretical programme also.

With regard to the programme of the "Alliance," therefore, it is not necessary for the General Council to submit it to a critical examination. The Council has not to examine whether it is an adequate, scientific expression of the working-class movement. It has only to ask if the *general tendency* of the

* A notification from the Geneva Russia section of the Bakunin "Alliance" of their desire to affiliate with the International.

programme is in opposition to the general tendency of the International Workingmen's Association—the complete emancipation of the working classes.

This reproach could only apply to one phrase in the programme, par. 2: "above all things it desires the political, economic and social equalisation of *the classes*." "The equalisation of the classes," literally interpreted, is nothing but another expression for the "harmony of capital and labour" preached by the bourgeois socialists. Not the logically impossible "equalisation of classes" but the historically necessary "abolition of classes" constitutes the final aim of the International Workingmen's Association. But from the context in which this phrase occurs in the programme it would appear that it is only a slip of the pen. The less, therefore, does the General Council doubt that this phrase, which might lead to serious misunderstanding, will be removed from the programme.

This being assumed, it is in accordance with the principle of the International Workingmen's Association to leave to each section the responsibility for its own programme. There is therefore nothing to prevent the transformation of the sections of the Alliance into Sections of the Workingmen's Association.

As soon as this has taken place, an enumeration of the newly joined sections according to country, locality and number must be sent to the General Council in accordance with the regulations.

This last point—the census of their legions—will especially tickle the gentlemen. Tell me everything you want altered in this draft of the reply when you return the letter.

123. MARX TO ENGELS

London, 15 April, 1869.

To-day I have discovered by accident that we have two copies of the *Neveu de Rameau** in our house and am therefore

* *Le Neveu de Rameau* [*Rameau's Nephew*], a satirical dialogue by Diderot (1713-1784), one of the leading French materialist philosophers of the 18th century. editor of the *Encyclopédie* and a brilliant man of letters. The passage from Hegel quoted here by Marx is from the *Phänomonolgie des Geistes* (*Phenomenology of Mind*), [*Ed. Eng. ed.*]

sending you one. This unique masterpiece will give you fresh pleasure again. Old Hegel says about it : " The mocking laughter at existence, at the confusion of the whole and at itself, is the disintegrated consciousness, aware of itself and expressing itself, and is at the same time the last audible echo of all this confusion. . . . It is the self-disintegrating nature of all relations and their conscious disintegration. . . . In this aspect of the return to self the *vanity of all things* is the self's *own vanity*, or the self is itself vanity . . . but as the indignant consciousness it is aware of its own disintegration and by that knowledge has immediately transcended it. . . . Every part of this world either gets its mind expressed here or is spoken of intellectually and declared for what it is. The *honest consciousness* (the rôle which Diderot allots to himself in the dialogue) takes each element* for a permanent entity and does not realise in its uneducated thoughtlessness that it is doing just the opposite. But the disintegrated consciousness is the consciousness of reversal and indeed of absolute reversal ; its dominating element is the concept, which draws together the thoughts that to the honest consciousness lie so wide apart ; hence the brilliance of its language. Thus the contents of the mind's speech about itself consist in the reversal of all conceptions and realities ; the universal deception of oneself and others and the shamelessness of declaring this deception is therefore precisely the greatest truth. . . . To the quiet consciousness, which in its honest way goes on singing the melody of the True and the Good in even tones, *i.e.*, on one note, this speech appears as 'a farrago of wisdom and madness,'" etc. (a passage from Diderot follows).

More amusing than Hegel's commentary is that of Mr. Jules Janin†, from which you will find extracts in the appendix to the little volume. This *cardinal de la mer* [sea-cardinal] feels the lack of a moral in Diderot's *Rameau* and has therefore set the thing right by the discovery that all Rameau's contrariness arises from his vexation at not being a " born gentleman."

* Each element in the dialectical movement, process of becoming. German : *Moment*. [*Ed. Eng. ed.*]

† Janin, Jules (1804-74). French bourgeois author and literary critic with a popular reputation in bourgeois circles.

The Kotzebue-ish rubbish which he has piled up on this cornerstone is being performed as a melodrama in London. From Diderot to Jules Janin is no doubt what the physiologists call regressive metamorphosis. The French intellect as it was *before* the revolution and *under Louis Philippe!* . . .

124. ENGELS TO MARX

Manchester, 6 July, 1869.

Nothing can in any case be done with Wilhelm [Liebknecht] until he has quite definitely separated his organisation from the People's Party and placed himself at most in a loose cartel relation with them. Very nice too his intending to put the International in the title of his little paper, which would then be the organ of the International Workingmen's Association *and* of the People's Party *at the same time!* The organ *both* of the German petty bourgeoisie and of the European workers!

Another fine idea of Wilhelm's, that one must neither accept nor even *force* concessions to the workers from the "present state." This will get him the hell of a long way with the workers. . . .

[In Tridon's pamphlet there is] the comic idea that the dictatorship of Paris over France, which was the reason why the first revolution went to pieces, could be carried out in just the same sort of way to-day but with a successful result.*

125. MARX TO ENGELS

[London] 10 August, 1869.

It cannot be denied that the section of the speech made by Wilhelm [Liebknecht] in *Berlin,* reprinted in the supplement, shows, beneath its stupidity, an undeniable cunning in arranging the affair to suit himself. This, by the way, is very fine! *Because* the Reichstag must *only* be used as a *means of agitation,* one must *never agitate* there for anything reasonable directly affecting the interests of the workers! The worthy Wilhelm's illusion

* Tridon's pamphlet: *Gironde et Girondins* (1869).

that because Bismarck " is fond of " using expressions friendly to the workers he would therefore not oppose *real measures on behalf of the workers* is really charming. " As if "—as Bruno Bauer would say—Herr Wagener had not declared in the Reichstag that he was *for* the factory laws in principle but against them in *practice* " because they were useless under Prussian conditions." " As if " Herr Bismarck, if he really wished or was *able* to do anything for the workers, would not *himself* enforce the *carrying out* of the existing laws in *Prussia itself!* The mere fact of this happening in Prussia would be enough to *force* the Liberal " Saxony " to follow suit. What Wilhelm does not grasp is that while the present governments coquette with the workers they are very well aware that their only support lies with the bourgeoisie ; they therefore scare the latter by phrases friendly to the workers but *cannot* ever really go against them.

The cow [Liebknecht] believes in the future "*Staat* DER *Demokratie* " [democratic state]. Privately this means at one moment constitutional England, at another the bourgeois United States, and at the next the wretched Switzerland. " It " has not the faintest idea of revolutionary politics. This is what he gives as a proof—according to Schwabenmayer—of democratic energy : the railway to California was built by the bourgeoisie *presenting* themselves, through Congress, with an enormous mass of " national land " ; that is to say, therefore, they *expropriated* the workers from it by importing a mob of Chinese to force down wages and finally formed a new branch of themselves, the " financial aristocracy."

¶SCHWABENMAYER-MAYER, KARL (1819-99). Swabian [Würtenburg] bourgeois journalist, a Democrat of 1848, " the verbose Swabian " (Marx). Editor of the Stuttgart *Beobachter* [*Observer*] in which the Preface to the first edition of *Capital* was reprinted. Mayer was a friend of the Bonapartist agent Karl Vogt and hostile to Prussia and Bismarck.

126. MARX TO ENGELS

[London] 18 August, 1869.

In Posen, as Zabicki reported, the *Polish* workers (joiners, etc.) have brought a strike to a victorious end by the help of their colleagues in Berlin. This struggle against Monseiur le Capital—even in the subordinate form of the strike—is a very different way of getting rid of national prejudices from that of the bourgeois gentlemen with their peace declamations.

127. MARX TO ENGELS

Hanover, 25 September, 1869.

This tour in Belgium, stay in Aix-la-Chapelle and voyage up the Rhine have convinced me that the priests, especially in the Catholic districts, must be energetically attacked. I shall work on these lines through the International. The curs (*e.g.*, Bishop Ketteler in Mainz, the parsons at the Düsseldorf Congress, etc.) are flirting, where they find it suitable, with the labour question. Indeed it was for them that we worked in 1848, they alone enjoyed the fruits of the revolution during the period of reaction.

¶In the 'fifties and 'sixties of the nineteenth century the Catholic Church developed a broad " socialistic " propaganda in west Germany under the leadership of the Jesuit, Bishop Ketteler of Mainz, and supported trade unions, protection of labour and even strikes. This was done in order to bring the rapidly growing workers' movement under the guidance of the Church and thus to create a mass basis for reaction in Germany —a move directed at the same time against the bourgeoisie. Lassalle did not combat this priestly demagogy—Bishop Ketteler even " recognised " the " iron law of wages "—but welcomed it because it was also aimed against his chief enemy, the liberal bourgeoisie. In his speech at Ronsdorf (May 1864) Lassalle said among other things : " But I am justified in attributing the greatest importance to the fact that a bishop, despite the gentleness and consideration natural to his position, should have been obliged by his conscience to express himself with as much sharpness as I used in my more ruthless capacity of people's tribune, and to accuse the Progressive Party, on account of its obstinate denial of the economic law proved by myself, of nothing less than deliberate deceit. Judge of the brilliant clarity to which I must have reduced that proof by the fact that it has provoked this language from a prince of the Church."

128. ENGELS TO MARX

Manchester, 24 October, 1869.

Irish history shows one how disastrous it is for a nation when it has subjugated another nation. All the abominations of the English have their origin in the Irish Pale.* I have still to work through the Cromwellian period, but this much seems certain to me, that things would have taken another turn in England but for the necessity for military rule in Ireland and the creation of a new aristocracy there.

129. ENGELS TO MARX

Manchester, 9 November, 1869.

I never thought that Mr. Carey would be such amusing reading. . . . The fellow imagines that the reason why rent is so high in South Lancashire and, among other places, in the Forest of Rossendale (a thickly-populated industrial centre) is because the land here is exceptionally good corn-producing land ! I am making a heap of marginal notes for you and as soon as I have read his theory of rent will write you my opinion and send the book back. Of course he explains the origin of rent by just as wild and senseless a story as Ricardo, and his idea too of *how it took place* is as absurd as the way in which all economists represent this sort of thing to themselves. But that has nothing to do with the theory of rent itself. What

* The section of Ireland in which the English laws, language, etc. were imposed before the conquest of the whole country was completed.

Carey calls the "best land" you can see from the fact that, according to his own statement, it is *exceptional* now for the so-called best land, even in the Northern States, to *yield a profit* when taken into cultivation.

130. MARX TO ENGELS

London, 18 November, 1869.

Last Tuesday I opened the discussion on Point No. 1, *the attitude of the British Ministry to the Irish Amnesty question.* Made a speech of about three-quarters of an hour, much cheered, and then proposed the following resolutions on Point No. 1 :

Resolved :

that in his reply to the Irish demands for the release of the imprisoned Irish patriots—a reply contained in his letter to Mr. O'Shea, etc., etc.—Mr. Gladstone deliberately insults the Irish nation ;

that he clogs political amnesty with conditions alike degrading to the victims of misgovernment and the people they belong to ;

that having, in the teeth of his responsible position, publicly and enthusiastically cheered on the American slaveholders' rebellion, he now steps in to preach to the Irish people the doctrine of passive obedience ;

that his whole proceedings with reference to the Irish Amnesty question are the true and genuine offspring of that "*policy of conquest*," by the fiery denunciation of which Mr. Gladstone ousted his Tory rivals from office ;

that the *General Council* of the "*International Workingmen's Association*" express their admiration of the spirited, firm and high-souled manner in which the Irish people carry on their Amnesty movement ;

that these resolutions be communicated to all branches of, and workingmen's bodies connected with, the "*International Workingmen's Association*" in Europe and America.*

* These resolutions are given in English by Marx.

¶The Irish Amnesty question—the demand for an amnesty for the Fenian political prisoners, coupled with a protest against their treatment as convicts. See notes on pp. 231 and (Jenny Marx) 392. For the discussion on the General Council, which Marx used to expose George Odger and his friends, see Note to Letter 133, for Marx's main object see Letter 134. [*Ed. Eng. ed.*]

GLADSTONE, WILLIAM EWART (1809-98). At first a Conservative, became a Liberal and the leader of the Liberal Party. Held office as President of the Board of Trade and Chancellor of the Exchequer; between 1868 and 1892 was four times Prime Minister. Gladstone was one of the most determined representatives of the class interests of the British bourgeoisie in opposition to those of the landowners and the workers and to those of the oppressed peoples in the British colonies. Despite his Liberal pacifist speeches he proceeded, where necessary, to the bloody suppression of colonial revolts (*e.g.*, Egypt). He also conducted a struggle against the Irish national revolutionary movement and it was only renewed rebellion which forced him to introduce into the House of Commons two Bills (1886 and 1893) promising Ireland certain minor rights of self-government within the framework of forcible union with Britain (Home Rule); the first Bill was rejected by the House of Commons and the second by the House of Lords. [Ireland only received Dominion status in 1921, after the revolutionary struggle, 1919-21.]

131. ENGELS TO MARX

Manchester, 19 November, 1869.

. . . And now for *Carey*.

The whole question at issue does not seem to me to have any direct connection with economics proper. Ricardo says, rent is the surplus yield of the more fertile pieces of land over that of the less fertile. Carey says just the same. . . . They are therefore agreed on what rent is. The dispute is only about how rent arises. Now Ricardo's description of the process by which rent originates (Carey, p. 104) is just as unhistorical as all the similar detailed stories of the economists and as Carey's own great Robinson-Crusoeade about Adam and Eve

(p. 96 seq.). In the older economists, including Ricardo, this is still excusable to a certain extent ; they do not want any historical knowledge, they are just as unhistorical in their whole conception as the other apostles of the eighteenth century Enlightenment, with whom such alleged historical digressions are nothing more than a manner of speech enabling them to represent the origin of this, that or the other to themselves in a rational way, and in which primitive man always thinks and behaves exactly as if he were an apostle of eighteenth-century Enlightenment. But when Carey, who wants to develop his own historical theory, proceeds to introduce Adam and Eve to us as Yankee backwoodsmen, he cannot expect us to believe him, he has not the same excuse.

There would be no dispute at all if Ricardo had not been naïve enough to call the more productive land simply "fertile." "The most *fertile* and *most favourably situated* land" is, according to Ricardo, the first cultivated. Just the way a thoughtful bourgeois in a land that has been cultivated for centuries would be bound to represent the thing to himself. Now Carey fastens on to the "fertile," foists on to Ricardo the assertion that the lands most capable of productivity in *themselves* are those taken into cultivation, and says : No, on the contrary, the most *naturally* fertile lands (the valley of the Amazon, the Ganges delta, tropical Africa, Borneo and New Guinea, etc.) are not cultivated even yet ; the first settlers, because they cannot help themselves, start cultivation on land *which drains itself*, namely, strips lying on hills and slopes, but these are by nature *poorer* land. And when Ricardo says : *fertile and the most favourably situated*, he is saying the same thing, without noticing that he is expressing himself loosely and that a contradiction can be introduced between these two qualifications connected by "*and*." But when Carey inserts a sketch on page 138 and declares that Ricardo puts his first settlers in the valley while Carey puts them on the hills (on bare crags and impracticable declivities of 45 degrees, in the sketch) he is simply lying about Ricardo.

Carey's historical illustrations, in so far as they refer *to America*, are the only useful thing in the book. As a Yankee he was able to live through the process of settlement himself and could follow it from the beginning ; here, therefore, he knows all about it. Nevertheless there is no doubt a lot of uncritical stuff here as well, which would have first to be sifted out. But when he gets to Europe he begins inventing and making himself ridiculous. And that he is not unprejudiced even in America is indicated by the eagerness with which he attempts to prove the worthlessness, indeed the *negative* quality, of the value of the uncultivated land (that in some respects it is worth minus 10 dollars an acre) and praises the self-sacrifice of the societies which, to their own certain ruin, make waste land serviceable for mankind. Related of the country of colossal land jobbery, this produces a humorous effect. Moreover, he never mentions the *prairie land* here and it is very lightly touched upon elsewhere. The whole story of the negative value of the waste land and all the calculation he gives to prove it are after all best contradicted by America itself. If the story were true, America would not only be the poorest of countries, but would be becoming *relatively* poorer every year, because more and more labour would be thrown away on this worthless land.

Now as to his definition of rent : " The amount received as rent is interest upon the value of labour expended, *minus* the difference between the productive power (the rent-paying land) and that of the newer soils which can be brought into activity by the application of the same labour that has been there given to the work "—pp. 165-6. This may, within certain limits, have a certain amount of truth here and there, especially in America. But rent is in any case such a complicated thing, to which so many other circumstances contribute, that even in those cases, this definition could apply only if other things were equal, only to two pieces of land *lying side by side.* That " interest for the value of labour expended " is also contained in rent, Ricardo knew as well as he. If Carey declares the land as such to be worse than worthless then rent is bound of course to be either " interest upon the value of labour expended," or, as it is called on p. 139, theft. But he has still to show us the transition from theft to interest.

The *origin* of rent in different countries and even in one and the same country seems to me to be by no means such a simple process as both Ricardo and Carey imagine. In Ricardo, as I said, this is excusable ; it is the story of the fishers and hunters in the sphere of agriculture. It is not in fact an economic *dogma*, but Carey wants to make a dogma out of his theory and prove it to the world—for which indeed historical studies of a very different sort from Mr. Carey's are necessary. There may even have been places where rent originated in Ricardo's way and others where it originated in Carey's way, and still others where its origin was entirely different. One might also remark to Carey that where fever has to be reckoned with, and above all tropical fever, economics pretty well cease to hold. Unless his theory of population means that with the increase of inhabitants the surplus population is obliged to begin work on the most fertile, *i.e.*, the most unhealthy pieces of land, an attempt in which they either succeed or perish. If so, he has successfully established a harmony between himself and Malthus.

In Northern Europe, rent originated neither in Ricardo's nor in Carey's way, but simply from the feudal burdens which were later reduced to their right economic level by free competition. In Italy different again, see Rome. To calculate how much of the rent in the old civilised countries is really original rent and how much is interest for labour invested is impossible, because every case is different. Moreover it has no importance at all once it has been proved that rent can also increase where no labour is put into the land. The grandfather of Sir Humphrey de Trafford, in Old Trafford near Manchester, was so laden with debt that he did not know what to do. His grandson, after paying off all the debts, has an income of £40,000 a year. If we subtract about £10,000 of this, which comes from building land, £30,000 remains as the yearly value of the agricultural estate, which eighty years ago brought in perhaps £2,000. Further, if £3,000 is taken as interest on invested labour and capital, which is a lot, there remains an increase of £25,000, or five times the former value, including the improvements. And all this, not because labour was put into it, but because labour was put into something else near by—because the estate lies close to a city like Manchester, where milk, butter and garden produce get a good price. It is just the same on a larger scale. From the moment England became a corn and cattle importing country, and even earlier, the density of population became a factor in the determination of rent, and particularly of rent-increases, quite independently of the labour invested in the land of England as a whole. Ricardo, with his " most favourably situated lands " includes the consideration of connection *with the market* as well, Carey ignores it. And if he were then to say that land itself only has a negative, but *situation* a positive value, he would have nevertheless admitted, what he denies, that land, just because it can be monopolised, has, or *can* have, a value independent of the labour invested in it. But on this point Carey is as quiet as a mouse.

It is equally indifferent whether the labour invested in the land in civilised countries pays regularly or not. More than 20 years ago I made the assertion that in our present society no instrument of production exists which can last from 60 to 100 years, no factory, no building, etc., which by the end of its existence has covered the cost of its production. I still think that one way and another this is perfectly true. And if Carey and I are both right, that proves nothing about the rate of profit or the origin of rent, it only proves that bourgeois production, even measured by its own standards, is rotten.

With these random comments on Carey you will no doubt have enough. They are very mixed because I made no extracts. As for the historical-materialistic-scientific trimming, its whole value = that of the two trees, the tree of life and the tree of knowledge, which he has planted in his Paradisical work, not indeed for Adam and Eve, who have to slave in the backwoods, but for their descendants. This wretched ignorant stuff can only be compared with the shamelessness which allows him to unburden himself of such nonsense.

132. MARX TO ENGELS

[London] 26 November 1869.

. . . In my book against Proudhon,* where I still fully accepted Ricardo's theory of rent, I already showed what was false in it, even from Ricardo's own point of view.

" Ricardo, after having presupposed bourgeois production as necessary for the determination of rent, nevertheless applies it to landed property in every epoch and every country. These are the errors of all the economists, who regard the conditions of bourgeois production as eternal categories." Mr. Proudhon had of course immediately transformed Ricardo's theory into an expression of equalitarian moralty and therefore discovered in Ricardo's determination of rent, " an immense land valuation, carried out by farmers and landlords in opposition to one another . . . in a higher interest of which the final result must be to equalise the possession of the land between the exploiters of the soil and the industrialists."

Upon this I remark, among other things :

" In order that any valuation whatever, determined by rent, should have a practical value, it is always necessary to remain within the actual conditions of society. Now we have shown that the *rent* paid for his farm by a farmer to his landlord roughly expresses the *rent* only in those countries which are most advanced industrially and commercially. And this farm rent often also includes the *interest* paid to the landlord for the capital invested in the land. The situation of the land, the neighbourhood of towns and many other circumstances have their effect on the farming and modify the rent. . . . On the other hand, rent cannot be a *constant index of the degree of fertility possessed by a piece of land*, since at each instant the modern application of chemistry comes in to change the nature of the soil, and it is precisely in the present day that geological knowledge is beginning to *upset the old estimates of relative fertility* . . . fertility is not such a natural quality as might well be believed ; it is intimately connected with existing social *relations*."

* *La Misère de la Philosophie* [Poverty of Philosophy], chap. II (4).

With regard to the progress of cultivation in the United States themselves, Mr. Carey ignores even the most familiar facts. The English agricultural chemist, Johnstone, for instance, shows in his Notes on the United States that the settlers who left New England for the State of New York left worse for better land (better not in Carey's sense, that the land has first to be made, but in the chemical and at the same time economic sense). The settlers from the State of New York who established themselves at first beyond the Great Lakes, say in Michigan, left better for worse land, etc. The settlers in Virginia exploited the land suited both in *situation* and *fertility* to their chief product, tobacco, so abominably that they had to move on to Ohio, where the land was less good for this product (though not for wheat, etc.). The nationality of the immigrants also asserted itself in their settlements. The people from Norway and from our high forest lands sought out the rough northern forest land of Wisconsin ; the Yankees in the same province kept to the prairies, etc.

Prairies, both in the United States and Australia, are, in fact, a thorn in Carey's flesh. According to him land which is not absolutely overgrown with forests is infertile by nature—including, therefore, all natural pasture land.

The best of it is that Carey's two great final conclusions (relating to the United States) stand in direct contradiction to his dogma. *First*, owing to the diabolical influence of England, the inhabitants, instead of socially cultivating the good model lands of New England, are disseminated over the poorer (!) lands of the West. Progress therefore from better land to worse. (Carey's "dissemination," in opposition to "association," by the by, is all copied out of Wakefield). *Second*, in the south of the United States there is the unfortunate fact that the slaveowners (whom Mr. Carey, as a harmonist, has hitherto defended in all his previous works) take the better land into cultivation too soon and leave out the worst. In fact just what ought not to be : starting with the better land ! If Carey had convinced himself by this instance that the real cultivators, in this case the slaves, were decided in this course neither by economic nor any other reason of their own, but by *external force*, it would have been obvious to him that this condition also exists in other lands.

According to his theory, cultivation in Europe should have started from the mountains of Norway and continued to the Mediterranean countries instead of proceeding in the reverse direction.

Carey tries, by a highly absurd and fantastic theory of money, to conjure away the awkward economic fact that, unlike all other improved machinery, the earth-machine, which according to him is *always a better* one, *increases*—(periodically at least)—*the cost* of its products instead of *cheapening* them. (This was one of the points which influenced Ricardo; he could see no further than his nose, namely, the history of corn prices in England from about 1780 to 1815).

As a harmonist, Carey first proved that there was no antagonism between capitalist and wage-labourer. The second step was to prove the harmony between landowner and capitalist, and this is done by taking landownership where it is *still* in an undeveloped state and representing this as *normal.* The great and decisive difference between the colonies and the old civilised countries, that in the latter the mass of the population is excluded from land and soil—whether fertile or unfertile, cultivated or uncultivated—by the system of *landed property*, while in the colony land can, relatively speaking, still be appropriated by the cultivator himself—this fact must not be mentioned whatever happens. It must have absolutely nothing to do with the rapid development of the colonies. The disagreeable "*question of property*" in its most disagreeable form, would indeed knock harmony off its feet.

As for the deliberate distortion that, because in a country with developed production the natural fertility of the soil is an important condition for the production of surplus value (or, as Ricardo says, affects the rate of profit), therefore the converse must also follow that the richest and most developed production will be found in the most naturally fertile lands, so that it must stand higher, *e.g.*, in Mexico than in New England, I have already answered this in *Capital*, p. 502 *et seq.**

* Vol. I. chap. XVI, page 562 (Kerr Edition).

Carey's only merit is that he is just as one-sided in asserting the progress from worse to better lands as Ricardo is in asserting the opposite. In reality, different kinds of land, unequal in their degrees of fertility, are always cultivated simultaneously, and therefore the Germans, the Slavs and the Celts took this into account and made a very careful division of the strips of land of different kinds among the members of the community; it was this which later made the breaking up of the common lands so difficult. As to the progress of cultivation throughout the course of history, however, this, influenced by a mass of circumstances, sometimes takes place in both directions at once, sometimes one tendency prevails for a period and sometimes the other.

Interest on the capital embodied in the land becomes a part of the *differential rent* just because of the fact that the landowner gets this interest from capital which not *he* but the *tenant-farmer* has put into the land. This fact, known throughout Europe, is supposed to have no economic existence because the tenant system is *not yet* developed in the *United States*. But there the thing takes place in another form. The land jobber and not the farmer gets paid in the end, in the *price* of the land, for the capital invested by the latter. Indeed the history of the pioneers and land jobbers in the United States often reminds one of the worst horrors taking place, *e.g.*, in Ireland.

133. ENGELS TO MARX

Manchester, 29 November, 1869.

The election in Tipperary* is an event. It forces the Fenians out of empty conspiracy and the fabrication of small coups into a path of action which, even if legal in appearance, is still far more revolutionary than what they have been doing since the failure of their insurrection. In fact, they are adopting the methods of the French workers and that is an enormous advance. If only the thing is carried on as intended. The terror which this new turn has produced among the philistines,

* The election of O'Donovan Rossa, one of the Fenian prisoners. See Note to Letter 134. [*Ed. Eng. ed.*]

and which is now being screeched throughout the whole Liberal press, is the best proof that this time the nail has been hit on the head. Typical is the *Solicitors' Journal*, which remarks with horror that the election of a political prisoner is *without precedent* in the realm of Britain ! So much the worse—where is there a country *except* England in which such a case is not a common event ! The worthy Gladstone must be horribly annoyed.

But you really ought to look at the *Times* now. *Three* leaders in eight days in which either it is demanded of the Government or the Government itself demands that an end be put to the excesses of the Irish Nationalist press.

I am very eager to hear about your debate to-morrow evening and its result, about which there can be no doubt. It would be very fine to get Odger into a hole. I hope Bradlaugh will stand for Southwark as well as he, and it would be much better if Bradlaugh were elected. For the rest, if the English workers cannot take an example from the peasants of Tipperary they are in a bad way. . . .

Last week I waded through the tracts by old Sir John Davies (Attorney-General for Ireland under James). I do not know if you have read them, they are the main source ; at any rate you have seen them quoted a hundred times. It is a real shame that one cannot have the original sources for everything ; one can see infinitely more from them than from the second-hand versions which reduce everything that is clear and simple in the original to confusion and complexity.

From these tracts it is clear that communal property in land *still existed* in full force in Ireland in the year 1600, and this was brought forward by Mr. Davies in the pleas regarding the confiscation of the alienated lands in Ulster, as a proof that the land did not belong to the individual owners (peasants) and therefore either belonged to the lord, who had forfeited it, or from the beginning to the Crown. I have never read anything finer than this plea. The division took place afresh every two to three years. In another pamphlet he gives an exact description of the income, etc., of the chief of the clan. These things I have *never* seen quoted and if you can use them I will send them you in detail. At the same time I have nicely caught Monsieur Goldwin Smith. This person has never read Davies and so puts up the most absurd assertions in extenuation of the English. But I shall get the fellow. . . .

¶" YOUR DEBATE . . . ODGER," etc. The debate in the General Council of the International on the Irish resolution. (See Letters 130, 134.) Marx had described the adjourned debate to Engels on November 26, 1869 :

" The meeting last Tuesday was very fiery, heated and violent. Mr. Muddlehead or whatever in the hell the fellow is called*—a Chartist and old friend of Harney's—had brought along Odger and Applegarth as a precaution. On the other side Weston and Lucraft were absent because they had gone to an Irish ball. *Reynolds* had published my resolutions in its Saturday issue, together with a summary of my speech . . . which was put right on the front page, after the first leading article. This seems to have scared the people who are making love to Gladstone. Hence the appearance of Odger and a long rambling speech from Muddershead, who got knocked on the head damned heavily by Milner (an Irishman himself). Applegarth was sitting next me and therefore did not dare to speak against the resolution, indeed he spoke *for* it, obviously with an uneasy conscience. *Odger* said that if the resolutions were forced to a vote he would be obliged to vote for them, but unanimity would surely be better, could be reached with a few small modifications, etc. To this, as *he* is the one I particularly want to put into a hole, I replied that *he* should bring forward his amendments next Tuesday ! At our last meeting, although many of our most reliable members were absent, we should have got the resolution through with *only one* vote against. Next Tuesday we shall be in full force."

Of the final discussion Marx reported to Engels on December 4 : " The resolutions unanimously carried, despite Odger's persistent *verbal* amendments. I only gave way to him on one point : to omit the word ' deliberate ' before ' insults ' in paragraph one. I did this on the pretence that everything a Prime Minister did publicly must be presumed *eo ipso* to be

* Mottershead. See also Letter 168.

deliberate. The real reason was that I knew that if once we got the essential point of paragraph one conceded all further opposition would be useless. . . . With the exception of Mottershead, who came out as John Bull, and Odger, who was as much of a diplomat as ever, the English delegates behaved splendidly." A general debate on the relation of the English working class to the Irish question was to follow. (See Letters 134, 136.) [*Ed. Eng. ed.*]

ODGER, etc. (See Note to Letter 71.) Eighteen months previously Marx had written to Kugelmann (April 6, 1868) : " The Irish question is dominant here just now. Of course it is only being exploited by Gladstone and Co. in order to get them into office, principally as an election cry for the forthcoming elections, which will be held on household suffrage. At the moment this turn of affairs is harmful for the workers' party, for the intriguers among the workers who want to get into the next parliament, like Odger and Potter, now have a new excuse for joining with the bourgeois Liberals." Gladstone came into office at the elections that autumn. [*Ed. Eng. ed.*]

APPLEGARTH, ROBERT (1833-1923). Secretary of the Amalgamated Society of Carpenters and Joiners (1862). Marx wrote to Engels (December 4, 1869) that Applegarth was " very important " because he was regarded by both Houses of Parliament as " the officially recognised representative of the English trade unions." Together with Odger and Allan (Amalgamated Society of Engineers) he was one of the so-called " Junta," the leading representatives of the " new model " trade unionism. Marx related to Engels (December 4.) that after the final debate on the Irish question Applegarth, " who had behaved very well," had informed him that " an eminent member of the House of Commons " had been commissioned by " an eminent member of the House of Lords " to ask Applegarth if he had voted for the abolition of all private property at the Basle Congress of the International. His answer would decide the attitude of his parliamentary patrons. Applegarth wanted to " give the fellows a decided answer " and commissioned Marx to draw up " the reasson " for him. Despite ill-health and press of work Marx wrote him " eight pages which will take him a long time to chew " on " landed property and the necessity of its abolition." " Odger and Applegarth," wrote Marx to Engels, April 5, 1869, " are both possessed with a mania for compromise and a thirst for respectability." Applegarth eventually became the owner of a flourishing business. See also Notes on Odger and on the *Beehive*, Letter 71. [*Ed. Eng. ed.*]

134. MARX TO KUGELMANN

London, 29 November, 1869.

You will probably have seen in the *Volksstaat* the resolution against Gladstone which I proposed on the question of the Irish amnesty. I have now attacked Gladstone—and it has attracted attention here—just as I formerly attacked Palmerston. The demagogic refugees here love to fall upon the Continental despots from a safe distance. That sort of thing only attracts me, when it happens *vultu instantis tyranni.**

Nevertheless both my coming out on this Irish Amnesty question and my further proposal to the General Council to discuss the relation of the English working class to Ireland and to pass resolutions on it, have of course other objects besides that of speaking out loudly and decidedly for the oppressed Irish against their oppressors.

I have become more and more convinced—and the only question is to bring this conviction home to the English working class—that it can never do anything decisive here in England until it separates its policy with regard to Ireland in the most definite way from the policy of the ruling classes, until it not only makes common cause with the Irish, but actually takes the initiative in dissolving the Union established in 1801 and replacing it by a free federal relationship. And, indeed, this must be done, not as a matter of sympathy with Ireland, but as a demand made in the interests of the English proletariat. If not, the English people will remain tied to the leading-strings of the ruling classes, because it must join with them in a common front against Ireland. Every one of its movements in England itself is crippled by the disunion with the Irish, who form a very important section of the working class in

* Before the face of the tyrant.

England. *The primary condition* of emancipation here—the overthrow of the English landed oligarchy—remains impossible because its position here cannot be stormed so long as it maintains its strongly entrenched outposts in Ireland. But there, once affairs are in the hands of the Irish people itself, once it is made its own legislator and ruler, once it becomes autonomous, the abolition of the landed aristocracy (to a large extent the *same persons* as the English landlords) will be infinitely easier than here, because in Ireland it is not merely a simple economic question, but at the same time a *national* question, since the landlords there are not like those in England, the traditional dignitaries and representatives, but are the mortally hated oppressors of a nation. And not only does England's internal social development remain crippled by her present relation with Ireland ; her foreign policy, and particularly her policy with regard to Russia and America, suffers the same fate.

But since the English working class undoubtedly throws the decisive weight into the scale of social emancipation generally, the lever has to be applied here. As a matter of fact, the English republic under Cromwell met shipwreck in —Ireland. *Non bis in idem !* [Not twice for the same thing]. The Irish have played a capital joke on the English government by electing the " convict felon " O'Donovan Rossa to Parliament. The government papers are already threatening a renewed suspension of the Habeas Corpus Act, a " renewed system of terror." In fact, England never has and never *can*— so long as the present relation lasts—rule Ireland otherwise than by the most abominable reign of terror and the most reprehensible corruption.*

¶O'DONOVAN ROSSA (born 1831). Irish politician and journalist. In 1865 founded in Dublin the organ of the Fenians, the *Irish People*. The revolutionary tendencies of this paper led to his being sentenced to life imprisonment. In 1869 he was elected while in prison as M.P. for Tipperary. (Letter 133.) The election was declared invalid but he was released and in

* *Letters to Dr. Kugelmann* (Martin Lawrence 1934) page 95.

1870 went to America. [For the Fenians compare Letters 102, 130, 133, 136.]

[HABEAS CORPUS ACT, supposed to guarantee personal freedom to British subjects. Can be suspended by Parliament.]

135. ENGELS TO MARX

Manchester, 9 December, 1869.

. . . Ireland still remains the Holy Isle whose aspirations must on no account be mixed with the profane class-struggles of the rest of the sinful world. This is no doubt partly honest madness on the part of the people, but it is equally certain that it is also partly a calculation on the side of the leaders in order to maintain their domination over the peasant. Added to this, a nation of peasants always has to take its literary representatives from the bourgeoisie of the towns and their intelligentsia, and in this respect Dublin (I mean *Catholic* Dublin) is to Ireland much what Copenhagen is to Denmark. But to these gentry the whole labour movement is pure heresy and the Irish peasant must not on any account know that the Socialist workers are his sole allies in Europe.

136. MARX TO ENGELS

London, 10 December, 1869.

As to the *Irish question*. . . . The way I shall put forward the matter next Tuesday is this: that quite apart from all phrases about "international" and "humane" *justice for Ireland*—which are to be taken for granted in the *International Council*—*it is in the direct and absolute interest of the English working class to get rid of their present connection with Ireland*. And this is my most complete conviction, and for reasons which in part I cannot tell the English workers themselves. For a long time I believed that it would be possible to overthrow the Irish regime by English working class ascendancy. I always expressed this point of view in the *New York Tribune*. Deeper study has now convinced me of the opposite. The English working class will *never accomplish anything* before it has got rid of Ireland. The lever must be applied in Ireland. That is why the Irish question is so important for the social movement in general.

I have read a lot of *Davies* in extracts. The book itself I had only glanced through superficially in the Museum. So you would do me a service if you would copy out the passages relating to *common property*. You must get *Curran's Speeches* edited by Davis, (London, James Duffy, 22 Paternoster Row.) I meant to have given it you when you were in London. It is now circulating among the English members of the Central Council and God knows when I shall see it again. For the period 1779-80 (Union) it is of decisive importance, not only because of *Curran's speeches* (especially the *legal* ones ; I consider Curran the *only great advocate*—people's advocate—of the eighteenth century and the *noblest nature*, while Grattan was a parliamentary rogue) but because you will find quoted there *all the sources* for the *United Irishmen*. This period is of the highest interest, scientifically and dramatically. Firstly, the foul doings of the English in 1588-89 repeated (and perhaps even intensified) in 1788-89. Secondly, it can be easily proved that there was a class movement in the Irish movement itself. Thirdly, the infamous policy of Pitt. Fourthly, which will annoy the English gentlemen very much, the proof that Ireland came to grief because, in fact, from a revolutionary standpoint, *the Irish were too far advanced for the English Church and King mob*, while on the other hand the English reaction in England had its roots (as in Cromwell's time) in the subjugation of Ireland. *This period* must be described in at least one chapter. John Bull in the pillory! . . . As to the present *Irish movement*, there are three important factors : (1) opposition to lawyers and trading politicians and blarney ; (2) opposition to the dictates of the priests, who (the *superior ones*) are traitors, as in O'Connell's time, from 1789-1800 ; (3) the *agricultural labouring class* beginning to come out against the farming class at the last meetings. (A similar phenomenon in 1795-1800.)

The rise of the *Irishman* was only due to the suppression of the *Fenian* press. For a long time it had been in opposition to Fenianism. Luby, etc., of the *Irish People*, etc., were educated men who treated religion as a bagatelle. The government put them in prison and then came the Pigotts and Co. The *Irishman* will only be anything until those people come out of prison again. It is aware of this although it is making *political capital* now by declaiming for the " felon-convicts."

¶CURRAN, JOHN PHILPOT (1750-1817). Irish barrister and politician who took part in the struggle for emancipation. Elected to the House of Commons in 1770, Curran attached himself to the opposition and protested against English policy in Ireland. Pitt tried to bribe him with position and a peerage but Curran would not be bribed. [In 1783 he became a member of the freed Irish Parliament ; he was a follower of Grattan's party. Curran's speeches in defence of Wolfe Tone and other Irish rebels made him famous.] Byron wrote of him : " He has fifty faces and twice as many voices when he mimics. . . . I have heard that man speak more poetry than I have ever seen written." His speeches were published in 1855.

GRATTAN, HENRY (1746-1820). Succeeded Flood as leader of the Protestant " patriot " party which carried on agitation for the emancipation of the Irish parliament. The measure of emancipation granted in 1783, however, (see Note to Letter 128,) was due to causes more powerful than the agitation of Grattan's party. Grattan, whom Fox called " the Irish Demosthenes," was a great figure in the Irish parliament (" Grattan's parliament "). He always protested his loyalty to the English Crown. [*Ed. Eng. ed.*]

137. ENGELS TO MARX

[Manchester] 1 February, 1870.

It is a real mercy that in spite of G. Flourens, there was *no* outbreak at Noir's funeral. The fury of the " *Pays* "* shows the bitter disappointment of the Bonapartists. Indeed what could be wished for better than to catch the whole of the

* *The Country*—a newspaper. (*Ed. Eng. ed.*]

revolutionary masses of Paris in flagrant delinquency in an open space *outside* Paris and even *outside the walls of the fortifications*, which have only a few entrances? Half a dozen cannons at the passages through the walls, a regiment of infantry in skirmishing formation and a brigade of cavalry to charge in and pursue—and in half an hour's time the whole unarmed crowd—the few revolvers that some of them may have in their pockets do not count—will be blown up, cut to pieces or taken prisoners. But as there are 60,000 troops at hand the crowd could even be allowed inside the fortifications, these could then be manned and the whole mass shot or ridden down in the open ground of the Champs Elysées and the Avenue de Neuilly. Mad! Paris, manned by 60,000 soldiers, is to be captured from the open fields by 200,000 unarmed workers!

¶NOIR, VICTOR (1848-70). French journalist. He was killed by Pierre Bonaparte, son of Lucien Bonaparte, Napoleon I's brother, in Pierre Bonaparte's own house. Noir's funeral served as the occasion for an immense demonstration against the Empire (Napoleon III).

FLOURENS, GUSTAV (1831-71). Revolutionary. Member of the Paris Commune and of its military commission. Killed April 3, 1871.

138. MARX TO ENGELS

[London] 10 February, 1870

I have read the first 150 pages of *Flerovsky's* book (they are taken up by Siberia, North Russia and Astrakhan). This is the first work to tell the truth about Russian economic conditions. The man is a determined enemy of what he calls "Russian optimism." I never held very rosy views of this communistic Eldorado, but Flerovsky surpasses all expectations. In fact it is wonderful and undoubtedly a sign of change that *such* a thing could be printed in Petersburg at all.

"Our proletariat is small in number but the mass of our

working class consists entirely of workers whose lot is worse than the lot of all other proletarians."*

The method of presentation is quite original, at times it reminds one most of Monteil. One can see that the man has travelled around everywhere and seen everything for himself. A glowing hatred of landlords, capitalists and officials. No socialist doctrine, no mysticism about the land (although in favour of the communal form of ownership), no nihilistic extravagance. Here and there a certain amount of well-meaning twaddle, which, however, is suited to the stage of development reached by the people for whom the book is intended. In any case this is the most important book which has appeared since your *Condition of the Working Class.* The family life of the Russian peasants—the awful beating to death of wives, the vodka and the concubines—is also well described. It will therefore come quite opportunely if you would now send me the imaginative lies of Citizen Herzen.

¶FLEROVSKY, VASSILI VASSILYEVITCH (1829-1918) Russian publicist, Narodnik. In 1862, having protested against the actions of the Government, he drew reprisals upon himself and was first banished to Astrakhan, then to Siberia (Kuznezk, Tomsk district) and later to the northern part of European Russia (Vologda, Tver). In the 'eighties he went abroad. The book which Marx is referring to, *The Condition of the Working Class in Russia*, was published in 1869. (See next letter).

Marx, in his letter to the members of the Committee of the Russian section in Geneva on March 24, 1870, said of *The Condition of the Working Class in Russia*, "this book was a real discovery for Europe." "The *Russian optimism* which was widely spread on the Continent, even among the so-called revolutionaries, is ruthlessly exposed in this work. I am doing the book no injury if I say that in certain places it cannot, from a purely theoretical point of view, be criticised altogether favourably. It is the production of an earnest observer, a fearless worker, a dispassionate critic, a great artist and above all of a man whom servitude of every kind enrages, who will not tolerate all manner of national hymns of praise and who

* Quoted by Marx in Russian.

passionately enters into all the sufferings and the struggle of the productive class. Works such as those of Flerovsky and those of their teacher, Chernyshevsky, really do the Russians honour and prove that their country is also beginning to participate in the general movement of our century."

MONTEIL, AMANS ALEXIS (1769-1850) French historian who defended the ideas of the great French Revolution. His chief work was his "*Histoire des Français des divers Etats.*" [*History of the French in their Different Orders.*]

¶HERZEN, ALEXANDER (1812-70). Russian author and revolutionary who "played a great part in the preparation of the Russian revolution." (Lenin.) He belonged to the generation of revolutionaries of the landowning class in the first half of the nineteenth century. "Herzen came close to dialectical materialism and stopped short—before historical materialism." (Lenin.) After the defeat of the Revolution of 1848, in "that period of history when the revolutionary spirit of bourgeois democracy was *already* dead and the revolutionary consciousness of the socialist proletariat was *not yet* mature" (Lenin), Herzen became a sceptic. He had been living abroad since the end of the 'forties and did not believe in the revolutionary movement in Russia, though in the free Russian press which he had established abroad he supported every revolutionary manifestation in Russia. "Herzen was the founder of 'Russian' socialism, of 'Narodnikism.'" (Lenin.) Marx criticised Herzen for idealising the Russian village commune and failing to see the signs of its decay.

139. MARX TO ENGELS

[London] 12 February 1870.

Your introduction is very good.* I know of nothing which should be altered or added. With your treatment of 1866 I agree word for word. The double thrust at Wilhelm [Liebknecht] with the People's Party and Schweitzer with his bodyguard of ruffians is very pretty! . . .†

* Introduction to second edition of Engels' *Peasant War in Germany*, 1870.

† The thrust against Wilhelm Liebknecht is the passage where Engels calls the National Liberals and the People's Party "the two opposite poles of the same narrow-mindedness." The thrust against Schweitzer—the passage in which Engels says that the only serious opponent of revolution remaining in Germany is—the Prussian government.

The title of N. Flerovsky's book is *The Condition of the Working Class in Russia*, Publishers, N. P. Polyakov, St. Petersburg, 1869.*

What amuses me very much among other things in Flerovsky is his polemic against the *direct dues* paid by the peasantry. It is a regular reproduction of Marshal Vauban and Boisguillebert. He feels too that the situation of the country people has its analogy in the period of the old French monarchy (after Louis XIV). Like Monteil, he has a great feeling for national characteristics—" the honest Kalmuck," " the Mordwin, poetical despite his dirt " (he compares him to the Irish), the " agile, lively, epicurean Tartar," " the talented Little Russian," etc. Like a good Russian he teaches his fellow countrymen what they should do to turn the *hatred* which all these races have for them into its opposite. As an example of this hatred he instances among other things a genuinely *Russian* colony which has emigrated from Poland to Siberia. These people only know Russian and not a word of Polish, but they regard themselves as Poles and devote a Polish hatred to the Russians, etc.

From his book it follows irrefutably that the present conditions in Russia can no longer be maintained, that the emancipation of the serfs only, of course, hastened the process of disintegration and that a fearful social revolution is approaching. Here too one sees the real basis of the schoolboy nihilism which is at present the fashion among Russian students, etc. In Geneva, by the by, a new colony of exiled Russian students has been formed whose programme proclaims opposition to Pan-Slavism, which is to be replaced by the International.

In a special section Flerovsky shows that the " Russification " of the alien races is a sheer optimistic delusion, *even in the East.*

140. MARX TO ENGELS

[London] 24 March, 1870.

I enclose a letter from the *Russian colony* in Geneva. We have admitted them and I have *accepted* their commission

* Quoted in Russian.

to be their representative in the General Council and have also sent them a short reply (official, with a private letter as well) and given them permission to publish it in their paper. A funny position for me to be functioning as the representative of young Russia! A man never knows what he may come to or what strange fellowship he may have to submit to. In the official reply I praise Flerovsky and emphasise the fact that the chief task of the Russian section is to work for Poland (*i.e.*, to free Europe from Russia as a neighbour). I thought it safer to say nothing about Bakunin, either in the public or in the confidential letter. But what I will never forgive these fellows is that they turn me into a "*vénérable*." They obviously think I am between eighty and a hundred years old.

¶Marx's official letter referred to was published in the *Narodnoye Dyelo* (*People's Cause*), No. 1, 1870. It began as follows: "Citizens, at its session on March 27, the General Council by a unanimous vote resolved that your programme and statutes are in agreement with the general statutes of the International Workingmen's Association. It hastened to admit your branch to the International. I accept with pleasure the honourable commission you give me to act as your representative on the General Council. You say in your 'programme' . . . that 'the tsarist yoke oppressing Poland is a hindrance to the political and social freedom of both peoples—the Russians as well as the Poles.' You might add that the violent seizure of Poland by Russia forms the pernicious support and the actual cause of the military regime in Germany and consequently on the whole Continent. Therefore, in bending their efforts towards smashing the chains of Poland the Russian socialists impose upon themselves the noble task of destroying the military regime, a task that is essential as a preliminary condition for the general emancipation of the European proletariat."

141. MARX TO MEYER AND VOGT*

[London] 9 April, 1870.

After occupying myself with the Irish question for many years I have come to the conclusion that the decisive blow against the English ruling classes (and it will be decisive for the workers' movement all over the world) cannot be delivered *in England but only in Ireland.* On December 1, 1869, the General Council issued a confidential circular drawn up by me in French (for the reaction upon England only the French, not the German, papers, are important), on the relation of the Irish national struggle to the emancipation of the working class, and therefore on the attitude which the International Workingmen's Association should take towards the Irish question.

I will here only give you quite shortly the decisive points.

Ireland is the bulwark of the English *landed aristocracy.* The exploitation of this country is not only one of the main sources of their material wealth, it is their greatest *moral* strength. They, in fact, represent the *domination of England over Ireland.* Ireland is therefore the great means by which the English aristocracy maintains *its domination in England* itself.

If, on the other hand, the English army and police were withdrawn to-morrow, you would at once have an agrarian revolution in Ireland. But the overthrow of the English aristocracy in Ireland involves and has as a necessary consequence its overthrow in England. And this would fulfil the prerequisite for the proletarian revolution in England. The destruction of the English landed aristocracy in Ireland is an infinitely easier operation than in England itself, because the *land question* has hitherto been the *exclusive* form of the social question in Ireland, because it is a question of existence, of *life and death,* for the immense majority of the Irish people and because it is at the same time inseparable from the *national* question. Quite apart from the passionate character of the

* Two German members of the North American section of the International living in New York. Both took part in the 1848 Revolution. See Letter 117, Note. [*Ed. Eng. ed.*]

Irish and the fact that they are more revolutionary than the English.

As for the English *bourgeoisie*, they have in the first place a common interest with the aristocracy in transforming Ireland into a mere pasture land which provides the English market with meat and wool at the cheapest possible prices. Hence they are interested in reducing, by expropriation and forcible emigration, the Irish population to such a small number that *English capital*, invested in land leased for farming, can function with "security." They have the same interest in *clearing the estate of Ireland* as they had in clearing the agricultural districts of England and Scotland. The £6000–£8000 absentee and other Irish revenues which at present flow annually to London have likewise to be taken into account.*

But the English bourgeoisie has also much more important interests in the present Irish regime. Owing to the constantly increasing concentration of farming, Ireland supplies its own surplus to the English labour market and thus forces down wages and lowers the moral and material position of the English working class. And most important of all: every industrial and commercial centre in England now possesses a working-class population *divided* into two *hostile* camps, English proletarians and Irish proletarians. The ordinary English worker hates the Irish worker as a competitor who lowers his standard of life. In relation to the Irish worker he feels himself a member of the *ruling* nation and so turns himself into a tool of the aristocrats and capitalists *against Ireland*, thus strengthening their domination *over himself*. He cherishes religious, social and national prejudices against the Irish worker. His attitude towards him is much the same as that of the "poor whites" to the "niggers" in the former slave states of the U.S.A. The Irishman pays him back with interest in his own coin. He regards the English worker as both sharing in the guilt for the English domination in Ireland and at the same time serving as its stupid tool.

This antagonism is artificially kept alive and intensified

* "£6000–£8000"—apparently refers to the average income of an absentee landlord. [*Ed. Eng. ed.*]

by the press, the pulpit, the comic papers, in short by all the means at the disposal of the ruling classes. It is the secret of the impotence of the English working class, despite their organisation. It is the secret by which the capitalist class maintains its power. And of this that class is well aware.

But the evil does not stop here. It continues across the ocean. The antagonism between English and Irish is the hidden basis of the conflict between the United States and England. It makes any honest and serious co-operation between the working classes of the two countries impossible. It enables the governments of both countries, whenever they think fit, to break the edge of the social conflict by their mutual threats and if need be by war with one another.

England, as the metropolis of capital, as the power which has hitherto ruled the world market, is for the time being the most important country for the workers' revolution, and moreover the *only* country in which the material conditions for this revolution have developed up to a certain point of maturity. Therefore to hasten the social revolution in England is the most important object of the International Workingmen's Association. The sole means of hastening it is to make Ireland independent.

Hence the task of the " International " is everywhere to put the conflict between England and Ireland in the foreground, and everywhere to side openly with Ireland. The special task of the Central Council in London is to awaken a consciousness in the English workers that for them the *national emancipation of Ireland* is no question of abstract justice or human sympathy but the first condition of *their own emancipation.*

¶In his pamphlet on *The Self-Determination of Nations*, Lenin writes : " The policy of Marx and Engels in the Irish question furnished a powerful example, which has retained its highly practical significance up to the present day, of the attitude which the proletariat of oppressing nations must adopt towards nationalist movements. . . . If the Irish and English proletariat had not accepted Marx's policy and had not issued the slogan of the separation of Ireland this would have been the worst opportunism on their part, forgetfulness of the tasks of democrats and Socialists, a concession to *English* reaction and the English bourgeoisie."

Marx and Engels developed the main lines of the national policy of the revolutionary proletariat in the period of pre-imperialist, pre-monopolistic capitalism, and gave a number of important examples of the correct application of these fundamental principles, always taking the whole of the national and international conditions and factors into consideration. The task of Communists in the period of imperialism consists in the correct application of these fundamental principles *under the changed conditions* of imperialistic capitalism, including the existence of a proletarian state which demonstrates how the proletariat solves the national question in practice. In its struggle for emancipation the attitude of the proletariat towards the movement for national liberation is not one of indifference, like that of Rosa Luxemburg even in 1915; the proletariat supports the national movement in the most determined and active way because that movement is objecttively revolutionary and leads to rebellion against imperialism in the very place where it has its "greatest reserve and most important source of strength," thus furthering the proletarian revolution. Hence Stalin writes: "Lenin is absolutely right when he says that the national movement of the oppressed countries must be regarded not from the standpoint of formal democracy, but from that of the real results of the struggle against imperialism, *i.e.*, not in isolation but on a world scale."

142. MARX TO ENGELS

[London], 18 May, 1870.

Our members in France are giving the French government ocular proof of the difference between a secret political society and a genuine workers' organisation. No sooner had the government jailed all the members of the Paris, Lyons, Rouen, Marseilles, etc., committees (some of them fled to Belgium and Switzerland) than *twice the number* of committees announced themselves as their successors with the most daring and provocative declarations in the newspapers (and as an additional precaution added their *private addresses* as well). At last the French government has done what we have so long wanted it to do and transformed the political question, Empire or Republic, into a question of life or death for the working-class.

143. MARX TO ENGELS

[London] 20 July, 1870.

But the paper* is also interesting on account of the leading article by old Delescluze. Despite his opposition to the government, the most complete expression of chauvinism—because France alone is the home of ideas—(of the ideas it has got about itself). The only thing that annoys these republican chauvinists is that the real expression of their idol—L. Bonaparte the long-nosed Stock Exchange shark—does not correspond to their fancy picture. The French need a thrashing. If the Prussians win, the centralisation of the state power will be useful for the centralisation of the German working class. German predominance would also transfer the centre of gravity of the workers' movement in Western Europe from France to Germany, and one has only to compare the movement in the two countries from 1866 till now to see that the German working class is superior to the French both theoretically and organisationally. Their predominance over the French on the world stage would also mean the predominance of *our* theory over Proudhon's, etc.

Finally, I am also enclosing the *criticism of my book*† in *Hildebrand's Journal of Economy and Statistics.* My physical state scarcely disposes me to merriment, but I have cried with laughter over this essay—bona fide tears of mirth. With the reaction and the downfall of the heroic age of philosophy in Germany the "*petty bourgeois*", inborn in every German citizen, has again asserted himself—in *philosophic* drivel worthy of Moses Mendelssohn, would-be clever and superior peevish

* *Le Réveil,* a democratic French newspaper.
† *Capital,* Volume I, 1867. Hildebrandt's *Zeitschrift für Okonomie und Statistik.*

nagging. And so now even *political economy* is to be dissolved into twaddle about "*conceptions of justice!*"

144. MARX TO ENGELS

[London] 8 August, 1870.

The Empire is made, *i.e.*, the German Empire. It seems as if all the trickery that has been perpetrated since the Second Empire has finally resulted in carrying out, by hook and crook, though neither by the path intended nor in the way imagined, the "national" aims of 1848—Hungary, Italy, Germany! It seems to me that this sort of movement will only come to an end as soon as the *Prussians and the Russians* come to blows. This is by no means improbable. The press of the Moscovite party (I have seen a lot of it at Borkheim's) has attacked the Russian government just as violently for its friendly attitude to Prussia as the French papers representing Thiers' point of view attacked Boustrapa* in 1866 for his flirtation with Prussia. Only the tsar, the German-Russian party and the official St. Petersburg *Journal* sounded a note hostile to France. But the last thing they expected was such a decided Prussian-German success. Like Bonaparte in 1866, they thought that the belligerent powers would weaken each other by a long struggle so that Holy Russia could intervene as supreme arbiter and dictate to them.

But now! If Alexander does not want to be poisoned, something must be done to appease the national party. Russia's prestige will obviously be even more "injured" by a German-Prussian Empire than the prestige of the Second Empire was by the North German Confederation.

Russia therefore—just as Bonaparte did in 1866-70—will intrigue with Prussia in order to get concessions in relation to Turkey, and all this trickery, despite the Russian religion of the Hohenzollerns, will end in *war between the tricksters*. However silly German Michael may be, his newly fortified national sentiment will hardly allow him to be pressed into the *service*

* Napoleon III.

of Russia without any remaining reason whatever, or so much as a pretext (especially now when he can no longer be lectured into putting up with everything in order that German unity may first be achieved). *Qui vivra verra* [who lives longest will see most]. If our Handsome William* lives on for a bit we may yet witness his proclamations to the Poles. When God wants to do something especially great, says old Carlyle, he always chooses out the stupidest people for it.

What troubles me at the moment is the state of affairs in France itself. The next great battle can hardly fail to turn against the French. And then ? If the defeated army retreats to Paris, *under* the leadership of *Boustrapa*, the result will be a peace of the most humiliating kind, perhaps with the *restoration* of the Orleans. If a revolution breaks out in Paris, the question is whether they have the means and the leadership to offer a serious resistance to the Prussians. One cannot conceal from oneself that twenty years of the Bonapartist farce have produced enormous demoralisation. One is hardly justified in reckoning on revolutionary heroism. What do you think about it ?

¶Engels, writing as a military expert, had sixty articles on the Franco-Prussian War published by the bourgeois *Pall Mall Gazette ;* these articles attracted great attention. In his article of August 8, 1870, he wrote :

" The French army has lost all initiative. Its movements are dictated less by military considerations than by political necessities. Here are 300,000 men almost within sight of the enemy. If their movements are to be ruled, not by what is done in the enemy's camp, but by what happens or may happen in Paris, they are half beaten already. Nobody, of course, can foretell with certainty the result of the general battle which is now impending, if not going on ; but this much we may say, that another week of such strategy as Napoleon III has shown since Thursday is alone sufficient to destroy the best and largest army in the world."

* Kaiser Wilhelm I.

145. ENGELS TO MARX

Manchester, 15 August, 1870.

The position seems to me to be this: Germany has been driven by Badinguet [Napoleon III] into a war for her national existence. If Badinguet defeats her, Bonapartism will be strengthened for years to come and Germany broken for years, perhaps for generations. In that case there can be no more question of an independent German working-class movement either, the struggle to restore the national existence will absorb everything, and at best the German workers will be dragged in the wake of the French. If Germany wins, French Bonapartism will at any rate be smashed, the endless row about the establishment of German unity will at last be got rid of, the German workers will be able to organise themselves on a national scale quite different from that hitherto, and the French workers, whatever sort of government may succeed this one, are certain to have a freer field than under Bonapartism. The whole mass of the German people of every class have realised that this is first and foremost a question of national existence and have therefore at once flung themselves into it. That in these circumstances a German political party should preach total obstruction *a la* Wilhelm [Liebknecht] and place all sorts of secondary considerations before the main consideration, seems to me impossible.

Added to this is the fact that Badinguet would never have been able to conduct this war without the chauvinism of the mass of the French population: the bourgeoisie, the petty bourgeoisie, the peasants and the imperialistic, Haussmannist* building workers' proletariat derived from the peasants, which Bonaparte created in the big towns. Until this chauvinism is knocked on the head, and that properly, peace be-

* *Haussmann:* French official and Prefect of the Seine under Napoleon III; many new streets were made and new buildings erected at his direction—Boulevard Haussmann. Engels (in his work *The Housing Question* II. 3) explains that what he calls "Haussmannism" took the form under Napoleon III of "breaking up the closely built working-class districts by long, straight, wide streets and enclosing them on each side with big luxury buildings, both with the strategical aim of making barricade fighting more difficult and with the object of forming a special Bonapartist building-workers' proletariat dependent on the government, and thus transforming the city into a pure luxury city." [*Ed. Eng. ed.*]

tween Germany and France is impossible. One might have expected that a proletarian revolution would have undertaken this work, but since the war is already there, nothing remains for the Germans but to do it themselves and quickly.

Now come the secondary considerations. For the fact that this war was ordered by Lehmann [Wilhelm I] Bismarck & Co., and must minister to their temporary glorification if they conduct it successfully, we have to thank the miserable state of the German bourgeoisie. It is certainly very unpleasant but cannot be altered. But to magnify anti-Bismarckism into the sole guiding principle on this account would be absurd. In the first place, Bismarck, as in 1866, is at present doing a bit of our work for us, in *his own* way and without meaning to, but all the same he is doing it. He is clearing the ground for us better than before. And then we are no longer at the year 1815. The South Germans are bound now to enter the Reichstag and this will develop a counterpoise to Prussianism. Then there are the national duties which will fall to Prussia and which, as you wrote, will from the outset forbid the Russian alliance. In general to try *à la* Liebknecht to set the clock back on all that has happened since 1866 is senseless. But we know our model South Germans. There is nothing to be done with these fools.

I think our people can:

(1) Join the national movement—you can see from Kugelmann's letter how strong it is—in so far as and for so long as it is limited to the defence of Germany (which does not exclude an offensive, in certain circumstances, before peace is arrived at).

(2) At the same time emphasise the difference between German-national and dynastic-Prussian interests.

(3) Work against any annexation of Alsace and Lorraine—Bismarck is now revealing the intention of annexing them to Bavaria and Baden.

(4) As soon as a non-chauvinistic republican government is at the helm in Paris, work for an honourable peace with it.

(5) Constantly stress the unity of interest between the German and French workers, who did not approve of the war and are also not making war on each other.

(6) *Russia*, as in the International Address.

Wilhelm's assertion that because Bismarck is a former accomplice of Badinguet's the correct position is to remain neutral, is amusing. If that were the general opinion in Germany, we should soon have the Confederation of the Rhine again and the noble Wilhelm should just see what sort of a part he would play in that, and what would happen to the workers' movement. A people that gets nothing but kicks and blows is indeed the right one to make a social revolution, and in Wilhelm's beloved X-petty states moreover! . . .

. . . The debacle in France seems to be awful. Everything squandered, sold, swindled away. The *chassepots* are badly made and fail when brought into action, there are no more there, the old flintlocks have got to be hunted out again. Nevertheless a revolutionary government, if it comes *soon*, need not despair. But it must leave Paris to its fate and carry on the war from the South. There would then still be a possibility of its holding out until arms have been bought and new armies organised with which the enemy would be gradually forced back again to the frontier. This would really be the true end of the war, both countries reciprocally furnishing proof that they are unconquerable. But if this does not happen quickly the game is up. Moltke's operations are a model—old Wilhelm seems to give him a perfectly free hand—and the four battalions are already joining the main army, while the French ones are not yet in existence.

If Badinguet is not out of Metz yet it may go badly with him. . . .

Wilhelm [Liebknecht] has obviously calculated on a victory for Bonaparte simply in order to get his Bismarck defeated. You remember how he was always threatening him with the French. *You*, of course, are *on Wilhelm's side* too!

¶Lenin cited this letter in his controversy with Plekhanov in 1915 when he branded the social patriotism of the latter. In his article, *Russian Sudekums*, Lenin, in demonstrating the difference between dialectics and sophistry, writes: " In 1870

Engels wrote to Marx that Wilhelm Liebknecht was mistaken in making anti-Bismarckism his *sole* leading principle. Plekhanov was glad when he found that quotation : The same is true, he argues, in relation to our anti-tsarism. But try to replace sophistry (*i.e.*, the method of clinging to the outward similarity of cases without a connection between the events, by dialectics (*i.e.*, by the study of all the concrete circumstances of an event and of its development). The unification of Germany was necessary, and Marx recognised this both before and after 1848. As early as 1859 Engels directly summoned the German people to a war for unification. When revolutionary unity failed, Bismarck achieved unity in a counter-revolutionary, *junker* fashion. Anti-Bismarckism as the *sole* principle became absurd since the necessary unification was an accomplished fact." (Lenin, *Collected Works*, English edition, Vol. XVIII, p. 113.)

The Address of the General Council of the International on July 23, 1870, declared : " If the German working class allows the present war to lose its strictly defensive character and to degenerate into a war against the French people, then victory and defeat will be equally harmful. All the disasters which befell Germany after the so-called wars of liberation will be revived with intensified violence. . . . In the background of this suicidal struggle lowers the mysterious figure of Russia. It is an evil omen that the signal for the present war was given at the very moment when the Russian government had completed its strategical railways and had already concentrated troops in the direction of the Pruth. Whatever sympathy the Germans can rightfully claim in a defensive war against a Bonapartist attack, they would as quickly lose if they allowed the German government to summon the aid of the Cossacks or even so much as to accept it. Let them remember that for decades after its war of independence against the first Napoleon, Germany lay helpless at the feet of the tsar."

146. MARX TO ENGELS

Ramsgate, 17 August, 1870.

. . . In such an important matter—it is not a question of Wilhelm [Liebknecht] but of *instructions as to the line of the*

German workers—I did not want to act without first referring to you.

Wilhelm infers his agreement with me :

(1) From the Address of the International, which he has of course first translated into Wilhelm's own language.

(2) From the circumstance that I approved the declaration made by Bebel and himself in the Reichstag. That was a "moment" when *Prinzipienreiterei* [stickling for principle] was an act of courage, but from this it by no means follows that the moment is still continuing, much less that the attitude of the German proletariat to a war which has become national is expressed in Wilhelm's antipathy to Prussia. It would be just as if we, because at a suitable moment we had raised our voices against the "Bonapartist" liberation of Italy, were to wish to redress the relative independence which Italy received as a result of that war.

The lust for Alsace and Lorraine seems to predominate in two circles, the Prussian camarilla and the South German beer-patriots. It would be the greatest misfortune which could befall Europe and above all Germany. You will have seen that most of the Russian newspapers are already talking of the necessity of European diplomatic intervention in order to maintain the balance of power in Europe.

Kugelmann confuses a defensive war with defensive military operations. So if a fellow falls upon me in the street I may only parry his blow but not knock him down, because then I should turn into an *aggressor* ! The want of dialectic comes out in every word these people utter. . . .

With the death knell of the Second Empire, that will end as it began, by a parody, I hit off my Bonaparte after all ! Can one imagine a finer parody of Napoleon's 1814 campaign ? I believe we two are the only people who grasped the *whole mediocrity* of Boustrapa from the beginning, regarded him as a mere showman and never allowed ourselves to be misled by momentary successes.

¶This letter refers to the fundamental differences of opinion which had broken out among the German Social-Democrats* with regard to their attitude to the Franco-Prussian war. On July 24 The Party Committee, whose centre was in Brunswick (Wolfenbüttel), issued a manifesto calling upon the German workers to support Prussia so long as the war remained a defensive war on the part of Prussia. This attitude provoked a sharp criticism from Liebknecht, who, since he regarded the Franco-Prussian war as a dynastic war between Bonaparte and Prussia, stood for the complete neutrality of the Party. In consequence of the conflict which arose between the Committee and Liebknecht, who was editor of the *Volksstaat* (the Party organ), the Committee appealed to Marx for enlightenment. Marx sent the materials he had received from the Committee to Engels with the letter printed above.

The Address of the General Council of the First International (July 23, 1870) declares: "On the German side the war is a defensive war. But who brought Germany into a position where she was forced to defend herself? Who gave Louis Bonaparte the possibility of making war on Germany? Prussia! It was Bismarck who conspired with this same Louis Bonaparte in order to break down popular opposition at home and annex Germany to the Hohenzollern dynasty. If the battle of Sadowa [Königgratz] had been lost instead of won, French battalions would have overrun Germany as allies of Prussia."

The following declaration was made by Bebel and Liebknecht in the Reichstag when the voting of war credits took place: "The present war is a dynastic war, undertaken in the interests of the Bonaparte dynasty, just as the war of 1866 was undertaken in the interests of the Hohenzollern dynasty. We *cannot grant* the financial resources demanded by the Reichstag for the conduct of the war, because this would be a vote of confidence in the Prussian government, which prepared the present war by its course of action in 1866. It is equally impossible for us to *refuse* the money demanded, for this might be taken as a justification of the vicious and criminal policy of Bonaparte. As opponents on principle of every war, as *social-republicans and members of the International Workingmen's*

* The Social-Democratic Workers' Party had been founded in August, 1869. See Notes to Letters 159, 161. [*Ed. Eng. ed.*]

Association, which fights against all oppressors without distinction of nationality and strives to unite all the oppressed in one great bond of brotherhood, we can neither directly nor indirectly declare ourselves for the present war, and we therefore abstain from voting, with an expression of our confident hope that the nations of Europe, enlightened by the present disastrous events, will make every sacrifice to win their own rights of self-determination and to abolish the present *rule of the sword and the class as the cause of all the evils of state and society*."

147. MARX TO SORGE

London, 1 September, 1870.

The miserable behaviour of Paris during the war—still allowing itself to be ruled by the mamelukes of Louis Bonaparte and of the Spanish adventuress Eugenie after these appalling defeats—shows how greatly the French need a tragic lesson in order to regain their manhood.

What the Prussian fools do not see is that the present war is leading just as inevitably to a war between Germany and Russia as the war of 1866 led to the war between Prussia and France. That is the *best result* I expect from it for Germany. Typical " Prussianism " never has had and never can have any existence except in alliance with and subjection to Russia. And a war No. 2 of this kind will act as the midwife to the inevitable social revolution in Russia.

148. ENGELS TO MARX

Manchester, 4 September, 1870.

" *Was schert mich Weib, was schert mich Kind,*
" *Ich trage höhres Verlangen ;*
" *Lass sie betteln gehn, wenn sie hungrig sind—*
" *Mein Kaiser, mein Kaiser gefangen !* "*

World history is surely the greatest of poets, it has even succeeded in parodying Heine. My Emperor, my Emperor a

* " What care I for wife or child, I have higher yearnings ; if they are hungry let them go and beg—my Emperor, my Emperor is a captive ! "

captive ! And of the " stinking Prussians," what is more. And poor William* stands by and assures everybody for the hundredth time that he is really quite innocent of the whole business and that it is a pure act of God. William appears just like the schoolboy : "Who created the world ? " " Please teacher, I did—but indeed I will never do it again ! "

And then the miserable Jules Favre comes along and proposes that Palikao, Trochu and a few Arcadians shall form the government. There never was such a lousy crew. But all the same it is to be expected now that when this becomes known in Paris something or other will happen. I cannot believe that this douche of news, which must surely be known to-day or to-morrow, will produce no effect. Perhaps a government of the Left, which after some show of resistance will conclude peace.

The war is at an end. There is no more army in France. As soon as Bazaine has capitulated, which will no doubt happen this week, half the German army will move in front of Paris and the other half across the Loire to sweep the country of all armed detachments. . . .

The Alsace swindle—apart from its purely Teutonic features—is mainly of a strategical nature and aims at getting the line of the Vosges and German Lorraine as border-country. (Language frontier : If you draw a straight line from Donon or Schirmeck in the Vosges to one hour east of Longwy, where the Belgian—Luxemberg and French frontiers meet, it is almost exactly the language frontier ; and from Donon down the Vosges to the Swiss frontier.) Northwards from Donon the Vosges are not so high and steep as in the South. Only the asses of the *Staatsanzeiger* and Brass and Co.† could suppose that France will be " throttled " by the snipping off of this narrow strip with its one and a quarter million or so inhabitants. The screams of the philistines for " guarantees " are altogether absurd, but they tell because they suit the rubbish of the Court people. . . . In Saarbrücken the French did as much

* Kaiser Wilhelm I.

† *Staatsanzeiger*, the official organ of the Prussian Government. Brass & Co., publishers of the *Norddeutsche Allgemeine Zeitung*, Bismarckians.

damage as they could. Of course the bombardment only lasted a few hours and not as in Strasbourg day and night for weeks. . . .

The defence of Paris, if nothing extraordinary happens in the course of it, will be an entertaining episode. These perpetual little panics of the French—which all arise from fear of the moment when they will really have to learn the truth—give one a much better idea of the Reign of Terror. We think of this as the reign of people who inspire terror ; on the contrary, it is the reign of people who are themselves terrified. Terror consists mostly of useless cruelties perpetrated by frightened people in order to reassure themselves. I am convinced that the blame for the Reign of Terror in 1793 lies almost exclusively with the over-nervous bourgeois, demeaning himself as a patriot, the small petty bourgeois beside themselves with fright* and the mob of riff-raff who know how to profit from the terror. These are just the classes in the present minor terror too.†

¶The war, as continued after the Emperor Napoleon III had been taken prisoner, changed its character. In his article of September 17, 1870, for the *Pall Mall Gazette*,‡ Engels wrote :

" At the present day, when the immense military strength of Germany, organised upon the Prussian system, is carrying everything before it, people begin to ask themselves who is in future, and how, to fight the Prussians. And when a war in which Germany, at the beginning, merely defended her own against French *chauvinisme* appears to be changing gradually, but surely, into a war in the interests of a new German *chauvinisme*, it is worth while to consider that question. . . . If the war be continued to that bitter end for which the German Philistines are now shooting, the dismemberment of France, we may depend upon it that the French *will* adopt that principle. They have been so far a warlike but not a military nation. . . ."

After the defeat of Sedan the monarchy was overthrown in

* *Hosenscheissenden.*
† See Note on the Jacobins, Letter 206.
‡ See Note to Letter 144.

Paris. A Government of National Defence was organised whose task it was to conduct the struggle against the occupation of further parts of France. On November 11, 1870, Engels wrote in the *Pall Mall Gazette :*

" During the last six weeks the character of the war has undergone a remarkable change. The regular armies of France have disappeared ; the contest is carried on by levies whose very rawness renders them more or less irregular. Wherever they attempt to come out in masses in the open, they are easily defeated ; wherever they fight under shelter of barricaded and loop-holed villages and towns they find they can offer a serious resistance. They are encouraged in this kind of fighting, in night surprises, and other coups of petty warfare, by proclamations and orders of the Government, who also command the people of the district in which they operate to support them in every possible way."

Against this petty warfare the Germans had recourse to the most intense terror (burning down of villages, slaughter of men taken in arms, etc.) In this connection Engels recalls the methods of armed resistance employed by the masses in the German wars of liberation, the " old half-revolutionary *Landsturm Ordnung* " [law of 1818] which " is drawn up . . . in this spirit of uncompromising national resistance, to which all means are justifiable and the most effective are the best. But then all this was to be done by the Prussians against the French, and if the French act in the same way towards the Prussians that is quite a different thing. What was patriotism in the one case becomes brigandage and cowardly assassination in the other."

149. ENGELS TO MARX

Manchester, 12 September, 1870.

If anything at all could be done in Paris, a rising of the workers before peace is concluded should be prevented. Bismarck will soon be in a position to make peace, either by taking Paris or because the European situation obliges him to put an end to the war. However the peace may turn out, it must be concluded before the workers can do anything at all. If they were victorious now—in the service of national defence

—they would have to inherit the legacy of Bonaparte and of the present lousy Republic, and would be needlessly crushed by the German armies and thrown back another twenty years. They themselves can lose nothing by waiting. The possible changes of frontier are in any case only provisional and will be reversed again. To fight for the bourgeoisie against the Prussians would be madness. Whatever the government may be which concludes peace, the fact that it has done so will eventually make its existence impossible, and in internal conflicts there will not be much to fear from the army, returned home after imprisonment. After the peace all the chances will be more favourable to the workers than they ever were before. But will they not let themselves be carried away again under the pressure of the external attack, and proclaim the Social Republic on the eve of the storming of Paris? It would be appalling if as their last act of war the German armies had to fight out a battle with the Parisian workers at the barricades. It would throw us back fifty years and delay everything so much that everybody and everything would get into a false position—and the national hatred and the domination by phrases which would *then* arise among the French workers!

It is a damnably bad thing that in the present situation there are so few people in Paris who are ready to dare to see things as they *really are*. Where is one man there who even dares to *think* that France's active power of resistance is broken where this war is concerned, and that with it the prospects of repelling the invasion by a revolution fall to the ground too! Just because people do not *want* to hear the real truth I am afraid that things may still come to this. For the apathy of the workers *before* the fall of the Empire will no doubt have changed by now.

150. MARX TO BEESLY*

[London] 19 October, 1870.

As to Lyons, I have received letters not fit for publication. At first everything went well. Under the pressure of the

* Written in English. Published in the *Social-Democrat*, London 1903. (Vol. VII, p. 233).

"International" section, the Republic was proclaimed before Paris had taken that step. A revolutionary government was at once established—*La Commune*—composed partly of workmen belonging to the "International," partly of Radical middle class Republicans. The *octrois* [internal customs dues] were at once abolished, and rightly so. The Bonapartist and Clerical intriguers were intimidated. Energetic means were taken to arm the whole people. The middle class began if not really to sympathise with, at least to quietly undergo, the new order of things. The action of Lyons was at once felt at Marseilles and Toulouse, where the "International" sections are strong.

But the asses, Bakunin and Cluseret, arrived at Lyons and spoiled everything. Belonging both to the "International," they had, unfortunately, influence enough to mislead our friends. The Hotel de Ville was seized for a short time—a most foolish decree on the *abolition de l'état* [abolition of the state] and similar nonsense were issued. You understand that the very fact of a Russian—represented by the middle class papers as an agent of Bismarck—pretending to impose himself as the leader of a *Comité du Salut de la France* [Committee for the Safety of France] was quite sufficient to turn the balance of public opinion. As to *Cluseret*, he behaved both as a fool and a coward. These two men have left Lyons after their failure.

At Rouen, as in most industrial towns of France, the sections of the International, following the example of Lyons, have enforced the official admisison into the "committees of defence" of the working-class element.

Still, I must tell you that according to all information I receive from France, the middle class on the whole prefers Prussian conquest to the victory of a Republic with Socialist tendencies.

¶BEESLY, EDWARD SPENCER (1831-1915). Professor of history and political economy at University College, London. A follower of August Comte (see Note to Letter 88) and "as such obliged to justify all sorts of crochets, but otherwise a very capable and courageous man." (Marx to Kugelmann,

December 13, 1870.) Beesly was chairman at the meeting in St. Martin's Hall, London (September 28, 1864) at which the International Workingmen's Association was founded. [He was associated with the early days of the Workingmen's College, St. Pancras. In March 1867 he published an article in the *Fortnightly Review* supporting the activities of the "new model" trade unions; this was republished as a pamphlet, *The Amalgamated Society of Carpenters and Joiners*. (See also Letter 155.) *Ed. Eng. ed.*]

CLUSERET, GUSTAVE PAUL (1823-1900). French officer who took part in the suppression of the Paris rising of June 1848; during the period of the Empire he was in the ranks of the bourgeois opposition. Military delegate of the Commune. From 1871-80 in emigration; in 1889 he joined the Nationalists.

151. MARX TO W. LIEBKNECHT

[London] 6 April, 1871.

It appears that the defeat of the Parisians was their own fault, but a fault which really arose from their too great *honnêteté* [decency]. The Central Committee and later the Commune gave the mischievous abortion Thiers time to centralise hostile forces, in the first place by their folly in trying not to start *civil war*—as if Thiers had not started it by his attempt at the forcible disarming of Paris, as if the National Assembly, which was only summoned to decide the question of war or peace with the Prussians, had not immediately declared war on the *Republic!* (2) In order that the appearance of having usurped power should not attach to them they lost precious moments—(they should immediately have advanced on Versailles after the defeat (*Place Vendôme*) of the reaction in Paris)—by the election of the Commune, the organisation of which, etc., cost yet more time.

You must not believe a word of all the stuff you may see in the papers about the internal events in Paris. It is all lies and deception. Never has the vileness of bourgeois journalism displayed itself more brilliantly.

It is highly characteristic that the German Unity-Emperor

Unity-Empire and Unity-Parliament in Berlin appear not to *exist at all* for the outside world. Every breath of wind that stirs in Paris excites more interest.

You must carefully follow what is happening in the *Danubian Principalities.** If the revolution in France is temporarily defeated—the movement there can only be suppressed for a short time—there will be a new business of war for Europe beginning in the East, and Rumania will offer the orthodox tsar the first pretext for it. So look out on that side.

¶In 1911 Lenin wrote in an article in commemoration of the Paris Commune :

" Only the workers remained true to the Commune to the end. The bourgeois republicans and the petty bourgeoisie generally fell away from it. . . . Forsaken by its allies of the days before and supported by no one, the Commune was bound inevitably to suffer a defeat. The whole bourgeoisie of France, all the landlords, stockholders, factory owners, all the big and little thieves, all the exploiters, united together against it. . . . But the chief thing which the Commune lacked was time, the freedom to look around and apply itself to the realisation of its programme. Hardly had it set to work before the government seated in Versailles, with the support of the whole bourgeoisie, opened military operations against Paris. Thus the Commune had above all to think about self-defence. And right to the very end, which came on May 21-28, it had no time to think seriously of anything else." (Lenin. Collected Works, Russian Edition. Vol. XV, pp. 158-9.)

The CENTRAL COMMITTEE was the highest organ of the National Guard, which consisted chiefly of workers.

PLACE VENDÔME. On March 22 a " train of fine gentlemen " tried to take the headquarters of the National Guard behind the Place Vendôme by a surprise attack ; the attack was repulsed but the attackers were not pursued and were thus enabled to escape to Versailles.

* Moldavia and Wallachia, now part of Rumania.

152. MARX TO KUGELMANN

London, 12 April, 1871.

If you look at the last chapter of my *Eighteenth Brumaire* you will find that I say that the next attempt of the French revolution will be no longer, as before, to transfer the bureaucratic-military machine from one hand to another, but to smash it, and that is essential for every real people's revolution on the Continent. And this is what our heroic Party comrades in Paris are attempting. What elasticity, what historical initiative, what a capacity for sacrifice in these Parisians! After six months of hunger and ruin, caused rather by internal treachery than by the external enemy, they rise, beneath the Prussian bayonets, as if there had never been a war between France and Germany and the enemy were not at the gates of Paris. History has no like example of a like greatness. If they are defeated, only their "good nature" will be to blame. They should have marched at once on Versailles, after first Vincy and then the reactionary section of the Paris National Guard had themselves retreated. The right moment was missed because of conscientious scruples. They did not want to *start* the *civil war*, as if that mischievous *abortion* Thiers had not already started the civil war with his attempt to disarm Paris. Second mistake: The Central Committee surrendered its power too soon, to make way for the Commune. Again from a too "honourable" scrupulosity! However that may be, the present rising in Paris—even if it be crushed by the wolves, swine and vile curs of the old society—is the most glorious deed of our Party since the June insurrection in Paris. Compare these Parisians, storming Heaven, with the slaves to heaven of the German-Prussian, Holy Roman Empire, with its posthumous masquerades, reeking of the barracks, the Church, cabbage-Junkerdom and, above all, of the philistine.

A propos. In the *official publication* of the list of those receiving direct subsidies from Louis Bonaparte's treasury there is a note that Vogt received 40,000 francs in August 1859. I have informed Liebknecht of this fact for further use.*

* *Letters to Dr. Kugelmann* by Karl Marx (Martin Lawrence 1934), page 123.

¶In *State and Revolution* (Chap. III. 1) Lenin wrote :

" In these words, 'to smash the bureaucratic-military state machine' is contained, briefly formulated, the principal lesson of Marxism in regard to the question of the tasks of the proletariat in relation to the state. And it is just this lesson which has not only been completely forgotten but also directly distorted by the prevailing Kautskyan 'interpretation' of Marxism ! . . .

" It is interesting to note especially two places in Marx's argument above quoted. Firstly, he confines his conclusions to the Continent. This was comprehensible in 1871, when England was still the model of a purely capitalist country, but without militarism and, in a large measure, without a bureaucracy. Hence Marx excluded England, where a revolution, and even a people's revolution, at that time appeared and was possible *without* the preliminary condition of the destruction of the 'ready-made state machine.'

" Now, in 1917, in the epoch of the first great imperialist war, this limitation of Marx no longer holds. Both England and America, the greatest and last representatives—in the whole world—of Anglo-Saxon 'liberty' in the sense of the absence of militarism and bureaucracy, have slid completely into the general European, dirty, bloody swamp of bureaucratic military institutions which subordinate everything to themselves and which crush everything under them. Now, both in England and in America, the *smashing* and *destruction* of the 'ready-made state machinery' (brought there in 1914-17 to 'European' general imperialist perfection) is the 'preliminary condition' of any real people's revolution." (Lenin. Collected Works. Russian Edition, Vol. I, XXI, p. 345.)

153. MARX TO KUGELMANN

London, 17 April, 1871.

How you can compare petty-bourgeois demonstrations *à la* June 13, 1849, etc., with the present struggle in Paris is quite incomprehensible to me.

World history would indeed be very easy to make, if the struggle were taken up only on condition of infallibly favourable chances. It would on the other hand be of a very mystical nature, if "accidents" played no part. These accidents themselves fall naturally into the general course of development and are compensated for, again, by other accidents. But acceleration and delay are very dependent upon such "accidents" which include the "accident" of the character of those who at first stand at the head of the movement.

The decisive, unfavourable accident this time is by no means to be found in the general conditions of French society, but in the presence of the Prussians in France and their position right before Paris. Of this the Parisians were well aware. But of this the bourgeois *canaille* of Versailles were also well aware. Precisely for that reason they presented the Parisians with the alternative of taking up the fight or succumbing without a struggle. In the latter case the demoralisation of the working class would have been a far greater misfortune than the fall of any number of "leaders." The struggle of the working class against the capitalist class and its state has entered upon a new phase with the struggle in Paris. Whatever the immediate results may be, a new point of departure of world-historic importance has been gained.*

154. MARX TO FRANCKEL AND VARLIN†

[London] 13 May, 1871.

Would it not be useful to put the documents which compromise the Versailles *canaille* [blackguards] in a safe place? A precaution of this kind could not do any harm. I hear in a letter from Bordeaux that four Internationalists were elected at the last municipal elections. The ferment is beginning in the provinces. Unfortunately the action there is only local and "pacific." I have written several hundred letters on behalf of your cause to every corner of the world in which we have branches. The working class, for the rest, was on the side of the Commune from the beginning. Even the bourgeois papers in England have given up their first ferocity. I have succeeded in slipping some favourable paragraphs into them from time to time.

* *Letters to Dr. Kugelmann*, page 125.
† This letter was written in French.

The Commune seems to me to be wasting too much time in trivialities and personal quarrels. One can see that there are other influences besides that of the workers. None of this would matter if you had time to make up for the time lost.

It is absolutely necessary that whatever you want to do outside Paris, in England or elsewhere, you should do quickly. The Prussians will not hand over the forts to the Versailles government, but after the final conclusion of peace (May 26) will allow it to invest Paris with its *gendarmes*. Since Thiers and Co. had, as you know, stipulated for a large commission for themselves in the treaty they concluded by Pouyer Quertier, they refused to accept the help from the German bankers which Bismarck offered them. Had they accepted it they would have lost their commission. The preliminary condition for the realisation of *their* treaty being the subjugation of Paris, they have asked Bismarck to postpone their payment of the first instalment until after the occupation of Paris. Bismarck has accepted this condition. Prussia, being herself in very urgent need of this money, will therefore give the Versailles government every possible facility for hastening the occupation of Paris. So take care!

¶FRANCKEL, LEO (1844-96). Hungarian Socialist, a worker in the jewellery trade. Was living in France at the end of the 'sixties and was one of the founders of the Lyons section of the First International and one of the leaders of the Paris Commune, in which he was made Minister of Labour. In this capacity Franckel appealed to Marx for advice in framing the laws for the protection of labour. After the fall of the Commune Franckel lived in London, where he was Corresponding Secretary for Hungary on the General Council; later he was active in the German and Hungarian workers' movement; after 1889 he returned to France; he was one of the founders of the Hungarian Social-Democratic Party.

VARLIN, LOUIS EUGENE (1839-71). French bookbinder, founder of the Co-operative Society of Bookbinders; one of the most active adherents of the First International; he was a member of the Paris Commune and was killed in the street fighting.

POUYER-QUERTIER, Augustin Thomas (1820-91). French statesman, owner of a cotton mill in Rouen. With Jules Favre he took part as an emissary in the Paris peace negotiations: "a passionate and even servile supporter of the Second Empire, he had never discovered anything wrong with it except its conclusion of the Trade Treaty with England which injured his own interests as a manufacturer...." A "man who regarded the counter-revolution as a means of forcing down wages in Rouen, and the cession of the French provinces as a means of forcing up the price of his goods in France." (Marx.)

155. MARX TO BEESLY*

London, 12 June, 1871.

Lafargue, his family and my daughter are in the Pyrenees, but on the French side of the Spanish frontier. As Lafargue was born in Cuba he was able to get a Spanish passport. I wish, however, that he would definitely settle on the Spanish side, as he played a leading rôle in Bordeaux.

Despite my admiration for your article in the *Beehive*, I am almost sorry to see your name in that paper. (And, by the way, you will allow me to observe that as a Party man I have a thoroughly hostile attitude towards Comte's philosophy, while as a scientific man I have a very poor opinion of it, but I regard you as the only Comtist, either in England or France, who deals with historical turning-points (crises) not as a sectarian but as an historian in the best sense of the word.) The *Beehive* calls itself a workers' paper but it is really the organ of the renegades, sold to Sam Morley and Co.† During the last Franco-Prussian war the General Council of the International was obliged to sever all connection with this paper

* Beesly (see Letter 150) gave this letter for publication in the German *Vorwärts*, (March 31, 1909) and it has here been re-translated from the German translation as the English original has not been traced. [*Ed. Eng. ed.*]

† For the *Beehive*, etc., see Note to Letter 71. Samuel Morley (1809-86) a woollen manufacturer (J. and R. Morley) was one of the wealthiest Englishmen of his time and the employer of thousands of workers. Supporter of Cobden and Bright and later of Gladstone. M.P. 1868-85. Promoted formation of Agricultural Labourers' Union. Famous as a "philanthropist." [*Ed. Eng. ed.*]

and publicly to declare that it was a sham workers' paper. The big London papers, however, with the exception of the London local paper, *The Eastern Post*, refused to print this declaration. In such circumstances your co-operation with the *Beehive* is a further sacrifice you are making to the good cause.

A woman friend of mine will be going to Paris in three or four days. I am giving her the proper passes for some members of the Commune, who are still living hidden in Paris. If you or one of your friends have any commissions there please write to me.

What comforts me is the nonsense which the *Petite Presse* publishes every day about my writings and my relations to the Commune ; this is sent me each day from Paris. It shows that the Versailles police is very hard put to it to get hold of genuine documents. My relations with the Commune were maintained through a German merchant who travels between Paris and London all the year round. Everything was settled verbally with the exception of two matters :

First, through the same intermediary, I sent the members of the Commune a letter in answer to a question from them as to how they could handle certain securities on the London Exchange.

Second, on May 11, ten days before the catastrophe, I sent them by the same method all the details of the secret agreement come to between Bismarck and Favre in Frankfort.

I had this information from Bismarck's right hand*—a man who had formerly (from 1848-53) belonged to the secret society of which I was the leader. This man knows that I have still got all the reports which he sent me from and about Germany. He is dependent on my discretion. Hence his continual efforts to prove his good intentions towards me. It was the same man who gave me the warning I told you about that Bismarck had decided to have me arrested if I visited Dr. Kugelmann in Hanover again this year.

If only the Commune had listened to my warnings ! I advised its members to fortify the northern side of the heights

* Lothar Bücher.

of Montmartre, the Prussian side, and they still had time to do this ; I told them beforehand that they would otherwise be caught in a trap ; I denounced Pyat, Grousset and Vesinier to them ; I demanded that they should at once send to London all the documents compromising the members of the National Defence, so that by this means the savagery of the enemies of the Commune could to some extent be held in check—thus the plan of the Versailles people would have been brought to nothing.

If these documents had been discovered by the Versailles people they would not have published forged ones.

The address of the International* will not be published before Wednesday. I will then at once send you a copy. Material for four to five sheets has been compressed into two. Hence arose numerous corrections, revisions and misprints. Hence also the delay.

156. MARX TO BOLTE†

London, 23 November, 1871.

The *International* was founded in order to replace the Socialist or semi-Socialist sects by a real organisation of the working class for struggle. The original Statutes and the Inaugural Address show this at the first glance. On the other hand the Internationalists could not have maintained themselves if the course of history had not already smashed up the sectarian system. The development of the system of Socialist sects and that of the real workers' movement always stand in inverse ratio to each other. So long as the sects are (historically) justified, the working class is not yet ripe for an independent historic movement. As soon as it has attained this maturity all sects are essentially reactionary. Nevertheless what history has shown everywhere was repeated within the International. The antiquated makes an attempt to re-establish and maintain itself within the newly achieved form.

* *The Civil War in France in* 1871.

† Bolte (U.S.A.), Member of the former Central Committee and at this time member of the Provisional Federal Council of the International in New York. [*Ed. Eng. ed.*]

And the history of the International was a *continual struggle on the part of the General Council* against the sects and amateur experiments which attempted to assert themselves within the International itself against the genuine movement of the working class. This struggle was conducted at the *Congresses*, but far more in the private dealings of the General Council with the individual sections.

In Paris, as the Proudhonists (Mutualists) were co-founders of the Association, they naturally had the reins in their hands there for the first years. Later, of course, collectivist, positivist, etc., groups were formed in opposition to them.

In Germany—the Lassalle clique. I myself went on corresponding for two years with the notorious Schweitzer and proved irrefutably to him that Lassalle's organisation is nothing but a sectarian organisation and as such hostile to the organisation of the *genuine* workers' movement striven for by the International. He had his " reasons " for not understanding this.

At the end of 1868 the Russian, Bakunin,* entered the *International* with the aim of forming inside it *a second International* called the " *Alliance of Social-Democracy*," *with himself as leader.* He—a man devoid of theoretical knowledge—put forward the pretension that this separate body was to represent the *scientific* propaganda of the International, which was to be made the special function of this second *International within the International.*

His programme was a superficially scraped together hash of Right and Left—EQUALITY of CLASSES (!), *abolition of the right of inheritance as the starting point* of the social movement (St. Simonistic nonsense), *atheism* as a *dogma* to be dictated to the members, etc., and as the main dogma (*Proudhonist*), *abstention from the political movement.*

This infant's spelling-book found favour (and still has a certain hold) in Italy and Spain, where the real conditions of the workers' movement are as yet little developed, and among a few vain, ambitious and empty doctrinaires in French Switzerland and Belgium.

For Mr. Bakunin the theory (the assembled rubbish he has

* See Note, page 165 and Letter 157.

scraped together from Proudhon, St. Simon, etc.) is a secondary affair—merely a means to his personal self-assertion. If he is a nonentity as a theoretician he is in his element as an intriguer.

For years the General Council had to fight against this conspiracy (which was supported up to a certain point by the French Proudhonists, especially in the *south of France*). At last, by means of Conference resolutions I (2) and (3), IX, XVI, and XVII*, it delivered its long prepared blow.

Obviously the General Council does not support in America what it combats in Europe. Resolutions I (2) and (3) and IX now give the New York committee legal weapons with which to put an end to all sectarian formations and amateur groups and if necessary to expel them.

The New York Committee will do well to express its full agreement with the decisions of the Conference in an *official communication to the General Council.*

Bakunin, personally threatened in addition by Resolution XIV (publication in *Égalité* of the Netchaev trial) which will bring to light his infamous doings in Russia, is making every possible effort to get a protest started against the Conference among the remnants of his followers.

For this purpose he has got into contact with the demoralised section of the French political refugees in Geneva and London (a numerically weak section, anyway). The slogan given out is that the Geneva Council is dominated by *Pan-Germanism* (especially Bismarckism). This refers to the *unpardonable* fact that *I* am by birth a German and do actually exercise a decisive intellectual influence on the German Council. (*N.B.* The *German* element on the Council is two-thirds weaker *numerically* than either the *English* or the *French.* The crime therefore consists in the fact that the English and French elements are

* Resolutions I (2) and (3) of the London Conference forbade all sectarian names for sections, branches, etc., and laid down that they should be exclusively designated as branches or sections of the International Workingmen's Association with the addition of the name of their locality ; Resolution IX stressed the necessity of the political activity of the working class and declared that their economic movement cannot be separated from their political activity. Resolution XVI declared the question of the Bakunist *Alliance of Socialist-Democracy* disposed of since its Secretary, Joukovsky, had declared the Alliance dissolved ; Resolution XVII permitted the Jura sections in Switzerland to adopt the name of *Jurassian Federation* and censured its organ, *Progress.*

dominated by the German element where *theory* is concerned (!) and find this domination, *i.e.*, German science, very useful and indeed indispensable.)

In Geneva, under the patronage of the bourgeois Madame Andrée Léo (who at the Lausanne Congress was shameless enough to denounce Ferré to his executioners in Versailles), they have published a paper, *La Révolution Sociale*, which conducts arguments against us in almost literally the same words as the *Journal de Genève*, the most reactionary paper in Europe.

In London they attempted to establish a French section, of whose activities you will find an example in No. 42 of *Qui Vive?* which I enclose. (Also the number which contains the letter from our French Secretary, Seraillier). This section, consisting of twenty people (including a lot of spies), has not been recognised by the General Council, but another much more numerous section has been.

Actually, despite the intrigues of this bunch of scoundrels, we are carrying on great propaganda in France—and in Russia, where they know what value to place on Bakunin and where my book on capital is just being published in Russian. . . .

N.B. as to political movement: The political movement of the working class has as its object, of course, the conquest of political power for the working class, and for this it is naturally necessary that a previous organisation of the working class, itself arising from their economic struggles, should have been developed up to a certain point.

On the other hand, however, every movement in which the working class comes out *as a class* against the ruling classes and attempts to force them by pressure from without is a political movement. For instance, the attempt in a particular factory or even a particular industry to force a shorter working day out of the capitalists by strikes, etc., is a purely economic movement. On the other hand the movement to force an eight-hour day, etc., *law* is a *political* movement. And in this way, out of the separate economic movements of the workers there grows up everywhere a *political* movement, that is to say a movement of the *class*, with the object of achieving its interests in a general form, in a form possessing a general social force of compulsion. If these movements presuppose a certain degree of previous organisation, they are themselves equally a means of the development of this organisation.

Where the working class is not yet far enough advanced in its organisation to undertake a decisive campaign against the collective power, *i.e.*, the political power of the ruling classes, it must at any rate be trained for this by continual agitation against and a hostile attitude towards the policy of the ruling classes. Otherwise it will remain a plaything in their hands, as the September revolution in France showed, and as is also proved up to a certain point by the game Messrs. Gladstone & Co. are bringing off in England even up to the present time.

157. ENGELS TO THEODOR CUNO

24 January, 1872.

Bakunin, who up till 1868 had intrigued against the International, joined it after he had made a fiasco at the Berne Peace Conference* and at once began to conspire *within it* against the General Council. Bakunin has a peculiar theory of his own, a medley of Proudhonism and communism, the chief point of which is in the first place that he does not regard capital, and therefore the class contradiction between capitalists and wage earners which has arisen through social development, as the main evil to be abolished—instead he regards the *state* as the main evil. While the great mass of the Social-Democratic workers hold our view that state power is nothing more than the organisation with which the ruling classes, landlords and capitalists have provided themselves in order to protect their social prerogatives, Bakunin maintains that it is the *state* which has created capital, that the capitalist has his capital *only by favour of the state*. As, therefore, the state is the chief evil, it is above all the state which must be done away with and then capitalism will go to hell of itself. We, on the contrary, say: do away with capital, the appropriation of the whole means of production in the hands of the few, and the

* Berne Conference of the League of Peace and Freedom.

state will fall away of itself. The difference is an essential one. Without a previous social revolution the abolition of the state is nonsense; the abolition of capital *is* in itself the social revolution and involves a change in the whole method of production. Further, however, as for Bakunin the state is the main evil, nothing must be done which can maintain the existence of any state, whether it be a republic, a monarchy or whatever it may be. Hence therefore *complete abstention from all politics.* To perpetrate a political action, and especially to take part in an election, would be a betrayal of principle. The thing to do is to conduct propaganda, abuse the state, organise, and when *all* the workers are won over, *i.e.*, the majority, depose the authorities, abolish the state and replace it by the organisation of the International. This great act, with which the millennium begins, is called *social liquidation.*

All this sounds extremely radical, and is so simple that it can be learnt by heart in five minutes; that is why this theory of Bakunin's has also speedily found favour in Spain and Italy, among young lawyers, doctors and other doctrinaires.

But the mass of the workers will never allow themselves to be persuaded that the public affairs of their country are not also their own affairs; they are by nature *political* and whoever tries to make out to them that they should leave politics alone will in the end get left in the lurch. To preach that the workers should in all circumstances abstain from politics is to drive them into the arms of the priests or the bourgeois republicans.

Now as, according to Bakunin, the International is not to be formed for political struggle but in order that it may at once replace the old state organisation as soon as social liquidation takes place, it follows that it must come as near as possible to the Bakunist ideal of the society of the future. In this society there will above all be no *authority*, for authority = state = an absolute evil. (How these people propose to run a factory, work a railway or steer a ship without having in the last resort one deciding will, without a unified direction, they do not indeed tell us.) The authority of the majority over the minority also ceases. Every individual and every community is autonomous, but as to how a society, even of only two people, is possible unless each gives up some of his autonomy, Bakunin again remains silent. The International, then, must also be reorganised according to this model. Every section, and in every section every individual, is autonomous. To hell with the *Basle resolutions*, which bestowed upon the General Council a pernicious authority demoralising even to itself!

Even if this authority is *voluntarily* bestowed it must cease simply *because* it is authority.

Here you have in brief the main points of the swindle.

¶Engels pointed out in a letter to Bernstein (January 28, 1884) that he and Marx "prophesied the destruction of the state before the anarchists even existed," and gives two quotations as evidence. One (from *The Poverty of Philosophy* (final section):

"As it develops, the working class will substitute for the old civil society an association which will exclude classes and their antagonism *and there will be no more political power*—properly *so-called*—since political power is an exact official summary of the antagonisms in civil society."

The other quotation is from *The Communist Manifesto*:

"When, in the course of development class distinctions have disappeared . . . the *public power will lose its political character.* Political power, properly so-called, is merely the organised force of one class for oppressing another."* [For anarchism see also Letter 186.]

CUNO, THEODOR (born 1847). German Social-Democrat. Engineer. Expelled from the country at the beginning of the 'seventies, took part in the organisation of a section of the International in Milan and stood for the line of the General Council. At the Hague Congress (1872) he was chairman of the commission which decided on the expulsion of Bakunin from the First International. Cuno later emigrated to America, where he collaborated in the *New York People's Paper*.

* English translation revised by Engels, 1888.

158. ENGELS TO MARX

[London], 30 May, 1873.

In bed this morning the following dialectical ideas on the natural sciences came into my head :

The subject of natural science—moving matter, bodies. Bodies cannot be separated from motion, their forms and kinds can only be known through motion, of bodies apart from motion, apart from any relation to other bodies, nothing can be asserted. Only in motion does a body reveal what it is. Natural science therefore knows bodies by considering them in their relation to one another, in motion. The knowledge of the different forms of motion is the knowledge of bodies. The investigation of these different forms of motion is therefore the chief subject of natural science.*

(1) The simplest form of motion is change of *place* (in time—to please old Hegel)—*mechanical* motion.

(a) There is no such thing as the movement of a *single* body, but relatively speaking, *falling* can be treated as such. Motion towards a centre common to many bodies. But as soon as an individual body moves in a direction *other* than towards the centre, while it is still subject to the laws of falling, these undergo modification†

(b) in the laws of orbits and lead directly to the reciprocal motion of several bodies—planetary etc., motion, astronomy, equilibrium—a modification temporarily or apparently in the motion itself. But the *real* result of this kind of motion is always ultimately—the *contact* of the moving bodies, they fall into one another.

(c) Mechanics of contact—bodies in contact, ordinary mechanics, levers, inclined planes, etc. *But the effects of contact are not exhausted by these.* Contact is directly manifested in two forms : friction and impact. Both have the property that at given degrees of intensity and under certain conditions they produce new, no longer merely mechanical effects : *heat, light, electricity, magnetism.*

* In the margin beside this paragraph Carl Schorlemmer wrote : " Very good ; my own view. C.S."

† Marginal note by Carl Schorlemmer : " Quite true."

(2) *Physics proper*, the science of these forms of movement, after investigation of each individuality, establishes the fact that under certain conditions they *pass into one another*, and ultimately discovers that all of them—at a given degree of intensity which varies according to the different bodies set in motion—produce effects which transcend physics, changes in the internal structure of bodies—*chemical* effects.

(3) *Chemistry.* For the investigation of the previous forms of movement it was more or less indifferent whether this was applied to animate or inanimate bodies. The inanimate bodies even displayed the phenomena in their greatest *purity*. Chemistry, on the other hand, can only distinguish the chemical nature of the most important bodies in substances which have arisen out of the process of life itself; its chief task becomes more and more to prepare these substances artificially. It forms the transition to the organic sciences, but the dialectical transition can only be accomplished when chemistry has either made the real transition or is on the point of doing so.*

(4) *Organism.* Here I will not embark on any dialectic for the time being.†

You being seated there at the centre of the natural sciences will be in the best position to judge if there is anything in it.

¶In a letter to Bernstein (February 27—March 1, 1883) Engels wrote: " After Marx, Schorlemmer is undoubtedly the most eminent man in the European Socialist Party. When I got to know him twenty years ago he was already a Communist. At that time a poor private assistant to English Professors, he is now a member of the Royal Society (the Academy of Science here) and the first authority in the world on his own speciality, the chemistry of the simpler hydro-carbons (paraffin and its derivatives). The great textbook of chemistry which he published jointly with Roscoe but wrote almost entirely himself (as all chemists know) now takes first place in England and Germany. And he has won this position abroad solely by real

* Marginal note by Carl Schorlemmer: " That's the point."
† Marginal note by Carl Schorlemmer: " Neither will I."

scientific work and without making a single concession to humbug, in a struggle with people who exploited him as long as it was possible to do so. With all this he makes no bones about coming out as a Socialist anywhere, reads out points from the *Social-Democrat* at the lecturers' dining-table, etc.,* but demands, and rightly so, that he should not be dragged into public, as Viereck has done, in this, that or the other way without his own consent. . . ."

159. ENGELS TO BEBEL

London, 20 June, 1873.

With regard to the attitude of the Party towards Lassalleanism, you can of course judge what tactics should be adopted better than we, especially in particular cases. But there is also this to be considered. When, as in your case, one is to a certain extent in the position of a competitor to the *Allgemeine Deutsche Arbeiter Verein* (General Association of German Workers)† it is easy to pay too much attention to one's rival and to get into the habit of always thinking about him first. But both the General Association of German Workers and the Social-Democratic Workers' Party together still only form a very small minority of the German working class. Our view, which we have found confirmed by long practice, is that the correct tactics in propaganda is not to draw away a few individuals and members here and there from one's opponent, but to work on the great mass which still remains apathetic. The primitive force of a single individual whom we have ourselves attracted from the crude mass is worth more than ten Lassallean renegades, who always bring the seeds of their false tendencies into the Party with them. And if one could only get the masses without their *local leaders* it would still be all right. But one always has to take a whole crowd of these leaders into the bargain, and they are bound by their previous public utterances, if not by their previous views, and have above all things to

* At Owen's College, Manchester, where, in the following year, 1874, he became Professor of Organic Chemistry, the chair being specially created for him. [*Ed. Eng. ed.*]

† See Note on Lassalle, Letter 29 and Letters 113, 161.

prove that they have not deserted their principles but that on the contrary the Social-Democratic Workers' Party preaches *true* Lassalleanism. This was the unfortunate thing at Eisenach, not to be avoided at that time, perhaps, but there is no doubt at all that these elements have done harm to the Party and I am not sure that the Party would not have been at least as strong to-day without that addition. In any case, however, I should regard it as a misfortune if these elements were reinforced.

One must not allow oneself to be misled by the cry for "unity." Those who have this word most often on their lips are those who sow the most dissension, just as at present the Jura Bakuninists in Switzerland, who have provoked all the splits, scream for nothing so much as for unity. These unity fanatics are either the people of limited intelligence who want to stir everything up together into one nondescript brew, which, the moment it is left to settle, throws up the differences again in much more acute opposition because they are now all together in one pot (you have a fine example of this in Germany with the people who preach the reconciliation of the workers and the petty bourgeoisie)—or else they are people who consciously or unconsciously (like Mühlberger, for instance) want to adulterate the movement. For this reason the greatest sectarians and the biggest brawlers and rogues are at certain moments the loudest shouters for unity. Nobody in our lifetime has given us more trouble and been more treacherous than the unity shouters.

Naturally every party leadership wants to see successes and this is quite good too. But there are circumstances in which one must have the courage to sacrifice *momentary* success for more important things. Especially a party like ours, whose ultimate success is so absolutely certain, and which has developed so enormously in our own lifetime and under our own eyes, momentary success is by no means always and absolutely necessary. Take the International, for instance. After the Commune it had its colossal success. The bourgeoisie, struck all of a heap, ascribed omnipotence to it. The great mass of the membership believed things would stay like that for all eternity. We knew very well that the bubble *must* burst. All the riff-raff attached themselves to it. The sectarians within it began to flourish, and misused the International in the hope that the most stupid and mean actions would be permitted them. We did not allow that. Well knowing that the bubble must burst some time all the same, our concern was not to delay the catastrophe but to take care that the International emerged from it pure and unadulterated. The bubble burst at the Hague, and you know that the majority of Congress members went home sick with disappointment. And yet nearly all these disappointed people, who imagined they would find the ideal of universal brotherhood and reconciliation in the International, had far more bitter quarrels at home than those which broke out at the Hague! Now the sectarian quarrel-mongers are preaching conciliation and decrying us as the intolerant and the dictators. And if we had come out in a conciliatory way at the Hague, if we had hushed up the breaking out of the split—what would have been the result? The sectarians, especially the Bakuninists, would have got another year in which to perpetrate, in the name of the International, much greater stupidities and infamies even; the workers of the most developed countries would have turned away in disgust; the bubble would not have burst but, pierced by pinpricks, would have slowly collapsed, and the next Congress, which would have been bound to bring the crisis anyhow, would have turned into the lowest kind of personal row, because *principles* had already been sacrificed at the Hague. Then the International would indeed have gone to pieces—gone to pieces through "unity"! Instead of this we have now got rid of the rotten elements with honour to ourselves—the members of the Commune who were present at the last decisive session say that no session of the Commune left such a terrible impression upon them as this session of the tribunal which passed judgment on the traitors to the European proletariat—we have left them to expend all their forces in lying, slander and intrigue for ten months—and where are they? They, the alleged representatives of the great majority of the International, now announce that they do not dare to come to the next Congress (more details in an article which is being sent off for the *Volksstaat* with this letter). And if we had to do it again we should not, taking it all together, act any differently—tactical mistakes are of course always committed.

In any case I think the efficient elements among the Lassalleans will fall to you of themselves in course of time and that it would therefore be unwise to break off the fruit before it is ripe, as the unity people want.

For the rest, old Hegel has already said: A party proves itself a victorious party by the fact that it *splits* and can stand the split. The movement of the proletariat necessarily passes through different stages of development; at every stage one section of people lags behind and does not join in the further advance; and this alone explains why it is that actually the "solidarity of the proletariat" is everywhere realised in different party groupings which carry on life and death feuds with one another, as the christian sects in the Roman Empire did amidst the worst persecutions.*

¶In the article referred to, which appeared in No. 53 of the *Volkstaat* (July 2, 1873) under the title "From the International," Engels wrote: "It is well known that the Jura Federation was always the soul of all the separatism in the International. At the Hague Congress† their delegates had already declared that they represented the real majority of the International and would prove this at the next Congress. . . . On April 27 and 28 the Jura Federation held its Congress in Neuchâtel. From the proceedings it is evident that the Federation includes *eleven* Swiss sections, of which *nine* were represented. As to what the position of these eleven sections is, how strong they are, etc., the Committee's report never says a word; on the other hand it announces that the whole International, so to speak, has joined in their separatism. Consequently this enormous majority will appear at the next General Congress and overthrow the Hague decisions? No, far from it. On the contrary, the same Committee proposes what is of course

* Compare Note, p. 382, and Letter 178.
† For the Hague Congress, see pp. 164. 330-31.

immediately agreed to by these 'autonomous' delegates, namely: in order that the new Congress shall not again fall into the dangerous aberrations of the Hague Congress, the separatist federations shall recognise a Congress of their own which might perhaps be summoned by the New York General Council. . . . The decision of the Jura Federation, therefore, means no more than a fresh retreat concealed behind high-sounding phrases."

EISENACH. In August 1869, as a counterpoise to the Lassallean *General Association of German Workers*, the *German Social-Democratic Workers' Party*, which was led by Bebel and Liebknecht, was founded at Eisenach. See also Note on *Bebel* below.

JURA BAKUNINISTS. Followers of Bakunin in the region of the Jura Mountains in Switzerland; Bakunin's followers were very numerous here among the handicraftsmen.

MÜHLBERGER, ARTHUR. A Würtemburg doctor, follower of Proudhon; the anonymous author of a series of articles on the housing question (1872) to which Engels replied in his book, *The Housing Question*.

BEBEL, AUGUST (1840-1913). One of the founders and chief leaders of German Social-Democracy and of the Second International. By trade a turner. From 1860 onwards Bebel took an active part in the movement of the workers' educational associations founded by the Liberals; in 1866, he, with Wilhelm Liebknecht, under whose influence he began to approach Marxism, founded the Saxon People's Party, which united petty bourgeoisie and workers on the basis of an anti-Prussian democratic programme. Bebel was the leader of the proletarian wing of this party, which formed the German Social-Democratic Workers' Party at Eisenach in 1869. He fought for the revolutionary way of unification for Germany and was an Internationalist during the Franco-Prussian war. Under the influence and guidance of Marx and Engels he took a proletarian-revolutionary line as a Party leader and conducted a fight on two fronts—against the "Right" and the "Left" opportunists and at times against Liebknecht's conciliatory attitude as well. For the "period in which the proletariat prepares and assembles its forces," he was "the model of a workers' leader" (Lenin.) But even in this period Bebel could never finally free himself of the vulgar economic prejudices regarding the state (see Lenin's *State and Revolution*) and permitted opportunist and conciliatory vacillations which Marx and Engels repeatedly criticised. (*E.g.*, 1877 : mistakes in the Dühring question ; 1878 : confusion and liquidatory tendencies when the Party became illegal ; 1891 : vacillations on the question of the fight with the remnants of Lassalleanism and with opportunism, etc.).

Bebel had to serve repeated sentences of imprisonment (1870-71 on account of his attitude on the war ; 1873-75 for "high treason," 1878 for insulting Bismarck, etc.). He was the author of a series of agitational books and pamphlets, of which the most important are : *Our Aims* (1870), *The Peasant War in Germany* (1876), *Woman and Socialism* (1879). From 1867 onwards (with one interval 1881-83) Bebel was a member of the Reichstag. After the Party again became legal (1890) Bebel was continuously the chairman of the Party Executive. After Engels' death he gradually began to deviate to the Right and became the leader of the Centrist tendency in the Party and the Second International.

160. ENGELS TO SORGE

London, 12 (and 17) September, 1874.

With your resignation the *old* International is entirely wound up and at an end.* And that is well. It belonged to the period of the Second Empire, during which the oppression reigning throughout Europe entailed unity and abstention from all internal polemics upon the workers' movement, then just reawakening. It was the moment when the common, cosmopolitan interests of the proletariat could be put in the foreground : Germany, Spain, Italy, Denmark had only just come into the movement or were just coming into it. Actually in 1864 the theoretical character of the movement was still very confused everywhere in Europe, that is, among the masses. German Communism did not yet exist as a workers' party, Proudhonism was too weak to be able to insist on its particular fads, Bakunin's new trash had not so much as come into being in his own head, even the leaders of the English trade unions

* For the International see Letters 71, 74, 83, 88, 100, 133, 142, 156, 157, 159.

thought the programme laid down in the Preamble to the Statutes gave them a basis for entering the movement. The first great success was bound to explode this naive conjunction of all fractions. This success was the Commune, which was without any doubt the child of the International intellectually, although the International did not lift a finger to produce it, and for which the International—thus far with full justification—was held responsible.

When, thanks to the Commune, the International had become a moral force in Europe, the row at once began. Every fraction wanted to exploit the success for itself. The inevitable collapse arrived. Jealousy of the growing power of the only people who were really ready to work further along the lines of the old comprehensive programme—the German Communists—drove the Belgian Proudhonists into the arms of the Bakuninist adventurers. The Hague Congress was really the end—and for both parties. The only country where something could still be accomplished in the name of the old International was America, and by a happy instinct the executive was transferred there. Now its prestige is exhausted there too, and any further effort to galvanise it into new life would be folly and waste of energy. For ten years the International dominated one side of European history—the side on which the future lies—and can look back upon its work with pride. But in its old form it has outlived itself. In order to produce a new International after the fashion of the old one—an alliance of all the proletarian parties in every country—a general suppression of the workers' movement like that which predominated from 1849-64 would be necessary. But for this the proletarian world has become too big, too extensive. I think that the next International—after Marx's writings have had some years of influence—will be directly Communist and will openly proclaim our principles. . . .

In Germany things are going splendidly in spite of all the persecution, and partly just *because* of the persecution. The Lassalleans have been so much discredited by their representatives in the Reichstag that the Government has had to start persecuting them in order to give this movement once more the appearance of being intended seriously. For the rest, since the elections the Lassalleans have found it necessary to come out in the wake of our people. It is a real piece of luck that Hasselmann and Hasenclever were elected to the Reichstag. They are discrediting themselves there visibly ; they will either have to go with our people or else perpetrate tomfooleries on their own. Both will ruin them.

¶Lenin writes in his article *Karl Marx :*

" After the fall of the Paris Commune (1871)—which Marx analysed as a man of *action*, a revolutionary, with so much penetration, pertinence and brilliance in his work *The Civil War in France, 1871*—and after the International had been split by the Bakuninists, it became impossible for that organisation to keep its headquarters in Europe. After the Hague Congress of the International (1872) Marx carried through the transfer of the General Council of the International to New York. The First International had accomplished its historic rôle, giving way to an epoch of an infinitely accelerated growth of the labour movement in all the countries of the world, precisely the epoch when this movement grew in *breadth* and *scope*, when *mass* socialist labour parties were created on the basis of individual national states." (Lenin, *Collected Works*, English edition, Vol. XVIII, p. 19.)

SORGE, FRIEDRICH ALBERT (1826-1906). German Communist. He took part in the Baden rising of 1849. In the U.S.A., where he lived as an emigrant, he played a prominent part in the German and North American labour movement. Sorge, who was in constant correspondence with Marx and Engels, fought for the line of the General Council in the American sections of the First International. After the transference of the General Council to New York (1872) Sorge became General Secretary of the International. He resigned this office in 1874.

HASSELMANN, WILHELM (born 1844). Lassallean : One of the representatives of the *General Association of German Workers* in the negotiations for unity—co-reporter on the programme question at the Unity Congress of the Party at Gotha (1875). Member of the Reichstag 1874-76 and 1878-80. After resigning from the editorial board of *Vorwärts* he founded an organ of his own in Elberfeld—*Die Rote Fahne*—in which he attacked the Party leadership from the "Left." He gradually went over to open anarchism and, together with Most, was therefore expelled from the Party at the Wyden Congress (1880). He then emigrated to America.

HASENCLEVER, WILHELM (1837-89). Lassallean. President of General Association of German Workers after Schweitzer's resignation. After the union between the Association and the Eisenachers in Gotha he was a member of the Executive of the united Social-Democratic Party. Editor of the Hamburg Party paper and, in 1876-78, with Liebknecht, of *Vorwärts*. Member of the fraction in the Reichstag 1874-87.

161. ENGELS TO BEBEL

London, 18—28 March, 1875.

You ask me what we think of the unification business.* Unfortunately our fate has been the same as yours. Neither Liebknecht nor anyone else has sent us any information and we too, therefore, only know what is in the papers, and there was nothing in them until the draft programme appeared, about a week ago! This has certainly astonished us not a little.

Our Party had so frequently made offers of reconciliation or at least of co-operation to the Lassalleans and had been so frequently and contemptuously repulsed by the Hasenclevers, Hasselmanns and Tölckes that any child must have drawn the conclusion: if these gentlemen are now coming and offering reconciliation themselves they must be in a damned tight fix. But considering the well-known character of these people it is our duty to utilise their fix in order to stipulate for every possible guarantee, so that they shall not re-establish their impaired position in the public opinion of the workers at the expense of our Party. They should have been received with

* The fusion of the Social-Democratic Workers' Party of Germany (the "Eisenachers," see Notes to Letter 159), led by Liebknecht and Bebel, with the General Association of German Workers (the Lassalleans, *cf.* Letters 29, 113) took place at the Gotha Unity Congress, May 22-27, 1875. The draft programme for the Congress, to which Engels is referring, had appeared in the organs of the two parties on March 7. Bedel was at this time in prison. [*Ed. Eng. ed.*]

extreme coolness and mistrust, and union should have been made dependent on the extent to which they were willing to drop their sectarian slogans and their state aid and to accept in essentials the Eisenach programme of 1869 or a revised edition of it adapted to the position at the present day.

Our Party had *absolutely nothing to learn* from the Lassalleans in the theoretical sphere and therefore in what is decisive for the programme, but the Lassalleans certainly had something to learn from our Party; the first condition of union was that they should cease to be sectarians, Lassalleans, and therefore that the universal panacea of state aid should be, if not entirely relinquished, at any rate recognised as a subordinate and transitional measure of less or equal importance to many other possible ones. The draft programme shows our people are a hundred times superior theoretically to the Lassalleans—but in the same measure removed from being equal to them where political cunning is concerned: the "honest" have been once more cruelly fleeced by the dishonest.

In the first place Lassalle's high-sounding but historically false phrase is accepted: in relation to the working class all other classes are only one reactionary mass. This statement is only true in particular and exceptional cases: for instance, in a proletarian revolution like the Commune, or in a country where state and society have not only been moulded by the bourgeoisie in their own image but where the democratic petty bourgeoisie have already followed suit by carrying out this re-casting down to its final consequences. If in Germany, for instance, the democratic petty bourgeoisie belonged to this reactionary mass, how could the Social-Democratic Workers' Party have gone hand in hand with it—with the People's Party—for years? How can the *Volksstaat* [People's State]* take almost the whole of its political contents from the petty-bourgeois democratic *Frankfurter Zeitung*? And how comes it that no less than seven demands are accepted in this programme which directly and literally coincide with the programme of the People's Party and petty-bourgeois democracy? I mean the

* The organ of the Social-Democratic Workers' Party, edited by Liebknecht. [*Ed. Eng. ed.*]

seven political demands, 1 to 5 and I to II, of which there is not a single one that is not *bourgeois* democratic.*

Secondly, the principle that the workers' movement is an international movement is completely disavowed in practice for the present day, and that by people who have upheld this principle in the most glorious way for five years and under the most difficult conditions.

The German workers' position at the head of the European movement is *essentially* based on their genuinely international attitude during the war; no other proletariat would have behaved so well. And now this principle is to be denied by them at the very moment when the workers everywhere abroad are emphasising it, in the same degree as the governments are striving to suppress every attempt at its realisation in an organisation!

What is left of internationalism to the workers' movement then? The faint prospect—not even of the future co-operation of the European workers for their emancipation—no, of a future "international brotherhood of nations"—of the bourgeois Peace League's "United States of Europe"!

It was of course quite unnecessary to speak of the International as such. But surely the very least would have been to make no retreat from the programme of 1869 and to say something to this effect: *although* the German Workers' Party is operating *for the time being* within the State boundaries laid down for it (it has no right to speak in the name of the European proletariat and especially not to say what is false), it is conscious of its solidarity with the workers of all countries and will always be ready in the future, as it has been hitherto, to fulfil the obligations imposed upon it by this solidarity. Obligations of that kind exist even if one does not exactly proclaim or regard oneself as a part of the "International"; for instance, help and abstention from blacklegging in strikes; care taken that the Party organs keep the German workers informed about the movement abroad; agitation against the threat or the outbreak of Cabinet-made wars, behaviour during such wars similar to that carried out in a model fashion in 1870 and 1871, etc.

* See Note, page 341. "One reactionary mass," see page 402.

Thirdly, our people have allowed the Lassallean " iron law of wages " to be foisted upon them, and this is based on a quite antiquated economic view, namely, that the worker only receives on the average the *minimum* of the labour wage, because, according to Malthus's theory of population, there are always too many workers (this was Lassalle's argument). Now Marx has proved in detail in *Capital* that the laws regulating wages are very complicated, that sometimes one predominates and sometimes another, according to circumstances, that therefore they are in no sense iron but on the contrary very elastic, and that the thing can by no means be dismissed in a few words, as Lassalle imagines. The Malthusian basis for the law which Lassalle copied from Malthus and Ricardo (with a falsification of the latter), as it is to be found for instance in the *Arbeiterlesebuch* [*Workers' Reader**], page 5, quoted from another pamphlet of Lassalle, has been refuted in detail by Marx in the section on the *Process of Capital Accumulation.* Thus by adopting Lassalle's " iron law " we commit ourselves to a false statement with a false basis.

Fourthly, the programme puts forward as its *sole social* demand—Lassalle's state aid in its most naked form, as Lassalle stole it from Buchez. And this after Bracke has very well exposed this demand in its entire nullity and after almost all, if not all, our Party speakers have been obliged to come out against this state aid in fighting the Lassalleans ! Lower than this our Party could not abase itself. Internationalism brought down to Armand Gögg and Socialism to the bourgeois republican Buchez, who put forward this demand *in opposition to the Socialists*, in order to supplant them !

In the best of cases, however, " state aid " in the Lassallean sense is only one *particular* measure among many others designed to attain the end here lamely described as " paving the way for a solution of the social question "—as if a theoretically *unsolved* social *question* still existed for us ! So if we say : the German workers' party strives for the abolition of wage labour, and with it of class differences, by the establishment of co-operative production on a national scale in industry and agriculture ;

* See Note, page 341.

it supports every measure adapted to the attainment of this end !—then no Lassallean can have anything against it.

Fifthly, there is not a word about the organisation of the working class as a class by means of the trade unions. And that is a very essential point, for this is the real class organisation of the proletariat, in which it carries on its daily struggles with capital, in which it trains itself, and which nowadays even amid the worst reaction (as in Paris at present) can simply no longer be smashed. Considering the importance which this form of organisation has also attained in Germany, it would be absolutely necessary in our opinion to mention it in the programme and if possible to leave open a place for it in the Party organisation.

All this has been done by our people to please the Lassalleans. And what has the other side conceded ? That a crowd of rather confused *purely democratic demands* should figure in the programme, of which several are a mere matter of fashion, as for instance the "legislation by the people" which exists in Switzerland and does more harm than good when it does anything at all. *Administration* by the people would be something different. Equally lacking is the first condition of all freedom : that all functionaries should be responsible for all their official actions to every citizen before the ordinary courts and according to common law. Of the fact that such demands as freedom for science, freedom of conscience, figure in every bourgeois liberal programme and have a somewhat strange appearance here, I will say nothing more.

The free people's state is transformed into the free state. Taken in its grammatical sense a free state is one where the state is free in relation to its citizens and is therefore a state with a despotic government. The whole talk about the state should be dropped, especially since the Commune, which was no longer a state in the proper sense of the word. The "*people's state*" has been thrown in our faces by the anarchists too long, although Marx's book against Proudhon* and later the *Communist Manifesto* directly declare that with the introduction of the socialist order of society the state will dissolve of itself

* *The Poverty of Philosophy.*

and disappear. As, therefore, the "state" is only a transitional institution which is used in the struggle, in the revolution, in order to hold down [*niederzuhalten*] one's adversaries by force, it is pure nonsense to talk of a "free people's state"; so long as the proletariat still *uses* the state, it does not use it in the interests of freedom but in order to hold down its adversaries, and as soon as it becomes possible to speak of freedom the state as such ceases to exist. We would therefore propose to replace the word "state" everywhere by the word *Gemeinwesen* [Community], a good old German word which can very well represent the French *commune*.

"Doing away with all social and political inequality" is also a very questionable phrase in place of "the abolition of all class differences." Between one country and another, one province and another and even one place and another there will always exist a *certain* inequality in the conditions of life, which can be reduced to a minimum but never entirely removed. Mountain dwellers will always have different conditions of life from those of people living on plains. The notion of socialist society as the realm of equality is a superficial French idea resting upon the old "liberty, equality, fraternity"—an idea which was justified as a *stage of development* in its own time and place but which, like all the superficial ideas of the earlier socialist schools, should now be overcome, for they only produce confusion in people's heads and more precise forms of description have been found.

I will stop, although almost every word in this programme, which has, moreover, been put together in a flat and feeble style, could be criticised. It is of such a character that if it is accepted Marx and I can *never* give our adherence to the *new* Party established on this basis, and shall have very seriously to consider what our attitude towards it—in public as well—should be. You must remember that abroad *we* are made responsible for any and every utterance and action of the German Social-Democratic Workers' Party. Thus Bakunin in his pamphlet, *Politics and Anarchy**—where we have to answer for every thoughtless word spoken or written by Liebknecht

* See Note, page 342.

since the *Demokratisches Wochenblatt* [*Democratic Weekly*] was started. People imagine, indeed, that we issue our orders for the whole business from here, while you know as well as I that we hardly ever interfere in internal Party affairs in the smallest way, and even then only in order to make good, so far as is possible, blunders, and only theoretical blunders, which have in our opinion been committed. But you will see for yourself that this programme marks a turning point which may very easily compel us to refuse any and every responsibility for the Party which recognises it.

As a rule, the official programme of a party is less important that what it does. But a *new* programme is after all a banner publicly raised, and the outside world judges the party from it. It should therefore on no account involve a step backwards, as this one does in comparison with the Eisenach programme. One should surely also take into consideration what the workers of other countries will say to this programme, what impression will be produced by this bending of the knee to Lassalleanism on the part of the whole German Socialist proletariat.

At the same time I am convinced that a union on *this* basis will never last a year. Are the best minds in our Party to lend themselves to grinding out repetitions, learnt off by rote, of the Lassallean statements on the iron law of wages and state aid? I should like to see you doing it, for instance! And if they did do this they would be hissed by their audiences. And I am sure the Lassalleans will insist on just *these* points of their programme like the Jew Shylock on his pound of flesh. The separation will come; but we shall have "made honest men" again of Hasselmann, Hasenclever, Tölcke & Co.; we shall come out of the separation weaker and the Lassalleans stronger; our party will have lost its political virginity and will never again be able to come out wholeheartedly against the Lassallean phrases which it will have inscribed for a time on its own banner; and if the Lassalleans then once more say that they are the most genuine, the only workers' party, while our people are bourgeois, the programme will be there to prove it. All the Socialist measures in it are *theirs*, and all *our* Party has put into it are the demands of that same petty-bourgeois democracy which is nevertheless *also* described *by it* in the same programme as a part of the " reactionary mass."

I had left this letter lying as you are only set free on April 1, in honour of Bismarck's birthday, and I did not want to expose it to the chance of being seized in any attempt to smuggle it in. And now a letter has just come from Bracke, who has also his grave doubts about the programme and wants to know our opinion. I am therefore sending this letter to him to forward, so that he can read it and so that I need not write all this stuff out over again. Moreover, I have also told the unvarnished truth to Ramm—to Liebknecht I only wrote shortly. I cannot forgive him for never telling us a *single word* about the thing (while Ramm and others thought he had given us exact information) until it was too late, so to speak. But indeed this is what he has always done—hence the large amount of disagreeable correspondence which both Marx and I have had with him—but this time it is really too much and *we are certainly not going to co-operate.*

¶Lenin attributed to this letter "*exceptionally* great importance on the question of the state," as he wrote in his preliminary studies for *State and Revolution.*

" This is probably the most striking and certainly the sharpest passage, '*against* the state,' so to speak, in Marx and Engels." " (1) It is necessary to drop the whole talk about the state." " (2) The Commune was no longer a state in the proper sense of the word." (But what then ? A transitional form from the state to no state, clearly !) (3) The anarchists have " thrown in our faces " the ' People's State ' long enough. (Marx and Engels, it is clear, were ashamed of this obvious error on the part of their German friends ; but they thought, and it is clear *under the circumstances then existing* rightly thought, that it was an incomparably less serious error than the error made by the anarchists. This *N.B. ! !*).

(4) The state " will decompose of itself (' dissolve ') *Nota Bene* (note well) and disappear " . . . (compare further on " will wither away ") " with the introduction of the socialist order of society. . . ." (5) The state is " a transitional institution "

which is needed in the struggle in the revolution . . . (needed *by the proletariat*, of course). . . . (6) The State is needed *not for freedom*, but to crush (? *Niederhaltung* is not crushing, properly speaking, but holding back from restoration, holding in subjection) *the adversaries of the proletariat*. (7) When there is freedom then there will be no state. (The concepts 'freedom' and 'democracy' are usually treated as identical and are often used interchangeably. Very often the vulgar Marxists with Kautsky, Plekhanov and Co. at their head treat them precisely in this way. In fact, democracy excludes freedom. The dialectic (process of development) is : from absolutism to bourgeois democracy ; from bourgeois democracy to proletarian ; from proletarian to none at all.) (8) " We " (*i.e.*, Engels and *Marx*) would suggest speaking " *everywhere* " (in the programme), instead of the " state," of the " community," the " commune " ! ! ! *N.B. ! ! ! !* From this it is clear how not only the opportunists, but also Kautsky, have vulgarised, defiled Marx and Engels. The opportunists have *not* understood a single one of these *eight* most fertile ideas ! ! They have grasped *only* the practical needs of the present : to make use of the political struggle, to make use of the *contemporary* state for the training, the education of the proletariat, for the " extraction of concessions." This is correct (as against the anarchists), but as yet it is only one-hundredth of Marxism, if it can be so expressed arithmetically.

Kautsky completely suppressed (or forgot, or did not understand) in his propagandist and throughout his publicist work, points 1, 2, 5, 6, 7, 8 and the " smashing " of Marx . . .* (Kautsky had already fallen into opportunism on this whole question).

We are distinguished from the anarchists by (*a*) the use of the state *now* and (*b*) at the time of the proletarian *revolution* (" the dictatorship of the proletariat ")—points of the greatest practical importance, just now.† (And Bukharin also has *forgotten* them !)

From the opportunists by the deeper, " more eternal " truths concerning (*aa*) the " temporary " character of the state, (*bb*) the *harm* of " talk " about it now, (*cc*) the dictatorship of the proletariat not having altogether the character of a state, (*dd*)

* Marx's statement that the bureaucratic-military state machine must be smashed. [*Ed. Eng. ed.*]

† January—February 1917. [*Ed. Eng. ed.*]

the contradiction between the state and freedom, (*ee*) the greater correctness of the idea (conception, programmatic term) "community" in place of state, (*ff*) the "smashing" of the bureaucratic-military machine. It must also not be forgotten that the *dictatorship of the proletariat* is directly repudiated by the open opportunists of Germany (Bernstein, Kolb and so forth) and *indirectly* by the official [Erfurt] programme and Kautsky, since they say nothing about it in everyday agitation, and tolerate the renegacy of the Kolbs and Co."

Marx wrote an extraordinarily deep and comprehensive criticism of the Gotha draft programme; it is one of the chief documents of Marxism, especially with regard to the theory of the state. On May 5, 1875 he wrote to Bracke:

"*Every step of real movement is more important than a dozen programmes.* If therefore it was not possible—and the conditions of the time did not permit of it—to go beyond the Eisenach programme, an *agreement for action* against the common enemy should simply have been concluded. But by drawing up a *programme of principles* (instead of postponing this until it has been prepared for by a considerable period of common activity) one sets up before the *whole world* a landmark by which the stature of the party movement is measured. The Lassallean leaders came because conditions forced them to come. If they had been told from the beginning that there would be no bargaining about principles they would have had to be content with a programme of action or a plan of organisation for common action."

The Social-Democratic leaders did not, however, follow Marx's advice and made, as Marx had foreseen, concessions to the Lassalleans on fundamental questions.

THE SEVEN POLITICAL DEMANDS of the draft concerned the introduction of universal suffrage, direct legislation by the people, the general arming of the people, democratic administration of justice, repeal of all emergency laws, "extension of rights and liberties" and a uniform progressive income tax.

WORKERS' READER. Two speeches made by Lassalle in Frankfurt on May 17-19, 1863. The "other pamphlet" is the *Open Letter in Reply to the Central Committee for the Summoning of a General German Workers' Congress in Leipzig* (Zurich, 1863). Engels is here referring to the following passage:

"The iron economic law which under present-day conditions, under the domination of supply and demand, determines the wages of labour, is this: that the average wage always remains reduced to the necessary subsistence which is required by a people according to its habits, for the maintenance of existence and reproduction." (Lassalle, *Gesammelte Reden u. Schriften*, III, S. 58.)

BAKUNIN'S PAMPHLET. In this pamphlet Bakunin calls Liebknecht an "agent of Herr Marx" and explains a series of mistakes in Liebknecht's public utterances as due to the direct influence of Marx.

BUCHEZ, PHILIPPE (1796-1865). French Catholic "socialist" who in the 'thirties and 'forties of last century propagated the theory of productive co-operatives by the aid of which he hoped to divert the workers from revolutionary struggle. Compare Letter 113.

GÖGG, ARMAND (1820-97). Petty-bourgeois democrat of Baden. Took part in the Revolution of 1848-49; in the 'sixties conducted pacifist propaganda; one of the leaders of the League of Peace and Freedom.

TÖLCKE, WILHELM (1817-93). Lassallean. President of the General Association of German Workers after B. Becker's resignation (1865); he took part in the negotiations for amalgamation with the Eisenachers in 1874-75.

BRACKE, WILHELM (1842-80). German Social-Democrat, bookseller and publisher. He was originally a Lassallean but took part in the foundation of the German Social-Democratic Workers' Party in Eisenach in 1869 and was a member of the Party Committee. In 1870, on account of the manifesto issued by the Party Committee against the war, he was arrested and imprisoned in a fortress. He criticised the draft programme submitted to the Gotha Congress; in 1878, owing to illness, he withdrew from Party work.

RAMM. Leipzig Social-Democrat, one of the editors of the *Volksstaat*.

162. ENGELS TO MARX

Ramsgate, 28 May, 1876.

It is all very well for you to talk. You can lie warm in bed and study ground rent in general and Russian agrarian conditions in particular with nothing to disturb you—but I am to sit on the hard bench, swill cold wine, suddenly interrupt everything again and get after the blood of the boring Dühring. However, there is doubtless nothing else for it, even if I involve myself in a controversy of which it is impossible to see the end ; after all, I shall have no peace otherwise, and then friend Most's panegyric on Dühring's *Course of Philosophy* has shown me exactly where and how to direct the attack. This book will have to be included because on many decisive points it better exposes the weak sides and weak foundations of the arguments put forward in the *Economy.* I am ordering it at once. There is no actual philosophy in it whatever—formal logic, dialectics, metaphysics, etc.—it is supposed rather to represent a general theory of science in which nature, history, society, state, law, etc., are treated in alleged inner interconnection. So again there is a whole section in which the society of the future, the so-called "free" society, is described in its less economic aspects, and among other things the scheme of education for the primary and secondary schools is already laid down. Here, therefore, one gets the banality in an even simpler form than in the economic book and taking both works together can expose the fellow from this side at the same time. For the noble gentleman's conception of history—that there was nothing but rubbish until Dühring arrived—this book also has the advantage that here one can quote his own crass words. Anyhow, I have him on the hip now.* My plan is ready —*J'ai mon plan.* First of all I shall deal with the trash in a purely objective and apparently serious way, and then the treatment will become sharper according to the degree in which the proofs of the nonsense on the one hand and of the platitudes on the other begin to pile up, until at last we get to a regular hailstorm. In this fashion Most and Co. are deprived of their excuse about "unkindness" and Dühring gets his deserts all the same. These gentlemen must be shown that there is more than one way by which one can settle accounts with people of this kind.

I hope Wilhelm [Liebknecht] will publish Most's article in

* This sentence was written in English.

the *Neue Welt*, for which it was obviously written. As usual Most cannot copy and so makes Dühring responsible for the most comic imbecilities in the way of natural science, *e.g.*, the breaking off of the *rings* (according to Kant's theory)—from the *fixed stars!*

With Wilhelm it is not merely the lack of manuscripts—that could be got over by other articles on questions of the day, etc., as was done in Hepner's and Blos's time. It is his passion for supplementing the deficiences of our theory, for having an answer to every philistine's objection and a picture of the society of the future because after all the philistine asks questions about it; and, in addition, for being as independent of us theoretically as possible (in which, owing to his total lack of all theory, he has always succeeded far better than he himself knows). But by all this he puts me into a position in which I cannot but say to myself that Dühring is at any rate an educated man compared with the theoretical bunglers of the *Volksstaat*, and his works are at any rate better than those of these subjectively and objectively obscure gentlemen. . . .

My re-reading of ancient history and my studies in natural science have been of great service to me for Dühring and make the thing much easier for me in many ways. Especially with natural science I find that the ground has become considerably more familiar to me and that, though I have to exercise great caution, I can nevertheless move on it with a certain amount of freedom and security. I am also beginning to see the end of this job too. The thing is beginning to take shape in my head, and bummelling here at the seaside where I can let the details go round in my mind has helped this on a good deal. In this enormous field it is absolutely necessary to interrupt one's regular grind from time to time and to digest what one has gulped down.

Herr Helmholz has never stopped chasing round the 'thing-in-itself' since 1853 and has still not got clear about it. The man is not ashamed of calmly allowing the nonsense he had printed *before* Darwin to be still reprinted over again.

¶This letter was written while Engels was working at his articles against Dühring, which were first printed in the Leipzig *Vorwärts* in 1877 and then published as a book under the title *Herr Eugen Dühring's Revolution in Science* (usually known as *Anti-Dühring*). The first edition was published in 1878.

MOST, JOHANN (1846-1909). German anarchist. A printer. At the beginning of his political activity a Social-Democrat. After 1867 he took part in the workers' movement in Vienna and was one of the leaders of the "Left" semi-anarchist wing there; in the German Social-Democratic Party he was an editor and member of the Reichstag. After the Anti-Socialist Laws (1878) he emigrated to London, where from January 1879 he published the paper *Freiheit* [*Freedom*], which gradually took on an anarchistic character. At the Wyden Party Congress (1880) he was expelled from the Social-Democratic Party. In 1882 he was expelled from England and emigrated to the United States, where he continued to publish *Freiheit*.

Marx wrote of Most in a letter to Sorge (September 19, 1879):

"The worthy Johann Most, a man of the most childish vanity, really believes that world conditions have suffered a vast transformation because this same Most is now housed in London instead of in Germany. The man is not without talent, but he kills his talent by too much writing. Added to which he has no intellectual stability. Every change of wind blows him first in one direction and then in another like a weathercock." Most, in his paper *Freiheit*, had criticised the opportunism of the Zürich *Sozial-Demokrat* (Bernstein, Höchberg, etc.) and the leaders of the German Social-Democratic Party. In the same letter to Sorge, Marx says that while Bernstein, Höchberg and Schramm criticise Most's paper for being "too revolutionary," he and Engels "reproach him because it (*Freiheit*) has no *revolutionary content* but only *revolutionary phraseology*. We reproach him, not for *criticising the German Party leaders*, but firstly for making a *public row* instead of conveying his opinions to them, as we do, in writing, *i.e.*, in *letters*; and secondly because he only uses this as an excuse for making himself important and putting the *idiotic secret conspiratorial plans* of Messrs. *Weber Junior and Kaufmann* into circulation." (Compare Letter 165.)

163. MARX TO ENGELS

[London] 18 July, 1877.

It would certainly be very pleasant if a really scientific socialist journal were to be published. It would provide an opportunity for criticisms or counter-criticisms in which we could discuss theoretical points, expose the utter ignorance of professors and lecturers and at the same time enlighten the minds of the general public—working class or bourgeois. But Wiede's periodical *cannot* possible be anything but sham-scientific; the same half-educated *Knoten** and dilettante literary men who make the *Neue Welt*, *Vorwärts*, etc., unsafe, necessarily form the majority of his collaborators. Ruthlessness—the first condition of all criticism—is impossible in such company; besides which constant attention has to be paid to making things easily comprehensible, *i.e.*, exposition for the ignorant. Imagine a journal of chemistry where the readers' ignorance of chemistry is constantly assumed as the fundamental presupposition. And apart from all that, the way the people who are necessarily Wiede's collaborators have behaved in the Dühring incident imposes the precaution of keeping oneself as separate from these gentlemen as political party conditions allow. Their motto seems to be: Whoever criticises his opponent by abusing him is a man of feeling, but whoever defames his opponent by genuine criticism is an unworthy character.

¶A plan had been made to start a theoretical journal for the Party. Liebknecht warned Marx and Engels against Wiede, whose scheme for a journal was a private affair; the official scientific organ of the Party was only to be the *Zukunft* [*Future*] which would be published in Berlin. (See Letter 164.)

WIEDE, FRANZ (born 1857). Bourgeois journalist, a Swede by origin, lecturer at Geneva University. His social reformist periodical (*Neue Gesellschaft*) [*New Society*] was published in Zürich 1877-79.

* See Note, page 87.

164. MARX TO ENGELS

[London] 1 August, 1877.

A few days ago the cheery little hunchback Wedde turned up—only to disappear again to Germany shortly after. He had a pressing commission from Geib to enlist you and me for the *Zukunft*. I made no secret to him whatever of our intentions of abstaining, to his great sorrow, and of our reasons for this, and explained to him at the same time that when our time allows or circumstances demand that we should again come forward as propagandists, we, as internationalists, are in no wise bound or pledged to attach ourselves to Germany, the beloved Fatherland.

In Hamburg he had seen Dr. Höchberg and ditto Wiede; the latter, he said, was rather tinged with Berlin superficiality and arrogance, but he liked Höchberg, who, however, was still suffering badly from "modern mythology." For when the little chap (Wedde) was in London for the first time I used the expression "modern mythology" as a designation for the goddesses of "Justice, Freedom, Equality, etc." who were now all the rage again; this made a deep impression on him, as he has himself done much in the service of these higher beings. He thought Höchberg rather Dühringised—and Wedde has a sharper nose than Liebknecht.

¶ WEDDE, JOHANNES (1843-180). Social-Democrat, one of the founders of the Social-Democratic papers, *Bürgerzeitung* (1881) and *Hamburger Echo* (1887). Expelled from Hamburg in 1887.

GEIB, AUGUST (1842-79). German Social-Democrat, trade union leader, one of the initiators and the chairman of the Eisenach Congress in 1869, Party treasurer from 1872. Member of the Reichstag 1874-76. In 1879 he strongly opposed the illegal organisation of the Party.

HÖCHBERG, KARL (1853-85). Bourgeois author. Son of a merchant. Philanthropist who attached himself to the German Social-Democrats in the second half of the 'seventies. He put material assistance at the disposal of the Party and tried to draw the movement into the path of reformism. He published a series of journals (*Zukunft* 1877-78; *Jahrbücher für Sozialwissenschaft und Sozialpolitik* 1879-82; *Staatswirtschaftliche Abhandlungen* 1879-82). At the beginning of the period of the Anti-Socialist Laws he organised around himself in Zürich a group of Social-Democratic literary men (Bernstein, Schramm, Kautsky, etc.); he also tried to get into touch with Engels whom he visited unexpectedly in London. Engels writing of this to J. Ph. Becker on September 15, 1879, says: "The poor lad, at bottom a good fellow, but *terribly naive*, was thunderstruck when I explained to him that we could never think of lowering the proletarian banner which we have held aloft for nearly forty years, and were equally far from agreeing with the general petty-bourgeois day-dream of fraternisation which we have now been fighting against for nearly forty years too." (See also Letters 166, 170.)

165. MARX TO SORGE

27 September, 1877.

This crisis* is a *new turning point* in European history. Russia has long been standing on the threshold of an upheaval, all the elements of it are prepared—I have studied conditions there from the original *Russian* sources, unofficial and official (the latter only available to a few people but got for me through friends in Petersburg). The gallant Turks have hastened the explosion by years with the thrashing they have inflicted, not only upon the Russian army and Russian finances, but in a highly personal and individual manner on the *dynasty commanding* the army (the Tsar, the heir to the throne and six other Romanovs). The upheaval will begin *secundum artem* [according to the rules of the art] with some playing at constitutionalism and then there will be a fine row. If Mother Nature is not particularly unfavourable towards us we shall still live to see the fun! The stupid nonsense which the Russian students are perpetrating is only a symptom, worthless in itself. But it is a symptom. All sections of Russian society are in complete disintegration economically, morally and intellectually.

* The Russo-Turkish war and Near Eastern crisis.

This time the revolution will begin in the East, hitherto the unbroken bulwark and reserve army of counter-revolution.

Herr Bismarck was pleased to see the thrashing, but it ought not to have gone so far. Russia too much weakened could not hold Austria in check again as she did in the Franco-Prussian War! And if it were even to come to revolution there, where would the last guarantee of the Hohenzollern dynasty be?

For the moment everything depends on the Poles (in the Kingdom of Poland) lying low. If only there are no risings there at the moment! Bismarck would at once intervene and Russian chauvinism would once more side with the Tsar. If on the other hand the Poles wait quietly till there is a conflagration in Petersburg and Moscow, and Bismarck then intervenes as a saviour, Prussia will find its—Mexico!

I have rammed this home again and again to any Poles I am in contact with who can influence their fellow-countrymen.

Compared with the crisis in the East, the *French crisis* is quite a secondary event. Still it is to be hoped that the bourgeois republic will be victorious or else the old game will begin all over again, and a nation can repeat the same stupidities once too often.

With the reforms of the 'sixties, which gave greater freedom to the development of capitalist conditions in Russia, class contradictions became intensified; the tsarist government tried to restrain the growth of revolutionary tendencies by the diversion of a war with Turkey—a method which it repeatedly employed later on (*e.g.*, 1914). After a gallant defence the Turks were defeated, but Russia could not make use of her victory because England threatened her with war if she annexed Constantinople. At the instigation of England a Conference of the various Powers was summoned in Berlin, its task being to reduce the advantages gained by Russia through her victory.

In France the monarchist President of the Republic, MacMahon, attempted in 1877 to prepare for a restoration of the monarchy and dissolved Parliament. At the elections in October, however, the victory was gained by a republican majority.

166. MARX TO SORGE

London, 19 October, 1877.

A rotten spirit is making itself felt in our Party in Germany, not so much among the masses as among the leaders (upper class and " workers ").

The compromise with the Lassalleans has led to compromise with other half-way elements too ; in Berlin (*e.g.*, Most) with Dühring and his " admirers ", but also with a whole gang of half-mature students and super-wise doctors who want to give socialism a " higher ideal " orientation, that is to say, to replace its materialistic basis (which demands serious objective study from anyone who tries to use it) by modern mythology with its goddesses of Justice, Freedom, Equality and Fraternity. Dr. Höchberg, who publishes the *Zukunft* [*Future*] is a representative of this tendency and has " bought himself in " to the party —with the " noblest " intentions, I assume, but I do not give a damn for " intentions." Anything more miserable than his programme of the " future " has seldom seen the light of day with more " modest " " presumption."

The workers themselves when, like Mr. Most and Co. they give up work and become *professional literary men*, always set some theoretical mischief going and are always ready to attach themselves to muddleheads from the alleged " learned " caste. *Utopian* socialism especially, which for tens of years we have been clearing out of the German workers' heads with so much toil and labour—their freedom from it making them theoretically, and therefore also practically, superior to the French and English—utopian socialism, playing with fancy pictures of the future structure of society, is now raging in a much more futile form, as compared not only with the great French and English utopians, but with—Weitling. Naturally utopianism, which *before* the time of materialistic-critical socialism concealed the germs of the latter within itself, coming now *after* the event can only be silly—silly, stale and basically reactionary.

¶WEITLING, WILHELM (1808-71) The first German socialist writer to come from the proletariat, a tailor by trade. After his years as a travelling journeyman in Germany (1828-35), he went to Paris and there became a member of the *League of the Just*, by which he was commissioned to write his pamphlet, *Humanity, As It Is and As It Should Be* (1838). His chief work, *Guarantees of Harmony and Freedom*, appeared in 1842. Weitling stands midway between utopian and proletarian socialism. He belonged to the oppressed class and understood the necessity for struggle, but he could not free himself from his utopian views. His theory is an attempt to combine the theory of the utopians with the revolutionary struggle of the working class. But his point of view remained that of the petty bourgeois. The basis of his theory is the petty-bourgeois demand for equality. He criticised bourgeois conditions from a moral point of view. In his understanding of history he was inferior to Saint Simon and Fourier.

In August 1844 Marx wrote in his article, *Kritische Randglossen* [*Critical Notes*] (*Marx-Engels Gesamtausgabe* Abteilung, I, Bd. 3, S. 18): "As to the degree of education or the capacity for education of the German workers in general, I would recall *Weitling's* brilliant writings, which often surpass even *Proudhon* where theory is concerned, greatly inferior though they are in presentation. Where can the bourgeoisie—including their philosophers and learned writers—point to a work relating to the emancipation of the bourgeoisie—their *political* emancipation—similar to Weitling's *Guarantees of Harmony and Freedom*? Compare the sober, timid mediocrity of German political literature with this *unmeasured* and brilliant literary *début* of the German workers: compare these giant *infant boots* of the proletariat with the dwarfish outworn political boots of the German bourgeoisie, and one is bound to prophesy an *athlete's stature* for this *German Aschenbrödel* [*Cinderella*]. It must be admitted that the German proletariat is the theoretician of the European proletariat, as the English proletariat is its *national economist* and the French proletariat its *politician*. It must be admitted that Germany possesses a *classic* mission for the *social* revolution in the same degree as she is incapable of a *political* one. . . . A philosophical nation can only find its corresponding practice in socialism and can therefore only find the active element of its emancipation in the *proletariat*." [See Note to Letter 1.]

167. MARX TO THE EDITOR OF THE *Otyecestvenniye Zapisky* [*Notes on the Fatherland*]*

(End of 1877).

The author† of the article *Karl Marx Before the Tribunal of M. Shukovsky* is evidently a clever man and if, in my account of primitive accumulation, he had found a single passage to support his conclusions he would have quoted it. In the absence of any such passage he finds himself obliged to seize upon an *hors d'oeuvre*, a sort of polemic against a Russian "literary man‡," published in the postscript of the first German edition of *Capital*. What is my complaint against this writer there? That he discovered the Russian commune not in Russia but in the book written by Haxthausen, Prussian Counsellor of State, and that in his hands the Russian commune only serves as an argument to prove that rotten old Europe will be regenerated by the victory of pan-Slavism. My estimate of this writer may be right or it may be wrong, but it cannot in any case furnish a clue to my views regarding the efforts "of Russians to find a path of development for their country which will be different from that which Western Europe pursued and still pursues," etc.§

In the postcript to the second German edition of *Capital*—which the author of the article on M. Shukovsky knows, because he quotes it—I speak of "a great Russian critic and man of learning"** with the high consideration he deserves. In his remarkable articles this writer has dealt with the question whether, as her liberal economists maintain, Russia must begin by destroying *la commune rurale* (the village commune) in order to pass to the capitalist regime, or whether, on the contrary, she can without experiencing the tortures of this regime appropriate all its fruits by developing *ses propres données historiques* [the particular historic conditions already given her]. He pronounces in favour of this latter solution. And my

* This letter was written in French.
† N. K. Michailovski, leading theoretician of the revolutionary petty-bourgeois socialist party of the Narodniki.
‡ Herzen.
§ Quoted in Russian.
** Chernyshevsky.

honourable critic would have had at least as much reason for inferring from my consideration for this " great Russian critic and man of learning " that I shared his views on the question, as for concluding from my polemic against the " literary man " and Pan-Slavist that I rejected them.

To conclude, as I am not fond of leaving " something to be guessed," I will come straight to the point. In order that I might be qualified to estimate the economic development in Russia to-day, I learnt Russian and then for many years studied the official publications and others bearing on this subject. I have arrived at this conclusion : If Russia continues to pursue the path she has followed since 1861, she will lose the finest chance* ever offered by history to a nation, in order to undergo all the fatal vicissitudes of the capitalist regime.

The chapter on primitive accumulation does not pretend to do more than trace the path by which, in Western Europe, the capitalist order of economy emerged from the womb of the feudal order of economy. It therefore describes the historic movement which by divorcing the producers from their means of production converts them into wage earners (proletarians in the modern sense of the word) while it converts into capitalists those who hold the means of production in possession. In that history, "all revolutions are epoch-making which serve as levers for the advancement of the capitalist class in course of formation ; above all those which, after stripping great masses of men of their traditional means of production and subsistence, suddenly fling them on to the labour market. But the basis of this whole development is the expropriation of the cultivators.

" This has not yet been radically accomplished except in England. . . . but all the countries of Western Europe are going through the same movement," etc. (*Capital*, French Edition, 1879, p. 315). At the end of the chapter the historic tendency of production is summed up thus: That it itself begets its own negation with the inexorability which governs the metamorphoses of nature ; that it has itself created the elements of a new economic order, by giving the greatest impulse at once to the productive forces of social labour and

* *I.e.* The finest chance of escaping capitalist development. [*Ed. Eng. ed.*]

to the integral development of every individual producer; that capitalist property, resting as it actually does already on a form of collective production, cannot do other than transform itself into social property. At this point I have not furnished any proof, for the good reason that this statement is itself nothing else than the short summary of long developments previously given in the chapters on capitalist production.

Now what application to Russia can my critic make of this historical sketch? Only this: If Russia is tending to become a capitalist nation after the example of the Western European countries, and during the last years she has been taking a lot of trouble in this direction—she will not succeed without having first transformed a good part of her peasants into proletarians; and after that, once taken to the bosom of the capitalist regime, she will experience its pitiless laws like other profane peoples. That is all. But that is not enough for my critic. He feels himself obliged to metamorphose my historical sketch of the genesis of capitalism in Western Europe into an historico-philosophic theory of the *marche genérale* [general path] imposed by fate upon every people, whatever the historic circumstances in which it finds itself, in order that it may ultimately arrive at the form of economy which will ensure, together with the greatest expansion of the productive powers of social labour, the most complete development of man. But I beg his pardon. (He is both honouring and shaming me too much.) Let us take an example.

In several parts of *Capital* I allude to the fate which overtook the plebeians of ancient Rome. They were originally free peasants, each cultivating his own piece of land on his own account. In the course of Roman history they were expropriated. The same movement which divorced them from their means of production and subsistence involved the formation not only of big landed property but also of big money capital. And so one fine morning there were to be found on the one hand free men, stripped of everything except their labour power, and on the other, in order to exploit this labour, those who held all the acquired wealth in possession. What happened? The Roman proletarians became, not wage labourers but a *mob* of do-nothings more abject than the former "poor whites" in the southern country of the United States, and alongside of them there developed a mode of production which was not capitalist but dependent upon slavery. Thus events strikingly analogous but taking place in different historic surroundings led to totally different results. By studying each of these forms of evolution separately and then comparing them one can easily find the clue to this phenomenon, but one will never arrive there by the universal passport of a general historico-philosophical theory, the supreme virtue of which consists in being super-historical.

¶On the Russian village commune Marx and Engels wrote in the preface to the Russian edition of *The Communist Manifesto* on January 21, 1882: "The question is now whether the Russian village commune—a form of primitive collective communal property which has indeed already been to a large extent destroyed—can pass immediately into the highest communist form of landed property or whether, on the contrary, it must go through from the beginning the same process of disintegration as that which has determined the historical development of the West. The only possible answer to this question to-day is as follows: If the Russian revolution becomes the signal for the workers' revolution in the West, so that the one supplements the other, then the present form of land ownership in Russia may be the starting-point of an historical development." (See letter 226.)

168. MARX TO W. LIEBKNECHT

[London] 11 February, 1878.

The Russians have achieved one good thing; they have exploded England's "great Liberal Party" and made it incapable of governing for a long time to come, whilst the trouble of committing suicide has been officially accomplished for the Tory Party through the traitors Derby and Salisbury (the latter the real driving force of Russia in the Cabinet).

The English working class had been gradually more and

more deeply demoralised by the period of corruption since 1848 and had at last got to the point when they were nothing more than the tail of the great Liberal Party, i.e., henchmen of the capitalists. Their direction had gone completely over into the hands of the corrupt trade union leaders and professional agitators. These fellows shouted and howled behind Gladstone, Bright, Mundella, Morley and the whole gang of factory owners etc., *in majorem gloriam* [to the greater glory] of the Tsar as emancipator of nations, while they never raised a finger for their own brothers in South Wales, condemned to die of starvation by the mineowners.* Wretches! To crown the whole affair worthily, in the last divisions in the House of Commons (on February 7 and 8, when the majority of the great dignitories of the "great Liberal Party"—Forster, Lowe, Harcourt, Goschen, Hartington and even [on Feb. 7] the great John Bright himself—left their army in the lurch and bolted away from the *division* in order not to compromise themselves too much altogether by voting)—the *only workers' representatives* in the House of Commons and moreover, *horribile dictu* [horrible to relate] direct *representatives of the miners*, and themselves originally *miners*—Burt and the miserable Macdonald—voted with the rump of the "great Liberal Party," the enthusiasts for the Tsar.

But the rapid development of Russia's plans suddenly broke the spell and shattered the "mechanical agitation" (five-pound notes were the main springs of the machinery); at the moment it would be "*physically dangerous*" for Mottershead, Howell, John Hales, Shipton, Osborne and the whole gang to let their voices be heard in a public meeting of workers; even their "corner and ticket meetings" are forcibly broken up and dispersed by the masses.

¶On February 7 and 8 the debate took place in the House of Commons on the vote of supplementary credits for the govern-

* Marx is referring to the suffering and starvation among the miners in South Wales, where, under the influence of the economic crisis, unemployment had reached enormous proportions. In January 1878 only 20 out of 500 pits were working in Monmouth and Glamorganshire.

ment in case of England's intervention in the Russo-Turkish war. The leaders of the Liberal Party, with Forster and Bright at their head, formerly bitter opponents of the voting of credits and in general of any action directed against Russia, altered their tactics and abstained from voting in the final division, which gave the Conservative Cabinet a considerable majority (328 to 124).

[For the Russian war, see also Note to Letter 165. In the final stages of the war against Turkey, in which the Tsar posed as the "emancipator" of the Southern Slav nations in the Balkans, Russia had completely gained the upper hand, and on Jan. 20 the Russian vanguard had entered Adrianople. The British imperialists were determined to prevent Russia from taking Constantinople or from making a separate peace with Turkey. At the date on which Marx was writing the Mediterranean fleet was waiting in Besika Bay and Turkey had appealed to Britain for intervention. Marx's consistent policy was that the defeat of Russian Tsarism, the bulwark of reaction in Europe, must always be put first, he was therefore in favour of a Turkish victory. "A *Russian defeat* would have greatly *hastened the social revolution in Russia*, for which the elements exist on a mass scale, and with it *the revolution throughout Europe*." (To Liebknecht, 4 Feb. 1878). *Ed. Eng. ed.*]

THOMAS BURT (1857-1922) and ALEXANDER MACDONALD (1821-81), the first working-class members of the House of Commons, had been elected in 1874. Both were leading officials of the National Union of Miners, of which Macdonald had been the chief founder (1863), remaining its President until his death. Burt (Northumberland Miners' Mutual Confident Society) became Parliamentary Secretary to the Board of Trade (1892-95) under the Liberal Government and was long known as the "father of the House of Commons." Macdonald was a leading member of the "Junta," a promoter of the "new model" and of the use of the trade union machine for parliamentary agitation. [*Ed. Eng. ed.*]

MOTTERSHEAD, THOMAS. Former member of the General Council of the International. Joined the opposition in the "British Federation" 1872. See Note on the Irish Debate, p. 276. [*Ed. Eng. ed.*]

HOWELL, GEORGE (1833-). Operative Bricklayers Society, Secretary of the London Trades Council, 1861, and of the

Parliamentary Committee of the T.U.C. 1872-75. One of the 14 "independent" Labour candidates returned with Keir Hardie in the elections of 1892. Author of many works on trade union history. [*Ed. Eng. ed.*]

HALES, JOHN. Member of the General Council of the International and Secretary in 1871 during the final period. After the Hague Congress (1872) formed one of the opposition in the "British Federation," which refused to accept the decisions of the Congress. [*Ed. Eng. ed.*]

SHIPTON, GEORGE. Associated with the "Junta," Secretary of the London Trades Council. Editor of the *Labour Standard* (1881-82). See Note to Letter 188 for Engels' dealings with him. [*Ed. Eng. ed.*]

169. MARX TO DANIELSON *

[London] April 10, 1879.

In regard to your most remarkable letter I shall confine myself to a few observations.

The railways sprang up first as the *couronnement de l'oeuvre*† in those countries where *modern industry was most developed*, England, United States, Belgium, France, etc. I call them the "*couronnement de l'oeuvre*" not only in the sense that they were at last (together with steamships for oceanic intercourse and the telegraphs) the *means of communication* adequate to the modern means of production, but also in so far as they were the basis of immense joint stock companies, forming at the same time a new starting point for all *other sorts* of joint stock companies, to commence by banking companies. They gave in one word, an impetus never before suspected to the *concentration of capital*, and also to the accelerated and immensely *enlarged cosmopolitan activity of loanable capital*, thus embracing the whole world in a network of financial swindling and mutual indebtedness, the capitalist form of "international" brotherhood.

On the other hand, the appearance of the railway system in the leading countries of capitalism allowed, and even forced,

* This letter was written in English.
† Crowning work.

states where capitalism was confined to a few summits of society, to suddenly create and enlarge their capitalistic superstructure in dimensions altogether disproportionate to the bulk of the social body, carrying on the great work of production in the traditional modes. There is, therefore, not the least doubt that in those states the railway creation has accelerated the social and political disintegration, as in the more advanced states it hastened the final development and therefore the final change, of capitalistic production. In all states, except England, the governments enriched and fostered the railway companies at the expense of the Public Exchequer. In the United States, to their profit, great part of the public land they received as a present, not only the land necessary for the construction of the lines but many miles of land along both sides the lines, covered with forests, etc. They become so the greatest landlords, the small immigrating farmers preferring of course land so situated as to ensure their produce ready means of transport.

The system inaugurated in France by Louis Philippe, of handing over the railways to a small band of financial aristocrats, endowing them with long terms of possession, guaranteeing the interest out of the public pocket, etc., etc., was pushed to the utmost limit by Louis Bonaparte, whose regime, in fact, was essentially based upon the traffick in railway concessions, to some of which he was so kind as to make presents of canals, etc.

And in Austria and Italy above all, the railways were a new source* of unbearable state indebtedness and grinding of the masses.

Generally the railways gave of course an immense impulse to the development of foreign commerce, but the commerce in countries which export principally *raw produce* increased the misery of the masses. Not only that the new indebtedness, contracted by the government on account of the railways, increased the *bulk of imposts* weighing upon them, but from the moment every local production could be converted into cosmopolitan gold, many articles *formerly cheap*, because invendible

* "M.S. course."

to a great degree, such as fruit, wine, fish, deer, etc., became *dear* and were withdrawn from the consumption of the people, while on the other hand, the *production itself*, I mean the special *sort of produce*, was changed according to its *greater or minor suitableness for exportation*, while formerly it was principally adapted to its consumption *in loco*. Thus, for instance, in Schleswig-Holstein agricultural land was converted into pasture, because the export of cattle was more profitable, but at the same time the agricultural population was driven away. All the changes very useful indeed for the great landed proprietor, the usurer, the merchant, the railways, the bankers and so forth, but very dismal for the real producer !

It is, to conclude by this my letter (since the time for putting it to post draws nearer and nearer), impossible to find real analogies between the United States and Russia. In the former the expenses of the government diminish daily and its public debt is quickly and yearly reduced ; in the latter public bankruptcy is a goal more and more appearing to become unavoidable. The former has freed itself (although in a most infamous way, for the advantage of the creditors and at the expense of the *menu peuple**) of its paper money, the latter has no more flourishing fabric than that of paper money. In the former the concentration of capital and the gradual expropriation of the masses is not only the vehicle, but also the natural offspring (though artificially accelerated by the civil war) of an unprecedented rapid industrial development, agricultural progress, etc.; the latter reminds you rather of the time of Louis XIV and Louis XV, where the financial, commercial, industrial superstructure, or rather the *façades* of the social edifices, looked (although they had a much more solid foundation than in Russia) like a satyre upon the stagnant state of the bulk of production (the agricultural one) and the famine of the producers. The United States have at present overtaken England in the rapidity of economical progress, though they lag† still behind in the extent of acquired wealth; but at the same time the masses are quicker, and have greater political means

* Small people.
† M.S. Lack.

in their hands, to resent the form of a progress accomplished at their expense. I need not prolong antitheses.

A propos. Which do you consider the best Russian work on credit and banking?

¶DANIELSON (NICOLAI-ON) NIKOLAI FRANZEVICH (1844-1918). Russian economist, Narodnik; translator of *Capital*; he completed the translation begun by G. A. Lopatin of the first volume, which was published in 1872. In this connection Danielson entered into correspondence with Marx. Danielson was one of the chief theoreticians of the Narodniki, who contested the necessity and possibility of the development of capitalism in Russia. In the first years of his activity Lenin conducted a sharp struggle against these false theories and against Danielson as their chief defender. In his first work, *What the 'Friends of the People' Are and How they Fight against the Social-Democrats*, Lenin writes of Danielson: "Nicolai-on's *fundamental error* is his failure to understand the class struggle, this necessary part of capitalism." "... This lack of understanding makes Nicolai-on into a *utopian*, for a socialist by ignoring the class struggle in capitalist society, *eo ipso* [thereby] ignores the whole real content of the social-political life of that society, and in order to realise his desires he inevitably takes refuge in the sphere of innocent dreams. This lack of understanding turns him into a *reactionary*, for the appeal to 'society' and to the 'state,' *i.e.*, to the ideologists and politicians of the bourgeoisie, confuses the socialist and leads him to take the worst enemies of the proletariat as his allies; it only obstructs the workers' struggle for emancipation instead of increasing its strength and clarity and the greater organisation of this struggle." (Lenin, *Collected Works*, Russian edition, Vol. I, pp. 202-3.)

With this letter compare also Lenin's *Imperialism as the Highest Stage of Capitalism* (Chap. VII) where the part played by railways in the imperialist epoch of capitalism is examined.

170. MARX AND ENGELS TO BEBEL, LIEBKNECHT, BRACKE AND OTHERS.

[London, Middle of September, 1879 (Draft).]

(1) *The negotiations with C. Hirsch.*

Liebknecht asks Hirsch if he will take over the editorship of the Party organ which is to be newly established in Zürich.* Hirsch wants information as to the finances of the paper: what funds are at its disposal and who provides them. The first, in order to know whether the paper will be bound to fade out after a few months. And then to make sure who holds the purse strings and with them the ultimate control over the line of the paper. Liebknecht's answer to Hirsch: "Everything all right, you will hear the rest from Zürich" (Liebknecht to Hirsch, July 28) does not reach him. But from Zürich comes a letter to Hirsch from Bernstein (July 24) in which Bernstein announces that "*we* have been charged with the launching and *supervision*" (of the paper). A discussion had taken place "between Viereck and *us*" in which it had been felt "that your position, owing to the differences which you had with individual conrades when you were a *Laterne* [*Lantern*] man would be made rather difficult; but *I* do not attach much weight to this objection." Not a word about the financing.

Hirsch replies by return on July 26, with the question as to the material position of the paper. What comrades have pledged themselves to cover the deficit? Up to what amount and for how long? The question of the editor's salary plays no part at all here, all Hirsch wants to know is if "the means are ensured for guaranteeing the paper for at least a year."

Bernstein answers on July 31: Any deficit will be covered by voluntary contributions, of which *some* (!) are already subscribed. To Hirsch's remarks about the line he thought of giving to the paper, dealt with below, he replies with disapproving remarks and *instructions:* "On which the *supervisory committee* must insist all the more since it is itself in its turn under

* The Social-Democratic Party had now become illegal in Germany by the operation of Bismarck's Socialist Law (1878-90). [*Ed. Eng. ed.*]

control, *i.e.*, responsible. On these points you will therefore have to come to an understanding with the *supervisory committee*." An early and if possible telegraphic reply desired.

Thus instead of an answer to his legitimate questions Hirsch receives the information that he is to edit the paper under a *supervisory* committee seated in Zürich, whose views differ very essentially from his own and whose members are not even named to him!

Justly indignant at this treatment, Hirsch prefers to come to an understanding with the Leipzig people. His letter of August 2 to Liebknecht must be known to you, as Hirsch *expressly required* that you and Viereck should be informed. Hirsch is even willing to submit to a supervisory committee in Zürich, up to the point of agreeing that it should have the right to make written observations to the editor and to appeal to the decision of the Leipzig control committee.

In the meantime Liebknecht writes on July 28 to Hirsch: "*Of course*, the undertaking is financed, as the whole Party + (including) Höchberg stands behind it. But I am not troubling myself about details."

Liebknecht's next letter again contains nothing about the finances, but the assurance instead that the Zürich committee is not an editorial committee at all but is only entrusted with the *management* and finances. Again on August 14 Liebknecht writes the same to me and demands that we persuade Hirsch to accept. Even on August 20 you yourself are so little informed of the true facts of the case that you write to me: "He (Höchberg) has no more voice in the editing of the paper than *any other well-known Party comrade*."

At last on August 11 Hirsch gets a letter from Viereck in which it is admitted that "the three residing in Zürich are to take the foundation of the paper in hand as an *editorial committee* and with the agreement of the three Leipzig members to choose an editor. . . . *So far as I recollect*, the decisions communicated to us also stated that the (Zürich) organisation committee mentioned in (2) should take over the *political as well as* the financial responsibility in relation to the Party! . . . From this position of affairs it seems to me to follow that . . . there can be no question of taking over the editorship without the co-operation of the three domiciled in Zürich who have been commissioned by the Party to start the paper." Here at last Hirsch had at least *something* definite, if only regarding the relation of the editor to the Zürich people. They are an *editorial committee* ; they also have the *political* responsibility ; without their co-operation no one can take over the editorship. In short, an indication is simply given to Hirsch that he should come to an understanding with the three people in Zürich whose names are still not given him.

To complete the confusion, however, Liebknecht writes a postscript to Viereck's letter : " S[inger] from B[erlin] has just been here and *reported :* the supervisory committee in Zürich is *not*, as Viereck thinks, an *editorial* committee but essentially a management committee financially responsible to the Party, *i.e.*, to us, for the paper ; naturally it is also the right and the duty of its members to discuss the editing with you (a right and a duty which belong, incidentally, to *every* Party member) : they have *not* the authority to act as your *guardians*."

The three Zürich and the one Leipzig committee members—the *only one* present at the negotiations—insist that Hirsch shall be under the official control of the Zürich people. A second Leipzig member directly denies this. And Hirsch is expected to come to a decision before the gentlemen are agreed among themselves ? That Hirsch had the right to be informed of the decisions come to, which contained the conditions he was expected to submit to, was thought of all the less because it never once seems to have occurred to the Leipzigers to get authentic information themselves about these decisions. How else could the above contradiction have been possible ?

If the Leipzigers cannot agree as to the powers conferred upon the Zürichers, the Zürichers themselves are perfectly clear about them.

Schramm to Hirsch, August 14 : " If you had not written at the time that you would do just the same in a similar case (to the Kayser case) and thus indicated the prospect of a similar style of writing, we should not waste a word over it.

But in view of your declaration we must reserve to ourselves the right of having a decisive vote in the acceptance of articles for the new paper."

The letter to Bernstein in which Hirsch is stated to have said this was dated July 26, that is to say *long* after the conference in Zürich at which the plenary powers of the three Zürichers were established. But the Zürichers are already revelling so much in the sense of their absolute bureaucratic power that in answer to this later letter of Hirsch they already claim further authority to *decide* upon the acceptance of articles. The editorial committee is already a *censorship* committee.

It was not until Höchberg came to Paris that Hirsch learned from him the *names* of the members of the two committees. If therefore the negotiations with Hirsch fell through, what was the reason?

(a) The obstinate refusal both of the Leipzig and the Zürich people to give him any concrete information as to the financial basis of the paper and therefore as to the possibility of maintaining the paper in existence, if only for a year. He first learnt the amount of the sum subscribed from me here (after your communication to me). It was therefore hardly possible to draw any other conclusion from the information already given (the Party+Höchberg) than that the paper was either already mainly financed by Höchberg or else would soon be completely dependent on his subsidies. And this latter possibility is still far from being excluded. The sum of 800 marks (£40), if I am reading correctly, is *exactly* the same as the Association here had to contribute to *Freiheit* in the *first half year*.

(b) The repeated assurances of Liebknecht, since proved totally false, that the Zürichers were to have no official control of the editing at all and the comedy of errors which arose from this.

(c) The certainty finally attained that the Zürichers were not only to control, but themselves to censor the editing and that the part allotted to Hirsch was that of a dummy.

When he thereupon refused the offer one can only say he was right. The Leipzig committee, as we heard from Höchberg, has been further strengthened by the addition of two members who do not live there ; so it can only intervene rapidly if the three Leipzigers are unanimous. This completely transfers the real centre of gravity to Zürich, and in the long run Hirsch would no more have been able to work with the people there than would any other editor of really proletarian and revolutionary views. On this later.

(2) *The proposed line of the paper.*

Bernstein has already informed Hirsch on July 24 that the differences he had had as a *Laterne* man with individual comrades would make his position difficult.

Hirsch replies that in his opinion the general line of the paper must be the same as that of the *Laterne*, *i.e.*, one which avoids prosecution in Switzerland and does not cause unnecessary alarm in Germany. He asks who the comrades are and continues : " I only know one, and I can promise you that in a similar case of *breach of discipline* I should treat him in exactly the same way."

To which Bernstein, conscious of his new official dignity as censor, replies : As to the line of the paper, the view of the supervisory committee is in fact that the *Laterne* should not be its model ; in our opinion the paper should not be so much taken up with political radicalism but rather kept socialist in principle. Cases like the attack on Kayser, which was disapproved of by every comrade without exception (!) must be avoided in all circumstances."

And so on and so on. Liebknecht calls the attack on Kayser " a blunder " and Schramm considers it so dangerous that he thereupon puts Hirsch under censorship.

Hirsch again writes to Höchberg, saying that a case like that of Kayser " cannot occur if an official party organ is in existence whose clear statements and well-intentioned indications *cannot* be so brazenly thrown to the winds by a deputy."

Viereck, too, writes that " a dispassionate attitude and the ignoring so far as possible of any differences which have occurred . . . are laid down " for the new paper, it is not to be an " enlarged *Laterne* " and Bernstein " could at most be reproached for a too moderate tendency, if that is a reproach at a time when we cannot after all sail under our full colours."

And what is this Kayser case, this unforgivable crime which Hirsch is supposed to have committed? Kayser is the only one among the Social-Democratic deputies who spoke and voted in the Reichstag for protective tariffs. Hirsch accuses him of having committed a breach of Party discipline because Kayser:

(1) Voted for indirect taxation, the abolition of which is expressly demanded in the Party programme;

(2) Voted supplies to Bismarck, thus breaking the first fundamental rule of all our Party tactics: not a farthing to this government.

On both points Hirsch is undeniably right. And after Kayser had trampled underfoot on the one hand the Party programme, to which the deputies are, so to speak, sworn by a Congress decision, and on the other hand the very first and most imperative fundamental rule of Party tactics, and voted money to Bismarck as *thanks for the Socialist Law*, Hirsch in our opinion was absolutely right to let fly at him as roughly as he did.

We have never been able to understand why this attack on Kayser could have aroused such violent wrath in Germany. Höchberg now informs me that the "fraction" gave Kayser *permission* to come out as he did and that this permission is considered to exonerate Kayser.

If this is the position of affairs it is really a bit strong. In the first place Hirsch could know no more of this secret decision than the rest of the world. Then the discredit for the Party, which previously could be diverted on to Kayser alone, is made all the greater by this business, as is also the service performed by Hirsch in openly exposing the disgusting phraseology and even more disgusting vote of Kayser to the whole world and thus saving the honour of the Party. Or is German Social-Democracy really infected by the parliamentary disease and does it believe that through election by the people the Holy Ghost is poured out upon the elected, fraction meetings are transformed into infallible Councils and fraction decisions into unassailable dogmas?

It is true that a blunder has been committed, not however by Hirsch, but by the deputies who covered Kayser by their resolution. If those whose special duty it is to pay attention to the maintenance of Party discipline themselves break Party discipline so glaringly by a decision of this kind, so much the worse. Still worse, however, when people advance to the belief that it was not Kayser by his speech and vote or the other deputies by their resolution who violated Party discipline, but Hirsch, because despite the decision, which, moreover, was still unknown to him, he attacked Kayser.

For the rest, it is clear that on the tariff question the Party took up the same confused and indecisive attitude as it had done hitherto on almost all economic questions which have become practical ones, *e.g.*, the imperial railways. This is due to the fact that the Party organs, especially *Vorwärts* [*Forward*], instead of thoroughly discussing these questions have preferred to concern themselves with the construction of the future order of society. When, *after* the Socialist Law, the tariff question suddenly became a practical one, the most varied shades of opinion arose and there was not a single person on the spot who possessed the prerequisite for the formation of a clear and correct judgment: knowledge of the conditions of German industry and its position on the world market. Among the electorate it was inevitable that tendencies in favour of protection should appear here and there and there was a wish to take these into consideration too. The only way of getting out of this confusion; by taking the question in a purely political way (as was done in the *Laterne*) was not decisively adopted; thus it was inevitable that in this debate the Party should have come out for the first time in a hesitating, uncertain and confused manner and finally, with and through Kayser, thoroughly discredited itself.

The attack on Kayser is now made the occasion for preaching to Hirsch in every key that the new paper must on no account copy the "excesses" of the *Laterne* and should not be so much taken up with political radicalism as kept to a dispassionate line, socialist in principle. And this by Viereck as much as by Bernstein, who, just because he is too moderate, seems to the former to be the right man, because one cannot after all sail under one's full colours at present.

But why emigrate at all, if not in order to be able to sail under one's full colours? There is nothing to prevent this abroad. The German Press, Assembly and Penal Laws do not exist in Switzerland. It is therefore not only possible but a duty to say things there which could not be said at home, under the ordinary German laws, even before the Socialist Law. For here we stand not only before Germany but before Europe, and it is a duty, so far as the *Swiss* laws permit of it, to state to Europe the methods and aims of the German Party without concealment. Anyone who wants to bind himself by *German* laws in Switzerland would only prove that he was worthy of these German laws and in fact had nothing to say which was not permissible in Germany before the Exceptional Laws. Nor should any consideration be paid to the possibility that the editors will be temporarily cut off from a return to Germany. He who is not ready to risk this is not fit for such an exposed post of honour.

And further. The Exceptional Laws have banned and outlawed the German Party precisely *because* it was the only serious opposition party in Germany. If, in an organ published abroad, the Party shows its gratitude to Bismarck by giving up this rôle of the only serious opposition party, by coming out nice and docile and accepting the kick with a dispassionate attitude, it only proves that it deserved the kick. Of all the German papers produced in emigration abroad since 1830, the *Laterne* is certainly one of the most moderate. But if even the *Laterne* was too bold—then the new organ can only compromise the Party in the eyes of its sympathisers in non-German countries.

(3) *The Manifesto of the three Zürichers.*

In the meantime Höchberg's *Yearbook* has reached us, containing an article: "The Socialist Movement in Germany in Retrospect," which, as Höchberg himself tells me, has been written by these same three members of the Zürich Commission. Here we have their authentic criticism of the movement up till now and with it their authentic programme for the line of the new organ, in so far as this depends on them.

Right at the beginning we read :

" The movement which Lassalle regarded as an eminently political one, to which he summoned not only the workers but all honest democrats, *at the head of which* were to march the independent representatives of science and *all who were imbued with a true love for humanity*, was diminished under the presidency of Johann Baptist Schweitzer into a *one-sided struggle for the interests of the industrial workers.*"

I will not examine whether or how far this is historically accurate. The special reproach here brought against Schweitzer is that he *diminished* Lassalleanism, which is here taken as a bourgeois democratic-philanthropic movement, into a one-sided struggle for the interests of the industrial workers, by *deepening* its character as a class struggle of the industrial workers against the bourgeoisie. He is further reproached with his " rejection of bourgeois democracy." And what has bourgeois democracy to do with the Social-Democratic Party? If it consists of " honest men " it cannot wish for admittance, and if it does nevertheless wish to be admitted this can only be in order to start a row.

The Lassallean party " chose to conduct itself in the most *one-sided* way as a *workers' party*." The gentlemen who write that are themselves members of a Party which conducts itself in the most one-sided way as a workers' Party, they are at present invested with offices and dignities in this Party. Here there is an absolute incompatibility. If they mean what they write they must leave the Party, or at least resign their offices and dignities. If they do not do so, they are admitting that they are proposing to utilise their official position in order to combat the proletarian character of the Party. If therefore the Party leaves them their offices and dignities it will be betraying itself.

In the opinion of these gentlemen, then, the Social-Democratic Party should *not* be a one-sided workers' Party but an all-sided Party of " everyone imbued with a true love of humanity." It must prove this above all by laying aside its crude proletarian passions and placing itself under the guidance of educated, philanthropic bourgeois in order to "cultivate good taste" and "learn good form" (page 85). Then even the "disreputable behaviour" of many leaders will give way to a thoroughly respectable "bourgeois behaviour." (As if the externally disreputable behaviour of those here referred to were not the least they can be reproached with!) Then, too, "*numerous adherents* from the circles of the *educated and propertied* classes will make their appearance. But *these* must first be won if the . . . agitation conducted is to attain *tangible successes.*"

German Socialism has "attached too much importance to the winning of the *masses* and in so doing has neglected energetic (!) propaganda among the so-called upper strata of society." And then "the Party still lacks men fitted to represent it in the Reichstag." It is, however, "desirable and necessary to entrust the mandate to men who have the time and opportunity to make themselves thoroughly acquainted with the relevant materials. The simple worker and small self-employed man . . . has the necessary leisure for this only in rare and exceptional cases." So elect bourgeois!

In short: the working class of itself is incapable of its own emancipation. For this purpose it must place itself under the leadership of "educated and propertied" bourgeois who alone possess the "time and opportunity" to acquaint themselves with what is good for the workers.

And secondly the bourgeoisie is on no account to be fought against but—to be *won over* by energetic propaganda.

But if one wants to win over the upper strata of society, or only its well-disposed elements, one must not frighten them on any account. And here the three Zürichers think they have made a reassuring discovery:

"Precisely at the present time, under the pressure of the Socialist Law, the Party is showing that it *is not inclined* to pursue the path of violent bloody revolution but is determined . . . to follow the path of legality, *i.e.*, of *reform.*" So if the 500,000 to 600,000 Social-Democratic voters—between a tenth and an eighth of the whole electorate and distributed over the whole width of the land—have the sense not to run their heads against a wall and to attempt a "bloody revolution" of one against ten, this proves that they also *forbid* themselves to take advantage at any future time of a tremendous external event, a sudden revolutionary upsurge arising from it, or even a *victory* of the people gained in a conflict resulting from it. If Berlin should ever again be so uneducated to have a March 18,* the Social Democrats, instead of taking part in the fight as " riff-raff with a mania for barricades " (page 88), must rather " follow the path of legality," act pacifically, clear away the barricades and if necessary march with the glorious army against the rough uneducated one-sided masses. Or if the gentlemen assert that this is not what they meant, what did they mean then ?

But still better follows.

" The more quiet, objective and well-considered the Party is, therefore, in the way it comes out with criticism of existing conditions and proposals for changes in them, the less possible will a repetition become of the present successful strategy (when the Socialist Law was introduced) by which the conscious reaction has intimidated the bourgeoisie by fear of the Red bogey." (Page 88.)

In order to relieve the bourgeoisie of the last trace of anxiety it must be clearly and convincingly proved to them that the Red bogey is really only a bogey, and does not exist. But what is the secret of the Red bogey if it is not the bourgeoisie's dread of the inevitable life-and-death struggle between it and the proletariat ? Dread of the inevitable decision of the modern class struggle ? Do away with the class struggle and the bourgeoisie and " all independent people " will " not be afraid to go hand in hand with the proletariat." And the ones to be cheated will be precisely the proletariat.

Let the Party therefore prove by its humble and repentant attitude that it has once and for all laid aside the " improprieties and excesses " which provoked the Socialist Law. If it voluntarily promises that it only intends to act within the limits of the Socialist Law, Bismarck and the bourgeoisie will surely have the kindness to repeal this then superfluous law !

" Let no one misunderstand us " ; we do not want " to give

* March 18, 1848. The street fighting in Berlin which opened the Revolution. [*Ed. Eng. ed.*]

up our Party and our programme, but think that for years hence we shall have enough to do if we concentrate our whole strength and energy upon the attainment of certain immediate aims which must in any case be achieved before the realisation of the more far-reaching ends can be thought of." Then the bourgeois, petty bourgeois and workers who are "at present frightened away . . . by the far-reaching demands will join us in masses."

The programme is not to be *given up* but only *postponed*—to an indefinite period. One accepts it, though not really for oneself and one's own lifetime but posthumously as an heirloom to be handed down to one's children and grandchildren. In the meantime one devotes one's "whole strength and energy" to all sorts of petty rubbish and the patching up of the capitalist order of society, in order at least to produce the appearance of something happening without at the same time scaring the bourgeoisie. There I must really praise the Communist, Miquel, who proved his unshakable belief in the inevitable overthrow of capitalist society in the course of the next few hundred years by heartily carrying on swindles, contributing his honest best to the crash of 1873 and so *really* doing something to assist the collapse of the existing order.

Another offence against good form was also the "exaggerated attacks on the company promoters," who were after all "only children of their time"; "the abuse of Strousberg and similar people . . . would therefore have been better omitted." Unfortunately everyone is only a "child of his time" and if this is a sufficient excuse nobody ought ever to be attacked any more, all controversy, all struggle on our part ceases; we quietly accept all the kicks our adversaries give us because we, who are so wise, know that these adversaries are "only children of their time" and cannot act otherwise. Instead of repaying their kicks with interest we ought rather to pity these unfortunates.

Then again the Party's support of the Commune had the disadvantage, nevertheless, "that people who were otherwise well disposed to us were alienated and in general the *hatred of the bourgeoisie* against us was increased." And further, "the Party is not wholly without blame for the introduction of the

October Law, for it had increased the *hatred of the bourgeoisie* in an unnecessary way."

There you have the programme of the three censors of Zürich. In clarity it leaves nothing to be desired. Least of all to us, who are very familiar with the whole of this phraseology from the 1848 days. It is the representatives of the petty bourgeoisie who are here presenting themselves, full of anxiety that the proletariat, under the pressure of its revolutionary position, may "go too far." Instead of decided political opposition, general compromise; instead of the struggle against the government and the bourgeoisie, an attempt to win and to persuade; instead of defiant resistance to ill-treatment from above, a humble submission and a confession that the punishment was deserved. Historically necessary conflicts are all re-interpreted as misunderstandings, and all discussion ends with the assurance that after all we are all agreed on the main point. The people who came out as bourgeois democrats in 1848 could just as well call themselves social-democrats now. To them the democratic republic was unattainably remote, and to these people the overthrow of the capitalist system is equally so, and therefore has absolutely no significance for practical present-day politics; one can mediate, compromise and philanthropise to one's heart's content. It is just the same with the class struggle between proletariat and bourgeoisie. It is recognised on paper because its existence can no longer be denied, but in practice it is hushed up, diluted, attenuated.

The Social-Democratic Party *is not to be* a workers' party, is not to burden itself with the hatred of the bourgeoisie or of anyone else; should above all conduct energetic propaganda among the bourgeoisie; instead of laying stress on far-reaching aims which frighten the bourgeoisie and are not, after all, attainable in our generation, it should rather devote its whole strength and energy to those small petty-bourgeois patching-up reforms which by providing the old order of society with new props may perhaps transform the ultimate catastrophe into a gradual, piecemeal and, so far as is possible, peaceful process of dissolution. These are the same people who under the pretence of indefatigable activity not only do nothing themselves but also try to prevent anything happening at all except chatter ; the same people whose fear of every form of action in 1848 and 1849 obstructed the movement at every step and finally brought about its downfall; the same people who see a reaction and are then quite astonished to find themselves at last in a blind alley where neither resistance nor flight is possible ; the same people who want to confine history within their narrow petty-bourgeois horizon and over whose heads history invariably proceeds to the order of the day.

As to their socialist content this has been adequately criticised already in the [*Communist*] *Manifesto*, chapter X, " German or True Socialism." When the class struggle is pushed on one side as a disagreeable " crude " phenomenon, nothing remains as a basis for socialism but " true love of humanity " and empty phraseology about " justice."

It is an inevitable phenomenon, rooted in the course of development, that people from what have hitherto been the ruling classes should also join the militant proletariat and contribute cultural elements to it. We clearly stated this in the [*Communist*] *Manifesto*. But here there are two points to be noted :

First, in order to be of use to the proletarian movement these people must also bring real cultural elements to it. But with the great majority of the German bourgeois converts that is not the case. Neither the *Zukunft* [*Future*] nor the *Neue Gesellschaft* [*New Society*] have contributed anything which could advance the movement one step further. Here there is an absolute lack of real cultural material, whether concrete or theoretical. In its place we get attempts to bring superficially adopted socialist ideas into harmony with the most varied theoretical standpoints which these gentlemen have brought with them from the university or elsewhere, and of which, owing to the process of decomposition in which the remnants of German philosophy are at present involved, each is more confused than the last. Instead of thoroughly studying the new science themselves to begin with, each of them preferred to trim it to fit the point of view he had already, made a private science of his own without more ado and at once came forward with the claim that he was ready to teach it. Hence there are about as many points of view among these gentry as there are heads ; instead of producing clarity in a single case they have only produced desperate confusion—fortunately almost exclusively among themselves. Cultural elements whose first principle is to teach what they have not learnt can be very well dispensed with by the Party.

Secondly. If people of this kind from other classes join the proletarian movement, the first condition is that they should not bring any remnants of bourgeois, petty-bourgeois, etc., prejudices with them but should whole-heartedly adopt the proletarian point of view. But these gentlemen, as has been proved, are stuffed and crammed with bourgeois and petty-bourgeois ideas. In such a petty-bourgeois country as Germany these ideas certainly have their own justification. But only *outside* the Social-Democratic workers' Party. If these gentlemen form themselves into a Social-Democratic Petty-Bourgeois Party they have a perfect right to do so ; one could then negotiate with them, form a *bloc* according to circumstances, etc. But in a workers' party they are an adulterating element. If reasons exist for tolerating them there for the moment, it is also a duty *only* to tolerate them, to allow them no influence in the Party leadership and to remain aware that a break with them is only a matter of time. The time, moreover, seems to have come. How the Party can tolerate the authors of this article in its midst any longer is to us incomprehensible. But if the leadership of the Party should fall more or less into the hands of such people then the Party will simply be castrated and proletarian energy will be at an end.

As for ourselves, in view of our whole past there is only one path open to us. For almost forty years we have stressed the class struggle as the immediate driving force of history, and in particular the class struggle between the bourgeoisie and the proletariat as the great lever of the modern social revolution ; it is therefore impossible for us to co-operate with people who wish to expunge this class struggle from the movement. When the International was formed we expressly formulated the battle-cry : the emancipation of the working class must be achieved by the working class itself. We cannot therefore co-operate with people who say that the workers are too uneducated to emancipate themselves and must first be freed from above by philanthropic bourgeois and petty bourgeois. If the new Party organ adopts a line corresponding to the views of these gentlemen, and is bourgeois and not proletarian, then nothing remains for us, much though we should regret it, but publicly to declare our opposition to it and to dissolve the solidarity with which we have hitherto represented the German Party abroad. But it is to be hoped that things will not come to *that.*

¶Engels wrote this letter in the name of himself and Marx to the members of the leading group of German Social-Democracy. It is among the most important documents in which the revolutionary proletarian line of Marx and Engels is revealed. Here we see what a consistent struggle was conducted by the founders of scientific Communism against opportunism in the German Social-Democratic movement. Marx and Engels had already long been following with growing mistrust the increasing influence of petty-bourgeois elements in the Party leadership and the insufficient fight put up by the Party against them. The open and organised emergence of the group around Höchberg, in connection with the foundation of the *Sozial-Demokrat* in Zürich, caused Marx and Engels to intervene. Especially the publication of the Zürich *Yearbook for Socialist Science and Politics* with the article " The Socialist Movement in Germany in Retrospect " (signed with three asterisks, as the disguise of Höchberg, Bernstein and Schramm) induced Marx and Engels to define their fundamental attitude to the opportunist danger in the German Party and to place before the Party leadership with the greatest sharpness the choice between a break with opportunism on their part or a break with the Party on the part of Marx and Engels. In his letter to Marx on September 9, 1879, Engels puts the question of the necessity for intervention : " I shall really have to answer Bebel at last . . . the *Yearbook* . . . fortunately enables us simply to give these people definitely the reasons why it is absolutely impossible for us to co-operate with an organ in which Höchberg has anything whatever to say. . . . I think you will also be of the opinion that after this business we should do well to define our standpoint at least to the Leipzigers [the Party Executive]. If the new Party organ sings Höchberg's tune it may become necessary to do this publicly. If you will send me the things . . . I will draft a letter to Bebel and send it you." Marx answered on September 10 and insisted that the most decided tone should be taken towards Leipzig. "Liebknecht has no judgment. The letters prove what they should refute, namely, our original view that the thing was given away in Leipzig, while the Zurichers proceeded according to the conditions laid down for them. . . . I fully share your opinion that there is no more time to be lost in announcing *bluntly* and *ruthlessly* our view of the *Yearbook* drivel. . . . If they carry on in the same way with their Party organ we must *publicly* repudiate them. In these matters there is no longer any question of good nature."

HIRSCH, CARL (1841-1900). German Social-Democrat, journalist, former Lassallean. In 1868 he edited the *Demokratisches Wochenblatt* [*Democratic Weekly*] with Liebknecht; in 1870 he was editor of the Social-Democratic *Bauern and Bürgerfreund* [*The Peasants' and Citizens' Friend*]. During Liebknecht's imprisonment in the winter of 1870-71 Hirsch replaced him as editor of the *Volksstaat.* In 1874 he settled in Paris where he took part in the workers' movement. After his expulsion from Paris he went to Belgium where he published a weekly called the *Laterne* (1878-79) in which he sharply criticised the opportunist attitude of a section of the German Social-Democratic leaders. In the 'eighties he lived in Paris. (See Letter 174.)

BERNSTEIN, EDUARD (1847-1932). German Social Democrat, bank clerk. He joined the Eisenachers at the beginning of the 'seventies. Was strongly under Dühring's influence 1874-78. In 1878 was Höchberg's private secretary and one of the authors of the article *Rückblicke auf die sozialistische Bewegung in Deutschland* [*The Socialist Movement in Germany in Retrospect*] one of the earliest documents of reformism in German Social-Democracy. In 1880, together with Bebel, he came to London to negotiate with Marx and Engels, and from then onwards corresponded with Engels. At the end of 1880 he was made editor of the *Sozial Demokrat* and remained in this position until the repeal of the Socialist Law (1890) when the *Sozial Demokrat* also ceased to appear. Under the influence and guidance of Engels he was able to give the paper a revolutionary proletarian character. In 1888, after his expulsion from Switzerland, he transferred himself, with the editorship of the *Sozial Demokrat*, to London. With Kautsky he assisted Engels in deciphering Marx's manuscripts. At the beginning of the 'nineties, influenced by English trade unionism and also by bourgeois economic literature, he began to deviate to reformism again ; after Engels' death he came out with an open criticism of the foundations of Marxism in his *Voraussetzungen des Sozialismus* [*Pre-requisites of Socialism*], 1898, which became the gospel of German and international revisionism. In 1901, in order to strengthen the Social-Democratic Right wing, the imperial government allowed Bernstein to return to Germany. He was elected to the Reichstag and took over the direction of the revisionist periodical *Socialistische Monatsheft* [*Socialist Monthly*]. During the imperialist war he was a social-pacifist. The influence of his theories, officially rejected by the Party decisions of 1899 (Hanover) and 1903 (Dresden), constantly increased among the Party and trade union bureaucracy and after the imperialist war became the official creed of German Social-Democracy. In his edition of the Marx-Engels Correspondence Bernstein specially omitted the passages in which the founders of Marxism criticised Lassalle and Lassalleanism.

VIERECK, LOUIS (1851-1921). German Social-Democrat, opportunist. At the end of the 'seventies an adherent of Dühring. From 1880 he edited the *Süddeutsche Post* [*South German Post*] in Münich ; this was suppressed in 1884. At the end of the 'eighties he emigrated to America where he left the labour movement. During the imperialist war he was a German chauvinist and carried on propaganda for Germany in America.

SCHRAMM, KARL AUGUST. German economist. Insurance inspector. Liberal. Took part in the Social-Democratic movement from the 'seventies onwards. Expelled from Berlin 1878. Came out in 1884-86 with a criticism of Marxism in which he represented Marx as a degenerate follower of Rodbertus and Lassalle. Later he withdrew from the Social-Democratic movement.

KAYSER, MAX (1853-83), German Social-Democrat, active in the Berlin and Dresden organisations from 1871. Reichstag deputy from 1878, attached himself to the Right wing of the Social Democratic fraction and represented an opportunist point of view on the tariff (1878) and steamship subsidies (1885) questions.

STROUSBERG, BÉTHEL-HENRI (1823-88). Big German financier who was specially active in the years of the great company swindles (1871-73).

171. ENGELS TO J. P. BECKER

London, 1 April, 1880

Here things are just as they were in 1850 again.* The Workers' Assoc. is splitting up into all sorts of parties—Most here, Rackow there—and we have trouble enough in preventing ourselves from being dragged into the whirl. It is all a storm in a teacup, which may in some ways have a very good influence on those who take part in it by contributing to their further education, but so far as the course of the world is concerned it is more or less indifferent whether a hundred German workers here declare themselves for one side or the other. If they could exercise *any influence on the English*—but there is *absolutely no question* of that. Most, in his confused anxiety to do something, can neither keep quiet nor accomplish anything whatever ; the people in Germany simply will not see that because Most has been expelled from the country the moment for revolution is now here. *Freiheit*, by main force, is to become the most revolutionary paper in the world, but this is not achieved by just repeating the word revolution in every line. Fortunately it does not much matter what is in the paper or not. The same is true of the Zürich organ, which one day preaches revolution and the next *declares that a revolution by force would be the greatest misfortune*, which is afraid on the one hand of being outdone by Most's big words and on the other that the workers may take its own big words seriously. So it is a choice between the empty shrieking of *Freiheit* and the narrow philistinism of the *Sozial Demokrat*.

I am afraid our friends in Germany are mistaken about the kind of organisation which should be maintained under present

* Engels is referring to the German colony in London, this time of exiles under the Socialist Law. [*Ed. Eng. ed.*]

conditions. I have nothing against the fact that the chief members of Parliament are taking the lead in the absence of any other leadership. But they can neither demand nor enforce the strict obedience which the old Party leadership—elected for this purpose—could insist upon. Least of all in the present circumstances, without a press, without mass meetings. The looser the organisation is now in appearance the stronger it will be in reality. But instead of this the old system is to be maintained, final decisions are in the hands of the party leadership (although there is no congress to correct it or if necessary to dismiss it), and anybody who attacks one of them is a *heretic*. And with it all the best of them know themselves that there are all sorts of incapable and in other ways not quite sound people among them, and they must surely be very limited if they do not realise that it is not they who have the command of their organ but Höchberg, thanks to his money-bags, and with him his fellow-philistines Schramm and Bernstein. In my opinion the *old Party*, together with its former organisation, has come *to an end*. If, as is to be expected, the European movement soon gets going again, the *great mass of the German proletariat* will enter it and then the 500,000 men of the year 1878 will join the trained and educated kernel of this mass ; but then too the old "strict organisation" handed down by Lassallean tradition will become a brake which might hold back a cart but cannot be applied to an avalanche.

Moreover these people are doing nothing but things well-calculated to break up the Party. First the Party is supposed constantly to provide for the old agitators and editors, thanks to which it gets saddled with a whole crowd of papers with nothing whatever in them beyond what can be read in every bourgeois gossip rag. And the workers are expected to co-operate with this indefinitely ! Secondly, they come out in the Reichstag and the Saxon Landtag in such a tame way, for the most part, that they discredit themselves and the Party before the whole world, making "*positive proposals*" to the existing government as to how to do things better in small questions of detail, etc. And the workers, who have been declared outside the law, who are delivered over bound hand and foot to the caprices of the police, are expected to regard this as proper representation ! Thirdly, the philistine petty-bourgeois tone of the *Sozial Demokrat*, which they sanction. In every letter they tell us not on any account to believe reports of any division or differences of opinion having broken out in the Party, but everybody who comes from Germany assures one that the people are completely bewildered by this behaviour on the part of their leaders and by no means in agreement with it. Indeed, considering the character of our workers, which has so splendidly maintained itself, anything else would be impossible. It is the peculiar characteristic of the German movement that all the mistakes of the leadership are invariably made good again by the masses, and so it will no doubt be this time too.

¶Engels in a letter to Bernstein (October 20, 1888) makes a very important remark about working class parties and the dialectic of their development :

" It seems that *every* worker's party, in a great country, can only develop itself by internal struggle, and this is based on the laws of dialectical development in general. The German Party became what it is in the struggle between the Eisenachers and Lassalleans, and this tussle itself played a chief part. Unity only became possible when the gang of ruffians whom Lassalle had deliberately cultivated as tools had worked themselves out, and there too it was accomplished with much too much haste on our side. In France, those people who while indeed sacrificing the Bakuninist theory are still carrying on the Bakuninist methods of struggle and at the same time trying to sacrifice the class character of the movement to their own particular ends, must also first work themselves out before unity is possible again. To try to preach unity in such circumstances would be sheer folly. Moral sermons are useless as treatment for infantile diseases, which, under present-day conditions, have got to be gone through some time anyhow." [Compare pages 327, 402.]

BECKER, JOHANN PHILIPP (1809-86). German revolutionary ; prominent member of the First International. Leader of the Geneva section. He began early on to take part in the revolutionary movement, participating in the Hamburg Festival of

May 27, 1832, and playing a leading part in the Baden rising of 1849. He was a typical partisan and also took part in the Italian revolution on the side of Garibaldi. Becker was a Communist whose whole soul was devoted to the workers' movement. From 1866 onwards he was editor of the *Vorbote*, the organ of the Geneva section of the International. After his death Engels wrote of Becker that " he was one of those rare people who have only to follow their instinct in order always to act correctly." Since he lived as an emigré and had a large family Becker suffered from poverty. Marx, who greatly valued Becker, wrote in one of his letters : " Be assured, dear friend, that nothing is more painful to me than to be obliged to watch helplessly and passively the struggle of a man like yourself. I admire your tenacity, your fiery zeal and your activity. The ancients, I think it was Æschines, say that one should desire to acquire worldly goods in order to spring to the help of one's friends in time of need. What deep human wisdom lies in this saying ! " (See also Note to Letter 185.)

172. MARX TO DANIELSON*

London, 19 February, 1881.

I have read with the greatest interest your article, which is in the best sense of the word " original." Hence the boycotting —if you break through the webs of routine thought, you are always sure to be " boycotted " in the first instance ; it is the only arm of defence which in their first perplexity the *routiniers* know how to wield. I have been " boycotted " in Germany for many, many years, and am still so in England, with that little variation that from time to time something so absurd and asinine is launched against me that I would blush to take any public notice of it. But try on ! The next thing to do—in my opinion—is to take up the wonderfully increasing *indebtedness of the landlords*, the upper-class representatives of agriculture, and show them how they are " crystallised " in the retort under the control of the " new pillars of society."

I am very anxious to see your polemics with the " *Slovo*." As soon as I shall sail in more quiet waters I shall enter more

* This letter was written in English.

fully upon your *Esquisse* [sketch]. For the present I cannot omit one observation. The soil being exhausted and getting not the elements—by artificial and vegetable and animal manure, etc. —to supply its wants, will, with the changing favour of the seasons, of circumstances independent of human influence—still continue to yield harvests of very different amounts, though, summing up a period of years, as for instance, from 1870-80, the stagnant character of the production presents itself in the most striking character. Under such circumstances the favourable climatic conditions pave the way to a *famine year* by quickly consuming and setting free the mineral fertilisers still potent on the soil, while *vice-versa*, a *famine-year*, and still more a series of bad years following it, allow the soil-inherent minerals to accumulate anew, and to work efficiently with returning favour of the climatic conditions. Such a process goes, of course, everywhere on, but *elsewhere* it is checked by the modifying intervention of the agriculturist himself. It becomes the *only regulating factor* where man has ceased to be a " power "—for want of means.

So we have 1870 as an excellent harvest in your country, but that year is a *climax year*, and as such immediately followed by a very bad one ; the year *1871*, the very bad harvest, must be considered as the starting point for a new little cycle, till we come to the new climax year 1874, which is immediately followed by the famine year 1875 ; then the upwards movement begins again, ending in the still worse famine year 1880. The summing up of the years during the whole period proves that the average annual production remained the same and that the mere natural factors have alone produced the changes, comparing the single years and the smaller cycles of years.

I wrote you some time ago, that if the great industrial and commercial crisis England has passed through, went over without the culminating financial crash at London, this *exceptional* phenomenon was only due to French money. This is now seen and acknowledged even by English *routiniers*. Thus the *Statist* (January 29, 1881) says : " The money market has only be[en] so easy as it has been during the past years *through an accident*. The *Bank of France* in the early autumn permitted its stock of gold bullion to fall from £30 millions to £22 millions . . . . *Last autumn undoubtedly there was a very narrow escape.*" (!)

The *English railway system* rolls on the same inclined plane as the European *Public Debt system.* The ruling magnates amongst the different railway-nets directors contract not only—progressively—new loans *in order to enlarge their network*, *i.e.*, the "territory," where they rule as absolute monarchs, but they enlarge their respective networks *in order to have* new pretexts *for engaging in new loans* which enable them to pay the interest due to the holders of obligations, preferential shares, etc., and also from time to time to throw a sop to the much ill-used common shareholders in the shape of somewhat increased dividends. This pleasant method must one day or another terminate in an ugly catastrophe.

In the United States the railway kings have become the butt of attacks, not only, as before this, on the part of the farmers and other industrial "*entrepreneurs*" of the *West*, but also on the part of the grand representative of commerce—the *New York Chamber of Commerce.* The Octopodus railway king and financial swindler *Gould* has, on his side, told the New York commercial magnates : You now attack the railways, because you think them most vulnerable considering their present unpopularity ; but take heed : after the railways *every sort of corporation* (means in the Yankee dialect joint stock company) will have its turn ; then, later on, all forms of associated capital ; finally *all forms of capital ;* you are thus paving the way to—*Communism* whose tendencies are already more and more spreading among the people. M. Gould "*a le flair bon.*"*

In *India* serious complications, if not a general outbreak, is in store for the British government. What the English take from them annually in the form of rent, dividends for railways useless to the Hindus ; pensions for military and civil service men, for Afghanistan and other wars, etc., etc.—what they take from them *without any equivalent* and quite apart from what they appropriate to themselves annually *within* India, speaking only of the *value of the commodities* the Indians have gratuitously and annually to *send over* to England—it amounts to *more than the*

* Monsieur Gould has a keen scent.

total sum of income of the sixty millions of agricultural and industrial labourers of India ! This is a bleeding process, with a vengeance ! The famine years are pressing each other and in dimensions till now not yet suspected in Europe ! There is an actual conspiracy going on wherein Hindus and Mussulmans co-operate ; the British government is aware that something is " brewing," but this shallow people (I mean the governmental men), stultified by their own parliamentary ways of talking and thinking, do not even desire to see clear, to realise the whole extent of the imminent danger ! To delude others and by deluding them to delude yourself—this is : *parliamentary wisdom* in a nutshell ! *Tant mieux !**

173. MARX TO DOMELA NIEUWENHUIS

London, 22 February, 1881

The " question " of the forthcoming Zürich Congress about which you inform me seems to me—a mistake. The thing to be done at any definite given moment of the future, the thing *immediately* to be done, depends of course entirely on the given historical conditions in which one has to act. But this question is in the *clouds* and therefore is really the statement of a phantom problem to which the only answer can be—the *criticism of the question* itself. No equation can be solved unless the elements of its solution are involved in its terms. Moreover the embarrassments of a government which has suddenly come into being through a people's victory have nothing specifically " socialist " about them. On the contrary. The victorious bourgeois politicians at once feel themselves embarrassed by their " victory " while the socialist can at least take action without any embarrassment. One thing you can at any rate be sure of : a socialist government does not come into power in a country unless conditions are so developed that it can above all take the necessary measures for intimidating the mass of the bourgeoisie sufficiently to gain time—the first *desideratum* [*requisite*]—for lasting action.

Perhaps you will point to the Paris Commune ; but apart

* So much the better.

from the fact that this was merely the rising of a town under exceptional conditions, the majority of the Commune was in no sense socialist, nor could it be. With a small amount of sound common sense, however, they could have reached a compromise with Versailles useful to the whole mass of the people—the only thing that could be reached at the time. The appropriation of the Bank of France alone would have been enough to dissolve all the pretensions of the Versailles people in terror, etc., etc.

The general demands of the French bourgeoisie laid down before 1789 were roughly just the same, *mutatis mutandis* [with corresponding alterations] as the first immediate demands of the proletariat are pretty uniformly to-day in all countries with capitalist production. But had any eighteenth-century Frenchman the faintest idea *a priori* beforehand of the way in which the demands of the French bourgeoisie would be accomplished? The doctrinaire and necessarily fantastic anticipations of the programme of action for a revolution of the future only divert us from the struggle of the present. The dream that the end of the world was at hand inspired the early Christians in their struggle with the Roman Empire and gave them confidence in victory. Scientific insight into the inevitable disintegration of the dominant order of society continually proceeding before our eyes, and the ever-growing passion into which the masses are scourged by the old ghosts of government—while at the same time the positive development of the means of production advances with gigantic strides—all this is a sufficient guarantee that with the moment of the outbreak of a real proletarian revolution there will also be given the conditions (though these are certain not to be idyllic) of its next immediate *modus operandi* [form of action].

It is my conviction that the critical juncture for a new International Workingmen's Association has not yet arrived and for this reason I regard all workers' congresses, particularly socialist congresses, in so far as they are not related to the immediate given conditions in this or that particular nation, as not merely useless but harmful. They will always fade away in innumerable stale generalised banalities.

¶NIEUWENHUIS, F. DOMELA (born 1846). Dutch socialist, later an anarchist. One of the leaders of the *Social-Democratic Federation* which had been formed from various Socialist Societies in 1881. Nieuwenhuis was originally a pastor but left the church in 1879. In 1888 he was elected to parliament. But when at the general election of 1892 he lost his seat, he gradually began to come out against the utilisation of parliament as a platform and turned more and more towards anarchism. He finally broke with the Marxist workers' movement at the London Congress of the Second International in 1896.

ZÜRICH CONGRESS. In May 1880 it was resolved at the Brussels Congress of the Belgian Socialists to organise a world congress of workers in the year 1884, in order to revive the International. The manifesto of the organisation commission appointed by the Congress laid down no concrete actual tasks. The German Social-Democrats, at their Wyden Party Congress (August 1880), decided to participate. Owing to the ban of the authorities the Congress could not take place in Zürich and was transferred to Chur. It had no practical results, as Marx had correctly foretold. The attempt to re-found the International did not succeed, as is well known, until the Paris Congress of 1889.

174. MARX TO HIS DAUGHTER JENNY

London, 11 April, 1881.

It is dull since you went away—without you and Johnny and Harra! and Mr. "Tea." I often run to the window when I hear children's voices that sound like our children's voices, forgetting for the moment that the little chaps are across the Channel.

One comfort is that you have good living-quarters, suitable for the children; otherwise everything seems rather worse than in London—except of course the climate, the beneficial effect of which, on asthma too, you will by and by discover.

I have got another new doctor for mother, recommended to my by Professor Lankester*—Dr. Donkin; he seems a bright and intelligent man but for mother's trouble one man really seems to me as good, and perhaps better, than another man.

* Professor Ray Lankester. See page 414. Marx's wife, Jenny, died on December 1881. [*Ed. Eng. ed.*]

However, the change of medical advisers is a distraction for her and for the first period—which does not as a rule last long—she is full of praise for the new Æsculapius. Longuet's eyeglasses turned up directly after you left, they were in fact reposing in your bedroom. Hirsch has been selected to bring them across, but this gossipmonger seems unable to tear himself away from London at a time when there is a lot to pry out. The "great" Most affair alone is an inexhaustable spring of fresh (if by no means joyously sparkling) water for this Hirsch. He is threatening now not to leave until April 18. And then he has found a companion in Kautsky—at whom he scowled so darkly; Engels too has taken a much milder view of this Kauz* since he has proved himself a very talented drinker. When this charmer first appeared at my place—I mean little Kauz—the first question which escaped me was: are you like your mother? Not in the very least, he assured me, and I silently congratulated his mother. He is a mediocrity with a small-minded outlook, superwise (only 26), very conceited, industrious in a certain sort of way, he busies himself a lot with statistics but does not read anything very clever out of them, belongs by nature to the tribe of the philistines but is otherwise a decent fellow in his own way. I turn him over to friend Engels as much as possible.

The day before yesterday the Dogberry Club was here; yesterday, in addition to the two Maitland girls—and for a moment Lankester and Dr. Donkin—an invasion from Hyndman and spouse, who both have too much staying power. I don't dislike the wife, for she has a brusque, unconventional and decided way of thinking and speaking, but it is funny to see how admiringly her eyes fasten upon the lips of her self-satisfied garrulous husband. Mother was so tired (it was nearly 10.30 p.m.) that she withdrew. But she was amused by some byplay. For Tussy has discovered a new *Wunderkind* among the Dogberries, a certain Radford; this youth is already a barrister at law, but despises the *jus* [law] and is working in the same line as Waldhorn. He looks well, a cross between Irving and the late Lassalle (though he has nothing in common with the

* Queer fellow, a pun on Kautsky's name. For Kautsky, see page 400.

cynically oily, obtrusive, ducal manners of the latter) an intelligent and somewhat promising boy. Well this is the point of the story—Dolly Maitland pays fearful court to him so that mother and Tussy are signalling to each other all through supper. Finally Mr. Maitland arrived as well, fairly sober, and also had a wordy duel with his instructive table companion—Hyndman—about Gladstone, in whom the spiritualist Maitland believes. I—rather annoyed by a bad throat— felt glad when the whole lot vanished. It is a strange thing that one cannot well live altogether without company, and that when you get it, you try hard to rid yourself of itself.*

Hartmann is working hard as a common workman in Woolwich ; the difficulty of talking to him in any language at all increases. The Russian refugees in Geneva are demanding that he should repudiate Rochefort, and publicly. This he will not and cannot do, and it is also impossible, if only on account of the exaggerated letter which the Petersburg Committee wrote to Rochefort and which he on his side published in the *Intransigeant*. The Genevans have in fact long been trying to persuade Europe that it is really *they* who direct the movement in Russia ; now when this *lie*, spread by themselves, is seized upon by Bismarck and Co. and becomes dangerous to them, they declare the opposite and vainly attempt to convince the world of their innocence. Actually they are mere doctrinaires, confused anarchist socialists, and their influence upon the Russian "theatre of war" is zero.

Have you been following the trial of the assassins† in Petersburg? They are sterling people through and through, *sans pose melodramatique* [no melodramatic pose], simple, businesslike, heroic. Shouting and doing are irreconcilable opposites. The Petersburg Executive Committee, which acts so energetically, issues manifestos of refined "moderation." It is far removed from the schoolboy way in which Most‡

* This and the preceding sentence, besides a number of words and phrases in this letter, were written by Marx in English. [*Ed. Eng. ed.*]

† The Russian revolutionaries of the *Narodnaya Volya* [People's Will] who had succeeded in their plot to kill the Emperor Alexander II on March 1, 1881. [*Ed. Eng. ed.*]

‡ Most. See page 345.

and other childish whimperers preach tyrannicide as a "theory" and "panacea" (that was done by such innocent Englishmen as Disraeli, [Walter] Savage Landor, Macaulay and Stanfield the friend of Mazzini); on the contrary they try to teach Europe that their *modus operandi* [method of action] is a specifically Russian and historically inevitable method about which there is no more reason to moralise—for or against—than there is about the earthquake in Chios.

This affair was the occasion of a fine row in the House of Commons. (You know that to please Bismarck and Gortchakov these miserable Gladstonians have embarked on an attack upon the freedom of the press in England, in the person of the wretched Most, an attack in which they are scarcely likely to succeed.) Lord Churchill (a cheeky Tory youngster of the Marlborough family) questioned Sir Charles Dilke and Brassey, both understrappers in the Cabinet, regarding financial subsidies to the *Freiheit*. These were flatly denied and Churchill was obliged to name his authority. He then named the inevitable Mr. Maltman Barry! I am enclosing you a cutting about this affair from the *Weekly Despatch* (Dilke's paper, edited by the "philosophical Radical," Ashton Dilke, brother of the great "Dilke") and a statement by Maltman Barry in the *Daily News*. Dilke is obviously lying; a miserable creature, this swaggerer who has nominated himself as the future "President of the British Republic" and who, for fear of losing his job, allows Bismarck to dictate to him which papers he is to favour with £1 and which not. If it were only known as well that immediately after Hartmann's arrival in London Ashton Dilke invited him to a luncheon! But Hartmann refused the invitation because he would not allow himself to be "exhibited."

About the Comtist renegade Maxse, by the way. *Justice** does him far too much honour and handles him with kid gloves. To this strange clique—of English Liberals and their even worse sub-species the so-called Radicals—it really seems a crime that, contrary to all tradition and in breach of agreement,

* Clemenceau's French radical bourgeois paper; Charles Longuet worked on its editorial staff.

Justice fails to treat these shams and humbugs in the traditional manner and to maintain the legend about them current in the Continental liberal press! When one considers the utterly shameless way in which the London press attacks the Socialist Party in every European country and how difficult it is, supposing one ever regards it as worth the trouble, to answer a word, to get even a few lines of reply into that press—then it is really going rather far to recognise the principle that if a Parisian paper entangles itself in a criticism of the "great" Gladstone, that arch hypocrite and casuist of an antiquated school, it is then obliged to put whole columns at the disposal of Herr Maxse and his prose in order that he may repay Gladstone in kind for the advancement received from him.

Assuming that the policy of Gladstone (the Coercion and Arms Acts man) with regard to Ireland were as correct as it is false, would this be a reason for talking about the "generosity" or "magnanimity" of this man? As if there were any question of this sort of thing between England and Ireland! It should really be explained to Maxse that Pecksniffian phrases of this kind have the rights of citizenship in London but not in Paris!

Let Longuet read *Parnell's* speech in Cork in *to-day's Times;* there he will find the heart of what there is to be said about *Gladstone's new Land Act;* and here it should not be overlooked that by his shameful preliminary measures (including the annulment of freedom of speech for members of the House of Commons) Gladstone prepared the conditions under which *the evictions in Ireland are now proceeding on a mass scale*, while the *Act* is mere shadow boxing, since the Lords—who get everything they want from Gladstone and no longer need to tremble at the Land League—will doubtless either reject it or else castrate it so much that the Irish themselves will eventually vote *against* it.

¶MARX-LONGUET, JENNY (1844-83), Marx's eldest daughter, married to Charles Longuet. In 1870 she took action in the Irish struggles by publishing in a French paper revelations of the treatment of the Irish political prisoners by the English bourgeoisie ; by this means she forced the Gladstone government to conduct an investigation into the question. She wrote under the name of "J. Williams."

JOHNNY, HARRA, MR. "TEA." The Longuets' children, of whom Marx was very fond. The eldest, "Johnny," is the well-known French centrist and 'patriot' Jean Longuet. At the French Socialist Party Congress at Tours in 1920 where the majority decided to found the Communist Party of France he remained with the minority which split off.

LONGUET, CHARLES (1833-1901), French journalist, Proudhonist. Delegate to the Lausanne Congress of the First International (1867) ; member of the Commune and editor of its official organ ; after the fall of the Commune he fled to London. In 1880 he returned to France and was elected a member of the Paris City Council. Longuet worked on the editorial staff of the bourgeois radical paper *La Justice*.

HYNDMAN, HENRY MAYERS (1842-1922). English Social-Democrat. Up to 1880, when he got to know Marx, Hyndman was a "democrat" of an indefinite type who had connections and sympathies with the Tories. "He achieved his turn to socialism after reading *Capital* (in the French translation) during one of the numerous voyages he made to America between 1874 and 1880." (Lenin.) [See Letter 176.] He was, in Lenin's words, "a bourgeois philistine, who belonging to the best of his class, eventually struggles through to socialism but never quite sheds bourgeois conceptions and prejudices." He was not capable of making the Social-Democratic Federation, which he founded in 1881, into a mass organisation. In a letter to Sorge (May 12, 1894), Engels writes that Hyndman's Social-Democratic Federation had succeeded "in reducing the Marxian theory of development to a rigid orthodoxy, which the workers are not to work their way up to by their own class feeling but to swallow instantly without development, as an article of faith." Engels, writing to Bebel on August 30, 1883 (Letter 188) mentions Hyndman's extreme chauvinism, which was a marked characteristic throughout his political life. In 1914 he was an ardent patriot ; after the October Revolution in Russia he was a supporter of intervention. (For Hyndman, the S.D.F., etc., see Letters 176, 188, 197, 200, 207.)

HARTMANN, LEO (1850-1913). Russian revolutionary. Member of the revolutionary petty-bourgeois Socialist Party *Narod-*

naya Volya (People's Will) in whose terrorist activities he took a prominent part. After the failure of the attempt on the Tsar's train he fled to Paris, where, at the request of the Russian government, he was arrested by the French police. His deportation to Russia was however prevented by the energetic efforts of the Russian emigrés and the French radical press. He then went to London where he occupied himself a great deal with inventions, and later to America. He was on friendly terms with Marx and Engels.

BARRY, MALTMAN (1842-1909). Journalist, member of the First International, later attached himself to the Conservatives. [See Letter 225.]

ROCHEFORT, HENRI (1831-1913). French journalist and politician, one of the leaders of the left Republican movement under the Empire ; sentenced to imprisonment on account of his sympathetic attitude to the Commune, he fled to London. After the amnesty he returned to Paris in 1880 and took over the direction of the radical paper *Intransigeant.* Later became a nationalist and monarchist.

PARNELL, CHARLES (1846-91). Leader of the Irish bourgeois Nationalist Party and of the Irish Land League. Leader of his Party in the House of Commons. The Irish Land League fought (1879-81) against the evictions of tenants from their farms, chiefly using the weapon of boycott. The League was prohibited in 1881.

175. MARX TO SORGE

London, 30 June, 1881.

Theoretically the man [Henry George] is utterly backward! He understands nothing about the nature of *surplus value* and so wanders about in speculations which follow the English model but have now been superseded even among the English, about the different portions of surplus value to which independent existence is attributed—about the relations of profit, rent, interest, etc. His fundamental dogma is that *everything would be all right* if ground rent were paid to the state. (You will find payment of this kind among the *transitional measures* included in *The Communist Manifesto* too.) This idea originally belonged to the bourgeois economists ; it was first put forward (apart from a similar demand at the end of the eighteenth century) by the earliest *radical* followers of Ricardo, soon after his death. I said of it in 1847, in my work against Proudhon: "We can understand that economists like Mill" (the elder, not his son John Stuart, who also repeats this in a somewhat modified form) "Cherbuliez, Hilditch and others have demanded that rent should be paid to the state in order that it may serve as a substitute for taxes. This is a frank expression of the hatred which the *industrial capitalist* dedicates to the *landed proprietor*, who seems to him a useless and superfluous element in the general total of bourgeois production."

We ourselves, as I have already mentioned, adopted this appropriation of ground rent by the state among numerous other *transitional measures*, which, as we also remarked in the *Manifesto*, are and must be contradictory in themselves.

But the first person to turn this *desideratum* [requirement] of the *radical* English bourgeois economists into a *socialist panacea*, to declare this procedure to be the solution of the antagonisms involved in the present method of production, was *Colins*, a former old Hussar officer of Napoleon's, born in Belgium, who in the latter days of Guizot and the first of Napoleon the Less, favoured the world from Paris with some fat volumes about this "discovery" of his. Like another discovery he made, namely, that while there is no God there is an "*immortal*" human soul and that animals have "no feelings." For if they had feelings, that is souls, we should be cannibals and a realm of righteousness could never be founded upon earth. His "anti-landownership" theory together with his theory of the soul, etc., have been preached every month for years in the Parisian *Philosophie de l'Avenir* [*Philosophy of the Future*] by his few remaining followers, mostly Belgians. They call themselves "rational collectivists" and have praised Henry George. After them and besides them, among other people, the Prussian banker and former lottery owner Samten from East Prussia, a shallow-brained fellow, has eked out this "socialism" into a thick volume.

All these "socialists" since Colins have this much in common that they leave *wage labour* and therefore *capitalist production* in existence and try to bamboozle themselves or the world into believing that if ground rent were transformed into a state tax *all the evils* of capitalist production would disappear of themselves. The whole thing is therefore simply an attempt, decked out with socialism, to *save capitalist domination* and indeed to *establish it afresh* on *an even wider basis* than its present one.

This cloven hoof (at the same time ass's hoof) is also unmistakably revealed in the declamations of Henry George. And it is the more unpardonable in him because he ought to have put the question to himself in just the opposite way: How did it happen that in the United States, where, relatively, that is in comparison with civilised Europe, the land was accessible to the great mass of the people and to a certain degree (again relatively) still is, capitalist economy and the corresponding enslavement of the working class have developed more *rapidly* and *shamelessly* than in any other country!

On the other hand George's book, like the sensation it has made with you, is significant because it is a first, if unsuccessful, attempt at emancipation from the orthodox political economy.

H. George does not seem, for the rest, to know anything about the history of the early *American anti-renters*,* who were rather practical men than theoretical. Otherwise he is a talented writer (with a talent for Yankee advertisement too) as his article on California in the *Atlantic* proves, for instance. He also has the repulsive presumption and arrogance which is displayed by all panacea-mongers without exception.

¶GEORGE, HENRY (1839-97). American bourgeois economist, earlier a sailor, gold-digger and printer. He was the founder of the petty-bourgeois land reform movement. See further Letters 202, 203 and Notes.

* Settlers in New York State in the 'thirties and 'forties of the 19th century who refused to pay rent for their land and shot down the sheriffs' officers who came to enforce payment. The no-renters numbered thousands and turned the scale at several elections.

176. MARX TO SORGE

London, 15 December, 1881.

The English have recently begun to occupy themselves more with *Capital*, etc. Thus in the last *October* (or November, I am not quite sure) number of the *Contemporary* there is an article on socialism by *John Rae*. Very inadequate, full of mistakes, but " fair " as one of my English friends told me the day before yesterday. And why fair ? Because* John Rae does *not suppose* that for the forty years I am spreading my pernicious theories, I was being instigated by " bad " motives. " *Seine Grossmuth muss ich loben*."† The fairness of making yourself at least sufficiently acquainted with the subject of your criticism seems a thing quite unknown to the penmen of British philistinism.

Before this, in the beginning of June, there was published by a certain Hyndman (who had before intruded himself into my house) a little book : *England for All*. It pretends to be written as an *exposé* of the programme of the " Democratic Federation " —a recently formed association of different English and Scotch radical societies, half bourgeois, half proletaires. The chapters on Labour and Capital are only literal extracts from, or circumlocutions of, the *Capital*, but the fellow does neither quote the book, nor its author, but to shield himself from exposure remarks at the end of his preface : " For the ideas and much of the matter contained in Chapters II and III, I am indebted to the work of a great thinker and original writer, etc., etc." Vis-à-vis myself, the fellow wrote stupid letters of excuse, for instance, that " the English don't like to be taught by foreigners," that " my name was so much detested, etc." With all that, his little book—so far as it pilfers the *Capital*—makes good propaganda, although the man is a " weak " vessel, and very far from having even the patience—the first condition of learning anything—of studying a matter thoroughly. All those amiable middle-class writers—if not specialists—have an itching to make money or name or political capital *immediately* out of any new thoughts they may have got at by any

* From here onwards this letter was written in English.
† " I must praise his magnanimity."

favourable windfall. Many evenings this fellow has pilfered from me, in order—to take me out and to learn in the easiest way.

Lastly there was published on the first December last (I shall send you a copy of it) in the monthly review, *Modern Thought*, an article : "Leaders of Modern Thought" ; No. XXIII—*Karl Marx*. By *Ernest Belfort Bax*.

Now this is the first English publication of the kind which is pervaded by a real enthusiasm for the new ideas themselves and boldly stands up against Brit. Philistinism. That does not prevent that the biographical notices the author gives of me are mostly wrong, etc. In the exposition of my economic principles and in his translations (*i.e.*, quotations of the *Capital*) much is wrong and confused, but with all that the appearance of this article, announced in large letters by placards on the walls of Westend London, has produced a great sensation. What was most important for me, I received the said number of *Modern Thought* already on the 30th of November, so that my dear wife had the last days of her life still cheered up. You know the passionate interest she took in all such affairs.

¶BAX, ERNEST BELFORT (1854-1926). Took part in the foundation of the Social Democratic Federation and collaborated in its organ, *Justice*, and in the monthly, *To-Day*, which he first tried to run independently but owing to lack of funds had to make over to Hyndman in 1884. Broke with Hyndman at the end of 1884 and together with Morris and Eleanor Marx-Aveling etc. helped to form the Socialist League, which, however, later fell under anarchist influence. Later resumed his relations with Hyndman and shared his chauvinistic position. Engels wrote of Bax and Aveling (to Kautsky 26 June and 20 October 1884) that they had "the best intentions and learn a lot too, but everything is confused and by themselves these literary people can do nothing;" "they are both thoroughly sound, intelligent and sincere although needing great assistance." This was at the period just before the formation of the Socialist League. Later (to Liebknecht 12 May 1886) Engels notes that "Bax and Morris are strongly influenced by the anarchists" and in 1889, see Letter 207, refers to Bax as "only a book-worm." [*Ed. Eng. ed.*]

177. ENGELS TO KAUTSKY

London, 12 September, 1882.

You ask me what the English workers think about colonial policy. Well, exactly the same as they think about politics in general: the same as what the bourgeois think. There is no workers' party here, there are only Conservatives and Liberal-Radicals, and the workers gaily share the feast of England's monopoly of the world market and the colonies. In my opinion the colonies proper, *i.e.*, the countries occupied by a European population, Canada, the Cape, Australia, will all become independent; on the other hand the countries inhabited by a native population, which are simply subjugated, India, Algiers, the Dutch, Portuguese and Spanish possessions, must be taken over for the time being by the proletariat and led as rapidly as possible towards independence. How this process will develop is difficult to say. India will perhaps, indeed very probably, produce a revolution, and as the proletariat emancipating itself cannot conduct any colonial wars, this would have to be given full scope; it would not pass off without all sorts of destruction, of course, but that sort of thing is inseparable from all revolutions. The same might also take place elsewhere, *e.g.*, in Algiers and Egypt, and would certainly be the best thing *for us*. We shall have enough to do at home. Once Europe is reorganised, and North America, that will furnish such colossal power and such an example that the semi-civilised countries will follow in their wake of their own accord. Economic needs alone will be responsible for this. But as to what social and political phases these countries will then have to pass through before they likewise arrive at socialist organisation, we to-day can only advance rather idle hypotheses, I think. One thing alone is certain: the victorious proletariat can force no blessings of any kind upon any foreign nation without undermining its own victory by so doing. Which of course by no means excludes defensive wars of various kinds.

The business in Egypt has been contrived by Russian diplomacy. Gladstone is to take Egypt (which he has not got yet by a long way and if he had it he would still be a long way from keeping it) in order that Russia may take Armenia, which according to Gladstone would be a further liberation of a Christian country from the Mohammedan yoke. Everything else about the affair is a sham, humbug, pretext. Whether the humbug will succeed will soon be seen.

¶In September 1882 the Egyptian army was destroyed at Tel-el-Kebir by the British, who then occupied Cairo. This was the final stage in Britain's forcible seizure of Egypt.

KAUTSKY, KARL (born 1854), German Social-Democrat, one of the best-known theoreticians of the Second International. By birth a Czech. He graduated at the University of Vienna and in 1874 joined the Austrian Social-Democratic Party, in which he attached himself to the "Left" semi-anarchist wing; at this time he began working in connection with the Democratic and Social-Democratic press, especially with the *Volkstaat;* he was still completely under the influence of Lassalle and the bourgeois economists at this period. In 1879 he associated himself with the "Left" opportunist *Freiheit* of Most* but in the same year, at the invitation of the reformist Höchberg,† he settled in Zürich in order to collaborate in Höchberg's periodicals. In the spring Kautsky was commissioned by Höchberg to go to London, where he made the acquaintance of Marx and Engels. (See Letter 174.) From 1883 onwards he was the editor of *Neue Zeit*, in 1885 he settled in Stuttgart. From the beginning of the 'eighties he began to make an approach to Marxism. Engels in his letters criticised the theoretical mistakes in Kautsky's works and his vacillations as editor of the *Neue Zeit.* (See Letter 195.) Kautsky later wrote a series of Marxist works, but even in his best works he made a number of important mistakes; he was never a consistent dialectical materialist and was equally far from ever adopting a revolutionary Marxist position on the question of the proletarian dictatorship. At the end of the 'nineties he led the fight against the revisionism

* See Letter 162, Note.
† See Letters 164, 166, 170.

of Bernstein (Note to Letter 170) in the course of which, however, he manifested great vacillations. Later he was the theoretical leader of centrism, the high priest of the "orthodoxy" of the Second International which attenuated Marxism and served as a cloak for revisionism. In the years of the first imperialist war Kautsky was a social pacifist. After the October Revolution he became the leading champion of the struggle against Marxism-Leninism and as a sworn foe of the proletarian revolution preached intervention against the Soviet Union. Since then he has published a great number of pamphlets and large Volumes in which he adulterates and distorts Marxism in the crudest way.

178. ENGELS TO BEBEL

London, 28 October, 1882.

I read [Vollmar's] second article rather hurriedly, with two or three people talking the whole time. Otherwise the way he represents the French Revolution to himself would have led me to detect the French influence and with it my Vollmar too, no doubt. You have perceived this side quite correctly. He at last is the dreamed-of realisation of the phrase about the "one reactionary mass." All the official parties united in one lump *here*, all the Socialists in one column *there*—great decisive battle. Victory all along the line at one blow. In real life things do not happen so simply. In real life, as you also remark, the revolution begins the other way round by the great majority of the people and also of the official parties massing themselves together *against* the government, which is thereby isolated, and overthrowing it; and it is only after those of the official parties whose existence is still possible have mutually and successively accomplished one another's destruction that Vollmar's great division takes place and with it the prospect of our rule. If, like Vollmar, we wanted to start straight off with the *final* act of the revolution we should be in a miserably bad way.

In France the long expected split has taken place. The original conjunction of Guesde and Lafargue with Malon and

Brousse was no doubt unavoidable when the party was founded, but Marx and I never had any illusions that it could last. The issue is purely one of principle: is the struggle to be conducted *as a class struggle* of the proletariat against the bourgeoisie, or is it to be permitted that in good opportunist (or as it is called in the Socialist translation: possibilist) style the class character of the movement, together with the programme, are everywhere to be dropped where there is a chance of winning more votes, more adherents, by this means. Malon and Brousse, by declaring themselves in favour of the latter alternative, have sacrificed the proletarian class character of the movement and made separation inevitable. All the better. The development of the proletariat proceeds everywhere amidst internal struggles* and France, which is now forming a workers' party for the first time, is no exception. We in Germany have got beyond the first phase of the internal struggle, other phases still lie before us. Unity is quite a good thing so long as it is possible, but there are things which stand higher than unity. And when, like Marx and myself, one has fought harder all one's life long against the alleged Socialists than against anyone else (for we only regarded the bourgeoisie as a *class* and hardly ever involved ourselves in conflicts with individual bourgeois), one cannot greatly grieve that the inevitable struggle has broken out.

¶On the "one reactionary mass" Engels wrote on June 12, 1883, to Bernstein: "Here indeed there is an end of the phrase about the one reactionary mass, which is as a rule only suitable for rhetoric (or, on the other hand, for a *really* revolutionary situation). For the irony of history, working on our side, lies in the very fact that the *different* elements of this feudal and bourgeois mass wear one another out, fight one another and devour one another for our advantage and so form the very opposite of the homogeneous mass which the *Knote* imagines he has dealt with if he calls them all "reactionaries." On the contrary, all these diverse scoundrels must first mutually

* Compare pages 327, 382.

smash up, discredit and utterly ruin one another, and prepare the ground for us by proving—one type after the other—their incapacity. It was one of Lassalle's greatest mistakes that as an agitator he utterly forgot the little dialectic he had learnt from Hegel. Here he could never see more than one side, just like Liebknecht, but as for certain reasons the latter by chance saw the right side, he was after all superior to the great Lassalle. . . . And parallel with this is the idea linked up with the idea of the one reactionary mass, that if existing conditions are overthrown, we should come into power. That is nonsense. A revolution is a lengthy process, compare 1642-46 and 1789-93, and in order that conditions may become mature for us and we for them, all the intermediate parties must come into power and do for themselves in turn. And then we shall come—and shall perhaps also get beaten again for the moment. Although if the thing proceeds normally I consider that scarcely possible."*

VOLLMAR, GEORG HEINRICH VON (born 1850). German Social-Democrat, former officer, who joined the Social-Democrats at the end of the 'seventies. He edited the Zürich *Sozial-Demokrat* 1879-80 and was a member of the Reichstag 1881-86 and 1890-1903; during the period of the Socialist Law a supporter of the revolutionary tactics. After the beginning of the 'nineties he became a reformist leader and ideologist. At the Erfurt Party Congress (1891) he came out in favour of the peaceful transition to socialism by means of "measures of state socialism"; at the Frankfort Party Congress (1894) he brought forward, on behalf of the Bavarian Social-Democrats, a full-blown reformist programme which foreshadowed an alliance with the well-to-do peasantry and a vote for a bourgeois state budget. Vollmar's articles—*Repeal of the Socialist Law*—mentioned in this letter were published in the *Sozial-Demokrat* of August 17 and 24, 1882; they expressed the view that the continuance of the Socialist Law was more favourable for Social-Democracy than its repeal and were couched in a very revolutionary tone, so that Bebel wrote to Engels: "The articles are well written and correct in principle though wrong in tactics. If we use the language recommended by Vollmar we shall be in quod in a month . . . with from five to ten years round our necks, and if the paper were to try to use this style

* For the "one reactionary mass" compare also page 333.

everyone caught distributing the paper would get the same. This language is simply impossible despite the principles it expresses; we should ruin ourselves with this language and therefore ought not to use it. . . . Nor do I hold the view that the repeal of the Exceptional Law and the sharpening of the general laws would do us harm and lead to a combination of our Party with the bourgeois opposition."

THE SPLIT IN THE FRENCH WORKERS' PARTY [*Parti ouvrier*] took place at the Congress at St. Etienne (September 25, 1882). The National Committee moved to exclude the Marxists from the Party as they could not "obey both the decisions of the Congress, and the will of a person who is himself located in London outside all Party control." The Marxist minority of the Congress, led by Guesde and Lafargue, retired from the Congress, at which the Possibilist majority had been obtained by falsifying the voting results, and opened their own Congress in Rouen. Engels wrote to Bernstein on November 28, 1882, with regard to the Possibilists: "These people are . . . anything but a workers' party. They are, however, in germ, what the people here [in London] are in full maturity: the tail of the bourgeois radical party. . . . They have no workers' programme at all. And in my opinion the workers' leaders who lend themselves to the production of a herd of working-class voting-cattle of this sort are guilty of direct treachery."

GUESDE, JULES (1845-1922). Leader of the Marxist wing of the French workers' movement. From 1877 onwards he published the socialist paper *Égalité*. In 1879-80, together with Lafargue, among others, he founded the French Workers' Party [*Parti ouvrier*], the programme of which, in its fundamental points, was formulated with Marx's help. In the 'eighties and 'nineties Guesde led the fight against the Possibilists and came out decidedly against Millerandism [Socialists taking office in bourgeois governments] but in the 'nineties he was already beginning to retreat to patriotism and reformism. Later he was one of the most prominent Centrist leaders in the Second International, during the war a social-patriot and in 1914-15 a member of the government.

LAFARGUE, PAUL (1842-1911). One of the leaders of the Marxist wing in the French workers' movement and co-founder of the French Workers' Party. From 1861 took part in the republican movement. Member of the First International.

Married in 1868 Laura, Marx's second daughter. In 1870-71 he carried on organisational and agitational work in Paris and Bordeaux; after the fall of the Commune he fled to Spain where he fought for the line of the General Council; he then settled in London. After the bloody May Day in Fourmis (1891) he was sentenced to a year's imprisonment. Lafargue fought against reformism and Millerandism; he wrote numerous propagandist works in which, despite many mistakes, he defended revolutionary Marxism.

MALON, BÉNOIT (1841-93). French petty-bourgeois Socialist, one of the founders and theoreticians of reformism. In 1865 a member of the First International. In 1871 a member of the Commune; after its fall he fled to Switzerland. He combated Marxism and stood for an eclectic theory of "integral socialism."

BROUSSE, PAUL (1854-1912). French petty-bourgeois Socialist. After the fall of the Commune he lived in Switzerland, where he joined the anarchists. In the beginning of the 'eighties he joined the French Workers' Party and there, as leader of the Possibilist line, soon took up the fight against Marxism.

179. ENGELS TO MARX

London, 8 December, 1882.

In order finally to get clear about the parallel between the Germans of Tacitus and the American Redskins I have made some gentle extractions from the first volume of your Bancroft.* The similarity is indeed all the more surprising because the method of production is so fundamentally different—here hunters and fishers without cattle-raising or agriculture, there nomadic cattle-raising passing into agriculture. It just proves how at this stage the type of production is less decisive than the degree in which the old blood bonds and the old mutual community of the sexes within the tribe have been dissolved. Otherwise the Thlinkeets in the former Russian America could

* Hubert Howe Bancroft (1832-1918). American historian. Author of *The Native Races of the Pacific States* (five volumes, 1874-76) and of the *History of the Pacific States from Central America to Alaska*, which began to appear in 1888. [*Ed. Eng. ed.*]

not be the exact counterpart of the Germanic tribes—even more so really than your Iroquois. Another riddle solved there is how the fact that the women are burdened with the main mass of the work is quite consistent with great respect for women. Moreover I have found my suspicion confirmed that the *Jus Primæ Noctis* [right to the first night] originally found in Europe among the Celts and the Slavs, is a remnant of the old sexual community: it subsists in two tribes, widely separated and of different races, for the medicine-man as the representative of the tribe. I have learned a great deal from the book, and with regard to the Germanic tribes enough for the time being. Mexico and Peru I must reserve for later on. I have given back the Bancroft but have taken the rest of Maurer's things, which are therefore now *all* at my place. I had to look through them on account of my concluding note on the *Mark*, which will be rather long and with which I am still dissatisfied although I have rewritten it two or three times. After all it is no joke to summarise its rise, flourishing and decay in eight or ten pages. If I can possibly get the time I will send it to you in order to hear your opinion. And I myself would like to be quit of the stuff and get back to the natural sciences.

It is funny to see from the so-called primitive peoples how the conception of *holiness* arose. What is originally holy is what we have taken over from the animal kingdom—*the bestial*; "human laws" are as much of an abomination in relation to this as they are in the gospel to the divine law.

This and the following letters refer to Engels' article, *The Mark*, in which he gives a short sketch of the history of the German peasant class. *The Mark* was first published in the *Sozial-Demokrat* (1883) and added as an appendix to Engels' pamphlet *The Development of Socialism from Utopia to Science.* [Now republished as an appendix to the *Peasant War in Germany.*]

180. Engels to Marx

London, 15 December, 1882.

Enclosed is the appendix on the *Mark*. Be so kind as to send it back on *Sunday*, so that I can revise it on Monday—I was not able to conclude the final revision to-day.

I consider the view expounded here regarding the conditions of the peasantry in the Middle Ages and the rise of a *second* serfdom after the middle of the fifteenth century is on the whole incontrovertible. I have been right through Maurer for all the relevant passages and find nearly all my assertions there, *supported, moreover, with evidence*, while alongside of them are exactly the opposite, but either unsupported by evidence or taken from a period which is *not* that in question at all. This particularly applies to *Fronhöfe* [lands liable to feudal dues], Volume 4, conclusion. These contradictions arise in Maurer: (1) from his habit of bringing in evidence and examples from all periods side by side and jumbled together; (2) from the remnants of his legalistic bias, which always gets in his way whenever it is a question of understanding a *development*; (3) from his great lack of regard for the part played by *force*; (4) from his enlightened prejudice that since the dark Middle Ages a steady progress to better things *must* surely have taken place—this prevents him from seeing not only the antagonistic character of real progress, but also the individual retrogressions.

You will find that my thing is by no means all of a piece but a regular patchwork. The first draft was all of one piece but unfortunately wrong. I only mastered the material by degrees and that is why there is so much patching together.

Incidentally the general re-introduction of serfdom was one of the reasons why no industry could develop in Germany in the seventeenth and eighteenth centuries. In the first place there was the *reversed* division of labour among the guilds—the opposite from that in manufacture: the work was divided *among the guilds* instead of inside the workshop. In England at this stage migration to the territory outside the guild took place, but in Germany this was prevented by the transformation of the country people and the inhabitants of the agricultural market towns into serfs. But this also caused the ultimate collapse of the trade guild as soon as the competition of foreign manufacture arose. The other reasons which combined with this in holding back German manufacture I will here omit.

181. ENGELS TO MARX

London, 16 December, 1882.

The point about the almost total disappearance of serfdom—legally or actually—in the thirteenth and fourteenth centuries is the most important to me, because formerly you expressed a divergent opinion on this. In the East Elbe region the colonisation proves that the *German* peasants were free ; in Schleswig-Holstein Maurer admits that at that time " all " the peasants had regained their freedom (perhaps rather later than the fourteenth century). He also admits that in South Germany it was just at this period that the bondsmen were best treated. In Lower Saxony more or less the same (*e.g.*, the new *Meier* [tenant farmers] who were in fact copyholders). He is only opposed to Kindlinger's view that serfdom first *arose* in the sixteenth century. But that it was newly reinforced after that, and appeared in a second edition, seems to me indubitable. Meitzen gives the dates at which serfs begin to be mentioned again in East Prussia, Brandenburg, Silesia : the middle of the sixteenth century ; Hanssen gives the same for Schleswig-Holstein. When Maurer calls this a *milder* form of serfdom he is right in comparison with the ninth and eleventh centuries, when the old Germanic slavery still continued, and right too with regard to the legal powers which the lord also had then and later—according to the law books of the thirteenth century—over his serfs. But compared with the *actual* position of the peasants in the thirteenth, the fourteenth and, in North Germany, the fifteenth centuries, the new serfdom was anything but an alleviation. Especially after the Thirty Years' War ! It is also significant that while in the Middle Ages the degrees of servitude and serfdom are innumerable, so that the *Mirror* *of Saxony** gives up any attempt to speak of *egen lüde recht* [rights over owned people—*i.e.*, bondsmen] this becomes remarkably simple after the Thirty Years' War.

182. ENGELS TO MARX

London, 19 December, 1882.

My idea of the Podolinsky† business is as follows. His real discovery is that human labour has the power of detaining solar energy on the earth's surface and permitting its activity longer than would be the case without it. All the economic conclusions he draws from this are wrong. I have not got the thing by me but recently read it in Italian in the *Plebe.*‡ The question is: how can a given quantity of energy in a given quantity of food leave behind it a greater quantity of energy than itself? I solve it in this way. Assume that the amount of food daily necessary for one person represents an amount of energy expressed as 10,000 H.U. (heat units). These 10,000 H.U. remain for ever = 10,000 H.U. and in practice, as is well known, lose in the course of their transformation into other forms of energy, through friction, etc., a part of their availability. In the human body this is even considerable. The *physical* work performed in economic labour can never therefore = 10,000 H.U. but is always less.

But this does not mean that physical labour is *economic* labour; far from it. The economic labour performed by the 10,000 H.U. in nowise consists of the *reproduction* of the same 10,000 H.U., wholly or partially, in this or that form. On the contrary, most of these are lost in the increased heat and radiation of the body, etc., and what remains available of them are the fertilising potentialities of the excrements. The economic labour which a man performs by the employment of these 10,000 H.U. consists rather in the fixation for a greater or less time of *new* H.U. radiated to him from the sun, which have

* *Der Sachsenspiegel*—the legal code of the period.
† Sergei Podolinsky, an Ukrainian Socialist.
‡ Official organ of the Italian section of the First International.

only this labour connection with the first 10,000 H.U. Whether, however, the *new* quantity of H.U. fixated by the application of the 10,000 H.U. of daily nourishment reaches 5,000, 10,000, 20,000 or 1,000,000 H.U., depends solely on the degree of development attained by the means of production.

This can only be represented arithmetically in the most primitive branches of production: hunting, fishing, cattle-raising, agriculture. In hunting and fishing new solar energy is not even fixated, only what has already been fixated is turned to use. At the same time it is obvious that, assuming the fisher or hunter to be normally nourished, the amount of albumen or fat he gets by hunting or fishing is independent of the amount of these foodstuffs which he consumes.

In cattle raising, energy is fixated in the sense that vegetable matter, which would otherwise rapidly wither, decay and decompose, is systematically transformed into animal albumen, fat, skin, bones, etc., and therefore fixated for a longer time. Here the calculation is already complicated.

Still more so in agriculture, where the energy value of the auxiliary materials, manures, etc., also enters into the calculation.

In industry all calculation comes to an end: in most cases the work added to the product can no longer be expressed in H.U. If, for instance, this is still possible with a pound of yarn because its toughness and capacity for resistance can just, with a lot of fuss and trouble, be reduced to a mechanical formula, here already this appears as an utterly useless piece of pedantry, and in the case of a piece of unbleached cloth, still more in the case of bleached, dyed and printed cloth, becomes absurd. The energy value of a hammer, a screw or a needle calculated according to the cost of production is an impossible quantity. In my opinion it is absolutely impossible to try and express economic relations in physical magnitudes.

What Podolinsky has entirely forgotten is that man as a worker is not merely a fixer of *present* solar heat but a still greater squanderer of *past* solar heat. The stores of energy, coal, ores, forests, etc., we succeed in squandering you know better than I. From this point of view even fishing and hunting appear not as the fixation of new sun heat but as the using up and incipient waste of solar energy already accumulated.

Further : what man does deliberately by work, the plant does unconsciously. Plants—and this is an old story already—are the great absorbers and depositors of sun heat in a changed form. By work, therefore, in so far as it fixates sun heat (which in industry and elsewhere is by no means always the case) man succeeds in uniting the natural functions of the energy-consuming animal with those of the energy-collecting plant.

Podolinsky has strayed away from his very valuable discovery into mistaken paths because he was trying to find in natural science a new proof of the truth of socialism, and has therefore confused physics and economics.

183. ENGELS TO MARX

London, 22 December, 1882.

To return once more to Podolinsky ; I must make a correction, namely, that storage of energy through work really only takes place in *agriculture* ; in cattle raising the energy accumulated in the plants is simply transferred as a whole to the animals, and one can only speak of storage of energy in the sense that without cattle-raising, nutritious plants wither uselessly, whereas with it they are utilised. In all branches of industry, on the other hand, energy is only *expended*. The most that has to be taken into consideration is the fact that vegetable products, wood, straw, flax, etc., and animal products in which vegetable energy is stored up, are put to use by being worked upon and therefore *preserved longer* than when they are left to decay naturally. So that if one chooses one can translate into the physical world the old economic fact that all industrial producers have to live from the products of agriculture, cattle-raising, hunting, and fishing—but there is hardly much to be gained from doing so. . . .

I am glad that on the history of serfdom we " proceed in agreement," as they say in business. It is certain that serfdom and bondage are not a peculiarly medieval-feudal form, we find them everywhere or nearly everywhere where conquerors have the land cultivated for them by the old inhabitants—*e.g.*, very early in Thessaly. This fact has even misled me and many other people about servitude in the Middle Ages ; one was much too much inclined to base it simply on conquest, this made everything so neat and easy. See Thierry among others.

The position of the Christians in Turkey during the height of the old Turkish semi-feudal system was something similar.

¶This was one of the last letters of Engels to Marx. In 1883 only two letters have been preserved.

In the last years of his life Marx made journeys for his health. In 1881-82 he went to France, Algiers and Switzerland as well as to the Isle of Wight. Engels wrote to him on August 26, 1882 :

" In the Waadt* country there is an excellent wine, Ivorne, which is much to be recommended, especially when old. Then people drink a red Neuchâteler, Cortaillod, which bubbles a little, the froth forms a star in the middle of the glass ; also very good. And finally Veltliner (Valtellina), the best wine in Switzerland. In my time the ordinary Burgundy, Macon and Beaujolais were also very good and not dear. Drink away gallantly at all these kinds, and if in the long run you get bored with all the wandering about remember that it is the only way for you to regain your old form ; it can be laid aside a little while longer, but the day will come when we shall need it only too badly."

184. ENGELS TO BERNSTEIN

London, 1 March, 1883.

From the outset we have always fought to the very utmost against the petty-bourgeois and philistine disposition within the Party, because this disposition, developed since the time of the Thirty Years' War, has infected *all* classes in Germany and has

* Marx was at this time at Lausanne in the Swiss canton of Vaud [*Waadt*]. [*Ed. Eng. ed.*]

become an hereditary German evil, sister to servility, abject subservience and all the hereditary German vices. This is what makes us ridiculous and despicable abroad. It is the main cause of the slackness and the weakness of character which predominate among us ; it reigns on the throne as often as in the cobbler's lodging. Only since a *modern* proletariat has been formed in Germany has a class developed there with hardly anything at all of this hereditary German disease about it, a class which has given evidence of a free outlook, energy, humour, tenacity in struggle. And are we not to fight against every attempt artificially to inoculate this healthy class—the only healthy class in Germany—with the old hereditary poison of philistine slackness and philistine narrow-mindedness ?

185. ENGELS TO SORGE

London, 15 March, 1883.

It was not possible to keep you regularly informed about Marx's state of health because it was constantly changing. Here, briefly, are the main facts.

Shortly before his wife's death, in October of '81, he had an attack of pleurisy. He recovered from this but when, in February '82, he was sent to Algiers, he came in for cold, wet weather on the journey and arrived with another attack of pleurisy. The atrocious weather continued, and then when he got better, he was sent to Monte Carlo (Monaco) to avoid the heat of the approaching summer. He arrived there with another, though this time a milder, attack of pleurisy. Again abominable weather. When he was at last better, he went to Argenteuil near Paris to stay with his daughter, Madame Longuet. He went to the sulphur springs near by at Enghien, in order to relieve the bronchitis from which he had suffered for so long. Here again the weather was awful, but the cure did some good. Then he went to Vevey for six weeks and came back in September, having apparently almost completely recovered his health. He was allowed to spend the winter on the south coast of England, and he himself was so tired of wandering about with nothing to do, that another period of exile to the south of Europe would probably have harmed him in spirit as much as it would have benefited him in health. When the foggy season commenced in London, he was sent to the Isle of Wight. There it did nothing but rain and he caught another cold. Schorlemmer and I were intending to pay him a visit at the New Year when news came which made it necessary for Tussy to join him at once. Then followed Jenny's death and he had another attack of bronchitis. After all that had gone before, and at his age, this was dangerous. A number of complications set in, the most serious being an abscess on the lung and a terribly rapid loss of strength. Despite this, however, the general course of the illness was proceeding favourably, and last Friday the chief doctor who was attending him, one of the foremost young doctors in London, specially recommended to him by Ray Lankester, gave us the most brilliant hope for his recovery. But anyone who has but once examined the lung tissue under the microscope, realises how great is the danger of a blood vessel being broken if the lung is purulent. And so every morning for the last six weeks I had a terrible feeling of dread that I might find the curtains down when I turned the corner of the street. Yesterday afternoon at 2.30—which is the best time for visiting him—I arrived to find the house in tears. It seemed that the end was near. I asked what had happened, tried to get to the bottom of the matter, to offer comfort. There had been only a slight hæmorrhage but suddenly he had begun to sink rapidly. Our good old Lenchen, who had looked after him better than a mother cares for her child, went upstairs to him and then came down. He was half asleep, she said, I might come in. When we entered the room he lay there asleep, but never to wake again. His pulse and breathing had stopped. In those two minutes he had passed away, peacefully and without pain.

All events which take place by natural necessity bring their own consolation with them, however dreadful they may be. So in this case. Medical skill might have been able to give him a few more years of vegetative existence, the life of a helpless being, dying—to the triumph of the doctors' art—not suddenly, but inch by inch. But our Marx could never have borne that. To have lived on with all his uncompleted works before him, tantalised by the desire to finish them and yet unable to do so, would have been a thousand times more bitter than the gentle death which overtook him. "Death is not a misfortune for him who dies, but for him who survives," he used to say, quoting Epicurus. And to see that mighty genius lingering on as a physical wreck to the greater glory of medicine and to the scorn of the philistines whom in the prime of his strength he had so often put to rout—no, it is better, a thousand times better, as it is—a thousand times better that we shall in two days' time carry him to the grave where his wife lies at rest.

And after all that had gone before, about which the doctors do not know as much as I do, there was in my opinion no other alternative.

Be that as it may, mankind is shorter by a head, and the greatest head of our time at that. The proletarian movement goes on, but gone is its central figure to which Frenchmen, Russians, Americans and Germans spontaneously turned at critical moments, to receive always that clear incontestable counsel which only genius and a perfect understanding of the situation could give. Local lights and lesser minds, if not the humbugs, will now have a free hand. The final victory is certain, but circuitious paths, temporary and local errors—things which even now are so unavoidable—will become more common than ever. Well, we must see it through. What else are we here for?

And we are not near losing courage yet.*

Engels also expressed himself upon the historic rôle and significance of Marx in other letters written during these days. Thus he wrote to Liebknecht on March 14: "Although I have seen him this evening laid out on his bed, the rigidity of death in his face, I cannot fully realise that this brilliant mind has ceased to impregnate the proletarian movement of both

* English translation taken from *The Fourteenth of March* 1883, Martin Lawrence, 1933.

worlds with its mighty thoughts. We all owe what we are to him ; and the movement as it is to-day is the creation of his theoretical and practical work. If it had not been for him, we should all still be groping in a maze of confusion." And to Bernstein Engels wrote on the same day : " What the worth of this man was to us, both theoretically and in all decisive moments in practice as well, only one who has long been together with him can realise. His mighty vision will be buried with him for years to come. It was something of which we others are not capable. The movement will go on its way, but it will lack that calm, timely, considered intervention which has saved it from so many tedious errors in the past." Finally, in a letter to J. Ph. Becker on March 15, 1883, Engels writes : *The greatest mind in our Party had ceased to think, the strongest heart* that I have ever known had *ceased to beat.* It was in all probability a case of internal hæmorrhage. You and I are now almost the last of the old guard of 1848. Well, *we'll remain in the breach!* The bullets are whistling, our friends are falling around us, but this is not the first time we two have seen this. And if a bullet hits one of us, let it come—I only ask that it should strike fair and square and not leave us long in agony."*

186. ENGELS TO VAN PATTEN

[London] 18 April, 1883.

Since 1845 Marx and I have held the view that *one* of the ultimate results of the future proletarian revolution will be the gradual dissolution of the political organisation known by the name of *state.* The main object of this organisation has always been to secure, by armed force, the economic oppression of the labouring majority by the minority which alone possesses wealth. With the disappearance of an exclusively wealth-possessing minority there also disappears the necessity for the power of armed oppression, or state power. At the same time, however, it was always our view that in order to attain this and the other far more important aims of the future social revolution, the working class must first take possession of the organised political power of the state and by its aid crush the resistance

* From *The Fourteenth of March* 1883.

of the capitalist class and organise society anew. This is to be found already in *The Communist Manifesto* of 1847, Chapter II, conclusion.

The anarchists put the thing upside down. They declare that the proletarian revolution must *begin* by doing away with the political organisation of the state. But after its victory the sole organisation which the proletariat finds already in existence is precisely the state. This state may require very considerable alterations before it can fulfil its new functions. But to destroy it at such a moment would be to destroy the only organism by means of which the victorious proletariat can assert its newly-conquered power, hold down its capitalist adversaries and carry out that economic revolution of society without which the whole victory must end in a new defeat and in a mass slaughter of the workers similar to those after the Paris Commune.

Does it require my express assurance that Marx opposed this anarchist nonsense from the first day it was put forward in its present form by Bakunin? The whole internal history of the International Workingmen's Association is evidence of this. From 1867 onwards the anarchists were trying, by the most infamous methods, to conquer the leadership of the International; the main hindrance in their way was Marx. The five-year struggle ended, at the Hague Congress of September 1872, with the expulsion of the anarchists from the International; and the man who did most to achieve this expulsion was Marx. Our old friend, F. A. Sorge, in Hoboken, who was present as a delegate, can give you further details if you wish.

And now for Johann Most.

If anyone asserts that Most, since he became an anarchist, has had any relations with Marx whatever or has received any kind of assistance from Marx, he has either been deceived or is deliberately lying. After the publication of the first number of the London *Freiheit*, Most did not visit Marx or me more than once, or at most twice. Equally little did we visit him—we did not even meet him by chance anywhere or at any time. In the end we did not even subscribe to his paper any more, because "there was really nothing" in it. We had the same contempt for his anarchism and his anarchistic tactics as for the people from whom he had learnt both.

While he was still in Germany Most published a " popular " account of Marx's *Capital*. Marx was asked to look through it for a second edition. I did this work in common with Marx. We found that it was impossible to do more than expunge Most's very worst blunders unless we were to rewrite the whole thing from beginning to end. Marx also allowed his corrections to be included only on the express condition that his name should never be brought into any connection even with this corrected edition of Johann Most's compilation.

¶This letter is the answer to a communication from the Secretary of the Central Labour Union in New York, Philipp van Patten, who had written to Engels on 2 April, 1883 :

" When all parties were united in connection with the recent memorial celebration in honour of Karl Marx, many loud declarations were made on the part of Johann Most and his friends that Most had stood in close relation to Marx and had popularised his work, *Capital*, in Germany and that Marx had been in agreement with the propaganda which Most had conducted. We have a very high opinion of the capacities and the activity of Karl Marx, but we cannot believe that he was in sympathy with the anarchistic and disorganising methods of Most, and I should like to hear your opinion as to the attitude of Karl Marx on the question of anarchism versus social-democracy. Most's ill-advised, stupid chatter has already done us too much harm here, and it is very unpleasant for us to hear that such a great authority as Marx approved of such tactics." (For Most see Letter 162.)

187. ENGELS TO J. P. BECKER

London, 22 May, 1883.

Our *lads in Germany* are really *magnificent fellows*, *now that the Socialist Law** *has freed them from the* " *educated* " *gentlemen* who had

* Bismarck's Anti-Socialist Law 1878-90. Compare Letter 190 and Note. [*Ed. Eng. ed.*]

tried before 1878 to schoolmaster the workers from the superior heights of their ignorant university-bred confusion, an attempt to which unfortunately only too many of the leaders lent themselves. That rotten trash has not been entirely got rid of as yet, but all the same the movement has come into a definitely revolutionary channel again. This is just the splendid thing about our boys, that *the masses are far better than almost all their leaders*, and now that the Socialist Law is forcing the masses to make the movement for *themselves* and the influence of the leaders is reduced to a minimum things are better than ever.

188. ENGELS TO BEBEL

Eastbourne, 30 August, 1883.

The Manifesto of the Democratic Federation* in London has been issued by about twenty to thirty little societies which under different names (always the same people) have for the last twenty years at least been repeatedly trying, and always with the same lack of success, to make themselves important. All that is important is that now at last they are obliged openly to proclaim our theory, which during the period of the International seemed to them to be dictated from outside, as their own, and that a crowd of young bourgeois intelligentsia are emerging who, to the disgrace of the English workers it must be said, understand things better and take them up more passionately than the workers. For even in the Democratic Federation the workers for the most part only accept the new programme unwillingly and as a matter of form. The chief of the Democratic Federation, Hyndman, is an arch-conservative and an extremely chauvinistic but not stupid careerist, who behaved pretty shabbily to Marx (to whom he was introduced by Rudolf Meyer) and for this reason was dropped by us personally.†

Do not on any account whatever let yourself be deluded into thinking there is a real proletarian movement going on here.

* The Manifesto of the Democratic Federation, "Socialism made Plain" (1883). The Democratic Federation (founded in 1881) took the name Social-Democratic Federation in 1884. For later references to the S.D.F. Hyndman, etc.; see index. [*Ed. Eng. ed.*]

† See Letter 176.

I know Liebknecht tries to delude himself and all the world about this, but it is not the case. The elements at present active may become important since they have accepted our theoretical programme and so acquired a basis, but only if a spontaneous movement breaks out here among the workers and they succeed in getting control of it. Till then they will remain individual minds, with a hotch-potch of confused sects, remnants of the great movement of the 'forties, standing behind them and nothing more. And—apart from the unexpected—a really general workers' movement will only come into existence here when the workers are made to feel the fact that England's world monopoly is broken.

Participation in the domination of the world market was and is the basis of the political nullity of the English workers. The tail of the bourgeoisie in the economic exploitation of this monopoly but nevertheless sharing in its advantages, politically they are naturally the tail of the " great Liberal Party," which for its part pays them small attentions, recognises trade unions and strikes as legitimate factors, has relinquished the fight for an unlimited working day and has given the mass of better placed workers the vote. But once America and the united competition of the other industrial countries have made a decent breach in this monopoly (and in iron this is coming rapidly, in cotton unfortunately not as yet) you will see something here.

¶Of the English labour movement as it was towards the close of the great period of industrial monopoly Engels wrote in a letter to Bernstein (June 17, 1879):

"The English labour movement has been revolving (now and) for a series of years in a narrow vicious circle of strikes for wages and shorter working hours, and this not merely as an expedient and a means of propaganda and organisation but as an end in itself.

" As a matter of principle even, and in accordance with their rules, the trade unions exclude all political action, and with it participation in every general activity of the working class as a class. The workers are divided politically into Conservatives and Liberal-Radicals, into adherents of Disraeli's (Beaconsfield's) administration and adherents of Gladstone's administration. A (real) workers' movement therefore can only be said to exist here in so far as strikes take place which, whether successful or not, do not bring the movement a step further. . . . The fact should not be concealed that no real workers' movement in the Continental sense exists here at the moment."

In a letter to Marx on August 11, 1881, Engels wrote :

"Yesterday morning I informed Mr. Shipton* that he will get no more leading articles from me. Kautsky had sent me a flat affair about international factory legislation, in a bad translation, which I corrected and sent to Shipton. Yesterday the proof arrived with a letter from Shipton, who found two places "too strong"—one of which he had misunderstood into the bargain—whether I would not soften them down? I did so and replied . . . if *this* was too strong for him my far stronger article would be much more so, hence it would be better for us both if I stopped. . . . I could not remain on the staff of a paper which lends itself to writing up these German trade unions, comparable only to those very worst English ones which allow themselves to be led by men sold to, or at least paid by, the middle class† . . . The most decisive reason of all I did not write him : the absolute lack of effect produced by my articles on the rest of the paper and on the public. If any effect is produced it is a hidden reaction on the part of the secret apostles of free trade. The paper remains the same hotch-potch of every possible and impossible crotchet, and in political details more or less, but predominantly, Gladstonian. . . . The British working man just will not budge, he must be shaken up by events, by the loss of the industrial monopoly. Meanwhile, let him have his own way."

In a letter to Kautsky (November 8, 1884) Engels wrote : "In England and France the transition to large-scale industry is more or less completed. The conditions in which the proletariat is placed have already become stable. Agricultural districts and industrial districts, large-scale industry and domestic industry have been separated and as much consolidated as modern industry itself permits. Even the fluctuations which the ten-

* George Shipton, Secretary of the London Trades Council and editor of the *Labour Standard*.

† This sentence was written in English.

year cycle of crises brings with it have become normal conditions of existence. The political or directly socialist movements which arose during the period of the industrial revolution—immature as they were—have collapsed, leaving behind them discouragement rather than encouragement : bourgeois capitalist development has shown itself stronger than the revolutionary counterpressure ; for a new revolt against capitalist production a new and powerful impulse is required, either perhaps the dethronement of England from its present dominance of the world market, or a particular revolutionary situation in France." See Letter 189. In Letter 193 Engels contrasts with the conditions just described the economic stage reached by Germany and its effect on the Labour movement there. [*Ed. Eng. ed.*]

189. ENGELS TO BEBEL

London, 18 January, 1884.

Here too industry has taken on a different character. The ten-year cycle seems to have been broken down now that, since 1870, American and German competition have been putting an end to English monopoly in the world market. In the main branches of industry a depressed state of business has prevailed since 1868, while production has been slowly increasing, and now we seem both here and in America to be standing on the verge of a new crisis which in England has not been preceded by a period of prosperity. That is the secret of the sudden—though it has been slowly preparing for three years—but the present sudden emergence of a socialist movement here. So far the organised workers—trade unions—remain quite remote from it, the movement is proceeding among " educated " elements sprung from the bourgeoisie, who here and there seek contact with the masses and in places find it. These people are of very varying moral and intellectual value and it will take some time before they sort themselves out and the thing becomes clarified. But that it will all go entirely to sleep again is hardly likely.

¶Engels, who had marked the onset of the " period of prosperity " in England (compare Letter 8) also discerned the beginning and the character of a new period—the period which proved to be the transition to the epoch of imperialism defined by Lenin. See Letters 197 and 199 and cf. page 500.

In the following year, in a letter to Bebel (July 24, 1885), Engels noted how the economic changes were reflecting themselves in the alignment of the political parties.

" Here the new franchise will overthrow the whole former party position. The alliance between the Whigs and Tories into one great Conservative Party having as its basis the *entire* body of landowners, which has hitherto been split up into two camps, and including all the conservative elements of the bourgeoisie : banking, high finance, trade, a section of industry ; beside it on the other hand the radical bourgeoisie, *i.e.*, the mass of large-scale industry, the petty bourgeoisie and, for the present still as its tail, the proletariat now re-awakening to political life—this is a revolutionary starting point such as England has not seen since 1689." [*Ed. Eng. ed.*]

190. ENGELS TO J. P. BECKER

London, 14 February 1884.

Things are by no means so bad with the agitation in Germany, even if the bourgeois press suppresses most of what is happening and only now and then lets out an involuntary groan of terror that the Party is gaining ground at a tearing rate instead of losing it.

The police have opened up a really splendid field for our people : the ever-present and uninterrupted struggle with the police themselves. This is being carried on everywhere and always, with great success and, the best thing about it, with great humour. The police are defeated—and made to look foolish into the bargain. And I consider this struggle the most useful in the circumstances. Above all it keeps the contempt for the enemy alive among our lads. Worse troops could not be sent into the field against us than the German police ; even where they have the upper hand they suffer a moral defeat, and confidence in victory is growing among our lads every day. This struggle will bring it about that as soon as the pressure is at last relaxed (and that will happen on the day the dance in Russia begins) we shall no longer count our numbers in hundreds of thousands but in millions. There is a lot of rotten stuff among the so-called leaders but I have unqualified confidence in our masses, and what they lack in revolutionary tradition they are gaining more and more from this little war with the police. And you can say what you like, but we have never seen a proletariat yet which has learnt to act collectively and to march together in so short a time. For this reason, even though nothing appears on the surface, we can, I think, calmly await the moment when the call to arms is given. You will see how they muster !

¶On the proletarian masses and the general conditions of political activity in Germany, Engels wrote to Bernstein on January 25, 1882 :

" I have never concealed my opinion that the masses in Germany are much better than the gentlemen who lead them, especially since the uses of the press and agitation had turned the Party for these gentlemen into a milch cow to provide them with butter—and this just when Bismarck and the bourgeoisie suddenly slaughtered the cow. The thousand individuals whose existence was thus temporarily ruined have the personal misfortune of not being transferred into a directly revolutionary situation, *i.e.*, into exile. Otherwise very many now bemoaning their fate would have gone over to Most's camp or would be finding the *Sozial-Demokrat* much too tame after all. The majority of these people stopped in Germany, and had to ; they went for the most part to rather reactionary places, remained socially respected, dependent on philistines for their existence, and became to a large extent infected by philistinism themselves. All hope very soon began to centre for them on the repeal of the Socialist Law. It is not surprising that under the pressure of philistinism the delusion, in reality absurd, should have arisen among them that this could be achieved by docility. Germany is a most infamous country for people without much strength of will. The narrowness and pettiness both of bourgeois and of political conditions, the provincialism even of the big towns, the small but constantly accumulating vexations of the struggle with police and bureaucracy, all this has a debilitating effect instead of exciting resistance, and thus many in the great "nursery" become childish themselves. Narrow conditions produce narrow views, so that it takes a lot of understanding and energy before anybody living in Germany can be in a position to see anything except what is in front of his eyes, to bear in mind the great interconnection of world events and not to sink into the self-satisfied "objectivity" which looks no further than its nose and just because of this is really the most limited subjectivity, even though it may be shared by thousands of these subjects.

But the more the development of this tendency to cover up their deficiency in insight and power of resistance by "objective" super-cleverness is a natural one, so much the more decisively must it be combated. And here the working masses themselves offer the best point of support. They alone in Germany live in something approaching modern conditions, all their miseries, small and big, centre in the oppression of *capital;* and while all other struggles in Germany, whether social or political, are wretched and petty and turn upon miserable trivialities elsewhere long overcome, their struggle is the only great one, the only one which stands on the heights of time, the only one which instead of enfeebling the fighter, endows him with perpetually renewed energy.

191. ENGELS TO KAUTSKY

London, 19 July, 1884.

That the *Neue Zeit* is to come to an end is no misfortune for the Party. It is becoming more and more apparent that the great majority of the *literary* Party people in Germany belong to the opportunists and cautious goers who, however disagreeable the Socialist Law may be to them from a pecuniary point of view, feel themselves quite in the right atmosphere under it from the *literary* point of view ; they can express themselves quite openly—we are prevented from giving them one in the eye. Hence the mere task of filling a journal of this kind every month demands very great tolerance, which results in its being gradually overrun with philanthropy, humanitarianism, sentimentality and whatever all the anti-revolutionary vices of the Freiwalds, Quarcks, Schippels, Rosuses, etc. are called. People who do not want to learn anything fundamentally and only make literature about literature and incidentally out of literature (nine-tenths of present-day German writing is writing about other writing), naturally achieve more printed pages per annum than those who grind at something and only want to write about other books when: (1) they have mastered these other books and (2) there is something in them worth the trouble. The preponderance of these former gentlemen which has been produced by the Socialist Law in the literature printed in *Germany* is inevitable while the Law lasts. Against it we have in the literature published abroad a weapon which strikes in a totally different manner.

¶In 1884 the further publication of *Neue Zeit* was in question. *Neue Zeit* was the theoretical organ of German Social-Democracy. Kautsky edited it from 1883 to 1917, the last number appeared in 1923. All the important leaders of the Second International wrote in *Neue Zeit*, but under Kautsky's editorship the Bolsheviks were almost entirely shut out from it while much space was granted to the criticism of Bolshevism (both on the part of the Russian Mensheviks and Trotskyists and of Rosa Luxemburg).

QUARCK (pseudonym, FREIWALD), SCHIPPEL, ROSUS. Collaborators in *Neue Zeit*. Quarck was a "Right" opportunist while Schippel at first attached himself to the "Left" opportunist tendency of the "Youth"; later he was one of the leading reformists and defenders of the imperialist policy of protective tariffs.

192. ENGELS TO BEBEL

London, 18 November, 1884.

The whole of the Liberal philistines have gained such a respect for us that they are screaming with one accord: Yes, if the Social-Democrats will put themselves on a *legal* basis and abjure *revolution* then we are in favour of the immediate repeal of the Socialist Law. There is no doubt, therefore, that this suggestion will at once be made to you in the Reichstag. The answer you give to it is important—not so much for Germany, where our gallant lads have given it in the elections, as for abroad. A *tame* answer would at once destroy the colossal impression produced by the elections.

In my opinion the case is like this :

Throughout the whole of Europe the existing political situation is the product of revolutions. The legal basis, historic right, legitimacy, have been everywhere riddled through and through a thousand times or entirely overthrown. But it is in the nature of all parties or classes which have come to power through revolution, to demand that the new basis of right created by the revolution should also be unconditionally recognised and regarded as holy. The right to revolution *did* exist—otherwise the present rulers would not be rightful—but from now onwards it is to exist no more.

In Germany the existing situation rests on the revolution which began in 1848 and ended in 1866. 1866 was a complete revolution. Just as Prussia only became anything by treachery and war against the German Empire, in alliance with foreign powers (1740, 1756, 1785), so it only achieved the German-Prussian Empire by the forcible overthrow of the German Confederation and by civil war. Its assertion that the others broke the Confederation makes no difference. The others say the opposite. There has never been a revolution yet which lacked a legal pretext—as in France in 1830 when both the king and the bourgeoisie asserted they were in the right. Enough, Prussia provoked the civil war and with it the revolution. After its victory it overthrew three thrones " by God's grace " and annexed their territories, together with those of the former free city of Frankfort. If that was not revolutionary I do not know the meaning of the word. And as this was not enough it confiscated the private property of the princes who had been driven out. That this was unlawful, revolutionary therefore, it admitted by getting the action endorsed later by an assembly—

the Reichstag—which had as little right to dispose of these funds as the government.

The German-Prussian Empire, as the completion of the North German Confederation which 1866 forcibly created, is a thoroughly revolutionary creation. I make no complaint about that. What I reproach the people who made it with is that they were only poor-spirited revolutionaries who did not go much further and at once annex the whole of Germany to Prussia. But those who operate with blood and iron, swallow up whole states, overthrow thrones and confiscate private property, should not condemn other people as revolutionaries. If the Party only retains the right to be no more and no less revolutionary than the Imperial Government has been, it has got all it needs.

Recently it was officially stated that the Imperial Constitution was not a contract between the princes and the people but only one between the princes and free cities, which could at any time replace the constitution by another. The government organs which laid this down demanded, therefore, that the governments should have the right to *overthrow the Imperial Constitution.* No Exceptional Law was enacted against them, they were not persecuted. Very well, in the most extreme case we do not demand more for ourselves than is here demanded for the governments.

The Duke of Cumberland is the legitimate and unquestioned heir to the throne of Brunswick. The right claimed by Cumberland in Brunswick is no other than that by which the King of Prussia is seated in Berlin. Whatever else may be required of Cumberland can only be claimed after he has taken possession of his lawful and legitimate throne.

But the revolutionary German Imperial Government prevents him from doing so by force. A fresh revolutionary action.

What is the position of the parties?

In November 1848 the Conservative Party broke through the new legal basis created in March 1848 without a tremor. In any case it only recognises the constitutional position as a provisional one and would hail any feudal-absolutist *coup d'état* with delight.

The Liberal Parties of all shades co-operated in the revolution of 1848-1866, nor would they deny themselves the right to-day to counter any forcible overthrow of the constitution by force.

The Centre recognises the church as the highest power, above the state, a power which might in a given case, therefore, make revolution a *duty*.

And these are the parties which demand from us that *we*, *we alone of them all*, should declare that in no circumstances will we resort to force and that we will submit to every oppression, to every act of violence, not only as soon as it is merely formally legal—legal according to the judgment of our adversaries—but also when it is directly illegal.

Indeed no party has renounced the right to armed resistance, *in certain circumstances*, without lying. None has ever been able to relinquish this ultimate right.

But once it comes to the question of discussing the *circumstances* for which a party reserves to itself this right, then the game is won. Then one can talk nineteen to the dozen. And especially a party which has been declared to have no rights, a party therefore which has had revolution directly indicated to it from above. Such a declaration of outlawry can be daily repeated in the fashion it has once occurred. To require an unconditional declaration of this kind from such a party is sheer absurdity.

For the rest, the gentlemen can keep calm. With military conditions as they are at present we shall not start our attack so long as there is still an armed force against us. We can wait until the armed force itself ceases to be *a force against us*. Any earlier revolution, even if victorious, would not bring *us* to power, but the most radical of the bourgeoisie, and of the petty bourgeoisie.

Meanwhile the elections have shown that we have nothing to expect from yielding, *i.e.*, from concessions to our adversaries. We have only won respect and become a power by defiant resistance. Only power is respected, and only so long as we are a power shall we be respected by the philistine. Anyone who makes him concessions can no longer be a power and is despised by him. The iron hand can make itself felt in a velvet glove but it must make itself felt. The German proletariat has become a mighty party; may its representatives be worthy of it.

¶The total Social-Democratic vote at the Reichstag elections had risen from 102,000 in 1871 to 493,000 in 1877, before the enactment of the Socialist Law (1878). In the first years of illegality when the Party had not as yet shown the broad mass of the workers, or had only shown it insufficiently, that it was carrying on the struggle and not submitting to the government, the total vote dropped (1881: 312,000). Then, however, a rapid growth of votes began. In 1884 the Party surpassed its previous highest figure and got 550,000 votes and in 1890, when the law was repealed, the number of Social-Democratic votes was almost one and a half million.

On November 11, 1884, Engels wrote to Bernstein:

" As to the result of the second ballots I only hear a little and that late. I hope that a great many of them have turned out well, because the more new elements that come into the fraction now the better. The worst (the " educated " ones) are already elected, the additional ones are mostly workers and they cannot but improve the company. The Socialist Law stands condemned. The state and the bourgeoisie have discredited themselves hopelessly in relation to us. But they live on none the less merrily for that, and anyone who thought the Law must come to an end because of this might be badly disappointed. . . . To do away with the Law a decision will always be necessary, and they will hardly bring themselves to that. In the most favourable case there will be penal clauses which will cost us greater sacrifices than the Socialist Law. We shall now have to make positive proposals for legislation. If they are resolute ones, *i.e.*, formulated without any consideration for petty-bourgeois prejudices, then they will be very good. . . . The 1884 elections are for us what 1866 was for the German philistine. At that date, without doing anything to bring it about, indeed against his own will, he suddenly became a 'great nation.' Now, however, by our own hard work and heavy sacrifices, we have become a 'great party.' *Noblesse oblige!* We cannot draw the mass of the nation over to us without this mass gradually developing itself. Frankfort, Münich and

Königsberg cannot suddenly become so definitely proletarian as Saxony, Berlin and the mining industrial districts. Here and there the petty-bourgeois elements among the leaders will temporarily find in the masses the background lacking to them hitherto. What has up till now been a reactionary tendency among individuals may now reproduce itself as a necessary element of development—locally—among the masses. This would necessitate a change of tactics in order to lead the masses further without by so doing leaving the bad leaders on top . . . for the time being, in fact, we shall get compliments right and left and these will not everywhere fall upon stony ground."

193. ENGELS TO BEBEL

London, 11 December, 1884.

About our proletarian masses I have never been deceived. This secure progress of their movement, confident of victory and for that very reason cheerful and humorous, is a model which cannot be surpassed. No European proletariat would have stood the test of the Socialist Law so brilliantly and have responded after six years of suppression with such a proof of increased strength and consolidated organisation; no nation would have achieved this organisation in the way it has been achieved without any conspiratorial humbug. And since I have seen the election manifestoes of Darmstadt and Hanover my fear that concessions might have become necessary in the new places (constituencies) has also vanished. If it was possible to speak in such a truly revolutionary and proletarian way in these two towns, then everything is won.

Our great advantage is that with us the industrial revolution is only just in full swing, while in France and England, so far as the main point is concerned, it is closed. There the division into town and country, industrial district and agricultural district is so far concluded that it only changes slowly. The great mass of the people grow up in the conditions in which they have later to live, are accustomed to them; even the fluctuations and crises have become something they take practically for granted. Added to this is the remembrance of the unsuccessful attempts of former movements. With us, on the other hand, everything is in full flow. Remnants of the old peasant industrial production for the satisfaction of personal needs are being supplanted by capitalistic domestic industry, while in other places capitalistic domestic industry is already succumbing in its turn to machinery. And the very nature of our industry, limping behind at the very end, makes the social upheaval all the more fundamental. As the great mass production articles, both mass commodities and articles of luxury, have already been appropriated by the French and English, all that remains for our export industry is chiefly small stuff, which, however, also runs into masses all the same, and is at first produced by domestic industry and only later, when the production is on a mass scale, by machines. Domestic industry (capitalistic) is introduced by this means into much wider regions and clears its way all the more thoroughly. If I except the East Elbe district of Prussia, that is to say East Prussia, Pomerania, Posen and the greater part of Brandenburg, and further Old Bavaria, there are few districts where the peasant has not been swept more and more into domestic industry. The region industrially revolutionised, therefore, becomes larger with us than anywhere else.

Furthermore. Since for the most part the worker in domestic industry carries on his little bit of agriculture, it becomes possible to depress wages in a fashion unequalled elsewhere. What formerly constituted the happiness of the small man, the combination of agriculture and industry, now becomes the most powerful means of capitalist exploitation. The potato patch, the cow, the little bit of agriculture make it possible for the labour power to be sold below its price ; they *oblige* this to be so by tying the worker to his piece of land, which yet only partially supports him. Hence it becomes possible to put our industry on an export basis owing to the fact that the buyer is generally presented with the whole of the surplus value, while the capitalist's profit consists in a deduction from the normal wage. This is more or less the case with all rural domestic industry, but nowhere so much as with us.

Added to this is the fact that our industrial revolution, which was set in motion by the revolution of 1848 with its bourgeois progress (feeble though this was), was enormously speeded up (1) by getting rid of internal hindrances in 1866 to 1870, and (2) by the French milliards, which were ultimately to be invested capitalistically. So we achieved an industrial revolution which is more deep and thorough and spatially more extended and comprehensive than that of the other countries, and this with a perfectly fresh and intact proletariat, undemoralised by defeats and finally—thanks to Marx—with an insight into the causes of economic and political development and into the conditions of the impending revolution such as none of our predecessors possessed. But for that very reason it is our *duty* to be victorious.

As to pure democracy and its rôle in the future I do not share your opinion. Obviously it plays a far more subordinate part in Germany than in countries with an older industrial development. But that does not prevent the possibility, when the moment of revolution comes, of its acquiring a temporary importance as the most radical *bourgeois* party (it has already played itself off as such in Frankfort) and as the final sheet-anchor of the whole bourgeois and even feudal regime. At such a moment the whole reactionary mass falls in behind it and strengthens it; everything which used to be reactionary behaves as democratic. Thus between March and September 1848 the whole feudal-bureaucratic mass strengthened the liberals in order to hold down the revolutionary masses, and, once this was accomplished, in order, naturally, to kick out the liberals as well. Thus from May 1848 until Bonaparte's election in France in December, the purely republican party of the *National*,* the weakest of all the parties, was in power, simply owing to the whole collective reaction organised behind it. This has happened in every revolution: the tamest party still remaining in any way capable of government comes to power with the others just because it is only in this party that the defeated see their last possibility of salvation. Now it cannot be expected that at the moment of crisis we shall already have the majority of the electorate and therefore of the nation behind us.

* See *The Eighteenth Brumaire*, Chapter II. [*Ed. Eng. ed.*]

The whole bourgeois class and the remnants of the feudal land-owning class, a large section of the petty bourgeoisie and also of the rural population will then mass themselves around the most radical bourgeois party, which will then make the most extreme revolutionary gestures, and I consider it very possible that it will be represented in the provisional government and even temporarily form its majority. How, as a minority, one should *not* act in that case, was demonstrated by the social-democratic minority in the Paris revolution of February 1848. However, this is still an academic question at the moment.

Now of course the thing may take a different turn in Germany, and that for military reasons. As things are at present, an impulse from outside can scarcely come from anywhere but Russia. If it does not do so, if the impulse arises from Germany, then the revolution can only start from the army. From the military point of view an unarmed nation against an army of to-day is a purely vanishing quantity. In this case—if our twenty to twenty-five-year-old reserves which have no vote but are trained, came into action—pure democracy might be leapt over. But this question is still equally academic at present, although I, as a representative, so to speak, of the great general staff of the Party, am bound to take it into consideration. In any case our sole adversary on the day of the crisis and on the day after the crisis will be the *whole collective reaction which will group itself around pure democracy*, and this, I think, should not be lost sight of.

If you are bringing forward motions in the Reichstag, there is one which should not be forgotten. The state lands are mostly let out to big farmers; the smallest portion of them is sold to peasants, whose holdings are, however, so small that the new peasants have to resort to working as day labourers on the big farms. The demand should be made that *the great demesnes which are not yet broken up should be let out to co-operative societies of agricultural labourers for joint farming*. The Imperial Government has no state lands and will therefore no doubt find a pretext for shelving such a proposition put in the form of a motion. But I think this firebrand must be thrown among the agricultural day labourers. Which can indeed be done in one of the many debates on state socialism. This and this alone is the way to get hold of the agricultural workers : this is the best method of drawing their attention to the fact that later on it is to be their task to cultivate the great estates of our present gracious gentlemen for the common account. And this will give friend Bismarck, who demands positive proposals from you, enough for some time.

Engels wrote of democracy in a letter to Bernstein (March 24, 1884) :

" This conception [of democracy] changes with every *demos* [people] and so does not get us a step further. In my opinion what should be said is this : the proletariat too requires democratic *forms* for the seizure of political power, but, like all political forms, these serve it as means. But if we want to make democracy an *aim* to-day, then we must support ourselves upon the peasants and petty bourgeoisie, that is upon classes in process of dissolution, which as soon as they try to maintain themselves artificially are *reactionary* in relation to the proletariat. Further, it must not be forgotten that the logical form of bourgeois domination is precisely the democratic republic, which has only become too dangerous owing to the development already attained by the proletariat, but which, as France and America show, is still possible as purely bourgeois rule. To speak therefore of the ' principle of liberalism ' as ' having become definitely past history ' is really only irrelevant ; the liberal constitutional monarchy is an adequate form of bourgeois domination : (1) at the beginning, when the bourgeoisie have not quite finished with the absolute monarchy, and (2) at the end, when the proletariat has already made the democratic republic too dangerous. And yet the democratic republic always remains the last form of bourgeois domination, that in which it is broken to pieces." (See also Note, page 486.)

194. ENGELS TO ZASULICH *

London, 23 April, 1885.

You asked for my judgment of Plekhanov's book, *Nashi Raznoglassiya* [*Our Differences*]. To deliver this I should have to read the book, and I can read Russian fairly easily when I have occupied myself with it for a week. But there are full half-years in which this is impossible for me ; then I lose practice and am obliged to learn it over again, so to speak. This has been the case with me over *Our Differences*. Marx's manuscripts, which I am dictating to a secretary, keep me busy the whole day ; in the evening come visitors whom one cannot after all turn out ; there are proofs to be read and much correspondence to be dealt with, and finally there are the translations of my *Origin*, etc.† (Italian, Danish, etc.) which I am asked to revise and the revision of which is at times neither superfluous nor easy. Well, all these interruptions have prevented me from getting further than to page 60 of *Our Differences*. If I had three days to myself the thing would be finished with and I should have refreshed my knowledge of Russian as well.

Meanwhile the piece of the book which I have read is enough, I think, to acquaint me more or less with the differences in question.

First of all I repeat to you that I am proud to know that there is a party among the youth of Russia which frankly and without ambiguity accepts the great economic and historic theories of Marx and which has decisively broken with all the anarchist and slightly Slavophil traditions of its predecessors. And Marx himself would have been equally proud of this had he lived a little longer. It is an advance which will be of great importance for the revolutionary development of Russia. To me the historic theory of Marx is the fundamental condition of all *reasoned* and consistent revolutionary tactics ; to discover these tactics one has only to apply the theory to the economic and political conditions of the country in question.

But to do this one must know these conditions ; and so far

* This letter was written in French.
† *The Origin of the Family.*

as I am concerned I know too little about the actual situation in Russia to presume myself competent to judge the details of the tactics demanded by this situation at a given moment. Moreover, the internal and intimate history of the Russian revolutionary party, especially that of the last years, is almost entirely unknown to me. My friends among the Narodovoltsy have never spoken to me about it. And this is an indispensable element towards forming one's opinion.

What I know or believe about the situation in Russia impels me to the opinion that the Russians are approaching their 1789. The revolution *must* break out there in a given time; it *may* break out there any day. In these circumstances the country is like a charged mine which only needs a fuse to be laid to it. Especially since March 13.* This is one of the exceptional cases where it is possible for a handful of people to *make* a revolution, *i.e.*, with one small push to cause a whole system, which (to use a metaphor of Plekhanov's) is in more than labile equilibrium, to come crashing down, and thus by one action, in itself insignificant, to release uncontrollable explosive forces. Well now, if ever Blanquism—the phantasy of overturning an entire society through the action of a small conspiracy—had a certain justification for its existence, that is certainly in Petersburg. Once the spark has been put to the powder, once the forces have been released and national energy has been transformed from potential into kinetic energy (another favourite image of Plekhanov's and a very good one)—the people who laid the spark to the mine will be swept away by the explosion, which will be a thousand times as strong as themselves and which will seek its vent where it can, according as the economic forces and resistances determine.

Supposing these people imagine they can seize power, what does it matter? Provided they make the hole which will shatter the dyke, the flood itself will soon rob them of their illusions. But if by chance these illusions resulted in giving them a superior force of will, why complain of that? People who boasted that they had *made* a revolution have always seen the next day that

* March 1, 1881, (Old Style) The day on which the Tsar Alexander II was assassinated.

they had no idea what they were doing, that the revolution *made* did not in the least resemble the one they would have liked to make. That is what Hegel calls the irony of history, an irony which few historic personalities escape. Look at Bismarck, the revolutionary against his will, and Gladstone who has ended in quarrelling with his adored Tsar.

To me the most important thing is that the impulse should be given in Russia, that the revolution should break out. Whether this fraction or that fraction gives the signal, whether it happens under this flag or that flag matters little to me. If it were a palace conspiracy it would be swept away to-morrow. There where the position is so strained, where the revolutionary elements are accumulated to such a degree, where the economic situation of the enormous mass of the people becomes daily more impossible, where every stage of social development is represented, from the primitive commune to modern large-scale industry and high finance, and where all these contradictions are violently held together by an unexampled despotism, a despotism which is becoming more and more unbearable to the youth in whom the national worth and intelligence are united—there, when 1789 has once been launched, 1793 will not be long in following.*

ZASULICH, VERA J. (1851-1919). Russian socialist; as a young student joined the Narodniki. In 1880 she emigrated and from then onwards worked with Plekhanov. Together with him she was one of the founders of the first Marxist group in the Russian workers' movement (the Emancipation of Labour group—1885) which began the struggle against the Narodniki for the creation of a proletarian revolutionary party. Zasulich was commissioned by the Emancipation of Labour group to translate a number of Marx's works into Russian. With Lenin and Plekhanov she was a member of the editorial board of *Iskra*. After the split in the Russian Social-Democratic Party (1903) she soon went over to the Mensheviks. During the imperialist war she was a social chauvinist. She maintained a hostile attitude to the October revolution.

* 1793. See Note on the Jacobins, page 459.

PLEKHANOV, G. V. (1856-1918). The leading Marxist in the Russian workers' movement before Lenin. After the split in the movement he soon went over to the Mensheviks. Even though at times he later moved away from them and approached the Bolsheviks again, he always stood near the Mensheviks, nevertheless. With the imperialist war he became a "defender of the Fatherland." He was hostile to the October Revolution. Plekhanov wrote a series of basic Marxist works, especially on philosophical questions. In his book, *Our Differences*, he took up the struggle against the petty bourgeois socialism of the Narodniki and fought for the leading rôle of the working class in the Russian revolutionary movement. At the end of the 'nineties he fought against revisionism (Bernstein). Lenin said of Plekhanov's philosophical writings: "It is impossible to become a real and conscious Communist without studying everything Plekhanov wrote on philosophy, studying it directly, for it is the best thing in the whole international Marxist literature." At the same time, however, Lenin fought most sharply against Plekhanov's important mistakes (*e.g.*, in the theory of the state and in the questions of dialectical materialism) and against his later betrayal of socialism.

195. ENGELS TO J. P. BECKER

London, 15 June, 1885.

Here in England things are going quite well, though not in the form originated in Germany. Since 1848 the English Parliament has undoubtedly been the most revolutionary body in the world and the next elections will open a new epoch, even if this does not reveal itself so very quickly. There will be workers in Parliament, in increasing numbers and each one worse than the last. But that is necessary in England. All the scoundrels who played the part of respectable bourgeois radicals here at the time of the International must show themselves in Parliament for what they are. Then the masses will turn socialist here too. Industrial over-production will do the rest.

The row in the German Party has not surprised me. In a petty-bourgeois country like Germany the Party is bound also to have a *petty bourgeois* "*educated*" *Right wing*, which it shakes off at the decisive moment. Petty bourgeois socialism in Germany dates from 1844 and was already criticised in *The Communist Manifesto*. It is as immortal as the German petty-bourgeois himself. So long as the Socialist Laws are in force I am not in favour of *our* provoking the split, because our weapons are unevenly matched. But if the gentlemen provoke a split themselves by suppressing the proletarian character of the Party and trying to replace it by a stick-in-the-mud* æsthetic-sentimental philanthropy without force or life, then we must just take it as it comes!

196. ENGELS TO BEBEL

London, 24 July, 1885.

You have exactly hit off Kautsky's decisive weakness. His youthful inclination towards hasty judgment has been still more intensified by the wretched method of teaching history in the universities—especially the Austrian ones. The students there are systematically taught to do historical work with materials which they know to be inadequate but which they are *supposed to treat as adequate*, that is, to write things which they themselves must know to be false but which they are supposed to consider correct. That has naturally made Kautsky thoroughly cocky. Then the literary life—writing for pay and writing a lot. So that he has absolutely no idea of what really scientific work means. There he has thoroughly burnt his fingers a few times, with his history of population and later with the articles on marriage in primitive times. In all friendship I rubbed that well into him too and spare him nothing in this respect: on *this* side I criticise all his things mercilessly. Fortunately, however, I can comfort him with the fact that I did exactly the same in my impudent youth and only first learnt the way one has got to work from Marx. It helps quite considerably, too.

* *Knotig*, see Note on *Knoten*, page 87. [*Ed. Eng. ed.*]

197. ENGELS TO BEBEL

London, 28 October, 1885.

The chronic depression in all the decisive branches of industry also still continues unbroken here, in France and in America. Especially in iron and cotton. It is an unheard-of situation, though entirely the inevitable result of the capitalist system: such colossal over-production that it cannot even bring things to a crisis! The over-production of disposable capital seeking investment is so great that the rate of discount here actually fluctuates between 1 and 1½ per cent. per annum, and for money invested in short term credits, which can be called in or paid off from day to day (money on call) one can hardly get ½ per cent. per annum. But by choosing to invest his money in this way rather than in new industrial undertakings the money capitalist is admitting how rotten the whole business looks to him. And this fear of new investments and old enterprises, which had already manifested itself in the crisis of 1867, is the main reason why things are not brought to an acute crisis.

But it will have to come in the end, all the same, and then it will make an end of the old trade unions here, let us hope. These unions have peacefully retained the craft character which clung to them from the first and which is becoming more unbearable every day. No doubt you suppose that the engineers, joiners, bricklayers, etc., will admit any worker in their branch of industry without more ado? Not at all. Whoever wants admission must be attached as an apprentice for a period of years (usually seven) to some worker belonging to the union. This was intended to keep the number of workers limited, but had otherwise no point at all except that it brought in money to the apprentice's instructor, for which he did absolutely nothing in return. This was all right up to 1848. But since then the colossal growth of industry has produced a class of workers of whom there are as many or more as there are "skilled" workers in the trade unions and who can do all that the "skilled" workers can or more, but who can never become members. These people have been *regularly penalised* by the craft rules of the trade unions. But do you suppose the unions ever dreamt of doing away with this silly bunk? Not in the least. I can never remember reading of a single proposal of the kind at a Trade Union Congress. The fools want to reform society to suit themselves and not to reform themselves to suit the development of society. They cling to their traditional superstition, which does them nothing but harm themselves, instead of getting quit of the rubbish and thus doubling their numbers and their power and really becoming again what at present they daily become less—associations of all the workers in a trade against the capitalists. This will I think explain many things in the behaviour of these privileged workers to you.

What is most necessary of all here is that masses of the official labour leaders should get into Parliament. Then things will soon go finely; they will expose themselves quickly enough.

The elections in November will help a lot towards this. Ten or twelve of them are certain to get in, if their Liberal friends do not play them a trick at the last moment. The first elections under a new system are always a sort of lottery and only reveal the smallest part of the revolution they have introduced. But universal suffrage—and with the absence of a peasant class and the start England had in industrialisation the new franchise here gives the workers as much power as universal suffrage would give them in Germany—universal suffrage is the best lever for a proletarian movement at the present time and will prove to be so here. That is why it is so important to break up the Social Democratic Federation as quickly as possible, its leaders being nothing but careerists, adventurers and literary people. Hyndman, their head, is doing his very best in this way; he cannot wait for the clock to strike twelve, as it says in the folk song, and in his chase after successes discredits himself more every day.* He is a wretched caricature of Lassalle.

¶The economic crisis—see Letters 189, 198, 199.

The elections in November-December, 1885, under the

* See Letter 200.

newly extended franchise, resulted in the return of 331 Liberals, including 11 "labour" candidates, 247 Conservatives and 82 Irish Nationalists.

"That . . . the official labour leaders should get into Parliament"- -compare Letter 195.

The craft unions—compare Letters 207, 208 on the rise of the "new unionism." [*Ed. Eng. ed.*]

198. ENGELS TO FLORENCE KELLEY WISCHNEWETSKY*

London, 7 January, 1886.

As to those wise Americans who think their country exempt from the consequences of fully expanded Capitalist production, they seem to live in blissful ignorance of the fact that sundry states, Massachusetts, New Jersey, Pennsylvania, Ohio, etc., have such an institution as a Labour Bureau from the reports of which they might learn something to the contrary.

¶Engels, in dealing with this subject a month later in a letter to Florence Kelley Wischnewetsky (February 3, 1886) wrote: "America will smash up England's industrial monopoly—whatever there is left of it—but America cannot herself succeed to that monopoly. And unless *one* country has the monopoly of the markets of the world, at least in the decisive branches of trade, the conditions—relatively favourable—which existed here in England from 1848 to 1870 cannot anywhere be reproduced, and even in America the condition of the working class must gradually sink lower and lower. For if there are three countries (say England, America and Germany) competing on comparatively equal terms for the possession of the *Weltmarkt* [world market] there is no chance but chronic over-production, one of the three being capable of supplying the whole quantity required. That is the reason why I am watching the development of the present crisis with greater interest than ever and why I believe it will mark an epoch in the mental and political history of the American and English working classes—

* Written in English.

the very two whose assistance is as absolutely necessary as it is desirable."* [*Ed. Eng. ed.*]

WISCHNEWETSKY, FLORENCE KELLEY (1859-1932). American social reformist. She translated Engels' *The Condition of the Working Class in England in 1844* into English.

199. ENGELS TO BEBEL

London, 20-23 January, 1886.

The disintegration of the German free thinkers in the economic sphere quite corresponds to what is going on among the English Radicals. The people of the old Manchester school *a la* John Bright are dying out and the younger generation, just like the Berliners, goes in for social patching-up reforms. Only that here the bourgeois does not want to help the industrial worker so much as the agricultural worker, who has just done him excellent service at the elections, and that in English fashion it is not so much the state as the municipality which is to intervene. For the agricultural workers, little gardens and potato plots, for the town workers sanitary improvements and the like—this is their programme. An excellent sign is that the bourgeoisie are already obliged to sacrifice their own classical economic theory, partly from political considerations but partly because they themselves, owing to the practical consequences of this theory, have begun to doubt it.

The same thing is proved by the growth of *Kathedersozialismus* [professorial socialism] which in one form or another is more and more supplanting classical economy in the professorial chairs both here and in France. The actual contradictions engendered by the method of production have become so crass that no theory can indeed conceal them any longer, unless it were this professorial socialist mish-mash, which however is no longer a theory but drivel.

Six weeks ago symptoms of an improvement in trade were said to be showing themselves. Now this has all faded away again, the distress is greater than ever and the lack of prospect too, added to an unusually severe winter. This is now already

* Written in English.

the eighth year of the pressure of overproduction upon the markets and instead of getting better it is always getting worse. There is no longer any doubt that the situation has essentially changed from what it was formerly ; since England has got important rivals on the world market the period of crises, in the sense known hitherto, is closed. If the crises change from acute into chronic ones but at the same time lose nothing in intensity, what will be the end? A period of prosperity, even if a short one, must after all return sometime, when the accumulation of commodities has been exhausted ; but how all this will occur I am eager to see. But two things are certain : we have entered upon a period incomparably more dangerous to the existence of the old society than the period of ten-yearly crises; and secondly, when prosperity returns, England will be much less affected by it than formerly, when she alone skimmed the cream off the world market. The day this becomes clear here, and not before, the socialist movement here will seriously begin.

200. ENGELS TO BEBEL.

London, 15 February, 1886.

The Social Democratic Federation which, despite all self-advertising reports, is an extremely weak organisation—containing good elements but led by literary and political adventurers—was brought to the verge of dissolution at the November elections by a stroke of genius on the part of these same leaders. Hyndman (pronounced Heindman) the head of the society, had taken money from the Tories (Conservatives) at the time, and with it put up two Social-Democratic candidates in two districts of London. As they had not even got any members in these two constituencies the way they would discredit themselves was to be foreseen (one got 27, the other 32 votes out of 4000—5000 respectively !). Hyndman, however, had no sooner got the Tory money than his head began violently to swell and he immediately set off to Birmingham, to Chamberlain, the present Minister, and offered him his "support" (which does not total 1000 votes in all England) if Chamberlain would guarantee him a seat in Birmingham by the help of the Liberals and would bring in an Eight Hour Bill. Chamberlain is no fool and showed him the door. Despite all attempts to hush it up, a great row about this in the Federation and threatened dissolution. So now something had to happen in order to get the thing going again.

In the meantime unemployment was increasing more and more. The collapse of England's monopoly on the world-market has caused the crisis to continue unbroken since 1878 and to get worse rather than better. The distress, especially in the East End of the city, is appalling. The exceptionally hard winter, since January, added to the boundless indifference of the possessing classes, produced a considerable movement among the unemployed masses. As usual, political wire-pullers tried to exploit this movement for their own ends. The Conservatives, who had just been superseded in the Government,* put the responsibility for unemployment on to foreign competition (rightly) and foreign tariffs (for the most part wrongly) and preached "fair-trade," i.e., retaliatory tariffs. A workers' organisation also exists which believes mainly in retaliatory tariffs. This organisation summoned the meeting in Trafalgar Square on February 8. In the meantime the S.D.F. had not been idle either, had already held some small demonstrations and now wanted to utilise this meeting. Two meetings accordingly took place; the "fair traders" were round the Nelson Column while the S.D.F. people spoke at the north end of the Square, from the street opposite the National Gallery, which is about 25 feet above the square. Kautsky, who was there and went away before the row began, told me that the mass of the real workers had been around the "fair traders," whilst Hyndman and Co. had a mixed audience of people looking for a lark, some of them already merry. If Kautsky, who has hardly been here a year, noticed this, the gentlemen of the Federation must have seen it still more clearly. Nevertheless, when everybody already seemed to be scattering, they proceeded to carry out a favourite old idea of Hyndman's,

* See page 442.

namely a procession of " unemployed " through Pall Mall, the street of the big political, aristocratic and high-capitalist clubs, the centres of English political intrigue. The enemployed who followed them in order to hold a fresh meeting in Hyde Park, were mostly the types who do not want work anyhow, hawkers, loafers, police spies, pickpockets. When the aristocrats at the club windows sneered at them they broke the said windows, ditto the shop windows ; they looted the wine dealers' shops and immediately set up a consumers' association for the contents in the street, so that in Hyde Park Hyndman and Co. had hastily to pocket their blood-thirsty phrases and go in for pacification. But the thing had now got going. During the procession, during this second little meeting and afterwards, the masses of the Lumpenproletariat, whom Hyndman had taken for the unemployed, streamed through some fashionable streets near by, looted jewellers' and other shops, used the loaves and legs of mutton which they had looted solely to break windows with, and dispersed without meeting with any resistance. Only a remnant of them were broken up in Oxford Street by four, say four, policemen.

Otherwise the police were nowhere to be seen and their absence was so marked that *we* were not alone in being compelled to think it intentional. The chiefs of the police seem to be Conservatives who had no objection to seeing a bit of a row in this period of Liberal Government. However the Government at once set up a Commission of Inquiry and it may cost more than one of these gentlemen his job.

¶"As to Hyndman," wrote Engels to Bebel a month later (18 March, 1886), "the way he came out in Trafalgar Square and Hyde Park on February 8 has done infinitely more harm than good. Shouting about revolution, which in France passes off harmlessly as stale stuff, is utter nonsense here among the totally unprepared masses and has the effect of scaring away the proletariat, only exciting the demoralised elements. It absolutely cannot be understood here as anything but a summons to looting, which accordingly followed and has brought discredit which will last a long time here, among the workers too. As to the point that it has drawn public attention to Socialism, you people over in Germany do not know how utterly blunted the public are with regard to such methods after a hundred years of freedom of the press and of assembly and the advertising bound up with them. The first alarm of the bourgeois was certainly very funny and brought in about £40,000 in contributions for the unemployed—in all about £70,000—but that has already been disposed of and nobody will pay more and the distress remains the same. What has been achieved—among the bourgeois public—is the identification of socialism with looting, and even though that does not make the matter much worse still it is certainly no gain to us."

The four leaders of the demonstration to Hyde Park, Hyndman, Champion, Williams and John Burns, were afterwards arrested, released on bail and, in April, tried and acquitted. "A fine advertisement for Hyndman, but it comes too late; he has succeeded in ruining his organisation hopelessly . . ." wrote Engels to Bebel (12 April 1886); "at the very most, the two organisations—Federation and League—have not 2,000 paying members between them nor their papers 5,000 readers between them—and of these the majority are sympathetic bourgeois, parsons, literary men, etc. As things are here it is a real mercy that these immature elements do not succeed in penetrating the masses. They must first ferment themselves clear, then it may turn out all right." [*Ed. Eng. ed.*]

---

201. ENGELS TO FLORENCE KELLEY WISCHNEWETSKY*

London, June 3, 1886.

Whatever the mistakes and the *Borniertheit* [narrow-mindedness] of the leaders of the movement, and partly of the newly-awakening masses too, one thing is certain: the American working class is moving, and no mistake. And after a few false starts, they will get into the right track soon enough. This appearance of the Americans upon the scene I consider one of the greatest events of the year.

What the downbreak of Russian Czarism would be for the

* This letter was written in English.

great military monarchies of Europe—the snapping of their mainstay—that is for the bourgeois of the whole world the breaking out of class war in America. For America after all was the ideal of all bourgeois ; a country *rich*, *vast*, *expanding*, with purely *bourgeois* institutions unleavened by feudal remnants or monarchical traditions and without a permanent and hereditary proletariate. Here everyone could become, if not a capitalist, at all events an independent man, producing or trading, with his own means, for his own account. And because there were not, *as yet*, classes with opposing interests, our—and your—bourgeois thought that America stood *above* class antagonisms and struggles. That dclusion has now broken down, the last Bourgeois Paradise on earth is fast changing into a Purgatorio, and can only be prevented from becoming, like Europe, an Inferno by the go-ahead pace at which the development of the newly fledged proletariate of America will take place. The way in which they have made their appearance on the scene is quite extraordinary : Six months ago nobody suspected anything, and now they appear all of a sudden in such organised masses as to strike terror into the whole capitalist class. I only wish Marx could have lived to see it !

¶A huge strike movement, based on the struggle for the eight-hour day, swept over the United States in the first half of 1886. Many of the strikes took on a political character. A number of new " Labour Parties " sprang into being under various titles. See Letter 202. [*Ed. Eng. ed.*]

202. ENGELS TO SORGE

London, 29 November, 1886.

The Henry George *boom* has of course brought to light a colossal mass of fraud and I am glad I was not there. But despite it all it has been an epoch-making day. The Germans have not understood how to use their theory as a lever which could set the American masses in motion ; they do not understand the theory themselves for the most part and treat it in a doctrinaire and dogmatic way, as something which has got to be learnt off by heart but which will then supply all needs without more ado. To them it is a *credo* [creed] and not a guide to action. Added to which they learn no English on principle. Hence the American masses had to seek out their own way and seem to have found it for the time being in the K(nights) of L(abour), whose confused principles and ludicrous organisation appear to correspond to their own confusion. But according to all I hear the K. of L. are a real power, especially in New England and the West, and are becoming more so every day owing to the brutal opposition of the capitalists. I think it is necessary to work inside them, to form within this still quite plastic mass a core of people who understand the movement and its aims and will therefore themselves take over the leadership, at least of a section, when the inevitably impending break-up of the present " order " takes place. The rottenest side of the K. of L. was their political neutrality, which resulted in sheer trickery on the part of the Powderlys, etc. ; but this has had its edge taken off by the behaviour of the masses at the November elections, especially in New York. The first great step of importance for every country newly entering into the movement is always the organisation of the workers as an independent political party, no matter how, so long as it is a distinct workers' party. And this step has been taken, far more rapidly than we had a right to hope, and that is the main thing. That the first programme of this party is still confused and highly deficient, that it has set up the banner of Henry George, these are inevitable evils but also only transitory ones. The masses must have time and opportunity to develop and they can only have the opportunity when they have their own movement—no matter in what form so long as it is only *their own* movement—in which they are driven further by their own mistakes and learn wisdom by hurting themselves. The movement in America is in the same position as it was with us before 1848 ; the really intelligent people there will first of all have the same part to play as that played by the Communist League among the workers' associations before 1848. Except that in America now things will go infinitely more quickly; for the movement to have attained such election successes after scarcely eight months of existence is absolutely unheard of. And what is still lacking will be set going by the bourgeoisie; nowhere in the whole world do they come out so shamelessly and tyrannically as here, and your judges have got Bismarck's smart practitioners in the German Reich brilliantly driven off the field. Where the bourgeoisie conducts the struggle by methods of this kind, things come rapidly to a decision, and if we in Europe do not hurry up the Americans will soon be ahead of us. But it is just now that it is doubly necessary to have a few people there from our side with a firm seat in their saddles where theory and long-proved tactics are concerned, and who can also write and speak English; for, from good historical reasons, the Americans are worlds behind in all theoretical things, and while they did not bring over any medieval institutions from Europe they did bring over masses of medieval traditions, religion, English common (feudal) law, superstition, spiritualism, in short every kind of imbecility which was not directly harmful to business and which is now very serviceable for making the masses stupid. And if there are people at hand there whose minds are theoretically clear, who can tell them the consequences of their own mistakes beforehand and make it clear to them that every movement which does not keep the destruction of the wage system in view the whole time as its final aim is bound to go astray and fail—then many a piece of nonsense may be avoided and the process considerably shortened. But it must take place in the English way, the specific German character must be cut out and for that the gentlemen of the *Sozialist* have hardly the qualifications, while those of the *Volkszeitung* are only more intelligent where *business* is concerned.*

¶In the November 1886 municipal elections in the U.S.A. many of the newly-formed Labour Parties polled big votes and

* The *Sozialist*, a German-American weekly (edited by Dietzgen), was the official organ of the Socialist Labour Party; the *New Yorker Volkszeitung*, a German daily paper, had been founded in 1878 by members of the S.L.P. (See Note, page 460). [*Ed. Eng. ed.*]

in some places even got their candidates elected. The most spectacular success was that in New York City where the United Labour Party, which had only been formed in July, put forward Henry George (Letter 175) as candidate for mayor. George took second place with over 68,000 votes to about 90,000 cast for the Democrat, Hewitt; Theodore Roosevelt, the Republican candidate, polled 60,000. Engels, in his Preface to the American edition of *The Condition of the Working Class in England in 1844*, written two months later (January 26, 1887), discussed the rise of the American Labour movement and gave a criticism of Henry George. See also Letter 201. [*Ed. Eng. ed.*]

THE KNIGHTS OF LABOUR. This organisation arose in 1869; in the first ten years of its existence it only continued with great difficulty and the number of its members was very insignificant. With the rising industrial development and the spread among the American working class of the eight-hour day movement, the Knights of Labour began to develop with unexpected rapidity. In 1886 the American working class was in the grip of a strong strike movement. The American bourgeoisie resorted to its usual methods: terrorist and provocative acts (the bomb attempt organised by the police in Chicago), a wild campaign of slander against the working-class movement in the corrupt press and the no less corrupt courts; gallows and prison for the most active and advanced leaders of the movement. Later the Knights of Labour became the prey of its own bureaucracy.

POWDERLY, TERENCE VINCENT (1849-1924). Irish leader of the Knights of Labour. Later lawyer and Immigration Commissioner.

203. ENGELS TO FLORENCE KELLEY WISCHNEWETSKY*

London, December 28, 1886.

My preface† will of course turn entirely on the immense stride made by the American working man in the last ten months, and naturally also touch H.G. and his land scheme. But it cannot pretend to deal exhaustively with it. Nor do I

* This letter was written in English.

† To the American edition of Engels' *The Condition of the Working Class in England in 1844*. "H.G."—Henry George.

think the time has come for that. It is far more important that the movement should spread, proceed harmoniously, take root and embrace as much as possible the whole American proletariate, than that it should start and proceed from the beginning on theoretically perfectly correct lines. There is no better road to theoretical clearness of comprehension than "*durch Schaden klug werden*" [to learn by one's own mistakes]. And for a whole large class, there is no other road, especially for a nation so eminently practical as the Americans. The great thing is to get the working class to move *as a class*; that once obtained, they will soon find the right direction, and all who resist, H.G. or Powderly, will be left out in the cold with small sects of their own. Therefore I think also the K[nights] of L[abour] a most important factor in the movement which ought not to be pooh-poohed from without but to be revolutionised from within, and I consider that many of the Germans there have made a grievous mistake when they tried, in face of a mighty and glorious movement not of their creation, to make of their imported and not always understood theory a kind of *alleinseligmachendes** dogma and to keep aloof from any movement which did not accept that dogma. Our theory is not a dogma but the exposition of a process of evolution, and that process involves successive phases. To expect that the Americans will start with the full consciousness of the theory worked out in older industrial countries is to expect the impossible. What the Germans ought to do is to act up to their own theory —if they understand it, as we did in 1845 and 1848—to go in for any real general working-class movement, accept its *faktische*† starting points as such and work it gradually up to the theoretical level by pointing out how every mistake made, every reverse suffered, was a necessary consequence of mistaken theoretical views in the original programme; they ought, in the words of *The Communist Manifesto*, to represent the movement of the future in the movement of the present. But above all give the movement time to consolidate, do not make the inevitable confusion of the first start worse

* Necessary to salvation.
† Actual.

confounded by forcing down people's throats things which at present they cannot properly understand, but which they soon will learn. A million or two of workingmen's votes next November for a *bona fide* workingmen's party is worth infinitely more at present than a hundred thousand votes for a doctrinally perfect platform. The very first attempt—soon to be made if the movement progresses—to consolidate the moving masses on a national basis will bring them all face to face, Georgites, K. of L., Trade Unionists, and all; and if our German friends by that time have learnt enough of the language of the country to go in for a discussion, then will be the time for them to criticise the views of the others and thus, by showing up the inconsistencies of the various standpoints, to bring them gradually to understand their own actual position, the position made for them by the correlation of capital and wage labour. But anything that might delay or prevent that national consolidation of the workingmen's party— no matter what platform—I should consider a great mistake, and therefore I do not think the time has arrived to speak out fully and exhaustively either with regard to H.G. or the K. of L.

204. ENGELS TO FLORENCE KELLEY WISCHNEWETSKY*

January 27, 1887.

The movement in America, just at this moment, is I believe best seen from across the ocean. On the spot personal bickerings and local disputes must obscure most of the grandeur of it. And the only thing that could really delay its march would be a consolidation of these differences into established acts. To some extent that will be unavoidable, but the less of it the better. And the Germans have most to guard against this. Our theory is a theory of evolution, not a dogma to be learned by heart and to be repeated mechanically. The less it is drilled into the Americans from outside and the more they test it with their own experience—with the help of the Germans—the deeper will it pass into their flesh and blood.† When we

* Written in English.
† This sentence was written in German.

returned to Germany, in spring 1848, we joined the Democratic Party as the only possible means of getting the ear of the working class; we were the most advanced wing of that party, but still a wing of it. When Marx founded the International, he drew up the General Rules in such a way that *all* working-class socialists of that period could join it—Proudhonists, Pierre Lerouxists and even the more advanced section of the English Trades Unions; and it was only through this latitude that the International became what it was, the means of gradually dissolving and absorbing all these minor sects, with the exception of the Anarchists, whose sudden appearance in various countries was but the effect of the violent bourgeois reaction after the Commune and could therefore safely be left by us to die out of itself, as it did. Had we from 1864 to 1873 insisted on working together only with those who openly adopted our platform where should we be to-day? I think that all our practice has shown that it is possible to work along with the general movement of the working class at every one of its stages without giving up or hiding our own distinct position and even organisation, and I am afraid that if the German Americans choose a different line they will commit a great mistake.

205. ENGELS TO SORGE

London, 7 January, 1888.

A war, on the other hand, would throw us back for years. Chauvinism would swamp everything, for it would be a fight for existence. Germany would put about five million armed men into the field, or ten per cent. of the population, the others about four to five per cent., Russia relatively less. But there would be from ten to fifteen million combatants. I should like to see how they are to be fed; it would be a devastation like the Thirty Years' War. And no quick decision could be arrived at, despite the colossal fighting forces. For France is protected on the north-eastern and south-eastern frontiers by very extensive fortifications and the new constructions in Paris are a model. So it will last a long time, and Russia cannot be taken by storm either. If, therefore, everything goes according to Bismarck's desires, more will be demanded of the nation than ever before and it is possible enough that partial defeats and the dragging out of the decisive war would produce an internal upheaval. But if the Germans were defeated from the first or forced into a prolonged defensive, then the thing would certainly start.

If the war was fought out to the end without internal disturbances a state of exhaustion would supervene such as Europe has not experienced for two hundred years. American industry would then conquer all along the line and would force us all up against the alternatives : either retrogression to nothing but agriculture for *home consumption* (American corn forbids anything else) or—social transformation. I imagine, therefore, that the plan is not to push things to extremities, to more than a sham war. But once the first shot is fired, control ceases, the horse can take the bit between its teeth.

¶Engels wrote on the coming war in his preface to Borkheim's *Zur Erinnerung für die deutschen Mordspatrioten 1806-1807* [*In Memory of the Supreme German Patriots 1806-1807*] :

" And finally no war is any longer possible for Prussia-Germany except a world war and a world war indeed of an extension and violence hitherto undreamt of. Eight to ten millions of soldiers will mutually massacre one another and in doing so devour the whole of Europe until they have stripped it barer than any swarm of locusts has ever done. The devastations of the Thirty Years' War compressed into three or four years, and spread over the whole Continent ; famine, pestilence, general demoralisation both of the armies and of the mass of the people produced by acute distress ; hopeless confusion of our artificial machinery in trade, industry and credit, ending in general bankruptcy ; collapse of the old states and their traditional state wisdom to such an extent that crowns will roll by dozens on the pavement and there will be nobody to pick them up ; absolute impossibility of foreseeing how it will all end and who will come out of the struggle as victor ; only one result absolutely certain : general exhaustion and the establishment of the conditions for the ultimate victory of the working class. This is the prospect when the system of mutual outbidding in armaments, driven to extremities, at last bears its inevitable fruits. This, my lords, princes and statesmen, is where in your wisdom you have brought old Europe. And when nothing more remains to you but to open the last great war dance—that will suit us all right. The war may perhaps push us temporarily into the background, may wrench from us many a position already conquered. But when you have unfettered forces which you will then no longer be able again to control, things may go as they will : at the end of the tragedy you will be ruined and the victory of the proletariat will either be already achieved or at any rate inevitable."

206. ENGELS TO VICTOR ADLER

London, 4 December, 1889

I recommended you to revise Avenel's *Cloots** for the following reasons :

In my opinion (and that of Marx) the book contains the first specific and correct account, based on a study of the archives, of the *critical period of the French Revolution*, namely from 10 August to 9 Thermidor.

Cloots and the Commune of Paris were for the propagandist war as the only means of salvation, whereas the Committee of Public Safety behaved like regular *statesmen*, were frightened of the European coalition and tried to get peace by *dividing* the allied powers. Danton wanted peace with England, that is with Fox and the English opposition, who hoped to come into power at the elections ; Robespierre intrigued with Austria and Prussia at Basle in the hope of coming to an understanding with *them*. Both united against the Commune in order above all to overthrow the people who wanted the propagandist war and the republicanisation of Europe. They succeeded, the Commune (Hébert, Cloots, etc.) was beheaded. But from that time onwards agreement became impossible between those

* Georges Avenel : *Anarcharsis Cloots, l'orateur du genre humain* [the orator of the human race]. Paris 1865.

who wanted to conclude peace only with England and those who wanted to conclude it only with the German powers. The English elections turned in favour of Pitt, Fox was shut out of the government for years, this ruined Danton's position, Robespierre was victorious and beheaded him. But—and Avenel has *not sufficiently* stressed this—while the reign of terror was now intensified to a pitch of insanity, because it was necessary in order to keep Robespierre in power under the existing internal conditions, it was rendered entirely superfluous by the victory of Fleurus on 24 June, 1794, which freed not only the frontiers but Belgium, and indirectly delivered over the left bank of the Rhine to France. Thus Robespierre also became superfluous and fell on July 24.

The whole French Revolution is dominated by the War of Coalition, all its pulsations depend upon it. If the allied army penetrates into France—predominant activity of the vagus nerves, violent heart-beat, revolutionary crisis. If it is driven back—predominance of the sympathetic nerves, the heart-beat becomes slower, the reactionary elements again push themselves into the foreground; the plebeians, the beginning of the later proletariat, whose energy alone has saved the revolution, are brought to reason and order.

The tragedy is that the party supporting war to the bitter end, war for the emancipation of the nations, is proved in the right, and that the Republic gets the better of all Europe, but only after that party itself has long been beheaded ; while in place of the propagandist war comes the Peace of Basle and the bourgeois orgy of the Directory.

The book must be completely revised and shortened—the rhetoric cut out, the facts taken from the ordinary histories supplemented and clearly emphasised. Cloots, meanwhile, can be put quite into the background, the most important things from the *Lundis révolut.** can be inserted and we may get a work on the revolution such as has never existed up till now.

* Georges Avenel : *Lundis Révolutionaires*, 1871-74.

¶In the great French Revolution, the Jacobins were the representatives of the consistent carrying through of the democratic revolution, *i.e.*, of the destruction of feudal fetters on the land and in the towns and the revolutionary defence of the country against the armies of intervention of the European counter-revolution. Marx wrote in 1848: "The proletariat and those fractions of citizens not belonging to the bourgeoisie either had [in the English and French revolutions] no interests apart from those of the bourgeoisie or else did not as yet form any independently developed classes or sections of classes. Hence when they clash with the bourgeoisie, as for instance between 1793 and 1794 in France, they are only fighting for the carrying out of the interests of the bourgeoisie, even though not after the fashion of the bourgeoisie. The whole French terror was nothing but a plebeian way of getting rid of the enemies of the bourgeoisie, of absolutism, feudalism and the petty bourgeoisie." (Marx: *Bilanz der preussischen Revolution* [*Balance of the Prussian Revolution*], *Literärischer Nachlass*, Bd. III, S. 211.)

After their victory over the counter-revolution, the Jacobins were, however, unable to solve the problems set them by the economic crisis, unemployment and high prices. Hence their social basis was greatly narrowed. Oppositional movements arose, above all from the Commune, the plebeian strata; these were indeed crushed, but the successes of the revolutionary armies, which consolidated the Republic, made the terror more and more superfluous and the bourgeoisie succeeded in overthrowing the Jacobins.

Lenin wrote in 1917 in his article, "Can Jacobinism Frighten the Working Class?" (*Collected Works*, Vol. 2, English Edition, p. 277.):

"The bourgeois historians see in Jacobinism a downfall (to "sink"). The proletarian historians regard Jacobinism as the greatest expression of an oppressed class in its struggle for liberation. The Jacobins gave France the best models of a democratic revolution; they repelled in an exemplary fashion the coalition of monarchs formed against the republic. The Jacobins were not destined to win a complete victory, chiefly because eighteenth-century France was surrounded on the Continent by countries that were too backward, and also because France itself was not possessed of the material requisites for socialism, since there were no banks, no capitalist syndicates, no machine industry, no railroads.

"Jacobinism" in Europe or on the boundary line between Europe and Asia in the twentieth century would be the rule of the revolutionary class, of the proletariat, which, supported by the poorest peasants and relying on the presence of the material requisites for an advance towards Socialism, could not only achieve the same, great, ineradicable, unforgettable things that were achieved by the Jacobins of the eighteenth century, but could also lead to a permanent triumph of the toilers on a universal scale.

It is natural for the bourgeoisie to hate Jacobinism. It is natural for the petty bourgeoisie to fear it. The class-conscious workers and toilers have faith in the transfer of power to the revolutionary oppressed class, for *that* is the essence of Jacobinism, and it is the only escape from the present crisis, the only way of stopping economic disintegration and the war."

ADLER, VICTOR (1852-1918). Founder and leader of Austrian social-democracy, originally a bourgeois radical; one of the leaders of reformism in the Second International; during the war a social pacifist. Father of Austro-Marxism.

207. ENGELS TO SORGE

London, 7 December, 1889.

Here in England one can see that it is impossible simply to drill a theory in an abstract dogmatic way into a great nation, even if one has the best of theories, developed out of their own conditions of life, and even if the tutors are relatively better than the S.L.P.* The movement has now got going at last and I believe for good. But it is not directly Socialist, and those English who have understood our theory best remain outside it: Hyndman because he is incurably jealous and intriguing, Bax because he is only a bookworm. Formally the movement is at the moment a trade union movement, but utterly different

* Socialist Labour Party of North America. This name was adopted in 1877 by the Social-Democratic Workingmen's Party of North America which had been founded in 1874, mainly by Germans. [*Ed. Eng. ed.*].

from that of the *old* trade unions, the skilled labourers, the aristocracy of labour.

The people are throwing themselves into the job in quite a different way, are leading far more colossal masses into the fight, are shaking society much more deeply, are putting forward much more far-reaching demands : eight-hour day, general federation of all organisations, complete solidarity. Thanks to Tussy* women's branches have been formed *for the first time*—in the Gas Workers and General Labourers' Union. Moreover, the people only regard their immediate demands themselves as provisional, although they themselves do not know as yet what final aim they are working for. But this dim idea is strongly enough rooted to make them choose *only* openly declared Socialists as their leaders. Like everyone else they will have to learn by their own experiences and the consequences of their own mistakes. But as, unlike the old trade unions, they greet every suggestion of an identity of interest between capital and labour with scorn and ridicule this will not take very long. . . .

. . . The most repulsive thing here is the bourgeois " respectability " which has grown deep into the bones of the workers. The division of society into a scale of innumerable degrees, each recognised without question, each with its own pride but also its native respect for its " betters " and " superiors," is so old and firmly established that the bourgeois still find it pretty easy to get their bait accepted. I am not at all sure for instance, that John Burns is not secretly prouder of his popularity with Cardinal Manning, the Lord Mayor and the bourgeoisie in general than of his popularity with his own class. And Champion—an ex-Lieutenant—has intrigued for years with bourgeois and especially with conservative elements, preached Socialism at the parsons' Church Congress, etc. Even Tom Mann, whom I regard as the finest of them, is fond of mentioning that he will be lunching with the Lord Mayor. If one compares this with the French, one can see what a revolution is good for after all. However, it will not help the bourgeoisie much if they do succeed in enticing some of the

* Eleanor Marx Aveling (1856-98), youngest daughter of Marx. See Note.

leaders into their toils. The movement has been far enough strengthened for this sort of thing to be overcome.

¶Engels is referring in this letter to the great movement among the unskilled workers of London which took place in 1889 and which led to the rise of the "New Unionism" described in Letter 208, Note, etc. The outstanding events were the Dock strike (led by John Burns, Tom Mann and Ben Tillett) and the formation of the Gas Workers' and General Labourers' Union, which, like the Dockers' strike, gained some immediate concessions from the employers. Eleanor Marx Aveling and Edward Aveling took a prominent and active part in the great developments in the East End (see also Note, pp. 468-69, agitating, under Engels' guidance, in the Radical clubs frequented by the workers. [*Ed. Eng. Ed.*]

BURNS, JOHN (born 1858). One of the chief leaders of the movement of "unskilled" workers and of the dock strike of 1889. At this time a member of the S.D.F. Entered Parliament as M.P. for Battersea, 1892. Deserted the workers' movement and took office in the Liberal Government (1906-14) as President of the Local Government Board, and finally as President of the Board of Trade. (See also Letter 208.) [*Ed. Eng. Ed.*]

MANN, TOM (born 1856). Engineering worker. First President of the Dockers' Union formed after the strike of 1889. Secretary of the I.L.P., 1894-96. One of the leaders of the great transport strike of 1911 (Liverpool). Secretary of the Amalgamated Engineering Union 1919-21. Chairman, from 1924, of the National Minority Movement affiliated to the Red International of Labour Unions. Delegate to first R.I.L.U. Congress. Member of the Communist Party. Imprisoned 1912 for his leaflet appealing to soldiers not to shoot down members of the working class and 1932-33 for agitation on behalf of the unemployed; tried for sedition in 1934 but acquitted owing to mass agitation. [*Ed. Eng. Ed.*]

208. ENGELS TO H. SCHLÜTER

London, 11 January, 1890.

The stormy tide of the movement last summer has somewhat abated. And the best of it is that the unthinking sympathy of the bourgeois gang for the workers' movement, which broke out in the dock strike, has also abated, and is beginning to make way for the far more natural feeling of suspicion and nervousness. In the South London gas strike, which was forcibly imposed on the workers by the gas company, the workers are once more standing entirely deserted by all the philistines. This is very good and I only hope Burns will some time go through this experience himself, in a strike led by himself—he cherishes all sorts of illusions in that respect.

Meanwhile there is all kinds of friction, as was only to be expected, between the gas workers and the dockers, for instance. But despite it all the masses are on the move and there is no holding them any more. The longer the stream is dammed up the more powerfully will it break through when the moment comes. And these unskilled are very different chaps from the fossilised brothers of the old trade unions ; not a trace of the old formalist spirit, of the craft exclusiveness of the engineers, for instance ; on the contrary, a general cry for the organisation of all trade unions in one fraternity and for a direct struggle against capital. In the dock strike, for instance, there were three engineers at the Commercial Dock who kept the steam-engine going. Burns and Mann, both engineers themselves and Burns a member of the Amalgamated Eng. Trade Union Executive, were summoned to persuade these men to go away, as then none of the cranes would have worked and the dock company would have had to climb down. The three engineers refused, the Engineers' Executive did not intervene and hence the length of the strike ! At the Silvertown Rubber Works, moreover, where there was a twelve-weeks' strike, the strike was broken by the engineers, who did not join in and even did labourers' work against their own union rules ! And why ? These fools, in order to keep the supply of workers low, have a rule that nobody who has not been through the correct period of apprenticeship may be admitted to their union. By this means they have created an army of rivals, so-called blacklegs, who are just as skilled as they are themselves and who would gladly come into the union, but who are forced to remain blacklegs because they are kept outside by this pedantry which has no sense at all nowadays. And because they knew that both in the Commercial Dock and in Silvertown these blacklegs would immediately have stepped into their place, they stayed in and so became blacklegs themselves against the strikers. There you see the difference: the new unions hold together; in the present gas strike, sailors (steamer) and firemen, lightermen and coal carters are all together, but of course not the engineers again, they are still working!

However, these arrogant old great trade unions will soon be made to look small; their chief support, the London Trades Council, is being more and more subjugated by the new ones, and in two or three years at most the Trade Union Congress will also be revolutionised. Even at the next Congress the Broadhursts will get the shock of their lives.

The fact that you have got rid of Rosenberg and Co. is the main point about the revolution in your American socialist tea-cup. The German party over there must be smashed up *as such*, it is the worst obstacle. The American workers are coming along already, but just like the English they go their own way. One cannot drum the theory into them beforehand, but their own experience and their own blunders and the evil consequences of them will soon bump their noses up against theory—and then all right. Independent nations go their own way, and of them all the English and their offspring are surely the most independent. Their insular stiff-necked obstinacy annoys one often enough, but it also guarantees that once a thing gets started what is begun will be carried out.

¶In his preface to the English edition (1892) of *The Condition of the Working Class in England in 1844*, Engels (January 11, 1892) wrote among other things:

" Needless to say that to-day there is indeed ' Socialism again in England,' and plenty of it—Socialism of all shades : Socialism conscious and unconscious, Socialism prosaic and poetic, Socialism of the working class and of the middle class, for, verily, that abomination of abominations, Socialism, has not only become respectable, but has actually donned evening dress and lounges lazily on drawing-room *causeuses*.* That shows the incurable fickleness of that terrible despot of 'society,' middle-class public opinion, and once more justifies the contempt in which we Socialists of a past generation always held that public opinion. At the same time we have no reason to grumble at the symptom itself.

" What I consider far more important than this momentary fashion among bourgeois circles of affecting a mild dilution of Socialism, and even more than the actual progress Socialism has made in England generally, that is the revival of the East End of London. That immense haunt of misery is no longer the stagnant pool it was six years ago. It has shaken off its torpid despair, has returned to life, and has become the home of what is called the 'New Unionism,' that is to say, of the organisation of the great mass of 'unskilled' workers. This organisation may to a great extent adopt the form of the old Unions of 'skilled' workers, but it is essentially different in character. The old Unions preserve the traditions of the time when they were founded, and look upon the wages system as a once for all established, final fact, which they at best can modify in the interest of their members. The new Unions were founded at a time when the faith in the eternity of the wages system was severely shaken ; their founders and promoters were Socialists either consciously or by feeling ; the masses, whose adhesion gave them strength, were rough, neglected, looked down upon by the working-class aristocracy ; but they had this immense advantage, that *their minds were virgin soil*, entirely free from the inherited 'respectable' bourgeois prejudices which hampered the brains of the better-situated 'old' Unionists. And thus we see now these new Unions taking the lead of the working-class movement generally, and more and more taking in tow the rich and proud 'old' Unions.†

SCHLÜTER, HERMANN. German Social-Democrat who after his expulsion from Dresden in 1883 conducted the publishing

* Sofas.
† Written in English.

house of the *Sozialdemokrat* in Zürich ; he was the first organiser of the German Social-Democratic Archive. In 1889, he emigrated to America where he worked in the German workers' movement. He wrote a history of Chartism and other studies of the English and American labour movement.

209. ENGELS TO SORGE

London, 8 February, 1890.

In my opinion we hardly lose anything worth counting by the going-over of the official Socialists there to the Nationalists.* If the whole *German* Socialist Labour Party went to pieces as a result it would be a gain, but we can hardly expect anything so good as that. The really serviceable elements will come together again in the end all the same, and the sooner the waste matter has separated itself the sooner this will happen ; when the moment comes in which events themselves drive the American proletariat forward there will be enough fitted by their superior theoretical insight and experience to take the part of leaders, and then you will find that your years of work have not been wasted.

The movement there, just like the one here and in the mining districts of Germany now as well, cannot be made by preaching alone. Facts must hammer the thing into people's heads, but then it will go quickly too, quickest, of course, where there is already an organised and theoretically educated section of the proletariat at hand, as in Germany. The miners are ours to-day potentially and necessarily : in the Ruhr district the process is proceeding rapidly, Aix la Chapelle and the Saar basin will follow, then Saxony, then Lower Silesia, finally the Polish bargemen of Upper Silesia. With the position of our party in Germany all that was needed in order to call the irresistible movement into being was the impulse arising from the miners' own conditions of life.

Here it is going in a similar way. The movement, which I now consider irrepressible, arose from the dockers' strike, purely out of the absolute necessity of defence. But here too the ground

* The followers of Edward Bellamy in the U.S.A.

had been so far prepared by various forms of agitation during the last eight years that the people without being Socialists themselves still only wanted to have Socialists as their leaders. Now, without noticing it themselves, they are coming on to the right theoretical track, they drift into it, and the movement is so strong that I think it will survive the inevitable blunders and their consequences and the friction between the various trade unions and leaders without serious damage. . . .

I think it will be the same with you in America too. The Schleswig-Holsteiners* and their descendants in England and America are not to be converted by lecturing, this pig-headed and conceited lot have got to experience it on their own bodies. And this they are doing more and more every year, but they are born conservatives—just *because* America is so purely bourgeois, so entirely without a feudal past and therefore proud of its purely bourgeois organisation—and so they will only get quit of the old traditional mental rubbish by practical experience. Hence the trade unions, etc., are the thing to begin with if there is to be a mass movement, and every further step must be forced upon them by a defeat. But once the first step beyond the bourgeois point of view has been taken things will move quickly, like everything in America, where, driven by natural necessity, the growing speed of the movement sets some requisite fire going under the backsides of the Schleswig-Holstein Anglo-Saxons, who are usually so slow; and then too the foreign elements in the nation will assert themselves by greater mobility. I consider the decay of the specifically German party, with its absurd theoretical confusion, its corresponding arrogance and its Lassalleanism, a real piece of good fortune. Not until these separatists are out of the way will the fruits of your work come to light again. The Socialist Laws were a misfortune, not for Germany, but for America to which they consigned the last *Knoten*. I often used to marvel at the many *Knoten* faces one met with over there† ; these have died out in Germany but are flourishing over yonder.

* Marx's name for Anglo-Saxons.

† Engels and his friend Schorlemmer visited Canada and the U.S.A. in 1888. *Knoten*, see Note, page 87. [*Ed. Eng. ed.*]

210. ENGELS TO SORGE

London, 19 April, 1890.

In a country with such an old political and labour movement there is always a colossal heap of traditionally inherited rubbish which has to be got rid of by degrees. There are the prejudices of the skilled Unions—Engineers, Bricklayers, Carpenters and Joiners, Type Compositors, etc.—which have all to be broken down; the petty jealousies of the particular trades, which become intensified in the hands and heads of the leaders to direct hostility and secret struggle; there are the mutually obstructive ambitions and intrigues of the leaders: one wants to get into Parliament and so does somebody else, another wants to get on to the County Council or School Board, another wants to organise a general centralisation of all the workers, another to start a paper, another a club, etc., etc. In short, there is friction upon friction. And among them all the Socialist League, which looks down on everything which is not directly revolutionary (which means here in England, as with you, everything which does not limit itself to making phrases and otherwise doing nothing) and the Federation,* who still behave as if everyone except themselves were asses and bunglers, although it is only due to the new force of the movement that *they* have succeeded in getting some following again. In short, anyone who only looks at the surface would say it was all confusion and personal quarrels. But *under* the surface the movement is going on, it is seizing ever wider sections of the workers and mostly just among the hitherto stagnant *lowest* masses, and the day is no longer far off when this mass will suddenly *find itself*, when the fact that it is this colossal self-impelled mass will dawn upon it, and when that day comes short work will be made of all the rascality and wrangling.

¶A fortnight after this letter was written, Engels was able to hail the first International May Day celebrations held in London (May 4, 1890). The fact that mass demonstrations (a procession to Hyde Park of over 100,000, etc.) were held in

* Social-Democratic Federation.

support of the eight-hour day, in accordance with the resolution passed by the Foundation Congress of the Second International (Paris 1889), constituted a triumph of the " new unionism " over the old craft unions (which supported an eight-hour day by " free agreement " and not by legislation). The London Trades Council, the representative of the " old " unions, and the S.D.F. (which had boycotted the Paris Congress and allied itself with the French Possibilists) tried both to prevent and to sabotage the demonstration but were eventually forced by the strength of the movement to take part in it—though with separate platforms. The story of this struggle, in which Eleanor Marx Aveling played a leading part, was told in full by Engels in his article *The Fourth of May in London* (Vienna *Arbeiter-zeitung*, May 23, 1890). He there wrote :

" And I consider this the grandest and most important part of the whole May Day festival, that on 4 May, 1890, the *English proletariat*, newly awakened from its forty years' winter sleep, *again entered the movement of its class*. . . .

" The general impression . . . which the numerous bourgeois politicians who were present as spectators have taken home with them is the conviction that the English proletariat, which has now been providing the great Liberal Party with its tail and its herd of voting cattle for over forty years, has at last awakened to new and independent life and action. And of that there can be no doubt. On May 4, 1890, the English working class joined up in the great international army. And that is an epoch-making fact. The English proletariat is based on the most advanced industrial development and also possesses the greatest political freedom of movement. Its long winter sleep—resulting from the collapse of the Chartist movement of 1836 to 1850 on the one hand and the colossal growth of industry in 1848 to 1880 on the other—is broken at last. The grandchildren of the old Chartists are entering the line of battle."

[*Ed. Eng. ed.*]

211. ENGELS TO AN UNKNOWN CORRESPONDENT*

19 April, 1890.

Anti-Semitism is the characteristic sign of a backward civilisation and is therefore only found in Prussia and Austria

* This fragment from a private letter was published with the consent of Engels and of the person to whom it was addressed, but without mentioning the name of the latter, in the Vienna *Arbeiterzeitung* of May 9, 1890.

or in Russia. If an attempt at anti-Semitism were made in England or America it would simply be ridiculed, and in Paris Herr Drumont after all only excites an ineffective little one-day sensation with his writings—which are incomparably superior in intelligence to those of the German anti-Semites. Added to which, now that he is coming out as a candidate to the City Council, he himself will have to declare that he is as much against Christian as Jewish capital! And even if he represented the opposite point of view people would still read Herr Drumont.

In Prussia it is the small nobility, the *junkers*—who with an income of 10,000 marks spend 20,000 and therefore fall into the hands of the usurers—who foment anti-Semitism, and both in Prussia and in Austria it is the petty bourgeois, the handicraftsman, the small shopkeeper, sinking into ruin owing to the competition of large-scale capitalism, who form the chorus and scream in unison with them. But if *capital* destroys *these* classes of society, which are reactionary through and through, then it is doing what it is its function to do and whether it is Semitic or Aryan, circumcised or baptised, is doing a good work; it is helping forward the backward Prussians and Austrians until at last they reach the modern position in which all the old social differences are resolved into the one great contradiction between capital and wage-labour. Only where this is not yet the case, where there is as yet no strong capitalist class and therefore also no strong wage-earning class, where capital, being still too weak to control the whole national production, has the Stock Exchange as the main scene of its activity, and where production is therefore still in the hands of peasants, landowners, handicraft workers and similar classes surviving from the Middle Ages—only here is capital predominantly Jewish and only here is anti-Semitism to be found.

In the whole of North America, where there are millionaires whose riches can hardly be expressed in our miserable marks, gulden or francs, there is *not a single Jew* among these millionaires, and the Rothschilds are regular beggars compared with these Americans. And even here in England, Rothschild is a man of modest means compared, for instance, with the Duke of Westminster. Even with us on the Rhine where, with the help of the French, we hunted the nobility out of the country ninety-five years ago and created a modern industry for ourselves, where are the Jews?

Anti-Semitism, therefore, is nothing but the reaction of the mediæval, decadent strata of society against modern society, which essentially consists of wage-earners and capitalists; under a mask of apparent socialism it therefore only serves reactionary ends; it is a variety of feudal socialism and with that we can have nothing to do. If it is possible in a country, that is a sign that there is not yet enough capital in that country. Capital and wage-labour are to-day inseparable. The stronger the capital the stronger also the wage-earning class and the nearer therefore the end of capitalist domination. To us Germans, therefore, among whom I include the Viennese, I wish a right merry development of capitalist economy and in no wise that it should sink into stagnation.

Added to this, anti-Semitism falsifies the whole position of affairs. It does not even know the Jews it howls down. Otherwise it would know that here in England, and in America, thanks to the Eastern European anti-Semites, and in Turkey, thanks to the Spanish Inquisition, there are thousands and thousands of *Jewish proletarians*, and that these Jewish workers are in fact the worst exploited and most wretched of all. Here in England we have had *three* strikes of Jewish workers within the last twelve months, and then we are expected to carry on anti-Semitism as a fight against capital?

And apart from this, we owe much too much to the Jews. To say nothing of Heine and Börne, Marx was of purest Jewish blood; Lassalle was a Jew. Many of our best people are Jews. My friend Victor Adler, who is at present paying in prison in Vienna for his devotion to the cause of the proletariat, Eduard Bernstein, editor of the London *Sozial-Demokrat*, Paul Singer, one of our best men in the Reichstag—people of whose friendship I am proud, are all Jews! Have I not been turned into a Jew myself by the *Gartenlaube?* And indeed if I had to choose, then rather a Jew than "Herr *von* . . ." !*

* *Von*, German prefix indicating aristocratic birth. *Gartenlaube* ["The Arbour"] periodical. [*Ed. Eng. ed.*]

DRUMONT, EDOUARD (1844-1917). French journalist. In 1886 published an anti-Semitic book, *La France juive* (Jewish France) which had a certain passing success. His later publications of the same kind awoke no response.

212. ENGELS TO CONRAD SCHMIDT

London, 5 August, 1890

I saw a review of Paul Barth's book* by that bird of ill-omen, Moritz Wirth, in the Vienna *Deutsche Worte* and *this* criticism left an unfavourable impression on my mind of the book itself as well. I will have a look at it, but I must say that if little Moritz is right when he quotes Barth as stating that the sole example of the dependence of philosophy, etc., on the material conditions of existence which he can find in all Marx's works is that Descartes declares animals to be machines, then I am sorry for the man who can write such a thing. And if this man has not discovered yet that though the material form of existence is the *primum agens* (primary agent) this does not exclude spheres of ideas from reacting upon it in their turn, though with a secondary effect, he cannot possibly have understood the subject he is writing about. However, as I have said, all this is second-hand and little Moritz is a fatal friend. And the materialist conception of history also has a lot of friends nowadays to whom it serves as an excuse for *not* studying history. Just as Marx used to say about the French " Marxists " of the late 'seventies : " All I know is that I am not a Marxist."

There has also been a discussion in the *Volkstribune* about the division of products in the future society, whether this will take place according to the amount of work done or otherwise. The question has been approached very "materialistically," in opposition to certain idealistic forms of phraseology about justice. But strangely enough it has never struck anyone that, after all, the method of division essentially depends on *how much* there is to divide, and that this must surely change with the progress of production and social organisation, so that

* Paul Barth : *The Philosophy of History of Hegel and of the Hegelians up to Marx and Hartmann* (1890).

the method of division may also change. But to everyone who took part in the discussion " socialist society " appeared not as involved in continuous change and progress but as a stable affair fixed once and for all, which must, therefore, have its method of division fixed once and for all. All one can reasonably do, however, is (1) to try and discover the method of division to be used *at the beginning*, and (2) to try and find the *general tendency* in which the further development will proceed. But about this I do not find a single word in the whole debate.

In general the word *materialistic* serves many of the younger writers in Germany as a mere phrase with which anything and everything is labelled without further study; they stick on this label and then think the question disposed of. But our conception of history is above all a guide to study, not a lever for construction after the manner of the Hegelians. All history must be studied afresh, the conditions of existence of the different formations of society must be individually examined before the attempt is made to deduce from them the political, civil-legal, æsthetic, philosophic, religious, etc., notions corresponding to them. Only a little has been done here up to now because only a few people have got down to it seriously. In this field we can utilise masses of help, it is immensely big and anyone who will work seriously can achieve a lot and distinguish himself. But instead of this only too many of the younger Germans simply make use of the phrase, historical materialism (and *everything* can be turned into a phrase), in order to get their own relatively scanty historical knowledge (for economic history is still in its cradle !) fitted together into a neat system as quickly as possible, and they then think themselves something very tremendous. And after that a Barth can come along and attack the thing itself, which in his circles has indeed been degraded into a mere phrase.

However all this will right itself. We are strong enough in Germany now to stand a lot. One of the greatest services which the Socialist Law did us was to free us from the officiousness of the German university student who had got tinged with socialism. We are strong enough now to digest the German university student too, who is giving himself great airs again.

You, who have really done something, must have noticed yourself how few of the young literary men who fasten themselves on to the Party give themselves the trouble to study economics, the history of economics, the history of trade, of industry, of agriculture, of the forms of society. How many know anything of Maurer except his name? The shamelessness of the journalist has to accomplish everything, and the result corresponds. It often seems as if these gentlemen think anything is good enough for the workers. If these gentlemen only knew how Marx thought his best things were still not good enough for the workers and how he regarded it as a crime to offer the workers anything less than the very best !

After the test they have so brilliantly sustained since 1848 I have unqualified confidence in our workers, and only in them. Like every great Party they will commit mistakes in particular points of their development, perhaps great mistakes. Indeed the masses only learn by the consequences of their own mistakes, by experiments on their own bodies. But all that will be overcome, and much more easily with us than elsewhere because our lads really are so indestructibly healthy, and then too because Berlin, which will not easily shed its particular Berlinishness so soon, is only our formal centre, like London, and not what Paris is to France. I have often enough got vexed with the French and the English workers (despite a realisation of the causes for their blunders) but with the Germans since 1870 never—with individuals who spoke in their name, yes, but never with the masses who set everything on to the right track again. And I would like to wager that it never will happen to me to get vexed with them.

¶SCHMIDT, CONRAD. German economist, Social-Democrat, revisionist. During his stay in London in 1887 he got to know Engels. Schmidt was gifted theoretically and had come near to solving independently the problem of the average rate of profit and some of the other problems solved by Marx in the third volume of *Capital*. Engels touched on a series of important theoretical questions in his letters to Schmidt. On October 17, 1889, he wrote :

"And yet in regard to theory there is still so much to be done, especially in the sphere of economic history and its connections with political history, with the history of law, of religion, of literature and of culture in general, where only a clear theoretical vision can guide the way through the labyrinth of facts."

Schmidt did not justify the hopes at first placed in him and later attached himself to revisionism. (See also Letter 232.)

213. ENGELS TO J. BLOCH

London, 21 September, 1890.

According to the materialist conception of history the determining element* in history is *ultimately* the production and reproduction in real life. More than this neither Marx nor I have ever asserted. If therefore somebody twists this into the statement that the economic element is the *only* determining one, he transforms it into a meaningless, abstract and absurd phrase. The economic situation is the basis, but the various elements of the superstructure—political forms of the class struggle and its consequences, constitutions established by the victorious class after a successful battle, etc.—forms of law—and then even the reflexes of all these actual struggles in the brains of the combatants: political, legal, philosophical theories, religious ideas and their further development into systems of dogma—also exercise their influence upon the course of the historical struggles and in many cases preponderate in determining their *form*. There is an interaction of all these elements, in which, amid all the endless *host* of accidents (*i.e.*, of things and events whose inner connection is so remote or so impossible to prove that we regard it as absent and can neglect it), the economic movement finally asserts itself as necessary. Otherwise the application of the theory to any period of history one chose would be easier than the solution of a simple equation of the first degree.

We make our own history, but in the first place under very definite presuppositions and conditions. Among these the

* *Moment*—element in the dialectical process of becoming. [*Ed. Eng. ed.*]

economic ones are finally decisive. But the political, etc., ones, and indeed even the traditions which haunt human minds, also play a part, although not the decisive one. The Prussian State arose and developed from historical, ultimately from economic causes. But it could scarcely be maintained without pedantry that among the many small states of North Germany, Brandenburg was specifically determined by economic necessity to become the great power embodying the economic, linguistic and, after the Reformation, also the religious differences between north and south, and not by other elements as well (above all by its entanglement with Poland, owing to the possession of Prussia, and hence with international, political relations—which were indeed also decisive in the formation of the Austrian dynastic power). Without making oneself ridiculous it would be difficult to succeed in explaining in terms of economics the existence of every small state in Germany, past and present, or the origin of the High German consonant mutations, which the geographical wall of partition formed by the mountains from the Sudetic range to the Taunus extended to a regular division throughout Germany.

In the second place, however, history makes itself in such a way that the final result always arises from conflicts between many individual wills, of which each again has been made what it is by a host of particular conditions of life. Thus there are innumerable intersecting forces, an infinite series of parallelograms of forces which give rise to one resultant—the historical event. This again may itself be viewed as the product of a power which, taken as a whole, works *unconsciously* and without volition. For what each individual wills is obstructed by everyone else, and what emerges is something that no one willed. Thus past history proceeds in the manner of a natural process and is also essentially subject to the same laws of movement. But from the fact that individual wills—of which each desires what he is impelled to by his physical constitution and external, in the last resort economic, circumstances (either his own personal circumstances or those of society in general)—do not attain what they want, but are merged into a collective mean, a common resultant, it must not be concluded that their value = O. On the contrary, each contributes to the resultant and is to this degree involved in it.

I would ask you to study this theory further from its original sources and not at second-hand, it is really much easier. Marx hardly wrote anything in which it did not play a part. But especially *The Eighteenth Brumaire of Louis Bonaparte* is a most excellent example of its application. There are also many allusions in *Capital*. Then I may also direct you to my writings : *Herr E. Dühring's Revolution in Science* and *Ludwig Feuerbach and the Exit of Classical German Philosophy*, in which I have given the most detailed account of historical materialism which, so far as I know, exists.

Marx and I are ourselves partly to blame for the fact that younger writers sometimes lay more stress on the economic side than is due to it. We had to emphasise this main principle in opposition to our adversaries, who denied it, and we had not always the time, the place or the opportunity to allow the other elements involved in the interaction to come into their rights. But when it was a case of presenting a section of history, that is, of a practical application, the thing was different and there no error was possible. Unfortunately, however, it happens only too often that people think they have fully understood a theory and can apply it without more ado from the moment they have mastered its main principles, and those even not always correctly. And I cannot exempt many of the more recent " Marxists " from this reproach, for the most wonderful rubbish has been produced from this quarter too.

214. ENGELS TO CONRAD SCHMIDT

London, 27 October, 1890

I think you would do very well to take the post in Zürich.* You could always learn a good deal about economics there, especially if you bear in mind that Zürich is still only a third-rate money and speculation market, so that the impressions which make themselves felt there are weakened or deliberately

* The position of editor of the *Zürich Post*.

distorted by twofold or threefold reflection. But you will get a practical knowledge of the mechanism and be obliged to follow the stock exchange reports from London, New York, Paris, Berlin and Vienna at first hand, and in this way the world market, in its reflex as money and stock market, will reveal itself to you. Economic, political and other reflections are just like those in the human eye, they pass through a condensing lens and therefore appear upside down, standing on their heads. Only the nervous system which would put them on their feet again for representation is lacking. The money market man only sees the movement of industry and of the world market in the inverted reflection of the money and stock market and so effect becomes cause to him. I noticed that in the 'forties already in Manchester: the London Stock Exchange reports were utterly useless for the course of industry and its periodical maxima and minima because these gentry tried to explain everything from crises on the money market, which were generally only symptoms. At that time the object was to explain away the origin of industrial crises as temporary overproduction, so that the thing had in addition its tendentious side, provocative of distortion. This point has now gone (for us, at any rate, for good and all), added to which it is indeed a fact that the money market can also have its own crises, in which direct disturbances of industry only play a subordinate part or no part at all—here there is still much, especially in the history of the last twenty years, to be examined and established.

Where there is division of labour on a social scale there is also mutual independence among the different sections of work. In the last instance production is the decisive factor. But when the trade in products becomes independent of production itself, it follows a movement of its own, which, while it is governed as a whole by production, still in particular cases and within this general dependence follows particular laws contained in the nature of this new factor; this movement has phases of its own and in its turn reacts on the movement of production. The discovery of America was due to the thirst for gold which had previously driven the Portuguese to Africa (compare Soetbeer's *Production of Precious Metals*), because the enormously extended European industry of the fourteenth and fifteenth centuries and the trade corresponding to it demanded more means of exchange than Germany, the great silver country from 1450 to 1550, could provide. The conquest of India by the Portuguese, Dutch and English between 1500 and 1800 had *imports from* India as its object—nobody dreamt of exporting anything there. And yet what a colossal reaction these discoveries and conquests, solely conditioned by the interests of trade, had upon industry: they first created the need for *exports to* these countries and developed large-scale industry.

So it is too with the money market. As soon as trading in money becomes separate from trade in commodities it has (under certain conditions imposed by production and commodity trade and within these limits) a development of its own, special laws and separate phases determined by its own nature. If, in this further development, trade in money extends in addition to trade in securities and these securities are not only government securities but also industrial and transport stocks and shares, so that money trade conquers the direct control over a portion of the production by which, taken as a whole, it is itself controlled, then the reaction of money trading on production becomes still stronger and more complicated. The money traders have become the owners of railways, mines, iron works, etc. These means of production take on a double aspect: their working has to be directed sometimes in the immediate interests of production but sometimes also according to the requirements of the shareholders, in so far as they are money traders. The most striking example of this is the American railways, whose working is entirely dependent on the stock exchange operations of a Jay Gould or a Vanderbilt, etc., these having nothing whatever to do with the particular railway concerned and its interests as a means of communication. And even here in England we have seen struggles lasting for tens of years between different railway companies over the boundaries of their respective territories—struggles in which an enormous amount of money was thrown away, not in the interests of production and communications but simply because of a rivalry which usually only had the object of facilitating the stock exchange dealings of the shareholding money traders.

With these few indications of my conception of the relation of production to commodity trade and of both to money trading, I have already also answered, in essence, your questions about "historical materialism" generally. The thing is easiest to grasp from the point of view of the division of labour. Society gives rise to certain common functions which it cannot dispense with. The persons selected for these functions form a new branch of the division of labour *within society*. This gives them particular interests, distinct too from the interests of those who gave them their office; they make themselves independent of the latter and—the state is in being. And now the development is the same as it was with commodity trade and later with money trade; the new independent power, while having in the main to follow the movement of production, also, owing to its inward independence (the relative independence originally transferred to it and gradually further developed) reacts in its turn upon the conditions and course of production. It is the interaction of two unequal forces: on one hand the economic movement, on the other the new political power, which strives for as much independence as possible, and which, having once been established, is also endowed with a movement of its own. On the whole, the economic movement gets its way, but it has also to suffer reactions from the political movement which it established and endowed with relative independence itself, from the movement of the state power on the one hand and of the opposition simultaneously engendered on the other. Just as the movement of the industrial market is, in the main and with the reservations already indicated, reflected in the money market and, of course, in inverted form, so the struggle between the classes already existing and already in conflict with one another is reflected in the struggle between government and opposition, but also in inverted form, no longer directly but indirectly, not as a class struggle but as a fight for political principles, and so distorted that it has taken us thousands of years to get behind it again.

The reaction of the state power upon economic development

can be one of three kinds: it can run in the same direction, and then development is more rapid; it can oppose the line of development, in which case nowadays state power in every great nation will go to pieces in the long run; or it can cut off the economic development from certain paths, and impose on it certain others. This case ultimately reduces itself to one of the two previous ones. But it is obvious that in cases two and three the political power can do great damage to the economic development and result in the squandering of great masses of energy and material.

Then there is also the case of the conquest and brutal destruction of economic resources, by which, in certain circumstances, a whole local or national economic development could formerly be ruined. Nowadays such a case usually has the opposite effect, at least among great nations: in the long run the defeated power often gains more economically, politically and morally than the victor.

It is similar with law. As soon as the new division of labour which creates professional lawyers becomes necessary, another new and independent sphere is opened up which, for all its general dependence on production and trade, still has its own capacity for reacting upon these spheres as well. In a modern state, law must not only correspond to the general economic position and be its expression, but must also be an expression which is *consistent in itself*, and which does not, owing to inner contradictions, look glaringly inconsistent. And in order to achieve this, the faithful reflection of economic conditions is more and more infringed upon. All the more so the more rarely it happens that a code of law is the blunt, unmitigated, unadulterated expression of the domination of a class—this in itself would already offend the "conception of justice." Even in the Code Napoleon the pure logical conception of justice held by the revolutionary bourgeoisie of 1792-96 is already adulterated in many ways, and in so far as it is embodied there has daily to undergo all sorts of attenuation owing to the rising power of the proletariat. Which does not prevent the Code Napoleon from being the statute book which serves as a basis for every new code of law in every part of the world. Thus to a great extent the course of the " development of law" only consists: first in the attempt to do away with the contradictions arising from the direct translation of economic relations into legal principles, and to establish a harmonious system of law, and then in the repeated breaches made in this system by the influence and pressure of further economic development, which involves it in further contradictions (I am only speaking here of civil law for the moment).

The reflection of economic relations as legal principles is necessarily also a topsy turvy one : it happens without the person who is acting being conscious of it ; the jurist imagines he is operating with *a priori* principles, whereas they are really only economic reflexes ; so everything is upside down. And it seems to me obvious that this inversion, which, so long as it remains unrecognised, forms what we call *ideological conception*, reacts in its turn upon the economic basis and may, within certain limits, modify it. The basis of the law of inheritance—assuming that the stages reached in the development of the family are equal—is an economic one. But it would be difficult to prove, for instance, that the absolute liberty of the testator in England and the severe restrictions imposed upon him in France are only due in every detail to economic causes. Both react back, however, on the economic sphere to a very considerable extent, because they influence the division of property.

As to the realms of ideology which soar still higher in the air, religion, philosophy, etc., these have a prehistoric stock, found already in existence and taken over in the historic period, of what we should to-day call bunk. These various false conceptions of nature, of man's own being, of spirits, magic forces, etc., have for the most part only a negative economic basis ; but the low economic development of the prehistoric period is supplemented and also partially conditioned and even caused by the false conceptions of nature. And even though economic necessity was the main driving force of the progressive knowledge of nature and becomes ever more so, it would surely be pedantic to try and find economic causes for all this primitive nonsense. The history of science is the history of the gradual clearing away of this nonsense or of its replacement by fresh but already less absurd nonsense. The people who deal with this belong in their turn to special spheres in the division of labour and appear to themselves to be working in an independent field. And in so far as they form an independent group within the social division of labour, in so far do their productions, including their errors, react back as an influence upon the whole development of society, even on its economic development. But all the same they themselves remain under the dominating influence of economic development. In philosophy, for instance, this can be most readily proved in the bourgeois period. Hobbes was the first modern materialist (in the eighteenth century sense) but he was an absolutist in a period when absolute monarchy was at its height throughout the whole of Europe and when the fight of absolute monarchy versus the people was beginning in England. Locke, both in religion and politics, was the child of the class compromise of 1688. The English deists and their more consistent successors, the French materialists, were the true philosophers of the bourgeoisie, the French even of the bourgeois revolution. The German petty bourgeois runs through German philosophy from Kant to Hegel, sometimes positively and sometimes negatively. But the philosophy of every epoch, since it is a definite sphere in the division of labour, has as its presupposition certain definite intellectual material handed down to it by its predecessors, from which it takes its start. And that is why economically backward countries can still play first fiddle in philosophy: France in the eighteenth century compared with England, on whose philosophy the French based themselves, and later Germany in comparison with both. But the philosophy both of France and Germany and the general blossoming of literature at that time were also the result of a rising economic development. I consider the ultimate supremacy of economic development established in these spheres too, but it comes to pass within conditions imposed by the particular sphere itself: in philosophy, for instance, through the operation of economic influences (which again generally only act under political, etc., disguises) upon the existing philosophic material handed down by predecessors. Here economy creates nothing absolutely new (*a novo*), but it determines the way in which the existing material of thought is altered and further developed, and that too for the most part indirectly, for it is the political, legal and moral reflexes which exercise the greatest direct influence upon philosophy.

About religion I have said the most necessary things in the last section on Feuerbach.

If therefore Barth supposes that we deny any and every reaction of the political, etc., reflexes of the economic movement upon the movement itself, he is simply tilting at windmills. He has only got to look at Marx's *Eighteenth Brumaire*, which deals almost exclusively with the *particular* part played by political struggles and events; of course, within their *general* dependence upon economic conditions. Or *Capital*, the section on the working day, for instance, where legislation, which is surely a political act, has such a trenchant effect. Or the section on the history of the bourgeoisie. (Chapter XXIV.) Or why do we fight for the political dictatorship of the proletariat if political power is economically impotent? Force (that is state power) is also an economic power.

But I have no time to criticise the book now. I must first get Vol. III out and besides I think too that Bernstein, for instance, could deal with it quite effectively.

What these gentlemen all lack is dialectic. They never see anything but here cause and there effect. That this is a hollow abstraction, that such metaphysical polar opposites only exist in the real world during crises, while the whole vast process proceeds in the form of interaction (though of very unequal forces, the economic movement being by far the strongest, most elemental and most decisive) and that here everything is relative and nothing is absolute—this they never begin to see. Hegel has never existed for them.

215. ENGELS TO KAUTSKY

Ryde, 29 June, 1891.

I have escaped here for a few days, the work storming in upon me was getting too much. Happy and content, I was just in the middle of group-marriage when I had the Party programme upon me and that *had to be* taken up. I wanted first to try and formulate rather more strictly the unity considerations, but from lack of time never got to this; also it seemed to me more important to analyse the partly avoidable and partly inavoidable deficiencies of the political part, as in so doing I found an opportunity to let fly at the conciliatory opportunism of *Vorwärts* and at the cheerful, pious, merry and free " growth " of the filthy old mess " into socialist society." Meanwhile I hear that you have proposed a new introduction to them ; so much the better.

¶This letter accompanied Engels' criticism of the draft of the new Party programme which was accepted at the Erfurt Party Congress of 1891 and which, under the name of the " Erfurt Programme," served as a model for nearly all the programmes of the parties in the Second International. Engels' criticism, however, was not published until ten years later. It was directed above all against the political demands of the draft. " The political demands of the draft have one great fault : what actually ought to be said *is not there* [namely the attitude towards the state]. . . . To touch on that is dangerous, however. And yet somehow or other the thing has got to be attacked. . . . How necessary this is is shown precisely at the present time by the inroads which opportunism is making in a great section of the Social-Democratic press. For fear of a revival of the Socialist Law and from recollection of all manner of premature utterances which were let fall during the reign of that Law, the present legal position of the Party in Germany is now all of a sudden to be treated as sufficient for the carrying out of all the demands of the Party by peaceful means. People talk themselves and the Party into the belief that ' the present society will grow into socialism ' without asking themselves if for this it is not equally necessary that society should grow out of its old social constitution and burst its old shell just as violently as the crab bursts its old shell—as if in Germany society had not in addition to smash the fetters of the still semi-absolutist and moreover indescribably confused political order. . . . General abstract questions have been put into the foreground, concealing thus the immediate concrete questions, the questions which at the first great events, the first political crisis, put themselves upon the agenda. What can result from this except that at the decisive moment the Party is suddenly without guidance, that unclarity and disunity reign on the most decisive points because these points have never been discussed.... This forgetfulness of the great main standpoints in the momentary interests of the day, this struggling and striving for the success of the moment without consideration for the later consequences, this sacrifice of the future of the movement for its present may be 'honestly' meant, but it is and remains opportunism, and 'honest' opportunism is perhaps the most dangerous of all. ... If one thing is certain it is that our Party and the working class can only come to power under the form of the democratic republic. This is even the specific form for the dictatorship of the proletariat, as the great French revolution has already shown. . . ."

"Of all these things not many can be put into the programme. I am also mentioning them chiefly in order to characterise both the conditions in Germany, where it does not do to say such things, and the self deception which wants to effect the transition from these conditions to Communist society by legal means. And further, in order to remind the Party Executive that there are still other political questions of importance besides 'direct legislation by the people' and 'gratuitous administration of justice'—without these we shall move on in the end all the same. Amid the general insecurity those questions may become burning ones any day, and what is to happen if we have not discussed them and come to an understanding about them?"

On these statements of Engels Lenin comments in *State and Revolution*:

"Engels repeats here in a particularly emphatic form the fundamental idea which runs like a red thread throughout all Marx's work, namely, that the democratic republic is the nearest approach to the dictatorship of the proletariat. For such a republic—without in the least setting aside the domination of capital, and, therefore the oppression of the masses and the class struggle—inevitably leads to such an extension, development, unmasking and sharpening of that struggle that, as soon as the possibility arises of satisfying the fundamental interests of the oppressed masses, this possibility is realised inevitably and solely in the dictatorship of the proletariat, in the guidance of these masses by the proletariat. These words have also been, for the whole of the Second International, 'forgotten' words of Marxism."

In the final programme only a small degree of consideration was paid to Engels' criticism ; above all it was not attended to on the main question. The question of the state was not formulated ; so too the Second International, with the exception of the Bolsheviks, evaded it throughout the whole period of its existence.

216. ENGELS TO CONRAD SCHMIDT

Ryde, 1 July, 1891.

I am very much disappointed with Barth's book. I had expected something rather less shallow and slap-dash. A man who judges every philosopher not by the enduring and progressive part of his activity but by what is necessarily transitory and reactionary—by the *system*—would have done better to remain silent. According to him, in fact, the whole history of philosophy is nothing but a pile of the " ruins " of broken-down systems. How high old Hegel stands above this alleged critic of his ! And then to imagine he is criticising Hegel because here and there he gets on the track of one of the false connections by means of which Hegel, like every other systematiser, has to get his system neatly constructed ! The colossal discovery that Hegel sometimes lumps contrary and contradictory oppositions together ! I could show him some more tricks very different from that if it was worth the trouble. The man is what we call on the Rhine a *Korinthenscheisser*—he turns everything into petty trash—and until he has got rid of this habit, he will, to use Hegel's language, " come from nothing through nothing to nothing."

His criticism of Marx is really funny. First he makes up a materialist theory of history for himself, which Marx is supposed, in his opinion, to have held, and then he finds something quite different in Marx's works. But from this he does not conclude that he, Barth, has foisted something distorted on to Marx: no, on the contrary, Marx contradicts himself and cannot apply his own theory! "Yes, if people could only *read!*" as Marx used to exclaim at criticisms of this kind.

I have not got the book here; if I had time I would show you hundreds more absurdities one by one. It is a pity: one sees that the man could accomplish something if he were not so hasty in passing his judgments. It is to be hoped that he will soon write something which will be attacked more; a regular dose of knocking about would do him a lot of good.

217. ENGELS TO SORGE

Helensburgh, Scotland, 14 September, 1891.

The Newcastle Trade Union Congress is also a victory. The *old* unions, with the textile workers at their head, and the whole of the reactionary party among the workers, had exerted all their strength towards overthrowing the eight-hour decision of 1890.* They came to grief and have only achieved a very small temporary concession. This is decisive. The confusion is still great, but the thing is in irresistible motion and the bourgeois papers recognise the defeat of the *bourgeois labour party* completely and with terror, howling and gnashing of teeth. The Scottish Liberals especially, the most intelligent and the most classic bourgeoisie in the kingdom, are unanimous in their outcry at the great misfortune and hopeless wrongheadedness of the workers.

218. ENGELS TO BEBEL

London, 29 September, 1891.

You are right, if it comes to war we must demand the general arming of the people. But in conjunction with the already existing organisation or that specially prepared in case of war. *Enlistment*, therefore, *of the hitherto untrained* in supplementary reserves and *Landsturm* and above all immediate emergency *training* besides arming and organisation into fixed cadres.

* Resolution in favour of the legal eight-hour day passed by the Liverpool Trade Union Congress. See Note pages 468-69. [*Ed. Eng. ed.*]

The proclamation to the French will have to come out rather differently in form. The Russian diplomats are not so stupid as to provoke a war in face of the whole of Europe. On the contrary, things will be so operated that either France appears as the provoking party or—one of the Triple Alliance countries. Russia always has dozens of *casus belli* [occasions for war] of this kind to hand ; the special answer to be given depends on the pretext for war put forward. In any case we must declare that since 1871 we have always been ready for a peaceful understanding with France, that as soon as our Party comes to power it will be unable to exercise that power unless Alsace-Lorraine freely determines its own future, but that if war is forced upon us, and morever a war in alliance with *Russia*, we must regard this as an attack on our existence and defend ourselves by every method, utilising all positions at our disposal and therefore Metz and Strasbourg also.

As to the conduct of the war itself, two aspects are immediately decisive : Russia is weak in attack but strong in defensive man-power. A stab in the heart is impossible. France is strong in attack but rendered incapable of attack, innocuous, after a few defeats. I do not give much either for Austrians as generals or for Italians as soldiers, so our army will have to lead and sustain the main push. The war will have to begin with the holding back of the Russians but the defeat of the French. When the French offensive has been rendered innocuous things may get as far as the conquest of Poland up to the Dvina and Dnieper, but hardly before. This must be carried out by *revolutionary* methods and if necessary by giving up a piece of Prussian Poland and the whole of Galicia to the Poland to be established. If this goes well revolution will doubtless follow in France. At the same time we must press for at least Metz and Lorraine to be offered as a peace offering to France.

Probably, however, it will not go so well. The French will not allow themselves to be so easily defeated, their army is *very good* and better armed than ours, and what we achieve in the way of generalship does not look as if very much would come of it either. That the French have learnt how to mobilise has been shown this summer. And also that they have enough officers for their *first field army*—which is stronger than ours. Our superiority in officers will only be proved with the troops brought up later into the line. Moreover the direct line between Berlin and Paris is strongly defended by fortifications on both sides. In short, in the most favourable case it will probably turn out a fluctuating war which will be carried on with constant drawing in of fresh reinforcements by both sides until one party is exhausted, or until the active intervention of England, who, by simply blockading corn imports can, under the then existing conditions, *starve out* whichever party she decides against, Germany or France, and force it to make peace. In the meantime what happens on the Russian frontier mainly depends on the way the Austrians conduct the war and is therefore incalculable.

So much seems certain to me: if we are beaten, every barrier to chauvinism and a war of revenge in Europe will be thrown down for years hence. If we are victorious our Party will come into power. The victory of Germany is therefore the victory of the revolution, and if it comes to war we must not only desire victory but further it by every means. . . .

What should have been categorically stated [by Bernstein] was that if France *formally* represents the revolution in relation to Germany, Germany, through its workers' Party, stands *materially* at the head of the revolution, and this is bound to come to light in the war—in which we, and with us the revolution, will either be crushed or else come to power.

¶In 1891 began the Franco-Russian *rapprochement*, and in conjunction with it the war danger, which Marx had already foreseen in 1870, began to draw nearer. . . . In a series of letters and in an article published in the *Calendar of the French Workers' Party for 1892* Engels dwelt on the question of this future war, its results and the attitude of the workers' parties, especially in Germany and France, to the war. (See also Letters 217, 218.)

219. ENGELS TO BEBEL

London, 24 October, 1891.

As I considered it necessary to tell the French the unvarnished truth about our position if it comes to war—a damned difficult task, certainly—I wrote a French article and sent it to Laura [Lafargue]. She writes to me to-day that both she and Paul [Lafargue] are quite enchanted with the article, that it is just what the French need, etc. If Guesde shares this opinion—he is still in Lille, where he is representing Lafargue with the electors—the article is to be published. It was originally written for the French Socialist *Calendar* but is possibly (I should say probably) too strong for the mishmash people who have to do with that, in which case it will be put in the *Socialiste*, which I hope you see. I say to the people : we have the almost absolute certainty of coming to power within ten years ; we could neither seize power nor retain it without making good the crimes committed by our predecessors towards other nationalities and therefore (1) opening the way for the reconstitution of Poland, (2) putting the North Schleswig population and Alsace-Lorraine in a position freely to decide where they shall belong. Between a Socialist France and a ditto Germany an Alsace-Lorraine problem has no existence at all. Hence there is no reason whatever for a war on account of Alsace-Lorraine. If, however, the French bourgeoisie begin such a war nevertheless, and for this purpose place themselves in the service of the Russian tsar, who is also the enemy of the *bourgeoisie* of the whole of Western Europe, this will be the renunciation of France's revolutionary mission. We German Socialists, on the other hand, who if peace is preserved will come to power in ten years, have the duty of maintaining the position won by us in the van of the workers' movement, not only against the internal but against the external foe. If Russia is victorious we shall be crushed. Therefore if Russia begins war—go for her ! go for the Russians and their allies, *whoever they may be*. Then we have to see to it that the war is conducted by every revolutionary method and that things are made impossible for any government which refuses to adopt such methods; also at a given moment to take the lead ourselves. We have not yet forgotten the glorious example of the French in 1793 and, if we are driven to it, it may come about that we celebrate the centenary of 1793 by showing that the German workers of 1893 are not unworthy of the *Sansculottes** of those days and that if French soldiers cross our frontiers then they will be greeted with the cry:

Quoi ces cohortes étrangères
Feraient le loi dans nos foyers? (Marseillaise)†

This is the general sequence of thought. As soon as the text is finally settled (I am of course expecting proposals for small alterations of detail) and the printing taken in hand I will translate the article into German and then we will see what can be done with it. I am not sure if your press conditions will allow of its being printed in Germany; perhaps if you make some reservations it can be all the same—this will be seen. *My* articles do not in any case tie the *Party*—very fortunate for us both, although Liebknecht imagines I regard it as unfortunate for myself, which never occurs to me.

According to the reports, you said that I had prophesied the collapse of bourgeois society in 1898. There is a slight error there somewhere. All I said was that we might possibly come to power by 1898. If this does *not* happen, the old bourgeois society might still vegetate on for a while, so long as a shove from outside does not bring the whole ramshackle old building crashing down. A rotten old casing like this can survive its inner essential death for a few decades, if the atmosphere is undisturbed. So I should be very cautious about prophesying such a thing. Our arrival at the possibility of power, on the other hand, is a pure calculation of probability according to mathematical laws.

For all that, I hope peace remains unbroken. In our present position we do not need to risk everything—but war would force us to do so. And then in another ten years we shall be quite differently prepared. And for the following reason.

* Sansculottes—literally: without breeches; name given to the revolutionary populace in the French Revolution of 1789. *The French in* 1793—see Letter 206.
† "What, shall these alien cohorts make the laws within our homes?"

In order to take possession of and set in motion the means of production, we need people with technical training, and masses of them. These we have not got, and up till now we have even been rather glad that we have been largely spared the "educated" people. Now things are different. Now we are strong enough to stand any quantity of educated Quarcks* and to digest them, and I foresee that in the next eight or ten years we shall recruit enough young technicians, doctors, lawyers and schoolmasters to enable us to have the factories and big estates administered on behalf of the nation by Party comrades. Then, therefore, our entry into power will be quite natural and will be settled up quickly—relatively. If, on the other hand, a war brings us to power prematurely, the technicians will be our chief enemies; they will deceive and betray us wherever they can and we shall have to use terror against them but shall get cheated all the same. It is what *always* happened, on a small scale, to the French revolutionaries; even in the ordinary administration they had to leave the subordinate posts, where real work is done, in the possession of old reactionaries who obstructed and paralysed everything. Therefore I hope and desire that our splendid and secure development, which is advancing with the calm and inevitability of a process of nature, may remain on its natural lines.

220. ENGELS TO SORGE

London, 24 October, 1891.

Despite the famine in Russia the danger of war is becoming greater. The Russians want to exploit the new French alliance rapidly and thoroughly, and although I am convinced that Russian diplomacy does not want a war, and the famine would make it look ridiculous, nevertheless military and pan-Slav tendencies (now supported by the *very strong* industrial bourgeoisie in the interest of extended markets) may get the upper hand and it is equally likely that some stupidity may be perpetrated in Vienna, Berlin or Paris which will cause war to

* See Letter 191.

break out. Bebel and I have been in correspondence on this point and we are of the opinion that if the Russians start war against us, German Socialists must go for the Russians and their allies, whoever they may be, *à l'outrance* [in a fight to the death]. If Germany is crushed, then we shall be too, while in the most favourable case the struggle will be such a violent one that Germany will only be able to maintain herself by revolutionary means, so that very possibly we shall be forced to come into power and play the part of 1793. Bebel has made a speech about this in Berlin which has aroused a lot of attention in the French press. I shall try to make this clear to the French in their own language, which is not easy. But although I think it would be a great misfortune if it came to war and if this brought us prematurely into power, still one has got to be armed for this eventuality and I am glad that here I have Bebel, who is by far the most capable of our people, on my side.

221. ENGELS TO CONRAD SCHMIDT

London, 1 November, 1891.

It is impossible, of course, to dispense with Hegel and the man also takes some time to digest. The shorter *Logic* in the Encyclopædia makes quite a good beginning. But you must take the edition in the sixth volume of the *Works*, not the separate edition by Rosenkranz (1845), because there are far more explanatory additions from the lectures in the former, even if that ass Henning has often not understood them himself.

In the Introduction you have the criticism, first (Par. 26, etc.) of Wolf's version of Leibnitz (metaphysics *in the historical sense*), then of English-French empiricism (par. 37, etc.) then Kant (par. 40, seq.) and finally (par. 61) of Jacoby's mysticism. In the first section (Being) do not spend too long over Being and Nothing; the last paragraphs on Quality and then Quantity and Measure are much finer, but the theory of Essence is the main thing: the resolution of the abstract contradictions into their own instability, where one no sooner tries to hold on to one side alone than it is transformed unnoticed into the other, etc. At the same time you can always make the thing clear to yourself by concrete examples ; for instance, you, as a bridegroom, have a striking example of the inseparability of identity and difference in yourself and your bride. It is absolutely impossible to decide whether sexual love is pleasure in the identity in difference or in the difference in identity. Take away the difference (in this case of sex) or the identity (the human nature of both) and what have you got left ? I remember how much this very inseparability of identity and difference worried me at first, although we can never take a step without stumbling upon it.

But you ought on no account to read Hegel as Herr Barth has done, namely in order to discover the bad syllogisms and rotten dodges which served him as levers in construction. That is pure schoolboy's work. It is much more important to discover the truth and the genius which lie beneath the false form and within the artificial connections. Thus the transitions from one category or from one contradiction to the next are nearly always arbitrary—often made through a pun, as when Positive and Negative (Par. 120) "*zugrunde gehen*" [perish] in order that Hegel may arrive at the category of "*Grund*" [reason, ground]. To ponder over this much is waste of time.

Since with Hegel every category represents a stage in the history of philosophy (as he generally indicates), you would do well to compare the lectures on the history of philosophy (one of his most brilliant works). As relaxation, I can recommend the Æsthetic. When you have worked yourself into that a bit you will be amazed.

Hegel's dialectic is upside down because it is supposed to be the "self-development of thought," of which the dialectic of facts therefore is only a reflection, whereas really the dialectic in our heads is only the reflection of the actual development which is fulfilled in the world of nature and of human history in obedience to dialectical forms.

If you just compare the development of the commodity into capital in Marx with the development from Being to Essence in Hegel, you will get quite a good parallel for the concrete development which results from facts ; there you have the abstract construction, in which the most brilliant ideas and often very important transmutations, like that of quality into quantity and *vice versa*, are reduced to the apparent self-development of one concept from another—one could have manufactured a dozen more of the same kind.

Engels returns to the subject of Hegel in his letter of February 4, 1892 to Conrad Schmidt:

" If you come to a ' bog ' with Hegel do not let it stop you; six months later in the same bog you will find firm stepping-stones and get across quite smoothly."

Engels further shows that the closed sequence of stages which is found in Hegel's development of the concept " belongs to the *system*, to what is transitory." As an example he again quotes from the *Encyclopædia* the transition of " Positive and Negative to the category of Ground," and says that these transitions would have to be made differently in every different language. " If you translate the sequence in the *Theory of Essence* into another language most of the transitions become impossible. This is not where Essence lies; it lies in the method, the principle, of universal movement and universal interaction, in a corresponding approach to the study of the object which leaves thought no peace, but forces it to express reality in its movement and its complexity in the most accurate way."

222. ENGELS TO SCHLÜTER

London, 30 March, 1892.

Your great obstacle in America, it seems to me, lies in the exceptional position of the native workers. Up to 1848 one could only speak of the permanent native working class as an exception: the small beginnings of it in the cities in the East always had still the hope of becoming farmers or bourgeois. Now a working class has developed and has also to a great extent organised itself on trade union lines. But it still takes up an aristocratic attitude and wherever possible leaves the ordinary badly paid occupations to the immigrants, of whom only a small section enter the aristocratic trade unions. But these immigrants are divided into different nationalities and understand neither one another nor, for the most part, the language of the country. And your bourgeoisie knows much better even than the Austrian Government how to play off one nationality against the other : Jews, Italians, Bohemians, etc., against Germans and Irish, and each one against the other, so that differences in the standard of life of different workers exist, I believe, in New York to an extent unheard of elsewhere. And added to this is the total indifference of a society which has grown up on a purely capitalist basis, without any comfortable feudal background, towards the human lives which succumb in the competitive struggle : "there will be plenty more, and more than we want, of these damned Dutchmen, Irishmen, Italians, Jews and Hungarians;" and beyond them in the background stands John Chinaman, who far surpasses them all in his ability to live on dirt.

In such a country, continually renewed waves of advance, followed by equally certain set-backs, are inevitable. Only the advancing waves are always becoming more powerful, the set-backs less paralysing, and on the whole the thing moves forward all the same. But this I consider certain : the purely bourgeois basis, with no pre-bourgeois swindle behind it, the corresponding colossal energy of the development, which manifests itself even in the mad exaggeration of the present protective tariff system, will one day bring about a change which will astound the whole world. Once the Americans get started it will be with an energy and violence compared with which we in Europe shall be mere children.

223. ENELS TO DANIELSON (NICOLAI—ON)*

London, 22 September, 1892.

So far, then, we agree upon this one point, that Russia, in 1892, could not exist as a purely agricultural country, that her agricultural population must be complemented by industrial production.

* This letter was written in English.

Now I maintain, that industrial production nowadays means *grande industrie*,* steam, electricity, self-acting mules, power-looms, finally machines that produce machinery. From the day Russia introduced railways, the introduction of these modern means of production was a foregone conclusion. You *must* be able to repair your own locomotives, waggons, railways, and that can only be done cheaply if you are able to *construct* those things at home, that you intend to repair. From the moment warfare became a branch of the *grande industrie* (ironclad ships, rifled artillery, quickfiring and repeating cannons, repeating rifles, steel covered bullets, smokeless powder, etc.), *la grande industrie*, without which all these things cannot be made, became a political necessity. All these things cannot be had without a highly developed metal manufacture. And that manufacture cannot be had without a corresponding development in all other branches of manufacture, especially textile.

I quite agree with you in fixing the beginning of the new industrial era of your country about 1861. It was the hopeless struggle of a nation, with primitive forms of production, against nations with modern production, which characterised the American War. The Russian people understood this perfectly; hence their transition to modern forms, a transition rendered irrevocable by the emancipation act of 1861.

This necessity of the transition from the primitive methods of production that prevailed in 1854, to the modern methods that are now beginning to prevail—this necessity once conceded, it becomes a secondary question whether the hothouse process of fostering the industrial revolution by protective and prohibitive duties was advantageous or even necessary, or otherwise.

This industrial hothouse atmosphere renders the process acute, which otherwise might have retained a more chronic form. It crams into twenty years a development which otherwise might have taken sixty or more years. But it does not affect the nature of the process itself, which, as you say, dates from 1861.

One thing is certain: if Russia really required, and was

* Large-scale industry based on machinery.

determined to have, a *grande industrie* of her own, she could not have it at all except under *some* degree of protection, and this you admit. From this point of view, too, then, the question of protection is one of *degree* only, not of principle ; the principle was unavoidable.

Another thing is certain : if Russia required after the Crimean War a *grande industrie* of her own, she could have it in one form only : the *capitalistic form.* And along with that form, she was obliged to take over all the consequences which accompany capitalistic *grande industrie* in all other countries.

Now I cannot see that the results of the industrial revolution which is taking place in Russia under our eyes, are in any way different from what they are, or have been, in England, Germany, America. In America the conditions of agriculture and landed property are different, and this *does* make some difference.

You complain of the slow increase of hands employed in textile industry, when compared with the increase of quantity of product. The same is taking place everywhere else. Otherwise, whence our redundant " industrial reserve " ? (*Capital,* C. 23, Sect. 3 and 4.) [Kerr edition, Vol. 1, Chap. 25.]

You prove the gradual replacing of men's work by that of women and children—*Capital,* C. 13 (Sect. 3a). [*Ibid,* Chap. 15.]

You complain that the machine-made goods supersede the products of domestic industry and thus destroy a supplementary production, without which the peasant cannot live. But we have here an absolutely necessary consequence of capitalistic *grande industrie :* the creation of the home market (*Capital,* C. 24, Sect. 5),* and which has taken place in Germany during my lifetime and under my eyes. Even what you say, that the introduction of cotton goods destroys not only the domestic spinning and weaving of the peasants, but also their *flax culture,* has been seen in Germany between 1820 and now. And as far as this side of the question : the destruction of home industry and the branches of agriculture subservient to it—as far as this is concerned, the real question for you seems to me this : that the Russians had to decide whether *their own grande industrie*

* *Ibid* Chapter 30.

was to destroy their domestic manufacture, or whether *the import of English goods* was to accomplish this. *With* protection, the *Russians* effected it, *without* protection, the *English.* That seems to me perfectly evident.

Your calculation that the sum of the textile products of *grande industrie* and of domestic industry does not increase, but remains the same and even diminishes, is not only quite correct, but would not be correct if it came to another result. So long as Russian manufacture is confined to the home market, its product can only cover home consumption. And that can only slowly increase, and, as it seems to me, ought even to decrease under present Russian conditions.

For it is one of the necessary corollaries of *grande industrie* that it *destroys* its own home market by the very process by which it *creates* it. It creates it by destroying the basis of the domestic industry of the peasantry. But without domestic industry the peasantry cannot live. They are ruined *as peasants* ; their purchasing power is reduced to a minimum ; and until they, as *proletarians*, have settled down into new conditions of existence, they will furnish a very poor market for the newly-arisen factories.

Capitalist production being a transitory economical phase, is full of internal contradictions which develop and become evident in proportion as it develops. This tendency to destroy its own market at the same time it creates it, is one of them. Another one is the insoluble situation* to which it leads, and which is developed sooner in a country *without* a foreign market, like Russia, than in countries which are more or less capable of competing on the open world market. This situation without an apparent issue finds its issue, for the latter countries, in commercial revulsions, in the forcible opening of new markets. But even then the *cul-de-sac* stares one in the face. Look at England. The last new market which could bring on a temporary revival of prosperity by its being thrown open to English commerce is China. Therefore English capital insists upon constructing Chinese railways. But Chinese railways mean the destruction of the whole basis of Chinese small agriculture and

* These two words in Russian.

domestic industry, and as there will not even be the counterpoise of a Chinese *grande industrie*, hundreds of millions of people will be placed in the impossibility of living. The consequence will be a wholesale emigration such as the world has not yet seen, a flooding of America, Asia and Europe by the hated Chinaman, a competition for work with the American, Australian and European workman on the basis of the Chinese standard of life, the lowest of all—and if the system of production has not been changed in Europe before that time, it will have to be changed then.

Capitalistic production works its own ruin, and you may be sure it will do so in Russia too. It may, and if it lasts long enough, it will surely produce a fundamental agrarian revolution—I mean a revolution in the condition of landed property, which will ruin both the *pomeshchik* and the *muzhik* [the landlord and the peasant], and replace them by a new class of large landed proprietors drawn from the *kulaki* [*kulaks*] of the villages and the bourgeois speculators of the towns. At all events, I am sure the conservative people who have introduced capitalism into Russia, will be one day terribly astonished at the consequences of their own doings.

224. ENGELS TO SORGE

London, 31 December, 1892.

Here in old Europe things are rather more lively than in your " youthful " country, which still refuses to get quite out of its hobbledehoy stage. It is remarkable, but quite natural, that in such a young country, which has never known feudalism and has grown up on a bourgeois basis from the first, bourgeois prejudices should also be so strongly rooted in the working class. Out of his very opposition to the mother country—which is still clothed in its feudal disguise—the American worker also imagines that the bourgeois regime as traditionally inherited is something progressive and superior by nature and for all time, a *non plus ultra* [not to be surpassed]. Just as in New England, Puritanism, the reason for the whole colony's existence, has become precisely on this account a traditional inheritance, almost inseparable from local patriotism. The Americans can strain and struggle as much as they like, but they cannot realise their future—colossally great as it is—all at once like a bill of exchange; they must wait for the date on which it becomes due; and just *because* their future is so great their present must mainly occupy itself with preparatory work for the future, and this work, as in every young country, is of a predominantly material nature and determines a certain backwardness of thought, a clinging to traditions connected with the foundation of the new nationality. The Anglo-Saxon race—those damned Schleswig-Holsteiners, as Marx always called them—is slow-witted anyhow and their history both in Europe and America (economic success and predominantly peaceful political development) has encouraged this still more. Only great events can be of use here and if, added to the more or less completed transition of the national property in land into private ownership, there comes the expansion of industry under a less crazy tariff policy and the conquest of foreign markets, then it may go well with you too. The class-struggles here in England too were more violent during the period in which large scale industry was *developing* and were enfeebled just in the period of England's unquestioned industrial domination of the world. In Germany, too, the development of large-scale industry since 1850 coincides with the rise of the Socialist movement, and it will be no different, probably, with America. It is the revolutionising of all traditional relations through industry *as it develops* which also revolutionises people's minds.

For the rest, Americans have for some time been providing the European world with the proof that a bourgeois republic is a republic of capitalist business men in which politics are only a business deal, like any other; and the French, whose ruling bourgeois politicians have long known this and practised it in secret, are now at last also learning this truth on a national scale through the Panama scandal. In order, however, that the constitutional monarchies should not be able to give themselves virtuous airs, every one of them has his little Panama: England the scandal of the building-societies, one of which, the

Liberator, has thoroughly "liberated" a mass of small depositors from some £8,000,000 of their savings; Germany the Baare scandals and Löwe Jüdenflinten (which have proved that the Prussian officer steals as he always did, but very, very little—the one thing he is modest about), Italy the *Banca Romana*, which already approaches the Panama scale, about 150 deputies and senators having been bought up; I am informed that documents about this will shortly be published in Switzerland—Schlüter should look out for everything which appears in the papers about the *Banca Romana.* And in holy Russia the old-Russian Prince Meshchersky is indignant at the indifference with which the Panama revelations are received in Russia and can only explain it to himself by the fact that Russian virtue has been corrupted by French examples, and "we ourselves have more than one Panama at home."

But all the same the Panama business is the beginning of the end of the bourgeois republic and may soon bring us into very responsible positions. The *whole* of the opportunist and the majority of the radical gang are shamefully compromised, the government is trying to hush it up but that is no longer possible; the documents containing the evidence are in the hands of people who *want* to overthrow the present rulers: (1) the Orleanists; (2) the fallen minister Constans, whose career has been ended by revelations about his scandalous past; (3) Rochefort and the Boulangists; (4) Cornelius Herz who, himself deeply involved in every sort of fraud, has obviously only fled to London in order to buy himself out by getting the others into a hole. All these have more then enough evidence against the gang of thieves, but are holding back, first in order not to use up all their ammunition at once, and secondly in order to give both the government and the *courts* time to compromise themselves beyond any hope of salvation. This can only suit us well; enough stuff is coming to light by degrees to keep up the excitement and compromise the *dirigeants** more and more while it also gives time for the scandal and the revelations to make their effect felt in the most remote

* The leaders, the wirepullers.

corner of the country before the inevitable dissolution of the chamber and new elections, which however ought *not to come too soon.* It is clear that this business brings the moment considerably nearer when our people will become the only possible leaders of the state in France. Only things ought not to move too quickly, our people in France are not ripe for power by a long way. But as things are at present it is absolutely impossible to say what intermediate stages will fill this gap. The old Republican parties are compromised to the last man, the Royalists and Clericals dealt in the Panama lottery bonds on a mass scale and identified themselves with them—if that ass Boulanger had not shot himself he would now be master of the situation. I am eager to know if the old unconscious logic of French history will assert itself again this time too. There will be plenty of surprises. If only some general or other does not swing himself to the top during the interval of clarification and start war—that is the one danger.

In Germany the steady irresistible progress of the Party goes quietly on. Small successes in every hole and corner, which prove the advance. If the essential part of the military Bill is accepted, new masses of the discontented will stream to us; if it is rejected there will be dissolution and new elections in which we shall get at least fifty seats in the Reichstag, which in cases of conflict may often give us the decisive vote. In any case the struggle, even if, as is possible, it also breaks out in France, can only be fought out in Germany. But it is good that the third volume [of *Capital*] will now at last be finished—when? Indeed I cannot yet say; the times are becoming disturbed and the waves are beginning to rise high.

¶In 1888 the French company which was financing the building of the Panama Canal went bankrupt. This event, known as the "Panama scandal," was utilised by the Nationalists in France to overthrow the Republican majority. In the course of the investigation a gigantic bribery scandal was discovered in which 150 deputies and the bourgeois press, etc., were involved. From this arose an intensification of the inner contradictions in France, and there was an imminent danger of the Nationalists, who demanded a war of revenge, coming into power and thus increasing the war danger. The trial was quashed in 1894 by the President of the Republic.

225. ENGELS TO SORGE

London, 18 January, 1893.

Here there has been a Conference in Bradford of the Independent Labour Party, which you know from the *Workman's Times*. The S.D.F. on the one hand and the Fabians on the other have not been able, with their sectarian attitude, to absorb the mass pressure for socialism in the provinces, so the foundation of a third Party was quite good. But the pressure has now become so great, especially in the industrial districts of the north, that the new Party came out already at this first Congress stronger than the S.D.F. or the Fabians, if not stronger than both put together. And as the *mass* of the membership is certainly very good, as the centre of gravity lies in the provinces and not in London, the home of cliques, and as the main point of the programme is ours, Aveling was right to join and to accept a seat on the Executive. If the petty private ambitions and intrigues of the London would-be-greats are slightly held in check here and the tactics do not turn out too wrong-headed, the Independent Labour Party may succeed in detaching the masses from the Social-Democratic Federation and in the provinces from the Fabians too, and thus forcing unity.

The Fabians are an ambitious group here in London who have understanding enough to realise the inevitability of the social revolution, but who could not possibly entrust this gigantic task to the rough proletariat alone and are therefore kind enough to set themselves at the head. Fear of the revolution is their fundamental principle. They are the "educated" *par excellence*. Their socialism is municipal socialism; not the nation but the *municipality* is to become the owner of the means of production, at any rate for the time being. This socialism of theirs is then represented as an extreme but inevitable consequence of bourgeois Liberalism, and hence follow their tactics of not decisively opposing the Liberals as adversaries but of pushing them on towards socialist conclusions and therefore of intriguing with them, of *permeating Liberalism with Socialism*, of not putting up Socialist candidates against the Liberals but of fastening them on to the Liberals, forcing them upon them, or deceiving them into taking them. That in the course of this process they are either lied to and deceived themselves or else betray socialism, they do not of course realise.

With great industry they have produced amid all sorts of rubbish some good propagandist writings as well, in fact the best of the kind which the English have produced. But as soon as they get on to their specific tactics of hushing up the class struggle it all turns putrid. Hence too their fanatical hatred of Marx and all of us—because of the class struggle.

These people have of course many bourgeois followers and therefore money, and have many active workers in the provinces who will have nothing to do with the S.D.F. But five-sixths of the provincial members agree more or less with our point of view and at the critical moment will certainly fall away. In Bradford, where they were represented, they several times decisively declared themselves against the London Executive of the Fabians.

You see that it is a critical moment for the movement here and something may come of this new organisation. There was a moment when it nearly fell into the clutches of Champion—who consciously or unconsciously works just as much for the Tories as the Fabians do for the Liberals—and of his ally Maltman Barry, whom you knew at the Hague (Barry is now an acknowledged and permanent paid Tory agent and manager of the Socialist wing of the Conservatives !)—see the *Workman's Times* for November and December. But in the end Champion preferred to start publishing his *Labour Elector* again and has thus placed himself in opposition to the *Workman's Times* and the new Party.

Hardie brought off a clever stroke by putting himself at the head of this new Party, while John Burns, whose complete inactivity outside his constituency has already done him a lot of harm, committed a fresh piece of stupidity by holding back here too. I am afraid he is heading straight for an impossible position.

The fact that here too people like Keir Hardie, Shaw-Maxwell and others are pursuing all sorts of secondary aims of personal ambition is of course obvious. But the danger arising from this becomes less according to the degree in which the party itself becomes stronger and gets more of a mass character, and it is already diminished by the necessity for exposing the weakness of the competing sects. Socialism has penetrated the masses in the industrial districts enormously in the last years and I am counting on these masses to keep the leaders in order. Of course, there will be stupidities enough, and cliques of every kind too, but so long as it is possible to keep them within decent limits——.

At the worst, the foundation of the new organisation has this advantage that unity will be more easily brought about between these competing sects than between two which are diametrically opposed.

THE INDEPENDENT LABOUR PARTY held its foundation Conference at Bradford, January 13, 14, 1893. In 1894 (November 10) Engels wrote to Sorge: "The Independent Labour Party is extremely indefinite in its tactics, and its leader, Keir Hardie, is a super-cunning Scotsman." [*Ed. Eng. ed.*]

THE FABIAN SOCIETY was founded in 1884. The name "Fabian" is taken from Fabius Cunctator (Fabius the Delayer) who was made dictator in Rome at the time of the Second Punic War and obtained successes against the Carthaginians and Hannibal by his slow, delaying tactics.

The Fabians became the theoreticians of the Labour Party, which in Engels' days did not as yet exist. They were among the most extreme Right leaders of British social-democracy and supported the line of British imperialism in the camp of the working class. [*Ed. Eng. ed.*]

226. ENGELS TO DANIELSON* (NICOLAI-ON)

London, 24 February, 1893.

We seem to be agreed upon all points except one, which you tackle in both your letters of 3rd October and 27 January, though in each from a different point of view.

In the first you ask: was the economic change which after 1854 had become unavoidable, of such a nature that it must, instead of developing the historical institutions of Russia, on the contrary attack them in their root? In other words, could not the rural commune be taken for the basis of the new economic development?

And, Jan. 27th, you express the same idea in this form: the *grande industrie*† had become a necessity for Russia, but was it unavoidable that it was developed in a capitalistic form?

Well, in, or about, 1854 Russia started with the commune on the one hand, and the necessity of the *grande industrie* on the other. Now, if you take the whole state of your country into account, as it was at that date, do you see any possibility of the *grande industrie* being grafted on the peasants' commune in a form which would, on the one hand, make the development of that *grande industrie* possible, and on the other hand raise the primitive commune to the rank of a social institution superior to anything the world has yet seen? And that while the whole Occident was still living under the capitalist regime? It strikes me that such an evolution, which would have surpassed anything known in history, required other economical, political and intellectual conditions than were present at that time in Russia.

No doubt the commune and to a certain extent the artel, contained germs which under certain conditions might have developed and saved Russia the necessity of passing through the torments of the capitalistic regime. I fully subscribe to our author's letter about Shukovsky.‡ But in his, as well as in my opinion, the first condition required to bring this about, was the

* This letter was written in English.
† Large-scale industry based on machinery.
‡ Marx's Letter about Shukovsky. See Letter 167.

impulse from without, the change of economic system in the Occident of Europe, the destruction of the capitalist system in the countries where it had originated. Our author said in a certain preface to a certain old manifesto, in January 1882, replying to the question whether the Russian commune might not be the starting point of a higher social development : if the change of economic system in Russia coincides with a change of economic system in the West, so that both supplement each other, then contemporary Russian landownership may become as the starting point of a new social development. *

If we in the West had been quicker in our own economic development, if we had been able to upset the capitalistic regime some ten or twenty years ago, there might have been time yet for Russia to cut short the tendency of her own evolution towards capitalism. Unfortunately we are too slow, and those economic consequences of the capitalistic system which must bring it up to the critical point, are only just now developing in the various countries about us : while England is fast losing her industrial monopoly, France and Germany are approaching the industrial level of England, and America bids fair to drive them all out of the world's market both for industrial and for agricultural produce. The introduction of an, at least relative, free trade policy in America, is sure to complete the ruin of England's industrial monopoly, and to destroy, at the same time, the industrial export trade of Germany and France ; then the crisis must come, *tout ce qui'il a de plus fin de siècle*. But in the meantime, with you, the commune fades away, and we can only hope that the change to a better system, with us, may come soon enough to save, at least in some of the remoter portions of your country, institutions which may, under those circumstances, be called upon to fulfil a great future. But facts are facts, and we must not forget that these chances are getting less and less every year.

For the rest I grant you that the circumstance of Russia being the *last* country seized upon by the capitalist *grande industrie*, and at the same time the country with by far the *largest peasant*

* Engels writes this passage in Russian. For the quotation from the preface to the Russian edition of *The Communist Manifesto* see Note to Letter 167. [*Ed. Eng. ed.*]

population, are such as must render the *bouleversement** caused by this economic change, more acute than it has been anywhere else. The process of replacing some 500,000 *pomeshchiki* (landowners) and some eighty million peasants by a new class of *bourgeois* landed proprietors cannot be carried out but under fearful sufferings and convulsions. But history is about the most cruel of all goddesses, and she leads her triumphal car over heaps of corpses, not only in war, but also in "peaceful" economic development. And we men and women are unfortunately so stupid that we never can pluck up courage to a real progress unless urged to it by sufferings that seem almost out of proportion.

227. ENGELS TO MEHRING

London, 14 July, 1893.

You have described the main things excellently and for any unprejudiced person convincingly. If I find anything to object to it is that you attribute more credit to me than I deserve, even if I count in everything which I might possibly have found out for myself—in time—but which Marx with his more rapid *coup d'oeil* (grasp) and wider vision discovered much more quickly. When one has the good fortune to work for forty years with a man like Marx, one does not usually get the recognition one thinks one deserves during his lifetime. Then if the greater man dies, the lesser easily gets overrated, and this seems to me to be just my case at present; history will set all this right in the end and by that time one will be safely round the corner and know nothing more about anything.

Otherwise there is only one other point lacking, which, however, Marx and I always failed to stress enough in our writings and in regard to which we are all equally guilty. We all, that is to say, laid and were bound to lay the main emphasis at first on the derivation of political, juridical and other ideological notions, and of the actions arising through the medium of these notions, from basic economic facts. But in so doing we neglected

* Upheaval.

the formal side—the way in which these notions come about—for the sake of the content. This has given our adversaries a welcome opportunity for misunderstandings, of which Paul Barth is a striking example.

Ideology is a process accomplished by the so-called thinker consciously, indeed, but with a false consciousness. The real motives impelling him remain unknown to him, otherwise it would not be an ideological process at all. Hence he imagines false or apparent motives. Because it is a process of thought he derives both its form and its content from pure thought, either his own or that of his predecessors. He works with mere thought material which he accepts without examination as the product of thought, he does not investigate further for a more remote process independent of thought; indeed its origin seems obvious to him, because as all action is produced through the medium of thought it also appears to him to be ultimately based upon thought. The ideologist who deals with history (history is here simply meant to comprise all the spheres—political, juridical, philosophical, theological—belonging to society and not only to nature), the ideologist dealing with history then, possesses in every sphere of science material which has formed itself independently out of the thought of previous generations and has gone through an independent series of developments in the brains of these successive generations. True, external facts belonging to its own or other spheres may have exercised a co-determining influence on this development, but the tacit pre-supposition is that these facts themselves are also only the fruits of a process of thought, and so we still remain within that realm of pure thought which has successfully digested the hardest facts.

It is above all this appearance of an independent history of state constitutions, of systems of law, of ideological conceptions in every separate domain, which dazzles most people. If Luther and Calvin "overcome" the official Catholic religion, or Hegel "overcomes" Fichte and Kant, or if the constitutional Montesquieu is indirectly "overcome" by Rousseau with his "Social Contract," each of these events remains within the sphere of theology, philosophy or political science, represents a stage in the history of these particular spheres of thought and never passes outside the sphere of thought. And since the bourgeois illusion of the eternity and the finality of capitalist production has been added as well, even the victory of the physiocrats and Adam Smith over the mercantilists is accounted as a sheer victory of thought; not as the reflection in thought of changed economic facts but as the finally achieved correct understanding of actual conditions subsisting always and everywhere—in fact if Richard Coeur-de-Lion and Philip Augustus had introduced free trade instead of getting mixed up in the crusades we should have been spared five hundred years of misery and stupidity.

This side of the matter, which I can only indicate here, we have all, I think, neglected more than it deserves. It is the old story: form is always neglected at first for content. As I say, I have done that too, and the mistake has always only struck me later. So I am not only far from reproaching you with this in any way, but as the older of the guilty parties I have no right to do so, on the contrary; but I would like all the same to draw your attention to this point for the future. Hanging together with this too is the fatuous notion of the ideologists that because we deny an independent historical development to the various ideological spheres which play a part in history we also deny them any effect upon history. The basis of this is the common undialectical conception of cause and effect as rigidly opposite poles, the total disregarding of interaction; these gentlemen often almost deliberately forget that once an historic element has been brought into the world by other elements, ultimately by economic facts, it also reacts in its turn and may react on its environment and even on its own causes. *E.g.*, Barth on the priesthood and religion on your page 475.

¶This letter deals with Mehring's article, *On Historical Materialism*, which was published as an appendix to the first edition of his book *Die Lessinglegende* [The Lessing Legend]. The quotation from Barth's book reads:

" In the East, religion everywhere created a specially

privileged order of priesthood, freed from physical labour by the obligation of paying tribute laid on other orders, and detached for intellectual activity; thus the utilisation of a portion of the economic product was determined by religion. Whilst in Græco-Roman culture priestly activity seldom devolved upon particular organs, Christianity led the way back to the Oriental differentiation, created a special order of priests which it richly endowed, and thus separated off a portion of economic goods as the material substratum of religious activity, which soon became general intellectual activity."

228. ENGELS TO DANIELSON (NICOLAI-ON)*

London, October 17, 1893.

When I received your letter of July 28, announcing your return home, I was on the point myself of going abroad for two months and am only just returned. This is the reason of my long silence.

Many thanks for the copies of the *Ocherki*† three of which I have forwarded to appreciative friends. The book, I am glad to see, has caused considerable stir and indeed sensation, as it well merited. Among the Russians I have met, it was the chief subject of conversation. Only yesterday one of them writes: "*With us in Russia a controversy is going on about the 'fate of capitalism in Russia.'*"‡

In the Berlin *Sozial-Politische Zentralblatt* a Mr. B. V. Struve has a long article on your book; I must agree with him in this one point, that for me, too, the present capitalistic phase of development in Russia appears an unavoidable consequence of the historical conditions as created by the Crimean War, the way in which the change of 1861 in agrarian conditions was accomplished, and the political stagnation in Europe generally. Where he is decidedly wrong is in comparing the present state of Russia with that of the United States in order to refute what he calls your pessimistic views of the future. He says the evil consequences of modern capitalism in Russia will be as easily

* This Letter was written in English.
† N-on: *Sketches of our Political Economy after the Reform* (1893).
‡ Italicized sentence written by Engels in Russian.

overcome as they are in the United States. There he quite forgets, that the U.S. are modern, bourgeois from the very origin; that they were founded by *petits* bourgeois and peasants who ran away from European feudalism to establish a purely bourgeois society. Whereas in Russia we have a groundwork of a primitive communistic character, a pre-civilisation *Gentilgesellschaft*,* crumbling to ruins, it is true, but still serving as the groundwork, the material upon which the capitalistic revolution (for it is a real social revolution) acts and operates. In America, *Geldwirtschaft*† has been fully established for more than a century, in Russia *Naturalwirtschaft*‡ was all but exclusively the rule. Therefore it stands to reason that the change, in Russia, must be far more violent, far more incisive, and accompanied by immensely greater sufferings than it can be in America.

But for all that it still seems to me that you take a gloomier view of the case than the facts justify. No doubt the passage from primitive agrarian communism to capitalistic industrialism cannot take place without terrible dislocation of society, without the disappearance of whole classes and their transformation into other classes; and what enormous suffering, and waste of human lives and productive forces that necessarily implies, we have seen—on a smaller scale—in Western Europe. But from that to the complete ruin of a great and highly gifted nation there is still a long way. The rapid increase of population to which you have been accustomed, may be checked; the reckless deforestation combined with the expropriation of the old landlords as well as the peasants may cause a colossal waste of productive forces; but after all, a population of more than a hundred millions will finally furnish a very considerable home market for a very respectable *grande industrie*,§ and with you as elsewhere, things will end by finding their own level—if capitalism lasts long enough in Western Europe.

You yourself admit that "the social conditions in Russia after the Crimean War were not favourable to the development

* The form of tribal society based on the *gens*, joint family.
† Money economy.
‡ Natural economy.
§ Large-scale industry.

of the form of production inherited by us from our past history." I would go further, and say, that no more in Russia than anywhere else would it have been possible to develop a higher social form out of primitive agrarian communism unless—that higher form was *already in existence* in another country, so as to serve as a model. That higher form being, wherever it is historically possible, the necessary consequence of the capitalistic form of production and of the social dualistic antagonism created by it, it could not be developed directly out of the agrarian commune, unless in imitation of an example already in existence somewhere else. Had the West of Europe been ripe, 1860-70, for such a transformation, had that transformation then been taken in hand in England, France, etc., then the Russians would have been called upon to show what could have been made out of their commune, which was then more or less intact. But the West remained stagnant, no such transformation was attempted, and capitalism was more and more rapidly developed. And as Russia had no choice but this: either to develop the commune into a form of production from which it was separated by a number of historical stages, and for which not even in the West the conditions were then ripe—evidently an impossible task—or else to develop into capitalism; what remained to her but the latter chance?

As to the commune, it is only possible so long as the differences of wealth among its members are but trifling. As soon as these differences become great, as soon as some of its members become the debt-slaves of the richer members, it can no longer live. The *kulaki* and *miroyedy* (kulaks and parasites) of Athens, before Solon, have destroyed the Athenian *gens* with the same implacability with which those of your country destroy the commune. I am afraid that institution is doomed. But on the other hand, capitalism opens out new views and new hopes. Look at what it has done and is doing in the West. A great nation like yours outlives every crisis. There is no great historical evil without a compensating historical progress. Only the *modus operandi* is changed. *Que les destinées s'accomplissent!* [Only the mode of operation is changed. Let fate be accomplished.]

The letters of Engels to Danielson on the question of the development of capitalism in Russia are particularly interesting because they contain the same refutation of the theories of the Narodniki which Lenin was providing independently almost at the same time in the writings he directed against the Narodniki, where he "further developed the principles of Marxism in harmony with the changing conditions and local peculiarities of different countries and further completed Marx's theory of dialectical materialism and of political economy." (Lenin.)

* * * *

In his principal economic work, *The Development of Capitalism in Russia* (1898), Lenin proved, from extensive material consisting of actual facts, the disintegration of Russian agriculture and the creation of an internal market for capitalism by means of this process. A comparison of the letters of Engels to Danielson with the writings of Lenin shows how Engels comes to the same conclusions as those which Lenin reached on the basis of his deep study of the development of capitalism in Russia, and by means of his masterly application of the method of Marx, which he enriched and concretised.

229. ENGELS TO H. STARKENBURG

London, 25 January, 1894.

Here is the answer to your questions!

(1) What we understand by the economic conditions which we regard as the determining basis of the history of society are the methods by which human beings in a given society produce their means of subsistence and exchange the products among themselves (in so far as division of labour exists). Thus the *entire technique* of production and transport is here included. According to our conception this technique also determines the method of exchange and, further, the division of products, and with it, after the dissolution of tribal society, the division into classes also and hence the relations of lordship and servitude and with them the state, politics, law, etc. Under economic conditions are further included the geographical basis on which they operate and those remnants of earlier stages of economic development which have actually been

transmitted and have survived—often only through tradition or the force of inertia ; also of course the external milieu which surrounds this form of society.

If, as you say, technique largely depends on the state of science, science depends far more still on the *state* and the *requirements* of technique. If society has a technical need, that helps science forward more than ten universities. The whole of hydrostatics (Torricelli, etc.) was called forth by the necessity for regulating the mountain streams of Italy in the sixteenth and seventeenth centuries. We have only known anything reasonable about electricity since its technical applicability was discovered. But unfortunately it has become the custom in Germany to write the history of the sciences as if they had fallen from the skies.

(2) We regard economic conditions as the factor which ultimately determines historical development. But race is itself an economic factor. Here, however, two points must not be overlooked :

(*a*) Political, juridical, philosophical, religious, literary, artistic, etc., development is based on economic development. But all these react upon one another and also upon the economic base. It is not that the economic position is the *cause and alone active*, while everything else only has a passive effect. There is, rather, interaction on the basis of the economic necessity, which *ultimately* always asserts itself. The state, for instance, exercises an influence by tariffs, free trade, good or bad fiscal system; and even the deadly inanition and impotence of the German petty bourgeois, arising from the miserable economic position of Germany from 1640 to 1830 and expressing itself at first in pietism, then in sentimentality and cringing servility to princes and nobles, was not without economic effect. It was one of the greatest hindrances to recovery and was not shaken until the revolutionary and Napoleonic wars made the chronic misery an acute one. So it is not, as people try here and there conveniently to imagine, that the economic position produces an automatic effect. Men make their history themselves, only in given surroundings which condition it and on the basis of actual relations already existing, among which the economic relations, however much they may be influenced by the other political and ideological ones, are still ultimately the decisive ones, forming the red thread which runs through them and alone leads to understanding.

(*b*) Men make their history themselves, but not as yet with a collective will or according to a collective plan or even in a definitely defined, given society. Their efforts clash, and for that very reason all such societies are governed by *necessity*, which is supplemented by and appears under the forms of *accident*. The necessity which here asserts itself amidst all accident is again ultimately economic necessity. This is where the so-called great men come in for treatment. That such and such a man and precisely that man arises at that particular time in that given country is of course pure accident. But cut him out and there will be a demand for a substitute, and this substitute will be found, good or bad, but in the long run he will be found. That Napoleon, just that particular Corsican, should have been the military dictator whom the French Republic, exhausted by its own war, had rendered necessary, was an accident; but that, if a Napoleon had been lacking, another would have filled the place, is proved by the fact that the man has always been found as soon as he became necessary: Cæsar, Augustus, Cromwell, etc. While Marx discovered the materialist conception of history, Thierry, Mignet, Guizot, and all the English historians up to 1850 are the proof that it was being striven for, and the discovery of the same conception by Morgan proves that the time was ripe for it and that indeed it *had* to be discovered.

So with all the other accidents, and apparent accidents, of history. The further the particular sphere which we are investigating is removed from the economic sphere and approaches that of pure abstract ideology, the more shall we find it exhibiting accidents in its development, the more will its curve run in a zig-zag. So also you will find that the axis of this curve will approach more and more nearly parallel to the axis of the curve of economic development the longer the period considered and the wider the field dealt with.

In Germany the greatest hindrance to correct understanding

is the irresponsible neglect by literature of economic history. It is so hard, not only to disaccustom oneself of the ideas of history drilled into one at school, but still more to rake up the necessary material for doing so. Who, for instance, has read old G. von Gülich,* whose dry collection of material nevertheless contains so much stuff for the clarification of innumerable political facts !

For the rest, the fine example which Marx has given in the *Eighteenth Brumaire* should already, I think, provide you fairly well with information on your questions, just because it is a practical example. I have also, I believe, already touched on most of the points in *Anti-Dühring* I, Chapters 9-11, and II, 2-4, as well as in III, 1, or Introduction, and then in the last section of *Feuerbach.*

Please do not weigh each word in the above too carefully, but keep the connection in mind ; I regret that I have not the time to work out what I am writing to you so exactly as I should be obliged to do for publication.

¶Starkenburg had put the following questions to Engels : (1) How far do economic conditions act *causally* ? (Are they an adequate ground, motive, permanent condition, etc., of development ?) (2) What part is played by the *racial* element and by historic *personality* in Marx and Engels' conception of history ?

230. ENGELS TO TURATI†

London, 26 January, 1894.

In my opinion the position in Italy is the following.

The *bourgeoisie*, which came to power during and after the national independence movement, would not and could not complete its victory. It neither destroyed the remains of feudal-

* G. van Gülich : *Historical Account of the Trade, Industry and Agriculture of the most Important Commercial States of Our Time* (1830).

† This Letter was written in French but is here translated from a German translation. [*Ed. Eng. ed.*]

ism nor transformed national production according to the modern capitalist pattern. Incapable of ensuring the relative and temporary *advantages* of the capitalist system to the country, they burdened it on the other hand with all the damage and the disadvantages of the system. And as if that were not enough, they forfeited the last remnant of respect and confidence by involving themselves in the dirtiest bank scandals.

The *labouring* population—peasants, handicraft workers, agricultural and industrial workers—finds itself in consequence in an oppressive position, on the one hand owing to old abuses inherited not only from feudal times but from an even earlier period (take, for instance, the *mezzadria* [share farming], or the *latifundia** of the south, where cattle are supplanting men); on the other hand owing to the most rapacious fiscal system ever invented by bourgeois policy. Here too one can say with Marx: "Like all the rest of continental Western Europe we are tortured not only by the development of capitalist production, but by the lack of its development. Side by side with modern distress we are oppressed by a whole sequence of inherited distress arising from the fact that ancient and antiquated methods of production, resulting in social and political conditions unsuited to the time, continue to vegetate among us. We suffer not only from the living but from the dead. *Le mort saisit le vif.* [The living are in the grip of the dead.]

This situation is pressing towards a *crisis*. Everywhere the producing masses are in a ferment: here and there they are rising. Where will this crisis lead?

The *Socialist Party* of Italy is obviously too young and, considering the whole economic position, too weak, to be able to hope for an *immediate victory of* Socialism. In this country the rural population far outweighs the urban; in the towns industry is only slightly developed and hence the real *typical* proletariat is small in number: here the majority is composed of handicraft workers, small masters and small merchants, a mass which fluctuates to and fro between the petty bourgeoisie and the proletariat. These are the petty and middle bourgeoisie of medieval times in their decay and dissolution—certain to be

* *Latifundia*; landed estates of exceptionally large extent. [*Ed. Eng. ed.*]

for the most part proletarians in the future, but at present not yet proletarianised. And this class, which sees ruin daily staring it in the face and is now driven to desperation, is the only class which can supply the fighters and leaders for a revolutionary movement in Italy. Along this path they will be followed by the *peasantry*, who are shut out from an effective initiative of their own by the fact that they live spatially scattered and cannot read and write, but who will in any case be strong and indispensable allies.

In the case of a more or less peaceful success, a change of Ministry will take place and the "converted" Republicans will come to the top; in the case of a revolution the bourgeois republic will triumph.

What should and must be the attitude of the Socialist Party in face of this situation?

The tactics which, since 1848, have brought Socialists the greatest success are those recommended by *The Communist Manifesto:* "In the various stages of development which the struggle of the working class against the bourgeoisie has to pass through, the Socialists always represent the interests of the movement as a whole . . . They fight for the attainment of the immediate aims, for the enforcement of the momentary interests of the working class, but in the movement of the present they also represent and take care of the future of that movement."

Consequently they take an active part in all the phases of the development of the struggle between the two classes without in so doing losing sight of the fact that these phases are only just so many preliminary steps to the first great aim: the conquest of *political* power by the *proletariat* as the means towards a new organisation of society. Their place is by the side of those who are fighting for the immediate achievement of an advance which is at the same time in the interests of the working class. They accept all these political or social progressive steps, but only as *instalments*. Hence they regard every revolutionary or progressive movement as a step further in the attainment of their own end; and it is their special task to drive other revolutionary parties ever further, and, in case one of them should be victorious, to guard the interests of the proletariat. These tactics, which never lose sight of the last great final aim, preserve us Socialists from the disappointments to which the other less clear-sighted parties, be they republicans or sentimental socialists, who confuse what is only a mere stage with the final aim of the advance, must inevitably succumb.

Let us apply what has been said to Italy.

The victory of the petty bourgeoisie, who are in process of disintegration, and of the peasantry, may perhaps bring a ministry of "converted" Republicans into power. This will give us universal suffrage and greater freedom of movement (freedom of the press, of organisation, and of assembly)—new weapons not to be despised.

Or it will bring us the bourgeois republic, with the same people and some Mazzinist or other among them. This would extend liberty and our field of action still further, at any rate for the moment. And Marx has said that the bourgeois republic is the only political form in which the struggle between proletariat and bourgeoisie can be resolved. To say nothing of the reaction which would make itself felt in Europe.

Thus the victory of the revolutionary movement which is being prepared cannot but strengthen us and place us under more *favourable* conditions. We should commit the greatest mistake if we refrained from sympathy with it or if in our attitude to the "related" parties we confined ourselves merely to negative criticism. There may come a moment when it would be our duty to co-operate in a positive way. What moment could that be?

Undoubtedly it is no business of ours directly to prepare a movement ourselves which is not strictly a movement of the class we represent. If the Republicans and Radicals believe the hour has come let *them* give free play to their desire to attack. As for ourselves we have been far too often disappointed by the large promises of these gentlemen to allow ourselves to be misused yet another time. Neither their proclamations nor their conspiracies will mislead us. If it is our duty to *support* every *real* movement of the people, it is not less our duty to protect the scarcely formed core of our proletarian Party, not to sacrifice it uselessly and not to allow the proletariat to be decimated in fruitless *local* risings.

But if, on the contrary, the movement is a really *national* one, our people will not keep themselves hidden and will need no password. . . .

But if it comes to this, we must be conscious of the fact, and openly proclaim it, that we are only taking part as an "*independent Party*," which is allied for the moment with Radicals and Republicans but is inwardly essentially different from them: that we indulge in absolutely no illusions as to the result of the struggle in case of victory; that this result not only cannot satisfy us but will only be a newly attained stage to us, a new basis of operations for further conquests; that from the very moment of victory our paths will separate; that from that same day onwards we shall form a *new opposition* to the new government, not a reactionary but a progressive opposition, an opposition of the most extreme Left, which will press on to new conquests beyond the ground already won.

After the common victory we might perhaps be offered some *seats in the new Government*—but always in a *minority. Here lies the greatest danger.* After the February Revolution in 1848 the French socialistic Democrats (the *Réforme* people, Ledru Rollin, Louis Blanc, Flocon, etc.) were incautious enough to accept such positions. As a minority in the Government they involuntarily bore the responsibility for all the infamy and treachery which the majority, composed of pure Republicans, committed against the working class, while at the same time their participation in the government completely paralysed the revolutionary action of the working class they were supposed to represent.

Here I am only expressing my personal opinion, which you asked me for, and I am doing this only with a certain amount of caution. As for the general tactics here communicated, I have convinced myself of their correctness throughout the whole of my life. They have never let me down. But with regard to their application in Italy under present conditions, the decision must be made on the spot and by those who are in the midst of the movement.

¶In the *Note* to Chapter 10 of his pamphlet *The Two Tactics of Social-Democracy in the Democratic Revolution* (1905) (*Collected Works*, Volume VIII) Lenin writes of the " correctness of the Marxian theory of the difference between the three main forces in the revolutions of the nineteenth century. According to this theory the forces which come out against the old social order, against absolutism, feudalism and serfdom are: (1) the liberal big bourgeoisie: (2) the radical petty bourgeoisie: (3) the proletariat. The first fights for the constitutional monarchy, the second for the democratic republic, the third for the social revolution.

" The Socialist who confuses the petty-bourgeois struggle for a complete democratic revolution with the proletarian struggle for a socialist revolution, is in danger of political bankruptcy. Marx's warning in this respect is quite justified.

" While absolutely recognising the bourgeois character of the revolution, which cannot *immediately* go beyond the bounds of a merely democratic revolution, our slogan, 'the revolutionary, democratic dictatorship of the proletariat and the peasantry, *pushes forward* this particular revolution and strives to mould it in forms most advantageous to the proletariat—consequently, it strives for the utmost utilisation of the democratic revolution for a most successful further struggle of the proletariat for socialism."

The strict and sharp distinction between the bourgeois-democratic revolution and the proletarian-socialist revolution, the latter lying before the working class as its immediate task after the more or less complete victory of the former, is one of the main pillars of the Marxist-Leninist theory of the proletarian revolution. But these revolutions are not separated from each other by a Chinese wall. Lenin in his article on *The Relation of Social-Democracy to the Peasant Movement* (1905) wrote: " With all our strength we will help the whole of the peasantry to carry through the democratic revolution *in order that* it may be so much the easier for us, the Party of the proletariat, to proceed as quickly as possible to the new and higher task, the socialist revolution." (*Collected Works*, Vol. VIII). In 1921 Lenin wrote in his article *For the Fourth Anniversary of the October Revolution* (*Collected Works*, Vol. VIII) that the socialist revolution " is not separated from the bourgeois-democratic revolution by a Chinese wall . . . that only *the struggle* will decide how far we shall succeed in moving forward."

TURATI, FILIPPO (1857-1931). Leader of Italian Social-Democracy. After the formation of the Communist Party of Italy he remained in the Party for a time in order " to put obstacles in its way when things really came to revolution there." (Lenin.) Lenin carried on an energetic struggle against Turati and demanded his expulsion from the party. Towards Fascism Turati adopted the cowardly and treacherous policy of capitulation and the disarming of the workers' movement. He died as an emigré abroad.

MEZZADRIA, *métayer* system, share farming. " A transitional form between the original form of rent and capitalist rent." Specially common in Italy. The landowner gives the farmer a portion of the working capital and receives in return a corresponding, but usually far larger portion of the farmers' produce. Hence the *métayer* system is a particularly intensive form of the exploitation of the poor peasant by the landowner. [See Letters 14, 15.]

231. ENGELS TO SORGE

London, 10 November, 1894.

On the Continent success is developing the appetite for more success, and catching the peasant, in the literal sense of the word, is becoming the fashion. First the French in Nantes declare through Lafargue not only (what I had written to them) that it is not our business to hasten by direct interference of our own the ruin of the small peasant which capitalism is seeing to for us, but they also add that we must directly *protect* the small peasant against taxation, usurers and landlords. But we cannot co-operate in this, first because it is stupid and second because it is impossible. Next, however, Vollmar comes along in Frankfort and wants to bribe the *peasantry as a whole*, though the peasant he has to do with in Upper Bavaria is not the debt-laden poor peasant of the Rhineland but the middle and even the big peasant, who exploits his men and women farm servants and sells cattle and grain in masses. And that cannot be done without giving up the whole principle. We can only win the mountain peasants and the big peasants of Lower Saxony and Schleswig-Holstein, if we sacrifice their ploughmen and day labourers to them, and if we do that we lose more than we gain politically. The Frankfort Party Congress did not take a decision on this question and that is to the good in so far as the matter will now be thoroughly studied; the people who were there knew far too little about the peasantry and the conditions on the land, which vary so fundamentally in different provinces, to have been able to do anything but take decisions in the air. But there has got to be a resolution on the question some time all the same.

¶At the Frankfort Congress of the German Social-Democratic Party Vollmar had come out in favour of an alliance with the big peasants.

In his article, *The Peasant Question in France and Germany* (1894), Engels writes:

"It is not to our interest to win the peasant to-day or to-morrow in order that if we are not able to keep our promise he should fall away from us again to-morrow or the next day. . . . Neither now nor at any future time can we promise the small peasants that individual property and individual working will be preserved in face of the supremacy of capitalist production. All we can promise them is that we will not forcibly intervene in the conditions of their ownership against their will. . . . And indeed we stand decidedly on the side of the small peasant; we will do everything in any way admissible to make his lot more bearable, to facilitate his transition to the co-operative, if he decides to take this step, and even, if he cannot as yet bring himself to this decision, to make a longer period of consideration possible for him on his holding. We do this, not only because we regard the small peasant who does his own work as virtually belonging to us, but also in the direct interests of the Party. The greater the number of peasants whom we can save from actual downfall into the proletariat and win for ourselves while they are still peasants, the more rapidly and easily will the social revolution take place. It can be of no service to us if we are obliged to wait for this transformation until capitalist production has developed itself everywhere up to its final consequences. . . . It is the duty of our Party to make clear to the peasants over and over again the absolute hopelessness of their position while capitalism rules, the absolute impossibility of preserving for them their small holdings as such, the absolute certainty that large-scale capitalist production will sweep over their impotent antiquated small-scale production as a railway train would sweep over a push-cart."

232. ENGELS TO SCHMIDT

London, 12 March, 1895.

Your letter gives me some light, I think, on how you have come to be side-tracked with the rate of profit. There I find the same way of going off into details, for which I put the blame on the eclectic method of philosophising which has made such inroads in the German universities since '48, and which loses all general perspective and only too often ends in rather aimless and fruitless argumentation about particular points.

Now of the classical philosophers it was precisely Kant with whom you had formerly chiefly occupied yourself, and Kant, owing to the position of German philosophising in his time and to his opposition to Wolf's pedantic form of Leibnitzism, was more or less obliged to make some apparent concessions in form to this Wolfian argumentation. This is how I explain your tendency, which also shows itself in the excursus on the law of value in your letter, to absorb yourself to such a degree in details, without always, as it seems to me, paying attention to the connection as a whole, that you degrade the law of value to a fiction, a necessary fiction, rather as Kant makes the existence of God a postulate of the practical reason.

The reproaches you make against the law of value apply to *all* concepts, regarded from the standpoint of reality. The identity of thought and being, to express myself in Hegelian fashion, everywhere coincides with your example of the circle and the polygon. Or the two of them, the concept of a thing and its reality, run side by side like two asymptotes, always approaching each other yet never meeting. This difference between the two is the very difference which prevents the concept from being directly and immediately reality and reality from being immediately its own concept. But although a concept has the essential nature of a concept and cannot therefore *prima facie* directly coincide with reality, from which it must first be abstracted, it is still something more than a fiction, unless you are going to declare all the results of thought fictions because reality has to go a long way round before it corresponds to them, and even then only corresponds to them with asymptotic approximation.

Is it any different with the general rate of profit? At each moment it only exists approximately. If it were for once realised in two undertakings down to the last dot on the *i*, if both resulted in *exactly the same rate of profit* in a given year, that would be pure accident; in reality the rates of profit vary from business to business and from year to year according to different circumstances, and the general rate only exists as an average of many businesses and a series of years. But if we were to demand that the rate of profit—say 14.876934 . . .—should be exactly similar in every business and every year down to the 100th decimal place, on pain of degradation to fiction, we should be grossly misunderstanding the nature of the rate of profit and of economic laws in general—none of them has any reality except as approximation, tendency, average, and not as *immediate* reality. This is due partly to the fact that their action clashes with the simultaneous action of other laws, but partly to their own nature as concepts.

Or take the law of wages, the realisation of the value of labour power, which is only realised as an average, and even that not always, and which varies in every locality, even in every branch, according to the customary standard of life. Or ground rent, representing a superprofit above the general rate, derived from monopoly over a force of nature. There too there is by no means a direct coincidence between real superprofit and real rent, but only an average approximation.

It is exactly the same with the law of value and the distribution of the surplus value by means of the rate of profit.

(1) Both only attain their most complete approximate realisation on the presupposition that capitalist production has been everywhere completely established, society reduced to the modern classes of landowners, capitalists (industrialists and

merchants) and workers—all intermediate stages, however, having been got rid of. This does not exist even in England and never will exist—we shall not let it get so far as that.

(2) Profit, including rent, consists of various component parts:—

(*a*) Profit from cheating—which is cancelled out in the algebraic sum.

(*b*) Profit from increased value of stocks (e.g., the remainder of the last harvest when the next one has failed). Theoretically this *ought* also to equalise itself out (in so far as it has not been already cancelled by the fall in the value of other commodities) either because the capitalist buyers have to contribute what the capitalist sellers gain, or, in the case of the workers' means of subsistence, because wages must also eventually increase. The most essential of these increases in value, however, are *not permanent*, and therefore the equalisation only takes place in an average of years, and extremely incompletely, notoriously at the expense of the workers; they produce more surplus value because their labour power is not fully paid.

(*c*) The total sum of surplus value, from which again, however, that portion is deducted which is *presented as a gift to the buyer*, especially in crises, when overproduction is reduced to its real value of socially necessary labour.

From this indeed it follows from the very first that the total profit and the total surplus value can only approximately coincide. But when you further take into consideration the fact that neither the total surplus value nor the total capital are constant magnitudes, but variable ones which alter from day to day, then any coincidence between rate of profit and the sum of surplus value* other than that of an approximating series, and any coincidence between total price and total value other than one which is constantly striving towards unity and perpetually moving away from it again, appears a sheer impossibility. In other words, the unity of concept and appearance manifests itself as essentially an infinite process, and that is what it is, in this case as in all others.

* Engels uses the formula $\frac{\Sigma\ S\ V}{\Sigma\ (O+V)}$

Did feudalism ever correspond to its concept? Founded in the kingdom of the West Franks, further developed in Normandy by the Norwegian conquerors, its formation continued by the French Norsemen in England and Southern Italy, it came nearest to its concept—in Jerusalem, in the kingdom of a day, which in the *Assises de Jerusalem** left behind it the most classic expression of the feudal order. Was this order therefore a fiction because it only achieved a short-lived existence in full classical form in Palestine, and even that mostly only—on paper?

Or are the concepts which prevail in the natural sciences fictions because they by no means always coincide with reality? From the moment we accept the theory of evolution all our concepts of organic life correspond only approximately to reality. Otherwise there would be no change: on the day when concepts and reality completely coincide in the organic world development comes to an end. The concept fish includes a life in water and breathing through gills: how are you going to get from fish to amphibian without breaking through this concept? And it has been broken through and we know a whole series of fish which have developed their air bladders further into lungs and can breathe air. How, without bringing one or both concepts into conflict with reality are you going to get from the egg-laying reptile to the mammal, which gives birth to living young? And in reality we have in the monotremata a whole sub-class of egg-laying mammals—in 1843, I saw the eggs of the duck-bill in Manchester and with arrogant narrow-mindedness mocked at such stupidity—as if a mammal could lay eggs—and now it has been proved! So do not behave to the conceptions of value in the way I had later to beg the duck-bill's pardon for!

In Sombart's otherwise very good article on Volume III I also find this tendency to dilute the theory of value: he had also obviously expected a somewhat different solution?

* *Assises de Jerusalem:* The statute book of Godefroi de Bouillon for the kingdom Jerusalem in the eleventh century.

KANT, IMMANUEL (1724-1804). German idealist philosopher. Professor in Königsberg. In the *Deutsche Ideologie* (1845-46) Marx writes:

"The condition of Germany at the end of last century is completely reflected in Kant's *Critique of Practical Reason.* Whilst the French bourgeoisie raised themselves to supremacy and conquered the European continent by the most colossal revolution known to history, whilst the English bourgeoisie, already politically emancipated, revolutionised industry and subjugated India politically and all the rest of the world commercially, the impotent German bourgeois could get no further than "the good will." Kant contented himself with the mere "good will" even when it remained without any result, and placed the *realisation* of this good will, the harmony between it and the needs and impulses of the individual, in the *Hereafter*.... Neither he nor the German bourgeois, whose euphemistic spokesman he was, noticed that the basis of these theoretical ideas of the bourgeoisie lay in material interests and in a *will* conditioned and determined by the material conditions of production: he therefore separated this theoretical expression from the interests it expresses...." "By his theory of the unknowable 'thing-in-itself' Kant contests the possibility of a knowledge of the world, or at least of an exhaustive knowledge." (Engels.)

In his chief philosophical work, *Materialism and Empirio-Criticism* (*Collected Works*, Vol. XIII, English Edition, p. 163), Lenin writes of Kant:

"The principal feature of the philosophy of Kant is an attempted reconciliation of materialism and idealism, a compromise between the claims of both, a fusion of heterogeneous and contrary philosophic tendencies into one system. When Kant admits that something outside of us—a thing-in-itself—corresponds to our perceptions, he seems to be a materialist. When he, however, declares this thing-in-itself to be unknowable, transcendent, 'trans-intelligible'—he appears to be an idealist."

This half and half character of Kant's philosophy makes it specially suitable and acceptable to the bourgeoisie and their agents in the camp of the working class, the Social Fascists.

SOMBART, WERNER (born 1863). German bourgeois economist. Professor. One of the sharpest opponents of Marxism. He attempted to get the Social-Democratic movement on to bourgeois lines. (See Rosa Luxemburg, *Against Reformism.*)

233. ENGELS TO VICTOR ADLER

London, 16 March, 1895.

. . . As you want to have a grind in prison at *Capital* [Volumes] II and III, I will give you a few hints to make it easier.

Volume II, *Section I.* Read Chapter I thoroughly, then you can take Chapters 2 and 3 more lightly; Chapter 4 more exactly again as it is a summary; 5 and 6 are easy and 6, especially, deals with secondary matters.

Section II. Chapters 7-9 important. Specially important 10 and 11. Equally so 12, 13, 14. On the other hand 15, 16, 17 need only be skimmed through at first.

Section III is a most excellent account of the entire circuit of commodities and money in capitalist society—the first since the days of the Physiocrats. Excellent in content but fearfully heavy in form because (1) it is put together from two versions which proceed according to two different methods and (2) because version No. 2 was carried to its conclusion by main force during a state of illness in which the brain was suffering from chronic sleeplessness. I should keep this *right to the end,* after working through Volume III for the *first time.* For your work too, it is not immediately indispensable.

Then the *third Volume.* Important here are: In Section I, Chapters 1 to 4; less important for the *general* connection, on the other hand, are Chapters 5, 6, 7, on which much time need not be spent at first.

Section II. Very important. Chaps. 8, 9, 10. Skim through 11 and 12.

Section III. Very important: the whole of 13-15.

Section IV. Likewise very important, but also easy to read: 16-20.

Section V. Very important, Chapters 21-27. Less so Chapter 28. Chapter 29 important. As a whole Chapters 30-32 are not important for your purposes; 33 and 34 are important as soon as paper-money is dealt with; 35 on international rates of exchange important, 36 *very interesting for you* and easy to read.

Section VI. Ground rent. 37 and 38 important. Less so, but still to be taken with them, 39 and 40. 41-43 can be more neglected (Differential rent II. Particular cases). 44-47 important again and mostly easy to read too.

Section VII. Very fine, but unfortunately a fragment and with very marked traces of sleeplessness as well.

Thus, if you go through the main things thoroughly and the less important ones superficially to begin with, following these indications (best first to re-read the main things in Volume I,) you will get an idea of the whole and can later also work through the neglected portions more easily.

In his letter to Kugelmann of November 30, 1867 Marx gave the following guidance for facilitating the understanding of *Capital*, Volume I.

"As those which can be read to begin with please point out to your wife the sections on the 'Working Day,' 'Co-operation,' 'Division of Labour and Machinery,' and finally on 'Primitive Accumulation.' You must give the explanation of incomprehensible terminology. In the case of any other doubts I am at your service."

Compare also Letter 67, in which Marx gives a short account of the reproduction process of the total social capital.

234. ENGELS TO KAUTSKY

London, 21 May, 1895.

I have learnt a great deal from the book,* it is an indispensable preliminary study for my new revision of the *Peasant War*. The main faults seem to be only two : (1) A very inadequate examination of the development and rôle of the declassed elements, almost like pariahs, who stood right outside the feudal organisation and were inevitably bound to come to the fore whenever a town was formed; who constitute the lowest stratum of the population of every mediaeval town, having no rights at all, detached from the *Markgenossenschaft*,† from

* *Forerunners of Modern Socialism* by K. Kautsky (1894).

† Group of villages sharing common land.

feudal dependence and from the craft guild. This is difficult, but it is the *chief basis*, for by degrees as the feudal ties are loosened, these elements become the *pre*-proletariat which in 1789 made the revolution in the suburbs of Paris, and which absorbs all the outcasts of feudal and guild society. You speak of proletarians—the expression is ambiguous—and bring in the weavers, whose importance you describe quite correctly—but only *after* declassed journeymen weavers existed outside the guilds, and only in so far as these existed, can you make them into your proletariat. Here there is still a lot to make good.

(2) You have not fully grasped Germany's position in the world market, her international economic position, in so far as it is possible to speak of this, at the end of the 15th century. This position *alone* explains why the bourgeois plebeian movement in religious form which was defeated in England, the Netherlands and Bohemia could have a *certain success* in Germany in the 16th century: the success of its *religious disguise*, whilst the success of the bourgeois content, . . .* of the new direction of the world market which had arisen in the meantime—was reserved for: Holland and England. This is a lengthy subject, which I hope to deal with *in extenso* [in full] in the *Peasant War*.—If only I were already at it! †

* The margin is cut off in the original here.

† A few months later, on August 6th, 1895, Engels died, of cancer in the throat; By his own wish his ashes were scattered in the sea at Eastbourne. [*Ed. Eng. ed.*]

INDEX

Numbers refer to pages except where otherwise stated. Italic figures refer to Biographical Notes.

* Letters mainly devoted to America are those numbered 55, 57, 58, 198, 201, 202, 203, 204, 209, 222, 224; there are of course many references in other letters.

* See especially letters numbered 8, 18, 19, 31 (and Notes), 35, 36, 41, 63, 71, 74, 83, 88, 90, 91, 116, 133 (and Notes), 134, 136, 141, 168, 174, 176, 177, 188 (and Notes), 189, 195, 197, 199, 200, 207, 208, 209, 210 (and Notes), 217, 225. There are of course other references

* See especially letters numbered 71, 74, 83, 87, 88, 91, 100, 122, 130, 133 (and Note), 136, 140, 141, 142, 156, 157, 159, 160, 186, 204.

* Letters dealing largely with Ireland are those numbered 32, 101, 102, 112, 128, 130, 133 (and Note), 134, 135, 136, 141.